PERCEPTION, KNOWLEDGE AND DISBELIEF

PERCEPTION, KNOWLEDGE AND DISBELIEF

A Study of Jayarāśi's Scepticism

ELI FRANCO

MOTILAL BANARSIDASS PUBLISHERS
PRIVATE LIMITED • DELHI

First Edition: Germany, 1987
Second Edition: Delhi, 1994

ISBN: 81-208-1119-4

Also available at:
MOTILAL BANARSIDASS
41 U.A. Bungalow Road, Jawahar Nagar, Delhi 110 007
120 Royapettah High Road, Mylapore, Madras 600 004
16 St. Mark's Road, Bangalore 560 001
Ashok Rajpath, Patna 800 004
Chowk, Varanasi 221 001

PRINTED IN INDIA
BY JAINENDRA PRAKASH JAIN AT SHRI JAINENDRA PRESS, A-45 NARAINA INDUSTRIAL AREA, PHASE I, NEW DELHI 110 028 AND PUBLISHED BY NARENDRA PRAKASH JAIN FOR MOTILAL BANARSIDASS PUBLISHERS PVT. LTD., BUNGALOW ROAD, JAWAHAR NAGAR, DELHI 110 007

In memory of my father

CONTENTS

Preface to the second edition

There are several reasons why the *Tattvopaplavasiṃha* deserves our special attention: It is the only Cārvāka or Lokāyata text which has come down to us; the only text where the Cārvāka is not a mere *pūrvapakṣin*, where he can speak for himself, where we can follow the detail of his arguments, rather than be presented with a bare skeleton of his position. It is also the only text where a full-fledged scepticism is propounded. Unlike the case of Nāgārjuna or Śrīharṣa, Jayarāśi does not use the sceptical arguments to arrive at a religious or dogmatic, nihilistic or monistic metaphysics. Further, even if we tend to slightly postpone Jayarāśi's date, his work belongs to one of the most interesting and creative periods of Indian philosophy. It contains one of the earliest and most devastating criticisms of philosophers like Uddyotakara, Kumārila and Dharmakīrti. Due to its extremely polemical character, highly diversified range of opponents, as well as the mode of criticism which is always accurately directed at a specific target - Jayarāśi never criticises a Buddhist or Nyāya position in general, but only as formulated by a specific philosopher in a specific passage - the text provides us with an unusually privileged perspective of the philosophical scene in the second half of the 8th century. Occasionally we may even catch a glimpse of doctrines we were completely unaware of (cf. e.g., nn. 139, 247 etc.). Unfortunately, the text is not very informative about the "usual," i.e., materialistic Lokāyata, but this lack of information is to some extent recompensated by the fact that if it were not for Jayarāśi we would probably not have been able to understand that there were at least two trends in the Lokāyata school or tradition, the one materialistic, the other sceptic. The fact that such divergent metaphysics and epistemologies could coexist under the wider umbrella of Lokāyata further indicates that the hard core of this school was not the pseudo-scientific doctrine of four or five material elements etc., but its anti-religious or anti-clerical ethics, which is common to both trends. But perhaps above all, the text deserves our attention and admiration by its own intrinsic merits. For Jayarāśi was an excellent logician with an ironical sense of humour and a fondness for the absurd. I cannot write these words without remembering Pt. Dr. Dalsukh Malvania, with whom I read the *TUS* for the first time, bursting into laughter on reaching an unexpected twist of argument, a surprising conclusion, or an ironical parody of an opponent.

With the exception of a single paper on the relationship between Bhāsarvajña and Jayarāśi, which is reprinted here as an appendix, I had no opportunity to continue my studies of the *TUS* in the five years that passed since this book was first published. This second edition, therefore, has nothing new to offer except for this appendix, corrections of typographical mistakes, which, I am sure, are not exhaustive, addition of some odd references, and occasional improvement of the translation. Some typographical and other errors have been pointed out by various reviewers, to whom I would like to express my gratitude at this place. Special thanks are due to Professors K.H. Potter and K. Rüping.

The following two notes, the one on Jayarāśi's date, the other on his affiliation to the Lokāyata school, are merely a short response to recent publications in the field. While reviewing the available information for the dating of Jayarāśi I felt that we could not make Sanghavi and Parikh's suggestion of the 8th century more precise (cf. p. 9ff.). Since then, however, two important works on Dharmottara's contribution to the theory of *prāmāṇya* were published, and our understanding of the historical development of the issue of general validity of the means of knowledge has improved significantly (cf. E. Steinkellner and H. Krasser, *Dharmottaras Exkurs zur Definition gültiger Erkenntnis im Pramāṇaviniścaya*, Wien 1989; H. Krasser, *Dharmottaras kurze Untersuchung der Gültigkeit einer Erkenntnis, Laghuprāmāṇyaparīkṣā*, 2 vols, Wien 1991; for the lack of a general definition of *pramāṇa* in Dharmakīrti's works cf. my "The Disjunction in the *Pramāṇavārttika, Pramāṇasiddhi* chapter 5c" in E. Steinkellner (ed.), *Studies in the Buddhist Epistemological Tradition*, Proceedings of the 2nd International Dharmakīrti Conference, Wien 1991). Even though I have failed so far to find a direct quotation of Dharmottara in the *TUS*, I now feel confident enough to suggest on terminological grounds (the use of *vyaktibheda*, "difference in manifestation," to account for the duality of the means of knowledge does not seem to appear in any text before Dharmottara), on contextual grounds (Jayarāśi uses a commentary on the *Pramāṇaviniścaya*), and historical or conceptual grounds (the doctrine of general validity criticized by Jayarāśi seems to have been developed for the first time by Dharmottara), that Jayarāśi does indeed refer to Dharmottara (cf. p. 416 below). H. Krasser (*op. cit.*, vol II, p. 5) has slightly modified Frauwallner's dating of Dharmottara from 750-810 to 740-800 by discovering a reference of Dharmottara to the *Tattvasaṅgraha* and to Dharmottara in the *Tattvasaṅgrahapañjikā*. Accordingly, the *TUS* could not have been written before the last third of the 8th c. On the other hand, the *TUS* is referred to by Vidyānanda (ca. 850). Following the convention of assigning a life span of sixty years to those philosophers about whose life we know nothing, we may suggest 770-830 as the most probable date of Jayarāśi. Certain fluctuations are still possible, of course. In fact, there is nothing to prevent us from assuming that Jayarāśi was a contemporary of Kamalaśīla (740-795), for it seems odd that neither the *TS* nor the *TSP* are ever mentioned in the *TUS*; the single apparent quotation from the *TS* is in fact a verse taken by both authors from the *Bṛhaṭṭīkā*.

Eversince its publication in 1940, the *TUS* was generally regarded as a genuine Cārvāka work for reasons which were clearly elaborated by Sanghavi and Parikh in their introduction to the text. This conclusion, which "created a great deal of furore in the academic world," has recently been challenged by the renowned Marxist historian D.P.

Chattopadhyaya (*In Defence of Materialism in Ancient India*, Delhi 1989, pp. 36ff.). (The furore was such that while writing his fascinating Marxist science fiction saga *Lokāyata*, Chattopadhyaya did not even know that the *TUS* existed.) Five arguments, such as they are, are raised to support the view that the *TUS* is not a genuine Cārvāka work: 1) "The word Bhaṭṭa in the name of the author cannot but remind us of a Brahmin... it is not easy to conceive a Brahmin of the 8th century... to write a book in defence of the Cārvāka view." 2) The title "the lion that domolishes (*sic*) all philosophies or philosophical views as such" implies a demolition of the Cārvāka view too. 3) The texts opens with a rejection of the materialist principles. 4) "[T]he author bragged that his work contained wisdom which was beyond the reach even of the preceptor of the gods. Could such a bragging of being wiser than Bṛhaspati himself be possible for a genuine follower of Bṛhaspati's view? In Indian tradition, at any rate, that is absolutely inconceivable." 5) A repetition of 3 in more detail, namely, Jayarāśi's rejection of matter as ultimate reality and of perception as a means of knowledge.

Having concluded that Jayarāśi is not a Cārvāka materialist, and having pointed out certain affinities with Śrīharṣa's *Khaṇḍanakhaṇḍakhādya*, Chattopadhyaya comes up with the absurd suggestion (p. 41) that Jayarāśi is to be affiliated to "extreme idealism." Rather than being persuasive, Chattopadhyaya manages to display an astonishing combination of ignorance with intellectual dishonesty. I do not wish to marshal here all the evidence to the contrary, about which he keeps silent, nor do I wish to analyse the incredible manner with which he dispenses with the counter arguments (notably his handling of Śaṅkaramiśra's testimony, p. 40). Let us just have a look at his own "positive" arguments. Arguments 2, 3 and 5 are simply based on an inference with a false major: All Cārvākas are materialists. Jayarāśi was not a materialist. Therefore Jayarāśi was not a Cārvāka. Chattopadhyaya spares no effort to prove the minor, but no one ever claimed that Jayarāśi was a materialist. On the other hand, the assumption that all Cārvākas are materialists is clearly refuted by the *TUS* itself and by other sources which are simply ignored. The other two arguments simply beg the question. The first is mildly amusing, because Sanghavi and Parikh (p. XI) used exactly the same argument to claim that Jayarāśi could not have been a Jaina or a Buddhist, and must have been a Brahmin Cārvāka. As for the fourth argument, it only shows the author's preconceived ideas as to what is conceivable or inconceivable in the Indian tradition, but since I have already dealt with the relationship between Jayarāśi and Bṛhaspati (p. 4 below), there is no need to repeat it here.

However, Jayarāśi's affiliation with the Cārvāka school need not obscure the fact that he has real affinities with the Madhyamakas, and with certain later trends in Advaita Vedānta. These affinities are obvious above all in the total rejection of the *pramāṇas*, but they are also apparent in a certain use of vocabulary. In an important note (*IIJ* 32, 1989, pp. 210-211) Professor de Jong pointed out some intriguing similarities between Buddhist texts from the 8th century onwards and the *TUS* in the usage of the terms *avicāritaramaṇīya* and *vyavahāra/saṃvṛtti*. De Jong is careful to conclude, and he is right of course, that "It is not possible to know whether Jayarāśi was the first to use the expression [*avicāritaramaṇīya*] or the Buddhists." Yet, my impression is that the latter is the case, and that the term has originated in the Madhyamaka tradition. This does not mean, of course, that we should try to equate the two; as de Jong puts it, "Jayarāśi maintains that one must be content with every day practice whereas the Buddhist denied all validity to *saṃvṛtti* from the point of view of absolute truth or reality (*paramārtha*)." Whatever the history of these terms may be (cf. also the Appendix on Bhāsarvajña's use of *vyavahāra*), it is certainly remarkable that Jayarāśi criticizes all schools of thought except one, the Madhyamaka.

It was with great pleasure that I accepted the generous offer of Mr. N.P. Jain from Motilal Banarsidass to issue an Indian edition of the annotated translation of the first half of the *TUS* (most of the second half is translated in the notes, cf. the Index Locorum). Jayarāśi was undoubtedly one of the most brilliant philosophers of classical India, and yet he remains almost completely unknown to his fellow countrymen. It is perhaps no exaggeration to say that he is better known among European and Japanese Indologists than he is among contemporary Indian philosophers or Indologists. If this book will help to restore Jayarāśi's due place as one of the most important Indian philosophers, I shall count my labor well-spent.

Vancouver, November '92

Acknowledgements

This book started to assume its present form during a seminar for advanced students arranged by Prof. A. Wezler at the Seminar für Kultur und Geschichte Indiens of the University of Hamburg, in which I prepared a tentative translation of the *Tattvopaplavasiṃha*, and in which everybody else's job was to criticize it. Although the experience of seeing my translation scrutinized, dissected and sometimes 'annihilated' (*upapluta*) was at times emotionally distressful, I would like to assure the participants of the seminar that I remember our weekly meetings as friendly, stimulating and with nothing but gratitude. It has been a privilege for me to be able to observe several highly competent Sanskritists, notably, Mrs. U. Plewnia-Erb, Dr. K. Preisendanz, Prof. C. Oetke and Prof. Wezler himself, tackling the same text, each from a different angle. I have learnt much from them all.

The translation of chapters 1 and 2 is to a large extent the result of this common endeavour. When the seminar ended I went on reading chapters 5 and 6 with Prof. Wezler, and numerous suggestions of his are incorporated in the present translation. Very special thanks are due to Prof. L. Schmithausen who read the translation of chapters 3 and 4, as well as an earlier version of the notes to chapter 3, and improved them in many ways. Some of the better conjectures in these chapters I owe to him. Most of all I am indebted to Dr. K. Preisendanz who read the entire manuscript and suggested a tremendous amount of corrections both to the translation and the notes. I dare not imagine in what shape this book would have been without her constant help and encouragement.

During the years I have been working on the *Tattvopaplavasiṃha* I profited from occasional discussions with

Prof. E. Solomon from Ahmedabad, Professors P.S. Filliozat and K. Bhattacharya from Paris, Professors G. Oberhammer and E. Steinkellner from Vienna, Prof. S.A. Srinivasan from Hamburg, and Prof. B.K. Matilal from Oxford. I would like to take this opportunity to thank them not only for their comments, but also for their collegiality and friendliness.

Apart from the common subject matter this book has hardly anything to do anymore with my thèse de doctorat de 3ème cycle: Lokāyata, la philosophie dite matérialiste de l'Inde classique; notwithstanding that I wish to express my gratitude for all those who helped me with the first steps of my work on Jayarāśi, especially Pt. N.R. Bhatt from the French Institute in Pondicherry, Pt. Dr. D. Malvania from the L.D. Institute of Indology, Ahmedabad, Prof. M. Hulin from the University of Paris, and above all my Doktorvater, Prof. C. Malamoud.

My stay in Hamburg, during which a considerable portion of this book was prepared, was made possible by a generous fellowship of the A. von Humboldt-Stiftung, for which I am most grateful. The last year of my work was spent under the auspices of the Van Leer Jerusalem Institute, and I owe a special debt of gratitude to its director, Prof. Y. Elkana, who assisted and supported me in so many ways.

The computerized final version of the book was prepared by Dr. K. Preisendanz using the t^3 word processor of the Computing Center of the Weizmann Institute, Rehovot. M. Moshitzky, S. Gamoran and I. Pereira rendered friendly assistance in this arduous task. The costs of the publication were undertaken by the Thyssen-Stiftung, Köln, arranged by the A. von Humboldt-Stiftung and by Prof. A. Wezler, who kindly accepted the book in the series under his editorship. It gives me a great pleasure to be able to thank all of them who gave me so generously of their help in various forms.

INTRODUCTION

Scepticism may be defined as a philosophical attitude which consists of doubting knowledge claims in all areas. As such it was often considered as the bankruptcy and end of philosophy; for if sceptics are right and dogmatics are wrong, then philosophy, as well as all other forms of human inquiry after truth and knowledge are impossible. It is perhaps the greatest merit of Richard H. Popkin, himself not only the most distinguished living historian of scepticism, but also a very distinguished sceptic, to have changed our apprehension of the development of modern (Western) philosophy from the renaissance onwards up to the 20th century. Thanks to his vast and fascinating work on the history of sceptical thought, we can no longer consider scepticism as an anti-intellectual attitude which discredits all intellectual efforts by relying on the sharpest intellectual tools and methods. Far from seeing scepticism as a deadly poison to philosophy and science, we have learnt to appreciate it as one of the most important driving forces behind the development of modern philosophy, a great deal of which can be described in terms of *crises pyrrhoniennes* and reactions to them. Furthermore, Hume's lasting influence has put scepticism at the basis of all modern schools of thought, from pragmatism and positivism to analytical philosophy, existentialism, and philosophy of science.

The study of scepticism in Indian thought is still in its infancy. Not that we didn't know that there were sceptics in India; on the contrary, this fact has become common knowledge by now. Even the *Encyclopaedia Britannica* (1974, p. 833) has a short section on "Scepticism in India." But so far, with the exception of a few short papers, not a single study was devoted to it. None of the Histories of Indian Philosophy has tried to follow its development throughout the centuries, or to deal with it in any other way. There are many reasons to this state of affairs, the most important of which is probably the fact that sceptics in India, unlike in Europe, never formed an independent school of their own. There were Vedānta sceptics, Lokāyata sceptics, Madhyamaka sceptics, but no sceptics *tout court*. And modern research is still very much bound to the traditional Indian scheme. We usually study Indian philosophers as representatives of this or that school, and not as independent original philosophers. Both approaches have their advantages and shortcomings. Not every philosophical text which has come down to us testifies an original contribution by its author, especially not in a traditional society which considers that knowledge is constantly decreasing and human faculties are constantly dwindling. Vācaspatimiśra I, for instance, is an outstanding example for a philosopher who should better be studied as an unoriginal representative of the many different schools presented in his writings, and we cannot see him transcending them in any way. Scepticism, however, obviously transgressed the boundaries of the different schools, and in my opinion deserves to be studied as a phenomenon independent of them.

It is my firm belief that the study of the sceptics and their influence on the so-called dogmatic philosophers will improve and deepen our understanding of the historical development of Indian thought, and that the evaluation of its role in India, compared to and contrasted with its role in Western philosophy, may turn out to be one of the most gratifying tasks for comparative philosophy. The present study, however, does not aim at that much. It should rather be considered as a first step in this direction. For before we can start checking the influence of scepticism on other philosophies, we need to have a better acquaintance than we have now with the sceptics' texts themselves[1].

The *Tattvopaplavasiṃha* (hereafter *TUS*) is a text unique of its kind. It is the only text of the Lokāyata or Cārvāka school which has come down to us, and it is also the only Sanskrit text in which full-fledged scepticism is propounded. The manuscript of the text which dates from the end of the 13th century, was discovered by Pt. Sukhlalji Sanghavi and Pt. Becherdas Doshi in the Sanghavinā Pādāno Bhandār at Patan in 1926. The text was meant to be published shortly afterwards in the Purātattvamandir Series, but due to some unspecified "adverse circumstances" it finally appeared in the Gaekwad Oriental Series in 1940[2]. Since then, surprisingly enough, the *TUS* has been almost completely ignored; and although one chapter, dealing with the Nyāya theory of inference, was translated for the extremely popular *Source Book in Indian Philosophy*, edited by Radhakrishnan and Moore, the *TUS* remains widely unknown almost fifty years after its publication. D.P. Chattopadhyaya, for instance, affirms in his 700 pages long *Lokāyata, A Study in Ancient Indian Materialism*, that "in the ocean of uncertainty concerning the lost Lokāyata the only piece of definite information is that we are left with no original work on it" (p. 6).

Being a text of the so-called materialistic school of Indian philosophy, the *TUS* attracted the attention of some Marxist indologists like Ruben and Dixit[3]. It is not at all surprising, of course, that they tried to emphasize the materialistic aspects of Indian philosophy, but this is also the reason why their interest in Jayarāśi quickly vanished, for, as mentioned above, Jayarāśi was not a materialist, but a radical sceptic. Instead of studying the *TUS* for what it is, their papers read more like a warning that Jayarāśi is not a true heir to the materialistic philosophy propounded in the now lost *Bṛhaspatisūtra*, which is rather obvious. This inevitably leads us to the problem of Jayarāśi's affiliation.

The relation of Jayarāśi to traditional Lokāyata

It is clear that there are important philosophical differences between Jayarāśi's views and what usually goes under the name of Lokāyata philosophy. Are we justified then to consider the *TUS* as a Lokāyata text? Already Sanghavi and Parikh attributed the *TUS* to the Lokāyata school: "... the *TPS* (=*TUS*) is a work of the Lokāyata or Chārvāka school or to be more precise - of a particular division of that school. Our reason for this statement is that J[ayarāśi] in support of his opinion quotes Bṛhaspati only and that with great regard, e.g. *idam eva cetasi samāropyāha bhagavān bṛhaspatiḥ paralokino 'bhāvāt paralokābhāvaḥ* (p. 45); and also on p. 88: *idam eva cetasi samāropyoktaṃ śarīrād eveti bṛhaspatiḥ*[4]."

What is implicit in these and other arguments adduced by Sanghavi and Parikh is that we should consider the *TUS* as a Lokāyata text, because Jayarāśi himself thought so; and this is, of course, an excellent reason. Indeed, there is no doubt that Jayarāśi regarded himself as a follower of Bṛhaspati, the *guru* of the gods and legendary founder of the Lokāyata. One can see that clearly in several passages in his work where he tries to show that there is no real difference of opinion between him and Bṛhaspati. However, the quotations from the *Bṛhaspatisūtra* which are scattered in the book are not raised by Jayarāśi "in support of his opinion," but rather in order to point out the total agreement with them.

Jayarāśi was an excellent dialectician, and he was quite conscious of that. Intellectually he was independent and self-reliant to a degree almost unmet with in India. As far as a critical analysis of a given philosophical position is concerned, he clearly considered himself as superior to Bṛhaspati (as is openly said in the concluding verses of his work[5]). When one examines the quotations from the *Bṛhaspatisūtra* in their context, one invariably finds them at the end of a discussion when the refutation of a position is already accomplished and needs no further support. At this point Jayarāśi proceeds to show that the opinion he was arguing for is also the opinion expressed in the *sūtra*. This is the reason why the quotations are preceded by *idam eva cetasi samāropyāha* (or similar formulations), namely, Bṛhaspati pronounced this *sūtra* while having in mind exactly what I (Jayarāśi) just said.

Jayarāśi explains at the very beginning of his work that there are no discrepancies between him and Bṛhaspati and clarifies further how he sees the relationship of his doctrine, namely, the annihilation of all principles (*tattvopaplava*), to the doctrine propounded in the *Bṛhaspatisūtra*. The *pūrvapakṣin* points out that Jayarāśi's doctrine is incompatible with the theory of the four material elements, earth, water, fire and wind, as sole constituents of the world. Jayarāśi flatly denies that there is such an incompatibility, and accuses the probably imaginary opponent of misunderstanding the *sūtra*'s intention (or meaning, or purpose - *artha*). To the question "What is the *sūtra*'s intention?" Jayarāśi answers in his typical laconic manner with one word: the *sūtra* has the purpose of reflecting (*pratibimbana*). And then he adds: "The principles, earth etc., are well known in the world, (but) they, too, when seriously examined, are not established; how much less the others."

The laconicism of Jayarāśi's answer has given rise to different interpretations of this sentence by Sanghavi and Parikh on the one hand, and by Ruben on the other[6]. Although the former do not try to explain how exactly they understand the word 'reflecting,' I believe they are right in concluding that "what Bṛhaspati really means is that when one thinks one finds that even that Tattvas like *pṛthivī* etc. do not stand."[7] Ruben, on the other hand, thinks that the word 'reflecting' does not refer to any statement or opinion, but rather means that matter itself is reflected (whatever that means!), and if I understand him correctly, he seems to think that reflecting matter means not to analyze matter philosophically ("Bṛhaspatis Lehre spiegelt die Materie wider, ohne sie philosophisch zu analysieren.")[8].

Neither Sanghavi and Parikh nor Ruben have noticed the close connection between the beginning of the *TUS* and a famous Lokāyata fragment which reads: *sarvatra paraparyanuyogaparāṇy eva bṛhaspateḥ sūtrāṇi.* "Everywhere (i.e., throughout the text) the *sūtras* of Bṛhaspati have the sole purpose of questioning [the opinions or doctrines] of others." The Jaina philosophers Anantavīrya and Vidyānanda, who - as we shall see later on - were thoroughly acquainted with the *TUS*, explicitly associate this fragment with Jayarāśi (*tattvopaplavakṛt, tattvopaplavavādin*) in *Siddhiviniścayaṭīkā*, *Pramāṇaparīkṣā* and *Tattvārthaślokavārttika*[9]. This fragment, however, does not appear in the *TUS*, and it would be useless to speculate whether it could have appeared in a lost work of Jayarāśi, such as the *Lakṣaṇasāra*. In any case, the ideological affinity between this fragment and Jayarāśi's interpretation of the *Bṛhaspatisūtra* is quite obvious. 'Reflecting' in Jayarāśi's sense would then mean to repeat an opponent's view, and that in order to question it, i.e., to raise doubts against it and refute it. The four principles, earth etc., are well known and are supposed to be firmly established, but even they cannot bear a serious examination. All the other principles are even more doubtful, and therefore Bṛhaspati did not bother about them, that is, they were not 'reflected' in the *sūtras* in order to be refuted.[10]

Jayarāśi's attitude towards Bṛhaspati is further reflected in the concluding verses of the *TUS* (p. 125. 13-18):

ye yātā na hi gocaraṃ suraguror buddher vikalpā dṛḍhāḥ,
prāpyante nanu te 'pi yatra vimale pākhaṇḍadarpacchidi /
bhaṭṭaśrījayarāśidevagurubhiḥ sṛṣṭo mahārthodayaḥ -
tattvopaplavasiṃha eṣa iti yaḥ khyātiṃ parāṃ yāsyati //
pākhaṇḍakhaṇḍanābhijñā jñānodadhivivardhitāḥ /
jayarāśer jayantīha vikalpā vādijiṣṇavaḥ //

"For even those firm (= invincible?) *vikalpas* which were not taken into consideration by the guru of the gods (or perhaps: which escaped his attention) are certainly met with in [this] spotless [treatise] which breaks the pride of the impostors.
[This very treatise] which gives rise to [something of] great significance (or: great utility[11]), [and] which will attain supreme fame, [people saying about it:] 'This is the lion which annihilates [all] principles,' was composed by [me] the guru Bhaṭṭa Śrī Jayarāśi Deva.
Skillful in destroying the impostors, made to prosper by [me] the ocean of knowledge, the *vikalpas* of Jayarāśi, vanquishing the disputants, are triumphant here [in this world]."

In these verses Jayarāśi reveals himself as boastfully proud of the force of his new arguments which did not even occur to Bṛhaspati, but by the same token he also puts himself in the position of a more or less faithful follower.

How sincere Jayarāśi was in his interpretation of the *Bṛhaspatisūtra* is a question which cannot be answered with any certainty. At least there is no evidence against his sincerity, and I cannot imagine any reason, external or internal, which could have compelled him to become an adept of the Lokāyata against his good faith or intellectual convictions. We, on the other hand, cannot take his interpretation to be faithful to the *Sūtra*; at the most we can consider it as a testimony for the *Sūtra*'s 'Rezeption.'

Whatever the case may be, one still wonders what has brought about this radical change from a rather primitive materialism to a highly sophisticated form of scepticism. It seems to me, as I suggested elsewhere,[12] that the answer lies in the weakness of the original epistemological position of the Lokāyata, namely, that perception is the only means of valid cognition (*pratyakṣam ekaṃ pramāṇam*). Bṛhaspati's rejection of all other means of cognition had a pragmatic purpose: to exclude any divine or supernatural factor from the foundation of social and ethical theories, and this meant fierce opposition to the religious Weltanschauung which had sacrifices at its center. The inherent difficulties in Bṛhaspati's position were probably not apparent before Dignāga's time, when logical and epistemological problems became the central preoccupation of Indian philosophers. Once every school had to establish, or at least give some justification for, the means of knowledge it recognized as valid, the Lokāyatikas found themselves in the embarrassing position of petitio principii (*ātmāśraya*). For by denying all other means of valid cognition, perception had to establish itself, or not to be established at all. The Lokāyata's opponents did not fail to point out this and similar problems. For instance, the theory of the four elements could not be arrived at by relying on perception alone; the negation of an eternal Soul which experiences the results of deeds done in a previous life, or in fact any negation, is not possible without having recourse to some form of reasoning. At least two ways were open to the Lokāyatikas to solve these problems: either inference had to be granted a limited validity, which would allow its use in everyday life, while denying its use for establishing non-perceptible entities such as God, Soul, etc., or, to be even more consistent, one had to forgo both perception and inference. The first solution was adopted by Lokāyatikas like Purandara;[13] Jayarāśi chose the second.

Date of Jayarāśi

Sanghavi and Parikh have confined Jayarāśi's lifetime to the 8th century,[14] and so far I have come across no evidence, which would either contradict this date or make it more precise. The editors' terminus a quo is based on the identification of quotations in the *TUS* itself. The only personal name which appears in the *TUS* is Bṛhaspati, and the only work mentioned by its title is the *Lakṣaṇasāra* (an unidentified lost work which may have been written by Jayarāśi himself). Jayarāśi never refers to his opponents by name, but only in general, often degrading, terms such as *naiyāyikapaśu* (the Naiyāyika beast), *śrutilālasa* (the fanatics of the revelation - a nickname for the Mīmāṃsakas), etc. Thus, the terminus a quo has to be based on those quotations whose origin we are able to identify. Among these, the latest in time are from Dharmakīrti's *Pramāṇavārttika* and *Pramāṇaviniścaya*, and from Kumārila's *Ślokavārttika* and *Bṛhaṭṭīkā*. Sanghavi and Parikh placed Dharmakīrti between 600 and 700, and concluded that Jayarāśi could not be earlier than the 8th century. Since then, Frauwallner suggested 600-660 as Dharmakīrti's date;[15] and according to this one could advance Jayarāśi's date to the second half of the 7th century. This dating was in fact suggested by the great Jaina scholar Mahendrakumar Jain, who claimed to have found a reference to Jayarāśi in the *Siddhiviniścaya* of Akalaṅka, and consequently placed Jayarāśi between 650 and 700.

The passage in question reads as follows:[16]

pramāṇābhāvena pratyakṣam ekaṃ nāparaṃ prameyatattvaṃ veti na tathā pratipattum arhati. pramāṇāntarapratiṣedhe pratyakṣalakṣaṇānupapatteḥ kiṃ kena vidadhyāt pratiṣedhayed vā yataś cāturbhautikam eva jagat syāt. yadi nāma svasaṃvedanāpekṣayā bahir antaś copaplutam iti; sūktam evaitan, nirā-

kṛtaparadarśanagamanāt. vibhramaikāntam upetya svasaṃvedane 'py apalāpopalabdher anyathā vipratiṣedhāc caturbhūtavyavasthām api lakṣaṇabhedāt kathayitum arhaty, anyathānavasthāprasaṅgāt.

It has to be noted, however, that the *Siddhiviniścaya* is lost, and that this passage was reconstructed by Mahendrakumar from *pratīkas* in Anantavīrya's commentary. Although the reconstruction is problematic in details, the general purport of the passage is quite clear: Akalaṅka argues against a Cārvāka who maintains that perception is the only means of knowledge. This position cannot be held, says Akalaṅka, because without accepting inference, perception cannot even be defined (for a definition is a kind of inference). Consequently one would be unable to deny or affirm anything, by virtue of which one could say that the world is composed only of the four elements. So far, there is nothing in this to evoke the *TUS*; on the contrary, the position argued against is incompatible with Jayarāśi's. The next sentence is quite obscure (*yadi nāma svasaṃvedanāpekṣayā bahir antaś copaplutam*). It contains a reference to the annihilation of external and internal objects in respect to, or in dependence on, self-apprehension. Although the word *upapluta* reminds, of course, of *upaplava*, I fail to see this sentence as a clear proof that Akalaṅka knew Jayarāśi as Mahendrakumar claims (cf. e.g., *PVA* 57.9f).

Mahendrakumar further supports his thesis by pointing out that Anantavīrya quotes Jayarāśi while commenting on the above passage by Akalaṅka. But this kind of evidence cannot be relied upon. Moreover, if we take a closer look at Anantavīrya's commentary we can see that sometimes he introduces the *TUS* as if Akalaṅka refers to it (p. 278.13), and sometimes as if Jayarāśi refers to Akalaṅka (p. 277.19).

As a last piece of evidence, Mahendrakumar tries to prove that Jayarāśi was known to Prajñākaragupta (English Introduction, p. 42): "Dharmakīrti attempts to establish the identity of happiness and knowledge, in his *PV* (III.252): -

> '*tadatadrūpiṇo bhāvās tadatadrūpahetujāḥ,*
> *tat sukhādi kim ajñānaṃ vijñānābhinnahetujam.*'

On the basis of this very argument Jayarāśi has established the identity of *rūpa* and *jñāna*, and has inserted the word '*rūpādi*' in the place of '*sukhādi*' in the said *Kārikā*. Prajñākara has given a reply to Jayarāśi, in his *Pramāṇavārtikālaṅkāra* (p. 313) citing the altered *Kārikā* of Jayarāśi in this way: -

anenaitad api nirastam -

> *tadatadrūpiṇo bhāvās tadatadrūpahetujāḥ,*
> *tad rūpādi kim ajñānaṃ vijñānābhinnahetujam.*"

Again, Mahendrakumar has taken things out of their context. When reading Prajñākaragupta's commentary on the altered verse it becomes clear that the opponent he has in mind cannot be Jayarāśi, because the opponent accepts several entities such as the Self (*ātman*) and inherence (*samavāya*) which are explicitly rejected by Jayarāśi. Since an implication (*arthāpatti*) is mentioned in the discussion, I would rather assume that the opponent is a Mīmāṃsaka, perhaps of the Prābhākara school, since *samavāya* was not admitted by the Bhāṭṭas. Furthermore, even if Prajñākaragupta knew Jayarāśi, this would not move his terminus ad quem to 700. Mahendrakumar's dating of Prajñākaragupta (ca. 700) is based on Sankrityayana's suggestion in the introduction to the *PVBh*. Professor Steinkellner, however, tells me in a personal communication that ca. 800 is a more probable date for Prajñākaragupta.

All this does not invalidate, of course, Jayarāśi's terminus a quo as 650. But it is probable that he lived some time after this limit. Dharmakīrti is supposed to have lived between 600 and 660 (so according to Frauwallner; this conclusion was recently challenged by Lindtner who wants to advance this date by some fifty years,[17] but as far as I know his opinion is not generally accepted), and

Kumārila was a younger contemporary of Dharmakīrti, since Dharmakīrti's influence can be traced in fragments of his now lost *Bṛhaṭṭīkā*.[18] As Jayarāśi refers to commentators of Dharmakīrti and Kumārila, we have to allow some span of time between them. I do not think that Jayarāśi could have lived before 700, unless, of course, our appreciation of Dharmakīrti's date will change.

The terminus ad quem was established by Sanghavi and Parikh with the help of references to Jayarāśi and his work in the Jaina literature. They convincingly showed that Jayarāśi was well known to almost all important Jaina philosophers between the 9th and 13th century, notably, Vidyānanda (or Vidyānandin), Anantavīrya, Prabhācandra, Abhayadeva Sūri and Malliṣeṇa Sūri. Of these, the earliest are Vidyānanda and Anantavīrya. Sanghavi and Parikh give as their date the 9th century following Vaṃśīdhara (the editor of the AS) for the date of Vidyānanda, and Vidyabhushana for the date of Anantavīrya. Potter, who follows the New Catalogus Catalogorum, places Vidyānanda ca. 850 and Anantavīrya ca. 980.[19] Thus, although Jayarāśi's dating was based on partly obsolete data, the conclusion reached at by Sanghavi and Parikh still holds; at most we could move Jayarāśi to the beginning of the 9th century. In fact, after the publication of the *TUS*, Sanghavi changed his mind and suggested 725-825 as a more probable date.[20]

Sanghavi and Parikh have confined their research of references to Jayarāśi mainly to Jaina sources. The only non-Jaina philosopher they mention who probably knew of Jayarāśi is the Vedāntin Śrīharṣa. The limitedness of their research is to a large extent a result of the material which was available at the time. Since the publication of the *TUS*, however, several non-Jaina works which contain references to Jayarāśi have been published, notably, the *Nyāyabhūṣaṇa* of Bhāsarvajña, the *Nyāyamuktāvalī* of Aparārkadeva, and the *Tarkarahasya* mistakenly attributed to Kamalaśīla. Unfortunately, none of these texts can modify our dating of Jayarāśi in any way. Aparārka wrote his *Nyāyamuktāvalī* ca. 1125, and Bhāsarvajña is roughly a contemporary of Jayanta (fl. 870). Thus, they do not increase our knowledge beyond what we already know. The evidence of the *Tarkarahasya*, on the other hand, would have been ideal for determining Jayarāśi's date if it were indeed written by Kamalaśīla (740-795), as its editor, P. Shastri, claims. Unfortunately, the attribution of the text to Kamalaśīla is absolutely impressionistic, Shastri having no better argument in its favour than the fact that the text often quotes from Śāntarakṣita without acknowledging the quotations as such, something which is proper, so he thinks, only for a direct disciple, for his guru will share his fame anyhow.[21] A closer examination of these quotations, however, reveals that most of them come from the *pūrvapakṣa* part of the *Tattvasaṅgraha*. Furthermore, the author of the *Tarkarahasya* quotes from later philosophers such as Dharmottara, Prajñākaragupta and Jñānaśrīmiśra (the latter is assigned to the first half of the 11th century).[22]

Although all this does not advance us beyond the original conclusion of Sanghavi and Parikh, these references are important from a different aspect. As more and more references to the *TUS* are gathered[23] our picture of Jayarāśi and his place in the historical development of Indian philosophy starts to change. From almost complete oblivion he slowly emerges as one of the three pillars on which Indian scepticism rests, the other two being the much more famous Nāgārjuna and Śrīharṣa.[24]

Perhaps the most interesting example of Jayarāśi's influence on posterity can be found in the *Vyomavatī*. Vyomaśiva never quotes from the *TUS*, nor does he mention Jayarāśi by name, although he was deeply influenced by him. As one reads through the *Vy* it is surprising to see how often Vyomaśiva owes his arguments to Jayarāśi, sometimes merely repeating them, sometimes using them creatively in new contexts.[25]

However, Jayarāśi's influence seems not to be confined to some specific arguments; an even greater effect was executed by his way of thinking or modes of argument. What I have in mind is this special mode of reasoning called *vikalpa* which consists in giving several (ideally all possible) interpretations of a given philosophical proposition, and then analyzing one interpretation after the other, showing that none of them is sound. Jayarāśi certainly did not invent this form of reasoning, but no one before him used this way of arguing with such persistence and ingenuity, and nowhere before was the full force of this reasoning brought to light. When Vyomaśiva raises his own *vikalpas*, one often feels that he follows in the footsteps of Jayarāśi.

Similarly, Jayarāśi seems to have played a role in the development of the *vikalpa* reasoning in the Jaina school. Of course, influence on a style of reasoning is not something which admits of rigorous proof. It is more a kind of intuition which develops slowly as one reads through these texts and is constantly reminded of Jayarāśi. However, as corroborative evidence, I would like to point out that Jaina philosophers who precede Jayarāśi or are his contemporaries like Mallavādin and Akalaṅka hardly ever use *vikalpas* the way he does. Philosophers who immediately follow him like Vidyānanda and Anantavīrya use them sporadically, and later philosophers like Prabhācandra and Abhayadeva constantly.

It is probably Jayarāśi's influence on the Jaina school which saved him from oblivion. There is no doubt that Jayarāśi represented a minority (*ekadeśa*) within the Lokāyata school. Although no other Lokāyata text survives today, we can safely conclude from numerous references in Hindu, Buddhist and Jaina sources that most Lokāyatikas remained materialists in one form or another. References to Lokāyata scepticism, on the other hand, are so scant that it was virtually unknown in the West before the publication of the *TUS*. One could expect, therefore, that if a single Lokāyata text survives, it would be of the materialistic and main branch of the school. The fact that this and no other text survives may be due, of course, to sheer chance or blind fate, but perhaps it is not merely that. While commenting on the 17th *śloka* of Hemacandra's *Anyayogavyavacchedadvātriṃśikā* Malliṣeṇa Sūri says (*SVM* p. 171.8): *vistaratas tu pramāṇakhaṇḍanaṃ tattvopaplavasiṃhād avalokanīyam*. "A refutation of the means of valid cognition in detail should be looked up from the *Tattvopaplavasiṃha*."

It seems from this recommendation that the *TUS* was well known at Malliṣeṇa's time, that is, more than 500 years after its composition, and that it was used as a standard refutation of the means of knowledge.[26] Repeating a metaphor Voltaire used for Bayle's Dictionary we can say that the book was used as an arsenal against the *pramāṇas*. In fact, Jayarāśi's scepticism is to a large extent compatible with the Jaina relativism, and the Jaina philosophers could easily use his critique of the theory of knowledge of all schools as the highroad to their *anekāntavāda*. Thus, the Jaina had an interest in studying (and consequently copying) the book. It is, therefore, probably not a mere coincidence that the manuscript of the *TUS* was found in the library of a Jaina temple and was edited by two Jaina scholars.

Jayarāśi on the criterion of truth and some methodological problems

Practically everybody is a sceptic in respect to some knowledge claims. One may dogmatically or undogmatically accept the knowledge claims made by the natural scientists or mathematicians, and raise serious doubts about the knowledge claims made by, say, theologians. Yet scepticism, at least in its purest or extreme form, consists in raising doubts about all knowledge claims, even those based on immediate experience. Most sceptics would argue that a necessary condition of knowing is that our impressions or cognitions would be the exact likeness of the object to which they correspond. But the real properties of an object cannot be known independently of the senses; and thus we can never be sure that our experience of an object is the exact copy of it. This idea is as old as philosophy, but let me quote a modern variant of it: "For if you know that no difference is made to a thing θ by the presence or absence of a certain condition c [c = the condition of knowing the object], you know what θ is like with c, and also what θ is like without c, and on comparing the two find no difference. This involves knowing what θ is like without c; in the present case, knowing what you defined as the unknown."[27]

If all we know is just how things appear to us, how could we distinguish between right and wrong cognitions? Do we have a criterion which will help us differentiating between them?

On the question "How can we know anything?" all Indian philosophers unanimously answer "By having a means of valid cognition (*pramāṇa*)." This answer is, of course, almost tautological, and perhaps no two philosophers understand this term in exactly the same manner, but it played an important role in structuring the Indian theories of knowledge. It is around this concept of *pramāṇa*, its nature, its definition and its varieties, that Indian philosophy ever since Dignāga's time developed. When we talk of validity of cognitions in the Indian philosophical context we usually mean *prāmāṇya*, a word which is sometimes explained as 'being a means of valid cognition,' but which in fact means 'being derived from a means of valid cognition,' since it does not apply to the means itself, but rather to the cognition which arises from it (*pramā*).

Note, however, that validity and truthfulness are not concepts which cover the same extension. A cognition may be true but not valid, and valid but not true. For instance, recollection may be true (*yathārtha*) but not valid for Jayanta, and for Dharmakīrti inference may be valid but not true (*bhrāntir api pramā*). Usually the notion of truthfulness is included in the notion of validity, but validity may include further conditions; for instance, a means of valid cognition may be required to be an agent of apprehension of an unapprehended object (*anadhigatārthagantṛ*).

Among the means of valid cognition, the one which appears first in every (or almost every) enumeration, which was considered as being at the basis of all the other means of knowledge and which was accepted by all Indian philosophers except the sceptics, is perception (*pratyakṣa*). Without (valid) perception, all the other means of knowledge such as inference and verbal testimony are useless and invalid. For what could be expected even from a simple inference like the one of fire from smoke if one mistakes dust for smoke; or from a verbal testimony if one cannot hear properly?

It is probably for this reason that problems of truthfulness are usually discussed in the context of perception. This can also be seen on the other side of the coin, namely, in the theories of error. As Schmithausen once observed,[28] it is the immediate deception of the senses which attracts most of the attention of Indian philosophers to the extent that it became an independent theme which had hardly anything to do anymore with other kinds of error such as false inferences.

Jayarāśi is no exception in this respect. He deals with the problem of truthfulness, or as he calls it (following the Nyāya) nonerroneousness (*avyabhicāritā*), not as a general problem common to all means of knowledge, but as a specific problem of sense perception. The discussion evolves around the Nyāya definition of perception, but it should be considered as applicable to other schools as well. For while discussing the same problem in the chapters on the Mīmāṃsā and the Sāṅkhya definitions of perception Jayarāśi refers the reader back to the chapter on Nyāya; and while discussing the Nyāya definition he already deals with theories of other schools, especially the one of the Mīmāṃsā.

Before presenting Jayarāśi's arguments I will have to go in some detail into his opponents' theories. For, obviously, before we can understand the criticism of some theory, we have to understand what is being criticized. Sometimes, a conscientious critic may take the trouble to present as faithfully as he can what he wants to examine and criticize. This, unfortunately, is not the case with Jayarāśi. The *TUS* is an extremely difficult text (one can tell that by seeing how often it was misunderstood by some very competent scholars), not because of its vocabulary, or syntax, or obscure compounds, or elusive thought, but because it is extremely laconic. Jayarāśi wrote for his contemporaries, that is, those who were acquainted with the theories he was criticizing. He, therefore, saw no need to repeat them; it was enough to refer to them. The type of sentence which appears most frequently in the *TUS* is the conditional: the 'if' part contains the position of the opponent in a nut shell, the 'then' part contains Jayarāśi's criticism and refutation of it. Thus, the opponent's position is hardly ever allotted more then a couple of words. This could have been sufficient for 8th century Indian philosophers. It is certainly not enough for most of us.

There is a further reason why Jayarāśi cannot be fully understood before we identify his opponents. He seems to have been a highly meticulous person, and he did not construe his arguments against a general philosophical position which might be common to a couple of philosophers or to a school of thought, but against a specific formulation of a position, as it appears in a specific text. His arguments often refer to a single word which he thinks his opponent uses in a dubious manner. Obviously, in such cases, if we don't know to exactly which text he was referring, we do not know what he is talking about. Most of the notes to the translation, therefore, (apart from translations of parallel passages from the *TUS* itself and references to Jayarāśi in later literature) deal with the identification of the opponents. Whenever I succeeded in identifying an opponent, Jayarāśi's arguments become clear and hardly need any further comment; in cases where I did not succeed, they are usually perplexing and only superficially understood. Unfortunately, the work of identification presented here is far from being completed. Partly it is due to my personal limitation: I obviously did not read everything. I tried to cover over a thousand years of philosophical literature, for there was no point in limiting myself to texts which precede the *TUS*, as older theories are often described in younger texts. The *Nyāyamañjarī*, for instance, is our best source for the appraisal of Nyāya theories after Vātsyāyana.[29]

Unlike in the case of the translation which was checked and read by many colleagues and friends, in identifying the opponents I was very much on my own. Thus, it is indeed possible that I did not succeed in identifying some of the most obvious opponents of Jayarāśi; I can only hope that such cases are not too numerous. One has to stop somewhere, and I will be more than happy to see someone else take up this work where I left it. However, apart from my personal limitations, the incompleteness of this work is a direct result of the available material. Indian philosophy today presents itself as the visible part of an iceberg, the rest of which can only vaguely be guessed about. Texts whose manuscripts will probably never be found on the one hand, and an oral tradition irrevocably lost on the other, leave of the intense and uninterrupted philosophical activity of the first millenium A.D. only a few big monuments, comparable to mountain summits which remain as isolated islands while all the rest is submerged under water.

In general outline Jayarāśi's apprehension of the philosophical scene is not very different from ours. The two most important antagonists are the Naiyāyikas and the Buddhists. The Mīmāṃsakas are partly treated together with the Naiyāyikas; only special Mīmāṃsā issues get an independent treatment. Sāṅkhya is dealt with briefly, and one can feel that it is already a dying system. Vedānta and Jaina philosophy are hardly noticed, since they did not yet occupy the outstanding positions they won after Śaṅkara and Akalaṅka. Perhaps the only discrepancy between our apprehension of Indian philosophy at the time and the way it is reflected in the *TUS* would be the relatively minor place allotted in the *TUS* to Bhartṛhari's philosophy of language.

So far for the broad outline. However, when we look into the details we see that Jayarāśi often uses texts which did not survive. The Nyāya philosophy is represented not so much by Uddyotakara himself, but by the Ācāryas, that is, a group of commentators on the *Nyāyavārttika*, the most important of which was the Rucikāra.[30] The Mīmāṃsā school is represented mainly by the Bhāṭṭas, however not by the *Ślokavārttika* or its commentaries, but by the *Bṛhaṭṭīkā* and commentaries thereupon. The Buddhists are represented mainly by Dharmakīrti, however not by any of his works which are extant in Sanskrit, but by the *Pramāṇaviniścaya* (in this case we are lucky to have a Tibetan translation of the work). The Sāṅkhya is represented not by the *Sāṅkhyakārikā* or the *Yuktidīpikā*, but by the *Ṣaṣṭitantra* of Vārṣagaṇya and Vindhyavāsin's commentary on it.

It should be expected, therefore, that Jayarāśi refers sometimes to theories of which we have only a vague idea, and to details of which we have no idea at all. In such cases his arguments usually seem tedious and gratuitous, for they are only superficially understood, but as soon as we find the opponent Jayarāśi had in mind the pieces of the puzzle start falling into their places, and the picture becomes clear in next to no time at all. Even when the assumption of a real opponent seemed at first sight unlikely for a certain passage, I often came to realize that it had one after all. Methodologically we can extrapolate from such cases and proceed as if Jayarāśi always aims at a real and specific target. Whenever we are unable to find such a target - and even if the intended position contradicts certain things we think we know - we have to assume that it is unknown to us, and not that it was invented by Jayarāśi for the sake of arguing.[31]

Fortunately, most of the protagonists whose criterion of truth Jayarāśi criticizes are easily identifiable. However, since I have already written on this subject[32] I refrain from presenting it here again with all the details which it implies. Instead, I shall confine myself, as a way of illustration, to a single example, that of the Mīmāṃsā criterion. It is the first one to be dealt with by Jayarāśi, and I believe it illustrates nicely the general flavour of the book. The context of the discussion is formed by *NS* 1.1.4 which contains the Nyāya definition of perception, and more specifically by the word 'nonerroneous' in that definition. How do you know that a cognition is nonerroneous, asks Jayarāśi, and enumerates four possible criteria: by being produced by a complex of faultless causal factors (*aduṣṭakārakasandohotpādyatva*), by the absence of sublation (*bādhārahitatva*), by the efficiency of the activity (*pravṛttisāmarthya*), and otherwise (*anyathā*).

Although one could expect from the context a discussion of the Nyāya theories, Jayarāśi prefers to start with the Mīmāṃsā. His arguments against the first two criteria are directed against the following passage of the *Vṛttikāragrantha*:[33] "The arising of cognition when the senses of a person are in contact with that [same object which appears in the cognition] is true perception. 4a.

The arising of cognition for a person when the senses are in contact with precisely that which the cognition has for [its] object is true perception. The cognition whose object is different from the one [with which the senses are] in contact is not perception. - But how is it apprehended that this [cognition arises when the senses are] in contact with that same [object which appears in the cognition], and that [cognition arises when they are] in contact with a different [object]? - That [cognition which arises when the senses are] not in contact with a different [object], [arises when they are] in contact with that [same object]. Its opposite [arises when the senses are] in contact with a different [object]. - How is it known? For even when someone takes a conch shell for silver, he thinks: ' My eye is in contact with silver.' - [It is known] for in respect to which [cognition] a sublating cognition is produced [which takes the form] 'This is not so, that is a false cognition,' this [cognition arises when the senses are] in contact with a different [object], [its] opposite when [the senses are] in contact with that [same object]. - [But] how is it apprehended before the production of the sublating cognition, at the time when there is no difference whatsoever between true cognition and false cognition? - When the mind is disturbed by hunger etc., or the sense by *timira* sickness etc., or the external object by fineness etc., [then] a false cognition [is produced] from these [kinds of disturbance]. When [they] are not disturbed, the cognition is true. For the contact between sense, mind and object is the cause of the cognition, because in its absence there is no cognition. A fault which intervenes with that [contact] is the cause of a false cognition, because when [the senses etc.) are faulty, the cognition arises as false. - How is it apprehended? - Because when the fault is gone, one sees an agreement [between the cognition and reality[34]]. - How is the apprehension of the faulty and faultless [brought about]? - If [in spite of] searching with effort we would not perceive [any] fault, [then] because there is no proof [for the opposite], we would think that [it is] not faulty. That is why only [the cognition] which has a faulty cause and about which [we have] the cognition '[It is] false' is an erroneous cognition; there is no other."

One can see a certain uneasiness of the Vṛttikāra about the criterion of truth. As the opponent's questions are raised, he piles two criteria one upon the other, and he does that, of course, because none of them is really satisfactory. The first criterion he uses is the sublation, or the assertion of falsity (*bādhā*), but as time intercalates between the cognition whose falsity is to be asserted and the cognition which asserts the falsity, he adds a second criterion: the production by faultless causes. By that he attempts to establish that the true cognition is made the normal one, the one we usually have, and that error is made an exception.[35] In other words, there is nothing inherently wrong with the cognitive process itself. But the fact that any particular cognition is produced by faultless causes is yet to be proved. The assertion that a valid cognition is produced by 'good' causes tells us what happens, but not when it happens. Thus, production by faultless causes needs in its turn another criterion which will tell us whether there is a production by faultless causes. (To say that it is known when a sublating cognition does not arise would result in a mutual dependence - *anyonyāśraya* - and will not solve the initial problem, i.e., to know whether a cognition is wrong before a sublating cognition arises.)

Here the Vṛttikāra seems to be at the end of his resources and says that if we make an effort to discredit or refute the cognition without success, we accept it as true. No further specification of what the effort should consist of is given. The last sentence, which is quoted by Jayarāśi on p. 76.7-9, concludes the discussion by putting the production by faultless causes and the absence of sublation side by side as a joint criterion of truth.

What the Vṛttikāra tried to do in the first half of this criterion is, I think, to take a definition of knowledge and turn it into a criterion of truth. The definition of knowledge in terms of the causal complex appears already in the Vaiśeṣikasūtra (VS 9.25-27): *indriyadoṣāt saṃskārāc cāvidyā. tad duṣṭaṃ jñānam. aduṣṭaṃ vidyā.* "Non-knowledge is due to a fault of the sense and to impressions [left by previous experience]. It is a faulty cognition. Faultless [cognition] is knowledge."

The difference between a definition of knowledge and its criterion is that the definition should tell us what knowledge is, while the function of the criterion is to tell us when and where it occurs. Taken as a criterion, the production by faultless causes should function as a reason, or a characteristic sign (*hetu*, *liṅga*) of an inference. One should be able to say "This cognition is true, because it is produced by faultless causes," just as one says "This cognition is true, because it is not sublated."

The difference between the two inferences is not in the nature of the *vyāpti*, but that in the first inference the occurrence of the middle term (*hetu*) in the minor term (*dharmin*) is unknown, whereas one always knows if a cognition is sublated or not; one has an immediate experience of it.

This is perhaps the most important difference between a definition and an inference. In every definition (that is, in every correct definition), there is a *vyāpti* between definiendum and definiens - or more precisely a *kevalavyatirekivyāpti*, since the definiendum has no *sapakṣa* - , but it does not indicate whether a particular substratum would possess the defining property or not.

The above interpretation of the *Vṛttikāragrantha* is also possible because of the ambivalence of the word *hetu*, which can be used both as an ontological and epistemological term. As an ontological term it can be used to denote a cause, something which actually produces; as an epistemological term, it denotes the reason, or the middle term of an inference. If the Vṛttikāra uses the production by faultless causes as a criterion, which I think he does, then both meanings of the word should be applicable to the text, when he says that a fault is the *hetu* of a false cognition. Jayarāśi's arguments are directed only against *hetu* as a middle term of an inference. He does not argue against a definition of knowledge in terms of the quality of its production, but he claims that it cannot be used as a criterion of truth:[36]

"In respect to these [alternatives], if the nonerroneousness of a cognition is known by being produced by a complex of faultless causal factors, [then] by which [means of valid cognition] is precisely that, [i.e.] the fact that the causes are faultless, apprehended? Not by perception, because the well-being etc., of the eye , are beyond [the apprehension by] the senses [themselves]. Nor [is it known] by inference, because there is no apprehension of another [inferential] sign (i.e., a sign which will prove that the causal complex is faultless, which proves, in its turn, that the cognition is nonerroneous).

[Objection:] It is precisely that cognition which is the sign; having arisen from that (i.e., from a faultless causal complex) it reveals its distinguished character (i.e., of being faultless).

[Reply:] If so, the insurmountable [fallacy of] mutual dependence follows necessarily.
Besides, the senses being substrata of qualities (i.e., good functioning) and faults, a cognition produced by them is not beyond the suspicion of faults, just like a cognition of a word produced by the activity of a person." (§ 1.11)

The first inference would be: this cognition is true, because it is produced by a faultless causal complex. The second inference would be: this causal complex is faultless, because it produces a true cognition. The interdependence is obvious.[37]

With this, Jayarāśi's criticism of the first part of the criterion is concluded, and he moves on to refute the second part, the absence of sublation.

Adopting a Western terminology, the absence of sublation looks at first sight as if it presupposes a coherence theory of truth, where truth is defined in terms of relations among statements, and not in terms of relations between statements and reality, as is the case in a correspondence theory of truth.

However, as far as I know, the basic assumption of all Indian philosophers is always a correspondence theory of truth. Even if the only way to assert the falsity of a cognition is by having another cognition which has a corrective function (e.g., that a cognition of water was nothing but a fata morgana), it can only do so because it corresponds to reality, and because the content of the previous cognition does not correspond to reality. In fact, the relation between the two cognitions always remained problematic; and in the final analysis unexplained. We saw that the main disadvantage of the absence of sublation as a criterion of truth is that a certain amount of time lapses before the sublation is produced. Consequently one can never be sure at any given moment which of one's cognitions are true and which are going to be proved false some time in the future. Moreover, in certain cases the falsity of the cognition will never be asserted: a deceptive sense may remain so, a disturbed mind may never be cured, an object may be too subtle to be rightly apprehended, or one may simply die before the sublation is produced:

"If the nonerroneousness [of a cognition] is known by the non-arising of sublation, we have the following doubt: Is the fact that a sublation of a cognition does not arise due to the fact that [the cognition] is true, or is it due to the deficiency of a causal factor which [could have] produced the sublating cognition? For it is seen [in some cases] that the sublation is not produced because of the deficiency of the causal factor which [could have] produced the sublating cognition. For instance, when a cognition of water is produced with reference to a faraway mass of sun-rays the sublation is not produced, [but] when a causal factor is produced additionally for [a person] who stands nearby, [the sublation] is produced. And being produced additionally it is produced with a difference in time, after a year etc., and sometimes, due to the deficiency of the causal factor, it is not produced at all; the nonerroneousness, however, of a [cognition] is not established by that much.

Besides, the absence [of a cognition] of sublation does not prove the real absence of sublation, because the apprehension of its real existence is due to its apprehension [but its inexistence is not proved by the absence of its apprehension]."[38] (§ 1.12)

In the last sentence Jayarāśi turns the practical difficulties into a matter of principle. If one apprehends a sublation, one can be sure that the sublation exists, and that the sublated cognition is false. But if one does not apprehend the sublation, it does not mean that the cognition is true, for it is always possible that the sublation is not produced because of the deficiency of one of the causal factors.

One of the basic principles in Popper's philosophy of science is that a hypothesis can never be confirmed. The scientific hypotheses we hold to be true are only those which are not yet refuted, but they are liable to be so sometime in the future. When we conduct a scientific experiment in order to check a hypothesis, we can either refute or corroborate it, but never confirm it. Jayarāśi's argument is based, I think, on a similar idea, but, of course, I do not mean to make a comparison between the two philosophers. This simply illustrates that similar ideas can arise in entirely different contexts.

While commenting on the *Vṛttikāragrantha* Kumārila had to deal with some problems which the Vṛttikāra had left open. For instance, what happens when a person who has an erroneous cognition is not in a position to rectify it?[39] (Umbeka ad loc., gives the example of a person whose sense is defective - *timiropahatacakṣuḥ* - , Sucarita that of a person who suffers from delusion about directions - *diṅmūḍha*; for an explanation of this phenomenon cf. SV(2) p. 53. 2-17) For such cases Kumārila introduces communication with other people, from whose opposite cognitions one can learn about one's own mistakes. This possibility does not appear in the *Vṛttikāragrantha*, but it could perhaps be subsumed under the 'searching with effort.'

However, apart from elaborating details as the above, or showing that sublation and sublating cognition are not mutually dependent (the fallacy of *anyonyāśraya*), Kumārila had to provide an answer to some problems of an altogether different order. The Buddhists, who traditionally had little original to say on problems of debate and epistemological theories which arose from them, started dealing with these topics around the 3rd century A.D. With Dignāga and Dharmakīrti they even became the leading school in this field, and occupied the center of the philosophical scene, in the sense that all the other schools had to react in some manner to the new theories they proposed. As we saw, the Vṛttikāra dealt with everyday errors such as mistaking a conch shell for silver. Kumārila had to go beyond that and deal with more radical types of error which are not due to a disturbance in the cognitive process, but rather are immanent to it, namely, the view that all everyday cognitions, including those we usually call 'true,' are essentially erroneous.

Dignāga's classification of cognitions into conceptual and non-conceptual, and his equation of conceptual cognitions, which include cognitions of empirical reality, with erroneous cognitions, raised philosophical problems which the Vṛttikāra did not have to face. Since reality, so claimed the Buddhists, cannot be conceptualized, all cognitions of empirical reality, which necessarily involve conceptual constructions, are necessarily false. To this we may add the traditional Buddhist mistrust against abstract entities such as the universal and the whole (*avayavin*) which were supposed to appear even in the simplest cognitions, where no error seemed possible at first sight, for instance 'This is a cow,' when you stand in front of such an animal. These cognitions were analyzed as containing two parts: the part 'this' referring to some individual, and the part 'cow' as referring to the universal 'cowness' or 'bovinity' (*gotva*).[40]

The Buddhists developed very early sharp arguments against the universal and the whole, or, more precisely, the residence of the universal in the individuals, and of the whole in its parts (*vṛttivikalpa*). And obviously the whole cognition would be false if it referred to inexistent entities and affirmed their existence. For instance, the universal cannot reside entirely in one of its individuals (or the whole in one of its parts), because it would not be able to reside in other individuals (or in other parts). Nor could it reside partly in them, because it has no parts. Such arguments appear already in the *Nyāyasūtra*.[41]

Now, if we apply all that to the criterion of the Vṛttikāra, we can indeed say that all cognitions are erroneous because they are produced by disturbed or faulty causes, namely, the conceptualization which intervenes with the process of perception. And we know that conceptualization is faulty, because it involves contradictory notions such as the universal, the whole, etc.

In order to defend the Vṛttikāra against such criticism Kumārila had to make room for exceptions. We saw that for the Vṛttikāra the production by faultless causes and the absence of sublation are proposed as a joint criterion, that is, if there is no sublation and no apprehension of a faulty cause, the cognition is considered as true; if, on the other hand, one of these conditions does not obtain, no matter which one of the two, the cognition is considered as false.

This, however, could no longer bear the Buddhist attack, because the Buddhists had adduced some very convincing arguments to show that all everyday cognitions which necessarily involve universals arise from faulty causes. In order to disarm the Buddhist attack Kumārila argued that the presence of sublation, or more precisely, what would seem to be a sublation, namely, a cognition which claims that another cognition is false, is not always enough to invalidate another cognition. There is, one might say, a sort of struggle between the sublating and the sublated cognition, as if each of them were trying to affirm and defend the reality of its own object.[42] In this struggle the sublating cognition does not always win, for sometimes it is not stronger than the sublated cognition.

However, Kumārila was careful enough to restrict this possibility only to extreme cases, which are, of course, precisely the cases which the Buddhists had in mind. Thus he says:[43]

sarveṣāṃ sarvadā yatra dhīḥ syāt tatra na bādhanam/
na hi kāraṇaduṣṭatvabuddhis tatra balīyasī//

"[An object] of which everybody has always a cognition, in respect to such [an object] there is no sublating,
for in this case the [alleged] cognition of the fact that the causes [such as the senses] are faulty is not stronger."

Jayarāśi has probably taken into consideration Kumārila's augmentations to the Vṛttikāra's theory as he proceeds to examine two interpretations of the absence of sublation:

1) If nobody experiences a sublation for a given cognition, the cognition is true.
2) If there is no sublation of a given cognition by further cognitions of one and the same person, the non-sublated cognition is true.

The first interpretation looks like a common sense argument ("How do I know that the water is real? Everybody says so."), and it raises the same difficulties, for even an absolute majority may be wrong. And, as Jayarāśi argues, one could hardly know what all people think on a given subject matter without being omniscient. For the second interpretation, the arguments given above (§ 1.12) apply equally. This explains the similarity between some of the arguments in the above quoted passage and in the following passage, which also concludes Jayarāśi's arguments against the absence of sublation as a criterion of truth:

"And there is another [argument]. Does the absence of sublation depend on all people or on the perceiver [alone]?

In respect to these [alternatives], if it depends on all people, ... [everybody] would be omniscient.[44]

[Objection:] Let everybody be omniscient, what is wrong with that?

[Reply:] One will not be able to talk about non-omniscient [people].

If the non-production of sublation depends on the perceiver [alone], [i.e., if] the perceiver does not have a sublating cognition [and] by this [fact knows] that [the cognition] is nonerroneous, [then] this [too] is not correct, because a false cognition of diamond-rays[45] etc., is observed even when there is no production of a sublating cognition for the perceiver, because he goes to another place or dies, etc. Or the false cognition arises in such a way by being subordinated to the nature of its source that it prevents the production of the sublating cognition. The destruction of this [false cognition] as well is of exactly the same kind (i.e., it as well prevents the production of the sublating cognition), just as a true cognition accepted by the opponent [prevents its own sublation]. Thus, to say: 'A cognition whose cause is faulty and about which one has the cognition 'It is false,' that cognition alone is untrue,'[46] is itself untrue." (§ 1.12a)

All this, of course, is nothing but a small fraction of what Jayarāśi has to say on the subject of perception in particular and of means of knowledge in general. The arguments presented here cover about one page of the book. Jayarāśi goes on analyzing and arguing against school after school, definition after definition, to erode not only every level of knowledge claim and certainty, but also the definitions themselves by paying attention to some of the more formal aspects of definitions, especially the rule of economy (i.e., every word in a definition must have a purpose; no word should be employed if its purpose is already fulfilled by another word). The definitions are dissected into their smallest constituent parts and every word receives an individual treatment to show that there is no justification for its employment. Most of the attention is naturally directed at the two most important means of knowledge, namely, perception and inference, but other means of knowledge, such as *arthāpatti* (negative implication or circumstantial evidence), *upamāna* (comparison or analogy), *abhāva* (absence or negation), *sambhava* (inclusion), *aitihya* (tradition) and *śabda* (verbal testimony) are also dealt with, albeit briefly, and found to be invalid. Consequently, as the title of the book (*tattvopaplava-*) already indicates, the general conclusion is that all the principles are annihilated.

As could be expected, this conclusion of Jayarāśi was criticized by some of his opponents as self-contradictory or self-refuting. Scepticism in its Indian context may be defined as the rejection of all *pramāṇas*. Thus, if scepticism (at least in its Indian version) is self-refuting, this means that the rejection of all *pramāṇas* implies the acceptance of some kind of *pramāṇa* after all. This is how Vidyānanda puts it:[47] "They want to prove only the annihilation of principles; consequently, [they] have to admit a proof. And this [proof] is nothing but a means of knowledge. And so, the following [can] be said: For the *tattvopaplavavādin*, too, there is a means of knowledge, for otherwise the proof of the desired [annihilation of all principles] would be impossible. If the desired [annihilation] is established even without a means of knowledge, everything would be established for everybody according to one's wish. Thus, why should a non-annihilated principle not be established as well, for there is no difference whatsoever [between the proof of anything whatsoever and your proof of annihilation of principles, in as much as both are established without a means of knowledge]."

In defense of scepticism

Scepticism is often charged to be logically self-refuting. To enter this topic here is to some extent outside the scope of this study, for Jayarāśi does not waste a word on it. However, since this charge was raised against Jayarāśi by later philosophers in various forms, and since such a charge is often not raised against a specific philosopher, or a specific form of scepticism, but rather against scepticism as such, and is thus applicable in principle to the *TUS* as well, a few words on this subject are not out of place here.

Consider, for instance, the following objection to scepticism made by a philosopher which I otherwise greatly admire:[48] "He (the sceptic) asserts that he has no philosophical doctrine of his own; but this assertion is belied by his practice, which implies two things, each in effect a constructive philosophical position.

He has condemned the philosophies of other people for showing certain characteristics which, he thinks, are faults. This implies a conception of what a constructive philosophy should be, and the use of this conception as a standard by which to condemn existing philosophies. Now, the idea of a philosophy is itself a philosophical idea; and the critic who uses such an idea as a standard is under an obligation to state it and defend it against criticism.

He has also a conception of what philosophical criticism should be; and this is a standard whose claims he thinks he can and does satisfy in his own philosophical practice. But this again is a philosophical conception; and hence a philosophical critic is bound to give us his theory of philosophical criticism, and satisfy us by positive or constructive argument that his principles are sound and that his practice faithfully follows them.

Scepticism in this form, as in all its forms, is in reality a covert dogmatism; ..."

A similar opinion is expressed by Uddyotakara while commenting on the *vitaṇḍāsūtra*. As is well known the *Nyāyasūtra* defined *vitaṇḍā* as a kind of debate (*kathā*) in which sophistical arguments (*chala*, *jāti*) and "points of defeat" (*nigrahasthāna*) are allowed, and in which a counterposition is not established (*NS* 1.2.3: *sa* (scil. *jalpaḥ*) *pratipakṣasthāpanāhīno vitaṇḍā*). In later times this *sūtra* was interpreted as if the protagonist who engages in this kind of debate must be a sceptic who never admits he has any position of his own. However, since the *sūtra* appears in a context which deals with the formal divisions of debate (note also, that it belongs to the earliest strata of the *NS*, that is, probably to a period before the appearance of the Madhyamaka school), and not with the philosophical positions of those who engage in a debate, I am inclined to believe that the *sūtra* was merely referring to the kind of debate in which one philosopher tries to establish a thesis, and another tries to refute him without establishing the opposite thesis or any other alternative thesis - an exercise not unworthy even of the most dogmatic of philosophers - and anyone would admit that the refutation of a certain position does not automatically prove its opposite which may be equally absurd.

Vātsyāyana's commentary on this *sūtra* points, I believe, in this direction. An opponent objects that the formulation of the *sūtra* is cumbersome, for one could simply say that *vitaṇḍā* lacks a counter-position, and thus the word "establishing" is superfluous. Vātsyāyana answers that in fact the *vaitaṇḍika* has a thesis (*pakṣa*) which consists in the negation of his opponent's thesis, but does not make a formal statement at the beginning of the debate of anything which has to be proved and then proceeds to prove it (*na tv asau sādhyaṃ kañcid arthaṃ pratijñāya sthāpayati*). Vātsyāyana does not say anything about the philosophical position of the *vaitaṇḍika* (literally, a person who engages in a *vitaṇḍā*-type of debate; and this does not necessarily imply a sceptic), but Uddyotakara already interprets *vaitaṇḍika* as a person who does not establish any position at all (*NV* p. 361.14: *vaitaṇḍiko na kañcit pakṣaṃ sthāpayati*) (that is, unlike Vātsyāyana who claims that in fact the *vaitaṇḍika* has a position, but does not formally announce anything in the form of a thesis - *pratijñā*). Arguing against some other philosophers (Vasubandhu?) who proposed to define *vitaṇḍā* as pure criticism (*dūṣaṇamātra*) Uddyotakara says that this definition is wrong because by the mere act of criticism the *vaitaṇḍika* does admit at least four things: there is a position to be criticized, he apprehends that it does not conform to reality, and that he as well as his opponent are present. It seems, therefore, that for Uddyotakara the *vaitaṇḍika* admits certain positions, at least for the sake of argument, but he will not even attempt to establish them.

However, is there anything in the above to convince us that a sceptic is inconsistent with himself as soon as he opens his mouth and engages in a philosophical debate? Is silence the only rescue of the sceptic as is sometimes suggested? Certainly sceptics themselves do not think so, for otherwise we would be completely ignorant of them. Obviously, everyone, including the sceptic, takes a lot of things for granted. And all that the above argument against scepticism[49] shows is that sceptics take certain things for granted. But does to take something for granted imply a knowledge claim regarding that thing? At least as far as my experience goes, one usually takes for granted precisely those things which one does not know. If the sceptic's opponent thinks that it is pertinent to the debate to establish the presence of the protagonists, he may turn to the sceptic and suggest they examine the question, and the sceptic, if he is well-disposed towards his interlocutor, may turn his undivided attention to the problem and arrive at the conclusion that one can't be sure of their presence. This is all there is to it. And if the reader thinks that the presence of oneself is impossible to doubt, let me remind him of Pierre Daniel Huet who dissected Descartes' *cogito* so deftly that he finally transformed it into "I thought, therefore, perhaps I was."[50]

However, most critics of scepticism may feel that this is too easy a way out and that one can formulate the argument of self-refutation in a more radical way. Consider the statement "No statement is true," which supposedly contains the sceptic's position in a nut shell. Is this statement itself true or not? If it is true, then it is not true, and the sceptic is refuted (and if it is not true, the sceptic is equally refuted). This is a simple argument based on self-reference,[51] and there are at least two well known ways to avoid it. One could say, like an academic sceptic, that all statements are false except the statement that all statements are false, somewhat like the case of Socrates who was considered the wisest of men because he was the only one who knew that he did not know. One could also say, like the Pyrrhonists, that all statements are false, and that the above statement is equally false, but the sceptic does not commit the fallacy of self-refutation, because he does not assert anything.

There are many ways to use a language, and assertion or affirmation is only one of them. The Greek sceptics used a great variety of terms for utterances which are not to be taken as asserting truth or expressing propositions. One can, for instance, report as a chronicler, or say something indicative of one's state of mind, or be inclined to believe, or acquiesce in and accept (in words) what appears, or even talk without a definite frame of reference.[52] Similarly, the Mādhyamikas developed the distinction between *paryudāsa-* and *prasajyapratiṣedha*[53], the first being a negation which affirms its opposite, the second being merely a negation which does not affirm anything at all.

Nāgārjuna must have been confronted with similar objections of self-refutation against his *Mūlamadhyamakakārikā*, and composed probably for this reason the *Vigrahavyāvartanī* to clarify the epistemological status of his arguments in the *MMK*. Very much like the Pyrrhonists he insists that he has no thesis (*pratijñā*) of his own, and that his statements are as void as his opponents' statements, for they are illusory as a magical trick. If any value is to be attributed to his writings, it is, I am tempted to say, not logical, but therapeutical; like an artificial person who prevents someone from taking an artificial woman for a real woman.[54] Nāgārjuna would probably agree with the Greek sceptics who compared their scepticism to a medicine which purges itself.

One could go into more and more details, but I think it is clear by now that sceptics both in India and in Europe were charged with certain forms of the fallacy of self-refutation, and that in both traditions this charge is mainly due to a misunderstanding of the sceptic's use of language and of his frame of mind.

Unfortunately, Jayarāśi does not say anything directly about his use of language, nor anything about the epistemological or logical status of his arguments. However, as I observed elsewhere,[55] he often seems to contradict himself, and the contradictions are sometimes so blatant, that it would be highly improbable to assume that he was unaware of them. I suggested, and I still think it is true, that all of Jayarāśi's statements or announcements or utterances are contextually bound, and are formulated against specific theories which he happens to deal with in a given context. Thus, if the opponent says "black," Jayarāśi says "white," and when another opponent says "white," Jayarāśi claims "black." If we combine two such passages, it may seem that he maintains both black and white, but this is unlikely in view of his elaborate arguments to refute both positions. I would rather interpret it as if he affirms neither, and that "black" means "white is not the case," or better, "you do not have sufficient reason for white, black is equally possible," and vice versa.

When we deal with specific theories, and when the context is well determined, this interpretation has the advantage to solve a number of riddles, but should we apply it as a matter of principle to every statement made by Jayarāśi? If we do so, it follows that no statement of Jayarāśi has any validity or truth or even meaning (for meaning depends on intention) outside the specific context, and even the specific time at which it was made. Perhaps the only thing that could be said about it is that it is indicative of Jayarāśi's state of mind at the time of the composition of the specific parts of the *TUS* in question. If this is accepted, then we are not in a position to make any generalization about Jayarāśi.

There are certain points in which Jayarāśi's scepticism seems unique of its kind. For instance, we usually tend to associate scepticism with doubt. The Oxford dictionary, for example, defines skepsis as philosophical doubt, and many Western sceptics considered that their professional activity consisted mainly in raising doubts. In a more personal vein I may add that in my mother tongue the word for "sceptic" is not "inquirer," but "doubter." Jayarāśi, however, argues in § 1.2 that there are no doubtful cognitions. Cognitions are either right or wrong, or even both, but never doubtful. Should we conclude that Jayarāśi does not allow doubtful cognitions in general? Or should we consider that his arguments intend only the Nyāya theory of certain doubtful cognitions which have to be excluded from the realm of the definition of perception, for the context of the discussion is formed by the word "*vyavasāyātmaka*" in *NS* 1.1.4?

Suppose that we find elsewhere in the book that Jayarāśi says "I doubt whether P because of Q or because of R." We would then tend to conclude either that his terminology is not rigorous or that his arguments against doubtful cognitions are not meant generally, but are intended only against specific doubtful cognitions of the Nyāya, say, only those which arise from a contact between sense and object.[66] But what if we do not have counterexamples? Should we then conclude that arguments adduced on certain topics are to represent Jayarāśi's thought in general? Surely, the absence of counterexamples in the *TUS* may be due to chance. This does not exclude, of course, the possibility that some statements were intended in a general manner (and those we suspect of being such are, of course, those which are repeated often enough, such as the statement that cognitions terminate in their own objects)[67]; but how are we to tell which is which? I am afraid that we are not in a better position than Clitomachus, Carneades' most assiduous student and his successor at the head of the Academy, who is said to have affirmed that he had never been able to find out what Carneades' own views were.[68]

At the present state of our knowledge, I think, we have no choice but to leave these questions open. We know no more about Jayarāśi than we would have known about Nāgārjuna, if all his works save the *MMK* were lost. Some day, I hope, further manuscripts of Jayarāśi's work shall be discovered and will shed new light on these and many other problems which remain unsolved. At the present we can only provide a general answer to the general question we asked above.

There are many ways in which sceptics can avoid the charge of self-refutation. The refusal to generalize is one of them, and even if it was not the one intended by Jayarāśi, we can safely assume that he was well acquainted with this problem and with the Madhyamaka response to it. Could it be that Jayarāśi did not deal with the charge of self-refutation, because he thought that it was already solved in a satisfactory manner by the *Prāsaṅgika-Mādhyamikas?[59]

I would like to conclude this introduction by considering another objection which is often raised against scepticism, namely, that scepticism may be logically coherent, but psychologically or practically impossible. In other words, can a sceptic live his scepticism? Non-sceptic philosophers repeatedly said that he could not, and the argument is probably as old as scepticism itself. Already the Epicurean philosopher Colotes wrote against his contemporary, the sceptic Arcesilas, a polemical tract called "On the fact that the doctrines of other philosophers make it impossible to live," claiming that a total *epoche* must result in total inaction. Galen asked whether a sceptic should stay in bed all day because he is uncertain whether it is day or night, or whether a sceptic should remain on board of a ship wondering whether what appears to be land really is land.[60] With the rediscovery of Sextus Empiricus' writings in the 16th century such arguments appeared again on the philosophical scene, and are repeated even today due to the lasting influence of Hume.[61] In his *Enquiry Concerning Human Understanding* (XII, 128) Hume says, rather dogmatically, that "he (the sceptic) must acknowledge, if he will acknowledge anything, that all human life must perish, were his principles universally and steadily to prevail. All discourse, all action would immediately cease; and men remain in total lethargy, till the necessities of nature, unsatisfied, put an end to their miserable existence. It is true; so fatal an event is very little to be dreaded. Nature is always too strong for principle ..."

There are several surprising things in this argument. It is surprising that it should come from the mouth of one of the greatest sceptics of modern philosophy. It is also surprising because Hume knew his Sextus Empiricus, and the *Outlines of Pyrrhonism* contain a detailed discussion of this problem. The sceptic does not cease to act, nor do his actions betray any belief. On the contrary, the sceptic acts because of bodily drives such as hunger and thirst, because of impressions, because of upbringing in a special society, etc.[62]

Astonishingly enough, the argument of practical impossibility of scepticism seems never to have been employed in Indian philosophy, whereas in European philosophy it is even more common than the argument of self-refutation. Why do we find that in similar philosophical contexts this argument is constantly repeated in one culture, and is completely lacking in another? This state of affairs may be partly due to the fact that Indian philosophers resorted rarely to personal sarcastic remarks.[63] But there is more to the matter. One of the advantages in studying a philosophical tradition which is not our own is that it helps us to see false associations, both ours and those of different civilizations. We all have a tendency to categorize, and to assume, consciously or unconsciously, that certain things go together naturally and necessarily; fortunately, however, different cultures categorize differently, and by comparing and contrasting different ways of thinking we have a chance of learning more about ourselves.

To go back to our subject matter here, as soon as we observe that the argument of the practical impossibility of scepticism is culturally bound, we realize not that Indian philosophers were too dull to think about it (as is clear from the *Kus*. cf. n. 63), but rather that it is neither obvious nor immanent to the nature of scepticism. We are then in a position to find out what affected the false association. When we look at the refutation of scepticism from this point of view, it is not hard to discover that they all presuppose (wrongly) that action is necessarily preceded by knowledge or by the belief that one knows. In India, on the other hand, this necessary connection between action and knowledge or belief in knowledge was not maintained. Not that the Indian epistemologists were cognitive anarchists; on the contrary, valid cognition, they claimed, will enable us to act successfully, to obtain objects we desire, and avoid or get rid of objects we distaste. But the assumption of knowledge was not considered a *conditio sine qua non* for action as such. In Indian "anthropology" action may follow upon desire, repulsion, delusion, doubt, disposition (*saṃskāra*), etc., alone,[64] and this is much more convincing than the connection between action and knowledge.

Thus, the real issue is not whether the sceptic can act or not, for he obviously can and does, nor whether the quest for knowledge is something desirable or not, for the sceptic agrees that it is. The trouble is that so far we have not reached this aim. In my opinion, the real issue is how to face and react to the lack of certainty in all matters from everyday life to religious beliefs and scientific theories. Should we suspend judgment on all matters, hold merely uncommitted opinions, accept higher and lesser probabilities, or take certain things to be true although the evidence at hand is surely not beyond doubt? Does scepticism stop with the conclusion that we do not know anything, or does it also provide some indications as to how life should go on after the sceptical conclusions are fully realized?

Different sceptics give, of course, different answers; as for Jayarāśi, he has little to say on this matter, but significantly enough he starts and ends his book with it. The *TUS* starts with the quotation of a verse which Jayarāśi attributes to those who know the absolute truth, or alternatively, to those who know the highest aim of life (*paramārthavid*). (Again, does this imply a knowledge claim, or is it a mere honorific?) According to this quotation the worldly path should be followed; the wise and the fool, or the learned and the ignorant, are similar in respect to everyday life. Matilal rightly points out that "One cannot miss an unintentional echo of Sextus in this comment: 'We live in accordance with the normal rules of life, undogmatically, seeing that we cannot remain wholly inactive.'"[65]

However, things are not so obvious. The above verse on the wise and the fool is not Jayarāśi's, and I do not even think that it comes from another Lokāyata work, as is sometimes assumed. But even if it came from a Lokāyata source, one would expect it to presuppose a materialistic, not sceptic point of view. What exactly is the similarity between the wise and the fool? Is it only that the wise and the fool behave alike in everyday life? Or do they behave alike because they are also similar in their ignorance and/or in their ability to manage in everyday life?

Vyomaśiva quotes twice the second half of this verse (if indeed it is a verse as Sanghavi and Parikh assume); in both cases it is quoted as a maxim (*nyāya*), and in both cases it is introduced into the discussion by a Buddhist opponent. It seems, therefore, that Jayarāśi is not quoting from a Lokāyata source, but is only referring to popular wisdom, and the assumption that it is a Buddhist saying has some probability in its favour.[66] Now, by looking at the context in the *Vyomavatī*, we can obtain some clues as to how this maxim was interpreted. In the first case it is used by a Buddhist who rejects the reality of the external world, but nevertheless undertakes actions such as bathing etc. He explains that "just as the common people act in as much as they apprehend the external objects because of ignorance, in the same way the inquiring people too [act] because, as the maxim says, in respect to everyday practice the wise and the fool are similar."[67] The second passage in which the maxim is quoted deals with the fact that words do not denote real objects. The interpretation of the maxim is basically the same (the wise knows about it, but nevertheless reacts upon verbal communication), but in addition it is stated that the activity is successful in some cases, just as in the case of a person who mistakes diamond-rays for the diamond itself, but is nevertheless successful in obtaining the diamond.[68]

In both contexts it is clearly implied that the wise, or the intelligent person, knows better, but nevertheless, for some unspecified reason, acts like the fool, as if wisdom did not bear upon everyday life. This, of course, could not have been Jayarāśi's interpretation of the maxim, for he does not think that the wise knows better. Or perhaps the sceptic takes the role of the wise, for Jayarāśi would agree with the Buddhist that everyday practice is without epistemic foundation. The wisdom in this case would consist in the understanding that all principles are annihilated. When this stage is reached (by the examination of the definitions of the means of knowledge), the wordly path is not only something which has to be followed by lack of choice (as in the above quotation from Sextus), but it becomes something delightful. This is how the book ends: "Thus, when the principles are completely annihilated, all everyday practice (or: all thinking, speaking and acting) can be delightful in as much as it no [longer has to be] deliberated" - *tad evam upapluteṣv eva tattveṣv avicārita-ramaṇīyāḥ sarve vyavahārā ghaṭanta iti.*[69]

There is a curious inversion which many sceptics report to have undergone. The sceptic starts with a search for truth and knowledge hoping that by obtaining them he will make his life better or happier; failing to obtain what he has set out to find he becomes disheartened, desperate, and inclined to dismiss everything as futile. But then at some point he realizes that the lack of knowledge can become the source of better life or happiness which he originally sought to obtain through knowledge. This sort of inversion is so often reported by European and Chinese sceptics, that I would like to assume a similar process for Jayarāśi as well. Perhaps he started as a traditional Lokāyatika hoping or believing that the materialistic principles could provide a firm basis for improving one's life in this (as opposed to the next) world. Gradually becoming aware that the materialistic principles, as well as all other principles, cannot bear a serious examination, he came to realize that the happy life which was traditionally promised by the Lokāyata[70] could be reached without taking the Lokāyata principles into the bargain, or even only without them.

One more thing in this connection: Granted that the wordly path or everyday practice should be followed, the question still remains which of the many practices should be followed.

European sceptics and men of letters with sceptical inclination were more often than not conservative. The reason for this is obvious, for never being sure of anything the sceptic should hesitate, act cautiously, and distrust any radical program for social reform. Of course, there is no innate relation between scepticism and conservatism; one can easily imagine a sceptic anywhere on the political spectrum except in those extremes where people think they know better not only for themselves, but also for you and me. However, the sceptic tendency to passivity is sometimes considered dangerous, for unable to fight for a principle (which he does not hold) the sceptic may become an instrument for criminal deeds. How would a sceptic behave under a totalitarian regime? Arguing against the Ethicists Sextus replies to the following dilemma: Should a sceptic become a subject of a tyrant and be compelled to do something despicable, he would either follow the natural impulse to save his skin and meekly surrender, or choose to die under torture, but then his behaviour will betray that he does hold on to some principle, and thus he would be no longer a sceptic. Sextus rejects the dilemma and says that the sceptic may choose either course of action according to his preconceptions which are due to ancestral laws and customs. However, he adds, it would be easier for the sceptic to oppose the tyrant, because unlike the dogmatist the sceptic does not have beyond the actual physical pain additional beliefs about suffering being evil etc.[71]

Now, if we apply the same question to Jayarāśi, where would he stand? Posed in these terms, surely the question cannot be raised, for political matters are never discussed in Indian philosophical texts. However, if we define conservatism in terms of *varṇāśramadharma*, Jayarāśi will have a clear stand, for he was after all a Lokāyatika. We saw above that Jayarāśi rejected some of the traditional Lokāyata doctrines, and interpreted some of the *sūtras* of Bṛhaspati as reflecting opinions which are not Bṛhaspati's own. But not all *sūtras* were submitted to this reinterpretation. Throughout the *TUS* Jayarāśi quotes two *sūtras* which represent in his opinion the true thought of Bṛhaspati and with which he agrees wholeheartedly. These are: *śarīrād eva* - "[Consciousness arises] from the body alone," and *paralokino 'bhāvāt paralokābhāvaḥ* - "There is no other world, because there is no [soul] which [transmigrates] to the other world." The purport of these *sūtras* is clear. They are not concerned with the problem of soul or consciousness per se, rather they form an attempt to remove the metaphysical foundations of ethical theories which claim that moral and immoral deeds bring about their corresponding results after death. Thus, in spite of the enormous differences in ontology and theory of knowledge, in ethical matters and in anti-clerical attitude, which formed the hard core of the Lokāyata, Jayarāśi remained a true heir to Bṛhaspati.

Notes to the Introduction

[1] This, of course, is only partly true. Nāgārjuna's scepticism is incomparably better studied than Jayarāśi's, and we are in a position to start evaluating its influence on other schools of thought. For an attempt to analyze Nāgārjuna's influence on Dignāga cf. Franco, "Once again on Dharmakīrti's deviation from Dignāga on *pratyakṣābhāsa*."

[2] Cf. *TUS*, preface.

[3] Cf. Ruben, "Über den Tattvopaplavasiṃha des Jayarāśi Bhaṭṭa, eine agnostizistische Erkenntniskritik"; Dixit, "The Ideological Affiliation of Jayarāśi, the Author of the Tattvopaplavasiṃha."

[4] Cf. *TUS*, introduction pp. XI-XII.

[5] Cf. *TUS* p. 125.13-14 quoted on p. 7.

[6] Cf. n. 6 on the translation.

[7] Cf. *TUS* p. XII.

[8] Ruben, ibid., p. 140, n. 5. To these we may add Jayatilleke's somewhat strange interpretation of reflecting as "indirectly referring to," cf. *Early Buddhist Theory of Knowledge*, p. 81.

[9] Cf. *SVṬ* p. 277.19f., *PrP* p. 62.12f., *Tattvārthaślokavārttika* p. 80 (not available to me, quoted in *TUS* p. VII): *tattvopaplavavādinaḥ paraparyanuyogamātraparatvād iti kaścit*.

[10] The metaphor of reflecting may have been borrowed by Jayarāśi from the Sāṅkhyas who use it to explain the relationship between *buddhi* and *puruṣa*. The consciousness of the *puruṣa* is reflected in the *buddhi*, which seems therefore to be conscious itself. In other words, just as the reflexion of consciousness in the *buddhi* may cause us to

attribute erroneously the consciousness of the *puruṣa* to the *buddhi*, the reflexion of the principles in the *Bṛhaspatisūtra* causes us to attribute to Bṛhaspati principles which are not his own. Note also that the word "reflexion" has strong connotations of error in Sanskrit (cf. for instance *MMK* 23.9), and one of the stock examples for error is the reflexion of the moon in water.

[11] I am not quite sure what Jayarāśi means by *mahārthodaya*. If something of great significance is promised to the reader as the outcome of reading a philosophical book, this usually means liberation, as for instance in the *maṅgalaśloka* of the *PDhS*: ... *padārthadharmasaṅgrahaḥ pravakṣyate mahodayaḥ*. On this Śrīdhara remarks (ad loc., p. 6.7f.): *mahān udayo mahat phalam apavargalakṣaṇaṃ yasmāt saṅgrahād asau mahodayaḥ saṅgrahaḥ*. Such a promise could certainly not be made by Jayarāśi. I am not sure whether he is not merely ironical, mocking such promises which are perhaps too lightly given, or whether he had something positive in mind. If the latter is the case, then this promise should probably be connected to the conclusion of the book (p. 125.11-12), namely, that when the principles are annihilated, all everyday practice becomes delightful.

[12] Cf. "Studies in *TUS* I," p. 148.

[13] Cf. Franco, "The *Paurandarasūtra*."

[14] Cf. *TUS* pp. IV-XI.

[15] Cf. Frauwallner, "Landmarks in the History of Indian Logic," pp. 137-38 = Kl. Schr. pp. 859-60.

[16] Cf. *SVṬ*, Hindi Introduction, pp. 28-29 (the main arguments are summarized in the English Introduction, pp. 42-43).

[17] Cf. Lindtner, "Apropos Dharmakīrti - Two New Works and a New Date."

[18] Cf. Frauwallner, "Kumārila's Bṛhaṭṭīkā," pp. 87-90 = Kl. Schr. pp. 332-35.

[19] Cf. *Encyclopedia of Indian Philosophies*, Vol. I, pp. 193, 209.

[20] Cf. Sanghavi, "Tattvopaplavasiṃha - Cārvākdarśan kā ek apūrv granth," Bhāratīya Vidyā, Vol. II,1 . This paper is not available to me; it is referred to by Mahendrakumar, SVṬ, Hindi Introduction, p. 28.

[21] Cf. *TR* p. XXXIII.

[22] These quotation have been identified by Bühnemann in "Tarkarahasya and Vādarahasya." Note that since Bühnemann has written her paper the *Vādarahasya* was edited by R.N. Pandey (Delhi 1984) under the erroneous title *Udayananirākaraṇa*. The attribution of the text to Ratnakīrti is highly doubtful.

[23] Among the Jaina works we may add the *Pramāṇaparīkṣā* (cf. *PrP* p. 62), and *Nyāyakumudacandra* (cf. *NKC* index, Vol. II, p. 919). It is probable that Jayanta as well knew Jayarāśi, but so far I have found no conclusive reference. Certain formulations, however, are very close; compare for instance *TUS* p. 125.11-12: *upapluteṣv eva tattveṣv avicāritaramaṇīyāḥ sarve vyavahārā ghaṭanta iti* with *NM* I p. 317. 10: *avicāritaramaṇīyataiva tattvaṃ, na tu lakṣaṇaniyamaḥ* ...; *ĀD* p. 60.17-18: *tad ayam avicārita eva ramaṇīyo vyavahāraḥ. etad eva ca tattvam iti tattvavidaḥ.*

[24] To these three Matilal adds Sañjaya as a forerunner, cf. *Logical and Ethical Issues of Religious Belief*, ch. 3.2.

[25] Cf. for instance nn. 75, 102, 121, 184, 330, 334 etc. on the translation.

[26] Cf. also *TUS* p. IV-V: "Chandraprabhasūri, in his Prabhāvaka-charita, chapter 16, mentions that the poet Dharma of the Kaula sect and a native of Broach had a dialectical duel with the great Jaina dialectician Śānti Sūri of Aṇahillapura Pattan and that he used the arguments taken from the TP (=*TUS*) for this purpose [verses 97, 101-2; Nirnaya Sagar Press ed. pp. 221-22]."

[27] Collingwood, *An Autobiography*, p. 44.

[28] Cf. *Vibhramaviveka*, p. 147.

[29] Cf. Frauwallner, "Beiträge zur Geschichte des Nyāya. I. Jayanta und seine Quellen."

[30] Cf. Wezler, "Zur Identität der 'Ācāryāḥ' und 'Vyākhyātāraḥ' in Jayantabhaṭṭas Nyāyamañjarī," pp. 137f.; Steinkellner, "Die Literatur des älteren Nyāya," p. 160.

[31] Granoff (*Philosophy and Argument in late Vedānta*, p. 53) is of a different opinion, as she claims that "Jayarāśi also uses fictitious *pūrvapakṣas* ... (see p. 18, l. 4; p. 19, l. 7ff.; p. 30; 34, l. 13; 35; 36; 49, l. 1; 51; 59, etc.)." I cannot undertake here a discussion of each of the passages she refers to; the reader is invited to check my notes on them and find out for himself whether the *pūrvapakṣas* are fictitious or not.
I do not mean, of course, that every single *vikalpa* must have an opponent behind it. Especially in the case of such

vikalpas as "Is A different from B or not?" or "Is A real or not?", one should not automatically assume (though sometimes it may be the case) that Jayarāśi has two opponents in mind, the one claiming that A is different from B, the other that it is not different. This kind of *vikalpa* is obviously a tool of philosophical analysis.

[32] Cf. "Studies in *TUS* I."

[33] Cf. *ŚBh* p. 26.1-21: *tatsamprayoge puruṣasyendriyāṇāṃ buddhijanma sat pratyakṣam.* 4a. *yadviṣayaṃ jñānaṃ, tenaiva samprayoga indriyāṇāṃ puruṣasya buddhijanma sat pratyakṣam. yad anyaviṣayaṃ jñānam anyasamprayoge bhavati, na tat pratyakṣam. - kathaṃ punar idam avagamyata "idaṃ tatsamprayoga, idam anyasamprayoga" iti? - yan nānyasamprayoge, tat tatsamprayoga, etadviparītam anyasamprayoga iti. - kathaṃ jñāyate? yadā hi śuktikāyām api rajataṃ manyamāno "rajatasannikṛṣṭaṃ me cakṣur" iti manyate. - bādhakaṃ hi yatra jñānam utpadyate "naitad evaṃ, mithyājñānam idam" iti, tad anyasamprayoge, viparītaṃ tatsamprayoga iti. - prāg bādhakajñānotpatteḥ katham avagamyate, yadā na tatkāle samyagjñānasya mithyājñānasya ca kaścid viśeṣaḥ? - yadā kṣudādibhir upahataṃ mano bhavati, indriyaṃ vā timirādibhiḥ, saukṣmyādibhir vā bāhyo viṣayas, tato mithyājñānam, anupahateṣu samyagjñānam. indriyamanorthasannikarṣo hi jñānasya hetur, asati tasminn ajñānāt. tadantargato doṣo mithyājñānasya hetuḥ. duṣṭeṣu hi jñānaṃ mithyā bhavati. - katham avagamyate? - doṣāpagame sampratipattidarśanāt. - kathaṃ duṣṭāduṣṭāvagama iti cet, - prayatnenānvicchanto na ced doṣam upalabhemahi, pramāṇābhāvād aduṣṭam iti manyemahi. tasmād yasya ca duṣṭaṃ karaṇaṃ yatra ca mithyeti pratyayaḥ, sa evāsamīcīnaḥ pratyayo nānya iti.*

[34] Cf. "Studies in *TUS* I," p. 165, n. 12.

[35] Cf. Schmithausen, *Vibhramaviveka*, p. 158.

[36] The following passage is also translated by Jayatilleke, op. cit., p. 87. The translation presented here differs in several points.

[37] Matilal, op. cit., p. 57, interprets this passage differently: "The *Pramāṇa* theorist may claim that the sensory experience is itself the evidence on the basis of which we can infer its special character, i.e., its truth or non-promiscuity with the facts. Jayarāśi rejects this by saying that it begs the question. For inference itself is another means of knowledge, and of course, the same question as regards its infallibility can be raised again." Jayatilleke's translation of this argument (ibid., p. 87) is not entirely clear to me: "Is not (then) this very knowledge the basis, which gives rise to the knowledge of its excellence? If so, the mutual dependence results in a difficulty. And what is it? A suspicion of defect in a cogni-

tion which arises in dependence on the virtues and defects of the senses, is not dispelled as in the case of a consciousness of sound produced by the effort of a person."

[38] For a different interpretation of this sentence cf. Matilal, op. cit., p. 58: " ...the lack of such a contradiction may (in a way) be a pointer to the possibility of such a contradiction."

[39] Cf. ŚV, *Vṛttikāragrantha* 23.

[40] Cf. ŚVV p. 193.19-23.

[41] Cf. *NS* 4.2.6f.

[42] According to Jayarāśi the opponent maintains that there is some sort of struggle even in the case of a **valid** cognition, i.e., a valid cognition has a certain kind of influence which pervents or obstructs its sublation. Moreover, this obstruction has to go on even after the cognition is destroyed, as if the *pradhvaṃsābhāva* (absence by destruction) of the cognition exercises such an influence which prevents the arising of a sublating cognition for a valid cognition. This theory is explicitly rejected by Bhāsarvajña (*NBhū* p. 37.3f.) who accuses Jayarāśi of attributing to his opponent theories which he does not hold. According to Bhāsarvajña, there can be no obstruction for the production of sublation, and, further, it is impossible that a cognition and its destruction (or absence) should obstruct the same thing.

[43] Cf. ŚV, *Vṛttikāragrantha* 24.

[44] The text is corrupted here, but the argument may be reconstructed from the parallel passages, cf. n. 15 on the translation.

[45] Cf. *PV pratyakṣa* 57.

[46] This is a quotation from *ŚBh* p. 26.9-10, quoted above n. 33.

[47] Cf. *PrP* p. 62.15-17: *teṣāṃ tattvopaplavamātram iṣṭaṃ sādhayituṃ, tadā sādhanam abhyupagantavyam. tac ca pramāṇam eva bhavati. tathā cedam abhidhīyate - tattvopaplavavādino 'py asti pramāṇam iṣṭasādhanānyathānupapatteḥ. pramāṇābhāve 'piṣṭasiddhau sarvaṃ sarvasya yatheṣṭaṃ sidhyed ity anupaplutatattvasiddhir api kiṃ na syāt sarvathā viśeṣābhāvāt.*

[48] Cf. Collingwood, *An Essay on Philosophical Method*, p. 140.

[49] Note, however, that Uddyotakara's purpose in *NV* 1.2.3 is not to refute scepticism, but to justify the presence of

the word *sthāpanā* in the *sūtra*. For his direct refutation of scepticism cf. *NV* 2.1.12-13.

[50] Cf. Popkin, *History of Scepticism*, p. 200.

[51] On self-reference and self-refutation cf. Passmore, *Philosophical Reasoning*, ch. 4.

[52] For an analysis and explanation of these terms cf. Naess, *Scepticism*, pp. 7-12.

[53] Cf. Kajiyama, "Three Kinds of Affirmation and two Kinds of Negation in Buddhist Philosophy," pp. 167-73.

[54] Cf. *VV* v. 27, cf. also v. 23.

[55] Cf. "Studies in *TUS* II," pp. 127f.

[56] This is how Bhāsarvajña must have understood the *TUS*, cf. *NBhū* p. 34.22: *na mayā pramāṇaṃ kvacid ucyate sarvatra sandehamātrapradarśanād iti*. "I do not pronounce [any] means of valid cognition anywhere, because everywhere [I] point out only doubt." Note also that a modern sceptic like Naess thinks that the sceptic must not doubt (cf. Naess, op. cit., pp. 53-54).

[57] Cf. *paryavasāyin* and *paryavasita* in the index.

[58] Cf. Cicero, *Academica* II 139, and Striker, "Sceptical Strategies," p. 55.

[59] Cf. *PrP* p. 63.1-2: *paraparyanuyogaparāṇi hi bṛhaspateḥ sūtrāṇiti vacanāt sarvatra svātantryābhāvād iti*. But this, of course, is no more than a hint.

[60] Cf. Burnyeat, "Can the Sceptic live his Scepticism?"

[61] For instance Strawson, *Skepticism and Naturalism*, pp. 14-17 and passim.

[62] Cf. *Outlines of Pyrrhonism* I. 23-24.

[63] This generalization has its exceptions. For instance Udayana says (*Kus* 3.6 p. 373.5-7) that a Cārvāka, who does not believe what he does not see, would not go back home after he has left the house, but rather should mourn his son, wife, etc., because he ascertains their inexistence when he does not see them. However, the argument is not intended against a Cārvāka sceptic, but a Cārvāka materialist. And the point of the argument is based on the fact that the Cārvāka materialist admits sense perception, and only sense perception, as means of knowledge. For as soon as the Cārvāka materialist admits sense perception, he cannot avoid such consequences without having recourse to some

form of reasoning. The case is perhaps similar to some forms of Academic scepticism which Sextus accuses of being covert dogmatism, for as soon as the sceptic will claim to **know** that nothing is known, he will have to explain how he does know it, and will have to make more and more knowledge claims. For as soon as you make one step into the epistemological pond you are bound to get all wet; the only way to remain dry is to keep clear off the water.

64 Cf. *CS śārīrasthāna* 5.10 p. 781.1: *mohecchādveṣakarmamūlā pravṛttiḥ*; cf. also *NBh* 1.1.18, 4.1.2; *NBhū* p. 43.2-4: *pravṛttir api puruṣasyābhilāṣādipūrvikārthaprāptyanarthaparihārānuṣṭhānalakṣaṇā bhavanti prāyeṇa pramāṇatadābhāsavivekaniścayaṃ nāpekṣate*; *NBṬ* p. 13.4: *saṃśayāc ca pravartante. arthasaṃśayo 'pi hi pravṛttyaṅgaṃ prekṣāvatām*; *NKan* p. 681.12-13: *kleśavāsanopanibaddhā hi pravṛttayaḥ*. Cf. also below p. 124.4-7 and *Kus* p. 372.24-26.

65 Cf. Matilal, op. cit., p. 59.

66 Cf. *TR* p. 35.10-12, quoted in n. 4 on the translation.

67 Cf. *Vy* p. 526.26-28: *yathā hy aparīkṣakā bāhyam artham avidyāvaśāt pratipadyamānāḥ pravartante tadvat parīkṣakā apīti "lokavyavahāraṃ prati sadṛśau bālapaṇḍitāv" iti nyāyāt.*

68 Cf. *Vy* p. 585.8-12. The example of the diamond-ray (l. 11-12) is a quotation of *PV pratyakṣa* 57.

69 Cf. *TUS* p. 125.11-12. Note that the expression *avicāritaramaṇīya* is used pejoratively in non-Cārvāka texts, cf. e.g., *PP* p. 373.1

70 As for instance in the famous half-verse (*SDS* p. 14.5 etc.):

yāvaj jīvet sukhaṃ jīved, ṛṇaṃ kṛtvā ghṛtaṃ pibet/

71 Cf. *Against the Ethicists* 160-67 and Naess, op. cit., p. 65.

Content and analysis of the text

The purpose of the analysis is to give the reader a quick glimpse of the structure of the work and of the subjects discussed. To make it less cumbersome I sometimes summarized only the thesis of a given section, not its conclusion. In other words, many of the statements in the analysis represent the *pūrvapakṣa* which is rejected by Jayarāśi. Any division of a text which originally contained none must remain to some extent arbitrary. In the broad division into chapters I follow Sanghavi and Parikh. The division within the chapters is my own.

Numbers on the left side of the point indicate chapters; letters on the left side of the point indicate digressions or appendices. Numbers on the right side of the point indicate a linear train of thought; letters on the right side of the point indicate aspects.
Example: 1.11 and 1.12 convey direct reasons to the statement of 1.1; 1.1a considers the statement of 1.1 from a different point of view. In order to save space the numbers appear in the text alone; the correspondence with the translation, however, should be easily discerned even by non-Sanskritist.

0. Introduction

0.1 The thesis of the book: All principles are annihilated; actions bear no result such as heaven etc.; the wordly path should be followed.

0.2 There is no contradiction between the book and the *Bṛhaspatisūtra*. The latter does not establish any principles, but merely reflects common believes spread among the people.

0.3 The principles are not established, because there are no correct definitions of valid means of knowledge.

1. Examination of the Nyāya definition of perception

1.1 Examination of the word nonerroneous (*avyabhicārin*)

1.11 Nonerroneousness is due to production by faultless causes (*aduṣṭakāraka*).

1.12 Nonerroneousness is known by absence of sublation (*bādhā*).

1.12a The absence of sublation depends neither on all people nor on the perceiver alone.

1.13 Nonerroneousness is known by the efficiency of the activity (*pravṛttisāmarthya*).

1.13a Specification: nonerroneousness of a water cognition is known by obtaining water;

1.13a1 by obtaining the water which appeared in the cognition;

1.13a2 by obtaining water which belongs to the same universal.

a. Digression: refutation of the universal

a.1 The universal is identical with the individuals.

a.2 The universal is different from the individuals.

a.2a Since the universal 'water' is ubiquitous, a cognition of water would be established by obtaining a cow etc.

a.2b The plurality of individual waters is not established; thus, there is no universal 'water' which differentiates them from other individuals.

a.2c The universal does not exist because something eternal cannot produce its cognition.

a.2d The universal is not proved by similarities among individuals.

a.3 The universal is both different and non-different from the individuals.

b. Digression: refutation of inherence (*samavāya*)

b.1 Inherence can be neither of distinct (*vyāvṛtta*) nor of recurrent (*anugata*) nature.

b.2 Inherence is not apprehended by perception:

b.21 neither by a cognition of relation,

b.22 nor by the cognition 'here' (in the threads there is a cloth),

b.23 nor by the cognition of inherence.

b.3 Inherence is not apprehended by inference.

1.13a3 Nonerroneousness of a water cognition is known by obtaining water which arises in the same series (*tadvaṃśaja-*).

1.13b Efficiency of activity can function neither as perception nor as inference.

1.14 Nonerroneousness is known by the cognition itself.

1.141 Nonerroneousness is a property (*dharma*) of the cognition.

1.142 Nonerroneousness is the cognition's own nature (*svarūpa*).

1.14a Nonerroneousness is not apprehended, because the cognition itself is not apprehended.

1.1a The word 'nonerroneous' is superfluous in the definition because of the word 'contact between sense and object' (*indriyārthasannikarṣa*).

1.1a1 The sun rays are the external object of a false cognition of water,

1.1a2 because one goes towards the place of the sun rays.

1.1b The word 'nonerroneous' is superfluous, because it cannot exclude cognitions of unreal objects.

1.1b1 Unreality = inexistence of the perceived object

1.1b2 Unreality = inexistence of the object is perceived

1.1ba Falsity of cognition is known by sublation (*bādhā*).

1.1ba1 The object is sublated.

1.1ba2 The cognition is sublated.

1.1baa-b The object of a false cognition produces the same efficient action (*arthakriyā*) as the object of a valid cognition.

c. Appendix: Examination of the theory of *smṛtipramoṣa*

1.2 The word 'which has the nature of determination' (*vyavasāyātmaka*) is useless in the definition, because there are no doubtful cognitions.

1.3 The word 'which cannot be designated' (*avyapadeśya*) is no good. (No discussion, just a reference to the *Lakṣaṇasāra*.)

1.4 The word 'which arises from contact between sense and object' (*indriyārthasannikarṣotpanna*) is not correct, because the production is not apprehended:

1.41 Production by contact is not apprehended.

1.42 Production by a sense is not apprehended.

1.43 Production by an object is not apprehended.

2. Examination of the Mīmāṃsā definition of means of valid cognition (*pramāṇa*) as agent of

apprehension of an unapprehended object (*an-adhigatārthagantṛ*)

2.1 The definition is not correct, because the first and second cognition of the same object are either both valid or both non-valid.

2.11 Recollection (*smṛti*) is the seventh means of valid cognition for the Mīmāṃsakas.

2.2 The definition is not correct, because inference would not be a *pramāṇa*.

2.21 The object of inference is a previously perceived universal 'fire'.

2.22 The object of inference is the nature of fire.

2.23 The object of inference is the possession (*matvartha*).

2.24 The object of inference is the existence of the universal at the time of inference.

2.25 The object of inference is the subordination of the universal to the inferential sign.

2.26 The object of inference is the dependence of the universal on the individual.

2.3 The definition is not correct, because the cognition of a word (*śabda*) would not be valid.

2.31 The substratum of a universal is not established by implication (*arthāpatti*).

2.4 The definition is not correct, because recognition would not be valid.

3. Examination of the Buddhist definition of means of valid cognition

3.1 The definition of *pramāṇa* as agent of apprehension of an unapprehended object (*anadhigatāthagantṛ*) excludes nothing, because no two cognitions have the same object:

3.11 neither two cognitions whose object is the particular,

3.12 nor two cognitions whose object is the universal.

3.1a The definition is not correct,

3.1a1 because two cognitions of the same object do not differ in their validity,

3.1a2 because the second cognition of the same object is another means of valid cognition.

3.2 *pramāṇa* defined as a cognition which does not belie its promise (*avisaṃvādin*)

3.21 *avisaṃvāda* = apprehension of an object as it really is

3.22 *avisaṃvāda* = absence of sublation

3.23 *avisaṃvāda* = production by the perceived object

3.24 *avisaṃvāda* = activity towards the perceived object

3.25 *avisaṃvāda* = obtaining the object

3.3 *pramāṇa* defined as twofold

3.31 Duality is not due to difference in individuals,

3.32 nor to difference in form,

3.33 nor to difference in object.

3.331 Examination of the object of inference

3.332 Examination of the object of perception

3.3a Duality is not established, because perception and inference do not apprehend one another.

4. Examination of the Buddhist definition of perception

4.1 Examination of the word 'conceptual construction' (*kalpanā*)

4.11 *kalpanā* = a cognition produced by qualifications such as quality, action, universal, etc.

4.12	*kalpanā* = a cognition which produces recollection
4.13	*kalpanā* has the nature of recollection.
4.14	*kalpanā* = a cognition produced by recollection
4.15	*kalpanā* = a cognition which appears as a blend of word and object
4.16	*kalpanā* = a cognition characterized by a word
4.17	*kalpanā* = a cognition with indistinct form
4.18	*kalpanā* has the nature of apprehension of an unreal object.
4.19	*kalpanā* itself is unreal.
4.1(10)	*kalpanā* is a cognition from a triform inferential sign.
4.1(10)a	Inference is conceptual construction, because it is indistinct.
4.1(10)a1	Indistinctness has been refuted in 4.17.
4.1(10)a2	Examination of vividness of perception
4.1(10)a21	Vividness = production by a particular
4.1(10)a22	Vividness = appearance of a particular
4.1(11)	*kalpanā* is an apprehension of a past or future object.
4.1a-d	Examination of *kalpanā* in other Buddhist propositions:
4.1a	Perception is free from conceptual construction, becaue it arises by the capacity of its object, just like a particular such as a visible etc.
4.1b	The conceptual cognition 'There is no pot on the ground' arises from the perception of the ground.
4.1c	The absence of conceptual construction is apprehended by perception.
4.1d	Conceptual construction is the cognition 'cow.'
4.1e	The form of conceptual construction is not beyond the form of cognition.

4.2	Examination of the word 'nonerroneous' (*avyabhicārin* = *abhrānta*)
4.21	Examination of unreality
4.211	Unreality = inexistence of the perceived
4.212	Unreality = inexistence itself is perceived
4.22	Examination of the object of a false cognition of water:
4.221	Object = water
4.222	Object = inexistence of water
4.223	Object = the cognition itself
4.224	Object = nothing at all
4.23	Examination of erroneousness
4.231	Erroneousness depends on the cognition alone.
4.232	Erroneousness depends on other causal factors.
4.24	Examination of validity
4.241	Validity depends on the cognition alone.
4.242	Validity depends on other causal factors.
4.25	Cognition and causality
4.251	Erroneous cognition produced by erroneous cognition
4.252	Erroneous cognition produced by nonerroneous cognition
4.25a	Cognition is not produced by its object: neither as an efficient cause, nor as a material cause.
4.25b	Cognition is not produced by its object: neither partly, nor entirely.
4.25c	The object does not produce the cognition: neither partly, nor entirely.
d.	Appendix: Critique of the Buddhist critique of the universal, the whole, etc.
d.1	The reductio ad absurdum of the residence (*vṛttivikalpadoṣa*) of the universal etc., in the individual etc., affects their relation alone, not the reality of the universal etc.

d.2 The non-apprehension of the universal in a place where the individual is not apprehended is no reason for its inexistence.

d.3 The non-apprehension of the universal when the individual is not apprehended is no reason for its inexistence (examination of empty subject terms).

d.4 The non-apprehension of the universal when the individual is seen for the first time is no reason for its inexistence.

d.5 The non-apprehension of the universal as distinct from the individual is no reason for its inexistence.

d.6 The universal is cognized by perception.

d.7 The universal produces efficient action both gradually and at once.

d.8 Rejection of the notion of commonness destroys Buddhist causality.

e. Appendix: Examination of the series of cognitions (*vijñānasantāna*)

e.1 The plurality of cognitions is not established.

e.2 If the cognition is real, the object is unreal, and vice versa.

e.3 Causality between cognitions is impossible, because a cognition stands in the same relation towards previous and posterior cognitions.

e.4 Causality between cognitions is impossible because of their momentary nature.

e.5 The first cognition in this life is not preceded by the la cognition in a previous life.

(4.) Conclusion

5. Examination of *Mīmāṃsāsūtra* 1.1.4

5.1 The *sūtra* considered as a definition of perception

5.11 The definition is not correct on grounds given in §§ 1.11-1.14.

5.12 The production of cognition by contact between sense and object cannot be known.

5.2 The *sūtra* considered as an enumeration of causal factors

5.3 The *sūtra* considered as a repetition

5.3a There is no motive for the repetition.

5.3b All valid cognitions apprehend an existent object.

5.a Examination of the part of the *sūtra* 'perception is production of cognition' (*buddhijanma*)

6. Examination of the Sāṅkhya definition of perception

6.1 Examination of the word 'functioning' (*vṛtti*)

6.11 If perception is the functioning of the senses, either false cognitions are included in the definition, or no cognition is excluded.

6.1a If the functioning is identical with the sense, an object would be perceived always or never.

6.1b Perception is impossible: neither of a perceptible object nor of a non-perceptible object.

6.2 The senses cannot be instruments of perception.

f. Appendix: Refutation of *prakṛti* and *puruṣa* based on *satkārya* causality

(0) General conclusion: Perception is not established as means of valid cognition.

The annotated translation presented here covers only the first half of the text (64 pages out of 125 in Sanghavi and Parikh's edition), which is devoted to the examination of perception and related topics. The remainder of the text deals almost exclusively with problems concerning inference. Sanghavi and Parikh divide it into the following chapters:

On the present edition

So far only a single manuscript of the *TUS* has been discovered. Sanghavi and Parikh (Introduction p. I) describe it as follows: "It consists of 176 leaves. Its length is 14" and breadth 1½". A few lines in the beginning and a few in the body of the work are illegible. It becomes clear from the colophon that the ms was copied in Samvat 1349 Marg. Vadi 11 Śanau (6th December 1292 A.D.) at Dholkā by Maham Narapāla. At the time Śāraṅgadeva (A.D. 1274-95) of the house of the Vāghelās was reigning."

Thanks to Dr D. Malvania I was able to obtain a microfilm of the manuscript in which, unfortunately, leaves 84-109 are missing. At the beginning I was reluctant to re-edit the text, for Sanghavi and Parikh have done an excellent job in deciphering the manuscript and have added some very useful conjectures. I do not think that any essential improvement on their work can be done before further manuscripts of the *TUS* will be discovered. However, many friends and colleagues have urged me to re-edit the text simply because it has long been out of print, and given the present policy of the GOS it is not likely to be reprinted in the foreseeable future. I therefore decided to re-edit the text for the reader's convenience.

However, this edition is not merely a reprint of the old one. By going back to the manuscript I was able to obtain some better readings, I corrected printing mistakes a few of which were misleading, added a number of new conjectures, pointed out possible lacunae, and took out some interpolations. On the whole I believe I present a more readable edition. It goes without saying that I do not offer a definitive critical edition, but only the best I could do with the available material.

TEXT & TRANSLATION

0.1 [S1, M1a][1]..*tāṃ muna ... tattvopaplavasiṃha eṣa viṣamo nūnaṃ mayā ...*[2]
... nāsti tatphalaṃ vā svargādi. satyaṃ, tāvad āttasya[3] *karmaṇaḥ sambhā ... uktaṃ ca paramārthavidbhir api -*

laukiko mārgo 'nusartavyaḥ a ...[4]/
lokavyavahāraṃ prati sadṛśau bālapaṇḍitau//

ityādi.

0.2 *nanu yady upaplavas tattvānāṃ kim āyā ...* [M1b]*athātas tattvaṃ vyākhyāsyāmaḥ. pṛthivy āpas tejo vāyur iti tattvāni. tatsamudāye śarīrendriyaviṣayasañjñetyādi. nānyārthatvāt. kimartham? pratibimbanārtham. kiṃ punar atra pratibimbyate? pṛthivyādīni tattvāni loke prasiddhāni. tāny api vicāryamāṇāni na vyavatiṣṭhante. kiṃ punar anyāni?*

0.3 *atha kathaṃ tāni na santi? tad ucyate - sallakṣaṇanibandhanaṃ*[5] *mānavyavasthānam. mānanibandhanā ca meyasthitiḥ. tadabhāve tayoḥ sadvyava-*

---

1 M refers to the Patan manuscript, S to the printed edition of Sanghavi and Parikh. Fol. 1a is broken at both ends, and one cannot even estimate the number of lost *akṣaras*. Roughly two thirds of the text are lost.

2 S conjectures [*sṛjyate*]

3 M: *tāvad ātasya*; S conjectures *etasya*

4 S: *a*[*ti?*]

5 M: °*vibadhanaṃ*

[Introduction]

This dreadful[1] [book], the lion of annihilation of [all] principles, was indeed [composed] by me ...
[Objection:] ... or it bears no fruit like heaven etc.[2]
[Reply:] True, of obtained karma ... . And even those who know the supreme reality[3] say:

> "The wordly path should be followed ...
> In respect to everyday practice the fool and the wise are similar."[4]

and so on.
[Objection:] If [all] principles are annihilated, isn't [there a contradiction with what Bṛhaspati says, namely] "Well, now we are going to explain the principles: Earth, water, fire and wind are the principles. The terms body, sense and object apply to their aggregates,"[5] and so on?
[Answer:] No, because [the *Bṛhaspatisūtra*] has another purpose.
[Question:] Which purpose?
[Answer:] The purpose of reflecting.[6]
[Question:] Then, what is reflected here (i.e., in the *Bṛhaspatisūtra*)?
[Answer:] The principles, earth etc., are well known[7] in the world; but even they, when seriously examined, are not established. How much less the others!
[Question:] Why don't they exist?
[Answer:] In respect to this [we] say: The establishment of means of valid cognition depends on [their] true definition.[8] And the establishment of objects of valid cognition depends on means of valid cognition.[9] When the one (i.e., a true definition) is absent, how could one talk about the other two (i.e., means of valid cognition and objects of

hāraviṣayatvaṃ kathaṃ ...[1] *tām. atha* ...[2] *na ba*...[3] *vyavahāraḥ kriyate, tadātmani rūpāstitva-vyavahāro*[4] *ghaṭādau ca sukhāstitvavyavahāraḥ pravartayitavyaḥ*

---

1 ≈ 8 *akṣaras* missing; S conjectures [*svayam eva*]

2 ≈ 2 *akṣaras* missing

3 ≈ 3 *akṣaras* missing

4 M: *rūpāstivyavahāro*

valid cognition) as real? ... If one talks[10] about [means and objects of valid cognition without a true definition of means of valid cognition], one could [as well] start talking about the existence of colour in the Soul and of pleasure in a pot etc.

1. [S2]a ... [1]indriyārthasannikarṣotpannaṃ jñānam avyapadeśyam avyabhicāri vyavasāyātmakaṃ pratyakṣam iti talla[M2a]kṣaṇam.

1.1 tac cāvyabhicāritvam ...[2] kim aduṣṭakārakasandohotpādyatvenāhosvid bādhārahitatvena pravṛttisāmarthyenānyathā vā?

1.11 tad yady aduṣṭakārakasandohotpādyatvenāvyabhicāritvaṃ, saiva kāraṇānām aduṣṭatā kenāvagamyate?

na pratyakṣeṇa, nayanakuśalāder atīndriyatvāt. nāpy anumānena, liṅgāntarānavagateḥ.

nanu idam eva jñānaṃ liṅgaṃ tadutthaṃ tasya viśiṣṭatāṃ gamayati.

yady evam itaretarāśrayatvaṃ duruttaram āpanīpadyate.

kiṃ cendriyāṇāṃ guṇadoṣāśrayatve tadutthe vi-

---

1 ≈ 6 akṣaras missing; i° conjectured by S

2 ≈ 9 akṣaras missing; M: cāvyabhicā ..., S: avyabhicā[ri]

[Chapter I
Examination of the Nyāya definition of perception]

... The [Nyāya] definition of [perception runs as follows]: "Perception is a cognition which arises from a contact between sense and object, cannot be designated [by words], is nonerroneous, [and] has the nature of determination."[11]

But [how is] the nonerroneousness [of a cognition known]? Is it [known] by being produced by a complex of faultless causal factors, or by being free from sublation, or by the efficiency of activity, or otherwise?

In respect to these [alternatives], if the nonerroneousness of a cognition is known by being produced by a complex of faultless causal factors, [then] by which [means of valid cognition] is precisely that, [i.e.] the fact that the causes are faultless, apprehended?

Not by perception, because the well-being etc., of the eye, are beyond [the apprehension by] the senses [themselves]. Nor [is it known] by inference, because there is no apprehension of another [inferential] sign (i.e., a sign which will prove that the causal complex is faultless, which proves, in its turn, that the cognition is nonerroneous).

[Objection:] It is precisely that cognition which is the sign: having arisen from that (i.e., from a faultless causal complex) it reveals its distinguished character (i.e., of being faultless).

[Reply:] If so, the insurmountable [fallacy of] mutual dependence follows necessarily.[12]

Besides, the senses being substrata of qualities (i.e., good functioning) and faults, a cognition produced by them jñāne doṣāśaṅkā nātivartate, puṃvyāpārotpādita-śabdavijñāna iva.

1.12 atha bādhānutpattyāvyabhicāritvaṃ jñāyate, bādhānutpattir vijñānasya kiṃ yathārthagṛhītitvenāhosvid bādhakajñānotpādaka[M2b]kārakavaikalyād iti sandihmaḥ. dṛśyate hi bādhakajñānotpādakakārakavaikalyād bādhānutpādaḥ. yathā dūre marīcinicaye jalajñāne jāte bādhā na sampadyate, 'bhyāsadeśāvasthitasya kārakopanipāte saty utpadyate. sā copajāyamānā saṃvatsarādikālavikalpena sañjāyate. kadācic ca kārakavaikalyān naiva[1] sampadyate. na caitāvatā tasya yathārtha[2]topapadyate.

api ca bādhāviraha eva <na>[3] bādhāsadbhāvāvedakas, tadupalabdhatvena tatsadbhāvopalabdheḥ.

1.12a anyac ca bādhāvirahaḥ kiṃ sarvapuruṣāpekṣayāhosvit pratipattrapekṣayā?

tad yadi sarvapuruṣāpekṣayā ...[4] [M3a]tadvirahopya ...[5]sarvajñāḥ syuḥ. bhavantu nāma sarve sarvajñāḥ, ko doṣaḥ? asarvajñavyavahārābhāvaprasaṅgaḥ.

[S3]atha pratipattrapekṣayā bādhānutpādaḥ - pratipattur bādhakaṃ vijñānaṃ notpadyate, tena

1 M: °vaikalyānaiva

2 M: yartha°

3 M & S om. na; note that the negation may also be obtained by reading avedaka

4 ≈ 12 akṣaras missing

5 ≈ 16 akṣaras missing; sa conjectured by S

is not beyond suspicion of faults, just like a cognition of a word produced by the activity of a person.

If the nonerroneousness [of a cognition] is known by the non-arising of sublation, we have the following doubt: Is the fact that a sublation of a cognition does not arise due to the fact that [the cognition] is true, or is it due to the deficiency of a causal factor which [could have] produced the sublating cognition?[13] For it is seen [in some cases] that the sublation is not produced because of the deficiency of the causal factor which [could have] produced the sublating cognition. For instance, when a cognition of water is produced with reference to a faraway mass of sun-rays the sublation is not produced, [but] when a causal factor is produced additionally for [a person] who stands nearby, [the sublation] is produced. And being produced additionally it is produced with a difference in time, after a year etc., and sometimes, due to the deficiency of the causal factor, it is not produced at all; but the non-erroneousness of a [cognition] is not established by that much.[14]

Besides, the absence [of a cognition] of sublation does not prove the real absence of sublation, because the apprehension of its real existence is due to its apprehension [but its inexistence is not proved by the absence of its apprehension].

And there is another [argument]: Does the absence of sublation depend on all people or on the [perceiver] alone?

In respect to these [alternatives], if it depends on all people, ... [everybody] would be omniscient.[15]

[Objection:] Let everybody be omniscient, what is wrong with that?

[Reply:] One will not be able to talk about non-omniscient [people].

If the non-production of a sublation depends on the perceiver [alone], [i.e., if] the perceiver does not have a sublating cognition [and] by this [fact knows] that [the *tad avyabhicāri. tad ayuktaṃ, pratipattur bādhakajñānānutpāde 'pi deśāntaragamanamaraṇādinā maṇimarīcyādiviparyayajñānadarśanāt. athavā tad viparyayajñānaṃ tathāvidham evotpannaṃ svaprabhavasvabhāvānupraveśena, yad bādhakavijñānotpādapratibandhakṛt. taddhvaṃso*[1] *'pi tathābhūta eva pareṣṭasamyagjñānavat. evaṃ sati yad uktaṃ yasya*[2] *ca duṣṭaṃ karaṇaṃ yatra ca mithyeti pratyayaḥ* [M 3b] *sa evāsamīcīnaḥ pratyaya ity etad evāsamīcīnam.*

1.13 *atha pravṛttisāmarthyenāvyabhicāritāṃ vetsi. pravṛttisāmarthyaṃ phalenābhisambandhaḥ, phalaṃ ca srakcandanavanitodakādi, teṣu satyaphalaniṣpattes teṣu phalopacāras, taddehasambandhaḥ pravṛttisāmarthyam. pravṛttiḥ kāyasthā kriyā, tatsāmarthyam avyabhicāritāṃ gamayati. tat kim avagatam anavagataṃ vā? yadi nāvagataṃ, tad astīti kathaṃ vetsi? athāvagataṃ, tadavagater avyabhicāritā katham avagamyata iti pūrvoktam anusartavyam.*

1.13a *udakaprāptyā pūrvotpannodakavijñānasyāvyabhicāritā vyavasthāpyate.*
kiṃ tatpratibhātodaka[M4a]*prāptyāhosvit tajjātīyodakaprāptyā*[3] *tadvaṃśajajalaprāptyā vā?*

---

1 M & S: *tadvaśo*, cf., however, *NBhū* p. 37.1f.

2 M & S: *yatra*

3 M: *tajjātīyodaprāpytā*

cognition] is nonerroneous, [then] this [too] is not correct, because a false cognition of diamond-rays[16] etc., is observed even when there is no production of a sublating cognition for the perceiver, because he goes to another place or dies etc. Or the false cognition arises in such a way by being subordinated to the nature of its source that it prevents the production of the sublating cognition. The destruction of this [false cognition] as well is of exactly the same kind, just as a true cognition accepted by the opponent. Thus, to say: "A cognition whose cause is faulty and about which one has the cognition 'It is false,' that cognition alone is untrue,"[17] is itself untrue.

You recognize the nonerroneousness [of a cognition] by the efficiency of activity.[18] The efficiency of activity is the connection with a fruit, and fruit [means] a garland, sandlewood, a beloved woman, water, etc. [The word] 'fruit' is used metaphorically for these [things], because in respect to them the real fruit is brought about. The efficiency of activity is the connection between the body and that [fruit]. Activity is a corporal action, its efficiency makes known the nonerroneousness [of a cognition]. Now, is [the efficiency of activity] apprehended or not? If it is not apprehended, how do you know that it exists? If it is apprehended, how is it apprehended that its apprehension is nonerroneous? Thus, the [argument] pronounced above should be followed.

[Objection:] The nonerroneousness of a cognition of water which has previously arisen is established by obtaining water.

[Reply: Is it established] by obtaining water which appeared in the [cognition], or by obtaining water belonging to the [same] universal as the [water which appeared in the cognition], or by obtaining water which arises in the [same] series as the [water which appeared in the cognition]?[19]

1.13a1 *tad yadi pratibhātodakaprāptyā, tad ayuktam. pratibhātodakasyāvasthānaṃ nopapadyate, jhaṣamahiṣaparivartanābhighātopajātāvayavakriyānyāyena pratyastamayasambhavāt.*

1.13a2 *atha tajjātiyodakaprāptyā, evaṃ tarhy asatyodakajñāne 'pi jāte kvacit toyam āsādayanti pumāṃsaḥ. tad apy avitathaṃ syāt.*

atha taddeśakālasaṃlagnam udakaṃ na prāpayati mithyājñānaṃ, samyagjñānaṃ tu taddeśakālasaṃlagnam udakaṃ prāpayati, tena tad avyabhicārīti ced,

yan na prāpayati, tad vyabhicāri; tarhi mumūrṣupadā[M4b]rthotpāditaṃ [S4]jñānaṃ candrārkagrahanakṣatratārakādisaṃvedanaṃ ca vyabhicāri prāpnoti. na ca taddeśakālasaṃlagnodakaprāpakatvam asti, deśasyāpy udakavad vināśasambhavāt.

a. *na ca jāteḥ sambhavo 'sti. sa eva katham? kathyate - sodakavyaktibhyo 'bhinnā bhinnā bhinnābhinnā veti.*

a.1 *tad yadi tādātmyavyavasthitā, tadeha tāsāṃ nānātvena tasyā api*[1] *nānātvopapattiḥ. tadekatve ca sarvāsām ekatāpattiḥ. ekatve ca niḥsāmānyatā*

1 M: *tasyāpi*

In respect to these [alternatives], if [the nonerroneousness of a cognition of water is established] by obtaining the [same] water which appeared [in the cognition], [then] this is not correct. The continuity of the water which appeared [in the cognition] is not established, because it may be destroyed by action in [its] parts produced by the turning around and hits of fish and buffalos.[20]

If [it is established] by obtaining water belonging to the [same] universal as the [water which appeared in the cognition], then even when a cognition of unreal water is produced people [may] obtain water somewhere, [and] that [false cognition of water], too, would be true.
[Objection:] A false cognition does not make one obtain water connected with [exactly] that place and time, but a true cognition does; by this [one knows that] it is nonerroneous.
[Reply: If] whatever [cognition] does not make one obtain [its object] is erroneous, then a cognition produced by a thing which is about to vanish, and the cognition of the sun, moon, planets, constellations, stars, etc., would be erroneous.[21] And [the cognition may] not make one obtain water connected with [exactly] that place and time, because the place, just like the water, may be destroyed.

And [on top of that] the universal can't exist.
[Question:] How is that?
[Answer: We] explain: This [universal 'water'] is either different from the water individuals, or not different, or both different and non-different.[22]

In respect to these [alternatives], if [the universal 'water'] is established as having the same nature [as the individuals],[23] then here (i.e., in this case), through their plurality, for it (i.e., the universal) too plurality is established. And if [the universal 'water'] is one, all [water individuals] would be one. And if they are one, [the *tādātmyavi[M5a]paryāso vā.*

a.2 *athārthāntarabhūtā*[1], *sā vyāvṛttākārānugatākārā vā.*

tad yadi vyāvṛttākārā, na tasyāḥ sāmānyarūpatvaṃ vyāvṛttaikasvabhāvatvāt toyādivat.

athānusyūtarūpā, tat kim ātmarūpānusyūtā pararūpānusyūtā vā?

tad yady ātmarūpānusyūtā, tad ayuktam, ātmany anugamābhāvāt.

atha pararūpānusyūtā, keyaṃ pararūpānusyūtatā kiṃ tattādātmyaṃ tatsamavāyo vā?

tad yadi tādātmyaṃ, sāmānyatadvator abhedaprasaṅgaḥ.

atha pararū[M5b]pasamavāyo 'nusyūtākāratā, tad ayuktam. sāmānyād bhinnaḥ samavāyaḥ. sāmānyasyānugataṃ rūpam ālocayitum ārabdhaṃ, na tato 'nyasya.

a.2a *yadi codakajātiyārthaprāptyāvyabhicāritā pūrvoditodakavijñānasya vyavasthāpyate, tadodakajāter gavādāv api sambhavo 'sti, gavādiprāptyāvyabhicā*[2]*ritodakavijñānasya syāt.*

athodakatvasya gavādāv abhāva iti cet,

kim itaretarābhāvaḥ prāgabhāvaḥ pradhvaṃsābhāvo 'tyantābhāvo vā?

---

1 M: °āntabhūtā

2 M: °ca°

universal] is not common [to many individuals]; or [the idea of] identity of nature is wrong.[24]

If [the universal is] something different [from the individuals], [then] it has either a distinct form or a recurrent[25] form.

If it has a distinct form,[26] it does not have the nature of a universal, because it has a distinct and unique nature, just like [an individual such as] water etc.

If [the universal] has a recurrent nature, then is it recurrent in its own nature or is it recurrent in the nature of something else?
If it is recurrent in its own nature, then this is not correct because there is no recurrence in oneself.
If it is recurrent in the nature of something else, [then] what is this recurrence in the nature of something else? Is it identity of nature with this [other thing][27] or is it inherence in it?[28]
If it is identity of nature, [then] the universal and [an individual] which is characterized by it would not be different.
If to have a recurrent form [means] to be inherent in the nature of something else, [then] this is not correct. Inherence is different from the universal. We undertook reflection upon the recurrent nature of the universal, not upon something which is different from it (i.e., from the universal).[29]

And if the nonerroneousness of a cognition of water which has previously arisen is established by obtaining an object which belongs to the universal water, then, [since] the universal of water may exist in cows[30] etc., too, the nonerroneousness of a cognition of water would be [established] by obtaining a cow etc.
[Objection: The universal] 'water' is absent in cows etc.
[Reply:] Is [this absence] a mutual absence, a previous absence, an absence by destruction, or an absolute absence?[31]

tad yaditare[S5]tarābhāvas tadodakādāv api samānam udakatvasyābhāvaprasaṅgaḥ. udakarūpatā nodakatvasyodakatvarūpatā ca noda[M6a]kasya[1].

atha prāgabhāvas tadodake[2] 'py udakatvasyā[3]bhāvaprasaṅgaḥ.

atha pradhvaṃsābhāvas tadodake 'py abhāvaprasaṅgaḥ.

athānyatrāsti, naikatra pratyastamitasyānyatra sambhava upapadyate.

athātyantābhāvas tadodake 'pi tasyābhāvaprasaṅgaḥ.

atha sambandhābhāvād gavādāv udakatvābhāva iti cet,

tatrāpi kim itaretarābhāvaḥ prāgabhāvaḥ[4] pradhvaṃsābhāvo 'tyantābhāvo veti pūrvavad vaktavyam.

nimittāntarābhāvād gavādā[M6b]v ud[5]akatvābhāva iti cet,

so 'trāpi samānaḥ.

a.2b na codakavyaktīnāṃ nānātvam upapādayituṃ pāryate. udakam anudakākārād udakākāratayā vyāvartata, udakākārāt tu kathaṃ vyāvartate? kim udakākāratayāhosvid ākārāntareṇa?

tad yady udakākāratayā vyāvartate, tadānyāsām udakavyaktīnām anudakākāratā prāpnoti rasāder iva.

athānudakākāratayodakākārān nivartate, tato dahanāder ivānudakatvaprasaṅgaḥ.

---

1 M & S: nodaka

2 M: tadedake

3 M & S: udakasyā°

4 M & S om. prāgabhāvaḥ

5 M: ad°

In respect to these [alternatives], if it is a mutual absence, then [the universal] 'water' would be equally absent in water etc., too. [The universal] 'water' does not have the nature of water, and water does not have the nature of [the universal] 'water.'

If it is a previous absence, then in water, too, there would be absence of [the universal] 'water.'[32]

If it is an absence by destruction, then in water, too, there would be absence [of the universal 'water'].

[Objection:] It exists elsewhere.[33]

[Reply:] What is destroyed at one place cannot exist elsewhere.

If it is an absolute absence, then in water, too, it would be absent.[34]

[Objection: The universal] 'water' is absent in cows etc., because there is no relation.

[Reply:] There again [we ask]: Is [this absence] a mutual absence, a previous absence, an absence by destruction, or an absolute absence?

One should answer as above.

[Objection: The universal] 'water' is absent in cows etc., because [some] other cause[35] is absent.

[Reply:] Here (i.e., in this case), too, [the argument] is the same [as above].

Nor can the plurality of water individuals be established. Water is differentiated from that which does not have the form of water by having the form of water, but how is it differentiated from that which has the form of water? Is it by having the form of water or by [having] another form?

If it is differentiated by having the form of water, then the other water individuals would not have the form of water, just like juice etc.

If [water] is differentiated from another water by not having the form of water, then, just like fire etc., it would not be water.[36]

athodakākārarūpatāviśeṣe 'py avāntaragaṇikākārabhedaparikḷptir iti cet.
satyam avāntaragaṇikākāras toyatādā[M7a]tmyavyavasthito 'tādātmyavyavasthito vā.

tad yadi tādātmyavyavasthitas, tadodakākāratayodakāntarād bhidyate. evaṃ cānyāsām udakavyaktīnām anudakarūpatā prāpnoti. pūrvoditam eva dūṣaṇam.

athātādātmyavyavasthitas, tarhy anudakatvaṃ rasāder iva.
athodakatvavyāvṛttyānudakākārād vyāvartate.
śṛṇvantu amī bālalapitaṃ vipaścitaḥ. yady udakatvavyāvṛttyānudakād vyāvartate toyam,[1] udakatvaṃ codakād anudakāc ca kathaṃ vyāvartate? na jātyantaraṃ vyāvartakam asti. abhyupagame vāniṣṭhopaplavānubandhaḥ [S6] syāt.
tasmāt svenaiva rūpeṇetaretarātmanā vyāvartate, na jātyā[M7b]dinā vyāvartate, jātyāder avyāvṛttiprasaṅgāt.
tasmāt sthitam etan nodakavyaktīnāṃ nānātvopa-

1 perhaps a lacuna at this point

[Objection:] Although there is no difference [among water individuals] in having the form of water, [nevertheless the different water individuals can be differentiated from one another because] a difference of forms belonging to the sub-classes [of water] is assumed.
[Reply:] True! [But] a form belonging to a sub-class [of water] is either determined as identical with [the form of] water or as not identical.

If it is determined as identical, then [a water individual belonging to a sub-class of water] differs from another water [individual] by having the form of water. And thus, the other water individuals would not have the nature of water. [This] criticism has already been raised above.

If [a form belonging to a sub-class of water] is determined as not identical [with the form of water], then [the individuals which have a form belonging to a sub-class of water would] not be water, just like juice etc.
[Objection: Water] is differentiated from that which does not have the form of water by a differentiation by means of [the universal] 'water.'[37]
[Reply:] One should listen to the childish babbling of the wise man! If water is differentiated from non-water by a differentiation by means of [the universal] 'water,' how is [the universal] 'water' differentiated from water and non-water? There is no other universal [which could be used as] a differentiator. Or if [a further universal] is admitted, the calamity of infinite regress would immediately follow.[38]
This is why [individuals][39] are differentiated [from one another] by their own form alone, [i.e.] by their respective natures; they are not differentiated by a universal etc., because [otherwise] there would not be a differentiation of the universal etc. [from other things].
Therefore the following is established: A plurality of water individuals is impossible. When this [plurality] is

pattiḥ. tadanupapattau nodakatvaṃ nāma sāmānyam asti svatvavat.

a.2c *ito 'pi na vidyate sāmānyaṃ - nityasya sato vijñānajanakatvāyogāt.*

tad eva katham? vyutpādyate - vijñānajanakāvasthāyāṃ yad eva svarūpaṃ sāmānyātmakaṃ śaktimac chaktirūpaṃ ca kāra[M8a]kāntarānapekṣayā[1] *ajanakāvasthāyāṃ tad eva rūpam, ataḥ pūrvam api kāryotpādaprasaṅgaḥ. anutpāde vā prāg ivedānim*[2] *api na*[3] *janayet.*

atha kārakāntaram apekṣyotpādayati[4] *kāryam.*

kiṃ tena kārakāntareṇa tasya kriyate kārakatvaṃ jñāpyate vā?

tad yady utpādyate[5] *susthitaṃ nityatvam. uta jñāpyate siddhaṃ tarhi kārakatvaṃ, tadabhāve 'pi vidyamānasyā[M8b]vadyotanāt.*

bhavatu nāma kārakatvaṃ, ko doṣaḥ?

kāryotpattiprasaṅgaḥ. atha kārakatve 'pi kāryaṃ na janayed, aho rājājñā garīyasī naiyāyikapaśoḥ.

---

1 *kārakāntarānapekṣayā* is probably an interpolation. There are several such interpolations in the manuscript which, I assume, were originally written as clarifying notes and mistakenly copied together with the text.

2 M: *evedānim*

3 M om. *na*

4 M: °*pādayati/*

5 M: *tad vyutpādyate*

impossible, there is no universal named 'water,' just as [the universal] Selfness [does not exist].

For the following [reason], too, the universal does not exist: because in as much as [the universal] is eternal, it cannot produce [its] cognition.[40]

[Question:] How is that?

[Answer: We] explain: The own-form consisting in the nature of a universal which possesses capacity and has the form of capacity[41] is the same in a state of affairs when [the universal] produces [its cognition] and in a state of affairs when it does not produce [its cognition]. Consequently, the production of [its] effect (i.e., its cognition) should take place also before [it actually occurs]. Or if there is no production [of cognition up to the present], [then] just as before, now as well [the universal] would not produce [its cognition].[42]

[Objection: The universal] produces the effect (i.e., its cognition) depending on other causal factors.

[Reply:] Is the fact that the [universal] is a causal factor [in the production of its cognition] effected by this other causal factor or is it made known [by it]?[43]

In respect to these [alternatives], if [the fact of being a causal factor] is effected, [then] the eternity [of the universal] is well established! If [the fact of being a causal factor is only] made known [by this other causal factor], then the fact of being a causal factor is established [even before], for [this causal factor] illuminates something which exists even when it (i.e., this other causal factor) is absent.

[Question:] Let [the universal] be a causal factor! What is wrong with that?

[Answer:] There would be [constant] production of the effect.[44] [Or] if [the universal] would not produce [its] effect in spite of being a causal factor, alas! [this must be] a heavy royal decree for the Naiyāyika beast.[44*] a.2d ito 'pi nāsti sāmānyaṃ - tadupapādakamānavyatirekāt.

nanu asti pramāṇam anayoḥ sādṛśyam, eṣāṃ sārūpyaṃ, tena sadṛśo 'yam, asau vā tena sadṛśa ityādijñānaṃ sāmānyasattāvabodhakam[1] apratipannasāmānyasya nopapadyate. asti tu idaṃ vijñānaṃ bādhāvikalaṃ jātitanuvyavasthāpakam.

tad etad ayuktam. kiṃ nimittabhūtena tenaivaṃvidhaṃ jñānam utpādyate karma[M9a]tāpannena vā?

tad yadi nimittabhūtenotpādyate, tadā na sāmānyaṃ kalpanīyam. asāmānyātmakam eva nimittam, itthambhūtasāmānyajñānotpādanāyālaṃ sāmānyakalpanayā.

atha karmatāpannenotpādyate, tad asat. naivāvabhāti vijñāne sāmānyaṃ dhūrtair aviparyāsitasaṃvidām.

nanu sādṛśyam avabhāti.

satyam, avabhāti, nāpahnūyate, 'pi tu dravyaguṇakarmātmakaṃ sat pācakādibhedeṣu yathaiṣāṃ pācakatvam, ete pācakās, [S7] tatpācakasadṛśo 'yam, asāv anena sadṛśa iti viśeṣādāv api [M9b] draṣṭavyam.

atrāpi sāmānyaparijñaptir[2] iti cen,

---

1 So in M, S's conjecture unnecessary

2 Perhaps -parikḷptir; cf. also p. 84.2

For the following [reason], too, the universal does not exist: because there is no proof which establishes it.
[Objection:] Of course there is a proof: cognitions [such as] "There is a similarity between these two," "They have the same form," "This is similar to it," or "That is similar to it," etc., which reveal the existence of the universal, are not possible for [someone] who has not apprehended the universal. But there are such cognitions which establish the existence of the universal in as much as they are free from sublation.[45]
[Reply:] This is not correct. Does the [universal] produce such cognitions as efficient cause or as object?

In respect to these [alternatives], if [the cognition] is produced by [the universal] as efficient cause, then [the existence of] the universal should not be assumed. [For] an efficient cause does not have the nature of a universal. [Thus] the assumption of [the existence of] the universal for the production of cognitions which have arisen thus (i.e., of cognitions of similarity) is superfluous.[46]

If [the cognition of similarity] is produced by [the universal] as object, [then] this is not true: the universal does not appear in the cognition of [people] whose consciousness has not been perverted by the [Naiyāyika] swindlers.
[Objection: But] the similarity appears!
[Reply:] True! It appears. We do not deny that, but in as much as [the similarity] consists in substance, quality, and action [it may appear] in respect to individuals [such as] cooks etc., for instance [in such cognitions as] "They share the property of being a cook," "These are cooks," "He resembles that cook," "This is similar to that"; thus, [similarity] may be observed among particulars etc., too.
[Objection:] Here [in particulars], too, a universal is ascertained!

na sūtravyāghātāt sāmānyaviśeṣeṣu sāmānyaviśeṣābhāvāt tata eva jñānam.

aniṣṭhā ca - viśeṣeṣu sāmānye parikalpyamāne sati sandehaḥ, sati sandehe teṣu viśeṣāntaraṃ parikalpanīyaṃ, punaḥ sāmānyam ity aniṣṭhety alam asad[1]*grahābhiniveśena.*

a.3 *atha bhinnābhinnaṃ sāmānyaṃ bhavadbhiḥ pratipādyata - ākārabhedena vyaktibhya upalabhyata ity arthāntaraṃ, deśabhedena* [M10a] *tu naivopalabhyata ity avyatiriktam*[2].

tad etan mahāsubhāṣitam. na deśabhedenaiva vastūnāṃ bhedo, 'pi tv ākārabhedenaiva bhāvā bhedam upayānti. yathā cākārabhedo nāsti tathānantaram eva niveditam.

b. *sāmānyaṃ samavāyavṛttyā vyaktiṣu vartata iti na cāsau vidyate.*

b.1 *samavāyo hi vyāvṛttaikasvabhāvo 'nugataikasvabhāvo vā.*

tad yadi vyāvṛttaikasvabhāvaḥ, kasyāsau samavāyaḥ sarvato vyāvṛtter nīlādivat?

athānugataika[M10b]*svabhāvaḥ, sāmānyaṃ*[3] *tarhi, na samavāyo, nityasya sato 'nekatra vṛtter gotvādivat.*

---

1 M: *asasado*

2 M: *avyatirikte*

3 M: *sāmānyaṃ/*

[Reply:] No, [it cannot be ascertained] because this contradicts [*Vaiśeṣika-*]*sūtra* [8.5]: "Because there are no universals and particulars in universals and particulars, [their] cognition [arises] from them[selves]."[47]
And [the assumption of universals in particulars is also impossible because this would lead to] an infinite regress: when a universal is assumed in particulars, a doubt [arises]; when there is a doubt, another particular has to be assumed in them, and again a universal; thus, [there would be] an infinite regress.[48] Therefore, enough with the obstinate attachment to the childish desire for [something] which does not exist!

Now, by you the universal is asserted to be both different and non-different [from the individuals]. It is apprehended with a difference in form from the individuals; thus it is something else. But it is never apprehended with a difference in place [from the individuals]; thus it is not something over and above [the individuals].[49]
This is very well said. [However] the difference among things is not simply due to a difference in place; rather by a difference in form alone do things attain difference.[50] And we have shown just above why there is no difference in form [between universal and individual].[51]

[Further, it is said:] "The universal resides in the individuals by way of inherence";[52] but this [inherence] does not exist.
For inherence has either a distinct unique nature or a recurrent unique nature.

In respect to these [alternatives], if it has a distinct unique nature,[53] [then] of what is it the inherence? [Of nothing at all] because it is distinct from everything, just like [a particular such as] a blue [object] etc.
If it has a recurrent unique nature, then it is a universal, not inherence, in as much as it is something eternal which resides in more than one [substratum], just like [the universal] 'cow' etc.

b.2 *upapādakapramāṇābhāvāc ca.*

b.21 *nanu pratyakṣabuddhyavaseyo 'sau.*

tad ayuktam. kiṃ sambandhabuddhyādhyavasīyata āhosvid ihabuddhyā[1] *samavāyabuddhyā vocyate?*

b.211 *tad yadi sambandhabuddhyā, ko 'yaṃ sambandhaḥ?*

kiṃ sambandha[2]*jātiyuktaḥ sambandha āhosvid anekopādānajanito 'nekāśrito vā sambandhabu[M11a]ddhiviśeṣo vā sambandhabuddhyutpādako vā sambandhākāro*[3] *vā?*

tad yadi sambandhajātiyuktas te sambandhaḥ, so 'nupapannaḥ, samavāyā[4]*sambandhatvaprasaṅgaḥ.*

athānekopādānajanitaḥ sambandhas, tadā kumbhāder api sambandhatvaprasaṅgaḥ.

athānekāśritaḥ [S8] sambandhas, tadā ghaṭajātyādeḥ sambandhatvaṃ prasajyate.

atha sambandhabuddhyutpādakas te sambandha ucyate, tadā locanāder api sambandhatvaprasaṅgaḥ.

atha sambandhabu[M11b]ddhyavaseyaḥ sambandho 'bhidhīyate, tadā kauleyakakarikumārādiṣv api sambandhaśabdavyutpādane sambandhatvaprasaṅgaḥ. sambandhetarayor eka[5]*vijñānaviṣayatva itarasya sambandharūpatā prāptā.*

---

1 M: °*buddhyo*

2 M: *saṃbaṃba*°

3 M: *sambaddhākāro*

4 perhaps: *samavāyasyā*°

5 M: *ekatva*°

And because there is no proof which establishes [its existence inherence does not exist].
[Objection: There is a proof;] it (i.e., inherence) may be determined by perceptual cognition.
[Reply:] This is not correct. Is it determined by a cognition of relation, or by the cognition 'here,' or is it said [to be determined] by the cognition of inherence?[54]

In respect to these [alternatives], if [inherence is determined] by a cognition of relation, [then] what is a relation?
Is a relation that which is connected to the universal 'relation,' or that which is produced by more than one material cause, or that which rests on more than one [substratum], or is it that which is distinguished by a cognition of relation, or that which produces a cognition of relation, or that which has the form of relation?

In respect to these [alternatives], if in your opinion a relation is that which is connected to the universal 'relation,' [then] this is impossible; inherence would not be a relation.[55]
If a relation is that which is produced by more than one material cause, then a pitcher etc., too, would be a relation.[56]
If a relation is that which rests on more than one [substratum], then a pot [as a 'whole'], a universal, etc., would be a relation.
If according to you a relation is said to be that which produces a cognition of relation,[57] then the eye etc., too, would be a relation.
If a relation is explained as that which is to be determined by a cognition of relation, then in the case of a dog, an elephant, a boy, etc., too, it would result that [they] are relations when one analyzes the relational words [that designate them].[58] When a relation and something else are object of the same cognition, this other thing [as well] would have the nature of relation.

atha sambandhākāraḥ sambandhaḥ, saṃyogābhedaprasaṅgaḥ.
avāntaragaṇikākāras tu yathā na bhedakas tathā purastād uktam eva dūṣaṇam.

b.212 *atheha tantuṣu paṭa itīhabuddhyādhyavasīyate,*
nehabuddher adhikaraṇasaṃvidrūpatvāt. na cānyasminn[1] *ākāre pratīyamāne 'nyat parikalpayituṃ nyāyyam atiprasaṅgāt.*

b.213 *atha samavāyabuddhyātmasātkriyate.*
so 'py anupapanna eva, samavāyabuddher anupapatteḥ. ayaṃ tantur ayaṃ paṭo 'yam anayoḥ samavā[M12a]ya iti na jātu jānate janāḥ.

b.22 *athānumānenānumīyate.*
dve anumāne - dṛṣṭaṃ sāmānyato[2] *dṛṣṭaṃ ca.*
na dṛṣṭaṃ, pratyakṣavyatirekāt.
sāmānyato dṛṣṭam api nāsti, tatprabhavakāryānupalabdheḥ.
nanv ihabuddhir eva samavāyajñāpikā - iha tantuṣu paṭa iti pratyayaḥ sambandhanimitto, 'bādhitehapratyayatvād iha kuṇḍe dadhīti pratyayavat. kim anenānumīyate? kiṃ nimittamātram uta sambandhaḥ?

---

1 M: *cāsminn*
2 M: *sāsāmānyato*

If relation is that which has the form of relation, there would be no difference between [inherence and] conjunction. As for the form belonging to a sub-class [of relation], the criticism why it [can]not distinguish [among individuals] has already been raised above.[59]

[Objection: Inherence] is determined by the cognition "here" [in cognitions such as] "Here, in the threads, there is a cloth."

[Reply:] No! [Inherence is not determined by it] because the cognition "here" has the nature of awareness of locus;[60] and it is not reasonable to assume one thing when the form of another is apprehended, because this is absurd.

[Objection: Inherence] is appropriated through the cognition of inherence.

[Reply:] This, too, is absolutely impossible, because the cognition of inherence is impossible: people never cognize [in such a way as] "These are threads," "This is a cloth," "This is the inherence between the two."

[Objection: Inherence is not determined by perception, but] it is inferred by inference.

[Reply:] There are two [kinds of] inference: 'seen' and 'seen on the basis of a common factor.'[61]

[An inference of the first kind, namely] 'seen' [can]not [establish inherence] because [inherence] is beyond perception.

Nor is there [an inference of the kind] 'seen on the basis of a common factor,' because the effect which arises from it (i.e., from inherence) is not apprehended.

[Objection:] It is precisely the cognition "here" which makes known inherence: the cognition "Here, in the threads, there is a cloth" is caused by a relation, because the cognition "here" is not sublated, just like the cognition "Here, in the bowl, are curds."[62]

[Reply:] What is inferred by this [cognition "here"]? Is it simply a cause or is it a relation?

yadi nimittamātraṃ, tataḥ siddhasādhyatayā sambodhayitavyaḥ.

atha sambandhaḥ, saṃyogaḥ samavāyo vā. saṃyogānumāna upagamahāniḥ. samavāyānumāne sambandhavyatirekaḥ. na cānyasya sambandhe 'nyasya gamakatvam atiprasaṅgāt. na jātu devadattanaya[M12b]*nakuṭasambandhe yajñadattendriyaṃ rūpādikam arthaṃ karaṇatvasāmyāt prakāśayad dṛṣṭam.*

evaṃ sati sāmānyasamavāyavirahe kathaṃ dravyādivyavastheti cintyate.

1.13a3 [S9]*atha tadvaṃśajajala*[1]*prāptyāvyabhicāritā jñāyate. tad ayuktam, antyāvayavidravyāṇāṃ janakatvavyatirekāt. na codakavyaktīnāṃ nānātvam*[2] *asti. yathā ca na vidyate tathā niveditaṃ purastāt.*

1.13b *kiṃ ca pravṛttisāmarthyenāvyabhicāritā pūrvoditajñānasya jñāpyate – kiṃ liṅgabhūtenāho 'dhyakṣātmakena?*

tad yadi liṅgabhūtena, tad ayuktaṃ, tena sākaṃ [M13a] *sambandhānavagateḥ. avagatau vālaṃ pravṛttisāmarthyena.*

---

1 M: *tadvastavyajala°*; S reads: *tadvat satyajala°*, but conjectures correctly, cf. *NBhū* p. 34.11-12

2 M: *nātvam*

If it is simply a cause, then you should be instructed that you prove what is already proved.

If it is a relation, [then it is] a conjunction or inherence.[63]

If it is an inference of conjunction, [then] you abandon your thesis.

If it is an inference of inherence, [then] there is no relation.[64] For when there is a relation of one thing [to another thing], [still] another thing does not make known [something else], because this is absurd. When there is a relation between the eye of Devadatta and a pot, one never observes that the sense of Yajñadatta illuminates an object [such as] a colour etc., just because there is a similarity [between both senses] in as much as [they] are instruments.[65]

Thus, when both universal and inherence do not exist, how can substance and the other [categories] be established? Think about it!

If the nonerroneousness [of a cognition of water] is known by obtaining water which arises in the [same] series as the [water which appeared in the cognition], then this is not correct, because substances which are final 'wholes' are not agent of production [of further 'wholes'].[66] Nor is there a plurality of water individuals. And why there is no [plurality] has been explained above.[67]

Further [you claim that] the nonerroneousness of a cognition [of water] which has previously arisen is made known by the efficiency of activity; [but] is it [made known by this efficiency of activity] as a [inferential] sign or as something which has the nature of perception?[68]

In respect to these [alternatives], if [the nonerroneousness is made known by the efficiency of activity] as a [inferential] sign, [then] this is not correct, because the relation [of nonerroneousness] with it is not apprehended. Or if it is apprehended, the efficiency of activity is superfluous [for the determination of nonerroneousness].

athādhyakṣātmakena, tad ayuktaṃ, pūrvoditapratyastamitena sākaṃ sannikarṣābhāvāt. tadviṣayavijñānaṃ na pratyakṣaphalaṃ nirālambanatvāt keśoṇḍukādisaṃvedanavat. na vijñānasyābhāvo 'vabhāti, na bhāvas tadabhāvāt.[1]

avidyamānasya viṣayārtho vaktavyaḥ - kim ākārārpakatvena vā mahattvādidharmopetatvena vā sattāmātreṇa vā sahotpādena vā?
sarvasya pratyastamitatvāt katham asau viṣayaḥ? tadviṣayatve keśoṇḍukādivijñānasyaiva[2] *mithyātve bi[M13b]jam anveṣaṇīyam. ātmasattāmātreṇa mithyātve sarvasya mithyātvam āpadyate. tatas tattvopaplavaḥ syāt.*

1.14 *athānyathāvyabhicāritvaṃ gṛhyata - ātmāntaḥkaraṇasambandhenotpannaṃ*[3] *vijñānam avyabhicāritāviśiṣṭaṃ pradyotyate.*
tad ayuktam. tad avyabhicāritvaṃ taddharmo vā tatsvarūpaṃ vā.

1.141 *tad yadi taddharmaḥ, sa nityo 'nityo vā.*

---

1 perhaps a lacuna at this point

2 M & S: *vijñānasyeva*

3 M: °*notpannaṃ/*

If [it is made known by the efficiency of activity] as something having the nature of perception, [then] this is not correct because there is no contact with [a cognition of water] which has previously arisen and has [already] vanished. The cognition which has the [cognition of water as nonerroneous] for its object is not the result of percep tion, because it does not have objective support, just like the [erroneous] cognition of the hair-net etc. The absence of the cognition does not appear, nor [its] presence, be-cause it does not exist [anymore].

[Or if you say that the absence of that cognition appears, then you] have to explain what [the word] 'object' means for something which does not exist. [Does it become object] by being that which provides [its] form [to the cognition], or by having properties such as magnitude etc., or by simply existing, or by arising together [with the cognition]?[69]
Since all these [qualifications] are destroyed [together with the thing thus qualified], how could this [inexistent thing be] an object [of a cognition which arises after it is destroyed]? If this [inexistent thing] is an object, a [new] reason for the falsity of the cognition of the hair-net etc., should be sought. If falsity is due to the mere existence [of the cognition] itself, all [cognitions] would be false, [and] consequently, [all] principles would be annihilated.

[Objection:] Nonerroneousness is apprehended other-wise: a cognition which has arisen by means of a relation between the Self and the inner organ appears as qualified by nonerroneousness.[70]
[Reply:] This is not correct. This nonerroneousness is either a property of that [cognition] or its own-nature.

In respect to these [alternatives], if it is its pro-perty, it is either eternal or not eternal.

yadi nityas, tadā jātidoṣeṇā[M14a]podito[1] *veditavyaḥ.*

athānityaḥ, sa pūrvotpannaḥ saha paścād vā jātaḥ.

tad yadi pūrvotpannas, tadā kasyāsau dharmaḥ? na hi dharmiṇam antareṇa dharmo bhavitum arhati. sarvato vyāvṛttarūpatvāt[2] *kaḥ kasyeti vaktavyam.*

atha sahotpannaḥ, kas tayoḥ sambandha iti vaktavyam. tādā[S10]tmyatadutpattisamavāyasambandhābhāve sati ṣaṣṭhyartho vaktavyas tasyāvyabhicāritvam iti

atha pṛṣṭhotpannas, tarhi [M14b] pūrvaṃ vyabhicāritā vijñānasya prāpnoti.[3] *na cādhyātmiko 'vyabhicārirūpo dharmo 'sti sukhādivyatiriktas, tatpratītyasambhavena svayam anabhyupagamāt.*

yadi cāvyabhicārādayo dharmā arthāntarabhūtā abhyupagamyante[4] *tair avacchinnaṃ vijñānaṃ sāmagryā avasthāpakam udghuṣyate. tac cānupapannaṃ, pratyekamanekaviśeṣaṇāvacchinnavijñānapratipatti*[5]*kālāvasthānāyogāt. jñāpyajñāpakayor abhāve kartṛmātraprabandhi jñānaṃ syāt.*

1.142 *atha tat*[6]*svarūpam avyabhicāritvaṃ - tat kiṃ*

---

1 M: °*doṣeṇāpopodito*

2 M: °*rūpatvāt/* (i.e., construes with *na ... arhati*, but cf. above p. 90, 19-20)

3 probably a lacuna at this point, cf. *TBV* p. 549.1-3

4 probably a lacuna at this point

5 M: °*pratipattiḥ*

6 M: *sat*°

If it is eternal, [you] should know that it is refuted by the [same] fallacies [which were found in the theory] of the universal.

If it is not eternal, it arises before, together with, or after [the cognition concerned].[71]

In respect to these [alternatives], if it arises before, then of what is it the property? For there can be no property without a property-possessor. Since it has a nature which is distinct from everything else, [you] should say what belongs to what.

If it arises together with [the cognition], [then you] should say what the relation is between the two. When there is neither a relation of identity, nor of causality, nor of inherence,[72] [you] should explain the meaning of the genitive inflection [when you say:] "**its** nonerroneousness."

If [nonerroneousness as a property of the cognition] arises after [the cognition], then the cognition would be erroneous before [this property has arisen]. And there is no property besides pleasure etc., which belongs to the Self[73] [and] which has a nonerroneous nature, because its apprehension is impossible, as you don't admit [it] yourself.

And if properties [such as] nonerroneousness etc., are admitted to be something different [from the property-possessor] (i.e., the cognition), <...> (?) the cognition which is delimited by these [properties] is proclaimed as establishing [the faultlessness of] the causal complex.[74] But this is impossible, because [a cognition can]not last for the time [necessary] for the apprehension of the cognition as delimited by several qualifications, one by one. When there is neither that which has to be made known, nor that which makes known, the cognition would be related to the agent alone.[75]

If nonerroneousness is the own-nature of the [cognition], then [is it determined] in dependence on its (i.e., *svasattāmātrānurodhenārthāntarasattānurodhena vā?*

tad ya[M15a]*di jñānasattāmātrataivāvyabhicāritvam ucyate, tadā keśoṇḍukasaṃvido 'py avyabhicāritā syāt. na ca jñānasattāmātrānurodhena jñānaṃ vyabhicāry avyabhicāri vodgīyate.*

athārthāntarasattānurodhenāvyabhicāritvaṃ - kim anupakārakārthāntarasattānurodhenāhosvid upakārakārthāntarasattānurodhena?

tad yadi tāvad anupakārakārthāntarasattānurodhena, tadā keśoṇḍukendudvayasaṃvido 'py avyabhicāritāprasaṅgaḥ.

athopakārakārthāntarasattānurodhenāvyabhicāritā - kiṃ pratīyamānārthāntaropakārakasattānurodhena tadviparītārthāntaro[M15b]*pakārakasattānurodhena vā?*

tad yadi pūrvapakṣābhyupagamas, tadātītānāgatānumānavijñānasya yogipratyakṣasya ca codanāvacanajanitavijñānasya vāvyabhicāritā na bhavet, tadavagatopakārakārthābhāvāt. bhāve vā vitāna[1]*-*

---

1 S notes that between *vitāna* and *kriyā akhila* is deleted

the cognition's) own existence alone or in dependence on the existence of something else?[76]

In respect to these [alternatives], if nonerroneousness is said to consist in only the existence of the cognition, then the [false] cognition of the hair-net, too, would be nonerroneous. And a cognition is not proclaimed [to be] erroneous or nonerroneous in dependence on the existence of the cognition alone.

If nonerroneousness [is determined] in dependence on the existence of something else, [then] is it in dependence on the existence of something else which does not participate in the production [of the cognition], or in dependence on the existence of something else which does participate in the production [of the cognition]?

In respect to these [alternatives], if [nonerroneousness is determined] in dependence on the existence of something else which does not participate in the production [of the cognition], then the cognitions of the hair-net and of the double moon would also be nonerroneous.

If nonerroneousness [is determined] in dependence on the existence of something else which participates in the production [of the cognition], [then] is it in dependence on the existence of something else which participates in the production [of the cognition and] which is perceived (i.e., appears in the cognition) or is it in dependence on the existence of something else which participates in the production [of the cognition and] which is contrary to that (i.e., which does not appear in the cognition)?

In respect to these [alternatives], if the first position is accepted, then inferential cognition of past and future objects and the perception of the yogi or a cognition which is produced by a Vedic injunction would not be nonerroneous, because the object which is apprehended by them and [should have] participated in [their] production does not exist [at the time when they arise]. Or if it *kriyālopaprasaṅgaḥ.*

athottaro matas, tadā keśoṇḍukendudvayasaṃvido 'vyabhicāritvaṃ prasajyata ity asadgṛhītam.

1.14a [S11]*kiṃ ca tad vijñānam avyabhicāry avagataṃ sāmagryā*[1] *jñāpakam anavagataṃ vā.*

yady avagataṃ tasyāvagatir ātmasaṃvidrūpā vā jñānāntaravedyā[2] *vā.*

tad yady ātmasaṃvedanarūpāvagatis, tad ayuktaṃ, sva[M16a]*yam*[3] *anabhyupagamāt. abhyupagame vopagamavirodhaḥ.*

atha jñānāntaravedyaṃ vetsi, vijñānayor bhede[4] *bījam anveṣṭavyam. jñànam ajñānākārāj jñānātmatayā vyāvartate, jñānāntarāt tu kathaṃ vyāvartate? kiṃ jñānātmatayā vyāvartata āhosvid ākārāntareṇa?*

tad yadi jñānātmatayā vyāvartate, tadānyasya jñānātmatā nivartate toyāder yathā.

athākārāntareṇa, ākārāntarasvīkaraṇe jñānākāravirahaḥ syād, ākārayos tādātmyāyogāt. tādātmye vaikaṃ tad vastu jñānam[5] *ajñānaṃ*[5] *vā.*
yadi jñānaṃ[5]*, na tarhy ākārāntareṇa vyāvartate, kiṃ tu* [M16b] *jñānātmatayaiva. anyasyājñānātma-*

---

1 M: *avagatasāmagryā*

2 perhaps: °*vedyaṃ*

3 M: *dvayam*

4 M: *bhade*

5 so in M; S's conjectures unnecessary

exists [at that time], the sacrificial actions would be annulled.[77]

If the latter [position] is adopted, then the cognition of the hair-net and of the double moon would [also] be nonerroneous. Thus, [the wish to show a difference between erroneous and nonerroneous cognitions] is a childish desire[78] [on the part of the Naiyāyikas and the Mīmāṃsakas].

Besides, this nonerroneous cognition which makes known [the faultlessness of] the causal complex is either apprehended or not apprehended.

If it is apprehended, [then] its apprehension has either the nature of self-apprehension, or [it] is apprehended by another cognition.

In respect to these [alternatives], if [its] apprehension has the nature of self-apprehension, [then] this is not correct, because you do not admit it yourself.[79] Or if [you] admit it, [you] contradict [your own] position.

If you consider [this cognition] as apprehended by another cognition, [then] you should account for the difference between two cognitions. A cognition is differentiated from that which does not have the form of cognition by having the nature of cognition, but how is it differentiated from another cognition?[80] Is it differentiated by having the nature of cognition or by having another form?

In respect to these [alternatives], if it is differentiated by having the nature of cognition, then the other [cognition] would not have the nature of cognition, just like water etc.

If [a cognition is differentiated] by having another form, [then] by adopting another form it would be devoid of the form of cognition, because the two forms cannot be identical. Or if [they] are identical, [then] this single thing is either a cognition or a non-cognition.
If it is a cognition, then it is not differentiated by having another form; on the contrary, [it is differentiated] exactly by having the nature of cognition. [Conse-

katvaprasaṅgaḥ.

athājñānaṃ[1] *siddhaṃ naḥ samīhitam.*

atha jñānatvaṃ vyāvartakaṃ, tat kena vyāvartata iti pūrvoktam anusartavyam. vijñānāntaravedyam api na sambhavati.

atha na vedyate, tad astīti kathaṃ punar vetsi?

anenaiva vartmanā satyetaravijñānayor vibhāgābhāvo 'bhyupagantavyaḥ. ato 'vyabhicāripadam apārthakam.

1.1a *ito 'py apārthakam - indriyārthasannikarṣapadenāpoditatvāt*[2]. *na hi keśoṇḍukavijñānasya nayanārthasannikarṣodbhūtir asti.*

nanu asti marīcyudakavi[M17a]*jñānasya, tadapanodāyāvyabhicāripadam.*

tan na, yata udakaṃ pratibhāti, na ca tena saha sambandho 'sti. vidyamānena sākaṃ sambadhyate, nāvidyamānena. tatsambandhe vā na tadviṣayajñānasya[3] *mithyātvam ihopapadyate satyodakasaṃvedanavat.*

[S12]*nanu yady api pratīyamānodakena saha sambandho nāsti cakṣuṣas, tathāpy*[4] *ālambya marīci-*

---

1 so in M; S's conjecture unnecessary

2 S conjectures °*āpohitatvāt*, but cf. below p. 112.5 (*TUS* p. 13.13)

3 M: *tadviṣayo*; S: *tadviṣaye*

4 M: *tathāpāpy*

quently] the other [cognition] would not have the nature of cognition.

If [this single thing] is a non-cognition, [then] what we have aspired is established.

If [the universal] 'cognition' differentiates [between cognitions and non-cognitions],[81] then by what is it [itself] differentiated? Thus, [the arguments] pronounced above should be followed. [Consequently, the nonerroneous cognition which makes known the faultlessness of the causal complex] can neither be apprehended by another cognition.

If [this cognition] is not apprehended, how do you know it exists?

In exactly this way it has to be admitted that there is no difference between true and false cognitions. This is why the word 'nonerroneous' is useless [in the definition of perception].

For the following reason, too, [the word 'nonerroneous'] is useless [in the definition]:[82] because [nonerroneous cognitions] are excluded [from the domain of the definition] by the word 'contact between sense and object.' For the cognition of the hair-net does not arise from a contact between the eye and an object.[83]

[Objection:] There is [origination of an erroneous cognition from a contact between eye and object, namely] of the cognition of water [which arises] from sun-rays. In order to exclude this [cognition from the domain of the definition] the word 'nonerroneous' [is employed].

[Reply:] This is not [correct], because water appears [in the cognition], but there is no contact with it.[84] [The sense] can have contact [only] with something existent, not with something inexistent. Or if there is a contact with this [inexistent water], [then] a cognition which has it for its object could not be false here (i.e., in this case), just like the cognition of real water.

[Objection:] Even if there is no relation between the eye and the perceived water, nevertheless, in as much as [the *nicayena sākaṃ sambandho 'sti, tasyaivālambanatvāt, taddeśaṃ prati pravṛtteḥ. ata eva mithyātvam - anyad ālambanam anyac ca pratibhāti.*

1.1a1 *ko 'yam ālambanārtho nā[M17b]ma yenedam udghuṣyate - 'nyad ālambanaṃ cānyat pratibhāti*[1]? *kiṃ vijñānajanakatvam ākārārpakatvaṃ vijñānādhikaraṇatvaṃ vijñānāvabhāsitatā vā?*

tad yadi vijñānajanakatvam ālambanārthas, tadā nayanālokāder apy ālambanatvaṃ prasajyate.
athākārārpakatvam ālambanatvaṃ, tad ayuktaṃ, naiyāyikasamaye 'nabhyupagamāt. yathā ca viṣayākāro vijñāne na yujyate tatho[M18a]pariṣṭāt pratipādayiṣyāmaḥ.
atha vijñānādhikaraṇatvam ālambanatvaṃ, na[2] *marīcicakrotkalitam udīyate jñānam, api tv ātmasamavetam ātmānam āsādayate.*
atha vijñānāvabhāsitatālambanatvaṃ, tadodakavijñāna udakaṃ pratīyate, na marīcayaḥ.
athodakākāratayā marīcaya eva pratīyante, sa udakākāro marīcibhyo vyatirikto 'vyatirikto [M18b] vā.

tad yady avyatiriktaḥ, sa tāttviko 'tāttviko vā.

---

1 S: *pratibhātīti*

2 S conjectures a second *na*

cognition] has an external object, there is a relation between [the eye and] the mass of sun-rays, because nothing but this [mass of sun-rays] is the external object. [This is known] because one goes towards the place of the [sun-rays]. This is precisely the reason why [the cognition] is false, [namely] one thing is the external object and another thing appears [in the cognition].[85]

[Reply:] What does it mean [to be] what is called external object by virtue of which it is proclaimed that one thing is the external object and another thing appears?

Is it the fact of being the producer of the cognition, or the fact of being that which provides [its] form [to the cognition], or the fact of being the locus of the cognition, or the fact of appearing in the cognition?

In respect to these [alternatives], if what is meant by external object is the fact of being the producer of the cognition, then the eye, light, etc., too, would be external objects.

If to be external object consists in being that which provides [its] form [to the cognition], [then] this is not correct, because it is not accepted in the established doctrine of the Naiyāyikas. And we shall show later on that the form of the object cannot [appear] in a cognition.[86]

If to be external object consists in being the locus of the cognition, [then this is not correct, for] the cognition does not arise as appearing in a mass of sun-rays; on the contrary, it arises as inherent in the Soul.[87]

If to be external object consists in appearing in the cognition, then [this is not correct, for] in the cognition of water water is perceived, not sun-rays.

[Objection:] The sun-rays are perceived as having the form of water.[88]

[Reply:] This form of water [has to be] either different or not different from the sun-rays.

In respect to these [alternatives], if it is not different, it [has to be] either real or unreal.

yadi tāttvikaḥ kathaṃ tadavagater mithyātvam? athātāttvikas, tadā marīcīnām apy atāttvikatvaṃ prasajyate. atāttvikodakatādātmye sati tad udakajñānam atathyaṃ kim uktaṃ bhavati? marīcivijñānam atathyam. ekasmiṃś codakākāre pratīyamāne kenaitad ākhyātaṃ - marīcayaḥ pratibhānti - devānāmpriyasya?[1]

athārthāntarabhūtas, tarhi na vaktavyaṃ marīcaya udakākāratayā pratīyanta, udakākārāntaritā marīcayaḥ.

atha keśoṇḍukavijñāne kim avabhāti? kim ālambate? keśo[M19a]ṇḍukasyaivālambanatvaṃ [S13] pratīyamānatvaṃ ca, tathodakasyaivālambanatvaṃ pratīyamānatvaṃ ca, nālambanāntaraṃ parikalpyam. na codakajñānasya pratīyamānodakānyālambanatvena[2] *mithyātvam, api tu abhāvāt tāttvikatvena*[3]. *anyathā keśoṇḍukasaṃvido 'pi mithyātvaṃ na prāpnoty, anyālambanavyatirekāt.*

1.1a2 *yad apy uktaṃ marīcideśaṃ prati gamanān marīcīnām ālambanatvam. yady evaṃ deśasyāpy ālambanatvam anayā rītyopapadyate. na cāvabhātodakabhinnārthasannikarṣajatvam udakavijñānasyopapadyate, satyodakajñāne 'dṛṣṭatvāt. anyathānumeyadaha[M19b]najñānasyāpīndriyārthasannikarṣajatvam āpanīpadyeta, ātmamanaḥsannikarṣajatvāt.*

---

1 Different interpretation of the syntax in S: *ākhyātaṃ - marīcayaḥ pratibhānti devānāmpriyasya!*

2 M: *°lambatvena*

3 M: *abhāvātāttvikatvena*

If it is real, why is its apprehension false?
If it is unreal, then the sun-rays, too, would not be real. When [the sun-rays] are identical with unreal water, [then] what does it mean to say that this cognition of water is false? The cognition of sun-rays is false! And when the form of water alone is perceived, who told [you], the beloved of the Gods (i.e., the fool),[89] that the sun-rays appear [in the cognition of water]?

If [the form of water] is different [from the sun-rays], then [you] should not say that the sun-rays are perceived as having the form of water [because in this case] the sun-rays are hidden (or perhaps: are excluded)[90] by the form of water.
What appears in the cognition of the hair-net? What is its external object? The hair-net itself is the external object and it is perceived; in the same manner water itself is the external object and is perceived, no other external object should be assumed. And the cognition of water is not false because its external object is something different from the perceived water, but because [this water] does not exist as a real thing. Otherwise, the cognition of the hair-net, too, would not be false, because there is no other external object [for it].

It has been said that the sun-rays are the external object [of the cognition of water], because one goes towards the place where the sun-rays [are]. If so, [then] in the same way (i.e., by the same reasoning) the place, too, is (i.e., can be) established as the external object.[91] And the origination from a contact with a thing different from the water which appeared [in the cognition] is not established for the [falṣe] cognition of water, because this is not observed in [the case of] a true cognition of water. Otherwise, the cognition of the inferred fire, too, will have to arise from a contact between sense and object, because it arises from a contact between the Soul and the mind.[92]

atha pratīyamānadahanena saha manaso nāsti sambandhas, tad ihāpi pratīyamānenāmbhasā saha nāsti sambandhaś cakṣuṣaḥ.

tasmād avyabhicāripadaṃ na yuktam indriyārthasannikarṣapadenāpoditatvāt.

1.1b *ito 'py anupapannam - apohyajñānāsambhavāt.*

atha marīcyudakavijñānāpaninīṣayo[1]*pādīyate, tat katham apanīyate?*

avidyamānoda[M20a]*kaviṣayatvāt.*

yady avidyamānaṃ, ko 'yaṃ viṣayārthaḥ? pūrvoditam anusaraṇīyam.

yadi tatrodakaṃ pratibhāti, kathaṃ nāsti?

satyaṃ, pratibhāti, kiṃ tv atathyaṃ pratibhāti.

atathyatā kā? kiṃ pratīyamānasyābhāva uta pratīyamāna evābhāvaḥ?

1.1b1 *tad yadi pratīyamānasyābhāvaḥ, sa kiṃ tadaivāhosvit kālāntareṇa?*

yadi tadaiva, sa kim avagato[2] *'navagato vā?*

yady avagataḥ, sa kenāvagamyate? kim udakavijñānena jñānāntareṇa vā?

---

1 M: °*avijñānāyanirnīṣayo*°, or perhaps °*nirbhīṣayo*°; the r seems to be deleted

2 M: *kimvavagato*

If [you object that] there is no contact between the mind and the cognized fire, then here, too, (i.e., in the case of an erroneous cognition) there is no contact between the eye and the perceived water.
Therefore, the word 'nonerroneous' is not correct [in the definition of perception] because [erroneous cognitions] are excluded [from the domain of the definition] by the word 'contact between sense and object.'

For the following [reason], too, [the word 'nonerroneous'] is not correct [in the definition of perception]: because a cognition to be excluded by it [from the domain of the definition] is impossible.
If [the word 'nonerroneous'] is employed because one wants to exclude the cognition of water [produced] by sun-rays, then [we ask] why it should be excluded.
[Answer:] Because it has inexistent water for its object.
[Question:] If [the water] does not exist, what does [the word] 'object' mean [for it]? [Thus] what has been said above should be followed.[93]
If water appears there (i.e., in the cognition), how is it possible that it does not exist?
[Objection:] True, [water] appears, but it is unreal [water] which appears.
[Reply:] What is unreality? Is it the inexistence of the perceived or is it the inexistence itself perceived?[94]

In respect to these [alternatives], if [unreality means] the inexistence of the perceived, is it [the inexistence of the perceived] at that time (i.e., at the time when the cognition arises) or at another time?
If it is [the inexistence of the perceived] at that time, [then] is this [inexistence] apprehended or not apprehended?
If it is apprehended, by what is it apprehended? [Is it apprehended] by [this very] cognition of water or by another cognition?

tad yady udakajñānena, tan na, tasyodakaviṣayatvāt. tadviṣayatve vā na tarhy udakajñānaṃ bhrāntam ity upapadyate, 'bhāva[S14]viṣayasya paramārthasattvā[M20b]t.

na codakākārāvagāhini vijñāne toyavinivṛttayo 'vabhānty atiprasaṅgāt.

atha jñānāntareṇa, na, jñānayaugapadyāsambhavāt. yadi cābhāvajñānenābhāvavyavasthā kriyate bhāvajñānena ca bhāvavyavasthā, tadodakasya bhāvābhāvāv ekakālau syātām.

atha bhāvajñānaṃ bhāvavyavasthāṃ na karoty abhāvajñānaṃ cābhāvavyavasthāṃ karoty, aho rājājñā naiyāyikapaśoḥ. yadi ca bhāvajñānaṃ bhāvavyavasthāṃ na karoti, tadā [M21a] sarvabhāveṣv anāśvāsaprasaṅgaḥ. tatprasaktāv abhāvasyāpy anavasthitiḥ. tadanavasthitau ca tattvopaplavaḥ syāt. athānavagataḥ, so 'stīti kathaṃ punar vetsi?

In respect to these [alternatives], if [the inexistence of the perceived at that time is apprehended] by [this very] cognition of water, [then] this is not [possible], because it (i.e., the cognition of water) has water for its object [and not the inexistence of water]. Or if it has the [inexistence of water] for its object, then it is impossible to say that the cognition of water is false, because the object inexistence is absolutely real.[95]

Nor do water and its inexistence appear in a cognition which apprehends the form of water [alone], because this is absurd.

If [you say that the inexistence of the perceived water exactly at that time is apprehended] by another cognition, [we answer:] no! [This is impossible] because [two] cognitions cannot exist simultaneously.[96]

[Or if you say that two cognitions can exist simultaneously, the one affirming the existence of water, the other denying it] and if the inexistence [of water] is established by the cognition of the inexistence [of water], and the existence [of water] established by the cognition of the existence [of water], then water would be both existent and inexistent at the same time.[97]

If the cognition of the existence [of water] does not establish the existence [of water], whereas the cognition of the inexistence [of water] establishes the inexistence [of water], [then] alas! [this must be] a royal decree for the Naiyāyika beast! For if the cognition of the existence [of something] does not establish [its] existence, then there would be insecurity in respect to everything. In this case inexistence, too, [would] not be established. And when these (i.e., existence and inexistence) are not established, [all] principles would be annihilated.

If [the inexistence of the perceived at the time of the cognition] is not apprehended, then how do you know that this [inexistence] exists?

atha kālāntare, tadā na kiñcid bādhyate, satyodakasyāpi kālāntare 'bhāvopapatteḥ.

1.1b2 atha pratīyamāna evābhāvaḥ, kathaṃ tadviṣayajñānasya mithyātvam upapadyate, pratīyamānasyaivābhāvasyopapatteḥ? na ca bhāvākāre pratīyamāne 'bhāvakalpanā nyāyyā[M21b]tiprasaṅgāt. anyathā rūpādau pratīyamāne rasādikalpanā kartavyā. na ca kriyate, tathehāpy udakaṃ pratīyate.

nanu pratīyate, kiṃ tv atathyam.

yady evam udakaprapañco 'yaṃ dīrghodakaṃ madhurodakam iti yathā.

nanv atra sarvāsv avasthāsūdakaṃ pratīyate, tena tāsv ambhaḥ prakalpyate.

yady evaṃ tad ihāpy avasthādvaye 'py udakaṃ pratīyate satyodakam asatyodakaṃ ca. satyodakajñāne satyodakam avabhāti, nāsatyodakam anudakaṃ vā. tathāsatyodakajñāne 'satyodakaṃ pratibhāti, na satyodakam anudakaṃ vā, svaviṣayaparyavasāyinyo hi buddhayaḥ.

1.1ba atha bādhyamānatve[M22a]na mithyātvam iti cet,

kiṃ bādhyate 'rtho jñānam ubhayaṃ vā?

1.1ba1 yady arthasya bādhā, sa kena bādhyate? kiṃ svayam evātmānaṃ bādhata āho 'rthāntareṇa jñānena vā?

If [the inexistence of the perceived means inexistence] at some other time (i.e., not at the time of the cognition), then nothing is sublated because real water, too, may not exist at another time.

If [unreality means that] the inexistence itself is perceived, how could the cognition which has it (i.e., the inexistence) for its object be false? [It cannot be false] since the inexistence which is indeed perceived is correct. And it is not reasonable to assume the inexistence [of something] when the form of [its] existence is perceived, because this is absurd. Otherwise flavour etc., would have to be assumed when colour etc., are perceived. But [this] is not done! In the same manner here [in our case], too, water is perceived. [Therefore, its existence should be assumed.]

[Objection: True,] it is perceived, but it is not real.

[Reply:] If so, [then] this is a kind of water, just as [the different kinds of water which appear in cognitions such as] "a long [patch of] water," "sweet water" [etc.].

[Objection:] Here, in all these cases, water is perceived; this is why [the existence of] water is assumed in them.

[Reply:] If so, then here, too, in both cases water is perceived: real water [in one case] and unreal water [in the other]. In a cognition of real water real water appears, not unreal water or something which is not water. In the same manner in a cognition of unreal water unreal water appears, not real water or something which is not water, for cognitions terminate in (i.e., convey no other information than)[98] their own objects.

[Objection:] Falsity is due to the fact of being sublated.

[Reply:] What is sublated? Is it the external object, the cognition, or both?[99]

If the external object is sublated,[100] [then] by what is it sublated? Is it sublated by itself, by another object, or by a cognition?

yadi [S15] *svayam evātmānaṃ bādhate, tadā bādhā tena kriyate jñāpyate vā.*
yadi kriyate, 'vyatiriktā vyatiriktā vā.
yady avyatiriktā, tadā bādhā kriyata ity ātmānenotpādyate. tac ca na jāghaṭīti svātmani kriyāvirodhāt.
atha vyatiriktā kriyate, tathāpi vidyamānasya kartṛtvaṃ, na pratīyamānasyāpalāpaḥ.
atha bādhā jñāpyate, sāpy abhinnā bhinnā vā.
yady abhinnā, tadā bādhā tena jñāpyate kim uktaṃ bhavati? udakaṃ jñā[M22b]*pyate.*
atha bhinnā, tadā vidyamānasya jñāpakatvaṃ siddhaṃ pratīyamānasya cāstitvam.

athārthāntareṇa bādhyate, tathāpi vidyamānayor bādhyabādhakabhāvo bhūpālayor iva, na caikasya bādhyabādhakabhāva upapadyate.

bādhāpi tena pratīyamānasya kiṃ kriyate jñāpyate vā?

If [the external object] sublates itself, then the sublation is either produced by it or made known [by it].
If [the sublation] is produced [by it], [then] it is either [produced as something] not different [from the object] or [as something] different.
If it is [produced as something] not different, then [to say] that the sublation is produced [means that the object] itself is produced by it (i.e., by the object). And this is totally impossible because action upon oneself is contradictory.
If [the sublation] is produced as different [from the object], even so [only] an existent thing [can] function as an agent [of production], [and therefore] there is no denial of what is perceived.
If the sublation is made known [by the object itself], once again it is either not different [from the object] or different [from it].
If it is [made known as something] not different, then what does it mean [to say] that the sublation is made known by it (i.e., by the object)? [It would mean that] the water is made known!
If [the sublation is made known as something] different [from the object], then making known [something] is established [only] for an existent thing, and [therefore] the perceived [water] exists.

If [the object] is sublated by another object, even so [both objects will exist, for] the relation of sublated and sublating [obtains] between two existent things, just like [the relation] between two kings, as the relation of sublated and sublating is not possible with reference to one thing alone.[101]

Is the sublation of the perceived [object], in its turn, produced by it (i.e., by the other object) or is it made known [by it]?

yadi kriyate, 'vyatiriktā vyatiriktā vā.
yady avyatiriktā, tadāvyatiriktā bādhotpādyate kim uktaṃ bhavet? udakam utpādyate. tadutpādane ca tatsaṃ[M23a]vido 'mithyātvam.
atha vyatiriktotpādyate, tathāpi toyasambandhitayopalabdher ambhasa upapattiḥ. na jātu devadattasyāsattve tannayanavyavahārasiddhiḥ.
atha jñāpyate, tadā sāvyatiriktā vyatiriktā vā.
yady avyatiriktā jñāpyate, tadā bādhā tena jñāpyate kim uktaṃ bhavati? udakaṃ jñāpyate.
atha vyatiriktā satī jñāpyate, tathāpy udakasyeyaṃ bādhety anyatantratayā pratibhāsanān nātyantābhāvopapattiḥ. tasmād arthā[M23b]ntareṇāpi na bādhopapattiḥ.

atha jñānena bādhyate kiṃ tadviṣayeṇānyaviṣayeṇa nirviṣayeṇa vā?
yadi tadviṣayeṇa, tadā tat svarūpaṃ vidhatte, na tu viparyāsayati tadākāraparyavasitarūpatvāt.

If it is produced, it is either [produced as] not different [from the perceived object] or [as] different [from it].
If it is [produced as] not different, then what does it mean [to say] that the sublation is produced as not different [from the object]? [It would mean that] the water is produced! And if it is produced, its cognition is not false.
If [the sublation] is produced as different [from the object], even so [the existence of] water is established, because [the sublation] is apprehended as related to water. [For] if Devadatta does not exist, talking/thinking about his eyes is never established.
If [the sublation of the perceived object] is made known [by the other object], it is either [made known as] not different [from the perceived object] or [as] different.
If [the sublation] is made known as not different [from the perceived object], then what does it mean [to say] that the sublation is made known by it (i.e., by the other object)? [It would mean that] the water is made known!
If [the sublation] is made known as different [from the perceived object], even so the absolute inexistence [of water] is not established because [the cognition] "This is the sublation of water" appears as dependent on something else (i.e., on water). That is why the sublation is not established by another object either.

If [the object] is sublated by a cognition, is it [sublated] by [the cognition] which has it for its object, by [a cognition] which has another object, or by [a cognition] which has no object?[102]
If [the object is sublated] by [the cognition] which has it for its object, then this [cognition] affirms the [reality of its] form (i.e., the form of the object), it does not overthrow [it], because [the cognition] has a form which terminates in (i.e., conveys no other information than) the form of its [object].

athānyaviṣayaṃ bādhakaṃ, tad api na yujyate. yad yadviṣayaṃ tat tasyaiva sattāṃ vidhatte, na tv anyasya vidhāyakaṃ pratiṣedhakaṃ vā. svaviṣaya-paryavasāyinyo hi buddhayaḥ.

[S16]*atha nirviṣayeṇa bādhyate, na kiñcid vidadhāti pratiṣedhati vā nirviṣayatvād eva.*

1.1ba2 *atha jñānaṃ bādhyate, tasyāpi bādhā kā? kiṃ svarūpavyāvṛttirūpā svarūpāpahnavarūpā vā viṣayāpahāralakṣa*[M24a]*ṇā vā?*

tad yadi svarūpavyāvṛttirūpā bādhā, tadā sarvaṃ bādhitaṃ syād, vijñānasya vijñānāntareṇa ni[1]*vartyamānatvāt.*

atha svarūpāpahnavarūpā[2]*, tad ayuktaṃ, mithyodakavijñānasyāpy anubhūyamānatvāt.*

atha viṣayāpahāralakṣaṇā bādhocyate, sāpi na yuktā. yathā ca viṣayāpahāro na śakyate kartuṃ tathānāntaram eva niveditam.

1.1baa *yadi na bādhyate kim ity asāv arthakriyāṃ na karoti bhāvaḥ?*

keyam arthakriyā yā tena na sampādyate[3] *puṃsām?*

kiṃ vijñānarūpā pravṛttirūpā prāptirūpā sukhaduḥkho[M24b]*tpādabhogarūpā vā?*

---

1 M: *niro*

2 M: *orūpaṃ*

3 M: *sampādyate/*

If [a cognition] which has another object is the sublating [cognition], [then] this is also not correct: whatever [a cognition] has for its object, it affirms the existence of that very [object], but it neither affirms nor negates [the existence of] another object. For cognitions terminate in their own objects.

If [the object] is sublated by [a cognition] which has no object, [then this is not correct, for a cognition without an object] neither affirms nor negates anything precisely because it has no object![103]

If the cognition is sublated, what is its sublation? Does it consist in the cessation of [the sublated cognition] itself, or does it consist in the denial of [the sublated cognition] itself, or is it characterized by the removal of the object [of the sublated cognition]?[104]

In respect to these [alternatives], if the sublation consists in the cessation of [the sublated cognition] itself, then every [cognition] would be sublated because [every] cognition is brought to an end by another cognition.[105]

If it consists in the denial of [the existence of the sublated cognition] itself, [then] this is not correct, because a false cognition of water, too, is experienced.[106]

If the sublation is said to be characterized by the removal of the object, [then] this [sublation], too, is not possible. It has just been shown that/why the object cannot be removed.[107]

[Objection:] If [a false cognition] is not sublated, why does this thing (i.e., the object of false cognition) not produce an efficient action?[108]

[Reply:] What is this efficient action which is not accomplished for the people by that [object]? Does it have the form of cognition, the form of activity [towards the object], the form of obtainment [of the object], or the form of experience which consists in the arising of pleasure and pain?

tad yadi vijñānalakṣaṇāṃ na karoti, tad ayuktaṃ, vijñānalakṣaṇām arthakriyāṃ karoty eva toyam.

atha pravṛttirūpāṃ na karoti, tad ayuktaṃ, pravṛttir hi puruṣecchānuvidhāyinī, nārthasvarūpabhāvābhāvāv anugamayati. puruṣo hi kāmataḥ pravartate vā na vā. na hy etāvatā tadabhāvasiddhiḥ.

atha prāptirūpām arthakriyāṃ na karoti, tenāsattvam.

tad apy ayuktaṃ, candrārkagrahanakṣatratārakādeḥ prā[M25a]ptyabhāve 'pi sattvasambhavāt.

atha sukhaduḥkharūpām arthakriyāṃ na karoti, kiṃ darśanajaṃ sukhaṃ na karoty āho dehasambandhajam?

tad yadi darśanajaṃ na karoti, tad ayuktaṃ, karoty eva.

atha dehasambandhajaṃ na karoti, tadā candrārkagrahanakṣatrādau vyabhicāras, teṣāṃ dehasambandhajasukhajanakatvaṃ nāsty, atha ca sattvam.

na cārthakriyākartṛtvena vastūnām asattvaṃ, svahetor eva vijñānajananamātrasyotpatteḥ, saha-

In respect to these [alternatives], if it does not produce [an efficient action] which is characterized as cognition, [then] this is not correct, [for even illusory] water does produce an efficient action characterized as cognition.

If it does not produce [an efficient action] which has the form of activity, [then] this is not correct, for activity follows (i.e., is due to) the volition of people; it does not follow the existence or inexistence of the object itself, for a person acts or does not [act] according to his desire. The inexistence of that [object] is not at all established by that much.

[Objection: The object of false cognition] does not produce an efficient action which has the form of obtainment; that is why [it is said to be] inexistent.

[Reply:] This is also not correct because existence is possible, even if there is no obtainment, [as in the case] of sun, moon, planets, constellations, stars, etc.

If [the object of false cognition] does not produce an efficient action which has the form of pleasure and pain, does it not produce a pleasure which arises from seeing [the object], or [a pleasure] which arises from a relation to (i.e., contact with) the body?

If it does not produce [a pleasure] which arises from seeing [the object], [then] this is not correct; it does [produce such a pleasure].

If it does not produce [a pleasure] which arises from a relation to the body, then this does not hold good for the sun, moon, planets, constellations, etc.; they do not produce a pleasure which arises from a relation with the body, but nevertheless they exist.

And it is not by their not being agents of efficient action that things do not exist, because [a thing may] be produced by its own cause [in such a way] that it produces nothing *kārivirahād vā na karoti.*

1.1bab *kiṃ cārthakriyāṃ na karoti - kim ekasya pratipattuḥ sarvapratipattṝṇāṃ vā?*

tad yady ekasya prati[M25b]pattur arthakriyāṃ na karoti [S17] tenāsattvaṃ, tadā candrārkagrahanakṣatratārakādau vyabhicāro, mumūrṣvarthe ca.

atha sarvapratipattṝṇām arthakriyāṃ na karoti tenāsattvam, evaṃ tarhi sarvabhāvānām asattvaprasaṅgaḥ. na hi sarve bhāvāḥ sarvapuruṣārthahetavaḥ. na ca sarvapuruṣārthakriyāvihīnam etad ity avagantuṃ pāryate 'rvāgvidā.

tasmāt sthitam etad avyabhicāripadam anarthakam.

c. *anye tu marīcyudakavijñānasya smṛtitvaṃ pratipadyante, na bhrāntirūpatām. tasya kathaṃ smṛtitvam? kim udakagṛhītitvena gṛhītodakagṛhītitvena vodakagrahaṇānantarakālabhāvitvena vā nirviṣayatvena vā yam aham adrākṣam ity anenākāreṇo[M26a]pajāyamānatvena vā?*

tad yady udakagṛhītitvena tadā sarvodakavijñānānāṃ smṛtitvaprasaṅgaḥ.

atha gṛhītodakagṛhītitvena smṛtitvaṃ, tadādyasyāpi gṛhītodakagṛhītitve[1] *smṛtitvaṃ prasajyate gṛhītodakagrāhitvāviśeṣāt.*

---

1 perhaps: °*gṛhītitvena*

but [its own] cognition;[109] or due to the absence of a co-producer [the thing] does not produce [anything at all].

Besides, does [the fact that a thing] does not produce an efficient action [refer] to one perceiver alone or to all perceivers?[110]

In respect to these [alternatives], if it does not produce an efficient action for one perceiver [and] therefore [is considered as] inexistent, then this would not hold good in [the case of] sun, moon, planets, constellations, stars, etc., nor in [the case of] an object which is about to vanish.

If [a thing] does not produce an efficient action for all perceivers [and] therefore is [considered as] inexistent, then all things would be inexistent. For nothing benefits all people. Nor can a person who does not possess superior faculties know that a certain thing is devoid of efficient action for all people.

Therefore it is settled: The word 'nonerroneous' is useless [in the definition of perception].

But others consider the cognition of water in respect to sun-rays as recollection, not as something having the nature of false cognition.[111] How is it a recollection? Is it by being an apprehension of water, or by being an apprehension of apprehended water, or by arising immediately after the apprehension of water, or by being without an object, or by being produced with the form "[This is the object] which I saw"?

In respect to these [alternatives], if it is [a recollection] by being an apprehension of water, then all cognitions of water would be recollections.

If its being a recollection [of water] is due to [its] being an apprehension of apprehended water, then the first [apprehension of water], too, would be recollection by being an apprehension of apprehended water, because there is no difference in the fact [that both cognitions] are apprehensions of apprehended water.[112]

athādyasya[1] gṛhītodakagrāhitvaṃ nāsti. tadānīṃ bhinnaviṣayatvam. bhinnaviṣayatve ca dvitīyasyāpi gṛhītagrāhitvaṃ vihīyate. athaikaviṣayatvam, āyātaṃ[2] tarhi prathamasyāpi gṛhītagrāhitvam aviśiṣṭārthagṛhītirūpatvāt prathamottaravijñānavat. yathaikanīlasvalakṣaṇagrāhakayugapadutpannānekavijñānānāṃ[3] nīlajñānarūpatā na bhidyate tathehāpi. ta[M26b]thā dhārāvāhivijñānānāṃ smṛtirūpatā prāpnoti. tathā pratyabhijñānasya ca gṛhītagrāhitvena smṛtitvaṃ prasajyate. atha pratyabhijñānasya gṛhītārthagrāhitvaṃ na vidyate, tadā pratyabhijñānatvaṃ nivartate. na hy ādyaṃ darśanaṃ sa evāyam ity upajāyate. tathānumānikam api vijñānaṃ[4] gṛhītārthagrāhitvena smṛtitvam āpadyate.

[S18] athodakagrahaṇottarakālabhāvitvena smṛtitvaṃ, tadā saṃskārasya smaraṇarūpatā prāpnoty, udakagrahaṇo[M27a]ttarakālabhāvitvena rasasaṃvedanasya ca.

atha nirviṣayatvena smṛtirūpatocyate, tad ayuktaṃ, pūrvoditānubhavāveditārthākārāvedakatvenodīyamānāyāḥ kathaṃ nirviṣayatvam?

atha pūrvānubhūtārthapratyastamaye sati samānakālārthābhāvān nirviṣayatā, tadā codanājanitavi-

---

1 M & S: ādyasya

2 M: āyātaṃ/ (i.e., construes with °viṣayatvam)

3 M: °vijñānān; S: °vijñānāt

4 M: vijñāna°

[Objection:] The first [cognition] does not apprehend apprehended water.
[Reply:] Then it has a different object, and having a different object the second [cognition], too, does not apprehend apprehended [water]. If [the two cognitions] have the same object, then the fact of apprehending apprehended [water] holds good for the first [cognition], too, because it has the form of apprehension of the same object, just like the cognition which is posterior to the first. Just as several cognitions which apprehend the same particular blue [object] and which arise at the same time do not differ in having the form of a cognition of a blue [object], so here too [the forms of the first and the second cognition of water do not differ]. In the same manner continuous cognitions would have the nature of recollection.[113] In the same manner recognition, too, would be recollection because it apprehends an apprehended [object]. If a recognition does not apprehend an apprehended object, then it is no longer a recognition. For a first cognition is not produced [with the form] "This is exactly that." In the same manner inferential cognition, too, would be a recollection because it apprehends an apprehended object.[114]
If [its] being a recollection is due to [its] arising after the apprehension of water, then a mental impression would have the form of recollection because it arises after the apprehension of water, and the cognition of taste [of water, too, would have the form of recollection when water is drunk after being seen].
If it is maintained that [it] has the form of recollection because it has no object, [then] this is not correct. How [is it possible] that something which is produced as making known the form of an object which has been made known by previous experience is without an object?
If it is without an object because there is no object at the same time [as the recollection], [assuming that] a previously experienced object has been destroyed [in the

jñānasya nirviṣayatvena smṛtitvam āpanīpadyate, kartavyatārūpārthasya tadābhāvāt. bhāve vā kartavyarūpatā nopapadyate. tadanupapattau saptatantukri[M27b]yāyā vilopaprasaṅgaḥ. yadi ca nirviṣayatvena smṛtitvaṃ, tadā vidyamānaghaṭajātyādeḥ smaraṇasyāsmṛtitvaprasaṅgaḥ.

athādrākṣam ity anenākāreṇopajāyamānatvena smṛtitvaṃ, tad ayuktam. ihodakam ity anenākāreṇopajāyamānāyāḥ katham adrākṣam ity evaṃrūpatopapadyate?

atha vipramuṣitatayānayā[1] *bhaṅgyopajāyate, ko 'yaṃ vipramoṣo*[2] *nāma? kim anubhavākārasvīkaraṇaṃ smaraṇākārapradhvaṃso vāpūrvārthagṛhītitvaṃ vendriyārthasannikarṣajatvaṃ vendriyārthāsannikarṣajatvaṃ vā?*

tad yady anubhavākārasvīkaraṇaṃ, [M28a] *tadā smṛtirūpatā nopapadyate. atha smṛtirūpatā, tadānubhavākārasvīkaraṇaṃ nopapadyate, smṛtyanubhavākārayor itaretaraparihārasthitilakṣaṇatvāt. atha smaraṇākārapradhvaṃsas, tad ayuktaṃ, vijñānasya svayaṃ smṛtitvenābhyupagamāt. pradhvaṃso hy avijñānātmakaḥ, kathaṃ smṛtirūpatāṃ vidhatte?*

---

1 M: *vipramuṣitānayā*; S: *vipramuṣi[ta]tā anayā*

2 M : *vimoṣo*

meantime], then a cognition produced by a Vedic injunction will necessarily be a recollection because it is without a [contemporaneous] object, since an object [of cognition] which consists in the fact that something has to be done does not exist at that time (i.e., at the time of the cognition produced by the Vedic injunction). Or if it exists, the fact that it has the form of something to be done is not possible. When this is not possible, sacrificial action would be annulled. And if being a recollection is due to being without an object, then remembering a [still] existing pot, a universal, etc., would not be a recollection.

If [its] being a recollection is due to [its] being produced with the form "I saw," [then] this is not correct. How is it possible that something which is produced with the form "There is water here" has the form "I saw"?

If [the recollection of water] arises in that manner (i.e., as a direct cognition of water) by being deprived [of the part "I saw"], what is this [thing] called deprivation? Is it the adaptation of the form of experience, or the destruction of the form of recollection, or the apprehension of an unprecedented object, or the arising from a contact between sense and object, or the arising without a contact between sense and object?[115]

In respect to these [alternatives], if it is the adaptation of the form of experience, then the fact of having the form of recollection is impossible. If it has the form of recollection, then the adaptation of the form of experience is impossible, because the forms of recollection and of experience are characterized by mutual exclusion.

If it is the destruction of the form of recollection, [then] this is not correct because the cognition is accepted as recollection by yourself. Since destruction does not have the character of cognition, how does it affirm the fact of having the form of recollection?

athāpūrvārthaviṣaya[1]*gṛhītitvaṃ smṛtipramoṣa ucyate, tadātyantānanubhūtakanakapanasādisaṃvittīnāṃ smṛtivipramoṣatvam āpadyate.*

athendriyārthasannikarṣajatvaṃ smṛtivipramoṣa ucyate, tadā saṃvittīnāṃ[2] *smṛtivipra*[S19]*moṣatva prasaṅgaḥ.*

athe[M28b]*ndriyāsannikarṣaja*[3]*tvaṃ smṛtivipramoṣa ucyate, tadā codanājanitavijñānasyānumānopamānavijñānasya ca smṛtivipramoṣatvam āpadyate.*

tasmād yathā yathā vicāryate smṛtivipramoṣas tathā tathā nyāyaṃ na viṣahata iti. tasmān marīcyudakavijñānasya na smṛtivipramoṣarūpatā, api tu viparītakhyātitvaṃ samyagjñānatvaṃ vā.

1.2 [M29a]*tathā vyavasāyātmakapadam api nopādeyam apaneyābhāvāt.*[4]

nanu sthāṇvādike 'rtha [5]*indriyārthasannikarṣāt*[5] *sāmānyamātradarśanād viśeṣānupalabdhau sandehajñānam upajāyate. tad apanīyate.*

tasmin sandehajñāne jāte kiñcit pratibhāty āho na pratibhāti. tad yadi pratibhāti, sa kiṃ dharmī dharmo vā?

tad yadi dharmī pratibhāti, sa tāttviko 'tāttvi[M29b]*ko vā.*

---

1 S deletes °*viṣaya*°

2 so in M; S's conjecture unnecessary

3 perhaps: °*endriyārthāsannikarṣa*°

4 M: *aprameyābhāvāt*

5 probably an interpolation

If being an apprehension which has an unprecedented thing as its object is called deprivation of recollection, then immediate cognitions of absolutely unexperienced [objects like] a golden jack fruit etc., would be [cases of] deprivation of recollection.
If arising from a contact between sense and object is called deprivation of recollection, then immediate cognitions would be [cases of] deprivation of recollection.
If arising without a contact between sense [and object] is called deprivation of recollection, then the cognition produced by Vedic injunction and the cognitions of inference and comparison would be [cases of] deprivation of recollection.
That is why in whatever way the deprivation of recollection is examined it does not stand to reason. Therefore, the cognition of water in respect to sun-rays does not consist in deprivation of recollection, but it is either the appearance of a different/wrong [object] or a valid cognition.[116]

In the same manner the word 'having the nature of determination' should not be employed [in the definition of perception] because there is no [cognition] which can be rejected [by it].[117]
[Objection:] In respect to an object such as a trunk[118] etc., a doubtful cognition arises [from a contact between sense and object], when the particular properties are not apprehended because one sees only the general features.[119] This [doubtful cognition] is rejected [by the word 'having the nature of determination'].
[Reply:] When this doubtful cognition arises, either something appears [in it] or not. In respect to these [alternatives], if [something] appears, [then] is it a property-possessor or a property?[120]

In respect to these [alternatives], if a property-possessor appears, it is either real or unreal.

yadi tāttviko, nāpaneyatā tadviṣayavijñānasya. athātāttvikas, tadāvyabhicāripadenāpanītatvān na vyavasāyātmakapadam upādeyam.

atha dharmaḥ pratibhāti, sa sthāṇutvalakṣaṇaḥ puruṣatvalakṣaṇa ubhayaṃ vā.

tad yadi sthāṇutvalakṣaṇo dharmaḥ pratibhāti, sa tāttviko 'tāttviko vā.
yadi tāttvikaḥ, kathaṃ tadbuddheḥ sandeharūpatā, tāttvikārthagṛhītirūpatvena satyodakasaṃvedanavat?
athātāttvikas, tadāvyabhicāripadenāpoditatvān na vyavasāyātmakapadam upādeyam.

atha puruṣatvalakṣaṇo dharmaḥ pratibhāty, asāv a[M30a]pi tāttviko 'tāttviko vā.
yadi tāttvikaḥ, kathaṃ tatbuddheḥ sandeharūpatā?
athātāttvikas, tadāvyabhicāripadenāpoditatvād vyavasāyātmakapadaṃ na sādhīyaḥ.

athobhayaṃ pratibhāti, tadobhayos tāttvikatvam atāttvikatvaṃ vāthaikasya tāttvikatvam anyasyātāttvikatvam.
tad yady ubhayos tāttvikatvaṃ, tadā tadvijñānasya tāttvikatvam eva, na [S20] sandehātmatā.
athobhāv[1] apy atāttvikau, tadā tadvijñānasya viparyayarūpatā, na sandehātmatā.
athaikasya tāttvikatvam anyasyātāttvikatvaṃ, tadā tad eva jñānaṃ vyabhicāri tad evāvyabhicāri. atāttvikārthagṛ[M30b]hītirūpatvād vyabhicāri, tāttvikārthagṛhītirūpatvād avyabhicāri.

---

1 M: athābhāve

If it is real, the cognition which has it for its object should not be rejected [from the domain of perception].
If it is unreal, then, since it is [already] rejected by the word 'nonerroneous,' the word 'having the nature of determination' should not be employed.

If a property appears [in the doubtful cognition], [then] this [property] is either characterized as 'being a trunk,' or as 'being a person,' or as both.

In respect to these [alternatives], if a property which is characterized as 'being a trunk' appears, it is either real or unreal.
If it is real, how could its cognition have the nature of doubt, considering that it has the nature of an apprehension of a real object, just like a cognition of real water?
If it is unreal, then, since it is [already] rejected by the word 'nonerroneous,' the word 'having the nature of determination' should not be employed.

If a property which is characterized as 'being a person' appears, it too is either real or unreal.
If it is real, how could its cognition have the nature of doubt?
If it is unreal, then, since it is [already] rejected by the word 'nonerroneous,' the word 'having the nature of determination' is no good.

If both [properties] appear, then they are both real, both unreal, or the one real, the other unreal.
In respect to these [alternatives], if they are both real, then their cognition is true indeed, it does not have the nature of doubt.
If they are both unreal, then their cognition has the nature of error, not the nature of doubt.
If the one is real, the other unreal, then one and the same cognition is both erroneous and nonerroneous: it is erroneous because it has the nature of apprehension of an unreal object; it is nonerroneous because it has the nature of apprehension of a real object.[121] In this [way] the cogni-

etena dvicandrajñānam udghāṭitam. tatra hi dravyākāraḥ pratibhāti, na guṇākāraḥ.
atha sandigdhārthākārapratibhāsi sandehajñānam iti cet,
sa sandigdho 'rtho vidyate vā na vā.

tad yadi vidyate, kathaṃ tatsaṃvedanasya sandeharūpatābādhitārthagṛhītirūpatvāt satyodakasaṃvedanavat?
atha na vidyate, tadāvyabhicāripadenāpoditatvād vyavasāyātmakapadam apārthakam.

atha na kiñcid api[1] *pratibhāti, na tarhi tasye[M31a]ndriyārthasannikarṣajatvaṃ*[2] *bhrāntodakavijñānavat.*
tasmād vyavasāyātmakapadam apy anupādeyam.

1.3 *avyapadeśyapadaṃ ca yathā na sādhīyas tathā lakṣaṇasāre draṣṭavyam.*

1.4 *tathendriyārthasannikarṣajatvam api nopapadyate tadgatyabhāvāt.*

1.41 *indriyārthasannikarṣo hi vyavahitārthānupalabdhiliṅgo vāvaraṇaliṅgo vā*[3] *tadutpāditaghaṭādijñānāvaseyo vā.*

tad yadi vyavahitārthānupalabdhiliṅgas, tad ayuktaṃ, tena saha sambandhānupapattes tadabhāve

---

1 M: *a...d api*; 3 akṣaras are missing

2 M: °*jaṃ*

3 M om. °*varaṇaliṅgo vā*; one can discern a marker for an addition between *vā* and *tad*°, but that part of the leaf on which the addition could be is broken off.

tion of the double moon is (i.e., has to be) explained, for there [in the cognition of the double moon] the form of substance appears, not the form of quality.[122]

[Objection:] Doubtful cognition contains the appearance of a doubtful object.

[Reply:] This doubtful object either exists or not.

In respect to these [alternatives], if it exists, how could its cognition have the nature of doubt? [It can't] since it has the nature of apprehension of a non-sublated object, just like the cognition of real water.

If [the doubtful object] does not exist, then, since [its cognition] is rejected by the word 'nonerroneous,' the word 'having the nature of determination' is useless.

If nothing at all appears [in the cognition], then it does not arise from a contact between sense and object, just as a false cognition of water.

Therefore the word 'having the nature of determination,' too, (i.e., not only the word 'nonerroneous') should not be employed [in the definition of perception].

And for the reason why the word 'which cannot be designated' is no good you should consult the *Lakṣaṇasāra* (The Essence of Definition).[123]

In the same manner the arising from a contact between sense and object, too, is not correct [in the definition of perception] because it is not apprehended.[124]

For the contact between sense and object has either the non-apprehension of objects separated [by a wall etc.] as its [inferential] sign, or it has obstruction as its [inferential] sign,[125] or it is determined by a cognition such as of a pot etc., which is produced by it (i.e., by the contact).

In respect to these [alternatives], if [the contact] has the non-apprehension of objects separated [by a wall etc.] as its [inferential] sign, [then] this is not correct, because the relation with it (i.e., with the contact) is not established, for one observes the existence of non-

'py anupalambhasadbhāvadarśanāt. yadabhāve 'pi yasya sadbhāvaḥ, [M31b] sa kathaṃ tatsadbhāvāvedakaḥ?

athāvaraṇaliṅgas, tad ayuktaṃ, tena saha saṅgater[1] abhāvāt, tadabhāve 'pi sadbhāvadarśanāt. tadbhāve vāvaraṇānarthakyam[2]. tadabhāve tadgatiḥ katham?

[S21]atha tadbhavakumbhādijñānenāvagamyate, tad ayuktaṃ, tadanavagatau tadudbhavatvasyānavagateḥ. piśācaparamāṇumaheśvarakalpo 'sau sannikarṣaḥ. kathaṃ tadāyattatā vedyate jñāne? [M32a] kathaṃ ca tadindriyārthasannikarṣam āvedayati jñānam? kiṃ vijñānākāratayāho kāryākāratayendriyārthasannikarṣajanyākāratayā vā?

tad yadi jñānasvabhāvatayā, tad ayuktaṃ, tadabhāve 'pi jñānākārasya sambhava upamānādijñāne.

atha kāryātmatayā gamayati, tad apy ayuktam, upamānānumānajñānamarīcinīlajalādau tasya sadbhāvopapatteḥ. yo yena vinā [M32b] bhavati, sa kathaṃ tasya jñāpako nāma? anyathā sattvāder api gamakatvaṃ syāt.

---

1 M: saṃmatigater

2 M: °arthajyam

apprehension even when this [contact] is absent.[126] When A exists even when B is absent, how can A reveal the existence of B?

If [the contact] has obstruction as its [inferential] sign, [then] this is not correct because there is no relation [of this sign] with this [contact]. For one observes the existence [of obstruction] even when there is no [contact]. Or if there is a [contact even when there is obstruction], the obstruction is inefficient. When there is no [efficiency of obstruction], how is it (i.e., the contact) apprehended [by obstruction]?

If [the contact] is apprehended by a cognition such as of a pot etc., which arises from it, [then] this is not correct, because when this [contact] is not apprehended the fact that [a cognition] arises from it is not apprehended [either]. This contact is like a demon, an atom, or God. How [could] the dependence on it be known in a cognition? Indeed, how [can] a cognition reveal this contact between sense and object? Is it by having the form of cognition, or by having the form of effect, or by having the form of something which arises from a contact between sense and object?

In respect to these [alternatives], if it [reveals this contact] by having the nature of cognition, [then] this is not correct, for the form of cognition is possible even when there is no [contact], [for instance] in cognitions [such as] comparison etc.
If [a cognition] reveals [this contact] by having the form of effect, [then] this, too, is not correct, because the existence of this [having the form of effect] is possible in cognitions [such as] comparison and inference [which arise without contact] and in [the cognition of] blue water in respect to sun-rays [which does not arise from contact with blue water] etc. If A exists without B, how should A make known B? Otherwise existence etc., too, would make known.[127]

athendriyārthasannikarṣajanyākāratayā saṃsūcayatīti ced,
asāv indriyārthasannikarṣajanyākāro jñānākārād avyatirikto vyatirikto vā.
yady avyatiriktas, tadā jñānātmatāmātraṃ, nākārātireko 'nyo 'sti vibhāvyamāno 'numānādijñāneṣu yathā. ākārāntarātireke vā jñānarūpatā hīyate.
atha vyatiriktas, tasyaiva tarhi gamakatvaṃ, na jñānākārasya. tasyāpy agamakatvaṃ tadavedanāt.

kiṃ ca tadutpannam [1]indriyārthasannikarṣād[1] vijñānaṃ svarūpeṇāvagāhanīyaṃ, tato vyā[M33a]ptismaraṇaṃ, tadanu parāmarśajñānaṃ, tato 'numeyāvagatir iti na caitāvantaṃ kālaṃ vijñānaṃ sthitipadaṃ badhnāty, āśubhāvitvena pratyastamitatvāt. atha buddhyārūḍhena dharmadharmi[2]nyāyena parikalpyate[3] 'numānaṃ, tadāvāstavaṃ prāpnoti sugatānumānavat.

1.42 tathendriyotpādyatvam api nopapadyata indriyotpādyatvātirekānavagateḥ. vijñānaṃ svabhāvatayaiva vedyate, nākārāntareṇa. tajjñaptau vā jñānākāravirahaprasaṅgaḥ. na ca jñānam indriya-

---

1 probably an interpolation introduced as an explanation to *tado*

2 M: *dharmidharmao*

3 M: *parikalpyate/*

[Objection: The cognition] indicates [the contact] by having the form of something which arises from a contact between sense and object.
[Reply:] This form of something which arises from a contact between sense and object is either something over and above the form of cognition or not.[128]
If it is not over and above [the form of cognition], then it is simply the nature of cognition, there is no other supplementary form which is manifested [in it], just as in cognitions [such as] inference etc. Or if there is another supplementary form, [the cognition] looses the nature of cognition.
If [the form of something which arises from a contact] is over and above [the form of cognition], then it is this [form] which makes known [the arising from a contact], not the form of cognition. [But this form] does not make known either because it is not apprehended.

Besides, the cognition which arises from it (i.e., from contact between sense and object) has to be apprehended by its own form, then the invariable concomitance is remembered, after this there is reflective cognition, and then the object to be inferred is apprehended. But the cognition does not last that long, for it has vanished [in the meantime] as it is characterized by quick transition.[129] If an inference is [mentally] constructed by reason of a conceptualized [relation between] property and property-possessor,[130] then [this inference] would be fictitious, just like the inference of the Buddhists.

In the same manner, being produced by a sense, too, is not established because the additional fact of being produced by a sense is not apprehended: a cognition is made known by its own nature alone, not by a different form.[131] Or if it is made known by that [different form], it would lack the form of cognition. And the cognition is not ob-

sambaddhaṃ [S22] *dṛṣṭaṃ, yena tad upalabhyamānam indriyaṃ gamayati.*

atha kriyānyatra karaṇasādhyā dṛṣṭā.

saiva gamikāstu, yasyāḥ karaṇasa[M33b]*mbandho 'vagataḥ. na cānyasya sambandhe 'nyasya gamakatvaṃ kiñcitsāmyād upapadyate. na jātu devadattanayananīlasambandhe sati yajñadattendriyaṃ ghaṭādikam artham asati sambandhe karaṇatvasāmyād prakāśayad dṛṣṭam.*

tathārthajanyākāro 'pi vijñāne 'nenaiva prakāreṇa paryudasto veditavyaḥ.

1.43 *tathārtho 'pi vijñānam utpādayaty anupajātātiśaya upajātātiśayo vāvyatiriktopajātātiśayo vā vyatiriktopajātātiśayo vā.*

tad yady anu[M34a]*pajātātiśayaḥ karoti, tadā sarvadā kuryān na vā. karaṇam akaraṇaṃ ca*[1] *nopapadyeta*[2] *tatsvarūpānativṛtteḥ.*

---

1 M & S: *vā*

2 M: *nopavidyeta*

served as related to a sense by virtue of which it makes known the sense, [when] being apprehended [itself].

[Objection:] Elsewhere [in other cases], an action is observed as realized by an instrument. [Thus, the act of cognizing has to be brought about by an instrument, namely, the sense.][132]

[Reply:] Only an [action] whose relation to an instrument is apprehended makes known [its instrument]. But it is not established that when there is a relation of one thing [to another thing], [still] another thing makes known [something else], [just] because there is some resemblance [between the two things]. When there is a relation between the eye of Devadatta and a blue [object], one never observes that the sense of Yajñadatta illuminates an object [such as] a pot etc., when there is no relation [with that object], [just] because there is a similarity [between both senses] in as much as [they] are instruments.[133]

In the same manner the form of something which is produced by an object, too, should be known as rejected for a cognition in exactly this way.

In the same manner [you say that] the object, too, produces the cognition, [but in order to do so] it is either [an object] in which a special excellence is not produced [at the time it produces the cognition], or it is [an object] in which a special excellence is produced [when it produces the cognition], [and if so] it is either [an object] whose special excellence is produced and is not something additional [to the object itself], or it is [an object] whose special excellence is produced and is something additional [to the object itself].[134]

In respect to these [alternatives], if [an object] in which a special excellence is not produced produces [the cognition], then it would do so always or never. That [it] produces [at one time] and does not produce [at another time] would be impossible, because [the object] does not (i.e., cannot) transgress its own nature.

tathāvyatiriktopajātātiśayo pi na karoty akāra-kākārasyānugateḥ. ananugatau vā na tarhi tada-vyatirikto 'tiśayaḥ.

atha vyatiriktopajātātiśayena janyate, tathāpi nopapadyate[1] *'kārakākārānativṛtteḥ. ativṛttau vāyātaṃ kṣaṇikatvam.*

tataś ca nendriyārthasannikarṣajaṃ vijñānaṃ pratyakṣalakṣaṇam.

---

1 M is illegible, S discerns *no* ... *te*

In the same manner [an object] in which a special excellence is produced which is not something additional [to the object] does not produce [the cognition] either, because [its] form of something which is not a causal factor subsists. Or if it does not subsist, then this special excellence is something additional [to the object].

If [the cognition] is produced by [an object] in which a special excellence is produced which is something additional [to the object], even so this is impossible, because [the object] does not transgress the form of something which is not a causal factor. Or if it does transgress it, momentariness would result.

And therefore the definition of perception is not "a cognition which arises from a contact between sense and object."

2. *anye tu anadhigatārthagantṛtvena pramāṇalakṣaṇam abhidadhati.*[1] *te* [M34b] *tu ayuktavādino draṣṭavyāḥ.*

katham ayuktavāditā teṣām iti ced,

ucyate - vibhinnakārakotpāditaikārthavijñānānāṃ yathāvyavasthitaikārthagṛhītirūpatvāviśeṣe 'pi pūrvotpannavijñānasya prāmāṇyaṃ nottarasyety atra niyāmakaṃ vaktavyam.

2.1 *atha yathāvyavasthitārthagṛhītirūpatvāviśeṣe 'pi pūrvotpannavijñānasya prāmāṇyam upapadyate, na prathamottaravijñānasya, tadānenaiva nyāyena prathamasyāpy aprāmāṇyaṃ prasaktaṃ gṛhītārthagrāhitvāviśeṣāt. ya*[M35a]*thaikanīlasvalakṣaṇāvabhāsitayugapadutpannānekanīlavijñānānāṃ nīlaikārtha*[S23]*gṛhītirūpatā na bhidyate, tathā pūrvāparotpannavijñānānām api gṛhītārthagṛhītirūpatā na nivartsyati.*

---

1 M: *abhidadhad iti*

[Chapter II
Examination of the Mīmāṃsā definition of valid cognition]

Others, however, claim that a means of valid cognition is defined as agent of apprehension of an object which has not been apprehended [before].[135] But they should be considered as people who hold incorrect views.
[Question:] Why do [you say that] they hold incorrect views?
[Answer: We] explain: The reason for the following restriction should be stated: Among [several] cognitions of the same object which arise from different causal factors the cognition which has arisen first is valid, [but] not the others, even though there is no difference [among them] in as much as [they all] have the nature of apprehension of this same object as it really is.

If, even though there is no difference in as much as [they] have the nature of apprehension of the object as it really is, the cognition which has arisen first is established as valid, [but] not the cognition which is subsequent to the first, then, by this very reasoning, the first [cognition], too, would be invalid because there is no difference [between it and the subsequent cognition] in as much as [both] apprehend an apprehended object.[136] Just as the fact of having the nature of apprehension of the same blue object is the same for several cognitions of a blue [object] which have arisen at the same time [in different persons and] in which the same particular blue [object] appears, in the same manner the fact of having the nature of apprehension of an apprehended object cannot disappear for [several] cognitions as well which have arisen one after the other.

atha[1] *niyataviṣayatvaṃ pūrvottaravijñānayoḥ - pūrvotpannavijñānam anadhigatārthākārasvīkaraṇamukhenopādīyata, uttaraṃ tv adhigatārthākāraviṣayam upajāyate.*

yadi gṛhītārthaviṣayatvaṃ kathaṃ pratiniyataviṣayatvam? atha pratiniyataviṣayatvaṃ kathaṃ gṛhī[M35b]*tārthagrāhitvaṃ, niyataviṣayatvagṛhītagrāhitvayor virodhāt? yadi ca niyataviṣayatvaṃ, tadobhayor api prāmāṇyam anadhigatārthagantṛtvāviśeṣāt. athaikaviṣayatvaṃ, tadobhayor api prāmāṇyam aprāmāṇyaṃ vā gṛhītagrāhitvāviśeṣāt. so 'yaṃ gaḍupraveśākṣitārakavinirgamanyāyopanipātaḥ śrutilālasānāṃ duruttaraḥ.*

2.11 *nanv adhigataviṣayatve saty api* [M36a] *prāmāṇyābhyupagame smṛter api prāmāṇyam anuṣajyate pramāṇaphalatā vā.*

ko 'tra nivārayitā? smṛtir ihopajāyamānādyānubhavāveditārthākāraviṣayā vānyaviṣayā vā nirviṣayā vā.

tad yadi pūrvoditānubhavāveditārthākāraviṣayā, tadā tasyāḥ pramāṇaphalatā naiva nivārayi-

---

1 M: *athā°*

[Objection:] A previous and a subsequent cognition have their respective objects: the cognition which has arisen first assumes its form principally by adopting the form of an unapprehended object, but the posterior [cognition] arises as having the form of an apprehended object for its object.

[Reply:] If [a posterior cognition] has an apprehended object for its object, how could [they] each have their respective objects? If each has its respective object, how could [the posterior cognition] be an apprehension of an apprehended object, since there is a contradiction between having respective objects and apprehending an apprehended [object]? And if [previous and posterior cognitions] have their respective objects, then both are valid, because there is no difference [between them] in as much as [they] are [both] agents of apprehension of an unapprehended object. If [they] have the same object, then both are valid or invalid, because there is no difference [between them] in as much as [they both] apprehend an apprehended [object]. This unexpected occurrence of [what is illustrated by] the maxim of the going out of the pupil because of the entrance of a tumor[137] can't be overcome by the Fanatics of the Revelation.

[Objection:] If the validity [of a cognition] is admitted, although it has an apprehended [object] for its object, [then] recollection, too, would be valid, or [more precisely] the result of a means of valid cognition.

[Reply:] Who [could] prevent it? A recollection which is produced here [in this world] either has the form of a thing which has been revealed by [its] first experience for its object, or it has another object, or it is without an object.

In respect to these [alternatives], if [recollection] has the form of a thing which has been revealed by a previous experience for its object, then in no way can it be prevented that it is the result of a means of valid cogni-

tuṃ pāryate gṛhītārthagrāhitvāviśeṣād ity uktam. [M36b] *evaṃ ca smṛtisañjñakaṃ saptamaṃ pramāṇaṃ prasaktaṃ mīmāṃsakānām.*

atha pūrvavijñānānavadhāritārthaviṣayā.

yady evaṃ kathaṃ tasyāḥ pramāṇaphalatvam apanetuṃ pāryate? ādyānubhavasyeva[1] *smṛtirūpatā ca*[2] *na prāpnoti. dṛṣṭaśrutārthaviṣayā hi smṛtir nāgṛhītārthaviṣayā.*

atha nirviṣayeṣyate, tadā na gṛhītārthagrāhitvena smṛter aprāmāṇyam, api tu keśoṇḍukasaṃvedanavan nirviṣayatvena.

api ca [S24] *yadi nirviṣayā, tadā gṛhītārthagrāhiṇī katham? gṛhītārthagrāhiṇīti cen, nirviṣayeti na vaktavyam. na ca nirviṣayā. mātaraṃ pitaraṃ śuśrūṣitavān ahaṃ, santi me pañcabhṛtyā* [M37a] *iti pūrvānubhavāveditārthākāraparyavasāyinyo hi smṛtayaḥ, smṛtijñānena pūrvānubhavāveditārthākārasya pratibhāsanāt.*

atha smṛtivijñānakāle pūrvaprabodhaviṣayīkṛtārthasya pratyastamitatvān na tadviṣayatvam.

evaṃ ca nirviṣayatvena smṛter aprāmāṇyaṃ na gṛhītārthagrāhitvenety uktam.

2.2 *yadi cāvadhāritārthaviṣayaṃ pramāṇam apra-*

---

1 M: °*bhavasyaiva*

2 *ca* should perhaps be deleted

tion, because there is no difference [between recollection and first experience] in as much as [they] apprehend an apprehended thing. This has [already] been explained [above]. And thus, there would be a seventh means of valid cognition for the Mīmāṃsakas, called recollection.

[Objection: Recollection] has a thing which has not been determined by a previous cognition for its object.

[Reply:] If so, how could it be denied that it is the result of a means of valid cognition? Moreover, just as the first experience [of an object], it would not have the nature of recollection. For recollection has a thing seen or heard [before] for its object, it does not have an unapprehended thing for its object.

If [recollection] is accepted as having no object, then recollection is not invalid because it apprehends an apprehended object, but [it is invalid] because it has no object, just as the cognition of the hair-net.

Besides, if [recollection] is without an object, then how does it apprehend an apprehended object? If you say that [recollection] apprehends an apprehended object, you shouldn't say that it is without an object. And [recollection] is not without an object. For recollections [such as] "I obeyed [my] mother [and] father," "I have five servants,"[138] [etc.] extend up to the form of an object made known by a previous experience, because a mnemonic cognition manifests the form of an object which has been made known by a previous experience.

[Objection:] Since at the time of the mnemonic cognition the thing which had become the object of the previous experience no longer exists, it is not the object of the [recollection].

[Reply:] And thus, recollection is invalid because it is without an object, not because it apprehends an apprehended object. This has [already] been explained [above].

And if a means of valid cognition which has a [previously] determined thing for its object is rendered inval-

māṇam upapādyate, tadānumānajñānasyāprāmāṇyam āpanīpadyeta.

tad eva katham? kathyate - yad evāvinābhāvasambandhagrahaṇakālāvadhāritam agnitvasāmānyaṃ [1]*liṅgājahadvṛttitvena pratyakṣeṇa*[1] *tad evānumānād avaga*[M37b]*cchaty āhosvit pāvakasvarūpaṃ matvarthaṃ vā liṅgavyāpārasamānakālīnāstitvaṃ*[2] *vā liṅgopasarjanatvaṃ vāgnivyaktipāratantryaṃ vāgnitvasāmānyasya?*

2.21 *tad yadi pūrvāvadhāritasāmānyaviṣayam abhyupeyate, tadā prāmāṇyaṃ naiva samāsādayati gṛhītārthagrāhitvena smṛtivad eva. tadaprāmāṇye nāgnimattvavyavasthopapattiḥ. tadanupapattau ca nārthā*[3]*pattyāgnivyaktisaṃsthitiḥ. tataś cāmutrāgnir agnir ānīyatām iti sakalalokavyavahāravirahaḥ syāt. atha mā bhūd etadvyavahārahānir iti cet pūrvāvadhārite 'py arthe 'numānasya prāmāṇyam*[4] *abhyupeyate, tadānadhigatārthagantṛviśeṣaṇam apā*[M38a]*rthakaṃ śrotriyāṇām iti.*

2.22 *atha pāvakasvarūpam anumimīṣe, tal liṅgājahadvṛttitvena pūrvam avadhāritaṃ vā na vā. yadi pūrvopalabdham adhigatārthaviṣayatvam āyātam anumānasya.*

---

1 probably an interpolation introduced as an explanation to °*āvadhāritam*

2 M: °*kālīnatāstitvaṃ*

3 M & S: °*pattau vārthā*°

4 M: *anumānasyāprāmāṇyam*

id, then an inferential cognition could not possibly be valid.

How is that?

[We] explain: Either exactly the same universal 'fire' which is determined at the time of the apprehension of the relation of invariable concomitance [between fire and smoke] is that which is apprehended by inference, or it is the nature of fire, or the possession, or the existence [of the universal 'fire'] at the same time as the functioning of the [inferential] sign, or the subordination [of the universal 'fire'] to the [inferential] sign, or the dependence of the universal 'fire' on the individual fire.[139]

In respect to these [alternatives], if [the inferential cognition] is acknowledged as having a previously determined universal for its object, then [it] certainly doesn't attain validity because it apprehends an apprehended object, just like recollection. When this [inferential cognition] is not valid, it is impossible to determine that [a certain place] possesses fire, and when this is impossible, the determination of the individual fire by implication is not [possible]. And thus, [we] would be deprived of all day-to-day activity [which involves statements such as] "There is fire up there [on the mountain]," "Please, bring [some] fire" [etc.]. If [you say that] this day-to-day activity should not be relinquished, [then] the validity of inference should be admitted, although [its] object has been previously determined. Consequently, the qualification [of means of valid cognition] as agent of apprehension of an unapprehended object is senseless for the Śrotrīyas (i.e., the Mīmāṃsakas).

If you infer the nature of fire,[140] then [the nature of fire] is either previously determined as invariably accompanying the [inferential] sign[141] or not.

If it is previously apprehended [as such], inference necessarily has an apprehended thing for its object.

atha na pūrvopalabdham, avyāpako 'gnir anumānāt tarhi pratīyate. tadabhyupagame tṛṇajalādiviṣayam apy anumānaṃ prasajyate.

2.23 [S25]*atha matvartho 'numīyate, sa pūrvāvadhārito vā na vā.*
yady avadhāritaḥ, katham anadhigatārthagantṛviśeṣaṇam anumāne sambhavati?
atha naivāvagatas, tadānīṃ jalatṛṇādiviṣayam apy anumānaṃ prasajyetety uktam.

2.24 *atha liṅgavyāpārasamānakālīnāstitvam agnitva*[1]*sāmānyasyānumīyate, tad anumānavyā*[M38b]*pārasamānakālīnāstitvam agnitvasāmānyād vyatiriktam avyatiriktaṃ vā.*
tad yady avyatiriktaṃ, tadānīṃ pūrvopalabdhāstitvaviṣayam evānumānam. katham anadhigatārthagantṛviśeṣaṇam apārthakaṃ na bhavet?
atha vyatiriktaṃ, tat kiṃ pūrvopalabdham anupalabdhaṃ vā?
yadi pūrvopalabdhaṃ tadviṣayatve 'numānasya nānadhigatārthagantṛviśeṣaṇam upapadyate.
atha nopalabdhaṃ, tat katham anumīyate[2] *jalādikalpaṃ dhūmena?*

---

1 S: *agni°*

2 M: *anumīyate/*

If it is not previously apprehended [as such], then fire which is not concomitant [with smoke] is apprehended by inference. When this is admitted, inference [on the basis of smoke] could also have grass, water, etc., for its object [because the absence of concomitance is the same].

If possession (i.e., that the mountain possesses fire)[142] is inferred, [then] this [possession] is either previously determined or not.

If it is [previously] determined, how is the qualification 'agent of apprehension of an unapprehended object' possible for inference?

If it is not at all [previously] determined, then inference [based on smoke as the inferential sign] could also have water, grass, etc., for its object. This has [already] been stated [above].

If the existence of the universal 'fire' at the same time as the functioning of the [inferential] sign[143] is inferred,[144] [then] this existence at the same time as the functioning of the inference is either different from the universal 'fire' or not different.

If it is not different, then the inference has a nothing but a previously apprehended existence for its object; how could [in this case] the qualification 'agent of apprehension of an unapprehended object' not be senseless?

If [the existence of the universal 'fire' at the same time as the functioning of the inferential sign] is different [from the universal 'fire'], then is it previously apprehended or not apprehended?

If it is previously apprehended, [then] given that inference has this [previously apprehended existence] for its object, the qualification 'agent of apprehension of an unapprehended object' does not apply [to it].

If [this existence] is not apprehended, how could [this existence] which is similar to water etc., [in as much as its connection with smoke is unknown] be inferred from smoke?

2.25 *atha liṅgopasarjanatvam agnitvasāmānya-[M39a]syānumānāt pratīyate, tal liṅgopasarjana-tvam agnitvasāmānyād*[1] *bhinnam abhinnaṃ vā. yady abhinnaṃ pūrvopalabdhāgnitva*[2]*sāmānyaviṣayam evānumānaṃ, kathaṃ prāmāṇyabhāg bhavati? atha bhinnaṃ, tadavinābhāva*[3]*sambandhagrahaṇakāle liṅgavyāpakatvenāvadhāritaṃ vā na vā. yady avadhāritaṃ katham anadhigatārthaviṣayam anumānam? atha liṅgavyāpakatvenānavagataṃ*[4]*, tadā tadviṣa-yatve 'numānasya parikalpyamāne tribhuvanāveda-katvaṃ dhūmasya kiṃ na parikalpyate sambandhā-bhāvāviśeṣāt?*

2.26 *athā[M39b]gnivyaktipāratantryam anumīyate dhūmenāgnitvasāmānyasyeti cet, tat pāratantryam agnitvasāmānyasya dhūmavyāpakatvenāvadhāritaṃ vā na vā. yady avadhāritaṃ, punar api gṛhītagrāhitvaṃ nātivartate*[5] *'numānam. atha nāvadhāritaṃ dhūmavyāpakatvena pāratantryam agnisāmānyasyeti cet, katham anumīyata ity uktaṃ purastāt.*

2.3 *[S26]etena pūrvopalabdhagotvādipratipādaka-tvena gośabdāder aprāmāṇyam udghāṭitam.*

---

1 M: °*sāmānyad*

2 M: °*labdhapragnitva*°

3 M & S: *avinābhāvi*°

4 M: °*tvenāvagataṃ*

5 M: *nātivartate/*

If the subordination of the universal 'fire' to the [inferential] sign is apprehended by inference, [then] this subordination to the [inferential] sign is either different from the universal 'fire' or not different.
If it is not different, [then] inference has nothing but the previously apprehended universal 'fire' for its object; how could it be valid?
If [this subordination] is different [from the universal 'fire'], then [this subordination] is either [previously] determined, at the time of the apprehension of the relation of invariable concomitance, as invariably accompanying the [inferential] sign or not.
If it is [previously] determined, how could inference not have an apprehended thing for its object?
If [this subordination] is not [previously] apprehended as invariably accompanying the [inferential] sign, then - while assuming that inference has the [thus defined subordination] for its object - why not assume that smoke makes known the three worlds, as there is no difference regarding the absence of relation [between inferential sign and inferred object]?

If the dependence of the universal 'fire' on the individual fire is inferred from smoke,[145] [then] this dependence of the universal 'fire' is either [previously] determined as invariably accompanying smoke or not.
If it is [previously] determined, then [here] again, inference is not beyond apprehending an apprehended [object].
If the dependence of the universal 'fire' [on the individual fire] is not [previously] determined as invariably accompanying smoke, [then] how is it inferred [from smoke]? This has [already] been stated above.

By this [very reasoning] the words 'cow' etc., are declared as not being a means of valid cognition, because they communicate the universal 'cow' etc., which have been previously apprehended.

tad eva katham? kathyate - kiṃ saṅketagrahaṇakālāvagatagotvārthavācakatvaṃ tadvyatiriktārthavācakatvaṃ vā pratipādyate gośabdasya?

tad yadi saṅketagrahaṇakālādhi[M40a]*gata*[1]*-gotvasvarūpāvedakatvaṃ jegīyate gośabdasya, tadā viditārthākārāvedakatvena na mānatvam āsādayati gośabdaḥ. atha veditārthākārāvedakatve 'pi prāmāṇyam āvahati, tadānadhigatārthagantṛviśeṣaṇasya viṣayo vaktavyaḥ.*

atha tadvyatiriktārthavācakatvaṃ, tadānīm asaṅketita[2] *evārthaḥ pratīyate gośabdāt. tataś ca svasiddhāntapratītivirodho durnivāraḥ.*
atha gotvam evāvagamyate gośabdeneti cet, tatrāpi prapañcitam evāprāmāṇyakāraṇaṃ[3] *gṛhītagrāhitvam. tadaprāmāṇye na gotvavyavasthitiḥ. tadanavasthitau nārthāpattyādhikaraṇavyavasthitiḥ.*

2.31 *ito 'pi nārthāpattyādhikaraṇavyavasthitir*

---

1 M & S: *°ādhikaraṇa-*

2 M: *asaṅketata*

3 so in M; S's conjecture unnecessary

How is that?
[We] explain: Is it maintained that the word 'cow' expresses the object, [namely] the [universal] 'cow' apprehended at the time of grasping the [linguistic] convention [that this sound should designate this object], or that it expresses an object which is different from this [universal 'cow']?[146]

In respect to these [alternatives], if it is declared that the word 'cow' makes known the nature of the universal 'cow' apprehended at the time of grasping the [linguistic] convention, then the word 'cow' does not obtain the status of a means of valid cognition because it makes known the form of an object which has [already] been made known. If [you say that] although [the word 'cow'] makes known an object which has [already] been made known, it is [nevertheless] accepted as a means of valid cognition, then [you] should explain what the realm of the qualification 'agent of apprehension of an unapprehended object' is.

If [the word 'cow'] expresses an object which is different [from the universal 'cow'], then an object concerning which there is no [linguistic] convention is apprehended from the word 'cow.' And thus, a contradiction to what is ascertained by your own established doctrine is unavoidable.
[Objection:] Nothing but [the universal] 'cow' is apprehended from the word 'cow.'[147]
[Reply:] In this [case] too the fact of apprehending an apprehended [object] is the already profusely explained reason for invalidity. When the [word 'cow'] is not a means of valid cognition, [the universal] 'cow' is not established. When this [universal 'cow'] is not established, [its] substratum (i.e., the individual cow) [can]not be established by implication.[148]

For the following [reason], too, the substratum [of the universal 'cow'] is not established by implication: is *upapa[M40b]dyate - kim arthāpattyā pūrvāvadhāritādhikaraṇapratyāyanaṃ kriyata āhosvid apūrvādhikaraṇapratyāyanam?*

tad yadi pūrvāvadhāritādhikaraṇaparyavasitārthāpattis, tadā pratipāditārthapratipādakatvena na pramāṇam.

athādṛṣṭapiṇḍāvedakatvaṃ tadā gotvānyathānupapattyā gajavājikalpanāpi kāryā.

atha pūrvāvadhāritasyedānīntanam astitvam arthāpattyāvasīyata iti cet

tad idānīntanam astitvaṃ pūrvāvadhāritād vyatiriktam avyatiriktaṃ vā.

tad yady avyatiriktaṃ, tadā pūrvāvadhāritārthapratipādakatvena katham arthāpatteḥ prāmāṇyaṃ vedavido vadanti?

athārthā[M41a]ntaraṃ, kathaṃ gotvānyathānupapattyā pratīyate? tatpratītyabhyupagame vā gajavājiviṣayāpi pratipattiḥ syād ity asakṛt pratipāditam.

evaṃ ca sati yad uktam [S27] idānīntanam astitvaṃ na hi pūrvadhiyā gatam iti tad bālavalgitam.

2.4 *etena pratyabhijñānasyāpi prāmāṇyaṃ pratyuktaṃ veditavyam.*

a substratum which has been previously determined made known by implication, or is it a substratum which has not been previously [determined]?[149]

In respect to these [alternatives], if implication extends up to a previously determined substratum, then [implication] is not a means of valid cognition because it makes known an object which has [already] been made known.

If [implication] makes known a [previously] unperceived object, then one could as well assume a horse or an elephant by the fact that [the universal] 'cow' is not possible otherwise.

[Objection:] The present existence of something previously determined is ascertained by implication.

[Reply:] This present existence is either different from [the substratum] which has previously been determined or not different.

In respect to these [alternatives], if it (i.e., this present existence) is not different [from the substratum which has previously been determined], then, as it makes known an object which has previously been determined, how could the Veda experts say that implication is a means of valid cognition?

If [the present existence] is something different [from the previously determined substratum], how is it apprehended by the fact that [the universal] 'cow' is not possible otherwise? Or if its cognition (i.e., of the present existence) [by means of this implication] is admitted, the apprehension [which arises from the fact that the universal 'cow' would not be possible otherwise] could also have an elephant or a horse for its object. This has [already] been explained several times.

And thus, what has been said, [namely] "for the present existence is not apprehended by a previous cognition,"[150] is the skipping of a child.

It should be known that by this [same reasoning] the validity of recognition,[151] too, is refuted.

3.1 *tathā tāthāgatānām apy anadhigatārthagantṛviśeṣaṇam apārthakam apohyajñānāsambhavāt. na hi pūrvāparakālabhāvinī vijñāne ekaviṣaye sto, na svalakṣaṇaikaviṣaye, na sāmānyaikaviṣaye*[1],

3.11 *svalakṣaṇasyābhinnai[M41b]kasvabhāvasya kramavṛttyanekavijñānajananaśaktivyatirekāt.*
atha yugapadekaviṣayotpannānekavijñānāpanodārtham,
tad apy ayuktam. ekaviṣayotpannānekapuruṣasaṃvedanasyāprāmāṇyam āpanīpadyeta.

3.12 *atha sāmānyaikaviṣayānekavijñānāpanodārtham viśe[M42a]ṣaṇam upādīyate, tad apy ayuktam. na sāmānya ekaṃ vijñānam asti, nāpy anekaṃ vijñānaṃ, tasya svayam asambhavāt. tadākāravirahe sāmānyaviṣayaṃ vijñānam iti pratikarmavyavasthāhetur vaktavyaḥ. tadākāre vā sāmānyasya sadātma-*

---

1 perhaps a lacuna at this point

[Chapter III
The Buddhist definition of means of valid cognition]

In the same manner the qualification of the Buddhists, too, of [a means of valid cognition as] agent of apprehension of an unapprehended object[152] is useless, because there is no cognition which could be excluded [by it from the domain of means of valid cognition]. For there are no two cognitions, one posterior to the other, which have the same object; neither two [cognitions] which have a particular as their common object, nor two [cognitions] which have a universal as their common object.[153]

[There are no two cognitions which have a particular as their common object] because an individual which has a unique and indivisible nature does not have the capacity to produce several successive cognitions.[154]

[Objection:] The purpose [of the above qualification] is to exclude several cognitions which have the same object [and] which are produced at the same time.[155]

[Reply:] This is also not correct, [for in that case] cognitions of several people produced [simultaneously] by the same object could not possibly be valid.

If [on the other hand] the qualification is employed to the purpose of the exclusion of several cognitions which have a universal as their common object, [then] this is also not correct: there is neither one [valid] cognition of a universal, nor several [valid] cognitions [of a universal], because the [universal] itself does not exist. If the form of the [universal] is missing (i.e., does not appear in the cognition), the reason for assigning [the cognition] to [its] object has to be explained [when you say:] "the cognition which has a universal for [its] object; or if [a *tā. atāttvikākāratādātmye vā jñānātāttvika-[M42b]tva*[1]*prasaṅgaḥ.*

3.1a *kiṃ caikaviṣaye pravartamānayor ekasyāprāmāṇyaṃ pramāṇāntaratvābhāvo vā.*

3.1a1 *tad yady aprāmāṇyaṃ, tad ayuktam. aviśiṣṭaikārthagṛhītirūpatva ubhayoḥ prāmāṇyam aprāmāṇyaṃ vā vikalpānupapatteḥ. vikalpe vaika*[2]*viṣayotpannānekapuruṣavijñānabhedaprasaṅgaḥ.*

3.1a2 *athāpramāṇāntaratvaṃ, tad apy anupapannam. kim ekaviṣayotpāditānekapratyakṣādijñānānāṃ vyaktinānātvaṃ nopapadyata āha ākāranānātvam?*

tad yadi vyaktinānātvaṃ na jāgha[S28]ṭīti, tad asad, ekanīlotpāditānekanīlālokavijñānānāṃ vyaktinānātvadarśanāt.

[M43a]athānekākāratā nopapadyate, tad ayuktaṃ, nīlālokavijñānām anekākāratvadarśanāt. na ca tadutpādako nīlaprapañco 'sty, ekātmatayā svayam abhyupagamāt[3]*.*

---

1 M: *jñānatāttvikatva*°

2 M & S: *bādhaka*°

3 M & S: *anupagamāt*

cognition] has as [its] form a [universal], [then] the universal has a real nature; or if [the form of the cognition has] the same nature as an unreal form, the cognition [itself] would be unreal.

Further, when two [cognitions] are coming forth in respect to the same object, [you either mean that] one [of them] is not valid, or [that] one [of them] is not a further means of valid cognition.[156]

In respect to these [alternatives], if [you mean that one of them] is not valid, [then] this is not correct: when [two cognitions] have the form of apprehension of one and the same object, either both of them are valid, or [both of them] are not valid, because a difference [in validity] is impossible.[157] Or if there is a difference [in validity], there would be a difference among cognitions of several people which arise from the same object (i.e., one would be valid, the other not).

If [you mean that one of the two] is not a further means of valid cognition, then this, too, is not adequate. Is it the plurality of individuals of several [valid] cognitions, perception etc., which are produced by the same object, which is impossible, or is it the plurality of forms?

In respect to these [alternatives], if it is the plurality of individuals which is not at all possible, [then] this is not true, for the plurality of individuals of several visual cognitions which are produced by the same blue [object] is evident.

If [you think that] it is not possible that [several cognitions of the same object] have several forms, [then] this is not correct, because it is evident that [several] visual cognitions of a blue [object] have several forms. And the blue [object] which produces these [cognitions] is not manifold, because you accept yourself [the particular blue object] as having a unique nature.

athaikaviṣayatve pratyakṣānumānavyapadeśānupapattiḥ[1].

tad etad ayuktaṃ, bhinnakaraṇa[2]*kāryatvena vyapadeśopapatteḥ*[3]. *yathaikanīlotpannānekadevadattādijñānānāṃ*[4] *bhinnakartṛkāryatvena devadattādijñānavyapadeśas tathehāpi.*

3.2 *anye tv avisaṃvādi jñānaṃ pramāṇam abhidadhati. ko 'yam avisaṃvādārthaḥ? kiṃ yathāvyavasthitārthagṛhī*[M43b]*titvaṃ bādhārahitatvaṃ vā pratīyamānārthajanyatā vā pratīyamānārthaṃ prati pravartakatvaṃ vārthaprāpakatvaṃ vā?*

3.21 *tad yadi yathāvyavasthitārthagṛhītitvaṃ, tad*[5] *anumānajñāne*[6] *nopapadyate.*

3.22 *atha bādhārahitatvaṃ, tad apy anumānajñāne nopapadyate.*

3.23 *atha pratīyamānārthotpādyatvaṃ, tad apy anumānajñānasya nopapadyate, sāmānyākārasya janakatvavyāvṛtteḥ.*

tathā rāgādisaṃvedanasyāpy avabhātārthotpādyatvaṃ nopapadyate, svātmotpādane sāmarthyavyati-

---

1 S: °*patti*

2 S: °*kāraṇa*°

3 M: *vyapadeśyopapatteḥ*

4 M: *yathaikanīlotpannānekadevadattajñānānāṃ bhinnakāraṇakāryatvena devadattavijñānānāṃ* ...; S suggests: *yathaikanīlotpannānekadevadattajñānānāṃ bhinnakāraṇakāryatvena* [*devadattavijñānānāṃ*]...

5 M & S: *tadā*°

6 M: °*jñānaṃ*

[Objection:] If [several cognitions] have the same object, a [different] designation for perception and inference is impossible [because the means of valid cognition are differentiated according to their respective objects].
[Answer:] This is not correct, because a [different] designation is possible by [their] being produced by different instruments. Just as several cognitions of Devadatta [,Yajñadatta] etc., which are produced by the same blue [object] are designated as cognitions of Devadatta [,Yajñadatta] etc., because of [their] being produced by different agents, in the same manner here (i.e., in this case) too [a different designation of perception and inference is possible because of their being produced by different instruments].[158]

Others, however, say that a means of valid cognition is a cognition which does not belie [its promise].[159] What does it mean not to belie? Is it to be an apprehension of the object as it really is, or to be free from sublation, or to be produced by the perceived object, or to prompt [the cognizer] to action towards the perceived object, or to make [the cognizer] obtain an object?[160]

In respect to these [alternatives], if [not to belie means] to be an apprehension of the object as it really is, [then] this is impossible in the case of inferential cognition.

If it [means] to be free from sublation, [then] this, too, is impossible in the case of inferential cognition.[161]

If it [means] to be produced by the perceived object, [then] this, too, is impossible for an inferential cognition, because that which has the form of a universal cannot be agent of production.
In the same manner a cognition of [a feeling like] affection etc., cannot be produced by the object which appears [in it], because nothing is capable of producing itself.[162]

rekāt. tathā yogipratyakṣasya[1] *pratīyamānārthajanyatā na sambhavati vyatītānāgatayor ajanakatvāt. janakatve*[2] *vātītānāgata*[M44a]*tā hīyate.*

3.24 *atha pratīyamānārthaṃ prati pravartakatvam avisaṃvādārthas, tad viparyayajñānasyāpi pravartakatvaṃ vidyate. viparītotpannodakabuddhiḥ pravartate, na ca tasyāvisaṃvādo 'sti. satyodakajñāne 'pi jāte na pravartate kenāpi hetunā, tad api visaṃvādi syāt.*

3.25 [S29]*athārthaprāpakatvam avisaṃvādas, tatra kim arthamātraprāpakatvam āho 'vabhātārthaprāpakatvaṃ tajjātīyodakaprāpakatvaṃ vā svotpādakārthaprāpakatvaṃ vātha svotpādakakārakāṇāṃ dhruvabhāvitvam avisaṃvādaḥ?*

yady arthamātraprāpakatvaṃ, keśoṇḍukenduduvayasaṃvedanasyāpy avisaṃvāditvam āpadyate.

a[M44b]*thāvabhātārthaprāpakatvaṃ, tadānumānajñānasyāvisaṃvāditvaṃ na labhyate 'vabhātārthāprāpakatvāt. anumānajñāne hi sāmānyākāro 'vabhāti, na cāsau prāpyate svayam asattvāt.*

---

1 M & S add *ca*

2 M: *janākatve*

In the same manner the perception of the yogis[163] cannot be produced by the perceived object, because past or future [objects] are not agents of production. Or, if [they] are agent of production, [they would] lose [their characteristic of] being past or future.

If not to belie means to prompt [the cognizer] to action towards the perceived object,[164] then [this is not correct because] there are false cognitions which prompt [the cognizer] to act: [a person] who has a cognition of water which arises from [an object] different [from water] acts, but he is bound to be disappointed. [Besides] even when a true cognition of water arises, [the cognizer may] not act because of some reason. This [cognition] would [have to be considered as] belying [its promise].

If not to belie [means] to make [the cognizer] obtain an object, does it mean to let [the cognizer] obtain any object, or to let [the cognizer] obtain the object which appeared [in the cognition], or to let [the cognizer] obtain [an object which belongs to the same universal, for instance in the case of water to let the cognizer obtain] water which belongs to the [same] universal as the [water which appeared in the cognition], or that [the cognition] lets [the cognizer] obtain a thing which produced it, or does not to belie [imply] the necessary existence of the causal factors which produce the [cognition]?[165]

If [it means] to let [the cognizer] obtain any object, the [false] cognition of the hair-net and of the double moon, too, would not belie [their promise].

If [it means] to let [the cognizer] obtain the object which appeared [in the cognition], then [all] inferential cognitions would belie [their promise], because [they] do not let [the cognizer] obtain the object which appeared [in them]. For in an inferential cognition the form of the universal appears, and this [form] is not [ever] obtained, because [the universal] itself does not exist.

tathā yogijñānasyātī[1]tānāgatārthe samutpannasyārthaprāpakatvaṃ na vidyate. tathā rāgādisaṃvedane 'pi jāte nāvabhātarāgādiprāptir asti. tathā pratyakṣe 'pi vijñāne nāvabhātārthaprāptir asti kṣaṇikatve[M45a]*nāstamitatvāt.*

atha tajjātīyodakaprāpakatvenāvisaṃvāditvam ucyate, tad ayuktam udakatvajāter abhāvāt. athānudakatvavyāvṛttir jātir ity ucyate, sodakavyaktibhyo 'vyatiriktā vyatiriktā vā. yady avyatiriktā tadā vyaktir eva na jātiḥ. atha vyatiriktā sā vastubhūtāvastubhūtā vā. yadi vastubhūtā tadā[2]bhyupetahāniḥ. athāvastubhūtā tadgatiḥ[3] katham? na codakavyaktīnāṃ nānātvam upa[M45b]*padyate. yathā ca nopapadyate tathā niveditaṃ naiyāyikapratyakṣalakṣaṇādhikāre.*

atha svotpādakārthaprāpakatvam avisaṃvādakatvaṃ, tad ayuktaṃ, nayanālokamanaskārādeḥ pratyastamitatvāt.

atha svotpādakakārakāṇāṃ dhruvabhāvitvam

---

1 M: °*jñāne syā 'tī*°

2 S om. *tadā*

3 M: *tadgatiḥ/*

In the same manner the cognition of the yogi, in as much as it arises in respect to past or future objects, does not let [the yogi] obtain [its] object. In the same manner in the case of cognitions of affection etc., too, in as much as they arise [in respect to affection etc.], there is no obtainment of affection etc., which appear [in them]. In the same manner in the case of perceptual cognitions, too, there is no obtainment of the object which appears [in them], because [the object] being momentary is destroyed [in the meantime].

If it is said that [a cognition of water] does not belie [its promise] because it lets [the cognizer] obtain water which belongs to the [same] universal as the [water which appeared in the cognition], [then] this is not correct because the universal 'water' does not exist.

[Objection:] The universal ['water'] is [nothing but] the exclusion of [all things] which are not water.[166]

[Reply:] This [exclusion] is either not different from the water individuals or different [from them].

If it is not different, then it is simply an individual, not a universal.[167]

If it is different, it is either a real thing or an unreal thing.

If it is a real thing, then you abandon your thesis.

If it is not a real thing, how could it [possibly] be apprehended?

And [on top of that] the plurality of water individuals is impossible. And why it is not possible was demonstrated in the chapter on the Naiyāyika's definition of perception.[168]

If not to belie [means that the cognition] lets [the cognizer] obtain a thing that produced it (i.e., the cognition), [then] this is not correct, because the eye, the light, attention, etc., are destroyed [in the meantime].

[Objection:] Not to belie [implies] the necessary existence of the causal factors which produce it (i.e., the *avisaṃvādas, tadabhāve tadabhāvaprasaṅgāt.*

yady evaṃ keśoṇḍukavijñānasyāpi dhruvabhāvikāraṇatvenāvisaṃvādo[1] *'sty anyathākasmikatvaprasaṅgāt.*

evaṃ cāvyavasthite yad uktaṃ na hy ābhyām arthaṃ paricchidya pravartamāno 'rthakriyāyāṃ visaṃvādyata iti tad bālavilasitam.

3.3 [S30]*tathā mānameyasaṅkhyāpi saugatamate nopapadyate.*

tad eva katham? ka[M46a]*thyate - dve eva pramāṇe, na mānāntaram asti. tad dvitvaṃ kiṃ vyaktibhedenākārabhedena viṣayabhedena vā?*

3.31 *yadi vyaktibhedena, tadāparisaṅkhyeyatvaṃ jñānavyaktīnām ānantyād, dvitvānupapattiḥ.*

na ca jñānānāṃ bhedo 'sty - ajñānād dhi jñānaṃ[2] *jñānātmatayā bhidyate, jñānāntarāt tu kathaṃ nivartate? kiṃ jñānātmatayākārāntareṇa vā?*

yadi jñānākāratayā bhidyate, tadānyeṣām ajñānātmakatvaprasaṅgo rasāder iva.

athākārāntareṇa vyāvartate, tadājñānātmatā tasyotpadyate rasāder iva.

---

1 M & S °*kāraṇāvisaṃvādo*

2 M: *ajñānād vijñānaṃ*

cognition), because if they were not existent, it (i.e., the cognition) would not exist.

[Answer:] If so, [then] the cognition of the hair-net, too, does not belie [its promise], because it has causal factors which exist necessarily, for otherwise it would be [produced] by chance (i.e., without a cause).

And thus, as none [of the above interpretations can be] established, what has been said [by Dharmakīrti] - "[The person] who acts after determining the object with these two (i.e., perception and inference) is not deceived/disappointed [by the cognition] in view of an efficient action,"[169] - is [nothing but] a child's play.

In the same manner the number of means and objects of valid cognition, too, is not established in the Buddhist system.

[Objection:] Why [can't it be established]?

[Reply: We] explain: [The Buddhists claim that] there are only two means of valid cognition, there is no other.[170] [Now] this duality, is it due to a difference of individuals, a difference of form, or a difference of objects?

If it is due to a difference of individuals, then [the means of valid cognition] are innumerable, because the individual cognitions are infinite; the duality [therefore] is not established.

Further, there is no difference among cognitions, for a cognition is differentiated from that which is not a cognition by [its] character of cognition; but how is it differentiated from another cognition?[171] Is it by [its] character of cognition or by another form?

If it is differentiated by the form of cognition, then [all] the other [cognitions] would have the character of non-cognition, just like flavour etc.

If [a cognition] is differentiated [from another cognition] by another form, then this [cognition] obtains the character of non-cognition, just like flavour etc.[172]

3.32 *athākārabhedena mānayor*[1] *bhedaḥ*, *so 'py anupa*[M46b]*panna eva. jñānākāravyatirekeṇa pratyakṣānumānayor nākārāntaram asti. tadupagame vā jñānākāravirahaḥ syāt. na cākārasamūhātmakaṃ jñānaṃ tasyābhinnātmakatvāt.*

3.33 *atha viṣayabhedena dvaividhyam upapādyate,*

3.331 *tadānumānajñānasya viṣayārtho vaktavyaḥ - kim agnyādisvalakṣaṇaviṣayaṃ vidyamānasāmānyaviṣayam apāramārthikasāmānyaviṣayaṃ vā nirviṣayaṃ vā svāṃśaviṣayaṃ vā?*

yady agnyādisvalakṣaṇaviṣayaṃ, tadā pratyakṣānumānayor bhedānupapattir abhinnaviṣayatvāt.

athānumānike jñāne 'gni[M47a]*mātraṃ pratīyate, pratyakṣe tu tārṇādiviśeṣātmatayā pratīyate.*

yady evaṃ svalakṣaṇaviṣayatvaṃ nātivartate[2] *'numānasya, yadi nāma vahner eva prapañcatā.*

atha satsāmānyaviṣayatvaṃ, tathāpi pratyakṣānumānayor na bhedo 'sti sāmānyasya svalakṣaṇarūpatvāt. na ca satsāmānyasya vijñānaviṣayatopapadyate nityatvena janakatvākārārpakatvānupapatteḥ.

---

1 M & S: °*bhede jñānayor*

2 M: *nātivartate/*

[Objection:] The difference between the two [kinds of] means of valid cognition is due to a difference in form. [Answer:] This [difference], too, is certainly not established. Perception and inference do not have another form over and above the form of cognition. Or if it (i.e., another form) is admitted, [they] would not have the form of cognition. And [it is not possible that the cognition has both the form of a cognition and another form, because] a cognition does not consist in multiple forms, for [as you admit] it has a unique nature.

If the duality is established as being due to a difference in objects, then it should be explained what the [word] 'object' in the case of inferential cognition means. Does it (i.e., inferential cognition) have a particular like fire etc., for its object,[173] does it have an existing universal for its object, or does it have an unreal universal for its object, or is it without an object, or does it have a part of itself for its object?[174]

If [the inferential cognition] has a particular like fire etc., for its object, then a difference between perception and inference is impossible, because [they] have the same object.

[Objection:] In inferential cognition only fire [in general] is apprehended; in perception, on the other hand, [fire] is apprehended as having a special character, [for instance fire] being produced by grass etc.[175]

[Answer:] If so, even though it is a special kind of fire (i.e., fire without special characteristics), inference is not beyond having a particular for its object.

If [inferential cognition] has an existing universal for its object, even so there is no difference between perception and inference, because the universal [would] have the nature of a particular.[176] And an existing universal cannot be the object of [any] cognition, because being eternal it can neither produce [the cognition][177] nor provide [its] *na ca satsāmānyaviṣayatve bhrāntatopapadyate. bhrāntir apy arthasambandhataḥ prame*[S31]*ti na vaktavyam.*

athāsatsāmānyaviṣayaṃ, na tarhi tasya bhrāntatā-sataḥ svena rūpeṇa vi[M47b]*dyamānatvāt. na cāsad viṣayabhāvaṃ pratipadyate janakatvākārārpakatva-vyatirekāt. avyatireke vā vastutvaprasaṅgaḥ. tatprasaktau ca pratyakṣānumānayor bhedānupapattiḥ.*

atha nirviṣayaṃ, na tarhi mānayor bhedo 'sty, anumānajñānasya viṣayāsambhavāt. nāpi bhrāntatā nirviṣayatvād eva. na ca jñānasya svasattāmātreṇa bhrāntatābhrāntatā copapadyate, kiṃ tu paropadhānavaśāt.

atha svāṃśaviṣayaṃ, tathāpi pratyakṣānumānayor na nānātvam, ubhayoḥ [M48a] *svalakṣaṇaviṣayatvāt. na cānumānajñānasya bhrāntatā svāṃśasyāvañcanāt.*

3.332 *tathā pratyakṣasyāpi viṣayo vaktavyaḥ - kiṃ rūpādisvalakṣaṇaviṣayam ātmaviṣayam ubhayaviṣa-*

form [to the cognition].[178] And if [the inferential cognition] has an existing universal for its object, [it] cannot be erroneous. [Thus] one should not say "Although [the inferential cognition] is erroneous, [nevertheless] it is a valid cognition, because of [its] relation to a [real] object."[179]

If [inferential cognition] has for its object an inexistent universal, then it is not erroneous, because an inexistent [object] exists as such.[180] And an inexistent thing cannot become object [of a cognition], because [it can] neither produce [the cognition], nor provide [its] form [to the cognition]. Or if it does [produce a cognition and provide its form to it], it would be a real thing, and in this case the difference between perception and inference cannot be established [according to their respective objects].

If [inferential cognition] is without an object, then there is no difference between the two means of valid cognition [which is due to their respective objects], because inferential cognition does not have an object. Nor is [inferential cognition] erroneous, precisely because it is without an object. For the erroneousness or nonerroneousness of a cognition are not established simply by its existence, but by force of [its] dependence on something else (i.e., the object).

If [inferential cognition] has for its object a part of itself, even so there is no difference between perception and inference, because both of them have a particular for their object.[181] Nor is the inferential cognition erroneous, because a part of itself [can]not lead [the cognition] astray (or: [the cognition] of a part of itself does not lead [the cognizer] astray).

In the same manner the object of perception, too, has to be explained:[182] does it (i.e., perception) have for its object a particular like something visible etc., does it

178

yaṃ vā?

tad yadi rūpādimātrālocakaṃ, tad ayuktaṃ tadanavagatāv etadgatyabhāvāt.

atha jñānamātrakāyāvagāhakaṃ, tad api nopapadyate, viṣayabhāvasya janakatvākārārpakatvena vyavasthiteḥ. na ca svātmani janakatvam ākārārpakatvaṃ copapadyate. viṣayiṇam apekṣya viṣayo bhavati, yathā kāra[M48b]ṇam apekṣya kāryaṃ kāryaṃ cāpekṣya kāraṇaṃ tathehāpi.

yadi ca pratyakṣajñānenātmamātram ātmasātkriyate, tadānumāne 'py etad asti, pratyakṣānumānayor bhedānupapattiḥ.

athobhayaṃ viṣayikriyate, tad apy ayuktam, ekopalambhasya dvitīyākāraparihāreṇa vyavasthitatvāt. yadi ca rūpagṛhītir eva jñānagṛhītis, tadā rūpasya jñānarūpatā, jñānasya vā rūparūpatā, rūpagṛhiter vā rūpāvyavasthāpakatvam. na caikasyākāradvayaṃ paśyāmaḥ.

180

3.3a *na ca dvitvāvadhāraṇam*[1] *iho[M49a]papadyate. pratyakṣaṃ jñānam ātmānaṃ gṛhṇad upajāyate, nānumānaṃ viṣayayati. tathānumānam apy ātmānam ātmasātkurvad upajāyate, na pratyakṣaṃ jñānam ava[S32]dyotayati. evaṃ dvitvasaṅkhyāvyavahārānupapattiḥ.*

atha vikalpena dvayāvadhāraṇam iti cet,

tad ayuktam, asāv apy ātmasaṃvedanaparyavasitatvān na dvayaṃ gṛhṇāti. grahaṇe vābhyupetahānam. tadanupapattau ca dve eveti jaḍaceṣṭitam.

---

1 M: °ṇām

have itself for its object, or does it have both for its object?

In respect to these [alternatives], if [perception] illuminates (i.e., apprehends) only [a particular] like something visible etc., [then] this is not correct, because when the one (i.e., cognition) is not apprehended, there is no apprehension of the other (i.e., the object).[183]

If [perception] makes known the body of the cognition alone, [then] this is also impossible, because to be object [of a cognition] consists [by definition] in producing [the cognition] and being that which provides [its] form [to the cognition]. And [nothing] can produce itself, or provide its own form [to itself]. [The object] becomes object in respect to something characterized by an object (i.e., to a cognition). Just as [the effect becomes] effect in respect to its cause, and [the cause becomes] cause in respect to its effect, in the same manner here too [the cognition becomes cognition in respect to its object which is different from itself].

And if perceptual cognition appropriates only itself [as object], then, [as] this is the case with inferential cognition too, the difference between perception and inference cannot be established.

If both [object and cognition] are made the object [of perception], [then] this is also not correct, because the apprehension of one [form] consists in the exclusion of [every] other form. And if [in order to avoid this exclusion you say that] the apprehension of cognition is nothing but the apprehension of the visible, then either the visible [would] have the form of cognition, or the cognition [would] have the form of the visible, or the apprehension of the visible [would] not establish the visible. And [on top of that] we [never] observe that one thing has two forms.

And [besides] the determination of duality [of the means of valid cognition] is impossible here [within the Buddhist system]: perceptual cognition arises as apprehending itself, it does not have inference for its object. In the same manner inferential cognition, too, arises as appropriating itself [for its object], it does not illuminate (i.e., apprehend) perceptual cognition. Thus [even] talking/thinking about two as the number [of the means of valid cognition] is impossible.[184]

[Objection:] The determination of duality is due to a conceptual construction.

[Answer:] This is not correct. This [conceptual construction] too, as it terminates in the apprehension of itself, does not apprehend the two [means of valid cognition]. Or if [you claim that] it apprehends [both], you abandon your own position.

And [thus], when this [determination of two means of valid cognition] is not established, [to say:] "There are only two [means of valid cognition]," is the gesticulation of a fool.

4.1 *tathā pratyakṣaṃ kalpanāpoḍham abhrāntam iti na vaktavyaṃ kalpanāpoḍhapadasyāpohyārthāsam[M49b]-bhavāt.*
nanu kalpanaivāpohyā.
keyaṃ kalpanā - kiṃ guṇacalanajātyādiviśeṣaṇotpāditaṃ vijñānaṃ kalpanāho smṛtyutpādakaṃ vijñānaṃ kalpanā smṛtirūpaṃ vā smṛtyutpādyaṃ vābhilāpasaṃsarganirbhāso vābhilāpavatī pratītir vā kalpanāspaṣṭākārā vātāttvikārthagṛhītirūpā vā svayaṃ vātāttvikī trirūpāl liṅgato 'rthadṛg vātītānāgatārthanirbhāsā vā?

4.11 *tad yadi guṇacalanajātyādiviśeṣaṇotpāditaṃ vijñā[M50a]naṃ kalpanā, tat kim avidyamānaguṇacalanajātyādiviśeṣanotpādyatvena kalpanota vidyamānotpādyatvena?*

tad yady avidyamānaguṇacalanajātyādiviśeṣaṇotpādyatvena kalpanātvaṃ, tad ayuktam avidyamā-

[Chapter IV

Examination of the Buddhist definition of perception]

In the same manner, one should not say "Perception is free from conceptual construction and nonerroneous,"[185] because there is nothing to be excluded by the word 'free from conceptual construction.'

[Objection:] Conceptual construction itself should be excluded.

[Reply:] What is conceptual construction? Is conceptual construction a cognition which is produced by qualifications [such as] quality, action, universal, etc., or is conceptual construction a cognition which produces recollection, or does it consist in recollection, or is it produced by recollection, or is it the appearance of a blend of [object and] word, or is conceptual construction a cognition which is characterized by a word, or is it [a cognition] which has an indistinct form, or does [conceptual construction] consist in the apprehension of an unreal object, or is it itself unreal, or is it the cognition of an object based on the triform sign, or is it [a cognition] in which a past or future object appears?

In respect to these [alternatives], if conceptual construction is a cognition which is produced by qualifications such as quality, action, universal, etc.,[186] is it a conceptual construction because it is produced by qualifications [such as] inexistent quality, action, universal, etc., or is it [a conceptual construction] because it is produced by existing [quality, action, universal, etc.]?

In respect to these [alternatives], if its being a conceptual construction is due to its being produced by qualifications such as inexistent quality, action, univer-

nasya janakatvābhāvād evākalpanātvam.

atha vidyamānaguṇacalanajātyādiviśeṣaṇotpādyatvena kalpanā, tat kiṃ saviṣayaṃ kalpanājñānaṃ nirviṣayaṃ vā?

tad yadi saviṣayaṃ sat kalpanājñānaṃ, tad ayuktaṃ, guṇacalanajātyādijanyatve 'pi [M50b] *na kalpanātvam arthasāmarthyasamudbhavatvasyānativṛtteḥ.*

atha nirviṣayaṃ sat kalpanā, tadā nirviṣayatvam eva kalpanātve kāraṇaṃ, na guṇacalanajātyādiviśeṣaṇajanyatvam. yadi ca tan nirviṣayaṃ, tadā na kalpanājñānaṃ nāpy akalpanājñānaṃ, jñānamātratā syāt. jñānātmatayā ca kalpanātve sarvaṃ jñānaṃ kalpanājñānaṃ syāt.

4.12 [S33]*atha smṛtyutpādakaṃ jñānaṃ kalpanā, tad ayuktaṃ, rūpādidarśanād api smṛtir utpadyate na ca kalpanātvaṃ, yatsannidhāne yo dṛṣṭas taddṛṣṭes taddhvanau*[1] *smṛtir iti vacanāt.*

4.13 *atha smṛtirūpatvena kalpanā, tatrāpi kiṃ gṛhītagrāhitvena nirviṣayatvenāpūrvārthagṛhīti-*

---

1 so in M; S's conjecture unnecessary

sal, etc., [then] this is not correct. No [cognition would] be conceptual construction, because what does not exist certainly does not produce.

If [a cognition is] a conceptual construction because [it] is produced by qualifications such as existing quality, action, universal, etc., then does the conceptual cognition have an object, or [is it] without an object?

In respect to these [alternatives], if [a cognition] is a conceptual cognition in as much as it has an object, [then] this is not correct: although it is produced by quality, action, universal, etc., it is not conceptual, because the fact of being produced by the capacity of [its] object remains.[187]

If it is a conceptual construction in as much as it is without an object, then it is simply the fact of being without an object which is the cause of being a conceptual construction, not the fact of being produced by qualifications such as quality, action, universal, etc. And if this [cognition] is without an object, then it is neither a conceptual cognition, nor a non-conceptual cognition; [it] would simply be a cognition. And if [a cognition] is a conceptual construction because of its nature of cognition, every cognition would be a conceptual cognition.[188]

If conceptual construction is a cognition which produces recollection,[189] [then] this is not correct: a recollection is produced by seeing a visible etc., too, and [seeing a visible etc.] is not conceptual construction, as it is said: "When a [word] is perceived in the presence of an [object], [later on] there occurs recollection of the word due to the seeing of that [object]."[190]

If [a cognition] is a conceptual construction because it has the nature of recollection, [then] in respect to this [alternative] too [we ask:] Is it [a conceptual construction] because it apprehends a [previously] apprehended [object], or because it is without an object, or because it *rūpatvena vā?*

[M51a]*tad yadi gṛhītārthagrāhitvena kalpanātvaṃ, tadā prathamānubhavasyāpi kalpanātvam āpadyate gṛhītārthagrāhitvāviśeṣād ity uktaṃ purastāt.*

atha nirviṣayatvena, tadā na kalpanākāratā nāpy akalpanākāratā jñānākāravyatirekeṇa.

athāpūrvārthagṛhītitvena kalpanātvaṃ, tad ayuktaṃ, na smṛter apūrvārthagṛhītitvam asti. tadabhāvān na kalpanātvam. yadi cāpūrvārthagṛhītitvena kalpanātvaṃ, rūpādijñānānāṃ kalpanātvam āpadyate.

4.14 *atha smṛtyutpādyatvena kalpanātvaṃ, tadā rūpādijñānasyāpi nirvikalpakatvenābhimatasya smṛtyutpādyatvam asti, tad astu kalpanājñānam.*

atha na bhavati tat kalpanājñānaṃ[1] [M51b] *smṛtyā bodhasvabhāvatayotpāditaṃ, kalpanājñānaṃ tu*[2] *smaraṇākāratayotpādyate.*

tad idaṃ madvikalpāndolitabuddher nirupapattikābhidhānam. na hy ekasya svabhāvadvayam upapaśyāmaḥ.

---

1 M: ◦*jñānaṃ/*

2 M & S: *na*

consists in the apprehension of a previously unperceived object?

In respect to these [alternatives], if [a cognition] is a conceptual construction because it apprehends a [previously] apprehended object, then the first experience [of an object], too, would be a conceptual construction, because, as we have explained above,[191] there is no difference in [their both] apprehending a [previously] apprehended object.

If [a cognition is a conceptual construction] because it is without an object, then it has neither the form of conceptual construction, nor the form of a non-conceptual cognition over and above the form of cognition.[192]

If [a cognition] is a conceptual construction because it is an apprehension of a previously unperceived object, [then] this is not correct. A recollection is not an apprehension of a previously unperceived object, [and] because it is not [an apprehension of an unperceived object, a recollection would] not be a conceptual construction. And if [a cognition] is conceptual because it is an apprehension of a previously unperceived object, the cognitions of a visible etc., would be conceptual constructions.

If [a cognition] is a conceptual construction because it is produced by recollection, then cognitions of a visible etc., too, accepted [by you] as free from conceptual construction, are produced by recollection; they would be conceptual cognitions.

[Objection:] These [cognitions of a visible etc.] are not conceptual cognitions, [because] they are produced by recollection in as much as it has the nature of cognition; a conceptual cognition, however, is produced [by recollection] in as much as it has the form of recollection.

[Reply:] This is the unreasonable talk of [a person] whose mind is confused by my argumentation, for we do not make out that one [thing] has a double nature.[193]

4.15 *athābhilāpasaṃsargapratibhāsā pratītiḥ kalpanā, sa saṃsargaḥ pāramārthiko 'pāramārthiko vā.*

yadi pāramārthiko, na tadā tasya kalpanātvaṃ rūpādijñānasyeva.

athāpāramārthikaḥ, kathaṃ tadābhaṃ vijñānaṃ nairātmyaprasaṅgāt? na cātāttvike viṣayārthaḥ kaścil labhyate janakatvākārārpakatvasahotpādasattāmātravyatirekāt. yadi cātāttvikārthagrhītirūpaṃ, [S34] *tadā vipa*[M52a]*ryayajñānam. tac cāvyabhicāripadenāpoditaṃ, na kalpanāpoḍhapadam upādeyam.*

4.16 *athābhilāpavātī pratītiḥ kalpanā, kim abhilāpātmikāho 'bhilāpotpādyābhilāpagrhītir vā?*

tad yady abhilāpātmikā, pratītiḥ katham? pratītiś ced abhilāpātmiketi na vaktavyaṃ, viruddhākārayos tādātmyavyatirekāt.

athābhilāpotpādyā, tadā śabdajñānānāṃ kalpanātvam āpadyate. teṣāṃ ca kalpanātve śabdavyavasthānupapattiḥ syāt.

athābhi[1]*lāpagrhītitve*[M52b]*na kalpanātvaṃ, tadā sarvāsām abhilāpagrhītīnāṃ kalpanātvam ā-*

---

1 M & S: *abhi*°

If conceptual construction is a cognition which appears as a blend of [object and] word,[194] [then] this blend is either real or unreal.
If it is real, then its [cognition] is not a conceptual construction, just like the cognition of a visible etc.
If [this blend] is unreal, how is the cognition in which this [blend] appears [possible], for it would be without a proper character (i.e., unreal)?[195] And [on top of that] in the case of an unreal [blend as object, the word] 'object' makes no sense at all, because [an unreal thing can] neither produce [a cognition], nor provide [its] form [to the cognition], nor arise at the same time [as the cognition], nor simply exist.[196] And if [conceptual construction] consists in the apprehension of an unreal thing, then it is a false cognition. And this (i.e., false cognition) is already excluded [from the domain of the definition of perception] by the word 'nonerroneous.'[197] [Thus] the word 'free from conceptual construction' should not be employed [in it].

If conceptual construction is a cognition which is characterized by a word,[198] does it have the nature of a word, or is it produced by a word, or is it an apprehension of a word?

In respect to these [alternatives], if [conceptual construction] has the nature of a word, how is it a cognition? If [you say that] it is a cognition, [you] should not say that [it] has the nature of a word, because there is no identity of nature between two contradictory forms.

If [conceptual construction] is produced by a word, then the cognitions of words would be conceptual constructions.[199] And if they are conceptual constructions, the determination of words [as related to their respective objects] would be impossible.[200]

If [a cognition] is a conceptual construction because it is an apprehension of a word, then all apprehensions of words would be conceptual constructions. If they (i.e., all *padyate. tatkalpanātve śabdavyavasthānupapattiḥ.*

4.17 *athāspaṣṭākārā pratītiḥ kalpanā, aspaṣṭatā kā? kim avijñānātmakatvam āho svalakṣaṇājanyatvam atha pratīyamānārthājanyatvaṃ pratīyamānāsatyatā vā svalakaṇāpratibhāsitā* [M53a] *vā?*

tad yady avijñānātmakatvam aspaṣṭatā, tad ayuktaṃ, pratītir ihāspaṣṭākārā gīyate, sā katham avijñānātmikā[1] *bhavitum arhati?*

atha svalakṣaṇājanyatāspaṣṭatā, tadā jñānākasmikatvaprasaṅgaḥ.

atha pratīyamānārthājanyatvaṃ, tadā rāgādisaṃvedanasyāspaṣṭatā prāpnoti, rāgādīnāṃ svātmasaṃve[M53b]*danotpādakatvāyogāt. svātmotpādakatvaṃ vastūnāṃ na dṛṣṭapūrvam. tathā keśoṇḍukavijñānasya pra*[2]*tīyamānakeśoṇḍukotpādyatvaṃ na vidyate. tad api spa*[3]*ṣṭābham upajāyate, na tv aspaṣṭābhaṃ, na vikalpānubaddhasya spaṣṭārthapratibhāsiteti vacanāt.*

atha svalakṣaṇāpratibhāsitvam aspaṣṭatā, tadā nirvikalpābhimatakeśoṇḍukavijñānasyāspaṣṭatā prāpnoti, tatra svala[S35]*kṣaṇasyāpratibhāsanāt, spaṣṭābhaṃ ca tad gīyate. na ca tāthāgate darśane tathābhūtaṃ jñānam asti yat svalakṣaṇā-*

---

1 S: *vijñānātmikā*

2 M: °*jñānasyāpra*°

3 M: *ted apy aspa*°

apprehensions of words) are conceptual constructions, the determination of words is impossible.

If conceptual construction is a cognition which has an indistinct form,[201] [then we ask] what indistinctness [means]. Does it [mean] not to have the nature of cognition, or not to be produced by a particular, or not to be produced by the perceived object, or [does it mean] the inexistence of the perceived [object], or not to contain the appearance of a particular?[202]

In respect to these [alternatives], if indistinctness [means] not to have the nature of cognition,[203] [then] this is not correct. It is asserted obstinately here [in this context] that the **cognition** has an indistinct form; how could it not have the nature of cognition?

If indistinctness [means] not to be produced by a particular, then the cognition would be produced by chance (i.e., without a cause).[204]

If [indistinctness means] not to be produced by the perceived object, then the cognitions of affection etc., would be indistinct, because affections etc., cannot produce their own cognitions.[205] [For] we have not yet seen that things produce themselves.[206] In the same manner the [false] cognition of the hair-net is not produced by the perceived hair-net; [nevertheless] it, too, is produced as [a cognition] which appears vividly, not as an indistinct [cognition], since [you] say [yourself]: "[A cognition] which is related to conceptual construction does not contain a vivid appearance of the object."[207]

If indistinctness is the fact that [a cognition] does not contain the appearance of a particular, then the cognition of the hair-net which is accepted [by you] as free from conceptual construction would be indistinct, because a particular does not appear in it, but [nevertheless] it is obstinately proclaimed as a vivid [cognition]. And [besides] in the Buddhist system there is no such thing as a cognition which does not contain the appearance of a par-

pratibhāsi, sarvasmin jñāne jñānakāyapratibhāsanā[M54a]*t.*

atha pratīyamānāsatyātā[1]*spaṣṭatā, tadā keśoṇḍukendudvayavijñānasyāspaṣṭatā prāpnoti. na ca pratīyamānasyāsatyatā vijñānakāyasya pratīyamānatvāt. na ca tasya visaṃvādo 'sti.*

4.18 *athātāttvikārthagṛhītirūpā kalpanā, tadā keśoṇḍukavijñānasyāpi kalpanātvam āpadyate.*

4.19 *atha svayam atāttvikī, tadā pratītiḥ katham? pratītiś ced, atāttvikī katham?*

4.1(10) *atha trirūpāl liṅgato 'rthadṛk kalpaneti cet,*

sāpi kiṃ liṅgajanyatvena kalpanāho nirviṣayatvena?

tad yadi liṅgajanyatvena kalpanātvaṃ, tadā liṅgā[M54b]*vagāhakanirvikalpakavijñānasyāpi kalpanātvam āpadyate. na cānumeyajñānasyāvyavadhānena liṅgotpādyatvam asti.*

atha nirviṣayatvena kalpanātvaṃ, tad api na yoyujyate, svāṃśaviṣayatvād anumānajñānasya.

atha svāṃśaviṣayavyatiriktaviṣayo nāsti, nirvi-

---

1 S: *pratīyamānā satyatā°*

ticular, because the body of cognition[208] appears in every cognition.

If indistinctness [means] the inexistence of the perceived [object], then the cognition of the hair-net and that of the double moon [etc.] would be indistinct. And the inexistence of the perceived is not [possible in the Buddhist system], because the body of the cognition is perceived [in every cognition], and in respect to it [the cognition] does not [ever] belie.[209]

If conceptual construction consists in the apprehension of an unreal object, then the cognition of the hair-net, too, would be a conceptual construction.

If [conceptual construction] itself is unreal,[210] then how is it a cognition? If [you say that] it is a cognition, how is it not real?

[Objection:] Conceptual construction is a cognition of an object based on the triform sign.[211]
[Reply:] This [cognition], too, is it a conceptual construction because it is produced by an [inferential] sign, or because it is without an object?

In respect to these [alternatives], if [the cognition which is based on the triform sign] is a conceptual construction because it is produced by an [inferential] sign, then the non-conceptual cognition which apprehends the [inferential] sign would also be a conceptual construction.[212] And [on top of that] the cognition of an inferred [object] is not directly produced by the [inferential] sign.[213]

If [the cognition which is based on the triform sign] is a conceptual construction because it is without an object,[214] [then] this, too, can in no way be correct, because inferential cognition has a part of itself as object. [Objection: Inferential cognition has] no object over and above a part of itself [and it is in this sense that] we *ṣayatvena kalpanātvam apadiśyate.*

tadā keśoṇḍukavijñānasyāpi kalpanātvam āpadyate.

4.1(10)a *atha yan nirvikalpakaṃ tad vispaṣṭatayopajāyata, ānumānikaṃ tv aspaṣṭābhaṃ, tena tat kalpanājñānam.*

4.1(10)a1 *tad ayuktam. aspaṣṭatā ca yathā na sambhavati, tathā prāg evoktā.*

4.1(10)a2 *pratyakṣajñānasya ca spaṣṭatā kā?* [M55a] *kiṃ svalakṣaṇajanyatāho svalakṣaṇapratibhāsitā?*

4.1(10)a21 *tad yadi svalakṣaṇajanyatā, kiṃ pratīyamānasvalakṣaṇajanyatā tadviparītasvalakṣaṇajanyatā vā?* [S36] *tad yadi pratītyārūḍhasvalakṣaṇajanyatā, pratītau kim avabhāti? kim artho jñānam ubhayaṃ vā?*

tad yady arthas, tad ayuktam apratītāyāṃ pratītau tadanavabhāsanāt.

atha jñānaṃ, na tarhi tad ātmānam utpādayati svātmani kriyāvyatirekāt.

athobhayaṃ pratibhāti, tad ayuktam, ekopalambha-

say that [an inferential cognition] is a conceptual construction because it is without an object.
[Reply:] Then the cognition of the hair-net would also be a conceptual construction.

[Objection: A cognition] which is free from conceptual construction arises vividly, but inferential [cognition] appears indistinctly. This is why it is a conceptual cognition.
[Reply:] This is not correct. [On the one hand] we just explained above that/why indistinctness is impossible (i.e., why it cannot be used as a criterion to distinguish between conceptual construction and non-conceptual cognitions).
And [on the other hand] what [does] vividness of a perceptual cognition [mean]?[215] Is it [due to] the fact of [the cognition's] being produced by a particular or the fact that it contains the appearance of a particular?
In respect to these [alternatives], if [vividness is due to] the fact of [the cognition's] being produced by a particular, is it the fact of being produced by a perceived particular or the fact of being produced by a particular other than this [perceived particular]?
In respect to these [alternatives], if [vividness is due to] the fact of [the cognition's] being produced by a particular which is perceived, what does appear in the cognition? Is it the object, the cognition, or both?

In respect to these [alternatives], if it is the object, [then] this is not correct because it does not appear [in a cognition] when the cognition [itself] is not perceived.[216]
If it is the cognition, then [the particular which appears in the cognition does not produce the cognition, because] the [cognition] does not produce itself, for there is no action upon oneself (i.e., nothing can produce itself).
If both [the object and the cognition] appear, [then] this is not correct, because the apprehension [of one form]

sya dvitīyākāraparihārasthitidharmatvāt. yadi cobhayaṃ pratibhā[M55b]*ti, tadārthavaj jñānenāpi jñānam utpādyata ity āpadyate. tac cāyuktaṃ svātmani kriyāvirodhāt.*

athāpratīyamānasvalakṣaṇajanyatā, tadgatiḥ[1] *katham?*

na pratyakṣeṇāpratīyamānatvād eva.

nāpy anumānena, svabhāvakāryaliṅgānavagateḥ.

na svabhāvānumānaṃ tatkāryatādātmye tadanavagatau tasyānavagateḥ.

nāpi kāryānumānaṃ tadbhūtakāryānupalabdheḥ. piśācaparamāṇumaheśvarakalpārthotpāditaṃ kāryaṃ nehopalabhyate.

atha jñānam eva tasya liṅgaṃ,

tad ayuktaṃ, tena saha tasya sambandhānavagateś cinmātratayaiva [2] *na tv anyo 'rthaḥ. na ca cid ātmānaṃ janaya*[M56a]*ti.*

---

1 M: *vadgatiḥ/*

2 perhaps a lacuna at this point; one could expext something like *cinmātratayaiva jñānam upalabhyate ...*

necessarily stands by the exclusion of [any] other form.[217] And if both [cognition and object] appear, [then] the following would be inevitable: the cognition [would] be produced by the cognition (i.e., by itself), just as by the object.[218] And this is not correct, because action upon oneself is contradictory.[219]

If [vividness is due to] the fact of [the cognition's] being produced by a particular which is not perceived, how is this known?

Not by perception, precisely because it (i.e., the particular) is not perceived.

Nor by inference, because neither a sign which is the own-nature [of the inferred], nor a [sign] which is the effect [of the inferred] is perceived.[220]

There is no inference by own-nature, because when this [sign] and the result (i.e., the inferred object)[221] are identical, when the one (i.e., the inferred object) is not perceived, the other (i.e., the sign) is [also] not perceived.

Nor is there an inference based on an effect [as sign], because the effect which is produced by it (i.e., the unperceived particular) is not perceived [as such].[222] That which is produced by a thing similar to a demon, the atom, or God is not apprehended here [in this world] as an effect [of this invisible thing].

[Objection:] The cognition itself is its sign (i.e., the sign of the unperceived particular).

[Reply:] This is not correct, because the relation between this [cognition which supposedly is the sign] and that [unperceived particular which supposedly produces it] is not apprehended. [The cognition is apprehended] only as a mental entity, something else is [therefore] not [apprehended]. [Consequently what you could do at most is to deduce a mental entity from it] but a mental entity does not produce itself. [Therefore you cannot deduce its cause.]

samanantarajñānaṃ tasya hetur iti cet,
tad ayuktaṃ, tadavagatau na mānam asti. [1] *para-santānajñānārthakalpaṃ tad api na svasaṃvedyaṃ tatkāryajñānasya, tato*[2] *bhinnatvāt parasantāna-jñānārthavat.*
nāpy anumānena, tadāyattatāyā anavagateḥ. cinmātratayaivātmānam avagāhayati, nānyāyattatayā, tato 'nyasya piśāceśvara[3]*tulyatvāt.*
yadi ca samanantaravijñānotpādyatvena spaṣṭatā, tadānumānajñānasyāpi samanantarajñānotpādyatvena nirvikalpakatvam anuṣaktam.

4.1(10)a22 *atha svalakṣaṇapratibhāsitā spaṣṭatā, tatra kiṃ pratibhāti - kim artho jñānam ubhayaṃ vā?*

tad yady arthas, tad ayuktam, aprasiddhāyāṃ[4] *pra*[M56b]*siddhau tatprasiddhyabhāvāt.*
atha jñānaṃ, tad anumāne 'pi pratibhāti, tad apy astu nirvikalpakam. tannirvi[S37]*kalpakatve tarhy apohyo mṛgyo 'dhunā kalpanāpoḍhapadasya.*

---

1 perhaps a lacuna at this point; one could expect *na pratyakṣeṇa* ..., cf. l. 6, also above pp.72.10-11, 196.7-8.

2 M: *tavo* (?)

3 M: *piśāceśvare*; perhaps: *piśāc<aparamāṇumah>eśvara*o

4 M: *aprasiddhāyāḥ*

[Objection:] The immediately preceding cognition is its cause.
[Answer:] This is not correct, [because] there is no means of valid cognition to apprehend it. Similar to an object of (?)[223] a cognition in another series, this [immediately preceding cognition], too, is not self-apprehended [by the following cognition], because the cognition which is its effect is different from it,[224] just like the object of (?) a cognition in a different series.
Nor [is the immediately preceding cognition established as cause of the following one] by inference, because the fact that [the cognition] depends on it (i.e., the previous cognition) is not apprehended. [The cognition] apprehends itself only as a mental entity, not as depending on something else, because that which is different from it (i.e., from the cognition) is similar to (i.e., just as imperceptible as) a demon or God.
And if [a cognition] is vivid because it is produced by the immediately preceding cognition, then inferential cognition, too, would be free from conceptual construction because it is produced by the immediately preceding cognition.

If vividness [means] the fact that [the cognition] contains the appearance of a particular, [then] there [we ask again:] What does appear [in the cognition]? Is it the object, the cognition, or both?

In respect to these [alternatives], if it is the object, [then] this is not correct, because when the cognition[225] [itself] is not apprehended there is no cognition of the [object].
If it is the cognition, [then this is not correct, because] it appears in an inference, too; [consequently] this [inferential cognition] too is free from conceptual construction. [And] if this [inferential cognition] is free from conceptual construction, then [you] have to search now [for something] which can be excluded [from the definition of

athobhayaṃ pratibhāti, tad ayuktam, ekopalambhasya dvitīyākāraparihārasthitidharmatvābhyupagamāt.

4.1(11) *athātītānāgatārthagṛhītirūpā kalpanā, tatra kim avabhāty - arthas tadabhāvo vā na kiñcid vā?*

yady atīto 'rthaḥ prati[M57a]*bhāti, na tarhi tasya kalpanātvaṃ vartamānanīlajñānavat. nāpy arthasyātītatā pratīyamānatvena nīlajalādivat. na hi pratīyamānasyātītatā nāma. yadi ca pratīyamānasyāpy atītatocyate, tadā sarvasya buddhyupalakṣitasyātītatā bhavet. tataś ca vartamānavyavahāravirahaḥ syāt.*

atha tadabhāvaḥ pratibhāti, tasyāpy atītatā nāsti, svena rūpeṇa vidyamānatvāt. nāpi tadviṣayavijñānasya kalpanātva[M57b]*m upapadyate 'bhāvārthasāmarthyena samudbhavāt. asāmarthye vā viṣayārthaś cintyaḥ.*

atha nirviṣayaṃ, na tarhi tad atītānāgatārthavijñānam atītānāgatārthopakārarahitam apadiśyate. na ca nirviṣayatve sati savikalpakatvaṃ nirvikalpakatvaṃ vāpi tu jñānātmatayaiva tasya vyavasthitiḥ[1]*. na ca jñānamātratayā tasya savi-*

---

1 M & S: *tasyāvyavasthitiḥ*

perception] by the word 'free from conceptual construction'!
If both [the object and cognition] appear, [then] this is not correct because you admit [yourself] that the apprehension of one [form] necessarily stands by the exclusion of [any] other form.

If conceptual construction consists in the apprehension of a past or future object, [then] there [again we ask]: What appears [in this cognition]? Is it the object, its inexistence [at present], or nothing at all?

If a past object appears, then this [cognition] is not a conceptual construction, just like the cognition of a present blue [object]. Nor is the object past, because it is perceived, just like blue water etc. For [you] don't call past what is perceived. And if what is perceived is also said to be past, then everything apprehended by a cognition would be past. And thus, one could not talk/think about something as present.

If the inexistence of the [object at present] appears [in the cognition of a past object], [then] this [inexistence], too, is not past, because it exists as such. Nor can a cognition which has it (i.e., inexistence at present) for its object be conceptual construction, because it is produced by the capacity of [its] object, [i.e.] the inexistence [at present].[226] Or if [the inexistence at present] has no capacity [to produce a cognition], [then you] should reflect on the meaning [of the word] 'object' (i.e., it has no meaning).

If [a cognition of a past or future object is said to be] without an object, then it [can]not be designated as a cognition of a past or future object in as much as it is devoid of the influence of a past or future object. And when [a cognition] is without an object, it is neither conceptual nor non-conceptual; on the contrary, it is determined as having only the nature of cognition.[227] And it is not by being simply a cognition that it [can be] accept-

kalpakatvam iṣyate sarvajñānānāṃ savikalpakatvaprasaṅgāt. yadi ca nirviṣayatvenātītānāgatārthavijñānasya savikalpakatvam abhyupeyate, nirvikalpakābhimatakeśoṇḍukavijñānasyāpi savikalpakatvam āpadyate. na cātītānāgata[M58a]*vijñānasya nirviṣayatvam asti svāṃśaparyavasitatvāt. nāpi svāṃśavyatirikto 'rtho 'nyo 'sty ekopalambhenāpohitatvāt*[1]. *na ca svāṃśasya vañcanopapadyate. tadabhāvāt sarvaṃ vijñānaṃ savikalpakaṃ nirvikalpakaṃ vā vaktavyaṃ bhedānupapatteḥ.*

4.1a *yad apy uktaṃ kalpanāpoḍhaṃ pratyakṣam arthasāmarthyena samudbhavād rūpādisvalakṣaṇavad iti*

tatra kiṃ pratīyamānasva[S38]*lakṣaṇodbhavatvaṃ vivakṣitam āho 'rthamātrodbhavatvam?*

tad yadi pratīyamānasvalakṣaṇodbhavatvaṃ vivakṣitaṃ, tadā rāgādisaṃvedanasya yogipratyakṣasya ca pra[M58b]*tīyamānasvalakṣaṇodbhavatvaṃ na labhyate.*

athendriyajapratyakṣavivakṣayedam apadiśyate [2]*arthasāmarthyena samudbhūtatvād iti sādhanaṃ*[2], *tatrāpi ...*[3]*sya bāhyārthanirākaraṇaparatvāt.*

---

1 M: *ekopalambhas tenāpohitatvāt*

2 probably an interpolation introduced as an explanation to *idam*

3 M is illegible for ≈ 7 *akṣaras*; S suggests [*pratīyamānārthasamudbhava*?]*sya*

ed as conceptual, because [in this case] all cognitions would be conceptual. And if [you] accept that a cognition of a past or future object is conceptual because it is without an object,[228] [then] the cognition of the hair-net which is accepted [by you] as non-conceptual would also be conceptual. And it is not [true that] the cognition of a past or future object is without an object, because it extends up to a part of itself (i.e., has a part of itself as object). And [you can't say that when the cognition has no other object except a part of itself, it is said to be without an object, because for every cognition] there is no other object over and above a part of itself, for by the apprehension of one [form the apprehension of any other form] is excluded. And [the apprehension of] a part of itself cannot deceive; since it does not [deceive], one may say either that all cognitions are conceptual or that [all cognitions] are non-conceptual, because a difference cannot be established.[229]

It has also been said: "Perception is free from conceptual construction, because it is produced by the capacity of a real thing, just like a particular [such as] a visible etc."[230]

In respect to this [inference, we ask]: Do [you] mean production by the perceived particular or production by any object?[231]

In respect to these [alternatives], if [you] mean a production by the perceived particular, then [this is not correct, because] the cognition of affection etc., and the perception of the yogi cannot be produced by the perceived particular.

[Objection:] This (i.e., the reason 'because it is produced by the capacity of a real thing') is formulated while having in mind perception produced by the senses [alone, and not in respect to all kinds of perception].

[Answer:] There, too, ... because ... has the purpose of refuting [the existence of] an external object.[232]

astu vā bāhyo 'rthas, tathāpi kiṃ tena nimittātmakenotpādyata āha upādānātmakena?

tad yadi nimittabhūtenotpādyate, tadā tad-utpāditarūpasya rūparūpatā na prāpnoti nimitta-bhūtarūpotpāditajñāna[M59a]vat.

athopādānātmakenotpādyate, tadānayā rītyā rūparūpatāpadyate jñānasya rūpotpāditarūpasyeva. tataḥ sarvam avijñānātmakaṃ jagat syāt. avijñā-nātmake ca jagati mānameyavyavahārābhāvaprasaṅ-gaḥ. tatprasaktau ca kasyedaṃ lakṣaṇaṃ prastūya-te?

athopādānabhūtena rūpeṇa rūpam utpādyate, nimit-tātmakena tu jñānam iti cet,

tad idaṃ mahānubhavasya darśanam. na hy abāliśa evaṃ vaktum utsaheta. na hy ekasyānekākāratā nāma. na cānekanāmakaraṇe meyādyanyatvam asti. a[M59b]nyatve vā na tarhidaṃ vaktavyaṃ - svavi-ṣayānantaraviṣayasahakāriṇendriyajñānena manovi-jñānaṃ niṣpādyate. tad evam indriyajñānasya pratīyamānārthasamudbhavatvābhāvaḥ.

dṛṣṭāntaś ca sādhanavikalo - na rūpādisvalakṣa-ṇasya rūparūpāvabhātārthodbhavatvam asti.

Or let us assume [the existence of] an external object. Even so [we ask]: Is [the perceptual cognition] produced by it (i.e., by the external object) as an efficient cause or as a material cause?[233]

In respect to these [alternatives], if it is produced [by it] as efficient cause, then a visible which is produced by it would not have the nature of a visible, just like the cognition which is produced by [this] visible as efficient cause.[234]

If [the cognition] is produced by [a visible] as material cause, then in this way the cognition would have the nature of a visible, just like a visible produced by [this] visible. Thus, the whole world would have the nature of non-cognition.[235] And if the world does not have the nature of cognition (i.e., if there is nothing in the world that has the nature of cognition), [then] one cannot talk/think about means and objects of valid cognition. And in this case the definition of what is the subject under discussion?

[Objection:] The visible is produced by the visible as material cause, the cognition on the other hand [is produced by the visible] as efficient cause.

[Answer:] This is the point of view of a great man! For a serious man wouldn't dare talk like that. For one thing certainly doesn't have several forms. And it is not by giving several names that one [thing] becomes different, [namely] object of valid cognition etc. Or if it does, then you shouldn't say that "Mental cognition is produced by the sensory cognition assisted by the object which immediately follows/is not different from its own object (i.e., the object of the sensory cognition)."[236] Thus, sensory cognition is not produced by the perceived object.

And [on top of that] the example is devoid of the reason:[237] a particular [like] a visible etc., is not [necessarily] produced by an object which appears [in a cognition] in the form of a visible.[238]

athāpratīyamānasvalakṣaṇodbhavatvaṃ me vivakṣitam,
tadātītānāgatānumānavikalpānām apratīyamānārthodbhavatvena nirvikalpakatvam āpadyate.

4.1b *yad apy anyad uktam ekopalambhasāmarthyād vikalpikāyāḥ samudbhava idam upalabha idaṃ nopalabha iti kīlaikabhūtalopalambhe* [S39] *sati vikalpikā buddhir utpa*[M60a]*dyata idam upalabha idaṃ nopalabhyata ityādikā*
etad api na yuktam. yathā rūpasvalakṣaṇasya savikalpakavijñānajanakatvaṃ nāsty avikalpakatvāt, tathā vijñānasvalakṣaṇam api na[1] *savikalpakavijñānotpādakatvam ativartate 'vicārakatvāviśeṣāt.*
athāvicārakatvāviśeṣe[2] *'pi nirvikalpakavijñānasya savikalpakavijñānodayadānasāmarthyaṃ jegīyate, tadā rūpādisvalakṣaṇasyāpy etad astu. tataś ca pratyakṣānumānayor bhedānupapattiḥ.*

4.1c *yad apy anyad uktaṃ - pratyakṣasādhana evendriyadhiyaḥ kalpanāvirahaḥ.*
[M60b]*atha ko 'yaṃ kalpanāviraho nāma? kiṃ jñānakāyatādātmyavyavasthitadehas tadviparīto vā?*

---

1 M & S om. *na*
2 M: °*viśeṣeṣe*

[Objection:] What I mean is that [perception] is produced by a particular which is not perceived.[239]
[Reply:] Then conceptual constructions, [like] inferences of past or future [objects], would not be conceptual, because they are not produced by the objects perceived [by them].

Something else has been said as well: "Conceptual [cognition which consists in a negation, for instance] 'I perceive this (e.g., the ground), I do not perceive that (e.g., a pot)' is produced by the capacity of the apprehension of only one (i.e., of the apprehension of the ground); indeed, when only the ground is perceived, a conceptual cognition [of both objects] arises: 'I perceive this [ground], that [pot] is not perceived,'"etc.[240]
This is also not correct. Just as [you say that] a particular that is a visible does not produce a conceptual cognition because it is not conceptual, in the same manner a particular that is a cognition, too, cannot produce a conceptual cognition, because there is no difference in the fact of [their both] being non-conceptual.
If [you] obstinately maintain that, although there is no difference in the fact of being non-conceptual, a non-conceptual cognition has the capacity of giving birth to a conceptual cognition, then this would be [the case] for a particular that is a visible etc., too, and thus the difference between perception and inference cannot be established [according to their different objects].

Something else has been said as well: "It is proved by perception itself that sensory cognition lacks conceptual construction."[241]
[This, too, is not correct.] Now, what is [this thing] called lack of conceptual construction? Does it have an essence (lit. body) which is established as having the same nature as the essence of cognition, or does it have [an essence] which is different [from the essence of cognition]?

tad yadi jñānatādātmyena vyavasthitas, tadā pratyakṣasādhanaḥ kalpanāviraha iti kim uktaṃ bhavati? pratyakṣasādhano vijñānākāraḥ pratyakṣadhiyaḥ. na kevalaṃ pratyakṣakalpanāvirahaḥ pratyakṣasādhano, 'nu[1]*mānadhiyo 'pi pratyakṣasādhana eva, jñānākārasyānumānajñāne 'pi bhāvāt. athānumānajñānasyāpy ātmasaṃvittau ka*[M61a]*lpanārahitatvaṃ, bāhyārthāpekṣayā kalpanātmakatvam iti cet,*

tad etan mugdhābhidhānaṃ[2] *dunoti mānasam. kathaṃ syur vividhākārās tadekasya vastunaḥ?*[3]

atha bhedena vyavasthitas, tadgatiḥ[4] *katham? na svasaṃvedyo 'sau jñānākāravyatirekāt. nāpi janakatvākārārpakatvena gṛhyate virahasya sāmarthyavyatirekāt. evaṃ ca sati yad uktaṃ - pratyakṣasādhana evendriyadhiyaḥ kalpanāviraha iti tad bālavalgitam.*

4.1d *atha gaur ityādijñānaṃ kalpanā, katham asya kalpanātvam?*

arthenājanitatvād - yadi gavāder arthasya [M61b] *gaur ityādijñānotpāda*[S40]*nasāmarthyaṃ syāt, tadā prathamākṣasannipātavelāyām api kuryāt tad-*

---

1 M: *sādhānu°*

2 M: *°ābhidhāna*

3 S considers *kathaṃ ... vastunaḥ* as a quotation

4 M: *tadgatiḥ/*

In respect to these [alternatives], if [this lack] is established as identical with the cognition, then what does it mean [to say]: "The lack of conceptual construction is proved by perception"? [It means that] it is proved by perception that sensory cognition has the form of cognition. [But in this case it follows that] not only it is proved by perception that perception lacks conceptual construction, [but also] that it is proved by perception itself that inferential cognition as well [lacks conceptual construction], because the form of cognition exists in an inferential cognition as well.

[Objection:] Inferential cognition, too, when it apprehends itself, is devoid of conceptual construction; [it is only] in respect to the external object [that] it has the nature of conceptual construction.

[Answer:] This stupid talk tortures [my] mind: how is it possible that one and the same thing would have multiple forms?[242]

If [the lack of conceptual construction] is established as different [from the cognition], how is it apprehended? It is not apprehended by itself, because it doesn't have the form/nature of cognition. Nor is it apprehended by producing [the cognition] and providing [its] form [to the cognition], because a [mere] absence does not have the capacity [to do it]. And when such is [the case], what has been said: "It is proved by perception itself that sensory cognition lacks conceptual construction," is the skipping of a child.

Now, [it has also been said that] conceptual construction is a cognition [such as] 'cow' etc.[243] Why is it a conceptual construction?

[Opponent:] Because it is not produced by the object. If an object [such as] a cow etc., had the capacity to produce a cognition [such as] 'cow' etc., then it would have done [so] already at the time of [its] first encounter with the *ātmano 'viśeṣāt. tad uktaṃ*

> *yaḥ prāg ajanako buddher upayogāviśeṣataḥ/*
> *sa paścād api tena syād arthāpāye 'pi netradhīḥ//*

atha śabdasmaraṇam apekṣyotpādayati, tad evāstu taddehānantaraphalatvād gaur ityādijñānasya. tad uktam

> *arthopayoge 'pi punaḥ smārtaṃ śabdānuyojanam/*
> *akṣadhī[M62a]r yady apekṣeta so 'rtho vyavahito bhavet//*

tad etad ayuktam. prāthamikam api jñānaṃ[1] *gaur iti jñānaṃ, gopiṇḍāvagāhini vijñāne gaur iti jñānasañjñā. tataś ca prathamākṣasannipātajam api*[2] *bhavati. evaṃ ca pūrvāparavijñānayor ekaviṣayatva ubhayor gaur iti jñānasañjñāviṣayatvam. nanv ekasya kramabhāvivijñānajanakatvaṃ kim ekena svarūpeṇa svarūpāntareṇa vā?*

---

1 S: *prāthamikajñānaṃ*

2 perhaps a lacuna at this point; one could expect *gaur iti jñānaṃ*

sense, because the nature [of the object] is not different at that time. It is said:[244]

> "That which did not produce the cognition before [would not produce it] afterwards either, because there is no difference in [its causal] efficiency. Consequently there would be a visual cognition even when the object has [already] disappeared."

If [you admit that the object] produces [the cognition] in dependence on the recollection of a word, [then we object:] this [recollection] alone should be [the cause of the cognition], because a cognition [such as] 'cow' etc., is the result which immediately follows the body (i.e., existence) of that [recollection]. It has been explained [by Dharmakīrti]: [If one admits that sensory cognition is produced by the object, it has to be non-conceptual, i.e., independent from the recollection of the word; otherwise it could not be produced by its object, because]

> "Even if [one admits] the capacity of the object [to produce this conceptual cognition], nevertheless if sensory cognition would depend on the remembered relation [of the object] with a word [as well], this object (i.e., the object of the sensory cognition) would be separated [in time] (i.e., the object would not exist immediately before the production of its cognition)."[245]

[Reply:] This is not correct. The first cognition [of a cow] as well is the cognition 'cow.'[246] A cognition which apprehends the thing cow is called "the cognition 'cow.'" And thus, [the cognition] which arises at the first encounter of sense [and object] is as well [the cognition 'cow']. And so, since the previous and the posterior cognition have the same object, both of them are the object of the designation "the cognition 'cow.'"

[Objection: If] one and the same [object] produces [several] cognitions which arise successively, does it [produce them] by having one and the same nature or by having a *ekenaiva svabhāvena janaya[M62b]tīti brūmaḥ.*

nanv ekakālīnatā pūrvāparavijñānayor ekasvabhāvāyattatve saty āpadyate.

yady evam ekanīlotpāditanayanālokavijñānānām ekadeśasambandhitvam ekākārataikavyaktitvam āpadyata ekanīlotpādyatvāviśeṣāt.

athaivambhūtaṃ tat tasya svarūpaṃ yac citrakāryakaraṇātmakam.

yady evaṃ mamake 'pi pakṣe kramabhāvyanekakāryakaraṇātmakam eva svarūpaṃ svahetusāmarthyaniyamitasyotpatteḥ.

athavā yathā tvadīye pakṣe manojñānaṃ svalakṣaṇaviṣayaṃ na ca prathamākṣasannipātajam, api tv indriyajñāne[M63a]na svaviṣayānantaraviṣayasahakāriṇotpādyate, tathā gaur ityādikam api jñānaṃ prathamākṣasannipātajena[1] *vijñānena svaviṣayānantaraviṣayasahakāriṇā smaraṇādyupahitena cotpādyata iti nirviṣayatvābhāvo viṣayāntarasya*[2] *svakāraṇasāmarthyānurodhena gaur ityādijñānaja-*

---

1 M: *thathamākṣajena*; S: *prathamākṣajena*

2 M: *viṣayāntara*°

different nature (i.e., by having different natures which correspond to the different cognitions)?
[Answer:] We say that [the object] produces [the different cognitions] by having one and the same nature.
[Objection:] If the previous and the posterior cognitions depend on [one object which has] one and the same nature, they would be simultaneous.
[Reply:] If so, [then] the eye, the light and the cognition (or perhaps: several visual perceptions?)[247] which are produced by the same blue [object] would be related to the same place, would have the same form and would be the same individual, because there is no difference in the fact of being produced by the same blue [object].
[Objection:] The nature of that [blue object] is such that it consists in producing various effects.
[Reply:] If so, [then] according to my position, too, the nature [of the object which produces the cognition 'cow' is such that it] consists in producing several effects which arise successively, because it arises as determined by the capacity of its own cause (i.e., the object is produced by its cause in such a way that it has the character of producing several successive cognitions).[248]
Or, just as according to your position the mental cognition has the particular for its object and does not arise from the first encounter of sense [and particular], but is produced by the sensory cognition assisted by the object which follows immediately/is not different from its own object,[249] in the same manner a cognition [such as] 'cow' etc., too, is produced by the cognition which arises at the first encounter [of the object] with the sense assisted by an object which immediately follows its own object/which is not different from its own object and dependent on the recollection [of the word 'cow'] etc. Thus [the cognition 'cow'] is not without an object,[250] because it is produced by an object different [from the word 'cow'] which is capable of producing a cognition [such as] 'cow' etc., in com-

nanayogyasyotpatteḥ. [S41]*smaraṇam api samartham utpannaṃ sad gaur ity utpādayati. evaṃ sati yad uktaṃ yaḥ prāg ajanako buddher ityādi, tad svaparamatam anālocyaiva jegīyate.*

4.1e *na ca jñānākaravyatirekeṇa vikalpākāro*[1] [M63b] *'nyo 'sti. kalpanākāro hi jñānatādātmyena vyavasthitaḥ. tataś ca kalpanāpoḍhaṃ pratyakṣaṃ kim uktaṃ bhavati? jñānāpoḍhaṃ pratyakṣam. yo yatsvabhāvopanibaddhaḥ, sa nivartamānas tam ādāya nivartate. tataś cājñānātmakaṃ pratyakṣaṃ bhikṣūṇāṃ prasaktam.*

4.2 *tathāvyabhicāripadam api nopādeyam apohyajñānāsambhavāt.*

nanu mārtaṇḍapādasaṅghātotpāditaṃ vijñānam apohyam asti - kathaṃ tad apohyam? - atathyodakaviṣayatvāt.

yady atathyodakaviṣayatvaṃ, kathaṃ tad apanīyate 'tathyodakākārasya svena rū[M64a]*peṇa vidyamānatvān madhurodakadīrghodakākāravat?*

atha tatra madhurodakaṃ vidyate, svena rūpeṇa pratīyamānatvāt,

tad ihāpy udakaṃ pratīyata udakaṃ gṛhṇāmīti vyavahāradarśanāt.

---

1 M: *vaikalpākāro*

pliance with its own cause (i.e., the cause of the cause of the cognition 'cow'). Recollection, too, in as much as it arises capable, produces [the cognition] 'cow.' Thus, what has been said - "That which did not produce the cognition before"[251] etc., - has been emphatically proclaimed without taking into view either one's own position or the rival's position.

And [on top of all that] there is no further form of conceptual construction over and above the form of cognition, for the form of conceptual construction is determined [by you] as identical with the cognition.[252] And thus, what does it mean [to say]: "Perception is free from conceptual construction"? [It means that] perception is free from cognition! [If] something which is necessarily related to the nature of something [else] disappears, it disappears while taking that [other thing along with it].[253] And thus it results that for the Buddhists perception does not have the nature of cognition.[254]

In the same manner the word 'nonerroneous'[255] as well should not be employed [in the definition of perception] because a cognition which should be excluded [by it] does not exist.

[Objection:] There is [a cognition] to be excluded, [namely] the cognition [of water] which is produced by a mass of sun-rays.

[Reply:] Why should it be excluded?

[Answer:] Because it has unreal water for its object.

[Reply: Even] if it has unreal water for its object, why is it excluded, since the form of unreal water exists as such, just like the form of sweet water, of a long [patch of] water [etc.]?[256]

[Objection:] There [in your example] sweet water exists, because it is apprehended as such.

[Reply:] Then here [in the case of unreal water], too, water is perceived, since one observes that [people] say "I perceive water."

satyaṃ, pratibhāty, atathyaṃ tu pratibhāti.

4.21 atathyatā kā? kiṃ pratīyamānasyābhāvo 'tha pratīyamāna evābhāvaḥ?

4.211 yadi pratīyamānasyābhāvaḥ, so 'tra nāvābhāty, udakākāra evāvabhāti.

4.212 atha pratīyamāna evābhāvaḥ so 'py anupapanna eva. na hi bhāvākāre pratīyamāne 'bhāvakalpanā yuktā. anyathā rasākāre pratīyamāne rūpākāraḥ pari[M64b]kalpayitavyaḥ. tataś cālūnaviśīrṇaṃ jagat syāt. yadi cābhāvaḥ pratibhāti, kathaṃ tad udakajñānaṃ mithyājñānaṃ[1] cocyate 'bhāvaviṣayasya svena rūpeṇa vidyamānatvāt?

4.22 [S42]tad etad udaka[2]jñānam udakaṃ viṣayayaty udakābhāvam ātmānaṃ na kiñcid vā.

4.221 tad yady udakaṃ viṣayayati, tadā na tasya mithyātvaṃ madhurodakasaṃvedanasyeva.
tatra tathyodakaṃ pratibhāti.
kiṃ yat pratibhāti tat tathyodakam, āho yat tathyaṃ [M65a] tat pratibhāti?
tad yadi yat pratibhāti tat tathyam, ihāpy udakaṃ pratibhāti, prāptā tasyāpi tathyatā.
atha yat tathyaṃ tat pratibhāti, tasya tathyatā kathaṃ jñāyate? kiṃ pratītyānyathā vā?

---

1 S: mithyā jñānaṃ

2 M: uka°

[Objection:] True, [water] appears, but [it is] unreal [water which] appears.
[Reply:] What is irreality? Does it [mean] the inexistence of the perceived [object] or the inexistence itself perceived?[257]

If [irreality means] the inexistence of the perceived [object], [it cannot be known because] this [inexistence] does not appear in this [cognition of unreal water]: it is precisely the form of water which appears [in it].

• If [it means] the inexistence itself perceived, [then] this, too, is completely impossible, for it is not correct to assume inexistence when the form of existence is perceived. Otherwise, when the form of flavour is perceived, the form of a visible would have to be assumed. And thus the world would disintegrate. And if the inexistence appears, why [do you] say that [on the one hand] it is a cognition of water, and that [on the other hand] it is a false cognition? [It is neither a cognition of water nor a false cognition] because the object, [namely] the inexistence, exists as such.

This cognition of water has water as its object, the inexistence of water, itself, or nothing at all.[258]

In respect to these [alternatives], if it has water as its object, then this [cognition] is not false, just like the cognition of sweet water.
[Objection:] There [in the cognition of sweet water] real water appears.
[Reply: Do you mean that] what[ever] appears [in the cognition of water] is real water, or [that] what is real [water] appears [in the cognition of water]?

In respect to these [alternatives], if what[ever] appears is real, then there, too, water appears; [therefore] it, too, would be real.
If what is real [water] appears, [then] how is its reality known? Is it by a cognition or otherwise?

yadi pratītyā, ihāpi pratītir utpadyate. astu tathyatā.

atha pratītim antareṇa tathyatopapādyate, tadā susthitāni vastūni. sarvavādasiddhiḥ syāt.

atha pratīyate yadi nāma bādhyate.

pratīyate bādhyate ceti citram. pratīyamānatvaṃ ca janakatvākā[M65b]rārpakatvena vyāptam. yac ca na janayati nākāram arpayati tan[1] *nāvabhāti yathā rūpajñāne rasaḥ. pratīyate cātrodakaṃ, janakatvākārārpakatvopapattiḥ. tadupapattau' ca na bādhopapattir, janakatvākārārpakatvasya sattvanibandhanatvāt.*

4.222 *athābhāvaṃ viṣayayati, na tarhy udakajñānarūpatābhāvagṛhītirūpatvāt. nāpi tasya mithyātvam abhāvaviṣayasyo*[2]*papatteḥ.*

na ca saugatamate 'bhāve kaścid viṣayārtha upapadyate janakatvākārārpakatvavyatirekāt.[3] *udakākāro hi pratītyutkalitaḥ. tadabhāvaś cāprātītika ihopapādyate mugdhabauddhaiḥ.*

---

1 M: *yan*

2 S: *abhāvaviṣayatvasyo°*

3 perhaps a lacuna at this point

If it is by a cognition, [then] here, too, a cognition arises; [therefore the water] would be real.
If the reality is being established without a cognition, then things are well founded: all doctrines would be proved!
[Objection:] Even though[259] [water] is perceived, it is sublated.
[Answer:] Perceived and sublated, this is marvelous! For being perceived is invariably attended by being the producer [of the cognition] and that which provides [its] form [to the cognition].[260] And what[ever] does not produce [the cognition and] does not provide [its] form [to the cognition] does not appear [in the cognition], for example flavour in a cognition of a visible. But water is perceived there [in the cognition], [consequently] it is established that it produces [the cognition] and provides [its] form [to the cognition]. And when this is established, the sublation is not established, because being the producer [of the cognition] and that which provides [its] form [to it] are dependent on existence (i.e., are restricted to existent things).

If [the false cognition of water] has the inexistence [of water] for its object, then it does not have the form of a cognition of water, because it has the form of an apprehension of inexistence. Nor is it false, because the object which consists in inexistence is established [by it].
And [on top of that] in the Buddhist system no meaning of [the word] 'object' applies to inexistence, because [inexistence can] neither produce [a cognition] nor provide [its] form [to the cognition]. [According to this definition, there would never be a false cognition] for the form of water becomes visible in the cognition, and it is being established here by the stupid Buddhists that its inexistence is imperceptible [because it cannot produce the cognition and provide its form to it].

4.223 athātmaviṣayaṃ, tathāpi vyabhicāritā nopapadyate, svāṃśa[M66a]syāvañcanāt. na hi jñānam ātmānaṃ visaṃvadati. nāpi tad udakajñānatvena vyapadeśyaṃ rāgādisaṃvedanavat. na hi nīlābhaṃ saṃvedanaṃ rasavijñānātmakatvena vyapadiśyamānaṃ dṛṣṭam.

4.224 [S43]atha nirviṣayaṃ, na tarhi tad udakajñānam, udakajñānatayā tu pratibhāti, tena jānīmo na nirviṣayam. yadi ca nirviṣayaṃ, kathaṃ tan mithyājñānam? jñānamātrānurodhena na mithyājñānaṃ nāpi samyagjñānam. na ca bhavatāṃ pakṣe jñānaṃ nirālambanam asti svāṃśaparyavasitatvāt.

4.23 vijñānasya vyabhicāritā kiṃ svasattāmātrānurodhenāho parasattānurodhena?

4.231 tad yadi svasattānurodhena, tadā sarvavijñānānāṃ vyabhicāritā prāpnoti jñānarūpa[M66b]tāyāḥ sarvatra bhāvāt. na kiñcid vijñānam avyabhicāri syāt.

4.232 atha parasattānurodhena vyabhicāritocyate, kim anupakārakaparasattānurodhenāho upakārakaparasattānurodhena?

If [the false cognition of water] has itself for its object, even so [its] erroneousness is impossible, because a part of itself[261] [can]not deceive [the cognition], since the cognition does not deceive itself. Nor should it be designated as a cognition of water, just like the cognitions of affection etc. [which apprehend themselves, and which are not designated as cognitions of water].[262] For it has not [ever] been seen that a cognition in which a blue [object] appears is being designated as having the nature of a cognition of flavour.

If [a false cognition of water] is without an object, then it is not a cognition of water; however, it appears as a cognition of water! By this [fact] we know that it is not without an object. And if it is without an object, how could it be a false cognition? Due to the mere [fact of being a] cognition (i.e., without a relation to an object) [a cognition] is neither a false cognition nor a valid cognition. And [besides] according to your position, there is no [such thing as a] cognition without an object, because [every cognition] extends up to a part of itself (i.e., has a part of itself as its object).[263]

Is the erroneousness of a cognition [determined] in dependence on its own existence alone, or is it [determined] in dependence on the existence of something else?[264]

In respect to these [alternatives], if it is [determined] in dependence on its own existence alone, then all cognitions would be erroneous, because the fact of having the nature of cognition occurs in every [cognition]. [Consequently] no cognition would be nonerroneous.

If the erroneousness is explained [as being determined] in dependence on the existence of something else, [then] is it [determined] in dependence on the existence of something else which does not assist [in the production of the cognition], or in dependence on the existence of something else which assists [in the production of the cognition]?

tad yady anupakārakaparasattānurodhena vyabhicāritā, tadā sarvasaṃvittīnāṃ vyabhicāritā prāpnoty anupakārakaparasattāviśeṣāt.

athopakārakaparasattānurodhena vyabhicāritābhidhīyate[1]*, kiṃ karaṇabhūtaparopakārakasattā*[2]*nurodhenāho karmatāpannopakārakaparasattānurodhena?*

tad yadi karaṇabhūtaparopakā[M67a]*rakasattānuvedhena, tadā sarvāsāṃ saṃvittīnāṃ mithyātvam āpadyate karaṇabhūtaparopakārakasattāviśeṣāt.*

atha karmakārakopakārakaparasattānuvedhena mithyātvaṃ, tad ayuktaṃ, na tasya mithyātvaṃ satyodakajñānasyeva karmakārakeṇopakriyamāṇatvāt.

4.24 *tathā samyag*[3]*jñānatvam api ka ham? kiṃ jñānasattāmātrānurodhenāho parasattānurodhena?*

4.241 *tad yadi jñānasattāmātrānurodhena samyak-*

---

1 M & S: *vyabhicāry abhidhīyate*

2 S: *karaṇabhūtaparopakārakaparasattā°*

3 M: *samya°*

In respect to these [alternatives], if erroneousness [is determined] in dependence on the existence of something else which does not assist [in the production of the cognition], then all cognitions would be erroneous, because there is no difference [between true and false cognitions] in respect to the existence of something else which does not assist [in the production of the cognition].
If it is affirmed that erroneousness [is determined] in dependence on the existence of something else which assists [in the production of the cognition], [then] is it in dependence on the existence of something else which assists [in the production of the cognition] as an instrument, or is it in dependence on the existence of something else which assists [in the production of the cognition] as an object?
In respect to these [alternatives], if [the erroneousness is determined] in dependence on the existence of something else which assists [in the production of the cognition] as an instrument, then all cognitions would be false, because there is no difference [between true and false cognitions] in respect to the existence of something else which assists [in the production of the cognition] as an instrument.
If falsity [is determined] in dependence on the existence of something else which assists [in the production of the cognition] as an object, [then] this is not correct. [In this case] that [cognition of water] is not false, because, just like in the case of the cognition of real water, one of the causal factors which assist [in its production] is [its] object.

In the same manner, how is the fact of being a valid cognition , in its turn [determined]?
Is it [determined] in dependence on the existence of the cognition alone, or is it [determined] in dependence on the existence of something else?

In respect to these [alternatives], if validity [is determined] in dependence on the existence of the cognition *tvaṃ, tadā sarvasaṃvittīnāṃ samyaktvaṃ prāpnoti jñānākārasyopapatteḥ.*

4.242 [S44]*atha parasattānurodhena samyaktvaṃ, tadā kim a*[M67b]*nupakārakaparasattānurodhena kiṃ vopakārakaparasattānurodhena?*
tad yady anupakārakaparasattānurodhena samyaktvaṃ, tadā sarvāsāṃ saṃvittīnāṃ samyaktvam āpadyate 'nupakārakaparasattāviśeṣāt.
athopakārakaparasattānurodhena kiṃ karaṇabhūtaparopakārakasattā[1]*nuvedhenāho karmatāpannopakārakaparasattā*[2]*nuvedhena?*
tad yadi karaṇabhūtaparopakārakasattānuvedhena, tadā sarvāsāṃ saṃvittīnāṃ samyaktvam āpadyate karaṇabhūtaparopakārakasattāviśeṣāt.
atha karmatāpannopakārakaparasattā[3]*nuvedhena samyaktvam abhidhīyate, tadā rāgādisaṃvedanasya samyaktvaṃ na prāpno*[M68a]*ty, atītānāgatārthaviṣayatve yogijñānasya ca.*

4.25 *yat tad vyabhicāri jñānaṃ, tat kiṃ vyabhicāribhūtenopādānajñānena janyata āho 'vyabhicā-*

---

1 M & S: *karaṇabhūtaparopakārakaparasattā°*

2 S: *karmatāpannopakārakasattā°*

3 M & S: *karmatāpannaparasattā°*

alone, then all cognitions would be valid, because the form of cognition is proved [for every cognition].

If validity [is determined] in dependence on the existence of something else, then is it [determined] in dependence on the existence of something else which does not assist [in the production of the cognition], or in dependence on the existence of something else which assists [in the production of the cognition]?

In respect to these [alternatives], if validity [is determined] in dependence on the existence of something else which does not assist [in the production of the cognition], then all cognitions would be valid, because there is no difference [between true and false cognitions] in respect to the existence of something else which does not assist [in the production of the cognition].

If [validity is determined] in dependence on the existence of something else which assists [in the production of the cognition], [then] is it in dependence on the existence of something else which assists [in the production of the cognition] as an instrument, or in dependence on the existence of something else which assists [in the production of the cognition] as an object?

In respect to these [alternatives], if it is [determined] in dependence on the existence of something else which assists [in the production of the cognition] as an instrument, then all cognitions would be valid, because there is no difference [between true and false cognitions] in respect to the existence of something else which assists [in the production of the cognition] as an instrument.

If validity is affirmed [as being determined] in dependence on the existence of something else assists as object, then the cognitions of affection etc., would not be valid, and the cognition of the yogi as well, in as much as it has a past or future thing for its object.

This [cognition] which is an erroneous cognition, is it produced by an erroneous cognition as its material cause *ribhūtenopādānajñānena janyate?*

4.251 *tad yadi vyabhicāribhūtenopādānajñānena janyate, tad api vyabhicāribhūtena, prāptā vyabhicāriparamparā. saṅgrāhyam avyabhicāri na labhyate.*

4.252 *athāvyabhicāribhūtenopādānajñānena janyate, tad upādānakāraṇam anukurvad vopajāyate 'nanukurvad vā.*

tad yady upādānakāraṇānukāreṇotpādyate, tadā kim āpnoti? avyabhicāri[1]svarūpānukāreṇotpādyate. katham? avyabhicārasya [M68b] jñāna[2]tādātmyena vyavasthiteḥ. na caikadeśānukāritvam asty upādānakāraṇasya niravayavatvāt. evaṃ sarvaṃ vijñānam avyabhicāri prasaktam, apohyajñānānupapattiḥ. na ca vyabhicārāvyabhicārau jñānād vyatiriktau staḥ. yathā rasākāro rūpākāro vā jñānākārād bhinno, na tathā vyabhicārāvyabhicārau jñānād vyatiriktau. tataś ca vyabhicārākāro 'tra nirākriyate kim uktaṃ [S45] bhavati? jñānākāro 'tra nirākriyate. tataś cājñā[M69a]nātmakaṃ pratyakṣaṃ prasaktaṃ saugatānām.

4.25a *api ca yathā rūpeṇopādānabhūtena janyate rūpaṃ, tathā jñānam apy upādānabhūtenaiva janya-*

---

1 S: *avyabhicāri svarūpā°*

2 M: *jāna°*

or is it produced by a nonerroneous cognition as its material cause?[265]

In respect to these [alternatives], if it is produced by an erroneous cognition as its material cause, [then] this [cognition which is its material cause], too, [is produced] by an erroneous [cognition as its material cause]. [Consequently] there results an uninterrupted series of false [cognitions], a nonerrroneous [cognition] could never be contained [in this series].

If [an erroneous cognition] is produced by a nonerroneous cognition as its material cause, then it is either produced while imitating its material cause or while not imitating [its material cause].

In respect to these [alternatives], if it is produced while imitating its material cause, then what does result? It is produced while imitating the nature of [its] nonerroneous [material cause]. Why? Because the nonerroneousness is established as identical with the cognition. And it [can]not imitate [only] a part [of its cause], because the material cause has no parts. Thus, every cognition would be nonerroneous, [and consequently] a cognition which could be excluded [from the domain of perception by the word 'nonerroneous'] is impossible. Nor are erroneousness and nonerroneousness [something] over and above the cognition. Unlike the form of flavour or the form of a visible which are different from the form of cognition, erroneousness and nonerroneousness are not over and above the cognition. And thus, what does it mean [to say that] the form of erroneousness is rejected in it (i.e., in the definition of perception)? [It means that] the form of cognition is rejected in it. And thus, for the Buddhists perception would have the nature of non-cognition.[266]

Besides, just as a visible is produced by a visible as material cause, in the same manner the cognition, too, is *te. ya eva tasya rūpotpādana ātmā, sa eva tasya jñānotpādane 'pi. na hi tasya jñānotpādana ātmānyatvam.*

atha nimittabhūtena jñānam utpādyata upādānabhūtena rūpam iti cet, tat katham ekasyānekākārayogitopapadyate? na ca sañjñānyatve meyādyanyatvam[1] *upapadyate. rūpavad vijñānasyāpi rūparūpatā prāpno*[M69b]*ti. tatprāptau ca na paraloky ātmā. tadabhāvān na paralokaḥ. idam eva*[2] *cetasi samāropyāha bhagavān bṛhaspatiḥ - paralokino 'bhāvāt paralokābhāvaḥ.*

atha rūpopādānajanyatve 'pi jñānarūpataiva, rūpasyāpi jñānarūpatā prāptā rūpopādānajanyatvāj[3] *jñānavat*[4].

atha jñā[5]*naṃ jñānenopādānabhūtena janya*[5]*te, rūpam api tenaiva janyate. na hi tasya rūpotpādana*[6] *ātmānyatvam. evaṃ ca*

tadatadrūpiṇo bhāvās tadatadrūpahetujāḥ/

---

1 M & S: *meyānyatvam*; perhaps a lacuna after *upapadyate*

2 M & S: *evaṃ*; cf. also *TUS* p. 88.8.

3 M: *rūpopādānatvāj*

4 M & S: *jñānarūpavad/t*

5-5 conjectured by S; M is broken

6 M & S: *rūpopādāna/e*, but cf. above l. 1-3.

produced [by it] exactly as material cause.[267] The [visible] has exactly the same nature when it produces [another] visible and when it produces a cognition. For [the visible] does not have a different nature when it produces the cognition.[268]

If [it is said that] the cognition is produced [by the visible as] an efficient cause [and that] the visible is produced by [the visible as] material cause, then [we ask]: How could one [thing] be connected to several forms? [And it is not enough to call the visible sometimes a material cause and sometimes an efficient cause] for it is not correct [to say that a single thing] becomes different, [namely] object of valid cognition etc., by [using] different designations [for it].[269] [If you say that the visible is the material cause of another visible, then] just like the visible [which is produced by it] the cognition, too, would have the nature of a visible. And in this case, there is no Self[270] which [transmigrates] to the other world; [and] because it does not exist, there is no other world. Having exactly this in mind the venerable Bṛhaspati said: "There is no other world, because there is no [Self] which [transmigrates] to the other world."[271]

If [you say that] although [the cognition] is produced by a material cause which is a visible, it must have the nature of cognition, [then] the visible, too, would have the nature of cognition because it is produced by a material cause which is a visible, just like the cognition.
If a cognition is produced by a cognition as material cause, [then] the visible, too, is produced exactly by it (i.e., the cognition as material cause), for the [cognition] does not have a different nature when it produces the visible [and when it produces the cognition]. And accordingly [Dharmakīrti himself said]:

"Things have this or that nature, [because] they arise from causes which have this or that nature.

tad rūpādi kim[1] ajñānaṃ vijñānābhinnahetujam//

atha rūpopādānajanyatve 'pi[2] vijñānasya na rūpātmatā, tathā jñānopādāna[3]janyatve 'pi vijñānasya na jñānarūpatā. tataś ca nairātmyaprasaṅgaḥ. atha jñānopādānajanyatve jñānākāraparikalpanā, tathā rūpopādānajanyatve rūpā[M70a]kārātālokopādānajanyatve cā[4]lokākāratā prāpnoti. tataś cākārakadambātmakaṃ jñānaṃ prasaktam. aniṣṭaṃ caitad advayarūpatvenābhyupagamāt.

4.25b *yat tad rūpotpādyaṃ vijñānaṃ, tat kim eka[S46]deśena rūpotpādyatvena sthitaṃ sarvātmanā votpādyatvena paryavasitam?*

tad yady ekadeśena sthitaṃ, tad ayuktam, akhaṇḍasyaikadeśavirahāt.

atha sarvātmanā rūpotpādyatvena paryavasitaṃ, tadā vijnānotpādyaṃ na prāpnoti, yathaikakārakasamūhotpādyatvena paryavasitasya kāryasya[5] saṅghātāntaro[6]tpādyatvaṃ na dṛṣṭam. tataś ca vijñānasaṅghātānupapattiḥ.

4.25c *[M70b]tathā rūpam api jñānam ekadeśena kur-*

---

1 M: *rūpādikam*

2 M & S om. *'pi*; perhaps *'pi jñānasya*

3 M: *jñānotpādana*°

4 M & S: °*janyatvenā*°

5 M & S: *kārakasaṅghātasya*

6 M: *saṃghāntaro*°

Therefore, how could a visible etc., not be a cognition, in as much as they arise from causes which are not different from [those of] the cognition?"[272]

If [you say that] although the cognition is produced by a material cause which is a visible, it does not have the nature of a visible, [then] in the same manner, even though a cognition is produced by a material cause which is a cognition, it [would] not have the nature of cognition, and thus it would not have [any] nature [at all] (or: would be unreal).

If the form of cognition is assumed when (i.e., because) [the cognition] is produced by a material cause which is a cognition, [then] in the same manner it would result that [the cognition] has the form of a visible when [it] is produced by a material cause which is a visible, and that [it] has the form of light when [it] is produced by a material cause which is light. And thus the cognition would have a multitude of forms as its nature. But this is not accepted [by you], because you hold that [the cognition] has a unique nature.[273]

This cognition which is produced by a visible, does it stand by being partially produced by the visible, or is it completed by being entirely produced [by the visible]?[274]

In respect to these [alternatives], if it stands by [being] partially [produced by the visible], [then] this is not correct because that which is indivisible has no parts.

If it is completed by being entirely produced by the visible, then it would not be produced by the [previous] cognition, just as it has not [ever] been seen that the effect which is completed by being produced by one collection of causes is [also] produced by another collection [of causes]. And thus a collection [of causes] of the cognition is impossible.

In the same manner the visible, in its turn, can either produce the cognition with a part [of itself], or it yāt sarvātmanā karaṇaparyavasitaṃ vā.

tad yady ekadeśena karoti, tad ayuktam, akhaṇḍasyaikadeśāyogāt.

atha sarvātmanā karoti, tadā rūpaṃ sarvātmanā vijñānakaraṇe paryavasitaṃ na rūpāntarakaraṇe pravartate. yathaikakārakasāmagry ekakāryotpādanaparyavasitā kāryāntarasavitrī na bhavati, tathā rūpam api rūpāntarotpādakaṃ na bhavati. tataś ca rūpāntarasyākasmikatvam. tadākasmikatve[1] kāryānumānaṃ vilupyate saugatānām.

athānekakāryotpādakatvena paryavasitaṃ rūpasvarūpaṃ, tadā ghaṭasaṅkhyā[M71a]sāmānyāder apy anekādhikaraṇāśritātmakaṃ rūpaṃ, vṛttivikalpadoṣānupapattiḥ.

d.1 ito 'pi vṛttivikalpadoṣānupapattir - vṛttivikalpadoṣeṇa vṛtter eva nirākaraṇaṃ kṛtaṃ, na ghaṭasaṅkhyāsāmānyādes, tato 'nyatvāt. na hy anyasyābhāve 'nyasyābhāvo 'sty asambandhāt. na hy anudakaḥ kamaṇḍalur ity ukte kamaṇḍalor abhāvaḥ pratīyate, kapālānāṃ tadudakasya vā, api tu

---

1 M: kathaṃ tadākasmikatve; perhaps kathaṃ ... **na** vilupyate

would be exhausted by producing [the cognition] with its entirety.

In respect to these [alternatives], if [the visible] produces [the cognition] with a part [of itself], [then] this is not correct, because that which is indivisible does not have parts.

If it produces [the cognition] with its entirety, then the visible, in as much as it is exhausted by producing the cognition with its entirety, [would] not undertake the production of another visible. Just as one collection of causes which is exhausted by the production of one effect does not produce another effect, in the same manner the visible, too, would not produce another visible. And thus the other visible would be [produced] by chance. When it is [produced] by chance, the inference which is based on the effect [as an inferential sign] is being ruined for the Buddhists.

If the nature of the visible extends up to the production of several effects, then the pot, the number,[275] the universal, etc., too, have a nature which consists in residing in several substrata. [Consequently] the reductio ad absurdum of the residence [of the whole in its parts, of certain qualities in several substances at once, and of the universal in all its individuals] is not established.

For the following [reason], too, the reductio ad absurdum of the residence is not established:[276] by the reductio ad absurdum of the residence only the residence is refuted, not the pot, the number, the universal, etc., because [they] are different from the [residence]. For when one thing does not exist, [this does] not [mean that] another thing does not exist, because there is no relation [between the inexistence of the one and the inexistence of the other]. For when one says "The pot is without water," the inexistence of the pot is not apprehended, nor [the inexistence] of the parts [of the pot], nor [the inexist-

kamaṇḍalunā sākam udakasya viśleṣamātraṃ pratīyate.

nanu naiyāyikair vṛttimad ghaṭasāmānyam abhyupeyate. tadabhāve kathaṃ tasya saṃsthi[M71b]*tiḥ?*

yady evaṃ rūparasavijñānānām api vṛttir abhyu-[S47]*peyate naiyāyikais, tadabhāve 'pi sadbhāvo 'bhyupagamyate teṣāṃ bhavadbhiḥ.*

atha tāni pratibhānti vṛttyabhāve 'pi, tena teṣām abhyupagamaḥ kriyate.

yady evaṃ ghaṭasaṅkhyāsāmānyāder api svarūpaṃ pratibhāty abhinnānugatātmatayā. na cānubhūyamānasya nihnavo yuktaḥ sarvāpalāpaprasaṅgāt. anupalabdhau vā saiva samarthā, alaṃ vṛttivikalpadoṣeṇa. yady upalabhyate, tadā[1] *vṛttivikalpadoṣo na vaktavyaḥ. atha nopalabhyate, tathāpi na vaktavyaḥ.*

d.2 *yad apy uktaṃ - deśabhedenāgrahaṇād ghaṭasāmānyānupapattis - tad apy ayuktam. na deśa-*[M72a]*bhedena vastūnāṃ bhedo, 'pi tv ākārabhedenā*[2]*bhinnānugatātmatayā tayoḥ svarūpam anubhūya-*

---

1 M: *tathā*

2 perhaps a lacuna at this point

ence] of that water; on the contrary, only the separation between pot and water is apprehended.[277]

[Objection:] The pot, the universal [etc.],[278] are accepted by the Naiyāyikas as characterized by residence [in the parts, the individuals, etc.]; when this [residence] does not exist, how could they be established?

[Reply:] If so, the residence of colour and flavour [in substances] and cognitions [in the Soul], too, is accepted by the Naiyāyikas, [and] although this [residence] does not exist, the real existence of these [cognitions and objects] is accepted by you.

[Objection:] They (i.e., colour, flavour and cognitions) appear [in the cognition], although the residence [in substances assumed by the Naiyāyikas] does not exist; this is [the reason] why their [existence] is accepted.

[Reply:] If so, [then] the own-form of the pot, the number, the universal, etc., too, appears [in the cognition] as not different [from one substratum to another] and recurrent [in several substrata]. And it is not correct to deny what is being experienced, because [otherwise] every [knowledge] would be denied. Or if [the pot etc.] are not apprehended, [then] this [non-apprehension] alone is capable (i.e., is enough in order to deny their existence); the reductio ad absurdum of the residence is superfluous. If [the pot etc.] are apprehended, [then] the reductio ad absurdum should not be pronounced. If [the pot etc.] are not apprehended, [then] even so it should no be pronounced.

What has been said as well: "The pot and the universal are not established, because [they] are not apprehended with a difference in place,"[279] is also not correct. The difference among things is not due to a difference in place, but to a difference in form.[280] [Consequently, the existence of the pot and the universal is established, because] the own-form of these two is experienced as non-different [from one substratum to another] and recurrent te. na deśabhedāgrahaṇena svāvayavādhikaraṇena saha tayos tādātmyaṃ sidhyaty asattvaṃ vā.

yady ākārabhedena grahaṇaṃ, tadā deśabhedenāgrahaṇasyāprayojakatvam, ākārabhedagrahaṇena svarūpānyatvasya prabodhitatvāt.

athākārānyatvena nāvabodho 'sti, sa evāstv asadvyavahārasamarthatvāt. kiṃ deśabhedāgrahaṇena? svahetor eva niyatadeśakālaniyamitasyotpatter na deśāntarādau grahaṇam. anyathā rūpāder asattvaṃ syād itaretaradeśa[1]lagnasyāgrahaṇāt.

d.3 ya[M72b]d apy uktaṃ - nāsti ghaṭasāmānyaṃ tadagrahe 'grahāt.

kim anena kriyate? kim avayavādhikaraṇāvyatirekapratipādanam āho 'sattvapratipādanam?

tad yady avyatirekapratipādanaṃ kriyate, ka-

---

1 S: itaradeśa°

[in several substrata]. And the identity of the [pot] with its parts and [that] of the [universal] with its substrata are not established [just] because [they are] not apprehended in a different place (i.e., different from the place of the parts of the pot and of the substrata of the universal); nor [is it established] that [the pot and the universal] do not exist.

If [the pot and the universal] are apprehended with a difference in form, then the non-apprehension with a difference in place is not a criterion [for their inexistence], because the fact that [things] have different natures is known by [their] apprehension with a difference in form.

If [the pot and the universal] are not apprehended as having a different form [from that of the parts and of the substrata], [then] this alone should be [enough to prove their inexistence or their identity with the parts and the substrata], because [the non-apprehension with a difference in form] is adequate for [their] being considered as unreal [objects]; of what use is the non-apprehension with a difference in place? [A thing] is not apprehended in a different place etc., because it is produced by its own cause as confined to a specific place and time. Otherwise [things like] something visible [,flavour] etc., would not exist, because [they] are not apprehended as connected to respectively different places.[281]

It has also been said: "The pot and the universal do not exist, because [they] are not apprehended when these (i.e., the parts of the pot and the substrata of the universal) are not apprehended."[282]

What is accomplished by this [statement]?

Does it communicate that [the pot] is not different from its parts and [that the universal is not different] from its substrata, or does it communicate that [the pot and the universal] do not exist?

In respect to these [alternatives], if the non-difference [between the pot and its parts etc.] is communicated, *syātra pakṣīkaraṇam? kiṃ ghaṭasāmānyasyāho tadavayavādhikaraṇasya?*

tad yadi ghaṭasāmānyasya pakṣīkaraṇaṃ, tat kim avagatasyānavagatasya vā?

tad yady anavagatasya, tad ayuktam. na hy anava-[S48]*gate dharmiṇi hetor utthānam asti. na cāśrayavaikalye*[1] *gamakatvam.*

athāvagatasya, tadā tenaiva bhinnākārāvagamenāvyatirekapratyāyakasādhanaṃ bādhyate.

atha tadavayavādhikaraṇasya [M73a] *pakṣīkaraṇaṃ, tatrāpi kiṃ svasmāt svarūpād avyatirekaḥ sādhyata* [2]*āho parasmād*[2] *iti?*

[2]*yadi svasmāt svarūpād avyatirekaḥ sādhyate*[2], *siddhasādhyatayā sambodhayitavyāḥ.*

atha parasmād avyatirekaḥ sādhyate, sa parātmā pratipanno 'pratipanno vā?

yadi pratipannaḥ, sa kiṃ bhinnākāratayāvagato 'bhinnākāratayā vā?

tad yadi bhinnākāratayopalabdhas, tadānenaiva bhinnākārāvagamenābhedapratyāyakaṃ sādhanaṃ bādhyate.

---

1 M: °*vaikalya*°

2 conjectured by S; cf. *TUS* p. 103.3f.

[then] what do [you] make the subject of the inference here (i.e., in this case)? Is it the pot as well as the universal, or the parts of the [pot] as well as the substrata of the [universal]?

In respect to these [alternatives], if [you] make the pot as well as the universal the subject of inference, then are [they] apprehended or not?

In respect to these [alternatives], if [they] are not apprehended, [then] this is not correct, because a reason [can]not be employed when the property-possessor is not apprehended.[283] For when [its] support is missing, [a reason] does not make [anything] known.

If [the pot and the universal] are apprehended, then by this very apprehension [of the pot and the universal] as having a different form the reason which [is supposed to] prove the non-difference [between the pot and its parts and between the universal and its substrata] is sublated.

If [you] make the parts of the [pot] as well as the substrata of the [universal] the subject of the inference, [then] here again [we ask]: Is it the non-difference from their own nature which is proved, or [the non-difference] from another nature?[284]

If it is the non-difference from their own nature which is proved, then [you] have to be instructed that [you] prove what is [already] proved.

If it is the non-difference from something else which is proved, [then] this other nature is either apprehended or not apprehended.

If it is apprehended, is it apprehended as having a different form or as having a non-different form?

In respect to these [alternatives], if it is apprehended as having a different form, then by this very apprehension of something having a different form the reason which [is supposed to] prove the non-difference [between the pot and its parts etc.] is sublated.

athābhinnākāratayāvagato, na tarhi parātmā. idānīṃ svasmāt svarūpād avyatirekaḥ sādhyata iti siddhasādhyatayā sambodhayitavyāḥ.
athānavagato, na tarhy ekatvaṃ rathaturagaviṣāṇayor iva.

athābhāvaḥ sādhyas, tatrāpi kasya pakṣīkaraṇam? kiṃ [M73b] *ghaṭasāmānyasyāho tad avayavādhikaraṇasya?*
tad yadi ghaṭasāmānyasya pakṣīkaraṇaṃ, tat kim avagatasyānavagatasya vā?
yady avagatasya, tadā tenaiva sadbhāvāvagamenābhāvahetor bādhyamānatvād agamakatvam.
atha nāvagataṃ, kathaṃ tasya pakṣīkaraṇaṃ svayam anavagatasya pakṣīkaraṇāyogāt?
athāvayavādhikaraṇasya pakṣīkara[M74a]*ṇaṃ* [1]*ghaṭasāmānyaṃ nāstīti pratijñā*[1] *tadagrahe 'grahād ity asya hetos tadabhāvena saha sambandho nāsti. tādātmyatadutpattisambandhābhāve sati kathaṃ gamakatvam?*

tadagrahe 'grahād ity asya ko 'rthaḥ? kim

---

1 probably an interpolation introduced as an explanation to *tadabhāvena*

If [this other nature] is apprehended as having a non-different form, then it is not another nature; now it is [again] the non-difference from its own nature which is proved, [and] thus [you] should [again] be instructed that [you] prove what is [already] proved.
If [this other nature] is not apprehended, then it is not one [with the parts of the pot as well as the substrata of the universal], just as the horse [is not one with its unperceived] horn.[285]

If the inexistence [of the pot as well as of the universal] is to be proved,[286] [then] here again [we ask]: What do [you] make the subject of inference? Is it the pot as well as the universal, or is it the parts of the [pot] as well as the substrata of the [universal]?
In respect to these [alternatives], if [you] make the pot as well as the universal the subject of inference, then [are they made the subject of inference] as apprehended or as non-apprehended?
If [they are made the subject of inference] as apprehended, then the [supposed] reason for [their] inexistence does not make [anything] known, because it is sublated by this very apprehension of the existence [of the pot as well as of the universal].
If [the pot as well as the universal are made the subject of inference] as not apprehended, how [can you] make them the subject of inference, since what is itself unapprehended (or: what is [accepted] by yourself as unapprehended) cannot be made the subject of inference?
If the parts [of the pot] as well as the substrata [of the universal] are made the subjects of inference, [then] there is no relation between the reason 'because [they] are not apprehended when these are not apprehended' and the inexistence of the [pot and of the universal].[287] When there is neither a relation of identity of nature nor a relation of causality,[288] how could [the reason] make [anything] known? What is the meaning of this [reason], [i.e.] 'because

avayavādhikaraṇagrahaṇam eva ghaṭasāmānyasya grahaṇam āho 'vayavādhikaraṇagrahaṇā[S49]nantaraṃ ghaṭasāmānyasya grahaṇaṃ kiṃ vā ghaṭasāmānya[M74b]syāgrahaṇam eva vivakṣitam?

tad yady avayavādhikaraṇagrahaṇam eva ghaṭasāmānyasya grahaṇaṃ vivakṣitaṃ, tadā nānenāvyatireko 'nyatarāsattvaṃ vā pratipādyate. yathā nīlataddhiyor ekopalambhe 'pi nānyatarābhāvo 'vyatireko vā, tathā nīlalohitayor ekopalambhe 'pi nānyatarābhāvo 'vyatireko vā.

athāvayavādhikaraṇagrahaṇānantaraṃ ghaṭasāmānyagrahaṇaṃ vivakṣitaṃ, tadā nānenāvyatirekaḥ sādhyate 'nyatarāsattvaṃ vā. yathā rūpagrahaṇānantaraṃ rasasaṃvedanaṃ na tayor ekatāṃ gamayaty 'nyatarāsattvaṃ vā.

athāgrahaṇam eva vivakṣitaṃ ghaṭasāmānyasya, tadā tadagra[M75a]he 'grahād ity etan na vaktavyam. agrahād ity etāvad astu. na hy anya-

[they] are not apprehended when these are not apprehended'? Does it [mean that] the apprehension of the pot as well as of the universal is nothing but the apprehension of the parts [of the pot] as well as of the substrata [of the universal], or [does it mean that] the apprehension of the pot as well as of the universal immediately follows the apprehension of the parts [of the pot] as well as of the substrata [of the universal], or does it mean that the pot as well as the universal are simply not apprehended?

In respect to these [alternatives], if it means that the apprehension of the pot as well as of the universal is nothing but the apprehension of the parts [of the pot] as well as of the substrata [of the universal], then neither the non-difference nor the inexistence of one of the two is made known by this [reason]. For example, although a blue [object] and its cognition are apprehended by one and the same [cognition], [this does not prove that] one of the two does not exist, or [that they are] not different.[289] In the same manner, although a blue and a red [object] are apprehended by one and the same [cognition], [this does not prove that] one of the two does not exist, or [that they are] not different.

If [the reason] means that the apprehension of the pot as well as of the universal immediately follows the apprehension of the parts [of the pot] as well as of the substrata [of the universal], then neither the non-difference nor the inexistence of one of the two is proved by this [reason]. For instance, a cognition of flavour [may] immediately follow an apprehension of a visible, [but this] does not make known that the two are one, or that one of the two does not exist.

If [the reason] means simply the non-apprehension of the pot as well as of the universal, then [you] should not say "because [they] are not apprehended when these are not apprehended." It would be enough [to say] "because [they] are not apprehended." For the non-apprehension of the [pot *syāgrahe tadanupalambhasiddhis tatsvabhāvavinivṛttinibandhanatvāt tadanupalambhasya. na cāyaṃ*[1] *vyatirekārtho labhyate tadagrahe 'grahād ity asya hetor* [2]*ghaṭasāmānyasyāgrahaṇam eva*[2], *api tv avayavādhikaraṇagrahaṇānantaraṃ ghaṭasāmānyasya grahaṇaṃ labhyate. tataś ca viparītasādhanād viruddho bhavati.*

d.4 *yad apy abhyadhāyy - ekapiṇḍagrahaṇakāla upalabdhilakṣaṇaprāptasyānupalabdher nāsti sāmānyam.*

ka evam āha - nopalabdhaṃ sāmānyam? api tūpalabdham eva. katham jñāyate? dvitīyādipiṇḍadarśane sati pūrve piṇḍe smṛtidarśanād, anena [M75b] *sadṛśo 'sāv evam anusmarati.*

athavaikapiṇḍagrahaṇakāle tad upalabdhilakṣaṇaprāptaṃ na bhavati tena nopalabhyate. upalabdhilakṣaṇaprāptir ihānekasahakāripiṇḍopanipātaḥ. yadi copalabdhilakṣaṇa[S50]*prāptaṃ, kathaṃ nopalabhyate? atha nopalabhyate, na tarhy upalabdhilakṣaṇaprāptam. upalabdhilakṣaṇaprāptir iha pratyayāntarasākalyaṃ*[3] *svabhāvaviśeṣaś ca*[4]. *etac*

---

1 M: *cāyao*

2 probably an interpolation introduced as an explanation to *ayaṃ vyatirekārtho*

3 M: *osākalyao*

4 M: *viśeṣas sa*

and the universal] is not proved when something else is not apprehended, because their non-apprehension is dependent on the disappearance (i.e., inexistence) of their own nature [alone]. Nor is this meaning, [namely] that there is no [apprehension of the pot as well as of the universal], obtained for the reason 'because [they] are not apprehended when these are not apprehended,' rather [the meaning which] is obtained [for this reason] is that the apprehension of the pot as well as of the universal immediately follows the apprehension of the parts [of the pot] as well as of the substrata [of the universal].[290] And thus, since the contrary is proved, [the reason] is contradictory.[291]

It has also been said: "The universal does not exist, because when [only] one individual is perceived, there is no perception of [the universal, although it] fulfills the conditions for perception."[292]

Who says that the universal is not perceived? On the contrary, it is very well perceived! Whence is it known? Because one observes the recollection of a previous individual when the second and further individuals [which belong to the same class] have been seen. One remembers [it] in the following manner: "This resembles that."

Or when [only] one individual is perceived, the [universal] does not fulfill the conditions for perception, [and] this is why it is not perceived. To fulfill the conditions for perception here [in this case] consists in the presence of more than one individual which assists in the production [of the perception]. And if [the universal] fulfills the conditions for perception [as just explained], how is it [possible that it is] not perceived? If it is not perceived, then it does not fulfill the conditions for perception. To fulfill the conditions for perception here [in this case] consists in the presence of [all] other causal factors, and in [having] a specific nature (i.e., a perceptible nature).[293] If these [two conditions] are [fulfilled], how [is it possible that the universal] is not *ced vidyate katham anupalabdhiḥ? evambhūtasyāpy anupalambhe parikalpyamāne sarvavastūnām anupalambhaprasaṅgaḥ. upalabdhau vānyat kāraṇam anveṣṭavyam.*

atha pratyayāntarasākalyamātraṃ vivakṣitaṃ, na tatsvabhāvavi[M76a]śeṣaḥ.

yady evam adṛśyasyaivānupalabdhir, na dṛśyānupalabdhir asti. yadi cānyakārakasākalyam upalabdhilakṣaṇaprāptir abhidhīyate, tadāpy[1] *upalabdhyā bhavitavyaṃ nānupalabdhyā. itarakārakasākalyaṃ hy upalambhajananasāmarthyam. tac ced vidyate, katham anupalabdhiḥ?*

tasmād anupalabdhilakṣaṇaprāptasyaivānupalabdhir[2]*, nopalabdhilakṣaṇaprāptasya.*

d.5 *yad apy uvāca - kṣīrodakavad vivekenāgrahaṇān nāsti sāmānyaṃ - tad apy ayuktam. viveko hy ākārānyatvaṃ*[3] *vyaktīnām ananugamarūpatā, sāmānyaṃ tv anugatākāram anayoḥ sārūpyaṃ taiḥ saha sārūpyam asyeti viviktākārāvagamadarśa[M76b]nāt.*

tathā kṣīrodakayor api viviktam eva grahaṇam. tatra kṣīrodakayor ekabhājananikṣepe sati, kiṃ kevalaṃ kṣīraṃ pratibhāty āha udakam ubhayaṃ vā?

---

1 perhaps: *tathāpi*

2 M: °*labdher*; perhaps a lacuna at this point

3 M: °*ānyatva*°; perhaps a lacuna at this point

perceived? If it is assumed that even such a thing [which fulfills the conditions for perception] is not perceived, all things would not be perceived. Or if [such things, but not the universal] are perceived, another reason [for their perception] must be looked for.[294]

[Objection: By fulfilling the conditions for perception we] mean only the presence of [all] other causal factors, not the specific nature (i.e., the perceptible nature) of the [universal].[295]

[Reply:] If so, [then] there is non-perception only of [a universal] which is not perceptible, not non-perception of [a universal] which is perceptible. And if to fulfill the conditions for perception is said to be [only] the presence of [all] other causal factors, even then perception must occur, not non-perception. For the presence of [all] other causal factors constitutes the capacity of producing the perception. If this [capacity to produce] exists, how is non-perception [possible]?[296]

This is why only [a thing] which does not fulfill the conditions for perception is not perceived, not [a thing] which does fulfill the conditions for perception.[297]

What has also been said: "The universal does not exist, because [it] is not apprehended with distinction [from the individuals], just like milk and water,"[298] is also not correct, for distinction consists in having a different form [and the universal and the individuals have different forms]: the individuals have a non-recurrent nature, the universal, on the other hand, has a recurrent form; for one observes the apprehension of [its] distinct form [in such cognitions as] "There is a similarity between these two," "That is similar to these" [etc.].[299]

In the same manner there is surely a distinct apprehension of milk and water, too. There, when milk and water have been poured into the same vessel, does only the milk appear [in the cognition], or [only] the water, or both?[300]

tad yadi kṣīram eva pratibhāti, kathaṃ tad udakākārān na viviktaṃ bhavati?
athodakaṃ kevalaṃ pratibhāti, tad api kathaṃ kṣīrān na viviktaṃ bhavati?
athobhayaṃ pratibhāti, tadobhayor itaretarākāraviviktayor grahaṇaṃ tādātmyavyatirekāt.

d.6 [S51]*yad apy anyad uktam -*

ekatra dṛṣṭo bhedo hi kvacin nānyatra dṛśyate/
na tasmād bhinnam asty anyat sāmānyaṃ buddhyabhedataḥ//

ity etad apy ayuktam. ekatra [M77a] *dṛṣṭasya*[1] *bhedasyānyatra darśanam asty eva. yathā ghaṭavastrāder ekāvayavoparidṛṣṭasyāvayavāntaralagnasyopalambhas*[2]*, tathā sāmānyam api bhinnam asty anugatākārasya buddhibhedenādhyavasīyamānatvāt.*

d.7 *yad apy anyad uktaṃ nityasya krametarābhyām arthakriyākaraṇasāmarthyaṃ nāstīty asat sāmānyaṃ.*
tad etad ayuktam. ubhayathāpy arthakriyāsampādanam upapadyate yugapat krameṇa ca.
nanu kramakartṛtvam abhinnasya nopapadyate, kāryasyaikakālīnatā prāpnoti.

---

1 M: *dṛṣṭesya*; perhaps *dṛṣṭe 'sya*

2 M & S: °*opalambhāt*; probably a lacuna at this point

In respect to these [alternatives], if only the milk appears, how is it not distinct from the form of water?
If only the water appears, then [in this case], too, how is it not distinct from the milk?
If both appear, then both are apprehended as distinct in form from each other, because there is no identity [when two forms appear].

What has also been said:

"Since an individual seen in one place is seen nowhere else;
there is no further [object] different from the [individual], [namely] the universal, because there is no difference of cognition (i.e., because the cognition of the universal is not different from the cognition of the individual),"[301]

is also not correct: an individual seen in one place is very well seen somewhere else, for example a pot, a cloth, etc., which have been seen on one part [of the ground, the body, etc., respectively] are apprehended as connected to another part [of the ground, the body, etc.] <...> In the same manner the universal, too, exists as different [from the individuals], because [it] is determined as having a recurrent form by a cognition different [from the one of the individuals].[302]

Something else has also been said: "An eternal [thing] is not capable of accomplishing an efficient action, neither gradually nor at once. This is why the universal does not exist."[303]
This is not correct: [an eternal thing] can accomplish an efficient action in both ways, at once and gradually.
[Objection: A thing which is eternal and] which is [therefore] not different [at the beginning and at the end of the action] cannot be agent [of efficient action] gradually. [If it would be agent, then all] effects would have to occur simultaneously.

etac cāsamīcīnam. yathā bhavatāṃ pakṣa ekaṃ nīlasvalakṣaṇam anekākāra[M77b]kāryaṃ niyatadeśasambandhi janayati nayanālokamanaskārādirūpaṃ, na ca kāryāṇām ekākārataikadeśasambandhitā vā vidyata ekasvabhāvasamudbhavatve 'pi, tathehāpy evambhūtaṃ tat sāmānyaṃ yat krametarābhyāṃ kāryotpādātmakam.

nanu yadi krameṇa kāryaṃ karoti, tadā tad eva janakaṃ tad eva cājanakam.

satyaṃ, tad eva janakaṃ tad eva cājanakam.

nanu janakājanakayor bhedaprasaṅgaḥ.

na prasaṅgo 'sti. yathā tvadīye pakṣa ekaṃ nīlasvalakṣaṇaṃ svakāryā[M78a]pekṣayā janakaṃ, svakāraṇātmāpekṣayā tv ajanakaṃ, na tasya svarūpabhedo 'sti.

atha svakāraṇam ātmānaṃ ca janayati,

tad ayuktam. tad ātmānaṃ kurvad utpannaṃ vā kuryād anutpannaṃ vā.

tad yady utpannaṃ[1] [S52] karoti, tad ayuktaṃ, kṛtasya karaṇāyogāt.

athānutpannaṃ karoty asataḥ kaḥ kārakārthaḥ?

tathā svakāraṇam api na janayatītaretarāśraya-

---

1 M: anutpannaṃ

[Reply:] But this is not true. Just as according to your position one particular blue [object] produces [several] effects which have several forms, namely, eye, light, attention, etc., [and] which are related to respectively different places, and the effects neither have the same form nor are related to the same place, although they are produced by [an entity] which has the same nature [when producing one or the other], in the same manner here, too, this universal is such a thing that it produces the effect gradually and at once.[304]

[Objection:] If [the universal] produces the effect gradually, then the same thing produces and does not produce.

[Reply:] True. The same thing produces and does not produce.

[Objection:] There would be a difference between that which produces and that which does not produce.

[Reply:] There would not be. For example, according to your position the same particular blue [object] produces in respect to its effect and does not produce in respect to its cause and itself, [but nevertheless] there is no difference in its nature.[305]

[Objection:] The [particular] produces its own cause and itself. [Therefore there is no difference in its nature.][306]

[Reply:] This is not correct. This [particular], while producing itself, would either produce as [something already] arisen or as [something] not [yet] arisen.

In respect to these [alternatives], if it produces [itself] as [something already] arisen, [then] this is not correct, because it is impossible to produce what is [already] produced.

If [it] produces [itself] as [something] not [yet] arisen, [then you should explain] what [the word] 'causal factor' means for [something] which does not exist.

In the same manner [the particular] does not produce its own cause either, because [in this case] the fallacy of *tvadoṣaprasaṅgāt. atas tad eva kārakaṃ tad eva cākārakam iti tathā sāmānyam api janakam ajanakaṃ ca.*

na cārthakriyākartṛtvābhāve 'sattvaṃ sidhyati. yathā vahner ayogolakāṅgārāvasthāyāṃ dhūmotpādakatvābhāve 'pi na nivartate[1] *vahni-*[M78b]*rūpatā, svahetor eva tathābhūtasyotpatter vahnisvabhāvasya dhūmājanakā*[2]*tmakasya ca, tathānyad api kāryaṃ svahetunotpāditaṃ yad vastusvabhāvaṃ kāryājanakātmakaṃ ca. tathā sāmānyam api vastubhūtaṃ na ca kāryam utpādayati.*

nanu yadi kāryaṃ notpādayati, tad astīti kathaṃ vetsi? tadupalabdhyā.

nanu tadanutpādyā kathaṃ tadgṛhītir bhavati?

svahetusāmarthyaniyamitāyās tadgṛhītyātmatayotpatteḥ. na ca tadutpādyatvena tadgṛhītitvaṃ, cakṣurāder api saṃvedyatvaprasaṅgāt. na ca viṣayākārayogitvena tadgṛhītitvaṃ[3] *vijñānātmatāvyatirekeṇa*[4] *viṣayākārasamāveśāyo*[M79a]*gāt.*

yo 'sāv ākāro viṣayārpitaḥ, sa kiṃ jñānākārād

---

1 M: *nivartate/*

2 M & S: *dhūmajanakā°*

3 M: *°gṛhītitva°*

4 M & S: *vijñānātmanā vyatirekeṇa*

mutual dependence would be inevitable. Therefore, the same thing is a causal factor and is not a causal factor. In the same manner the universal, too, produces and does not produce.

And [besides, even if the universal does not accomplish an efficient action, neither gradually nor at once, this does not mean that it does not exist, because] when [a thing] is not agent of an efficient action, this does not prove [its] inexistence.[307] For instance, although fire in a state of [extreme] heat in an iron ball does not produce smoke, [it] does not cease to have the nature of fire. [The fire does not produce smoke] because [in this case it] is produced from its own cause as such a thing, [i.e.] as having the nature of fire and the nature of a non-producer of smoke. In the same manner another effect, too, is produced from its own cause [in such a way] that it has the nature of a real thing and the nature of a non-producer of an effect. In the same manner the universal, too, is a real thing and does not produce an effect.

[Objection:] If [the universal] does not produce an effect, how do you know it exists?

[Answer:] Because it is apprehended.

[Objection:] How does its apprehension come about in as much as it is not produced by it (i.e., by the universal)?

[Answer: It comes about] because [a cognition] which is determined by the capacity of its own cause [which is not the universal] arises as having the nature of the apprehension of it (i.e., of the universal).[308] And the fact of being an apprehension of something is not due to the fact of being produced by this [thing], because [otherwise] the eye etc., too, would have to be perceived. Nor is the fact of being the apprehension of something due to the fact of being connected to the form of [that] object, because it is impossible that the form of an object enters the cognition without having the nature of cognition.

[We are going to prove it:] Is the form which is provided

bhinno 'bhinno vā?
yadi bhinnaḥ, sa tāttviko 'tāttviko vā.
yadi tāttvikas, tadgatiḥ katham? kiṃ svasaṃvedyatvenāho janakatvākārārpakatvena?

tad yadi svasaṃvedyatvena, tad ayuktam, avijñānā[1]*tmatayā svasaṃvedyatvāyogāt.*
atha janakatvākārārpakatvena, tadā prāptākāraparamparā.
athātāttvikas[2]*, tadgatir nopapadyate svasaṃvedyatvajanakatvavyatirekāt.*

athāvyatiriktaḥ, sa tāttviko 'tāttviko vā.
yadi tāttvikaḥ, sa jaḍātmā tadviparīto vā.
yadi jaḍātmā, na tarhi citā saha tādātmyam. cidacitos tādātmyānu[S53]*papattiḥ.*
atha tadviparītas, tadā jñānamātratā syāt. [M79b] *jñānarūpatā ca sarvajñānasādhāraṇā*[3] *-pratikarmavyavasthānupapattiḥ.*
athātāttvikas, tadā jñānasyāpy atāttvikatvaṃ prāpnoti.
yadi ca vijñānatādātmyenākārotpattir bhavati,

---

1 S: *ajñānā°*

2 M: *paramparātāttvikaḥ*; S: *paramparā/ atāttvikaḥ*

3 M: *°jñānāvadhāraṇāt/* (*t/* seems to be deleted)

by the object different from the form of cognition or not different?[309]

If it is different, it is either real or unreal.

If it is real, how is it known? Is it [known] by self-apprehension, or by producing [the cognition] and providing [its] form [to the cognition]?

In respect to these [alternatives], if it is [known] by self-apprehension, [then] this is not correct, because in as much as it does not have the nature of cognition self-apprehension is impossible.

If it is [known] by producing [the cognition] and providing [its] form [to the cognition], then there would be an uninterrupted series of forms [which leads to an infinite regress].[310]

[If the form provided by the object] is unreal, [then] its apprehension is impossible, because [what is unreal] is neither self-apprehended nor producer [of a cognition].

If [the form provided by the object] is not different [from the form of cognition], [then] it is either real or unreal.

If it is real, it has either an unconscious nature or its opposite.

If it has an unconscious nature, then [it] is not identical with the conscious (i.e., cognition). The identity between the conscious and the unconscious is impossible.

If [the form provided by the object] is its opposite (i.e., if it has a conscious nature), then it would be nothing but cognition. And [since] the fact of having the nature of cognition is common to all cognitions, it [would] be impossible to assign [a specific cognition] to [its] corresponding object.

If [the form provided by the object is identical with the cognition and] is not real, then the cognition, too, would not be real.

Further, if the form [provided by the object] arises as identical with the cognition, [then, since] the cognition *vijñānaṃ sarvakārakaniṣpādyatvena*[1] *sādhāraṇaṃ - pratikarmavyavasthānupapattiḥ.*

evaṃ ca sati yad uktam

arthena ghaṭayaty enāṃ na hi muktvārtharūpatām/

tasmād arthādhigateḥ[2] *pramāṇaṃ meyarūpatā//*

tan mugdhavilasitaṃ saugatānām.

d.8 *tad evaṃ vṛttivikalpādidūṣaṇaṃ sāmānyādau na sambhavati -* [3] *yathaikaṃ rūpam anekakāryotpādakatvena*[4] *sādhāraṇaṃ, tathaikaṃ sāmānyam anekādhārasādhāraṇam.*

athaikaṃ[5] *rū[M80a]paṃ nānekaṃ kāryaṃ janayaty, api tv ekam eva, tatrāpi kiṃ rūpam eva kevalam utpādayaty uta jñānam eva?*

tad yadi rūpam eva kevalam utpādayati, tadā rūpasyāgrahaṇaṃ prāpnoti vijñānājananāt.

atha jñānam eva kevalam utpādayati, tathāpi mānasaṃ pratyakṣaṃ na prāpnoti. svaviṣayānantaraviṣayasahakāriṇendriyajñānena yaj janyate, tan mānasaṃ pratyakṣam. na ca svaviṣayānantarabhāvī viṣayo 'sti rūpāntarājananāt[6]*. tasmād ekam eva rūpaṃ vijñānanīlādikāryasādhāraṇaṃ pratipattavyam.*

cakṣūrūpālokādīni kāraṇāni vijñānam utpādayanti, tāni ki[M80b]m ekasvabhāvayuktāny āho ni-

---

1 M & S: °*niṣpādyena*

2 PVin I 34: *prameyādhigateḥ*

3 perhaps a lacuna at this point

4 M: °*otyādakatvena*

5 M & S: *athaika*°

6 S: °*ājanakāt*

is common [to all causal factors] in as much as it is produced by all causal factors, it [would] be impossible to assign [a specific cognition] to [its] corresponding object.

And thus, what has been said:

> "For [nothing] except the fact of having the form of the object relates the [cognition] to an object.
> This is why the means of valid cognition for the apprehension of an object is the fact of having the form of the object."[311]

is [only] a stupid gesticulation of the Buddhists.

Now, in the following manner [too] the reductio ad absurdum of the residence etc.,[312] is not applicable to the universal etc.: just as one [and the same] visible is common [to several effects] because it produces several effects, in the same manner one [and the same] universal is common to several substrata.

If [you say that] one visible does not produce several effects, but only one,[313] [then] in this [case], too, [we ask:] Does it produce only [another] visible or only a cognition?

In respect to these [alternatives], if it produces only[314] [another] visible, then the visible would not be apprehended, because it does not produce a cognition.[315]

If it produces only a cognition, even so there would be no mental perception. Mental perception is that [cognition] which is produced by the sensory cognition assisted by the object which immediately follows its own object (i.e., the object of the sensory cognition).[316] But there is no object which immediately follows its own object, because [the visible] does not produce another visible. This is why it has to be acknowledged that one [and the same] visible is common to [several] effects, [such as] the cognition, the blue [object], etc.

[Several] causes, [such as] the eye, the visible, light, etc., produce the cognition. [Now] are they con-

yatasvabhāvayuktāni?

tad yady ekasvabhāvatayotpādayanti[1], *tadā*[2] *kārakaikatvaṃ prāpnoty abhinnasvabhāvayogitvāt. atha niyatasvabhāvayuktāni* [S54] *jñānarūpaṃ kāryaṃ janayanti, tadā vijñānasyābhedarūpatā nivartate niyatasvabhāvakārakajanyatvād rūpaśabdādivat*[3].

atha vividhād api kāraṇād akhaṇḍitarūpaṃ kāryaṃ bhavati.

evaṃ ca kāryabhedād bhinnakāraṇānumānaṃ nivartate. [4] *ekasvabhāvād api vijñānād anekaṃ nayanālokādikāryam utpadyate. anekasmād apy ekaṃ bhavati. evaṃ ca sati niyatakāryadarśane niyatakā-*[M81a]*raṇānumānaṃ nivartate.*

athaikasmād eva kāraṇād ekaṃ kāryaṃ bhavati na bahūnāṃ saṅkalitānām ekaphalotpādakatvam. tataś ca niyatakāryadarśane niyatakāraṇānumānaṃ kena nivāryate?

tad etad asamīcīnam. yady ekaṃ kāraṇam ekaṃ kāryaṃ janayati tadābhyupagamavirodhaś - caturbhyaś cittacaittā bhavanti bodhād bodharūpatā viṣayād[5] *viṣayākāratetyādi.*

ekam eva janayati, kiṃ samānajātīyatvenāho tadā-

---

1 M: °*yati*

2 M: *tataḥ*

3 M: °*ādhivat*

4 perhaps a lacuna at this point

5 M & S om. *viṣayād*

nected to one nature or are they connected to respectively different natures?[317]

In respect to these [alternatives], if they produce [a common effect] while having the same nature, then [all] causal factors would be one because they are connected to the same nature.

If [the causes] as connected to respectively different natures produce an effect consisting in a cognition, then the cognition ceases to have a unique form, because it is produced by causal factors which have respectively different natures, like the visible, sound, etc. [which do not have the same causes and, therefore, not the same nature].[318]

[Objection:] Although from various causes, the effect arises having a unique form.[319]

[Reply:] And so, the inference of [respectively] different causes based on [respectively] different effects [as inferential signs] disappears. [On the one hand, you say that] from [one] cognition, although it has a unique nature, several [different] effects, [such as] the eye, light, etc., arise. [On the other hand, you say that] from several [causes], too, one [effect] arises. And thus, the inference of respective causes, when one sees respective effects, disappears.[320]

[Objection:] One effect [only] arises from only one cause, several [causes] joint together do not produce one result. And thus, what [would] impede the inference of respective causes, when one sees respective effects?

[Reply:] This is not true. If one cause [alone] produces [only] one effect, then [your] position is contradicted, [namely] "The cognition and [its accompanying] mental factors arise from four [causes]: having the nature of cognition [results] from a cognition, having the nature of an object [results] from an object,"[321] etc.

[If] one [cause] alone produces [only one effect], [then]

kāratvena kiṃ vā pūrvāparakālabhāvitvena?

tad yadi samānajātīyatvena janakatvaṃ, tadā samānajātīyaṃ[1] paścād utpannam api janaye[M81b]t.

atha tadākārānukāritvena janakaṃ, tatrāpy etad eva dūṣaṇam.

atha pūrvāparakālabhāvitvena janakaṃ, na tarhīdaṃ vaktavyam ekam eva janakaṃ cakṣūrūpālokamanaskārāṇāṃ pūrvakālabhāvitvāviśeṣāt. evaṃ cānekopādānotpādyatvenākārakadambakasvarūpaṃ vijñānaṃ prasaktam. rūpādyākāraparihāre vā vijñānākārasyāpy anupapattiḥ. tadanupapattau nairātmyaprasaṅgaḥ.

kiṃ ca jñānaṃ kāryaikasvabhāvaṃ kāraṇaikasvabhāvam ubhayasvabhāvaṃ vā.

tad yadi kāraṇaikasvabhāvaṃ, tadā kāryarūpatā na sambhavati. tadabhāve na vastutvaṃ saṃskṛtānāṃ vastutvābhyu[M82a]pagamāt. nāpi kāraṇarūpatopapadyate 'nādhīyamānātiśaya[S55]tvena janakatvāyogāt.

atha kāryaikasvabhāvaṃ, tathāpi na sadātma-

1 M & S: samānakālīnaṃ

is it by being of the same kind, or by having the same form, or by existing [respectively] before and after?[322]

In respect to these [alternatives], if [something is considered as] producer because it is of the same kind [as the effect without any reference to time], then - being of the same kind - even that which has arisen afterwards would produce [that which has arisen before].

If [something is considered as] producer because [the effect] imitates its form, [then] in respect to this [alternative], too, [we raise] exactly the same criticism.

If [it is considered that something] produces [the effect, i.e., the cognition] because it exists before and [the effect] afterwards,[323] then it should not be said that only one [cause] produces [the cognition], because the eye, the visible, light, attention, [etc.] equally exist before [the cognition]. And thus the cognition would have a multitude of forms as its nature, because it is produced by several material causes. Or if the form of the visible etc., is rejected [for the cognition], [then] the form of cognition, too, [would] be impossible. [And] when [even] the [form of cognition] is impossible, [the cognition] would not have a proper nature (i.e., would be unreal).

Moreover, the cognition has either a unique nature of an effect, or a unique nature of a cause, or the nature of both.

In respect to these [alternatives], if it has a unique nature of a cause, then it cannot have the nature of an effect. When this [nature of an effect] is absent, [the cognition] is not a real thing, because you accept [only things] which are produced [by several factors] jointly as real.[324] Nor is it possible that [the cognition] has the nature of a cause [alone], because it can't be producer without a [special] excellence being added [to it].

If [the cognition] has a unique nature of an effect, even so it [can]not have the nature of something real, be-

kam arthakriyākaraṇe vastutvavirahāt.

athobhayātmakam.

ekam anekātmakaṃ bhavati. kena tvaṃ vipralambhitaḥ? na hy ekasyānekanāmakaraṇe nānātopapadyate. na cānekanāmakaraṇam[1] *upapadyate nimittasyāvicitratvāt. evaṃ vijñānasyāsambhave sati santānānupapattir abhrāntabhrāntadvaitasyānupapattiś ca.*

e.1 *ito 'pi santānasyāsiddhir - vijñānasyaikatvāt. tadekatvaṃ cākārāntarasyānupapatteḥ. upapattau vā jñānākāravirahaprasaṅgaḥ. tatprasaktau ca san*[M82b]*tānānupapattiḥ.*

e.2 *ito 'pi vijñānasantānānupapattir - vijñānam asaddharmāt sadātmatayā nivartate, svarūpāntarāt tu kathaṃ vyāvartate? kiṃ sadātmatayāha ākārāntareṇa?*

tad yadi sadātmatayā vyāvartate, tadā rūpāder asadākāratā prāpnoti vājiviṣāṇayor iva. athākārāntareṇa nivartate, tadā jñānasyāsatsvabhāvatā prāpnoti turagaviṣāṇavad iti

atha vijñānākāratayā nivartate rūpādibhyo vijñānaṃ, sā vijñānākāratā satsvabhāvāsatsvabhāvā vā[2].

---

1 M: °*kāraṇam*

2 M om. *vā*

cause [you say that] if [a thing] does not accomplish an efficient action, it is not real.
[Objection: The cognition] has the nature of both [cause and effect].
[Reply:] One [thing] has several natures! Who deceived you? For it is not by giving several names to one [thing] that [its] plurality [of nature] is established. And it is not correct to give several names [to the cognition], because the cause [of the denomination] is not diversified. Thus, when the cognition is impossible, a series [of cognitions, too] is impossible, and the duality of nonerroneous and erroneous [cognitions] is [also] impossible.

For the following [reason], too, a series [of cognitions] is not proved: because the cognition is one. And it is one, because another form is impossible.[325] Or if [it] is possible, [then] it (i.e., the cognition) would lack the form of cognition. And in this case a series [of cognitions] is impossible.

For the following [reason], too, a series of cognitions is impossible: the cognition is differentiated from that which has an unreal character by having the nature of something real; but how is it differentiated from something which has another nature? Is it by having the nature of something real or by another form?[326]

In respect to these [alternatives], if it is differentiated by having the nature of something real, then the visible etc., would have the nature of something unreal, just like the two horns of a horse.
If it is differentiated by another form, then the cognition would have the nature of something unreal, just like the [two] horns of a horse.

If the cognition is differentiated from the visible etc., by having the form of cognition, [then] this having the form of cognition has either the nature of something real or the nature of something unreal.

tad yadi satsvabhāvā, tadā jñānākāratayā nivartata iti kim uktaṃ bhavati? sadātmatayā nivartate vijñānasadākārayor avyatirekāt. tataś ca rūpāder asadākāratā prāpnoti turagaviṣāṇavad iti pūrvoditam eva dūṣaṇam āpadyate.

athāsatsvabhāvā, [M83a] *tadā kharaviṣāṇavad vijñānarūpatāṃ parityajati. tyāge vijñānasantānānupapattiḥ. tadanupapattau caityavandanādikriyānarthakyam.*

e.3 *ito 'pi vijñānasantānānupapattis – tadutpādakavijñānasya pūrvāparasahotpannavijñānaṃ prati svarūpāviśeṣāt. yad eva pūrvasahotpannavijñānāpekṣayā svarūpaṃ tad evāparavijñānāpekṣayāpi* [S56] *svarūpaṃ vijñānasya niravayavatvena*[1]. *tataś ca yathā pūrvasahotpannavijñānasya hetur na bhavaty, evam aparavijñānasyāpi hetur na bhavati tatsvarūpavyatiriktavyāpārātiśayasyānupalabdheḥ.*

atha pūrvakālabhāva evātiśayas tena tasya hetutvam upapādyate.

---

1 M: *niravayatvena*

In respect to these [alternatives], if it has the nature of something real, then what does it mean [to say:] "[The cognition] is differentiated by having the form of cognition"? [It means that] it is differentiated by having the form of something real, because there is no difference between the form of cognition and [the form] of something real. And thus, the visible etc., would have the form of something unreal, just like the [two] horns of a horse. Thus, the criticism which has already been raised above is inevitable.

If [having the form of cognition] has the nature of something unreal, then just like the horns of a donkey it would loose the nature of cognition. When [the nature of cognition] is lost, a series of cognitions is impossible. When this [series of cognitions] is impossible, actions like the adoration of funerary monuments etc., are useless.

For the following [reason], too, a series of cognitions is impossible: because a cognition which produces in it (i.e., in the series) has the same nature in respect to cognitions which are previous, posterior, or which have arisen together [with it].[327] Exactly that which is the nature [of cognition] in respect to cognitions which are previous or which have arisen at the same time is the nature [of cognition] in respect to a posterior cognition, too, because the cognition has no parts. And thus, just as [a cognition] is not the cause of [another] cognition which is previous or which has arisen at the same time, in the same manner it is not the cause of a posterior cognition either, because a special excellence [responsible] for the activity (i.e., the production of another cognition), additional to the nature of that (i.e., of cognition), is not apprehended.

[Objection:] The special excellence is nothing but the existence before [the next cognition]; this is why the [cognition which exists before] is established as the cause [of the cognition which arises at the next moment].

yady evaṃ yathā devadattajñānapūrvakālabhāvi devadattajñānaṃ[1] *devadattajñānakāraṇaṃ, tathā sarvapuruṣajñānānāṃ devadattajñānapūrva*[2]*kālotpannānāṃ devadattajñānaṃ prati* [M83b] *hetutvaṃ prasaktam. tatprasaktāv anekadvīpadeśāntaritapuruṣānubhūtā*[3]*rthānusmaraṇaṃ syāt. tathā svajanabhujaṅgamādāv*[4] *ananubhūte 'py arthe 'nusmaraṇaṃ syāt. tathā tathāgatāvadātajñānajanyatve devadattādi*[5]*jñānānām avadātatā syāt. tataś ca sarve sarvajñāḥ syuḥ. atha naivāvadātatā devadattādijñānānāṃ tathāgatāvadātajñānopādānajanyatve 'pi devadattādijñānenāpi janitatvāt, tajjanyatvenaiva tathāgatajñānasyāpy avadāta*[M84a][6]*rūpatā na prāpnoti. tataś cāsāv apy avītarāgaḥ syād asarvajñaś ca.*

e.4 *itaś ca santānānupapattir - vijñānayoḥ sahotpāde hetuphalabhāvānupapatteḥ. yadaiva kāraṇajñānaṃ vinaśyati, tadaiva kāryajñānaṃ jāyata iti vaḥ siddhāntaḥ. kāraṇajñānasya ca vināśas tadutpāda eva. tataś ca kāraṇajñānavināśakāle kāryajñānaṃ bhavati kim uktaṃ bhavati? kāraṇajñānotpādakāla eva bhavati. tataś ca sahotpannayor hetuphalabhāvānupapattir ekakālodga-*

---

1 M & S om. *devadattajñānaṃ*; one could read perhaps: *devadattajñānaṃ pūrvakālabhāvi* and avoid the conjecture

2 M & S om. °*pūrva*°

3 M: °*ānusyūtā*°

4 M: °*bhujaṅgamādau 'nubhūte*; perhaps a lacuna at this point

5 S om. °*ādi*°

6 Folios 84a - 108b (= *TUS* pp. 56.13-74.12) are missing on the microfilm in my possession; from here on the text is based on S alone.

[Reply:] If so, just as a cognition of Devadatta which exists before [another] cognition of Devadatta is the cause of [this very next] cognition of Devadatta, in the same manner the cognitions of all people which have arisen before a [certain] cognition of Devadatta would be the cause of [that later] cognition of Devadatta. In this case [a person who lives here] would remember an object experienced by people who are separated [from him] in place by several continents. In the same manner one would recollect objects, although not experienced [by oneself], such as relatives, serpents, etc.[328] In the same manner the cognitions of Devadatta etc., would be pure, because they [would be] produced by the pure cognition of the Tathāgata. And thus, all [people] would be omniscient.[329] If the cognitions of Devadatta etc., are not pure, because - although produced by the pure cognition of the Tathāgata as material cause - they are produced by the [impure] cognition of Devadatta etc., as well, [then] the cognition of the Tathāgata, too, would not have a pure nature, precisely because it is produced by the [impure cognition of Devadatta etc.]. And thus, he (i.e., the Tathāgata) as well would not be [a person] free from passions and [therefore he would] not be omniscient.

For the following [reason], too, a series [of cognitions] is impossible: because the relation of cause and effect is impossible between two cognitions when they arise together (i.e., when they arise at the same time). Your established tenet is: Precisely at the time when the cause-cognition perishes the effect-cognition arises. And the perishing of the cause-cognition [constitutes] exactly the production of it (i.e., the effect-cognition). And thus, what does it mean [to say that] the effect-cognition arises at the time of the perishing of the cause-cognition? [It means that the effect-cognition] arises exactly at the time of the production of the cause-cognition. And thus, the relation of cause and effect is impossible between these two [cognitions] in as much as they have arisen together, *tayor goviṣāṇayor iva.*

kāraṇajñānasya cānutpanna[1]*syotpattivad anutpannasya vināśaprasaṅgaḥ. tataś ca kṣaṇam api nopalabhyeta. upalabdhau vā satatopalambhaprasaṅgas tadātmabhūtavināśasyopalambhavighātākartṛtvāt. vighātakartṛtve vaikakṣaṇopalambhasyāpy anupapattiprasaṅgaḥ.*

athaikakṣaṇopalabhyasvabhāvakaṃ sañjātaṃ tena na[2] *satatopalabdhir anupalabdhir vā.*

yady evaṃ dvādaśāṣṭakṣaṇopa[S57]*labhyasvabhāvakaṃ sañjātaṃ kiṃ na kalpyate?*

kiṃ cotpādavināśayor abhede sati kāryakāraṇayoḥ samaṃ vināśaḥ syāt.

e.5 *yad apy anyad uktaṃ - mātur udaraniṣkramaṇānantaraṃ yad ādyaṃ jñānaṃ taj jñānāntarapūrvakaṃ jñānatvād dvitīyajñānavat.*

nāsiddhatvād dṛṣṭāntasya. dvitīyādijñānasyāpi yathā jñānapūrvakatvaṃ nāvagāhayituṃ pāryate, tathā prāg evāveditam. kiṃ ca yadi[3] *jñānatvāj jñānapūrvakatvānumānaṃ, na kilāvabodhātmakakāra-*

---

1 M acc. to S: °*cānupapanna*°

2 M acc. to S om. *na*

3 S conjectures *yad dhi*

just like (i.e., not any more than) between the two horns of a cow which appear at the same time.[330]
And [since arising and perishing must occur at the same time, it follows that] just as the cause-cognition which has not [yet] arisen arises, [a cause-cognition] which has not [yet] arisen would perish [as well] (i.e., it would perish before it arises). And thus, not even for a moment would [the cognition] be apprehended. Or if it is apprehended, [then] there would be constant apprehension [of it], because perishing which has such a nature does not cause an impediment to the apprehension. Or if it does cause an impediment [to the apprehension], [then] even an apprehension for one moment would not be possible.
[Objection: The cognition] arises as having the nature of something apprehensible for [only] one moment; this is why [the cognition] is neither constantly apprehended nor not apprehended at all.
[Reply:] If so, why not assume that it arises as having the nature of something apprehensible for twelve or eight moments?
Besides, when there is no difference [in time] between arising and perishing, the cause and the effect would perish together.

Something else has also been said: "The first cognition immediately after the exit [of the newborn] from the womb of the mother is preceded by another cognition, because it is a cognition, just like the second cognition [of the newborn]."[331]
[This inference] is not [correct], because the example is not established. It has been explained already above[332] why it is not conceivable for the second and further cognitions, too, that they are preceded by [another] cognition. Besides, if one infers that [a cognition] is preceded by [another] cognition from the fact that it is a cognition, [then] supposedly (i.e., this presupposes the opinion that) an effect which has the nature of cognition is impossible

ṇam antareṇa bodhātmakaṃ kāryam upapadyate. etac cāvadyam. abodhātmakād api nīlālokalocanādikāraṇād upajāyate. tathā[1] *garbhādau yad ādyaṃ vijñānaṃ, tad bhūtasaṅghātād eva bhaviṣyati, na jñānāntaraṃ parikalpanīyam.*

yasyānantaraṃ yad bhavati, tat tasya kāraṇaṃ, nāparidṛṣṭasāmarthyam. vijñānābhāve vijñānajanyākāratā nivṛttā, na tu jñānākāratā. yathendriyavyāpāram antareṇopajāyamāne manovijñāna indriyajanyākāratā nivartate, na tu jñānākāratā.

yadi ca sadṛśāt sadṛśasyotpattir niyamyate, tadā dhūmena dahanānumānaṃ na prāpnoti, dahanasya dhūmasārūpyam antareṇopādānakāraṇatvāyogāt.

atha rūparūpatā sārūpyam ubhayor iti cet,

tad ihāpi svalakṣaṇarūpatā sārūpyaṃ bhūtavijñānayor, alaṃ paralokavijñānakalpanayā.

atha vijñānarūpatā bhūtānāṃ na vidyate tena teṣām upādānakāraṇatvaṃ nāsti vijñānaṃ pratīti ced[2]*,*

ihāpi dhūmarūpatā nāsti dahanasya, nopādānakāra-

---

1 S & M acc. to S: *tadā*

2 M acc. to S: *pratītiś ced*

without a cause which has the nature of cognition. But this is faulty. [The cognition] is produced from causes, [such as] a blue [object], light, the eye, etc., although they do not have the nature of cognition. In the same manner the first cognition of a foetus etc., should arise only from the aggregate of the [four] elements (i.e., the body), another (i.e., previous) cognition should not be assumed.

The cause of something is that which immediately precedes it, not something the capacity of which has not been observed. When the [previous] cognition is absent, [the cognition] does not have the form of something which is produced by a cognition, but it does have the form of cognition. Just as when a mental cognition is produced without the activity of a sense it does not have the form of something which is produced by a sense, but does have the form of cognition.

And if [in order to establish that a cognition is necessarily produced by a cognition you] make the restriction that [things only] arise from something to which they are similar,[333] then there would be no inference of fire from smoke, because without similarity with smoke the fire could not be [considered as] the material cause [of smoke].

[Objection:] The fact of having the nature of a visible is the similarity between the two (i.e., fire and smoke).

[Reply:] Then here, too, the fact of having the nature of a particular is the similarity between the [four] material elements and the cognition. The assumption of a cognition which belongs to another world (i.e., a former life) is [therefore] superfluous.

[Objection:] The material elements do not have the nature of cognition; this is why they are not the material cause of the cognition.

[Reply: Then] here, too, fire does not have the nature of smoke, [and therefore it would] not be the material cause [of smoke]. [And] when [fire] is not the [material cause of *ṇatvam. tadabhāve na dahanānumānam.*

tathānubhavajñānād anubhavajñānasyaiva niṣpattir abhyupeyopādānakāraṇānukāritvena kāryasya niṣpattyabhyupagamāt. na caikadeśānukāritvam asti tadbījasyāvicitratvāt. anubhavā[S58]*kārānanukāritve ca jñānākāratāvirahaḥ syāt. anukaroti ca vijñānarūpatāṃ tena kathaṃ nānubhavātmakam? tadupapattau ca prāptānubhavaparamparety ataḥ smaraṇānupapattiḥ. tadanupapattau cānumānajñānasyāpy anupapattiḥ. tataś ca sarvavyavahāravilopaprasaṅgaḥ.*

(4.) *evaṃ ca*[1] *na santānasiddhir, nāpi savikalpakanirvikalpakajñānadvairāśyam asti, nāpi vyabhicārāvyabhicāradvaividhyam upapadyate saugate mate.*

---

1 M acc. to S: *prasaṅgaś ca evaṃ*

smoke], there is no inference of fire [from smoke].[334]

In the same manner it has to be admitted that only a cognition which is an experience (i.e., not a recollection) is produced from a cognition which is an experience, because [you] accept that the effect is produced as imitating [its] material cause.[335] And [it] does not imitate [only] a part [of its cause], because its cause is not diversified. And if [the effect] does not imitate the form of experience, it would not have the form of cognition [either]. But it does imitate the fact of having the nature (i.e., form) of cognition; therefore, how could it not have the nature of experience?

And when this is established, an uninterrupted series of experiences results. Consequently, recollection [would be] impossible. And when this (i.e., recollection) is impossible, inferential cognition is also impossible.[336] And thus, all day-to-day activities would disintegrate.

[Conclusion:] And thus, in the Buddhist system, a series [of cognitions] is not proved; nor are there two groups of cognitions, [i.e.] conceptual and non-conceptual; nor are the two kinds [of cognitions according to] erroneousness and nonerroneousness possible.

5. *tathā satsamprayoge puruṣasyendriyāṇāṃ buddhijanma tat pratyakṣaṃ tad api pratyuktam. katham? etat sūtraṃ kadācil lakṣaṇaparaṃ kadācic ca kārakasaṅkhyāpratipādanaparaṃ kadācic cānuvādaparam.*

5.1(1) *tad yadi lakṣaṇaparaṃ, tadāvabodhasyāvyabhicāritvaṃ nāvagantuṃ pāryate - nāduṣṭakāraṇajanyatvena nāpi pravṛttisāmarthyena nāpi bādhārahitatvena nānyathā vā. sarvaṃ pūrvoditam anusmṛtya vaktavyam.*

5.12 *nāpīndriyārthasamprayogajatvaṃ vijñānasyāvabodhasya cārvāgbhāgavidāvagamyate tadatīndriyatvena tadāyattatānadhigateḥ. nāpīndriyajanyatvam avagantuṃ pāryata indriyāṇām atīndriyatvād eva.*

[Chapter V
Examination of *Mīmāṃsāsūtra* 1.1.4]

In the same manner the [statement] "Perception is the arising of cognition when the senses of a person are in contact with an existent [thing]"[337] is refuted as well.
Why [is it refuted]?
This *sūtra* [is] sometimes [explained] as having the purpose of a definition [of perception], sometimes as having the purpose of communicating the number of the causal factors [of perception], and sometimes as having the purpose of a repetition [of the definition of perception].[338]

In respect to these [alternatives], if [the *sūtra*] has the purpose of a definition, then [we reply that] the non-erroneousness of a cognition cannot be known: neither by its being produced by faultless causes, nor by the efficiency of activity, nor by its being free from sublation, nor otherwise. All what has been said above [in respect to these alternatives] should be remembered and pronounced [again].[339]

Moreover, a person who does not have superior faculties does not apprehend that a cognition or apprehension[340] arises from a contact between sense and object; for the dependence [of a cognition] upon that [contact] is not apprehended, because that [contact] is beyond [the reach of] the sense.[341]
One cannot apprehend either that [a cognition] is produced by a sense, precisely because the senses are beyond [the reach of] the senses.

athāvabodhānyathānupapattyā sannikarṣaparikalpanā kriyate.

avabodhasyānyathānupapattir na bhavati. kānumā?

5.2 *atha kārakasaṅkhyārthaṃ, kiṃ tena parisaṅkhyānena*[1] *prayojanam? ālokādīnām api kārakatvāt tāny api parisaṅkhyeyāni bhavanti.*

5.3 *athānuvādaparatā, prasiddhasyānuvādo nāprasiddhasya. na cādhyakṣaṃ kvacid viditam.*

nanu loke viditam.

na vidi[S59]*tam iti brūmo 'vyabhicāritayānavagateḥ. nāpi satsamprayogajatvaṃ viditam. tataś ca pratyakṣānadhigatiḥ. tadanavagatau cānuvādānupapattiḥ.*

5.3a *ito 'py anuvādānupapattiḥ - prayojanābhāvāt. na hi prayojanaṃ vinānuvādaḥ pravartata, 'nūdya kvacit kiñcid vidhīyate pratiṣidhyate vā.*

nanv atrāpi dharmaṃ prati nimittatvaṃ pratiṣidhyate. tad uktaṃ - dharmaṃ praty animittaṃ pratyakṣaṃ vidyamānopalambhanatvāt samprayogajatvāc ca.

tatra kim anyapadārthāvabhāsotpannaṃ pratyakṣaṃ dharmaṃ prati nimittatvena pratiṣidhyate kiṃ vā dharmāvabhāsotpannam anutpannaṃ vā?

---

1 S & M acc. to S: *parisaṃkhyātena*

[Objection:] Contact is assumed because otherwise the apprehension would be impossible.[342]

[Reply: We claim that] it is not [true that] an apprehension is not possible otherwise. What is the proof [for it]?

If [the *sūtra*] has the purpose of [communicating] the number of the causal factors, [then] what is the purpose of this enumeration? Since light etc., too, are causal factors, they should also be enumerated.

If [the *sūtra*] has the purpose of a repetition, [then] this is not correct because one repeats what is well known, not what is unknown. But perception is not known (i.e., mentioned) anywhere [else in the *Mīmāṃsāsūtra*].

[Objection:] It is known among the people.[343]

[Reply:] We say that it is not known, because it is not apprehended as nonerroneous.[344] Nor is it known that [perception] is produced by a contact with an existent [thing], and therefore, perception is not apprehended. And when it is not apprehended, [its] repetition is impossible.

For the following [reason], too, a repetition is impossible: because there is no motive [for it]. For one does not undertake a repetition without a motive: by repeating one affirms or negates something in respect to something.

[Objection:] Here [in this *sūtra*], too, it is negated that [perception] is a means for [the apprehension of] *dharma*. This has been stated [by us]: "Perception is not a means for [the aprehension of] *dharma*, because it apprehends an existing [object] and because it arises from a contact [between sense and object]."[345]

[Reply: Do you mean] in this [sentence that] a perception which arises containing the appearance of an object other [than *dharma*] is negated as a means for [the apprehension of] *dharma*, or [do you mean that a perception] which arises containing the appearance of *dharma* [is negated as the means for its apprehension], or [a perception] which does not arise?[346]

tad yady anyapadārthāvabhāsotpannapratyakṣavyāvṛttiḥ kriyate, tadāvipratipattyā sambodhayitavyā jaḍamatayaḥ.

atha dharmāva[1]bodhakotpannapratyakṣavyāvṛttiḥ kriyate, tadā virodhena pratyavastheyo bhavati. dharmāvabodhakotpannaṃ pratyakṣaṃ na ca dharmanimittam iti vyāhatam apadiśyate. anyathā codanāvacanajanitavijñānasyāpi dharmāvabodhakatvenotpannasyātannimittatvaṃ syāt.

athānutpannasya dharmāvabodhakatvaṃ nāsti, kenātra pratipadyate yan notpannaṃ tad dharmāvabodhakam ? nāpi kamaladalāvabodhakaṃ svayam asattvāt.

yad apy uktaṃ - satsamprayogajatvād iti, tad apy ayuktam. satsamprayogajatvaṃ yathā na bhavati tathā prāg evoktam.

5.3b yad apy anyad uktaṃ - vidyamānopalambhanatvāt kila pratyakṣaṃ vijñānaṃ vidyamānam avabodhayati. yady evaṃ na kevalaṃ pratyakṣam, api tu sarvapramāṇotpāditaṃ vijñānaṃ vidyamānāvabodhakam.

atha codanājanitaṃ vijñānam avidyamānakartavyārthāvabodhakam.

---

1 M acc. to S: dharmyavaº

In respect to these [alternatives], if a perception which arises containing the appearance of an object other [than *dharma*] is excluded [from the means for apprehension of *dharma*], then [you] blockheads should be informed that [we] do not disagree.

If perception which arises as making known *dharma* is excluded [from the means for apprehension of *dharma*], then [you] should be confronted with a contradiction: [on the one hand] perception arises as making known *dharma*, and [on the other hand] it is not a means for [the apprehension of] *dharma*; thus, something contradictory is indicated [by this proposition]. Otherwise, (i.e., if you don't consider this as a contradiction) a cognition arisen from a Vedic injunction which has arisen as making known *dharma* would also not be a means for [the apprehension of] *dharma*.

If [a perception] which does not arise does not make known *dharma*, [then the proposition is superfluous, for] who claims here (i.e., among sensible people) that [a perception] which does not arise makes known *dharma*? It does not make known a lotus leaf either, since it does not exist itself.[347]

It has also been said: "because it arises from a contact with an existent [thing]." This, too, is not correct. It has been explained already above[348] that there is no (i.e., that it cannot be known that there is) arising from a contact with an existent [thing].

Something else has also been said: "Perceptual cognition makes known an existing [thing] because, as is well known, it apprehends an existing [thing]."[349] If so, [then] not only perception, but cognitions which are produced by all means of valid cognition make known an existing [thing].

[Objection:] A cognition which arises from Vedic injunction makes known a thing which does not exist [as it] has [still] to be done.

yady avidyamānaṃ, katham avabodhyate? athāvabodhyate, [S60] katham avidyamānatā? avabodhyamānatvenaiva vidyamānatā pratyakṣapramāṇāvabodhitārthavad iti nāpy avabodhanam avabodhyam antareṇopajāyate pratyakṣāvabodhanavat.

api ca codanāvacanajanitavijñānasya mithyātvam upapadyate 'vidyamānaviṣayatvāt keśoṇḍukajñānavat. keśoṇḍukavijñānasyāpi pratīyamānopakārakārthābhāve mithyātvam. tad ihāpi pratīyamānopakārakārtho nāsty[1] *eva, kathaṃ na mithyātvam? tadanvaye vā kartavyārthaviṣayatvaṃ pratihīyeta codanāvacasaḥ.*

kiṃ ca codanājanitaṃ vijñānaṃ kartavyatārthaviṣayaṃ vā tadabhāvaviṣayaṃ nirviṣayaṃ vā.

tad yadi kartavyatārthaviṣayaṃ, tadā tasya vartamānataiva pratītyutkalitatvād vidyamānatoyādivat. [2]*toyāder apratīyamānatvaṃ svasattādhūmād agnau sati janakatvādinā nimittena*[2]. *etac ced vidyate, katham avidyamānatā?*

atha tadabhāvaviṣayaṃ, tasyāpi svena rūpeṇa vidyamānatvān na kartavyatā.

atha nirviṣayaṃ, na tarhi codanā kartavyā-

---

1 M acc. to S: 'sty

2 does not seem to make sense

[Reply:] If it does not exist, how is it made known? If it is made known, how [is it possible that] it does not exist? [One knows that] something exists only by its being made known, just like a thing which is made known by perception which is a means of valid cognition. Nor does an apprehension arise without an apprehended [thing], just like a perceptual apprehension.

Moreover, the cognition which arises from Vedic injunction is established as false, because it has for its object an inexistent [thing], just like the cognition of the hair-net. The cognition of the hair-net too is [only] false, when the apprehended co-producing object does not exist. Thus here, too, the apprehended co-producing thing certainly does not exist; how could [the cognition arising from Vedic injunction] not be false? Or if there is a [causal] connection between [the cognition and its object], the Vedic injunction would not have a thing which has to be done for its object.[350]

Besides, the cognition which arises from Vedic injunction either has the object of duty[351] for its object, or the absence of that [object of duty], or it is without an object.

In respect to these [alternatives], if it has the object of duty for its object, then this [object] must exist because it appears in a cognition, just like existing water etc. ... When this is the case, how [is it possible that the object of duty] does not exist?

If [the cognition from Vedic injunction] has the absence of that [object of duty] for its object, [then] this [object, namely, the absence of the object of duty] is not something [still] to be done, because it, too, exists in its own form.[352]

If [the cognition from Vedic injunction] is without an object, then [you] should not say that the Vedic injunction makes known [an object] which has to be done, but that it *vabodhikā, api tu nirviṣayety evaṃ vaktavyam. evaṃ sthite yathā pratyakṣaṃ vidyamānopalambhakaṃ tathānyāny api pramāṇāni.*

5.a *buddhijanma pratyakṣaṃ, na ca buddhyavagame pramāṇam asti. pratyakṣāvaseyā sā na bhavati svayam anabhyupagamāt. anumānagamyāpi na bhavati tayā pratibaddhaliṅgānavagateḥ. athārthāpattyā pratīyate, kiṃ ghaṭārthānyathānupapattyāho tadupādānaparityāgānyathānupapattyā ghaṭāvabodhānyathānupapattyā vā?*

tad yadi ghaṭārthānyathānupapattyā, tad ayuktam. na buddhikāryo ghaṭo, 'pi tu buddhir iha tatkāryā.

atha ghaṭopādānaparityāgānyathānupapattyā buddhiparikalpanā kriyate, tad ayu[S61]*ktam, buddhisvarūpasyānekakālāntarāvasthānāyogād arthāpatter nirviṣayatvam. kenāpi balavatā prerito buddhim antareṇa vā tadupaplavād vā ghaṭopādānaparityāgāya ghaṭate tena sandigdhārthāpattiḥ. na ca sambandhagrahaṇam antareṇa niyatāyāṃ buddhau pratipattir upapadyate. arthāpattitas tu tadanu-*

is without an object. When this is the case, just as perception apprehends an existing [thing], in the same manner [all] the other means of valid cognition, too [apprehend an existing thing].

[You say that] perception is the arising of cognition,[353] but there is no means of valid cognition for the apprehension of cognition. It (i.e., cognition) cannot be ascertained by perception, since [you] do not admit it yourself.[354] Nor can it be apprehended by inference,[355] because there is no apprehension of an [inferential] sign which is connected with it (i.e., with the cognition). If [the cognition] is apprehended by implication,[356] is it because the object, [for instance] a pot, would be impossible otherwise, or because obtaining and getting rid of/avoiding that [object] would be impossible otherwise, or because the apprehension of the pot would be impossible otherwise?

In respect to these [alternatives], if [you claim that the cognition must exist] because otherwise the object pot would be impossible, [then] this is not correct. The pot is not the effect of the cognition, on the contrary, the cognition is its effect here [in this world].

If [you] assume a cognition because otherwise obtaining and getting rid of/avoiding the pot would be impossible,[357] [then] this is not correct: the implication is without an object, because the cognition itself cannot subsist for several intervals of time. [A person] who is impelled by someone who prevails [over him] strives to obtain the pot [even] without a [prior] cognition [of that pot], or [he may strive] to get rid of [the pot], because it (i.e., the pot) has been destroyed; therefore the implication is doubtful. And the apprehension of a determined cognition is impossible without the apprehension of the relation [between cognition and object]. But when this papattāv indriyakalpanāpi durghaṭā.

athāvabodhānyathānupapattyā buddhiparikalpanā kriyate, tasyāpi buddhyā saha sambandho nāsti, katham avabodhayati? avabodhe cāvagate pratyakṣāvagataiva buddhir nāvabodhagamyā. avabodhabuddhivijñānaśabdānāṃ paryāyatvād avabudhyate jñāyata ity eko 'rthaḥ.

[apprehension of the cognition] is not established by implication, the assumption of the senses, too, is impossible.[358]

If [you] assume a cognition because otherwise the apprehension [of an object] would be impossible,[359] [then this is not correct, since] for this [apprehension] as well there is no relation to a cognition. How could [implication] make known [the cognition]? And when an apprehension is apprehended, [it means that] a cognition is apprehended by perception, not [that] it is apprehended by an apprehension. Since the words 'apprehension' (*avabodha*), 'cognition' (*buddhi*), and 'cognition' (*vijñāna*) are synonyms, 'is apprehended' and 'is cognized' have the same meaning.

6. *tathā śrotrādivṛttir avikalpikā, etad api pratyuktam.*

6.1 *śrotrādikaraṇānāṃ*[1] *śabdādiviṣayākāratayā vipariṇāmo vṛttiśabdenābhidhīyate. sā cānekaprakārā bhavati - samyagjñānarūpā viparyayajñānasandeharūpā ca. tad uktaṃ - tamo moho mahāmohas tāmisro 'ndhatāmisra ityādi.*

6.11 *tad yadi śrotrādivṛtteḥ pratyakṣatvaṃ, tadā viparyayādivṛtter api pratyakṣatvaṃ prāpnoti. athābādhitapadopādānaṃ kriyate.*

tat sūtre na śrūyate. bhavatu vā tasya kalpanā, tathāpy avyabhicāritvaṃ jñātuṃ na śakyate. tac ca naiyāyikapratyakṣalakṣaṇādhikāre prapañcitam. yadi cāvyabhicāripadena viparyayarūpā vṛttir apodyate, tat tadātmatayā vyavasthitā samyagrūpāpi vṛttir apoditā bhavati. tataś ca saṅgrāhyā

---

1 M acc. to S: °*kāraṇānāṃ*

[Chapter VI

Examination of the Sāṅkhya definition of perception]

In the same manner the [definition of perception as] "the functioning of the ear etc., which is not conceptual"[360] is refuted as well.

What is expressed by the word 'functioning' is the transformation[361] of the instruments (i.e., the senses), [such as] the ear etc., into the form of an object, [such as] sound etc.[362] And this [functioning] is of several sorts: it has the form of valid cognition (i.e., it equals perception) and it has the form of false cognition and doubt[363] (i.e., it is not perception). This has been said [by you]: "Obscurity, delusion, great delusion, darkness and blind-darkness"[364] etc.

Now, if the functioning of the ear etc., is perception, then the functioning [in the form of] error etc., would be perception as well.

[Objection:] The word 'not sublated' is employed [in order to exclude false cognition etc., from the realm of the definition].

[Reply:] This [word] is not mentioned (lit. heard) in the *sūtra*.[365] Or let it be assumed [as contained in the *sūtra*]: nevertheless the nonerroneousness [of a cognition] cannot be known. This has been explained in detail in the chapter on the Naiyāyikas' definition of perception.[366] And if the functioning which takes the form of error is excluded by the word 'nonerroneous,' then a functioning which takes the form of valid [cognition], too, is excluded [from the realm of the definition], in as much as it is established as identical with the [functioning which has the form of er-

na labhyate vṛttiḥ.

atha samyagrūpā vṛttir iha saṅgrāhyā, tadāpohyā na labhyate vṛttīnāṃ svarūpaikatābhyupagamāt. bhedābhyupagame[1] *vā*[2]*bhyupetahānam. na hi bhavatāṃ pakṣa indriyād bhidyante vṛttayas,* [S62] *tac ced abhinnaṃ, kathaṃ vṛttīnāṃ bhedaḥ? bhedābhyupagama indriyaikatvaṃ hīyate. indriyāvyatirekitvaṃ vā*[3] *na vaktavyam.*

6.1a *indriyāvyatirekitve 'bhyupagamyamāne nīlalohitaghaṭādīnāṃ sarvadopalambhaḥ syād, indriyāvasthāne tadavyatiriktāyā vṛtter avasthānasambhavāt. tatsambhave ca ghaṭādyanupalambhānupapattiḥ. atha vṛttisadbhāve 'py anupalabdhir, na kadācid upalabdhiḥ syāt. na hi bhavatāṃ pakṣe kiñcid apūrvaṃ jāyate pūrvaṃ vā nirudhyate. tataś ca sarvasyāstitva upalabdhyanupalabdhī kiṅkṛte? sadopalabdhir anupalabdhir*[4] *vā. na hy evaṃvādino dvitīyā gatir asti.*

6.1b *kiṃ ca śabdādaya upalabhyante kim anupalabhyasvabhāvā upalabhyanta āhosvid upalabhyasvabhāvāḥ*[5]*?*

---

1 S & M acc. to S: *bhedānabhyupagame*; perhaps: *bhedenābhyupagame*

2 S & M acc. to S: *cā°*

3 S & M acc. to S om. *vā*

4 M acc. to S: *anulabdhir*

5 M acc. to S: *°svabhāvā*

ror]. And thus, a functioning which can be included [in the realm of the definition] cannot be found.

If [on the other hand] the functioning which takes the form of valid [cognition] can be included here [in the realm of the definition], then [a functioning] which could be excluded [from it] cannot be found, because [you] admit [yourself] that [all] functioning has the same nature.

Or if [you] admit that [functioning] is differentiated, [then you] abandon your position. For according to you [all] functioning is not different from the sense; if it (i.e., the sense) is not different [from one moment to another], how could the functioning be differentiated? If [you] admit the difference [in functioning], the unity of the sense would be lost. Or [you] should not say that [the functioning] is not different from the sense.[367]

If [you] admit that [the functioning] is not different from the sense, [then objects such as] a blue [object], a red [object], a pot, etc., would always be perceived: given the continuity of the sense, there is also continuity of the functioning which is not different from it.[368] And when there is this [continuity of functioning of the sense], the non-apprehension of the pot etc., would be impossible. If there is no apprehension [of the pot etc.] in spite of the existence of the functioning, [then] there would never be an apprehension [of the pot etc.], for according to your position nothing is produced which [has] not [existed] before, and nothing which [has existed] before is destroyed.[369] And thus, when everything exists, how could apprehension and non-apprehension [both] be effected? [There must be] either apprehension or non-apprehension at all times, for there is no other way for him who holds such a doctrine (i.e., *satkāryavāda*).

Besides, [when you say that objects such as] sound etc., are apprehended, are they apprehended in as much as they have an imperceptible nature or in as much as they have a perceptible nature?

tad yady anupalabhyasvabhāvā upalabhyante, tadopalabdhiḥ katham? [1]yady anupalabhyasvabhāvāḥ, katham upalabhyeran?[1] anyathātmāder apy upalabdhiḥ syāt.

athopalabhyasvabhāvā upalabhyante, 'nupalabdhiḥ katham? kiṃ tenaivākāreṇāhosvid ākārāntareṇa?

yadi tenaivākāreṇānupalabdhir, ātmāder apy anupalabdhir na prāpnoti. upalabdhau vā bījāntaraṃ vacanīyam.

athākārāntareṇa nopalabhyante, tathāpy upalabhyamānānupalabhyamānayor naikatvaṃ śabdātmākārayor iva. na hy upalabhyasvabhāvāc chabdād anupalabhyasvabhāva ātmāvyatirikto dṛṣṭaḥ.

atha tasyaivābhivyaktasyopalabdhiḥ.

tatsvarūpavad abhivyakteḥ sarvadāvasthānāt[2] satatopalabdhiprasaṅgaḥ.

atha tirodhāne saty anupalabdhis, tadā tatsvarūpatādātmyāt satatānupalambhaprasaṅgaḥ. ubhayor vāvasthāne samam upalambhānupalambhau [S63] syātām. tataś cedānīm upalabhe pūrvaṃ nopalabha[3]

---

1 perhaps an interpolation

2 M acc. to S: *sarvadānavasthānāt*

3 S: *upōlabha* (M?)

In respect to these [alternatives], if [objects such as sound etc.] which have an imperceptible nature are apprehended, how is [their] apprehension possible? If they have an imperceptible nature, how could they be apprehended? [They cannot be apprehended, for] otherwise the Self etc., too, would be apprehended.

If [sound etc.] which have a perceptible nature are apprehended, how is [their] non-apprehension possible? Is it because of exactly this form (i.e., because of their perceptible nature) or because of another form?
If [their] non-apprehension is due to exactly this form, [then] non-apprehension of the Self etc., too, would be impossible. Or another reason for apprehension should be stated.
If [sound etc.] are not apprehended because of another form, even so there is no identity between what is being perceived (i.e., sound) and what is not perceived (i.e., that which has the other form), just as [there is no identity] between the forms of sound and the Self. For the Self which has an imperceptible nature is not regarded as identical with a sound which has a perceptible nature.
[Objection:] There is an apprehension only of that [which has a perceptible nature] in as much as it is manifested.[370]
[Reply:] Since the manifestation, just as this [perceptible] nature, subsists at all times, there would be constant apprehension [of the object].
If [you say that there would be no constant apprehension, because] there is no apprehension when [the perceptible manifested object] disappears,[371] then there would never be an apprehension, because [the disappearance and] this [perceptible] nature [of the object] are identical. Or if both [manifestation and disappearance] subsist, there would be apprehension and non-apprehension at the same time. [Since this is impossible, only one of them can take place, and that constantly.] And thus, one could not say: "I perceive

iti vyavahāravirahaḥ syāt. tathā pūrvam upalabha[1] *idānīṃ nopalabha ity etad api na prāpnoti.*
athāvayavopacaye saty upalambhaḥ.
tasya sarvadā bhāvāt sarvadopalambhaprasaṅgaḥ.
atha svalakṣaṇapuṣṭau satyām upalambhaḥ.
tasyāḥ sarvadā sattvāt satatopalambhaprasaṅgaḥ.
atha saṃsthānotkarṣe saty upalambhaḥ.
tasyāpi sarvadā vidyamānatvāt satatopalabdhiḥ syāt.
tasmād yena yena nimittenopalambhaparikalpanā, tasya tasya sarvadā bhāvāt satatopalambhaprasaṅgaḥ. atha deśakālakārakāpabandhād[2] *anupalambhas, tadā tasyāpabandhasya sarvadā bhāvād anupalambhānuparamaḥ syāt.*

6.2 *tathendriyāṇām api karaṇarūpatā nopalabhyate phalavaikalyāt.*
nanv asti vijñānaṃ phalam.
na tasya sarvadā vidyamānatvāt. sarvadā vidyamānayor hetuphalabhāvo nopapadyate, yathā guṇānāṃ parasparam ātmabhedānāṃ vā. na hy ātmātmāntarasya hetur bhavati tatphalaṃ vā, tathehāpy anādyantā sattā na phalaṃ hetur vocyate.

f. *kiṃ ca bhūjalādy anekaṃ kāryaṃ, tat kiṃ guṇatrayād vyatiriktam avyatiriktaṃ vā?*
tad yadi vyatiriktaṃ, tat kiṃ tāttvikam atāttvikaṃ vā?

---

1 S: *upālabha* (M?)

2 perhaps: *deśakālākārakārakāpabandhād*

now, I did not perceive before." Nor could [one say]: "I perceived before, I do not perceive now."[372]

[Objection:] There is apprehension when a part is increasing.[373]

[Reply:] Since this [increase] exists always, there would always be apprehension.

[Objection:] There is apprehension when the particular characteristic is fully developed.[374]

[Reply:] Since this [full development] exists always, there would be constant apprehension.

[Objection:] There is apprehension when there is a [special] excellence in the configuration.[375]

[Reply:] Since this [excellence], too, exists always, there would be constant apprehension.[376]

Therefore, since the cause of apprehension, whatever you assume it to be, exists at all times, there would be constant apprehension. If [on the other hand] non-apprehension is due to being tied down by the causal factors place and time,[377] [then] non-apprehension could not be stopped, because this being tied down [too] exists always.

In the same manner, it cannot be apprehended that the senses have the nature of instruments [for the production of cognition], because [their] effect is missing.[378]

[Objection:] There is an effect, [namely] the cognition.

[Reply:] No! For this [cognition] exists always. The relation between cause and effect is impossible between two things which always exist. For instance, [there is no such relation] among the [three] *guṇas* or the different Selves. For a Self is neither the cause nor the effect of another Self. In the same manner here, too, (i.e., in the case of senses and cognitions) a thing which has neither beginning nor end is said to be neither effect nor cause.

Besides, there are many effects, earth, water, etc.; are they different from the three *guṇas* or not?

If they are different, then are they real or not?

tad yadi tāttvikaṃ, na tarhi guṇatrayopādānapūrvakaṃ, tato bhinnatvād ātmasvarūpavat. na ca guṇatrayeṇa sahānyatamo 'pi sambandha upapadyate tadbhinnakāryasya. na mātrāmātrikasambandho nāpi sahacarasahacaritabhāvo[1] *nāpi nimittanaimittika*[2]*bhāva upakāryopakārakabhāvo vā.*

athātāttvikaṃ, kathaṃ tena guṇatrayaṃ pratīyate guṇatrayeṇa saha sambandhānupapatteḥ? na ca sadasatoḥ sambandha upapadyata ātmakharaviṣāṇayor iva. tadabhāvān nānumānād guṇatrayaprati-[S64]*pattiḥ.*

nāpi pratyakṣeṇa guṇāvadhāraṇaṃ svayam anabhyupagamāt. tad uktaṃ -

> *guṇānāṃ paramaṃ rūpaṃ na dṛṣṭipatham ṛcchati/*
> *yat tu dṛṣṭipathaprāptaṃ tan māyeva sutucchakam//*

tadanavagame ca na bhogyena bhoktur anumānam. tataś ca nātmā na guṇatrayam.

athāvyatiriktaṃ, tat kiṃ tāttvikam atāttvikaṃ vā?

yadi tāttvikaṃ, tadā kāryāṇām aparisaṅkhyeyatve guṇānām apy aparisaṅkhyeyatā. tataś ca trayo guṇā iti na vaktavyam. atha guṇānāṃ tritvaṃ, tadā kāryasyāpi tritvaṃ prāpnoty, ānantyaṃ hīyate. tathā kāryasya pratyakṣatve guṇānām api pratyakṣatvam. kiṃviṣayaṃ pradhānānumānam? guṇa-

---

1 M acc. to S: *°sahacaribhāvo*

2 M acc. to S: *nimittanimittika°*

If they are real, then they are not preceded by a material cause consisting in the three *guṇas*, because [they] are different from the [three *guṇas*], just like the nature of the Self. For not even one of the many relations is possible between the three *guṇas* and an effect which is different from them: neither the relation between portion and total, nor the relation between companion and accompanied, nor the relation between efficient cause and its effect, nor the relation between accessory cause and its effect.[379]

If [the many effects] are not real, how are the three *guṇas* apprehended through them, since a relation with the three *guṇas* is impossible? For a relation between a real and an unreal [thing] is impossible, just as [the relation] between the Self and the horn of a donkey. [And] because this [relation] is absent, there is no apprehension of the three *guṇas* on the basis of inference.
Nor are the [three] *guṇas* determined by perception, since you do not admit it yourself. This has been said [by you]:

> "The highest form of the *guṇas* does not fall into the reach of perception.
> That which falls into the reach of perception is futile as an illusion."[380]

And when these [*guṇas*] are not apprehended, there is no inference of [the Self] as experiencing subject from the experienced [manifestations of the three *guṇas*].[381] And thus, there is neither a Self nor the three *guṇas*.

If [the many effects] are not different [from the three *guṇas*], then are they real or unreal?
If they are real, then - the effects being innumerable - the *guṇas*, too, would be innumerable. And therefore, [you] should not say that the *guṇas* are three. If the *guṇas* are three, then the effects, too, would be triple; [their] infinity is [therefore] lost. In the same manner, when the effect is perceived, the [three] *guṇas*, too, would be perceived. What [would] the inference of the primordial matter have as its object [in that case]? [For] the primordial

matter is [nothing but] the three *guṇas*; and [if] they are apprehended [the primordial matter is also apprehended]. [Thus] the proof [of the primordial matter] by pervasion, capacity, limitation, omniformity, the relation between accessory cause and its effect, etc.,[382] is superfluous. If the primordial matter is not apprehended, [then] the effects which are not different from it are not apprehended either. Because there is no [apprehension of the effects], the proof of the Self is impossible.

If [the many effects] are not real, then the three *guṇas*, too, would not be real. Because they do not exist, there is no means of valid cognition for the proof of consciousness. When this [consciousness] is not proved, there is no other world, because there is no [Self] which transmigrates to the other world.[383]

Thus, perception is not established.

NOTES

[1] This is a pun on *viṣama*: the book is difficult, and the lion terrifying. If the conjecture *sṛjyate* is correct (cf. *TUS* p. 125.15), the pun may be stretched further: the book is composed, and the lion set free.

[2] The folio is broken, and nothing certain can be said about the purport of this sentence. However, Indian philosophers often start their work by assuring the reader of its importance for obtaining liberation, or even all the aims of life. In compliance with the Lokāyata doctrine, Jayarāśi may have done just the opposite. The meaning of the objection would then be: If your book does not bring about any results such as heaven etc., why bother to read it?

[3] An alternative translation may be suggested by taking *artha* as aim or purpose (i.e., as *puruṣārtha*): those who know the supreme or ultimate aim in life. As is well known the Lokāyatikas rejected *dharma* and *mokṣa*, and maintained that *kāma* and *artha* are the only aims in life (cf. for instance *SDS* p. 2.7-8).

[4] Namai, "Bārhaspatya Philosophy," p. 41, considers this quotation as a Lokāyata fragment. Note, however, that Vyomaśiva quotes it twice (*Vy* pp. 526.27-28, 585.9-10), in both cases as a *nyāya* (maxim), and in both cases the context of the discussion has nothing to do with Lokāyata. The *Tarkarahasya* quotes a variant of the second half-verse which is attributed explicitly to a *śāstrakāra*, a title often given to Dignāga, but highly doubtful in this context; cf. *TR* p. 35.10-12: *śāstrakārair api ... vyavasthitaṃ*

vikalpavyavahāreṣu samānau bālapaṇḍitau/

For a discussion of this verse cf. introduction, pp. 43-44.

[5] This is a quotation from the famous *Bṛhaspatisūtra*, the basic text book of Lokāyata. In fact, these three

sūtras probably formed the very beginning of the text, which is unfortunately lost to us. The second and the third *sūtra* are quoted extremely often, the first more rarely. Namai, loc. cit., p. 38, n. 11, already mentions *NM* I p. 168.12 (Kashi p. 59.27), *Bhāskarabhāṣya* 3.3.53 p. 196, *TSP* pp. 633.21-22, 634.14, *Madhyamakālaṅkārapañjikā* 99b 2-3, *TRD* p. 307, 13-15 and Jñānaśrībhadra's *Āryalaṅkāvatāravṛtti* 236b 1-3. To these we may add *NKC* p. 341.19-20, *SVR* pp. 1075.19, 1086.24-25, *Siddhitraya* p. 8.12, and *Lokatattva-nirṇaya* p. 290.2. This is by no means an exhaustive list.

[6] It is not quite clear what Jayarāśi means by 'reflecting' (*pratibimbana*). From the context it would seem to be 'repeating something without taking it as true.' There has been some difference of opinion as to what exactly is reflected in this passage. Ruben ("Über den Tattvopaplava-siṃha," p. 140, n. 5) said while criticizing Sukhlalji that "Diese Stelle hat Sukhlalji S. XII anders aufgefasst: Nicht die Materie wird in der materialistischen Philosophie widergespiegelt, sondern Bṛhaspati 'is merely reflecting in his statement the belief of the people'. Ich meine, der Sinn ist, Bṛhaspatis Lehre spiegelt die Materie wider, ohne sie philosophisch zu analysieren. Dieser Materialismus des Bṛhaspati vertritt also gleichsam die in Indien fehlende Naturwissenschaft, die die Materie widerspiegelt, während die materialistische Philosophie ihre Lehren aus den Naturwissenschaften abstrahiert."

Personally, I find Sukhlal's interpretation much more convincing. Besides, the verb 'vertritt' is surely inappropriate in this context. In any case, Jayarāśi denies that there is a discrepancy between the *TUS* and the *Bṛhaspati-sūtra*. If I understand him correctly, he claims that everything in the *sūtra*, or at least the theory of the four material elements, is brought up as a kind of *pūrvapakṣa* which has to be refuted. This is of course an extremely radical and highly improbable interpretation of Bṛhaspati, and I don't think it should be taken seriously. At most we may consider it as a testimony of the sūtra's 'Rezeption.' Indeed, there is a well known Lokāyata fragment which says that the purpose of the *Bṛhaspatisūtra* is to question the opinion of others, and not to affirm anything positively, for instance *TBV* pp. 69.39, 74.11: *sarvatra* <*para*>*paryanuyogaparāṇy eva sūtrāṇi bṛhaspateḥ*. It is interesting to note that Anantavīrya associates this fragment with Jayarāśi (*tattvopaplavakṛt*), but it is not to be found anywhere in the *TUS*. Cf. SVṬ p. 277.19-23: *atra tattvopaplavakṛd āha - cārvākaiś cāru carcitaṃ svayam evaṃ*(perhaps: *eva*)*lakṣaṇatas tad*(i.e., *pratyakṣa-*)*anupapattis teṣāṃ na doṣāya* (perhaps: *doṣo 'yaṃ*) *pratyakṣopagamas tu vyavahāreṇeti - ... na kenacid vidadhyāt kuryāc cārvākaḥ. na hi pramāṇam antareṇa tad api kartuṃ śakyaṃ yataḥ paraparyanuyogaparāṇi bṛhaspateḥ sūtrāṇiti sūktaṃ syāt*. This does not mean, of course, that Anantavīrya attributes this fragment to Jayarāśi, but the ideological affinity is quite clear. Cf. also introduction p. 6f.

7 There is an interesting distinction between *siddha* and *prasiddha*: *siddha* is something proved, whereas *prasiddha* is something so well known that it does not require a proof anymore. I am indebted for this remark to Professor Srinivasan.

8 Clearly the concept of definition is crucial to the whole book. It may be reminded that every definition can function as an inference in which the *sādhya* and the *hetu* are reversible: if one defines A as B, one should be able to say 'x is A because it is B' and 'x is B because it is A.' Otherwise, the definition is either too narrow (*avyāpti*) or too broad (*ativyāpti*). Further, the definition

forms a *kevalavyatirekihetu*, because it cannot have a *sapakṣa*; cf. *NVTṬ* 1.1.3 p. 84.14: *lakṣaṇaṃ nāma vyatirekihetuvacanam* ... . For a discussion of the variants to Vātsyāyana's definition of definition cf. Biardeau, "La définition dans la pensée indienne," pp. 372-76.

[9] Partly quoted *TBV* p. 73.40-74.1: *tathā hi 'pramāṇanibandhanā prameyavyavasthitir ' iti*.

[10] 'Talk' should be taken here in a broader sense. The word *vyavahāra* usually includes a threefold activity: thinking, speaking, and acting; cf. Steinkellner, *HB* II, p. 156, n. 3. For a fourfold division of *vyavahāra* cf. Schmithausen, *Vibhramaviveka*, p. 268, n. 215. Jayatilleke (*Early Buddhist Theory of Knowledge*, p. 82) takes this sentence to mean something completely different: "On pragmatic grounds (*vyavahāraḥ kriyate*) he [Jayarāśi] says that we should believe in the existence of the body, of physical objects (*ghaṭādau*) and of pleasure (*sukha-*)... ."

[11] This is a quotation of *NS* 1.1.4. Jayarāśi will undertake an examination of each and every term in this definition except for the word 'cognition' (*jñāna*). For an analysis of this term and a comparison with modern Western philosophy cf. Matilal, *The Navya-Nyāya Doctrine of Negation*, ch. 2.

Some of the arguments concerning the word 'nonerroneous have been explained in the introduction and need not to be repeated here. In what follows I simply quote some parallel passages from later literature which refer to Jayarāśi's arguments against the word *avyabhicārin*. Since these are not likely to be of interest to the nonspecialist, and in order to avoid tiresome repetition, I leave them untranslated.

Cf. *NBhū* p. 33.23f.: *api cābhrāntatvasya liṅgaṃ kim aduṣṭakārakotpādyatvam uta bādhānutpādaḥ kiṃ vā pravṛtti-*

sāmarthyam iti na tāvad aduṣṭakārakotpādyatvaṃ, nayanādṛṣṭādikāraṇānām atīndriyatvenāduṣṭatvasyāniścayāt. na hi svayam asiddhaṃ liṅgaṃ liṅginaḥ pratipādakam. na ca tadudbhūtaviśiṣṭajñānād eva kārakāduṣṭatvasiddhir, itaretarāśrayatvadoṣeṇobhayor asiddher iti...

AS p. 38.4f.: *kathaṃ pramāṇasya prāmāṇyam? kim aduṣṭakārakasandohotpādyatvena, bādhārahitatvena, pravṛttisāmarthyenānyathā vā? yady aduṣṭakārakasandohotpādyatvena tadā saiva kārakāṇām aduṣṭatā kuto 'vasīyate? na tāvat pratyakṣān nayanakuśalādeḥ saṃvedanakāraṇasyātīndriyasyāduṣṭatāyāḥ pratyakṣīkartum aśakteḥ. nānumānāt, tadavinābhāviliṅgābhāvāt. vijñānāṃ tatkāryaṃ liṅgam iti cen, na, vijñānasāmānyasya tadavyabhicāritvābhāvāt. pramāṇabhūtaṃ vijñānaṃ talliṅgam iti cet, kutas tasya pramāṇabhūtatāvasāyaḥ? tadaduṣṭakāraṇārabdhatvād iti cet, so 'yam anyonyāśrayaḥ. siddhe vijñānasya pramāṇabhūtatve nirdoṣakāraṇārabdhatvasiddhis tatsiddhau ca pramāṇabhūtatvasiddhir iti. kiṃ ca cakṣurādikāraṇānāṃ guṇadoṣāśrayatve tadupajanitasaṃvedane doṣāśaṅkānivṛttir na syād guṇadoṣāśrayapuruṣavacanajanitavedanavat...*

SVṬ p. 278.7f.: *aduṣṭakāraṇārabdhatvasya jñātum aśakter atīndriyasyendriyasya duṣṭatvasyetarasya vā pratyakṣato 'jñānāj jñāne 'pi pūrvacodyānivṛttiḥ, punas tatrāpy aduṣṭakāraṇārabdhatvakalpane tad eva codyaṃ tad evottaram ity anavasthā. jñānaprāmāṇyāt tadavagame 'nyonyasaṃśrayaḥ...*

PKM p. 63.17f.: *aduṣṭakāraṇārabdhatvam apy ajñātaṃ, jñātaṃ vā taddhetuḥ? prathamapakṣo 'yukto, 'jñātasya sattvasandehāt. nāpi jñātaṃ, karaṇakuśalāder atīndriyasya jñapter asambhavāt. astu vā tajjñaptis, tathāpy asāv aduṣṭakāraṇārabdho jñānāntarāt, saṃvādapratyayād vā? ādyavikalpe 'navasthā. dvitīyavikalpe 'pi saṃvādapratyayasyāpi hy aduṣṭakāraṇārabdhatvaṃ tathāvidhād anyato jñātavyaṃ tasyāpy anyata iti...*

TBV p. 547.5f.: *yad api vyabhicārijñānanivṛttyartham avyabhicāripadam upāttaṃ, tad apy ayuktaṃ, tatpratipādya-*

syārthasya paramatenāsaṅgateḥ. tathā hy aduṣṭakāraṇaprabhavatvaṃ bādhārahitatvaṃ vāvyabhicāritvaṃ pravṛttisāmarthyāvagamavyatirekeṇa na jñātuṃ śakyam iti ...; cf. also pp. 9.2f., 13.7f.

NMuk p. 65.18f.: *kim aduṣṭakārakotpādyatvam atra liṅgam uta bādhānutpādaḥ kiṃ vā pravṛttisāmarthyam iti na tāvad ādyo nayanādikārakāṇām aduṣṭatvaniścayāyogāt. vibhramahetudoṣāṇāṃ ca vicitratopapatter aśeṣadoṣaniṣedhasyāśakyatvāt. aniścitasya cāliṅgatvāt. na ca tajjanitavijñānavaiśiṣṭyād eva kārakāduṣṭatvam avasīyata iti sāmpratam. parasparāśrayāpātāt*...

Cf. also *Tattvārthaślokavārttika* (Nirnayasagar Press), p. 279, which is not available to me.

[12] *āpanīpadyate* is the intensive of *āPAD*.

[13] Jayarāśi uses the same argument while argueing against the validity of the Veda, cf. *TUS* p. 118.20-22: *kiṃ ca bādhāśabdena viparītavijñānam apadiśyate. tac ca notpadyate kiṃ codanājanitavijñānasya yathārthatvenota tadutpādakakāraṇavaikalyeneti sandihyate.* "Furthermore, with the word 'sublation' a cognition of an opposite [object] is designated. But if the [sublation] is not produced, there is a doubt: is it because the cognition which arises from Vedic injunction is true, or is it because of the deficiency of the cause [which may have] produced the [sublation]?"

[14] Cf. also *TUS* p. 118.23-119.2: *api ca bādhārahitatve 'py aprāmāṇyaṃ dṛṣṭaṃ, bādhakavijñānotpatteḥ pūrvam. bādhāpy upajāyamānā kālavikalpenopajāyate - kvacid ardhamāsena kvacin māsavyavadhānena kvacic cābdadvayatrayavyavadhānena, anyatra tu kārakavaikalyān naiva sampatsyate. na caitāvatā pramāṇaṃ codanājanitā buddhiḥ.*

"Besides, it is observed that there are false [cognitions] even when they are free from sublation, [namely] before the sublating cognition arises. As for the sublation, in as much as it arises, it arises with a difference in time: in some cases after half a month, in some cases after a month, and in some cases after two or three years. However, in other cases, due to the deficiency of the cause, it will not arise at all. And the cognition which arises from Vedic injunction is not valid by that much (i.e., by the mere non-arising of sublation)."

Cf. also AS pp. 38.23-39.3: *dṛśyate ca sandehaḥ, kiṃ yathārthagrahaṇān no 'tra bādhānutpattir āhosvit svakāraṇavaikalyād ity ubhayasaṃsparśipratyayotpatteḥ, kvacid dūre marīcikāyāṃ jalajñāne svakāraṇavaikalyād bādhakapratyayānutpattiprasiddher abhyāsadeśe tatkāraṇasākalyād bādhakajñānotpādāt. kiṃ cārthasaṃvedanānantaram eva bādhānutpattis tatprāmāṇyaṃ vyavasthāpayet sarvadā vā? na tāvat prathamavikalpaḥ sambhavati, mithyājñāne 'pi kvacid anantaraṃ bādhānutpattidarśanāt. sarvadā bādhānutpatteḥ saṃvidi prāmāṇyaniścayaś cen, na, tasyāḥ pratyetum aśakyatvāt, saṃvatsarādivikalpenāpi bādhotpattidarśanāt...*

"And one observes that there is a doubt, because a cognition which touches both [alternatives] arises: is it because the apprehension is correct that the sublation does not arise for us in respect to it, or is it because of the deficiency of its cause? For it is well known that the sublating cognition of a cognition of water in respect to a mirage does not arise [when the perceiver stands] at some remote place, because the cause of [the sublating cognition] is deficient. For [when he stands] in a place nearby the sublating cognition arises, because [its] cause is complete. Besides, would the validity of the apprehension of an object be established when the sublation does not arise immediately after it, or [when it] never [arises]? The first alternative is impossible, for one sees that in the case of some false cognitions, too, the sublation does not arise immediately. If the validity of a cognition is determined because the sublation never arises, [we answer:] no, because this cannot be known, for one sees that sublation arises with a difference [in time], afer a year etc., too."

[15] The manuscript is defective at this point, but, fortunately, we can reconstruct the argument from parallel passages; cf. *TUS* p. 119.3-9: *kiṃ ca bādhārahitatvam api kim aśeṣapuruṣāpekṣayā katipayapuruṣāpekṣayā vā? yady aśeṣapuruṣāpekṣayā, tadāvagantuṃ na śakyate paracittavṛttināṃ duranvayatvāt. atha katipayapuruṣāpekṣayā bādhārahitatvaṃ, tadānekāntiko hetur - yathāsatyodake jātodakabuddhis tasmād deśād deśāntaraṃ yadā prayāti tatraiva daśārdhatām upayāti na ca tasya bādhakāṃ vijñānam utpannam. kim etāvatā tat pramāṇaṃ bhavatu?*

"Moreover, the fact of being free from sublation, in its turn, is it with regard to all people, or is it with regard to some people? If it is with regard to all people, then it cannot be known, for the mental activities of [all] other [people] can hardly be followed. If [you mean] the fact of being free from sublation with regard to some people, then the reason [of the inference] is not conclusive. For instance, [a person] for whom a cognition of water arises in respect to unreal water goes from that place to another [place], there meets his death, and the sublating cognition has not arisen for him. Would that [false cognition of water] be valid by that much?"

Cf. also p. 117.12-18: *api ca kim aśeṣajanasmaraṇa-⟨vi⟩nivṛttir iha hetutvena vivakṣitāhosvit katipayapuruṣasmaraṇavinivṛttiḥ? tad yadi sakalajanasmaraṇavinivṛttis, tadāsiddhā, avadhārayitum aśakyatvāc ca (?) arvāgbhāgavidbhiḥ. avadhāraṇe vā ta eva sarvajñāḥ syur arvāgbhāgavido na bhaveyuḥ. atha katipayapuruṣāpekṣayā, tadānekāntiko hetur, vidyamānakartṛkeṣv api kartā na smaryate kaiścit.*

"Besides, is the disappearance of remembrance of all people meant here as a reason [for the inference that the

Veda is authorless], or is it the disappearance of remembrance of some people? In respect to these [alternatives], if it is the disappearance of remembrance of all people, then this is not established, because it cannot be determined by people with limited faculties. Or if it is determined, they (i.e., people of limited faculties) would be omniscient; [thus] there would be no people with limited faculties. If it is with regard to some people [alone], then the reason is not conclusive because even in the case of [books] the author of which is [still] alive some [people] do not remember the author."

Further passages of this argument against the Veda have been assembled by Mahendrakumar Jain in *NKC* p. 728, n. 2. Cf. also *TUS* p. 68.14-24, where the same arguments are applied to non-apprehension of destruction, and § 1.1bab. For more parallel passages cf. those already mentioned in n. 11, notably *AS* p. 39.8f.: *kiṃ ca kasyacid bādhānutpattiḥ, sarvasya vā?* ...; *NBhū* p. 34.1f.: *api ca sarvapuruṣabādhānutpatter asarvavidāvagantum aśakyatvāt* ...; *PKM* p. 63.12f.: *kiṃ ca kvacit kadācit kasyacid bādhāviraho vijñānapramāṇatāhetuḥ, sarvatra sarvadā sarvasya vā?* ...; *NMuk* p. 66.3f.: *kiṃ ca bādhānutpādo liṅgaṃ bhavat sarvapuruṣāvacchinnaṃ, kiṃ vā katipayapratipattṛvartī?* ...

[16] For the example of the diamond-rays cf. *PV pratyakṣa* 57. It may be added here that Umbeka made similar use of Dharmakīrti's example, probably independently of Jayarāśi; cf. *ŚVV* p. 65.7-8: *arthakriyāsaṃvādāc ca pūrvaprāmāṇye maṇiprabhāyām api maṇibuddhiḥ pramāṇaṃ syāt*. Cf. also ibid., p. 195.13-14.

[17] This is a quotation from *ŚBh* 1.1.5 (p. 26.20-21); cf. above pp. 49-50 and n. 33.

[18] The efficiency of the activity as a criterion of truth appears for the first time in the *Nyāyabhāṣya* (introduction pp. 1, 21): *pramāṇato 'rthapratipattau pravṛttisāmarthyād arthavat pramāṇam. pramāṇam antareṇa nārthapratipattir, nārthapratipattim antareṇa pravṛttisāmarthyam. pramāṇena khalv ayaṃ jñātārtham upalabhya tam artham abhīpsati jihāsati vā. tasyepsājihāsāprayuktasya samīhā pravṛttir ity ucyate. sāmarthyaṃ punar asyāḥ phalenābhisambandhaḥ.*

"A means of valid cognition is fruitful, because the activity is efficient when the object is apprehended by means of a valid cognition. There is no apprehension of the object without a means of valid cognition, [and] there is no efficiency of the activity without the apprehension of the object. When the cognizer apprehends the object by a means of valid cognition, he wants to obtain or avoid that object. The endeavour of this [person] who is lead by the wish to obtain or avoid that [object] is called 'activity.' Efficiency, on the other hand, is the connection between that [activity] and the result (lit. fruit)."

For a more detailed discussion of this criterion cf. Franco, "Studies in *TUS* I," pp. 157ff., the main points of which are repeated in the following notes.

It should be added here that Jayarāśi's explanation of 'fruit' is based on *NS* 4.1.53: *tatsambandhāt phalaniṣpattes teṣu phalavad upacāraḥ.* "Because the [real] fruit [namely, pleasure (*prīti*)] arises from a connection with them (i.e., a son, cattle, a woman, property, gold, etc., mentioned in the previous *sūtra*; note the sequence!) one talks about them metaphorically as [if they were] the fruit." Having found this parallel I realized that I was wrong to criticize Ruben regarding the interpretation of *phala*.

The gist of Jayarāśi's arguments can be explained as follows. In order to confirm a cognition, the efficiency of the activity in itself is not enough. One has to know that the activity is efficient, and to know means to apprehend through a veridical cognition, i.e., a cognition which has to be confirmed, in its turn, by an efficiency of activity, which has to be apprehended, and so on ad infinitum.

Jayarāśi's argument raises the same objection one uses to criticize pragmatism. To repeat James' example once more (cf. James, *The Meaning of Truth*, ch. 2, "The Tigers of India"), if one believes that there are tigers in India, one is prepared to find tigers there. And if one goes to India and does not find any tigers there, one is surprised or dissatisfied. The trouble with such a criterion of truth, as Chisholm for instance points out (cf. Chisholm, *A Theory of Knowledge*, p. 97), is that it is not true that a cognition will give satisfaction if and only if it is true. One may go to Syria, find some tigers, and think one is in India, or one may go to India, find tigers, and mistake them for cats. The cognition which is supposed to confirm another cognition has to be confirmed in its turn.

Vidyānanda repeats Jayarāśi's arguments as follows (AS p. 39.13f.): *nāpi pravṛttisāmarthyena, anavasthāprasakteḥ. pravṛttisāmarthyaṃ hi phalenābhisambandhaḥ sajātīyavijñānotpattir vā. yadi phalenābhisambandhaḥ, so 'vagato 'navagato vā saṃvidaḥ prāmāṇyaṃ gamayet. na tāvad anavagato, 'tiprasaṅgāt. so 'vagataś cet tata eva pramāṇād anyato vā. na tāvat tata eva parasparāśrayānuṣaṅgāt. sati phalenābhisambandhasyāvagame tasya pramāṇatvaniścayāt tasmiṃś ca sati tena tadavagamāt. anyataḥ pramāṇāt so 'vagata iti cet tad anyat pramāṇaṃ kutaḥ prāmāṇyavyavasthām āstighnute? pravṛttisāmarthyād iti cet tad api pravṛttisāmarthyaṃ yadi phalenābhisambandhas tadāvagato 'navagato vā saṃvidaḥ prāmāṇyaṃ gamayed ityādi punar āvartata iti cakrakaprasaṅgaḥ* ...

"Nor [is nonerroneousness known] by the efficiency of activity, because it results in infinite regress. For the efficiency of activity is either the connection with a fruit, or the production of a cognition of the same kind. If it is the connection with a fruit, [then] it makes known the validity of a cognition in as much as it is [itself] apprehended, or in as much as it is not apprehended. It does not [make it known] in as much as it is not apprehended [itself], because this is absurd. If it is apprehended, [it is apprehended] by that [cognition] itself as a means of valid cognition, or by another [means of valid cognition]. It is not [apprehended] by the [cognition] itself, because a mutual dependence would follow. For the validity of the [cognition] is determined when there is an apprehension of the connection with a fruit, and when the [validity is determined] the [connection with a fruit] is apprehended by it.

[Objection:] The [connection with a fruit] is apprehended by another means of valid cognition.

[Reply:] Where from does this other means of valid cognition obtain [its] validity? If [you say that it obtains it] from the efficiency of activity, [then] if this efficiency of activity too consists in a connection with a fruit, then [the alternatives] 'It makes known the validity of the cognition either in as much as it is apprehended, or in as much as it is not apprehended' etc., would recur again ;thus, there would be an [infinite] going around in a circle."

Cf. also *NBhū* p. 34.4f.: *nāpi pravṛttisāmarthyam. pravṛttisāmarthyaṃ hy arthaprāptyanarthaparihāralakṣaṇam. tac ced anavagataṃ, katham asiddhaṃ gamakaṃ bhavet? athāvagataṃ, tadavagater avyabhicāritvaṃ katham avagamyata ity aparihāryā pūrvoktavikalpaparamparā syād iti ...*

"Nor [is nonerroneousness known] by the efficiency of activity. For the efficiency of activity is defined as obtaining a desired object and avoiding an undesired one. If this [efficiency] is not apprehended, how could something which is [itself] unproved make known [anything]? If it is known, how is the nonerroneousness of its cognition apprehended? Thus, an [infinite] succession of the alternatives put forth above is unavoidable." Cf. also *NMuk* p. 66.6f.

[19] The opponent raises the concept of *arthaprāpti*, the obtaining of the object. I do not see any essential difference between the efficiency of activity and the obtaining of the object. The second is perhaps more precise, and has a narrower focus. The efficiency of activity was defined as obtaining a desirable object or avoiding an undesirable one, whereas the obtaining of the object can be interpreted as applying to the first possibility alone. One could easily argue that by perceiving water and avoiding it the cognition of water is not established to be veridical, because one can be successful in avoiding water whether water is there or not.

There are four possible relations between a cognition and the obtainment of its object:

(1) true cognition - object obtained

(2) false cognition - object unobtained

(3) true cognition - object unobtained

(4) false cognition - object obtained

Jayarāśi's opponent argues that only relations (1) and (2) are found in reality. This is clearly implied by the *Nyāyabhāṣya*, and the *Vārttika* states it explicitly (*NV*, introduction p. 8, 3-4): *so 'yaṃ pramātā yadā pramāṇenāvadhārya pravartate tadāsya pravṛttiḥ samarthā bhavati, yadā punaḥ pramāṇābhāsenārtham avadhārya pravartate tadāsamarthā* ... . "When the cognizer acts after determining [the object] with a means of valid cognition, his activity is efficient. On the other hand, when he acts after determining the object with a pseudo means of valid cognition, [his activity] is not efficient."

Against that Jayarāśi argues that relations (3) and (4) are equally possible, but first he diversifies the obtainment of the object into three *vikalpas*. The first possibility (*tatpratibhātodakaprāpti*) is, of course, the most desirable for the Nyāya, but it could not be applied to the example of water, because a change in the arrangement of the parts of a substance, i.e., a disjunction, brings about the destruction of the substance (*avayavavibhāga = vināśahetu*). Therefore, the Nyāya needed some guiding principle in order to bridge the gap between the object of cognition and the obtained object. Thus, although one might not obtain exactly the same water, if one obtains water that is similar, it is good enough. For the Naiyāyika, the universal is responsible for the similarity among the individuals; due to the universal 'water' we recognize that different individuals are all water. Therefore, one can define the obtaining of the object not as obtaining the same object, but as obtaining an object which belongs to the same universal. This definition, however, is too wide and tco narrow, as is clearly shown by Jayarāśi's arguments.

Another way to bridge the gap between the cognition's object and the obtained object is to say that the water, i.e., the *avayavin*, may be destroyed, but that the parts (*avayava*) of that water produce in their new arrangement a new water. This second water-substance belongs to the same series of production as the first. Thus, if we obtain an object produced in the same series as the object which appeared in the cognition, the cognition is true. This principle, argues Jayarāśi, is untenable, because it contradicts another Nyāya principle, namely, that final wholes (*antyāvayavin*) do not produce any further wholes.

The argument is quite convincing when we deal with solid objects which have a definite form like a cloth and a pot, but it looks rather strange in our context, where the example under discussion is water. I do not know whether the Naiyāyikas accepted the possibility of water being *antyāvayavin*, nor what it could possibly mean. (Perhaps all water in the world?) According to D.N. Shastri there was no definite criterion as to which objects should be regarded as final wholes (cf. Shastri, *The Philosophy of Nyāya-Vaiśeṣika*, pp. 240-41).

Bhāsarvajña mentions this *antyāvayavin* argument at the end of his summary of Jayarāśi's arguments concerning the criterion of truth (*NBhū* p. 34.11-13; cf. n. 19), but although he accepts the principle of production in the same series (p. 37.21-23), he does not answer Jayarāśi's objection, at least not directly. He brings forth a *vyavahāra* argument, i.e., that people recognize the object produced in the same series, which he defines as the immediate production of a similar object (*tatsadṛśanirantarotpāda*), as exactly the same object which appears in the cognition (*tad evedam iti*). But he does not say if and how it should be reconciled with the principle that *antyāvayavins* do not produce a further *avayavin*. Whatever the case may be, even if the concept of *antyāvayavin* cannot be applied to water, it does not change much in Jayarāśi's argumentation, because he also refutes the plurality (*nānātva*) of water individuals.

Abhayadeva repeats Jayarāśi's arguments as follows (*TBV* p. 547.8-18): *tac ca viṣayaprāptyā vijñānasyāvyabhicāritvaṃ jñāyamānaṃ kiṃ pratibhātaviṣayaprāptyāvagamyata āhosvid apratibhātaviṣayaprāptyā? yadi pratibhātaviṣayaprāptyā tadodakajñāne kim udakāvayavī pratibhātaḥ prāpyata uta tatsāmānyam āhosvid ubhayam iti pakṣāḥ. tatra yady avayavī pratibhātaḥ prāpyata iti pakṣaḥ sa na yukto 'vayavino 'sattvena pratibhāsaṃ prati viṣayatvāsambhavāt. sattve 'pi na tasya parābhyupagamena pratibhātasya prāptir jhaṣādivivartanābhighātopajātāvayavakriyādikrameṇa dhvaṃsasambhavāt. athāvasthitavyūhair avayavair ārabhyasya tasya tajjātīyatayā pratibhātasyaiva prāptir, nanv evam apy anyaḥ pratibhāto 'nyaś ca prāpyata iti kathaṃ tadavabhāsino jñānasyāvyabhicāritā, na hy anyapratibhāsane 'nyatra prāptāv avyabhicāritā. anyathā marīcikājalapratibhāse daivāt satyajalaprāptau* [*tadavabhāsinas*] (interpolation?) *tasyāvyabhicāritā bhavet. na ca taddeśajalaprāpakasyāvyabhicāriteti nāyaṃ doṣo yato deśasyāpi bhāskarakarānupraveśādināvayavakriyā<di>krameṇa nāśāt tattvānupapattiḥ. na caivamavyabhicāravādinaś candrārkādijñānaṃ vinaśyadavasthapadārthotpāditatvā (ditaṃ vā) tad avyabhicāri bhavet.*

"And this nonerroneousness of a cognition which is known by obtaining the object, is it apprehended by obtaining the object which appeared [in the cognition], or by obtaining an object which did not appear [in it]? If it is by obtaining an object which appeared [in the cognition], then is water as the whole (*avayavin*) which appeared in the cognition of water that which is obtained, or is it [water which is] similar to it, or both? These are the alternatives.

In respect to these [alternatives], if the [first] alternative, [namely] 'The whole which appeared is obtained' [is opted for], [then] this is not correct, for in as much as the whole does not exist, it cannot be the object of cognition. Even if it existed, one does not obtain that [whole] which appeared according to the opponent's doctrine, because it can be destroyed by the succession of movement [,disjunction] etc., in its parts produced by the turning around and hits by fish etc.

[Objection:] One obtains indeed that [water] which appeared [in the cognition, namely] as belonging to the [same] kind [as that] of the [destroyed water-whole] in as much as it is brought about by parts which have a fixed structure.

[Reply:] Even so, one thing appeared, and another is obtained. Thus, how could the cognition in which this [water] appears be nonerroneous? For when one thing appears [and] another is obtained the [cognition] is not nonerroneous. Otherwise, when there is a cognition of water in respect to a mirage [and] by chance real water is obtained, the [cognition] in which this [illusory water] appears would not be erroneous. And it is not so that this is no fault as nonerroneousness is [determined] for [a cognition] which makes [the cognizer] obtain water in exactly that place, because this cannot be true, as the place, too, can be destroyed by the succession of movement [disjunction] etc., in its parts by intrusion of fire etc. And [on top of that], for one who holds such a theory of nonerroneousness, the cognition of the moon, sun, etc., or that which is produced by an object in the state of vanishing, would not be nonerroneous."

The compound *tajjātīyodakaprāptyā* in the *TUS* has to be understood as 'obtaining water which belongs to the universal water' and not as 'obtaining water of the same kind,' as Abhayadeva (*TBV* p. 547, quoted above) seems to take it. Cf. p. 80, 18-22: *yadi codakajātīyārthaprāptyāvyabhicāritā pūrvoditodakavijñānasya vyavasthāpyate, tadodakajāter gavādāv api sambhavo 'sti, gavādiprāptyāvyabhicāritodakavijñānasya syāt*. Cf. also p. 170, 6-7: *tajjātīyodakaprāpakatvenāvisaṃvāditvam ucyate, tad ayuktam udakatvajāter abhāvāt*.

[20] Jayarāśi seems to refer to *VS* 5.2.1: *nodanād abhighātāt saṃyuktasaṃyogāc ca pṛthivyāṃ karma*. "In earth, movement [arises] from a push, a blow and conjunction with something connected [to something else pushed or beaten]." Therefore, *parivartana* may be understood as a special kind of *nodana*. One of the differences between *abhighāta* and *nodana* is that the first creates noise, whereas the second is silent (cf. *Upaskāra* p. 309, 5-6 on 5.2.1). Thus, we have here a *yathāsaṅkhya* correspondence, i.e., the fish turn the water silently, whereas the buffalo splash it.

[21] Cf. *NBhū* p. 34.7-11: *api ca candrādipratibhāsasyābhrāntatvaṃ na sidhyec, candrādyarthasya prāptyasambhavāt. na codakārthasyāpi pratibhātasya prāptiḥ sambhavati, tasya vāyvādibhiḥ prāṇiviśeṣaiś cāvayavakriyotpādanadvāreṇa pra-*

tikṣaṇaṃ vinaśyamānatvāt. tajjātiyārthaprāptes tv anekāntikatvān na gamakatvam.

"Besides, the validity of a cognition of the moon etc., would not be established, because an object such as the moon cannot be obtained. And even an object [such as] water which appeared [in the cognition] cannot be obtained, because it is being destroyed at every moment, as the wind etc., and certain living beings (i.e., fish) cause a movement in its parts. As for obtaining water of the [same] uni versal [as that] of the [water which appeared in the cognition], it does not make known [the validity oi a cognition], because it is not conclusive [as a reason]." Cf. also *NMuk* p. 66.13f.

[22] These three alternatives are not an enumeration of mere logical possibilities, but each represents the position of a real opponent. In Sāṅkhya and Yoga it is maintained that the universal is not different from the individuals, in Nyāya-Vaiśeṣika and Prābhākara-Mīmāṃsā that it is different, and by some Jainas and Bhāṭṭa-Mīmāṃsakas that it is both different and not different.

Kamalaśīla who is roughly a contemporary of Jayarāśi presents the positions of the different schools as follows (*TSP* p. 323.18-20): ... *vaiśeṣikādibhir vyaktito jātir ekāntabhinneṣṭā ... abhinnām ubhayarūpāṃ ca jātim icchanti jainajaiminīyasāṅkhyādayaḥ...*

For a general survey of the different theories of universal cf. Dravid, *The Problem of Universals in Indian Philosophy*; cf. also D.N. Shastri, *The Philosophy of Nyāya-Vaiśeṣika*, ch. 9; Jha, *Pūrva-Mīmāṃsā in its sources*, ch. 9, *The Prābhākara School*, pp. 94-101; Mookerjee, *Jaina Philosophy of Non-Absolutism*, ch. 9; Sinha, *Cognition*, ch. 10.

[23] Very little is known about the theory of universal in Sāṅkhya and Yoga. From the scanty references collected by Chakravarti in *Origin and Development of the Sāṃkhya System*

of *Thought*, pp. 247-51, we may distinguish three closely related, but quite distinct realms of reference:

1) *sāmānya* = *svarūpa*: the five elements, earth etc., have specific (*viśeṣa*) and general (*sāmānya*) characteristics. The latter are illustrated by hardness in earth, liquidity in water, heat in fire, motion in wind, and pervasiveness in ether; cf. *YBh* 3.44.

2) *sāmānya* = *sārūpya*: the similarity among individuals is called *sāmānya*; however, *sāmānya* is not hypostatized as a separate entity which resides in the individuals, but it is identified with the substance; cf. *YD* p. 64.12 (Chakravarti's ed. p. 76.14-15): *na hi vaḥ sāmānyaṃ dravyād arthāntarabhūtam asti sārūpyamātre sāmānyaparikalpanāt*. Cf. also *ŚV ākṛti* 65cd: *sārūpyam eva sāmānyaṃ piṇḍānāṃ yena kalpyate*.

3) *sāmānya* and *viśeṣa* as relative terms: earth, for instance, is *sāmānya* in respect to a pot, and *viśeṣa* in respect to the *gandhatanmātra*. In this meaning *sāmānya* and *viśeṣa* seem to be almost interchangeable with *dharmin* and *dharma*, cf. *YD* pp. 75.29-76.3.

Still another meaning of *sāmānya* is given *YD* p. 76.5-7, where *sāmānya* is defined as *śakti*, or more specifically the *śakti* of *sukha*, *duḥkha*, and *moha*.

[24] This kind of argument is often raised against the Sāṅkhya, for instance *NKan* p. 751.6f.

[25] On the concept of *anugama* and its relation to *jāti* cf. Matilal, *Negation*, pp. 83-84; cf. also *NK* s.v. I could not detect any difference in meaning between *anugata* and *anusyūta*, and it seems to me that Jayarāśi switches from the one to the other for purely stylistical reasons; the distinction, if there is any, is lost in the translation.

[26] I failed to identify the opponent who holds this position. It could fit with the theories of certain Jainas such

as Prabhācandra and Vādideva Sūri who consider the universal as 'similar transformation' (*sadṛśapariṇāma*), or perhaps better, the result of a similar transformation which consists in being connected to similar properties. According to them the universal is not an eternal all-pervasive entity which resides in many individuals; every universal is specific to one individual only, cf. *PKM* p. 479.19: *vibhinnaṃ hi prativyakti sadṛśapariṇāmalakṣaṇaṃ sāmānyam* (on *pariṇāma* cf. *Jaina Lakṣaṇāvalī* s.v.). Note, however, that for Prabhācandra and Vādideva the universal is not something completely different from the individual, and thus their position does not fit in the context; cf. also Dravid, op. cit., p. 142f.

[27] The opponent here is probably Kumārila, cf. for instance *ŚV ākṛti* 46-47:

sāsnādibhyas tu piṇḍasya bhedo nātyantato yadā/
sāmānyasya ca piṇḍebhyas tadā syād etad uttaram//
kasmāt sāsnādimatsv eva gotvaṃ yasmāt tadātmakam/
tādātmyam asya kasmāc cet svabhāvād iti gamyatām//

"When there is no absolute difference between the individual [cow] and the dewlap etc.,
nor between the universal and the individuals, then this should be the answer
[to the question] why bovinity [is found] only in [individuals] possessing a dewlap etc.: because [bovinity] has the nature of that [individual].
And if [one asks:] 'Wherefrom the identity with it?', you should know that [it comes] from the own-nature [of things]."

Note, however, that this alternative, namely, identity of nature, is introduced by Jayarāśi as a sub-alternative to the one which considers the universal as different from the individual, whereas Kumārila is usually said to claim that the universal is both different and non-different from the individual, and thus he may be the opponent in § a.3. This possibility cannot be completely excluded, but in my opinion it is not very probable, for the criteria for identity and difference which appear in § a.3 are found, to the best of my knowledge, nowhere in the ŚV or in any of the existing commentaries upon it.

It should also be noted that the expression *bhinnābhinna* or *bhedābheda* does not occur, again to the best of my knowledge, in the ŚV. Kumārila's terminology is still in a fluctuating state, and the use of these terms by all modern scholars who wrote on this subject seems to be based on the rather late commentaries of Sucarita Miśra and Pārthasārathi Miśra. Umbeka, on the other hand, who is our earliest commentator on the ŚV, uses a different terminology. For him the universal is completely identical with the individual; cf. ŚVV p. 156.13: *jātyādīnāṃ dravyād abheda eva ...*; p. 156.18: *na tu jātyādayaḥ svalakṣaṇaviviktāḥ svalakṣaṇaṃ vā jātyādiviviktam upalabdham.*

Thus, together with Jayarāśi's, we may have three different interpretations of Kumārila's terminology: the universal is not different from the individuals, both different and not different, and different, but with identical nature.

All this does not mean to exclude the Jainas as equally possible opponents, for they too maintain that the universal is 'somehow identical' (*kathañcit tādātmyam*) with the individual, cf. ĀM p. 31.24 = AS p. 216.15.

[28] Nyāya-Vaiśeṣika and Prābhākara-Mīmāṃsā agree that the universal inheres the individual, but while in Nyāya inherence is one, eternal, and directly perceptible, in Vaiśeṣika it is not perceptible, and in Prābhākara-Mīmāṃsā it is neither one nor eternal. For Jayarāśi's refutation of inherence cf. § b.

[29] The argument is not quite clear to me; Jayarāśi seems to accuse his opponent of defining the universal as inherence, but this seems to involve at some stage of the argument a switch from that which inheres to the relation inherence itself.

[30] Technically speaking, the body of the cow, as of all living beings in this world (as opposed to *varuṇaloka* etc.), is made of earth alone (cf. *NS* 3.1.26; *VS* 4.2.1-3), but all the other elements are found in it by conjunction.

[31] On different aspects of *abhāva* cf. Shastri, op. cit., ch. 11; Matilal, *Negation*, ch. 11.

[32] According to Nyāya an individual does not obtain its identity before the universal resides in it; cf. *NV* 2.2.64 p. 669.9-13: *atha manyase yad idaṃ gotvaṃ goṣu anuvṛttipratyayakāraṇaṃ tat kiṃ gavi vartata āhosvid agavi? yadi tāvad gavi, prāg gotvayogād gaur eva asāv iti vyarthaṃ gotvam. athāgavi, na, aśvādy api gotvayogād gauḥ prāpnoti. na cānyā gatir asti. tasmān na gotvād anuvṛttipratyaya iti. na, vikalpānabhyupagamāt. na gavi gotvaṃ nāgavi. prāg gotvān nāsau gaur nāpy agaur iti.*

"Now you [may] think: This [universal] 'cow' which is the cause of the cognition of recurrence in respect to cows, does it reside in a cow, or in a non-cow? If it resides in a cow, [then] before the connection [of the individual cow] with [the universal] 'cow,' it is already a cow. Thus, [the universal] 'cow' would be useless. If it [resides] in a non-cow, [then this is] not [possible]: a horse etc., too, would be cows by connection with [the universal] 'cow.' And there is no other way [except residing in a cow, or residing in a non-cow]. Therefore the cognition of recurrence is not due to [the universal] 'cow.'

No, [you are wrong] because [we] do not accept the dichotomy. [The universal] 'cow' [resides] neither in a cow, nor a non-cow. Before [the connection with the universal] 'cow,' this [individual] is neither a cow, nor a non-cow."

In other words, as soon as the individual is produced, the universal already resides in it, and before it is produced, it does not exist, and a non-existing thing is neither a cow, nor a non-cow.

[33] The opponent seems to argue that the universal is absent where one of the individuals of its class is destroyed, but it continues to exist in all other individuals of the class. If so, then the argument presupposes that the universal is not ubiquitous. This opinion was held by a minority among the Nyāya-Vaiśeṣika writers; the only ones who seem to adher to it are Uddyotakara and Śrīdhara. Cf. *NV* 2.2.64 p. 667.13-14: *kena sarvagatatvaṃ jāter abhyupagamyate? api tu svaviṣaye sarvatra vartata iti sarvagatety ucyate*; cf. also *NKan* p. 755.13.

D.N. Shastri, op. cit., p. 335, refers to three Nyāya theories on the ubiquity of the universal:

1) Universals are omnipresent and reside in all individuals, but they are manifest only in the individuals of their class (cf. *NM* II p. 8-b.18 = Kashi I p. 273.20; *Vy* p. 678).

2) Universals are omnipresent, but they reside only in individuals of their class through inherence. This view which is propounded already by Praśastapāda (cf. *PDhS* p. 753.3f. and *Vy* ad loc., p. 689.31-690.3) was accepted by most Nyāya-Vaiśeṣika philosophers.

3) Universals are not omnipresent (*NV* and *NKan*, see above).

In this connection, Shastri raises the problem of how ubiquity should be interpreted in Vaiśeṣika terms. He maintains that it has to be understood as *vibhu-parimāṇa* which is a quality (*guṇa*), and which, therefore, cannot reside in a universal (op. cit., p. 334, n. 82). In fact, the problem may be extended to every entity except substances; for instance, if inherence is one, it should have the *guṇa* number one residing in it by way of another inherence, etc., etc. This is obviously absurd, and as far as I know, no Nyāya-Vaiśeṣika writer claims that *jāti* has the quality *vibhu-parimāṇa*, or for that matter, any quality at all. Shastri, for one, fails to reproduce any such passage. It seems to me, therefore, that he simply mistakes a *dharma* for a *guṇa*. Unlike *guṇas*, *dharmas* are not ontologically separable from their *dharmins*. This point is clearly explained by Halbfass in "Praśastapāda's concept of substance."

[34] Commenting on this passage of Jayarāśi, Granoff says (*Philosophy and Argument in Late Vedānta*, p. 66, n. 26): "There is a question of how to interpret the argument '*athātyantābhāvaḥ, tadodake 'pi tasyābhāvaprasaṅgaḥ*'. Does Jayarāśi intend that this is so since *atyantābhāva* cannot be distinguished from *saṃsargābhāva*? Or because of the type of *vikalpa* which the Buddhists propose against the Naiyāyika category of universals - a universal cannot move from one place to the next, and so could never exist in the substratum in question? In either case, the hint is given in the *Tattvopaplavasiṃha* that if another type of *abhāva* be taken, then the definition will still apply to that which it meant to exclude."

This interpretation seems highly unlikely to me. As far as I understand it, Jayarāśi's argument is much more simple : given that the cow contains water, whatever the absence of the universal 'water' in a cow may be, it would also be absent in the water contained in the cow; thus, there would be a water individual without the universal 'water.' The key for understanding the different arguments on *abhāva* is given by Jayarāśi at the very beginning of the discussion: the universal 'water' exists in cows.

[35] The reasons given by Praśastapāda for the occurrence of universals in all and only individuals which are their realms are restriction by *upalakṣaṇa* and causal complex (*PDhS* pp. 753-754: *yady apy aparicchinnadeśāni sāmānyāni bhavanti, tathāpy upalakṣaṇaniyamāt kāraṇasāmagrīniyamāc ca svaviṣayasarvagatāni*). As for the word *upalakṣaṇa*, it is explained differently by Vyomaśiva and Śrīdhara; the one interprets it as the recurrent cognition (*Vy* p. 689.25: *upalakṣyate 'nenety upalakṣaṇam anugatajñānam eva*), the other as a special arrangement of structure of the parts of an individual which manifests the universal (*NKan* p. 754. 12: *tathāpy upalakṣaṇasyābhivyañjakasyāvayavasaṃsthānaviśeṣasya ...*).

[36] Jayarāśi seems to be very pleased with this argument as he repeats it several times, cf. p. 104.11-106.4; §§ e.1, e.2, *TUS* p. 120.22f., etc. I was unable to find a definition or explanation of *ākāra* in Nyāya texts which could correspond to Jayarāśi's arguments. As it appears in this passage, the concept of *ākāra* seems self-contradictory, for, on the one hand, it has to be common to a group of individuals, and, on the other hand, it has to be specific to only one individual. This second requirement clearly stands in contradiction to *NV* 1.1.14 p. 205.4, where *ākāra* is explained as a common property of one thing with another (*atathābhūtasya tathābhūtena sāmānyam ākāraśabdasyābhidheyam*). Independently of that, one is reminded of the Nyāya concept of *ākṛti* which contains exactly the same contradiction presupposed by Jayarāśi, for, on the one hand, it is specific to one individual (*NV* p. 667.26-27), and, on the other hand, it is the sign (*liṅga*) of the universal (*NS*, *NBh*, *NV* 2.2.68). (For an analysis of *ākṛti* cf. Biardeau,

Théorie de la Connaissance, especially pp. 46-62, 162-173, 229-241.) Even though we may translate both *ākṛti* and *ākāra* with 'form,' it is doubtful whether we may equate the two. *ākṛti* in *NBh* and *NV* means a physical structure, an arrangement of the parts of an object and the parts of its parts; *ākāra* in the *TUS* is closely related to such words as *rūpa*, *svarūpa*, *svabhāva*, *ātma(ka)*, etc., which are roughly translated by 'nature.' (The chief advantage of this translation is, of course, that it is as ambiguous as our understanding of the original.)

[37] The argument is not quite clear. Perhaps the opponent means that the water individuals are differentiated from one another by their respective forms, and that they are all differentiated from non-water by a differentiation for which the universal 'water' is responsible.

[38] The text seems to contain a lacuna here. Perhaps the intended argument was as follows: if something is differentiated from something else by a universal, then a universal - being an entity - has to be differentiated as well; but the Naiyāyikas do not accept universals for universals, and even if another universal would be assumed, this would lead to an infinite regress.

[39] I supplemented as the subject of this sentence 'individuals' in general and not, as could be expected, 'water individuals,' because this would contradict the conclusion, namely, that there are no water individuals. By putting the two together, the resulting notion is that the world is composed of individuals which do not form any classes and which are differentiated from one another by their own forms. A universal, of course, is superfluous in such a world.

[40] There is nothing original to this argument: something eternal can produce either always or never. This argument is often employed by the Buddhists against the Naiyāyikas, for instance *PV pratyakṣa* 21-22, *TS(P)* v. 793-94, cf. also *NM* II p. 301.6f., *PP* p. 69.1f. (= Ch. ed. p. 19.4), etc. As such it applies, of course, to any eternal entity; Vasubandhu uses it against God (*AKBh* p. 101.25f. on II. 64d), Dharmakīrti against the Veda (*PVin* II(2) p. 67), etc. Cf. also Jayarāśi's counterarguments in § d.7, but then again *TUS* p. 121.16-17: *na ca nityasyānupajātavikārasya vijñānodayadānasāmarthyam asti.* "Something eternal in which no transformation is produced is not capable of giving birth to a cognition."

[41] The expression *śaktimac chaktirūpaṃ ca* refers to a Vaiśeṣika theory which does not seem to be preserved in the extant Vaiśeṣika writings; however, it is shortly referred to in *VP sādhanasamuddeśa*, v. 9f. (translation p. 153f.). According to this theory, when a thing is produced its cause is *śaktimat*, and the coproducers are *śakti*: *sahakāriṇaḥ śaktiḥ, kāraṇaṃ śaktimat*. The *śakti* is not conceived as something different from the coproducers as is the case for the Mīmāṃsakas. The things themselves are *śakti* and *śaktimat* to one another (ibid., p. 241.21: *itthaṃ parasparaṃ śaktiśaktimanto bhāvāḥ*). When a thing is conceived as helping something else, it is *śakti*; when it is conceived as being helped by something, it is *śaktimat* (ibid., p. 239.12: *upakārāvasthāyāṃ śaktitvam, upakāryāvasthāyāṃ tu śaktimattvam ...*). As far as the universal is concerned, it is both *śakti* and *śaktimat* in respect to its substratum. For instance, when a quality such as flavour is apprehended, its apprehension depends on the universal 'flavour' which qualifies it; thus, the universal is *śakti*. In the same manner, when the universal 'flavour' is apprehended, its apprehension depends on, or 'is helped by,' its substratum;

thus, the universal is *śaktimat*. Cf. also Iyer, *Bhartṛhari, A Study*, pp. 288f.

[42] This argument may have been construed in analogy to the Vaiśeṣika explanation why a single atom cannot be productive; cf. for instance *NKan* pp. 79.10-80.2: *sa (paramāṇuś) caiko nārambhaka, ekasya nityasya cārambhakatve kāryasya satatotpattiḥ syād apekṣaṇīyābhāvāt*. "And this [atom] alone is not productive: if one single and eternal [thing] were productive, the effect would arise constantly, because there is nothing [else] to be dependent upon."

Cf. also *TUS* p. 72.2-6 where the same argument is adjusted to the theory of momentariness: *janakatvayogena janakam apadiśyate. yathā daṇḍayogena daṇḍī, dravyatvayogena dravyam. na bhavatāṃ pakṣe janakatvayuktasyānekakālāntarāvasthānam asti, kāryānekatvaprasaṅgāt. atha janakatve saty api na janayati, sarvadaivāhetuḥ syāt.*

"Something is designated as producer because of the connection with the fact of being a producer, just as [a person] who holds a stick [is designated so] because of the connection with the stick, [or] a substance because of the connection with the fact of being a substance. [But] according to your (i.e., Buddhist) position, nothing connected to the fact of being a producer lasts for more than one interval of time, because there would result more than one effect. If [a thing] does not produce in spite of being a producer, it would never be a cause."

[43] In other words, under the first alternative the other causal factors change the universal from a non-causal factor into a causal factor; under the second alternative the universal is constantly a causal factor, and the other causal factors merely reveal this fact. Jayarāśi is perhaps referring to the theory of *vyañjaka* according to which the universal is manifested by the individuals. In this connec-

tion Uddyotakara says that the individual is *sādhana* (means of realization?) of the universal; cf. *NV* 2.2.64 p. 667.16: *kaḥ punar nitye gotve goḥ sādhanārthaḥ? yat tena vyajyate.*

[44] Jayarāśi obviously assumes that a causal factor (*kāraka*) must bring about its results immediately, otherwise it is not a causal factor. This presupposition may have been taken from the doctrine of *kāraka* as propounded by Uddyotakara: a cook, for instance, is only a cook when he is actually cooking; otherwise he is no longer a cook in the proper sense of the word. Cf. *NV* 2.1.16 p. 440.10-13: *kā punar iyaṃ śaktiḥ? kriyākartṛvyatiriktaḥ kartṛdharmaḥ. sāmarthyam upāyaparijñānaṃ ca kriyāsambandhena vyavatiṣṭhate. yadopāyavijñānasāmarthyakriyāsambandhās tadā mukhyataḥ kārakaśabdaḥ pravartate pacati pācaka iti, yadā tu kriyāsambandham antareṇopāyaparijñānasāmarthyamātropādāne 'nyatamavaikalyāt pācakaśabdaḥ pravartate tadopacārato 'pākṣīt pācakaḥ pakṣyati pācaka iti.*

"What then is this *śakti*? It is a property of the agent which is different from the action and from the agent [himself]. The capacity and the knowledge of means [namely, of how to cook] are established by the connection [of the agent] with the action. When there are the knowledge of means, the capacity, and the connection [of the agent] with the action, then the word denoting the causal factor [namely, 'cook'] is used in its principal meaning: 'The cook cooks.' On the other hand, when the word 'cook' is used without a connection to an action, because by being employed in respect to the knowledge of means and capacity alone one of the three is missing, then [the word 'cook' is used] metaphorically: 'The cook just cooked,' 'The cook will cook.'"

Note also that in § d.7 Jayarāśi argues for the opposite position, namely, that something eternal can produce both gradually and at once, but there, of course, the opponent is a Buddhist. For an interpretation of such contradictory statements cf. my "Studies in *TUS* II," pp. 128f.

[44]* The expression *rājājñā* is perhaps not self-evident. It means roughly that no one in his right mind could say such a stupid thing, unless there is some arbitrary force such as a royal decree which compels him to utter such nonsense.

[45] Jayarāśi's arguments are probably directed against *NV* 2.2.64, as can be judged from the example of the cook, together with the quotation of VS 8.5. Cf. *NV* 668.1-18: *na hy asati sāmānye samānapratyayaṃ paśyāma iti. asaty api sāmānye dṛṣṭaḥ sāmānyapratyaya iti ced - atha manyase yathā sāmānyeṣv asati sāmānyāntare 'nuvṛttapratyayo dṛṣṭo, gotvādiṣv idaṃ sāmānyam idaṃ sāmānyam iti, tasmād anekāntikatvād anuvṛttipratyayo 'sādhanam arthāntarapratipādana iti nānabhyupagamān - na mayā gotvaghaṭatvāśvatveṣu nirnimittaḥ sāmānyapratyayo 'bhyupagamyate, tasmād anuttaram etad. sūtravyāghāta iti ced - yadi manyase sāmānyeṣv api sāmānyam astīti nanu sūtravyāghātaḥ "sāmānyaviśeṣeṣu sāmānyaviśeṣābhāvāt tata eva jñānam" iti, na, sūtrārthāparijñānāt. ayaṃ sūtrārtho yathā dravyam iti pratyayo dravyatvaviśeṣaṇo* (perhaps: *-viśeṣaṇe*) *dravye bhavati na punaḥ sāmānyaviśeṣeṣv evam iti. na punar ayaṃ sūtrārtho nirnimitto 'nuvṛttipratyaya iti. kiṃ nimittam iti ced - atha manyase gotvādiṣv anuvṛttipratyayasya kiṃ nimittaṃ yataḥ sāmānyam iti bhavati? kutaḥ sāmānyam iti bhavati? anekārthasamavāyād - yathā gotvam anekārthasamavāyi tathāśvatvādity anekārthais tatsamavāyasya samānatvād gotvādiṣv anuvṛttipratyaya iti. pācakādiśabdavad iti ced - atha manyase yathā pācakādiśabdā anuvṛttapratyayāś ca bhavanti, na ca pācakatvaṃ nāma sāmānyaviśeṣo 'sti tathā gavādiṣv anuvṛttapratyayā iti, na hetvarthāparijñānād - viśeṣapratyayānām anākasmikatvād ity asya hetoḥ piṇḍapratyayavyatiriktasya pratyayasya nimittāntarād utpāda ity ayam artho na punaḥ sarvo 'nuvṛttipratyayaḥ*

sāmānyād eva bhavatīti. evaṃ sati pacanakriyāyāṃ yat pradhānaṃ sādhanaṃ tat pācakaśabdenocyate. tac ca prādhānyaṃ pācakāntare 'py astīti na doṣaḥ.

"...For we do not see a cognition of something common when there is no universal.

[Objection:] A cognition of a common property is seen, even though there is no [further] universal.

[Reply:] Now you [may] think: [There is no need of a universal for such a cognition] just as a recurrent cognition in respect to universals is seen, even though there is no further universal [common to all universals], namely, in respect to cowness [horseness] etc., 'This is a universal,' 'This is a universal.' Therefore, the cognition of recurrence is no proof for establishing [the universal as] something different [from the individual (*piṇḍa*)], because it is inconclusive [as a reason]. [The answer to this objection is:] No, because [I] do not admit [this]. I do not admit that the cognition of a common property in respect to cowness, potness, horseness, etc., is without a cause. Therefore, this (i.e., the recurrent cognition in respect to universals) is no defence [of our position].

[Objection: This constitutes] a contradiction with the *sūtra*.

[Reply:] Now you [may] think: There is a universal in universals, too; thus, wouldn't there be a contradiction with the *sūtra* [namely] 'Because there are no universals and particulars in universals and particulars, [their] cognition [arises] only from them[selves]'? [In this case we answer:] No, because [you] do not understand the meaning of the *sūtra*. This is the meaning of the *sūtra*: Unlike the cognition 'substance' which arises in respect to a substance as qualified by substanceness, [the cognition 'universal' and 'particular'] in respect to universals and particulars does not [arise] in this manner. The *sūtra* does not mean that the cognition of recurrence [in respect to universals and particulars] is without a cause.

[Objection:] What is the cause?

[Reply:] Now you [may] think: What is the cause of the cognition of recurrence in respect to [universals such as] cowness etc., because of which [the cognition] '[This is] a universal' arises? Where from does [the cognition] '[This is] a universal' arise? [In this case we answer: It arises] because of inherence in more than one thing. Just as cowness is characterized (*-in*) by inherence in more than one thing, in the same manner horseness etc., [too, inhere more than one thing]. Thus, because their inherence in more than one thing is common [to all universals], the cognition of recurrence [in the form of 'This is a universal,' 'This is a universal,' arises] in respect to cowness etc.

[Objection: This is] just like [in the case of] the word 'cook' etc.

[Reply:] Now you [may] think: Just as the words 'cook' etc., and the recurrent cognitions ['This is a cook,' 'This is a cook,' etc.] arise, although there is no differentiating universal called 'cookness,' in the same manner the recurrent cognitions in respect to cows etc., [arise without a universal]. [In this case we answer:] No, because [you] do not understand the meaning of the reason [mentioned above = p. 667.22]. The meaning of the reason 'because cognitions of particulars are not accidental' is that a cognition which is different from the cognition of an individual arises from another cause [than the cause of the cognition of the individual], but not that all cognitions of recurrence arise from a universal only. Thus, that which is the predominant means of realization in the action of cooking is expressed by the word 'cook.' And this predominance is present in other cooks, too [and gives rise to the recurrent cognition 'This is a cook,' 'This is a cook']. Therefore, there is no fault."

It is indeed disconcerting to observe that long after the Naiyāyikas admitted that not all cognitions of similarity are due to universals, and the distinction between *jāti* and *upādhi* was firmly established, they still went on claiming that recurrent cognitions or cognitions of similarity prove the existence of universals; cf. Shastri, op. cit., pp. 327f., *NBhū* p. 262.10f.; cf. also *TS(P)* v. 749ff. (note the quotation of *NV* 2.2.64 in *TSP* on v. 761), *SDDP* p. 94.9f. (= Th. ed. p. 11.8f., translated by Shastri, op. cit., p. 328f.), *PKM* p. 477.18f., etc.

[46] To judge from the editors' punctuation in *TUS* p. 6.23, they prefer to construct *utpādanāya* with *nimittam*; according to this interpretation the translation runs as follows: "The efficient cause for the production of the cognition of universal which arises in this manner does not have the nature of a universal." This interpretation seems both semantically and syntactically unacceptable to me. I should add, however, that a friend, who certainly read more Sanskrit than I did, sided with it.

[47] This is a quotation of VS 8.5. The translation is, as usual with the VS, highly problematic. I thought it safe to follow Frauwallner's interpretation, cf. *Geschichte der Ind. Phil.* II, p. 182, cf. also Biardeau, *Théorie de la Connaissance*, p. 244. Note, however, that Candrānanda gives a different interpretation. For him *tataḥ* refers to 8.4 and means a contact with a substance, and not universals and particulars in them; cf. VSVṛ p. 62.19-20: ... *dravyasannikarṣād eva jñānam utpadyate, na sāmānyaviśeṣebhyas, teṣu tadabhāvāt*. In the *Upaskāra* a more differentiated interpretation than Candrānanda's is given, but basically it is the same. (The anonymous VSV*yākhyā* does not comment on this *sūtra*).

Another question which arises in this context is how Uddyotakara understood the *sūtra*, for it is the *NV* and not the VS which forms the context of our discussion. As far as the word *viśeṣa* is concerned, it is clear that he does not take it as *antyaviśeṣa*, as Candrānanda does. The interpretation of the word *tataḥ* is less obvious. It seems that he interprets it as *anekārthasamavāyāt* (p. 668.12), but if so, the topic of the discussion changes completely; for, obviously, the problem faced by Uddyotakara is not how the cognition of this or that specific universal arises, but rather how the recurrent cognition in respect to universals arises, that is, how we cognize that all universals are universals. As far as I can see this problem is not dealt with in the *sūtra* at all.

[48] I do not know what the doubt consists in. Note that the same argument appears *NKan* p. 49.12-13: *viśeṣeṣv api sāmānyasadbhāve saṃśayasyāpi sambhavāt. nirṇayārthaṃ viśeṣānusaraṇe 'py anavasthaiva.* "[Why are there no universals in particulars?] Because if there were a universal in particulars as well, a doubt might also arise. If in order to settle [this doubt, the assumption of another] particular also follows, there would be an infinite regress."

Jha interprets this passage as follows (translation of *NKan* p. 46): "In the case of Individualities (Ultimate Individualities) also, if we had any Generality applying to them, in as much as there would always be a doubt as to the particular Generality to which a number of Individualities with similar properties would belong, it would be necessary to follow up the series of Individualities, step by step: and this would lead us to an endless series of these Individualities."

Potter, in his summary of this passage, gives another interpretation (*Encyc. of Ind. Phil.* II, p. 488): "Individuators have no universals, since if they did there would be an infinite regress, for we should need an individuator to tell which class a given individuator belongs to, etc."

[49] I failed to identify the opponent who holds this position, which seems to be a combination of, or a compromise between, the positions of the Naiyāyikas and the Buddhists. The Buddhists argue that the universal is not something different from the individual, because it is not apprehended where the individual is not apprehended (cf. §§ d.2-d.3). The Naiyāyikas, on the other hand, claim that location cannot be used as a criterion for identity or difference. In *NBhū* (pp. 561.21f.) and *Vy* (p. 193.9f.) this position of difference and non-difference is shortly referred to, but I cannot determine on the basis of the context whether the opponent is a Jaina, or a Mīmāṃsaka; both positions might have been intended. (Note that the passage in the *Vy* is corrupt; the manuscript (fol. 33b) reads: *apekṣayā a̲bhinnam* (l. 12); *rūpabhedena katha<m>*(?)(l. 13); *vastuno dvyātmakatvam* instead of *vastubodhātmakatvam* (l. 14).) The difference in form and the non-difference in place appear also in the *AS* (p. 213.8-9, 16-18), but are parts of two different *pūrvapakṣas*; and even though Vidyānanda maintains that the universal is neither completely different from nor completely identical with the individual, he does not attempt to reconcile the two.

[50] Cf. also *TUS* p. 77.24-25: *tena na kāraṇabhedena vastūnāṃ bhedo, nāpi kāryabhedena, api tv ākārabhedenaiva bhedaḥ*. "Therefore the difference among things is not due to difference in cause, nor to difference in effect, but only to difference in form."

TUS p. 113.23-24: *na tāvat tādātmyalakṣaṇas (śabdārthayoḥ sambandhas), tayor ākārabhedāt*. Cf. also *YD* p. 80.21-22, *NM* II p. 35.7 (= Kashi I p. 285.7), *Vy* p. 698.22.

[51] Jayarāśi probably refers to § a.2b, although there the difference, or rather non-difference, in form obtains among individuals, and not between universal and individuals. Note also that in § a.2a he seems to have said the opposite, although there he uses the word *rūpa* and not *ākāra* (p. 82.2-3).

[52] On inherence cf. Shastri, op. cit., ch. 10.

[53] The Nyāya-Vaiśeṣika position is, of course, that inherence has a recurrent form; Jayarāśi could be referring to the Prābhākara position according to which inherences are many, not eternal, and specific to each individual (cf. *PP* pp. 92.1f = Ch. ed. pp. 26.21f.), but the facility with which he disposes of this position indicates that perhaps he has no real opponent in mind.

[54] Jayarāśi's influence on Prabhācandra is clearly seen in the following passage. *NKC* p. 300.1-9: *kiṃ ca, tadrūpatayāsau sambandhabuddhau pratibhāsata, ihedam ity anubhave, samavāya iti pratyaye vā. tatrādyavikalpe ko 'yaṃ sambandho nāma yadbuddhāv asau pratibhāseta - kiṃ sambandhatvajātiyuktaḥ sambandho, 'nekopādānajanito, 'nekāśritaḥ, sambandhabuddhyutpādakas, tadbuddhiviṣayo vā? na tāvat sambandhatvajātiyuktaḥ, samavāyasyāsambandhatvaprasaṅgāt, samavāyāntarāsattvenātra sambandhatvajāter apravartanāt. atha saṃyogavad anekopādānajanitas, tarhi samavāyasyāsambandhatvaprasaṅgas, tasya nityatvābhyupagamatas tadasambhavāt, paṭādeś ca tatprasaṅgas tatsambhavāt. nāpy anekāśrito, gotvāder api sambandhatvānuṣaṅgāt. nāpi sambandhabuddhyutpādakaś, cakṣurāder api tattvaprasakteḥ. nāpi sambandhabuddhiviṣayaḥ, sambandhasambandhinor ekajñānaviṣayatve sambandhino 'pi tadrūpatānuṣaṅgān, na ca prativiṣayaṃ jñānabhedo mecakajñānābhāvaprasaṅgāt.*

"Besides, this [inherence] appears as such in the cognition of relation, or [it appears] in an immediate experience [in the form] 'This is here,' or in a cognition [in the form]'[This is] inherence.' There, under the first alternative, what is this thing called relation, in the cognition of which this [inference] would [presumably] appear?

Is a relation that which is connected with the universal 'relation,' is it that which is produced by more than one material cause, that which rests on more than one [substratum], that which produces the cognition of relation, or is it that which is the object of a cognition of [relation]?

It is not, to begin with, that which is connected with the universal 'relation,' because inherence would not be a relation. For, in as much as there is no other inherence, the universal 'relation' does not set foot in it. If, like conjunction, [relation] is that which is produced by more than one material cause, then inherence would not be a relation, for this is impossible because it is admitted as eternal. Moreover, a [piece of] cloth etc., would be a [relation], because it is [produced by more than one material cause]. Nor is [relation] that which rests on more than one [substratum], because [the universals] 'cow' etc., too, would be relations. Nor is [relation] that which produces the cognition of relation, because the eye etc., too, would be [relations]. Nor is [relation] that which is the object of a cognition of relation, because in as much as the relation and the related [thing] are the object of the same cognition the related [thing] too would have the nature of [relation]. And the difference among cognitions is not according to their objects, because there would be no cognition of the peacock's [multicoloured] tail."

[66] If inherence would be connected to a universal, an infinite regress would result, as inherence would have to be connected to the universal by another inherence, which

would have to be connected to the universal as well by another inherence, etc. Besides, in the whole world there is only one single all-pervading inherence (*PDhS* p. 777. 4f.); thus, there can be no group of inherences to which the universal would be common.

[56] The two halves of the pot (*kapāla*) are its material cause as well as its substrata.

[57] Note that the fourth and fifth alternative are treated in reversed order.

[58] The word *kauleyaka* (dog) is derived from *kula* (family). The affix *ḍhakaṅ* is added to *kula* when the word so formed means 'a dog'; otherwise, the derivatives are formed as *kaula*, cf. Aṣṭādhyāyī 4.2.96. The word *karin* (elephant) is derived from *kara* (hand). The derivation of *kumāra* is unclear. The *PW* (s.v.) derives it from *ku-* and *māra* in the meaning of 'leicht sterbend, hinfällig.' Mayerhofer (*Etym. Wörterbuch*, s.v.) points out that in that case one would rather expect *sumāra*, and suggests, as more probable, a derivation from *mlāyati* 'becomes weak' to which *ku-* is prefixed to strengthen the meaning of small, lesser, frail. Mayerhofer is no doubt right in his objection to the analysis in the *PW*, but nevertheless is seems to me that the *PW*'s analysis is more convincing, even though its interpretation by Böhtlingk and Roth is not acceptable. It is probably based on a misunderstanding of the Indian grammarians who explain *kumāra* not as 'the one whose death is easy,' but rather as 'the one whose death is bad, deplorable.' According to other interpretations *kumāra* is derived from a verb *kumāraya* which means 'to play,' cf. Kṣīrataraṅgiṇī X.331: *kumāraḥ krīḍāyām. kumārayatīti kumāraḥ, kutsito māro yasya vā.* Cf. also *Uṇādisūtra* III.138.

Whatever the case may be, I failed to discover any further connection between the words, and the fact that they all start with *k* is probably due to alliteration. The argument, however, is quite clear: If relation is defined as that which appears in a cognition of relation, then the definition is too wide, because the related terms equally appear in the cognition.

[59] Cf. § a.2b.

[60] Cf. *Vy* p. 699.1-4: *athehabuddhiḥ pramāṇam. na tasyāḥ samavāyālambanatvam, ādhāraviṣayatvāt. tad uktam -*

iheti cānayā buddhyā samavāyo na gṛhyate/
ādhāragrāhiṇī caiṣā samavāyāpratiṣṭhitā//

"If the cognition 'here' is the proof [for inherence], [then this is not correct;] it does not have inherence for its object, since it has location for its object. This has been said [in the following verse]:

And inherence is not apprehended by the cognition 'here.'
For in as much as it apprehends location, it is not based on inherence [as its object]."

Though later in time, it is unlikely that Vyomaśiva repeats Jayarāśi's argument; on the contrary, Jayarāśi is probably repeating a Vaiśeṣika argument against the Nyāya position. The perception of inherence is one of the points on which Nyāya and Vaiśeṣika disagree (cf. Shastri, op. cit., pp. 386-88): in Nyāya inherence is directly perceptible (by *viśeṣaṇaviśeṣyabhāva*, cf. for example *NV* 1.1.4 p. 97.8-9), according to Vaiśeṣika it can only be inferred (by the cognition 'here'). Cf. *PDhS* p. 784.4f.: *ata evātīndriyaḥ, sattādīnām iva pratyakṣeṣu vṛttyabhāvāt, svātmagatasaṃvedanābhāvāc ca. tasmād ihabuddhyanumeyaḥ samavāya iti.* I owe this reference to Rüping's review in *OLZ* 86 (1991) 3, p. 320.

Prabhācandra presents Jayarāśi's argument as follows (*NKC* p. 300.10-18): *atha 'ihedam' ity anubhave samavāyaḥ pratibhāsate, na, asyādhārādheyabhāvalakṣaṇasambandhākārollekhitvāt. na cānyākāre 'rthe pratīyamāne 'nyākāro 'rthaḥ kalpayituṃ yukto 'tiprasaṅgāt. atha kuṇḍabadarādau tatsambandhaḥ sambandhāntarapūrvako dṛṣṭo, 'to 'vayavāvayavyādāv apy asau sambandhāntarapūrvaka eva sidhyatīti samavāyasiddhiḥ. nanv evam anavasthā syāt; dadhikuṇḍādisambandhasya sambandhāntarāt tatparatantratopalambhād avayavāvayavyādisambandhasyāpi tadantarāt tatparatantratāprasaṅgāt. atha samavāyabuddhyāsau pratīyate; tan na, tadbuddheḥ kasyacid apy asambhavāt. na hy 'ete tantavo,' ''yaṃ paṭo,' ''yaṃ ca samavāya' iti tritayam anyonyaviviktaṃ kasyacit svapne 'pi pratibhāsate. tan na pratyakṣagamyaḥ samavāyaḥ.*

"If [you claim that] inherence appears in an immediate experience [in the form] 'This is here,' [we answer:] No, because this [experience] makes known the form of a relation defined as the relation between location and located. And when something which has one form is perceived, it is not correct to assume something which has another form, because this is absurd.

[Objection:] In the case of berries and the plate [upon which they rest] etc., it is observed that the relation between them [which appears in the cognition] is preceded by another relation [in reality]. Therefore, in the case of the parts and the whole etc., too, it is established that this [relation between them] is indeed preceded by another relation. Thus, inherence is established.

[Reply:] In this way, there would be an infinite regress; because in the case of the relation between curds and bowl etc., one apprehends its dependence on another [real] relation, in the case of the relation between the parts and the whole etc., too, it (i.e., the relation) would be dependent on another [relation].

If [inherence] is apprehended by a cognition of inherence, [then] this is not [correct], because no one has the cognition of it (i.e., inherence). For the three [cognitions] 'These are threads,' 'This is a cloth,' and 'This is the inherence [between the two]' appear to nobody as distinct from one another, not even in a dream. Therefore, inherence is not apprehended by perception."

For further parallel passages cf. Mahendrakumar Jain's notes on the text.

61 In compliance with his opponent's theory Jayarāśi refers to the twofold division of inference in Vaiśeṣika, and not to the threefold division in Nyāya, for, as mentioned above, unlike the Naiyāyikas, the Vaiśeṣikas denied that inherence can be directly perceived (unless one is a yogi, of course). The examples given by Praśastapāda for these two kinds of inference are (*PDhS* p. 507.2f.): the inference of a cow from the dewlap (*dṛṣṭa*), and the inference of the results of the rites for people who perform them from the fact that in other cases, too, activity produces results (*sāmānyato dṛṣṭaḥ*). The VS does not contain a definition of inference, but the distinction between *dṛṣṭa* and *sāmānyato dṛṣṭaḥ* is clearly referred to in several *sūtras*; cf. Randle, *Indian Logic in the Early Schools*, p. 149. On *sāmānyato dṛṣṭaḥ* in the *NS* cf. Wezler, "Die dreifache Schlussfolgerung in *Nyāyasūtra* 1.1.5."

62 Cf. *PDhS* p. 774.4f.: *yatheha kuṇḍe dadhīti pratyayaḥ sambandhe sati dṛṣṭas, tatheha tantuṣu paṭaḥ ... iti pratyayadarśanād asty eṣāṃ sambandhaḥ.*

While commenting on this passage Vyomaśiva formulates a syllogism very close to the one reproduced by Jayarāśi (*Vy* p. 109.2-5): *tathā h[i]*<*iha*, according to Ms folio 18a 2>*tantuṣu paṭa ityādihapratyayaḥ sambandhakāryo, 'bādhyamānehapratyayatvāt. yo yo 'bādhyamānehapratyayaḥ, sa sambandhakāryo yatheha kuṇḍe dadhīti* [*juhuyāt*](?)(The Ms folio 18a 2 reads: *dadhītiha<pratya>(?)yas tathā cāyam* ...) *tathā cāyam abādhyamānehapratyayas, tasmāt sambandhakāryaḥ.*

"For the cognition 'here' such as 'Here in the threads there is a cloth' etc., is caused by a relation, because it is a cognition [in the form] 'here' which is not sublated. Whatever is a cognition 'here' which is not sublated, that [cognition] is caused by a relation, just like the cognition 'here' [in the form] 'Here in the bowl there are curds.' And similarly this [cognition, namely, 'Here in the threads there is a cloth'] is a cognition 'here' which is not sublated. Therefore, it is caused by a relation."

This type of inference is, of course, *sāmānyato dṛṣṭaḥ*.

[63] Vyomaśiva is perhaps answering Jayarāśi as follows (Vy p. 109.5-9): *na cātra samavāyapūrvakatvaṃ sādhyate dṛṣṭāntasya sādhyavikalatāprasaṅgāt. nāpi saṃyogapūrvakatvaṃ, kiṃ tarhi sambandhamātrakāryatvam. sa ca saṃyogādivilakṣaṇatvāt samavāya eveti vakṣyāmas tatparīkṣāyām.*

"And there (i.e., in the inference of *samavāya*, cf. the preceding note) it is not proved that [the cognition] is preceded (i.e., caused) by inherence, because the example (i.e., the cognition of curds and bowl) would be devoid of the property to be inferred (i.e., to be produced by inherence). Nor [is it proved that the cognition] is preceded by conjunction. What then? [It is proved that the cognition 'here'] is simply caused by a relation. And because [this relation] is different from conjunction etc., it must be (*eva*) inherence; we shall explain this in the examination of [inherence] (cf. p. 698.28-29)."

[64] The argument is not clear, for Jayarāśi does not say which relation he has in mind. By comparing this passage with Vy p. 109.5-9, it seems that he claims that there is

no relation between the example and the property to be proved (*dṛṣṭāntasya sādhyavikalatāprasaṅgaḥ*). This is also how Prabhācandra interprets it, and, unlike in the case of the Vy, we can be sure that he refers directly to Jayarāśi. Cf. *NKC* p. 301.7-14: *kiṃ ca - ato 'numānāt tantupaṭādau sambandhamātraṃ prasādhyate, tadviśeṣo vā. prathamapakṣe siddhasādhyatā, tādātmyalakṣaṇasambandhasyeṣṭatvāt. nanu tantupaṭayos tādātmye saty anyatarad eva syāt, tathā ca sambandhinor ekatve kathaṃ sambandhaḥ syād asya dviṣṭhatvād ity apy ayuktam; yo hi dviṣṭhaḥ sambandhas tasyetthamabhāvo yukto, yas tu tatsvabhāvatālakṣaṇaḥ kathaṃ tasyābhāvaḥ? tantūnāṃ svātmabhūto 'vasthāviśeṣa eva hi paṭo nārthāntaram, ātānavitānībhūtatantuvyatirekeṇa deśabhedādinā tasyānupalabhyamānatvāt. atha sambandhaviśeṣaḥ sādhyate, kiṃ saṃyogaḥ, samavāyo vā? saṃyogaś ced, abhyupagamabādhā. atha samavāyo, dṛṣṭāntasya sādhyavikalatā, pakṣasya cāprasiddhaviśeṣaṇatvaṃ samavāyasya kvacid apy aprasiddheḥ.*

"Besides, either it is simply a relation between threads and cloth etc., which is proved from this inference, or it is a particular [relation]. Under the first alternative [you] prove what is [already] proved, for a relation defined as identity is accepted [by us].

[Objection:] If there were identity between threads and cloth, there would be only one of the two (i.e., either only threads, or only cloth). And so, if the two related [things] were one, how is a relation [possible], since a [relation] obtains between two [things]?

[Answer:] This is also not correct. A relation which obtains between two [things] cannot be in this manner (i.e., cannot apply to one and the same thing), but why can [a relation] which is characterized as being the own-nature of a [thing], not be [applied to one thing]? For the cloth is nothing but a special disposition of the threads which is its own-nature, it is not something different [from the threads], for the [cloth] is not perceived with a difference in place [time] etc., as something over and above these threads when they become a spread of [interwoven] strings.

If a particular relation is proved [by that inference], is it conjunction, or inherence? If it is conjunction, [your] position is sublated. If it is inherence, the example is devoid of [the property] to be proved, and the subject is qualified by something which is unknown, for inherence is known nowhere."

[65] Cf. § 1.41; cf. also *TUS* pp. 65.22-66.1: *athāvinābhāvasambandhagrahaṇakālopalakṣitakatipayavyaktīnāṃ sambandhāvadhāraṇaṃ, na sarvāsām iti cet; yady evaṃ tāsām eva gamakatvaṃ nānyāsām. na hy anyasya sambandhe 'nyasya gamakatvam asty, atiprasaṅgāt. na jātu devadattanayanaghaṭasambandhe jāte jalādau jñānam utpadyate niyatadeśakālasvabhāvayogitvāt svabhāva* ... (corrupt manuscript).

"[Objection:] The relation of [only] some individuals, [namely, the ones] which are apprehended at the time of the apprehension of the relation of invariable concomitance, [to the thing to be inferred] is determined, not of all [individuals].

[Reply:] If so, only these [individuals] make known [the thing to be inferred], not the others. For when there is a relation of one thing [to another], another thing does not make known [something else], because this is absurd. When there is a relation between the eye of Devadatta and a pot, a cognition of water etc., never arises [for Yajñadatta], for [individuals] are connected to respectively different places, times, and natures ... ."

[66] Cf. n. 19 and my "Studies in *TUS* I," pp. 160-62.

Cf. also *NBhū* p. 34.11-13: *tadvaṃśajārthaprāptir gamiketi cen; na, antyāvayavinām ajanakatvena tadvaṃśajārthā-*

sambhavāt. na ca tadasiddhau tadvaṃśajo 'yam artha ity anumānaṃ kiñcid asti.

[Objection:] Obtaining an object which arises in the [same] series [as that] of the [object which appeared in the cognition] makes known [that the cognition is not erroneous]. [Reply:] No, because an object which arises in the same series is impossible, as final wholes are not productive [of further wholes]. And when it (i.e., an object which arises in the same series) is not established, there is no inferential sign whatsoever [which takes the form] 'This object arises in the same series.'"

[67] Cf. § a.2b.

[68] In other words, does the efficiency of activity function as a sign in an inference, i.e., one infers from its presence the nonerroneousness, or does it reveal the nonerroneousness directly, just as a contact between sense and object makes known the object?

Cf. *TBV* p. 548.6-11: *kiṃ ca, pravṛttisāmarthyenāvyabhicāritā pūrvoditajñānasya kiṃ liṅgabhūtena jñāyata utādhyakṣarūpeṇa? yady ādyaḥ pakṣaḥ, sa na yuktas tena saha sambandhānavagater avagatau vā na pravṛttisāmarthyena prayojanam. atha dvitīyaḥ, so 'pi na yukto dhvastena pūrvajñānena sahendriyasya sannikarṣābhāvāt. tadviṣayajñānasyādhyakṣaphalatānupapatteḥ keśoṇḍukādijñānavat tasya nirālambanatvāc ca katham avyabhicāritāvyavasthāpakatvam? na cāvidyamānasya kathañcid viṣayabhāvaḥ sambhavati janakatvākārārpakatvamahattvādidharmopetatvasahotpādasattvamātrādīnāṃ viṣayatvahetutvena parikalpitānām asati sarveṣām abhāvāt.*

"Besides, is the nonerroneousness of a previously arisen cognition known by the efficiency of activity as an [inferential] sign, or as something which has the nature of perception? If the first alternative [is accepted], this is not correct, because the relation [of nonerroneousness] with this [sign] is not apprehended. Or if it is apprehended, the efficiency of activity does not serve any purpose. If the second [alternative is accepted], this is also not correct, because there is no contact between the senses and a previous cognition which is [already] destroyed. Because the cognition which has this [previous cognition] for its object cannot be the result of perception, and because it is without an object, just like the cognition of the hairnet etc., how could it establish the nonerroneousness [of the cognition]? Nor could something inexistent be an object in any way as none [of the conditions] assumed as reasons [for something] to be an object [of perception] is present in something that doesn't exist: neither to be producer [of the cognition], nor to be that which provides [its] form [to the cognition], nor to be endowed with properties such as magnitude etc., nor to arise together [with the cognition], nor simply to exist, etc."

[69] Cf. *TUS* p. 91.21-26: *avidyamānaṃ sāmānyaṃ kathaṃ buddher viṣayabhāvaṃ pratipadyate - kiṃ sattāmātreṇa, sahotpādena vā, janakatvākārārpakatvena vā? sarvasyāsambhave viṣayārtho bhaṇanīyaḥ. yadi ca janakatvādyabhāve 'pi buddhau pratibhāti sāmānyaṃ, tadā rūpāder api janakatvaṃ na kalpanīyaṃ - rūpaṃ vijñānam akurvat pratyakṣaṃ syāt.*

"How could an inexistent universal become an object of cognition? Is it simply by existing, or by arising together [with the cognition], or by being the producer [of the cognition] and that which provides [its] form [to it]? Since all these [alternatives] are impossible, the meaning of [the word] object should be explained. And if a universal appears in a cognition even without being [its] producer etc., then for the visible etc., as well it should not be assumed that [they] produce [their cognition, etc.]. [Thus,] a visible, [although] not producing [its] cognition, would be perceived."

[70] The opponent here is difficult to identify. It seems from the following discussion that Jayarāśi deals here with some sort of *svataḥ prāmāṇyam* theory, even though the expression itself does not occur in it. In this case, we have two potential oppenents: a Sāṅkhya who claims that both validity and falsity are intrinsic to the cognition, or a Mīmāṃsaka who claims that validity is intrinsic, but falsity extrinsic. (Vaṃśīdhara's identification of the opponent as a Buddhist can be safely discarded for he was simply misled by the discussion in the *Aṣṭasahasrī*, cf. AS p. 38, n. 10.) Unfortunately, falsity is not discussed here by Jayarāśi, and thus the main difference between the Sāṅkhya and the Mīmāṃsā positions cannot be used as a criterion.

However, we do have some hints which, if not conclusive, at least point in the same direction. First, the use of the expression *ātmāntaḥkaraṇasambandha*: the Sāṅkhyas usually accept three internal organs and deny that there is a contact between *puruṣa* and *prakṛti*. But the expression itself is not conclusive, for Vindhyavāsin, whose definition of perception Jayarāśi quotes in ch. 6, accepts only one internal organ (cf. Frauwallner, *Geschichte der ind. Phil.* I, p. 401), and the word *sambandha* could perhaps be stretched to mean a relation between the reflected and the matter in which it is reflected, i.e., the *puruṣa*'s consciousness (*caitanya*) and *buddhi* (cf. Frauwallner, ibid., p. 397; Chakravarti, *Sāṃkhya System of Thought*, pp. 185ff.), for Vindhyavāsin *manas*.

Second, the word *anyathā* ("otherwise") appears only once more as denoting a means for the determination of validity (*TUS* p. 116.1-2), and there Jayarāśi clearly refers to Kumārila's followers: *anye tu kumatimatānusāriṇo vadanti "vedasya prāmāṇyam anyathā - apauruṣeyatvena ... ."* "Others who follow the opinion of the numbskull (*kumati* certainly mocks Kumārila) say: 'The validity of the Veda [is known] otherwise - by its not being of human origin.'"

This quotation seems to come from some unknown commentary on the *Bṛhṭṭīkā* (cf. Frauwallner, "Kumārila's Bṛhaṭṭīkā"), and it is my guess that here and throughout the *TUS* Jayarāśi refers to Kumārila's positions as they appear in the *Bṛhaṭṭīkā*, and not in the *ŚV*.

Third, one of the arguments presupposes an opponent who takes the cognition to be momentary; and as is well known Mīmāṃsakas accepted cognitions as momentary (for instance *ŚV* 4.55a), whereas the Sāṅkhyas did not.

Fourth, some of the *prasaṅgas* involve Vedic injunctions and sacrifices; this kind of argument is usually used against the Mīmāṃsā. (Note, however, that *yogipratyakṣa* is also employed in this same argument, and it is not accepted in Mīmāṃsā.)

Thus, the assumption of a Mīmāṃsā opponent has a higher probability, but further material is needed in order to solve the question definitively. It has to be noted that the possibility that Jayarāśi refers to a Naiyāyika opponent cannot be completely discarded. While argueing against Jayarāśi, Bhāsarvajña propounds, at least as a possible alternative, a very similar theory. Whether Bhāsarvajña's exposé was conceived as a response to Jayarāśi or whether he refers to a theory accepted by certain Naiyāyikas, I cannot say; cf. *NBhū* p. 35.14-24:

tatra jñānodayānantaram eva nirvikalpakaṃ pratyakṣaṃ bhrāntatvādiviśiṣṭajñānagrāhakam abhyupagantavyam. anyathā hy ayaṃ bhrāntābhrāntavyavahāro nirmūlaḥ syāt. na ca viparyastasyāpravṛttiprasaṅgas, tadbhrāntatvagrahaṇasyāvyaktatvād dhāvataḥ kaṇṭakādigrahaṇavat. vyaktaṃ hi jñānaṃ smaraṇātmakam anubhavātmakaṃ vāniṣṭaviṣayanivṛttinimittaṃ dṛṣṭam. avyaktagrahaṇe 'pi nimittaviśeṣād vyaktā smṛtir dṛṣṭā. yathā prathamagopiṇḍagrahaṇakāle gotvasyānugatavyāvṛttasvarūpāvyaktagrahaṇe saty uttarakālaṃ sajātīyavijātīyapiṇḍadarśanāt spaṣṭā smṛtir bhavaty anena sadṛśo mayā dṛṣṭa, etadvilakṣaṇo mayā dṛṣṭa, etatsādṛśyaṃ tasya, etadvailakṣaṇyam iti. evaṃ bhrāntatvābhrāntatvayor aspaṣṭagrahaṇottarakālaṃ bādhakasaṃvādakajñānanimittāt spaṣṭā smṛtir bhavati mithyā samyag vā jñānaṃ tad iti.

"One has to admit that immediately after the arising of a cognition there is a non-conceptual perception which apprehends the cognition [which has arisen a moment before] as qualified by erroneousness etc. For otherwise thinking/speaking of erroneous and nonerroneous [cognitions] would have no basis. And it would not follow that a mistaken [cognizer] would [therefore] not act [towards the object], because the apprehension of the erroneousness of the [previous cognition] is not [always] distinct, just as the apprehension of thorns and other [obstacles on the way is not distinct] for a running [person]. For it is observed that the distinct cognition, [and it does not matter now] whether it has the nature of recollection or of direct experience, is a condition for escape from an undesired object. [And] a recollection is observed to be distinct because of some special cause even when the [former] apprehension [of the now recollected object] was not distinct. For instance, when one apprehends an individual cow for the first time there is an indistinct apprehension of the recurrent nature of the universal 'cow' and of its distinct nature (i.e., distinct from the individual); later on, by seeing similar and dissimilar individuals a clear recollection [of the universal] arises: 'I saw something similar to that,' 'I saw something dissimilar to that,' 'This is similar to that,' '[This] is dissimilar to that.' Thus, after the indistinct apprehension of erroneousness and nonerroneousness a clear recollection arises because of sublating and confirming [cognitions respectively]: 'This is a false [cognition],' or 'This is a valid cognition.'"

The possibility that Jayarāśi was referring to a Naiyāyika is corroborated to some extent by a parallel passage in the

TBV. Abhayadeva's presentation clearly indicates that he interprets this passage as directed against the Naiyāyikas (cf. for instance the use of *vyavasāyātmaka* in the arguments). However, the context does not allow us to determine Abhayadeva's sources, and there are several significant points in which he deviates from the *TUS*; cf. *TBV* pp. 548.11-549.14:

athātmāntaḥkaraṇasambandhenāvyabhicāritāviśiṣṭajñānam utpannaṃ gṛhyata iti tadavyabhicāritāvagamo; nanv atrāpy avyabhicāritvaṃ kiṃ jñānadharma uta tatsvarūpam? yadi taddharmas tadā na nityaḥ sāmānyadūṣaṇenāpoditatvāt. anityo 'pi yadi jñānāt prāg utpannas tadā na taddharmo dharmiṇam antareṇa tasya taddharmatvāyogāt. sahotpāde 'pi tādātmyatadutpattisamavāyādisambandhābhāve 'tasya dharma' iti vyapadeśānupapattiḥ. paścād utpāde pūrvaṃ vyabhicāri taj jñānaṃ syāt. kiṃ ca, avyabhicāritādiko dharmo jñānād vyatirikto 'vyatirikto vā. yadi vyatiriktas tadā tasya jñānena saha sambandho vācyaḥ. sa na samavāyalakṣaṇas tasyāsiddheḥ siddhāv api jñānasya dharmatayāvyabhicāritādidharmādhikaraṇatāyogād dharmāṇāṃ dharmādhikaraṇatānabhyupagamād, abhyupagame vā tasyāpi dharmirūpatāprasaktiḥ. atha samānadharmādhikaraṇatā dharmāṇāṃ nābhyupagamyate, vijātiyadharmādhikaraṇatā tv iṣyata eva. anyathā jñāne 'vyabhicārityādivyapadeśānupapattir bhavet, tarhy avyabhicāritādīnām api dharmāṇāṃ sattvaprameyatvajñeyatvādyanekadharmādhikaraṇatayā dharmirūpataiva prasakteti kasyacid dharmasyāparadharmānadhikaraṇasyābhāvāt. dharmābhāvato dharmiṇo 'py abhāvaprasaktiḥ. nāpi viśeṣaṇaviśeṣyabhāvalakṣaṇo 'sau tasyāpy aparasambandhakalpanayā sambandha(ddha)tve 'navasthāprasakter asambaddhatve tatsambandha iti vyapadeśānupapatteḥ. nāpy asāv ekārthasamavāya ātmany evāvyabhicāritādidharmakalāpasya prasakteḥ. na ca samavāyābhāva ekārthasamavāyaḥ sambhavi na cānyaḥ sambandho 'tra parair abhyupagamyate. kiṃ ca, yady avyabhicāritādayo dharmā arthāntarabhūtā jñānasya viśeṣaṇatvenopeyante tadaikaviśeṣaṇāvacchinnajñānapratipat-

tikāle nāparaviśeṣaṇāvacchinnasya tasya pratipattir ity aśeṣaviśeṣaṇānavacchinnaṃ tat sāmagryā vyavacchedakaṃ bhaved aparaviśeṣaṇāvacchinnatatpratipattikāle jñānasya jñānāntaravirodhitayā tasyāsattvāt. atha nirvikalpake yugapad anekaviśeṣaṇāvacchinnasya tasya pratibhāsān nāyaṃ doṣas tarhi vyavasāyātmakam iti padam adhyakṣalakṣaṇe nopādeyam aniścayātmakasyāpy adhyakṣaphalatvenābhyupagamāt. atha viśeṣajanitaṃ vyavasāyātmakaṃ, nanv evaṃ sāmānyajanitaṃ viśeṣaṇajñānam adhyakṣaphalaṃ na bhavet. yadi cānekaviśeṣaṇāvacchinnaikajñānādhigatir ekaṃ jñānaṃ katham ekānekarūpaṃ vastu nābhyupagataṃ bhavet? athāvyatiriktas tarhi jñānam eva nāvyabhicāritādi tad eva vā na jñānam ity anyatarad eva syāt. na sāmagrīvyavacchedas tato bhavet. athāvyabhicāritādi jñānasvarūpam eva tadā viparyayajñāne 'py avyabhicāritāprasaktiḥ. atha viśiṣṭaṃ jñānam avyabhicāritādisvabhāvaṃ, nanu viśeṣaṇam antareṇa viśiṣṭatā katham upapattimatī? viśeṣaṇasya caikāntato bhede saiva sambandhāsiddhir, abhede na viśiṣṭatā, kathañcid bhede parapakṣasiddhiḥ. tan nāvyabhicāritāpadopādānam arthavat.

"[Objection:] A cognition qualified by nonerroneousness is apprehended, as [soon as] it has arisen, by a relation between the Self and the internal organ; thus, its nonerroneousness [as well] is apprehended.

[Reply:] In this case, too, is nonerroneousness a property of the cognition, or is it its own-nature? If it is its property, then it is not eternal, because [this possibility] is rejected by the critique of the universal. Even as non-eternal, if [the property] has arisen before the cognition, then it is not its (i.e., the cognition's) property, because without a property-possessor it cannot be a property. Even if [the nonerroneousness] arises at the same time [as the cognition], [it] cannot be called 'its property,' as there is no relation such as identity, causality, inherence, etc., [between them].

If [the property nonerroneousness] is produced after [the cognition], then before [that] this cognition would be erroneous. Besides, properties such as nonerroneousness etc., are either different from the cognition, or not. If they are different, then their relation with the cognition should be explained. This [relation] is not characterized as inherence, because it (i.e., inherence) is not established. (Note that at this point the discussion starts to deviate from the *TUS*.) [Or] even if [inherence] were established, [still it could not serve here as the relation] for in as much as the cognition [itself] is a property (viz., a quality of the Self) it cannot be a substratum of [another] property like nonerroneousness etc., because it is not admitted that properties are substrata of [further] properties. Or if [it] is admitted, this [cognition], too, would have the nature of a property-possessor.

[Objection: We] do not admit that properties are substrata for [further] common properties, but [we] do accept that [they] are substrata for specific properties (lit.: of different kinds). Otherwise, one would not be able to say that a cognition is nonerroneous etc.

[Reply:] In that case, since properties such as nonerroneousness etc., are substrata for several [common] properties such as to be existent, to be object of valid cognition, to be known, etc., [these properties such as the property nonerroneousness etc.] would have the nature of property-possessors. Consequently, as there is no property which is not a substratum for further properties, [all properties would be property-possessors, and thus] there would be no properties; [and when there are no properties] there would be no property-possessor either.

Nor is this [relation between cognition and nonerroneousness] characterized as a relation between qualifier and qualified, because - given that this [relation], too, is connected [to the relata] by presupposing another relation - there would be an infinite regress. For if the [relation] is not connected [with the relata] by another [relation], it cannot be said to be **their** relation.

Nor is this [relation between cognition and nonerroneousness] an inherence in one and the same thing, because there would be a bundle of properties such as nonerroneousness etc., in the Self (i.e., nonerroneousness would inhere the Self, and not the cognition, because the cognition inheres the Self). Nor is inherence in one and the same thing possible when inherence [itself] does not exist, and no other relation is accepted by the opponents in this case.

Besides, if properties such as nonerroneousness etc., which are something different [from the cognition] are accepted as a qualification of the cognition, then at the time of apprehension of the cognition as delimited by one qualification, it (i.e., the cognition) is not apprehended as delimited by [all its] other qualifications. Thus, the [cognition] would have to determine [the nature of] the causal complex without being [apprehended as] delimited by all [its] qualifications, because at the time, [when] the apprehension of that [cognition] as delimited by [its] other qualifications [would be possible], the [cognition] does not exist [anymore], as a cognition excludes another cognition [in the same Self at the same time].

If [you claim that] this is no fault because when [a cognition] is free from conceptual construction (i.e., is indeterminate), it appears as delimited by several qualifications at the same time, then the word 'has the nature of determination' should not be employed in the definition of perception, because [a cognition] which does not have the nature of determination is equally accepted as a result of perception.

[Objection: The word] 'has the nature of determination' [does not mean that perception is always determinate, but that] it is produced by a particular.

[Reply:] If so, a cognition of a qualification which is produced by a universal would not be the result of perception. And if there is apprehension of one cognition as delimited by more than one qualification, how could it not be admitted that one and the same cognition is something which has both one and more than one form?

If [nonerroneousness etc.] are not different [from the cognition], then only one of the two could be: either there is only cognition, [and then] no [properties] such as nonerroneousness etc., or there are only [properties], [and then] no cognition; a determination of the causal complex would not be possible from it.

If nonerroneousness etc., are the own-nature of the cognition, then [since the nature of cognition exists in false cognitions, too] a false cognition would not be erroneous either.

[Objection: Only] a qualified cognition has nonerroneousness for its own-nature.

[Reply:] How is it possible to be qualified without a qualification?

[To sum up:] And if the qualification is absolutely different, the relation [with the qualified cognition] is not established; if it is not different, [the cognition] is not qualified; if it is somewhat different [and somewhat not different], the position of the opponent [namely, of the Jaina] is established. Therefore, the employment of the word 'nonerroneousness' [in the definition of perception] does not serve [any] purpose."

[71] While commenting on the word *buddhijanma* in *MS* 1.1.4, Kumārila says that the word is employed in the *sūtra* in order to indicate that, unlike other causal factors which first arise and then bring about their results, the cogni-

tion becomes valid, or more precisely, a means of knowledge, as soon as it arises. Cf. *ŚV* 4.53cd-54:

buddhijanmeti cāpy āha jāyamānapramāṇatām//
vyāpāraḥ kārakāṇāṃ hi dṛṣṭo janmātirekataḥ/
pramāṇe 'pi tathā mā bhūd iti janma vivakṣyate//

Cf. also *ŚVV* p. 133.12-13: *jāyamānā buddhiḥ pramāṇaṃ, na bhūtā nāpi bhāvinī*. On *buddhijanma* cf. also n. 338.

[72] There is no identity, for otherwise the nonerroneousness would be the own-nature of cognition (this alternative is treated later on); there is no causality, since under the present alternative they arise at the same time; there is no inherence, since inherence has been refuted in § b., or because the opponent himself, if indeed the opponent is a Mīmāṃsaka, himself does not accept it. Abhayadeva takes some more relations into consideration, such as the relation between qualified and qualifier (cf. *TBV* quoted in n. 70); it is hard to say, however, to what extent he develops the theme independently of the *TUS*, or whether the *TUS* originally dealt with further relations which do not appear in our manuscript.

[73] According to Abhayadeva (*TBV* p. 549.1f., quoted in n. 70) it seems that the relation presupposed by this argument is inherence in one and the same thing (*ekārthasamavāya*). Thus, in as much as the cognition inheres the Self, the property nonerroneousness also inheres the Self, and not the cognition. This sudden switch in presuppositions seems to indicate that the manuscript contains a lacuna here.

[74] This theory inverts the logical relation between the validity of cognition and the nature of its causal complex. We saw in § 1.11 that the Vṛttikāra uses the production by faultless causes as a reason for inferring the validity of a cognition. The opponent here does exactly the opposite.

The validity, according to him, is directly apprehended, as a property of the cognition, and one can infer from it that the causes which produced the cognition were faultless. In order to do that, according to Jayarāśi, one has to apprehend the cognition together with several of its qualifications (i.e., the apprehension of nonerroneousness alone would not be enough), and according to Abhayadeva (quoted in n. 70), the cognition has to be apprehended together with all its qualifications. Unfortunately, neither of them tells us what other qualifications, besides nonerroneousness, he has in mind. I suppose they mean that the cognition has to be apprehended as produced from each single one of the causal factors which constitute the causal complex, but this is no more than a supposition.

[75] The argument is not quite clear. Perhaps an analogy may be drawn with *Vy* p. 525.7-11 (note the special use of *paryavasāna* which is so typical of Jayarāśi), where a Buddhist opponent argues that the relation between apprehended object and apprehending cognition (*grāhyagrāhakabhāva*) is impossible. Since at the time of cognition the object does not exist, and at the time of the object the cognition does not exist, there can be no relation of apprehended and apprehender between them, since a relation does not obtain between something existent and something inexistent. If, on the other hand, the cognition and the object arise at the same time, there is no relation of apprehended and apprehender between them, because it is impossible to conceive the dependence of the cognition on the object. In our case, of course, we are not concerned with the relation between cognition and external object, but with a relation between two cognitions the one of which apprehends the other; this, however, does not alter the purport of the argument.

[76] Cf. also § 4.23.

[77] Cf. also § 5.3b.

[78] *asadgṛhīta* is used idiomatically, cf. *MW* s. *asadgraha*, also above p. 90.6.

[79] The Mīmāṃsakas, as well as the Naiyāyikas, do not accept that the cognition is apprehended by itself. For the different theories of apprehension cf. Sinha, *Cognition*, pp. 199-221; Matilal, "Knowing that one knows."

[80] Cf. § a.2b.

[81] That is, every cognition would have a particular form which differentiates it from everything else, including other cognitions, and the universal 'cognition' would be responsible for grouping all cognitions together, by differentiating them as a class from all other things which are not cognitions.

[82] At this point the examination of the four criteria for nonerroneousness raised in § 1.1 is brought to a conclusion. Jayarāśi undertakes a different line of argument now, diametrically opposed to what we saw so far. Up to now he examined valid cognitions, and tried to prove that they cannot be determined as such and, therefore, the word 'non-erroneous' in the definition of perception is useless. From now on he will examine false cognitions, and will try to show that they cannot be excluded from the realm of the definition.

The best study of Indian theories of error is found in Schmithausen's *Vibhramaviveka*; those theories which are criticized by Jayarāśi are explained at some length in my "Studies in *TUS* II," and I shall try as much as I can not to repeat myself here.

Unfortunately, the original Nyāya texts which Jayarāśi had before him are lost to us. His opponents belong mainly to the Ācārya school, for which the best source of information is still the *NM* (cf. Frauwallner, "Beiträge zur Geschichte des Nyāya"). The only representative of the Vyākhyātṛ school dealt with by Jayarāsi seems to be Prabhākara (cf. § c.; note, however, that Jayarāśi does not seem to use the *Bṛhatī* while presenting Prabhākara's position).

The basic principle of the Ācārya theory of knowledge (with the possible exception of the theory of the so-called 'archaic' Ācāryas) is that the cognition's content (or internal object) is not equivalent to the cognition's external object. For instance, one and the same object appears differently when perceived from different points in space. The Vyākhyātṛs, too, would admit that, of course, but they would analyze the cognition's content differently, and claim that it is no longer the same object, for the object's space-time determinants have changed. In other words, there is no difference of opinion as to what actually appears in a cognition, but in the analysis of its content. The Ācāryas' conception of object is narrower than that of the Vyākhyātṛs: according to the latter, qualifications like space-time determinants belong to the object, according to the former, they belong to the causal complex. This accepted disparity between external object and content of the cognition allowed the Ācāryas to maintain what could be called the common sense position, namely, that the external object in the case of a mirage of water are the sun-rays. The Ācāryas may disagree among themselves about the details - some maintain that the sun-rays are perceived as having the form of water, others that simply water is perceived - but the basic position remains that the sun-rays are the external object for the illusion of water. One thing which put the Ācāryas in a relatively advantageous position was the fact that some of the very terms used for mirage, fata morgana, false cognition of water, etc., which were certainly coined before this issue became a topic of discussion, already contain references to sun-rays (*marīcikā*, *marīcyudakajñāna*, etc.). As far as the arising of false cognitions is concerned, the Ācāryas used the model of doubt, cf. n. 88.

[83] Jayarāśi's arguments are paraphrased by Abhayadeva as follows (*TBV* pp. 549.15-550.5): *ito 'py apārthakam indriyārthasannikarṣapadenaiva tadvyāvartyasyāpoditatvāt. tathā hi marīcyudakajñānavyavacchedāyāvyabhicāripadopādānam. tajjñāne codakaṃ pratibhāti. na ca tenendriyasambandho 'vidyamānena saha sambandhānupapatteḥ. vidyamānatve vā na tadviṣayajñānasya vyabhicāritā vidyamānārthajñānavat. atha pratibhāsamānodakasambandhābhāve 'pi [marīcibhiḥ sambandhād indriyasya]* (perhaps an interpolation) *tatsannikarṣaprabhavam. tad ata eva marīcīnāṃ tadālambanatvaṃ, tasya tadanvayavyatirekānuvidhānāt taddeśaṃ prati pravṛtteś ca. mithyātvam api tajjñānasyānyad ālambanam anyat pratibhātīti kṛtvā, nanv apratibhāsamānaṃ katham ālambanam? yadi jñānajanakatvād indriyāder apy ālambanatvaprasaktiḥ. ākārārpakatvatadadhikaraṇatvādikaṃ tv ālambanatvaṃ na parasyābhimatam. tasmāt tadavabhāsitvam evālambanatvam. na ca marīcyudakajñāne marīcayaḥ pratibhānti. athodakākāratayā tā eva tatra pratibhānti, nanu tābhya udakākāratā yady avyatiriktā paramārthasatī ca tadā tatpratipatter na vyabhicāritvam. athāparamārthasatī tadā tāsām apy aparamārthasattvaprasaktiḥ. kiṃ ca, aparamārthikodakatādātmye marīcīnāṃ tadudakajñānavan marīcijñānam api vitathaṃ bhavet. na codakākāra ekasmin pratīyamāne marīcayaḥ pratīyanta iti vaktuṃ śakyam atiprasaṅgāt. atha vyatiriktā tābhya udakākāratā, tarhi tatpratipattau kathaṃ marīcayaḥ pratibhānty anyapratibhāse 'py anyapratibhāsābhyupagame 'tiprasaṅgāt? kiṃ ca, keśoṇḍukajñāne kim ālambanaṃ kiṃ vā* (read: *ca*) *pratibhātīti vaktavyam. atha keśoṇḍukādikam evālambanaṃ pratibhāti ca tad eva tatra, tarhi marīcyudakajñāne 'pi tad evālambanaṃ tad eva pratibhātīti kiṃ na bhavet? na ca tajjñānasya pratīyamānān-*

yālambanatvena mithyātvam, api tu pratibhāsamānasyāsatyatvena. anyathā keśoṇḍukajñānasya mithyātvaṃ na bhavet. na ca marīcideśaṃ prati pravṛtter marīcyālambanatvaṃ taddeśasyaivam ālambanatvaprasakteḥ. na ca pratibhāsamānānyārthasannikarṣajatvaṃ tajjñānasya satyodakajñāne 'syādṛṣṭeḥ. na cā(vā)(read: *ca*)[*pratīyamānasannikarṣajatvasya*](perhaps an interpolation) *tasya tajjatvam abhyupagantuṃ yuktam. anyathānumeyadahanajñānasyāpīndriyārthasannikarṣajatvaṃ syāt. atha mana eva tatrendriyaṃ tasya ca dahanena saha pratīyamānena nāsti sambandha, ihāpi tarhi pratīyamānenodakena na sambandhaś cakṣuṣaḥ. marīcīnāṃ tu na pratīyamānatvam iti tābhir api kathaṃ tasya sambandhaḥ?*

"For the following [reason], too, [the word 'nonerroneousness'] is useless [in the definition of perception]: for that which has to be excluded by it, is already excluded by the word 'contact between sense and object.' For one employs the word 'nonerroneous' in order to exclude the cognition of water in respect to sun-rays.

But in this cognition water appears, and there is no relation between the sense and this [water], because a relation is not possible with something which does not exist. Or if [the water] exists, the cognition which has it for its object is not erroneous, just like a cognition of an existing object.

[Objection:] Even though there is no relation [of the sense] with the water which appears [in the cognition], [nevertheless] this [false cognition] arises from a contact between these (i.e., between the sense and the sun-rays). This is exactly [the reason] why the sun-rays are the external object of that [cognition of water], for there is a positive and negative concomitance between them (i.e., whenever there is a false cognition of water the sun-rays are present, and whenever the sun-rays are absent there is no false cognition of water), and because of the activity towards the place of the [sun-rays]. The falsity of this cognition [is determined], in its turn, by considering that one thing is the external object, [and] another thing appears [in the cognition].

[Reply:] In as much as [the sun-rays] do not appear, how could [they] be the external object? If it is by producing the cognition, the eye etc., too, would be external objects. However, [other definitions of] being external object such as to be that which provides [its] form [to the cognition], to be the locus of the [cognition], etc., are not accepted by the opponent. Therefore, to be an external object [means] nothing but to appear in the [cognition]; but the sun-rays do not appear in the cognition of water in respect to sun-rays.

[Objection:] They (i.e., the sun-rays) do appear in the [cognition, but they appear] as having the form of water.

[Reply:] If the fact of having the form of water is not different from these [sun-rays] and is absolutely real, then its (i.e., the water's) apprehension is not erroneous. If [the fact of having the form of water] is not real, then the [sun-rays] too would not be real. Besides, if the sun-rays are identical with unreal water, [then] just as the cognition of that water, a [true] cognition of sun-rays, too, would be false. And when the form of water is the only thing which is being apprehended, [you] cannot say that the sun-rays are apprehended, because this is absurd.

If the fact of having the form of water is different from these [sun-rays], then how do the sun-rays appear in its (i.e., the water's) apprehension? For it is absurd to maintain that one thing appears, even though another thing appears.

Furthermore, you should explain what the external object in the cognition of the hair-net is, and what appears in it. If the external object is nothing but the hair-net etc., and precisely this [hair-net] appears in the [cognition], then why shouldn't in the case of the cognition of water in respect to sun-rays as well one and the same thing be the object and appear in the [cognition]? And this cognition [of water] is not false, because the external object is different from the one which appears [in it], but because that which appears is unreal. Otherwise the cognition of the hair-net would not be false. (Some manuscripts add: *na hi keśoṇḍukajñānasya pratīyamānāt keśoṇḍukād anyat kiñcid ālambanam asti. tato 'syāpi mithyātvaṃ na syāt.* "For the cognition of the hair-net does not have any other external object different from the hair-net which is apprehended. Therefore, it would not be false either.")

And [the false cognition of water] does not have the sun-rays as its external object because one proceeds towards the place of the sun-rays, for in this way their place [too] would be the external object. Nor does this cognition arise from a contact with an object different from the one which appears [in it], because this is not observed in the case of a true cognition of water. For it is not correct to admit that this [false cognition] arises from that (i.e., a contact with something which does not appear in it). Otherwise, the cognition of inferred fire, too, would arise from a contact between sense and object. If the mind is the sense in this case, and there is no connection between it and the apprehended fire, then here, too, there is no connection between the apprehended water and the eye. As for the sun-rays, they are not apprehended; thus, how could the connection between them and the [eye] be possible?"

Cf. also *PKM* p. 48.18f.

[84] This argument has already been raised by Dignāga in *PS* I.16 (Hattori's translation p. 36). Jayanta replies to this objection (*NM* I p. 226.6-8) by establishing a positive and negative concomitance between sense and object, on the one

hand, and the false cognition on the other hand: a false cognition of water occurs only when the sun-rays are present, and it never occurs when they are absent; similarly, when a person's eyes are closed, he does not have an illusion of water in the desert (*NM* p. 226.9-11):

tasyendriyārthajanyatvaṃ siddhaṃ tadbhāvabhāvataḥ/
na hy anumīlitākṣasya marau salilavedanam//
artho 'pi janakas tasya vidyate nāsataḥ prathā/

[85] Cf. *NM* I p. 228.2-3:

anyad ālambanaṃ cānyat pratibhātīti kecana/
ālambanaṃ dīdhitayas toyaṃ ca pratibhāsate//

"Some [Ācāryas] say: 'One thing is the external object, and another thing appears [in the cognition];
the sun-rays are the external object, and the water appears.'"

For an analysis of this theory cf. "Studies in *TUS* II," p. 116; cf. also *NM* I pp. 456.10f.

[86] Cf. § d.7.

[87] Jayarāśi plays on the ambiguity of the word *adhikaraṇa*; the opponent means, of course, that to which the cognition refers, and not the substratum of the cognition itself. Note that *adhikaraṇa* and object are not always equivalent terms: for the Ācāryas they are equivalent, but for the Vyākhyātṛs the cognition refers to the sun-rays (or the place of the sun-rays), whereas its object is water.

[88] Cf. *NM* I p. 227.1-5: *tatra taraṅgādisāmānyadharmagrahaṇe sati na sthāṇupuruṣavad ubhayaviśeṣāḥ smaraṇapatham avataranti. na ca sannihitamarīciviśeṣāḥ smaraṇapatham avataranti, kiṃ tu pūrvopalabdhaviruddhasalilavartino viśeṣāḥ. tatsmaraṇāc ca sthagiteṣu svaviśeṣeṣu marīcayaḥ svarūpam upadarśayitum aśaknuvantas toyarūpeṇāvabhāsante.*

"There [in the case of a mirage] where common properties [of sun-rays and water like] waves etc., are apprehended, unlike [in the case of a doubtful cognition in the form] 'Is it a trunk or a man?', the particular properties of both objects are not remembered. For the particular properties of the sun-rays [which are found] in proximity are not remembered, but [only] the particular properties which occur in water which has been previously perceived and which stands in contradiction [to the sun-rays]. And the sun-rays, unable to reveal their nature when their own particular properties are concealed because of the remembrance of these (i.e., the particular properties of water), appear with the form of water."

It is clear that this explanation of error is based on the model of doubt. In both, doubt and error, one perceives properties common to two things, but in the case of doubt one is aware that the information at hand does not permit the decision as to which of the two possible property-possessors is present, because one remembers that the perceived common properties apply equally to both things. In the case of error, the cognitive process is disturbed, because one does not remember the particular properties of that thing which is actually present, and thus jumps to the wrong conclusion, namely, that the perceived common properties must belong to the other thing which is not present. The theory does not explain what happens in a case when one jumps by chance into the right conclusion, that is, when one does not remember the particular properties of water, but of the sun-rays.

89 On the expression *devānāmpriya* cf. Hara, "A Note on the Sanskrit-phrase *devānām priya*."

90 Jayarāśi uses the word *antarita* sometimes in the meaning of 'excluded' (for instance *TUS* p. 79.1-2: *athābhāvākā-*

ratayopalabhyate, tadā bhāvo 'nyo nāsty, abhāvākārāntaritatvāt), and sometimes in the meaning of 'hidden/covered' (for instance *TUS* p. 81.20: *yathā paṭāntarite ghaṭe ghaṭabuddhir na bhavati*). The context here does not permit to choose between the two meanings, but if a rapprochment is to be made with Jayanta's exposé of the same theory (cf. NM I p. 227 quoted in n. 88), the meaning of 'hidden' is to be preferred.

[91] Jayarāśi probably repeats an argument which was used by the Vyākhyātṛs, who argue for *asatkhyāti*, against the Ācāryas, who hold the position of *viparītakhyāti*; cf. *NM* I p. 458.11-13:

na hy ālambanatā yuktā sannidhānanibandhanā/
tatraiva bhūpradeśasya tathābhāvaprasaṅgataḥ//
tad evālambanaṃ buddher yad asyām avabhāsate/

"For it is not correct that being an external object depends on proximity;
for the spot of ground [which is] exactly there (i.e., in proximity) would be such [an external object].
[Therefore] only that which appears in a cognition is its external object."

Cf. also Jayanta's definition of object as that at which one points with a finger and which produces the cognition as the object (*NM* I p. 474.16-21), which was developed as a reply to such objections as those raised by Jayarāśi and the Vyākhyātṛs.

[92] What makes this argument possible is the fact that in Nyāya-Vaiśeṣika the mind (*manas*) was considered as a sense. Vyomaśiva is aware of this argument, and consequently denies that the mind is a sense for inferential cognition. According to him the mind is a sense only for immediate internal cognitions such as the cognition of pleasure and pain; cf. Vy p. 556.4-7: *athendriyaṃ mano 'rthaś cātmā*

tatsannikarṣād anumānādijñānam api bhavatīti pratyakṣaphalaṃ syāt. na, jñānamātrotpattāv antaḥkaraṇasyendriyatvānupapatteḥ. karaṇatvādiviśeṣaṇasyāparokṣajñānajanakatvam indriyalakṣaṇam ity uktam.

"Now [you may object:] The mind is a sense, and the Self is an object, [and] from a contact between these two inferential cognition etc., also arise; thus, [this inferential cognition] would be a result of perception. [In this case we answer:] No, because the internal organ is not established as sense in the production of cognition as such (i.e., in the production of every cognition). It has been said that the definition of a sense is to be [the thing] qualified [by properties such as] being an instrument etc., which produces an immediate cognition."

Another reason why the opponent cannot adduce the fact that in the case of inference there is no contact with the inferred object is that it does not apply to the case of the inference of the Self.

[93] Cf. p. 98.6-13.

[94] I failed to discover the context to which these alternatives could refer. It is possible that Jayarāśi had a compound in mind (*pratīyamānābhāva*), and that he analyzes it in two different manners: under the first alternative as a genitive *tatpuruṣa*, and under the second alternative as a *karmadhāraya*. However, the repetition in § 4.21 makes such an assumption doubtful. Another possibility is to assume that with *pratīyamāna evābhāvaḥ* Jayarāśi refers to some kind of *asatkhyāti* theory.

[95] Or perhaps: "because [the cognition] which has the inexistence [of the perceived water] for its object is absolutely true."

[96] Cf. for instance *NS* 1.1.16 and *VS* 3.2.3.

[97] Cf. for instance *NM* I p. 453.10-14.

[98] For this usage of the word *paryavasāyin* cf. p. 122.3-4, *TUS* p. 67.19-20, *ŚVV* p. 246.13, *ŚD* pp. 95.2, 5, 10-11, 97.6, etc.

[99] Note that the third alternative is not discussed in the refutation.

[100] Jayarāśi criticizes here a theory which is little known, for none of the texts which have come down to us opts for it; it is usually shortly mentioned, just in order to be repudiated. According to this theory, the phenomenon of error is due to some sort of modification which occurs in the external object. To use Uddyotakara's expression, the object deviates (*vyabhicārin*) from the way it usually or really is; cf. *NV* 1.1.4 p. 113.6f.

Moreover, it seems that we do not deal here with a single theory , but rather with a group of theories which all used this basic idea; the modification, however, is accounted for in different ways. In *NM* I p. 226.15 it is said that the form of the sun-rays is hidden (*nigūhita*, the cause is not specified), and that the sun-rays which appear in a false cognition of water bear the form of water. Padmapāda, on the other hand, reports a theory according to which the object is transformed (*pariṇāma*), just like milk is transformed into curds, or a lotus bud into a flower, and vice versa; cf. *Pañcapādikā* pp. 49.7-50.1, cf. also Hacker, *Vivarta*, pp. 36-37, Schmithausen, *Vibhramaviveka*, pp. 167-68, Franco, "Studies in *TUS* II," pp. 106-8.

It should be reminded that the word *bādhā*, just like the word 'sublation,' can be used as both an epistemological and an ontological term. As an epistemological term, which is the much more common use of it, it means an assertion of falsity (*mithyeti bādhakaṃ jñānam*); as an ontological term it simply means 'obstruction,' for instance the subtlety of an object may obstruct its apprehension. Having failed to find any other word which conveys both meanings, I decided to conform with the indological tradition which translates and uses the word 'sublation,' even though it is indeed an unfortunate translation, for, apparently, most English native speakers do not know what it means. The Hegelian associations of this word should be disassociated, of course.

101 Cf. also *TUS* p. 108.6-7: *bhinnayoḥ sambaddhayoḥ sambandho dṛṣṭo, na hy ekasya sambandha upapadyate.* "A relation is observed [to take place] between different relata, for a relation for one [thing] is not possible."

102 Cf. Vy p. 526.1-6: *atha jñānenaiva jñānaṃ bādhyate, tatrāpi na vibhinnaviṣayeṇa rūpajñānena rasādijñānasyāpi bādhaprasaṅgāt. samānaviṣayatve tu sampādakatvam eva syān, na bādhakatvam. na ca vijñānasyotpattir* (note, however, that the manuscript reads: *vijñānasyānutpattir*) *vināśo vā bādhāt* (read with the manuscript: bādhā), *sarvasyāpi tathābhāvaprasaṅgāt. atha viṣayāntaropasarpaṇā<n>* (with manuscript? cf. folio 158b 2) *mithyā<tvā>pattir bādhā, tad asad, viṣayasya karmakārakarūpatvāt. yatrotpadyate jñānaṃ sa eva tasya viṣaya iti viṣayāntaropasarpaṇam asiddham.*

"If a cognition is sublated by a cognition, in this case, too, it [can] not [be sublated] by [a cognition] which has a different object, for a cognition of flavour etc., too, would be sublated by a cognition of colour. If, however, [the sublating cognition] has the same object [as the sublated cognition], then [it] would corroborate it, not sublate [it]. Nor does sublation [consist in] production or destruction of a cognition, for [in this case] every [cognition] would be so (i.e., sublated). If sublation is the fact that falsity [of the cognition] occurs [to a person] because [he] moved (lit.: crept) towards another object [than the one which appeared in his previous cognition], [then] this is not true, because the object has the nature of the objective causal factor: the object of [cognition] is that in respect to which the cognition arises. Thus, moving towards another object is not established."

In spite of some dissimilarities in formulation and structure, the most important of which is the fact that Jayarāśi is talking about a sublation of the object by a cognition, whereas Vyomaśiva employs the arguments in respect to a sublation of a cognition by a cognition, it is quite probable that Vyomaśiva refers to Jayarāśi, all the more so as the conclusion in the Vy fits perfectly with Jayarāśi's general standpoint (*Vy* p. 526.7-8: *vijñāne bādhyabādhakasadbhāvasyaivāprasiddher na mithyājñānam astīti. nāpi saṃvidi samyaktvaṃ pramāṇābhāvāt.* "Since neither the fact of being sublated, nor the fact of sublating is known for [any] cognition, there is no false cognition. There is no valid cognition either, because there is no means of valid cognition."

Cf. also *NM* I p. 454.2-6.

[103] Jayarāsi uses the same arguments while refuting the inference of fire from smoke. One cannot infer fire from smoke, because the destruction of the smoke cannot be perceived, and what is not destroyed is not an effect. The opponent who claims that the destruction of smoke is directly perceived has to face the same *vikalpas* as those used against sublation: is it perceived by a cognition of smoke, by a cognition of another object, or by a cognition without an object? The cognition of smoke confirms the existence of smoke, and not its destruction; the cognition of another object confirms the existence of another object, and has nothing to do with the negation of smoke; and a cognition without an object neither affirms nor denies anything at all (cf. *TUS* pp. 66.21-67.24, translated by

Shastri and Saksena in *Source Book of Ind. Phil.*, ed. Radhakrishnan and Moore, p. 239).

[104] According to the first alternative the sublation destroys the false cognition, according to the second it denies that the false cognition existed, and according to the third it denies that the object of the false cognition existed. All three alternatives presuppose that the sublation is effected by a cognition; the possibility of sublation by an object is not taken into consideration as in the preceding discussion. Accordingly, the meaning of the word 'sublation' changes, for it is used now as an epistemological term, cf. n. 100.

[105] Cf. *NM* I p. 452.15-17: *ka ivottarajñānena pūrvajñānasya bādhaḥ? bādhārtham eva na vidmaḥ.' yadi tāvan nāśa eva bādhaḥ, sa na teṣām eva, buddher buddhyantarād virodha iti sakalabodhasādhāraṇatvāt.*

"What is the sublation of a previous cognition by a posterior cognition like? We don't even know the meaning of [the word] 'sublation.' If, to begin with, sublation is simply the destruction [of cognition], then it is not [restricted] to them (i.e., false cognitions) only, for [destruction] is common to all cognitions, as [it has been said:] 'A cognition is opposed to another cognition [in the same Self].'" (This is a partial, slightly modified quotation of *NS* 3.2.24 which reads: *anityatvagrahād buddher buddhyantarād vināśaḥ śabdavat.*)

Note that the same argument is used by Umbeka who may have lived earlier than Jayarāśi (cf. *ŚVV* p. 58.3-4). Thus, it seems improbable that Jayanta was referring to the *TUS*; from the context in the *NM* it would rather seem that the opponent there belongs to the Prābhākara school.
Cf. also *PVBh* pp. 4.24-5.4.

[106] Cf. *NM* I p. 453.15-17: *atha phalāpahāro bādhaḥ, so 'pi na sambhavati, saṃvidaḥ pramāṇaphalasyotpannatvenānapaharaṇīyatvāt. na hi yad utpannaṃ tad anutpannam iti vadati bādhakaḥ.* "If sublation removes the result, this is also not possible, for a cognition, in as much as it has arisen as the result of a means of valid cognition (i.e., is apprehended by a means of valid cognition?), cannot be removed. For the sublating [cognition] does not state: 'That which has arisen has not arisen.'"

Cf. also *ŚVV* p. 58.7f.

[107] Cf. the sublation of the object by a cognition; cf. also *NM* I p. 454.2-4: *sa (=bādho) hi samānaviṣayayor vā jñānayor iṣyate, bhinnaviṣayayor vā. na samānaviṣayayor, dhārāvāhijñāneṣv adṛṣṭatvāt. nāpi bhinnaviṣayayoḥ, stambhakumbhopalambhayos tadanupalambhāt.*

"[Sublation] is accepted either between two cognitions which have a common object, or between two which have different objects. It cannot be between two which have a common object, because it is not seen in the case of continuous cognitions [which have a common object and do not sublate each other]. Nor is it between two [cognitions] which have different objects, for [sublation] is not apprehended between a cognition of a pillar and a cognition of a pot."

For another interpretation of *viṣayāpahāra* cf. *NM* I p. 453.7-9.

[108] The concept of *arthakriyā* has strong Buddhist connotations, but it is not exclusively a Buddhist term, and it is clear from the context that the opponent is a Naiyāyika. The main difference between the Nyāya and the Buddhist (epistemological, not ontological) concept of *arthakriyā* is that for a Buddhist an efficient action does not prove the reality of the object; an inferential cognition, for example, may lead to an efficient action without its object,

the universal, being considered as real. For the Naiyāyika, however, an efficient action does prove the reality of the object. It seems, therefore, that there is no essential difference between the Nyāya concept of *arthakriyā* and the more usual one of *pravṛttisāmarthya* (cf. for instance *NM* I p. 450.11-12: *sthitam etad - arthakriyājñānāt prāmāṇyaniścaya iti. tad idam uktaṃ - pramāṇato 'rthapratipattau pravṛttisāmarthyād arthavat pramāṇam* (*NBh* p. 1) *iti*).

As far as I can see, *arthakriyā* may be used more vaguely, and has a larger semantical field than *pravṛttisāmarthya* which is sometimes reduced to strict *arthaprāpti*, the actual obtaining of the object. Thus, the efficient action of an object can be the production of its cognition, and this enables the Naiyāyikas to consider the cognitions of the sun, the moon, and other such objects which cannot be obtained to be valid.

[109] Note that *arthakriyā* in this conclusion cannot include *vijñānarūpārthakriyā*.

[110] Cf. § 1.12a.

[111] We saw that the basic principle of the Ācārya theory of knowledge was that internal and external object are not equivalent, and that they based their theory of error on the model of doubt (cf. n. 88). The Vyākhyātṛs, on the other hand, maintain that internal and external object are equivalent, and they based their theory of error on the model of recollection. Note, however, that there was no quarrel between the two schools concerning the appearance of the cognition; they differ merely in the analysis of that appearance. Take, for instance, the cognition 'I see a pot here on the ground.' According to the Ācāryas, the external object of such a cognition is the pot alone; there are further causal factors, namely, space, time, light,

etc., which are responsible for the way in which the pot appears in the cognition, and these causal factors are responsible for the fact that the pot is apprehended as 'here and now.' These further causal factors are not considered by the Ācāryas as part of the external object, but only as a part of the causal complex (*sāmagrī*) which produces the cognition. This analysis the Vyākhyātṛs could not accept; for if external and internal object are equivalent, then, obviously, whatever appears in the cognition, that alone is its external object. The Vyākhyātṛs would not deny, of course, that the pot appears in the cognition as related to a certain place and time, but they do deny that place and time are something over and above the object itself. On the contrary, it is the object (pot) which appears with its space-time qualifications (*viśeṣaṇa*). In other words, the Vyākhyātṛs' concept of external object is broader than the Ācāryas', and includes things which the Ācāryas subsume under the causal complex.

Bearing this analysis of valid cognition in mind, we can easily see the difficulties which arise for the Vyākhyātṛs in its application to false cognitions. In an illusory cognition of water, the internal object is of course water; therefore, the external object must be water too. Since there is no water in the present (for otherwise the cognition would not be illusory), the water must come from the past; thus, its cognition must be a recollection of a previously perceived water. This is why the Vyākhyātṛs based their explanation of error on the model of recollection. The sun-rays which were considered by the Ācāryas as the external object of the illusory cognition of water could no longer form any part of the cognition; they cannot even be one of its immediate causal factors. However, they were not dropped altogether; their role was limited to what one may call association provoked by similarity, that is, the sun-rays merely remind us of water, because some of their properties are similar to some of the properties of water.

However, there is an essential difference between recollection and illusion. A recollection of water appears as 'that water which I saw at that time at that place,' whereas an illusion of water appears as having a present object. Therefore, something must have changed the space-time determinants of the recollection when it is mistaken for perception. The Vyākhyātṛs had to be very cautious in postulating anything which could deform the content of the cognition, for we must remember that both the Ācāryas and the Vyākhyātṛs formulated their theory of error in view of the menace of the Buddhist *nirālambanānumāna*. Nothing immanent or inherent to the process of cognizing could be assumed as responsible for error, for the Buddhist opponents would have been only too glad to infer from it that all cognitions are illusory. It is probably Prabhākara who first thought of a quite ingenious solution to this problem; since cognitions are absolutely transparent (*svaccha*), they cannot bring about any change in the apprehension of the object, not even in its space-time determinants. What the cognition could do at most is not to apprehend some of the properties of the object, but it could not exchange one property of the object with another (e.g., turn apprehended past water into present water). The illusion of water as present is, therefore, nothing but the **non**-apprehension of the (past) space-time determinants (cf. *Bṛhatī* p. 52.6: *kathaṃ tarhi viparyayaḥ? agrahaṇād eveti vadāmaḥ*). The assumption that certain properties are not apprehended by the cognition does not imply that there is anything inherently wrong in the cognitive process, for not even a valid cognition apprehends its object with all its properties. This point is well expressed by Jayarāśi, when he says that the wrong cognition of water does not have the nature of a false cognition, but of recollection (cf. also *NM* I pp.

454.12-455.12). Illusions, therefore, do not appear as something positively new; they are only recollections in which something is missing, namely, that part which is presented to consciousness as 'I remember ...' (cf. *Bṛhatī* p. 55.6: *smarāmīti jñānaśūnyāni smṛtijñānāny etāni*). To describe this lack Prabhākara used the term *smṛtipramoṣa* which probably owes to the definition of recollection in *YS* 1.11 (cf. *Bṛhatī* p. 53.8-9: *śuktikāyāṃ rajatajñānaṃ smarāmīti pramoṣāt smṛtijñānam uktam*).

The advantage of this theory for establishing the reality of the world and the validity of the Veda is quite clear: a recollection of water could not have been possible without an experience of water, that is, without real water having left the impressions (*saṃskāra*) necessary for the production of its recollection. This is why errors of objects which never existed, such as a flower in the sky, never occur. Thus, a cognition without a present real object presupposes a past real object. In other words, true cognitions and their real objects have a logical priority over errors. As for the Veda, the advantage of the theory consists in the fact that there is no such thing as a false cognition (in the sense explained above), and thus all cognitions are valid; therefore, they are intrinsically valid. Now, if all cognitions are intrinsically valid, then the Vedic injunctions, too, should be intrinsically valid means of cognition (cf. *NM* I p. 464.13-18).

Jayarāśi's criticism against this theory is basically twofold. First he points out that recollections are not as purely imitative as Prabhākara perhaps assumes them to be. If one defines recollection as a cognition of an object which has previously been experienced, then the difference between recollection and immediate experiences is bound to disappear, for recollections always contain new elements which were not present in the first experience of an object. Indeed, recollection does not arise with the same form as perception, since its object is a **remembered** object, and '**being remembered**' must be a new qualification of the object. The fact that the object is being remembered cannot appear in the first experience of an object, for otherwise the first experience, too, would be a recollection. If, on the other hand, the fact that the object is remembered appears for the first time in a recollection, then it is not something of which one has had an experience before, or, in other words, it is not recollected. For, obviously, one apprehends that the object is recollected, one does not recollect that the object is recollected. Thus, the definition of recollection as a cognition of a previously perceived object breaks down, for it is too narrow. It may be added that by insisting that recollection contains new elements, Jayarāśi argues on safe lines, for the Naiyāyikas themselves used the phenomenon of recollection for the proof of the *ātman* as eternal, and in doing so argued with the fact that recollection is not a mere awareness of an object; it contains the cognizer as the conscious agent of his past experiences (cf. *NBh* 3.1.14).

Yet there is another definition of recollection which seems to be more acceptable to Jayarāśi, namely, a cognition which takes the form 'This is the object which I saw.' Jayarāśi has nothing to say against this definition as such, but he argues that the theory of *smṛtipramoṣa* is incompatible with it. For no matter how *smṛtipramoṣa* is interpreted - as destruction of the form of recollection, as adaptation of the form of experience, etc. - it cannot account for the fact that the illusion of water is experienced as an immediate awareness. In other words, Prabhākara cannot hold the stick at both ends; he cannot describe a cognition with the characteristic marks of an experience, and nevertheless claim that it has the nature of recollection.

I would like to add that although I presented Prabhākara's theory of *smṛtipramoṣa* as it appears in the *Bṛhatī*, I do not believe that Jayarāśi was referring to it in his critique, because some of the *vikalpas* cannot be derived from the context in the *Bṛhatī* (and thus we cannot fully understand them, for we don't know which statements prompted Jayarāśi to put forth his *vikalpas*). Perhaps Jayarāśi was referring to the *Lāghavī*, or some other lost work of Prabhākara.

112 Cf. also §§ 2.1 and 4.13.

113 Cf. *PP* p. 124.9-125.2 (= Ch. ed. p. 42.15-20): "*pramāṇam anubhūtiḥ." na ca smṛteḥ prāmāṇyāpattir iti darśayati - "sā smṛter anyā" iti. atha kā smṛtiḥ? "smṛtiḥ punaḥ pūrvavijñānasaṃskāramātrajaṃ jñānam ucyate." na caivaṃ dhārāvāhikajñānānāṃ smṛtitvam, indriyārthasannikarṣajatvāt pūrvavat. mātragrahaṇāc ca pratyabhijñānasya na smṛtitvam indriyasacivasaṃskārajatvāt.*"

"'Immediate experience is a means of valid cognition.' And recollection would not become a means of valid cognition [according to this definition]. [Prabhākara] shows this [with the words]: 'This [immediate experience] is different from recollection.' Now, what is recollection? 'Recollection again is said to be a cognition which arises only from impressions of previous cognitions.' And thus, continuous cognitions are not recollections, because they arise from a contact between sense and object, just as the previous [cognition of the same object]. And because [Prabhākara] employs [the word] 'only,' recognition is not a recollection, because it arises from impressions assisted by the senses."

114 This point is proved elaborately in § 2.2.

[115] Cf. *NKC* p. 58.1f. and further parallel passages assembled by Mahendrakumar Jain in n. 1 thereupon.

[116] For an interpretation of this conclusion cf. my "Studies in *TUS* II," p. 128f.

[117] What Jayarāśi has in mind is the old interpretation of the word *vyavasāyātmaka* according to which its role is to exclude doubtful cognitions from the realm of the definition of perception; cf. *NBh* 1.1.4 p. 121.2-4: *dūrāc cakṣuṣā hy ayam arthaṃ paśyan nāvadhārayati dhūma iti vā reṇur iti vā. tad etad indriyārthasannikarṣotpannam anavadhāraṇajñānaṃ pratyakṣaṃ prasajyata ity ata āha - vyavasāyātmakam iti.* "For somebody who sees with the eye an object from far away does not determine whether it is smoke or dust. This indeterminate cognition which has arisen from the contact between sense and object would be perception; thus [in order to exclude this possibility the *sūtrakāra*] says: 'which has the nature of determination.'"

It is interesting to note that later interpretations which used the word *vyavasāyātmaka* in order to introduce the distinction between *savikalpaka-* and *nirvikalpakapratyakṣa* into the *sūtra* seem to be unknown to Jayarāśi. The distinction does not appear in the *NV*, and Uddyotakara still follows Vātsyāyana on this point; however, starting with the 9th century, it is already taken for granted in Nyāya texts (*NM*, *NBhū*, and *NVTṬ*). In any case, it would be incautious to conclude that the concept of *savikalpakapratyakṣa* was introduced into Nyāya after Jayarāśi's time, especially as we do not know what Jayarāśi had to say on the word *avyapadeśya* (cf. § 1.3).

[118] *sthāṇu* is usually translated as 'pillar,' and, of course, *sthāṇu* sometimes means 'pillar.' This may even be its principal meaning, but in the context of doubtful cog-

nition where it is always compared with a person, the translation as 'pillar' does not only go against our common sense, but also against the understanding of most Indian commentators. For among the differentiating properties which are not perceived the hollow of a tree (*koṭara*) is sometimes mentioned (for instance Candrānanda on VS 2.2.19, *NKan* p. 422.12, but cf. also Kir p. 174.8). In another context Kumārila mentions *kākavattva*, 'possessing crows,' as a property of sthāṇu, cf. ŚV *anumāna* 95b.

119 The word *sāmānya* cannot be translated here as 'universal'; for the common property which provokes the doubtful cognition cannot be a universal such as uprightness (*ūrdhvatva*), because such universals reside in qualities, namely, extension (*parimāṇa*), and not in substances. It can neither be a quality, because qualities are not common. Therefore, *ūrdhvatva* etc., were considered as properties (*dharma*) which are ontologically inseparable from their property-possessors. Cf. *NV* 1.1.23 p. 235.5f.: *kiṃ punar atra sādhāraṇaṃ, kiṃ guṇa āho sāmānyam iti? yadi guṇaḥ, sa na sādhāraṇaḥ ... sāmānyam api na yuktaṃ dravyāvṛttitvān, na hy ūrdhvatvaṃ dravye vartate, kiṃ tu guṇe parimāṇe ... na brūmo guṇaḥ sādhāraṇa iti. nāpi sāmānyam, api tu sādṛśyārtho, yāvad aham arthau pūrvam adrākṣaṃ tayor yo dharma ūrdhvatvalakṣaṇo vartate tena dharmeṇa sadṛśo 'yaṃ dharma upalabhyata iti.*

120 Abhayadeva summarizes Jayarāśi's arguments as follows (*TBV* p. 551.17-31): *tatra ca kiṃ pratibhāti dharmimātraṃ dharmo vā? yadi dharmī vastu san pratibhāti tadā nāsyāpaneyatā samyagjñānatvāt. athāvastu sann asāv atra pratibhāti tadāvyabhicāripadavyāvartitatvān na tadvyāvartanāya vyavasāyapadopādānam arthavat. atha dharmaḥ pratibhāti tadātrāpi vaktavyaṃ kim asau sthāṇutvapuruṣatvayor anyatara ubhayaṃ vā? yadi sthāṇutvalakṣaṇo vastu san katham asya jñānasya*

vyavacchedyatā samyagjñānatvād iti. athāparamārthiko 'sau tatra pratibhāti tathāpy avyabhicāripadāpohyataiva mithyājñānatvāt. evaṃ puruṣatvalakṣaṇapratibhāse 'py etad eva dūṣaṇaṃ vācyam. ubhayasyāpi tāttvikasya pratibhāse na tajjñānasya sandeharūpateti nāpohyatā. ubhayasyāpy atāttvikasya pratibhāse tadviṣayajñānasya viparyayarūpatā na sandehātmakatety avyabhicāripadāpohyataiva. athaikasya dharmasya tāttvikatvam aparasyātāttvikatvam evam api tāttvikadharmāvabhāsitvāt tajjñānam avyabhicāry atāttvikadharmāvabhāsitvāc ca tad eva vyabhicārīty ekam eva jñānaṃ pramāṇam apramāṇaṃ ca prasaktam. na ca sandigdhākārapratibhāsitvād sandehajñānam iti vācyaṃ yato yadi sandigdhākāratā paramārthato 'rthe vidyate tadābādhitārthagṛhītirūpatvān na sandehajñānatā satyārthajñānavat. atha na vidyate tadāvyabhicāripadena tadgrāhijñānasyāpoditatvād vyavasāyagrahaṇaṃ tadvyavacchedāyopādīyamānaṃ nirarthakam. atha na kiñcid api tatra pratibhāti na tarhi tasyendriyārthasannikarṣajatvam iti na tadvyavacchedāya vyavasāyātmapadopādānam arthavat. tan na tad api pratyakṣalakṣaṇa upādeyam.

"And what does appear there [in the doubtful cognition]? Just a property-possessor, or a property? If a property-possessor, being real, appears, then its [cognition] should not be excluded [from the realm of the definition of perception], because [it] is a valid cognition. If this [property-possessor], being unreal, appears in the [doubtful cognition], then, since [it] is excluded by the word 'nonerroneous,' the employment of the word 'determination' is not useful for its exclusion. If a property appears, then in this case, too, it should be said whether this [property] is one of the two, [namely] being a trunk and being a person, or both. If [a property] characterized as 'being a trunk,' being real, [appears], why should its cognition be excluded, as [it] is a valid cognition? If this [property], being unreal, appears in the [cognition], even so, [it] should already be excluded by the word 'nonerroneous,' because [it] is a false cognition. In the same manner, as well in the [case of] the appearance of a [property] characterized as 'being a person,' exactly this criticism should be raised. If both, being real, appear, their cognition does not have the nature of doubt; thus, [it] should not be excluded. If both, being unreal appear, [then] the cognition which has them for its object has the nature of a false cognition, not the nature of doubt; thus, [it] should already be excluded by the word 'nonerroneous.' If one property is real and the other unreal, even so, this cognition is not erroneous, because a real property appears in it, and the very same [cognition] is erroneous, because an unreal property appears in it; thus, one and the same cognition would be valid and not valid. And it should not be said that the cognition is doubtful because a doubtful form appears in it; for, if the fact of having a doubtful form really occurs in the external object, then [its cognition] is not a doubtful cognition, because [it] has the nature of an apprehension of an object which is not sublated, just as a cognition of a real object. If [the external object] does not have [a doubtful form], [then] since the cognition which apprehends it is excluded by the word 'non-erroneous,' the employment of 'determination' in order to exclude it is nonsensical. If nothing whatsoever appears in the [cognition], then it does not arise from a contact between sense and object; thus, the employment of the word 'having the nature of determination' is not useful to exclude it. Therefore, it too should not be employed in the definition of perception."

Cf. also SVR pp. 143.25-144.8: *tathā hi saṃśayajñāne dharmī dharmo vā pratibhāsate. yadi dharmī sa tarhi tāttviko 'tāttviko vā. yadi tāttvikaḥ, kathaṃ tarhi tadbuddheḥ saṃśayarūpatā? tāttvikārthavyavasitirūpatvāt karatalakalitakuvalayādivyavasāyavat. athātāttvikas, tadāpy atāttvikārthagocaratvāt keśakūrcādijñānavad viparyaya eva saṃśayaḥ prāptaḥ. atha dharmaḥ, sa sthāṇutvalakṣaṇaḥ puruṣatvalakṣaṇa ubhayaṃ vā. pakṣatraye 'pi tāttvikātāttvikapakṣayoḥ pūrvavad doṣaḥ. athaikasya tāttvikatvam anyasyātāttvikatvaṃ, tathāpi tadviṣayaṃ jñānaṃ bhrāntam abhrāntaṃ cety ubhayarūpaṃ prāptam. atha sandigdho 'rthas tatra pratibhāsate, tatrāpi tāttvikātāttvikatvavikalpayoḥ sa eva doṣaḥ.*

Note, however, that unlike in the case of Abhayadeva it is not certain whether Vādideva knew Jayarāśi; the above summary of Jayarāśi's arguments is probably borrowed from Prabhācandra's *PKM* (p. 47.10-21): *saṃśayajñāne hi dharmī dharmo vā pratibhāti. dharmī cet, sa tāttviko 'tāttviko vā. tāttvikaś cet, kathaṃ tadbuddheḥ saṃśayarūpatā, tāttvikārthagṛhītirūpatvāt karatalādinirṇayavat? athātāttvikas, tathāpy atāttvikārthaviṣayatvāt keśoṇḍukādijñānavad bhrāntir eva saṃśayaḥ. atha dharmaḥ, sa sthāṇutvalakṣaṇaḥ puruṣatvalakṣaṇa ubhayaṃ vā. yadi sthāṇutvalakṣaṇas, tatra tāttvikātāttvikayoḥ pūrvavad doṣaḥ. atha puruṣatvalakṣaṇas, tatrāpy ayam eva doṣaḥ. athobhayaṃ tathāpy ubhayasya tāttvikatvātāttvikatvayoḥ sa eva doṣaḥ. athaikasya tāttvikatvam anyasyātāttvikatvaṃ tathāpi tadviṣayaṃ jñānaṃ tad eva bhrāntam abhrāntaṃ ceti prāptam. atha sandigdho 'rthas tatra pratibhāsate, so 'pi vidyate na vetyādivikalpe tad eva dūṣaṇam. tan na saṃśayo ghaṭate.*

[121] Vyomaśiva mentions a very similar argument, perhaps inspired by Jayarāśi, but in it the doubtful cognition consists of two different cognitions; cf. Vy p. 537.15-18: *atha kim idam ekaṃ jñānam āhosvid anekam iti. yady anekaṃ krameṇotpadyate sthāṇur ity ekaṃ puruṣa iti cānyat, tarhi yat tasmiṃs tad iti rūpaṃ tat samyagjñānaṃ, viparītaṃ tu mithyājñānam iti saṃśayocchedaḥ.* "Is this [doubtful cognition] one cognition, or more than one? If it is more than one [and consequently] arises successively, [namely] one [in the form] '[This is] a trunk,' and the other [in the form] '[This is] a person,' then the one which has the form

'this' in respect to this (i.e., the one which has the form 'This is a person' when there is a person, or 'This is a trunk' when there is a trunk) is a valid cognition, whereas the other [one] is a false cognition. Thus, [the notion of] doubt is destroyed."

122 The quality meant here is the number 'two' (*dvitva*) which the Nyāya-Vaiśeṣikas considered as a *guṇa*.

123 The *Lakṣaṇasāra*, "Essence of Definition," is probably another work of Jayarāśi (cf. *TUS*, introduction, p. XI). So far no manuscript of this work has been discovered.

124 Having done away with the first three qualifications of perception in *NS* 1.1.4 (*avyapadeśya*, *avyabhicārin*, *vyavasāyātmaka*) Jayarāśi proceeds to refute the last qualification, namely, the compound 'which arises from a contact between sense and object.' His method is to take the first three members of the compound and analyze them separately; the word 'which arises,' or production, governs the whole discussion. Thus, he starts with the production by contact (§ 1.41), continues with the production by a sense (§1.42), and concludes with the production by an object (§ 1.43). Central to this discussion is the issue of *prāpyakāritva*, i.e., whether the senses, especially the eye, come in contact with the objects they apprehend. This problem was vehemently debated for more than a thousand years between the Naiyāyikas who affirmed it and the Buddhists who denied it. The Mīmāṃsakas and the Sāṅkhyas sided with the former, whereas the Jainas agreed with the latter. For a general background to this problem cf. Sinha, *Cognition*, pp. 21f., for a detailed treatment cf. Preisendanz, *Nayatattvāloka*, nn. 146, 147, 155, 159, 185, 189, 191.

[125] Is there any real difference between these two alternatives? It seems to me that there is only a difference in formulation; consider, for instance, the following passage from the *NV* in which *āvaraṇa* and *vyavahitārthānupalabdhi* appear side by side, and which may have been Jayarāśi's reference (*NV* 1.1.4 p. 105.7-10): *kathaṃ punar avagamyate kālabhedāgrahaṇanimitta eṣa yugapadpratyayo na punar ekakāla eva? idam anumānam āvaraṇānupapatter iti. yady aprāpyakāri cakṣur bhavati, na kuḍyakaṭāder āvaraṇasya sāmarthyam astity āvaraṇānupapattiḥ syāt. na ca vyavahitārthopalabdhir asti. tasmān nāprāpyakāriti.* "How is it known that the cognition [of the moon and of the branch of a tree] at the same time is conditioned/caused by the non-apprehension of the difference in time [between two cognitions, one of the moon, the other of the branch], but does not really occur at the same time? This is the inferential sign [for it]: 'obstruction would be impossible.' If the eye operates without reaching [its object], obstructions such as walls, screens of straw, etc., would possess no capacity [to obstruct] (i.e., we could see the objects behind them); thus, obstruction would be impossible. But there is no apprehension of an object which is separated [from the sense by walls, screens, etc.]. Therefore, [the eye] does not operate without reaching [its object]."

āvaraṇaliṅga is used by Vātsyāyana as if it were the inferential sign for the contacts between sense and object (cf. *NBh* 2.1.19 p. 443.8: *indriyārthasannikarṣās tv āvaraṇena liṅgenānumīyante*), but, obviously, it should not be taken literally; that is, the inference cannot be formulated with the reason *āvaraṇāt*. The correct formulation of the reason is *vyavahitārthānupalabdhi*, and *āvaraṇa* is nothing but a technical abbreviation for it (cf. *NV* 3.1.34 p. 763. 9-11, *NM* I p. 191.14-16). Jayarāśi is probably aware of this, for he repeats exactly the same arguments for the two alternatives. But even the better formulation *vyavahitār-*

thānupalabdhi is not entirely satisfactory. For if the non-apprehension of a hidden object is the *liṅga*, and the contact is the *sādhya*, then whenever there is a non-apprehension of a hidden object, there should be a contact. This is obviously absurd, and the Naiyāyika can be accused of a sloppy formulation. In fact, we find that Nyāya-Vaiśeṣika authors a century or so after Jayarāśi's time - whether by Jayarāśi's influence or not I cannot say - are much more careful in their formulations of this inference; cf. *Vy* p. 159.3-4: *cakṣuḥ prāptārthaparicchedakaṃ vyavahitāprakāśakatvāt* (quoted and criticized *SVR* p. 318.13f.), *NVTṬ* 1.1.4 p. 105.23-24: *prayogas tu cakṣuḥśrotre prāpya svaviṣaye kāryaṃ kuruto,* ***janakatve sati*** *tadaprāptāv ajanakatvāt*. However, these later formulations are unknown to Jayarāśi, and they cannot be dealt with here.

Of course, it is not the ocular globe which goes out of its socket to meet the object. The visual sense is a special ray of light, and the visible eye is only its support or seat (*āśraya, adhiṣṭhāna*). Cf. *NBh* 3.1.34 p. 763. 2-3: *raśmyarthasannikarṣaś cāvaraṇaliṅgaḥ. cākṣuṣo hi raśmiḥ kuḍyādibhir āvṛtam arthaṃ na prakāśayati yathā pradīparaśmir iti.* "The contact between the ray [of light] and the object has the obstruction for its [inferential] sign. For the ocular ray [of light] does not illuminate an object separated [from it] by a wall etc., just like the ray of a lamp."

126 Note how Jayarāśi uses the arguments he rejects here in order to refute the Vedānta theory of the blissful *ātman*, cf. *TUS* p. 81.22-24: *paṭāntarite ghaṭe ghaṭabuddhir na bhavati paṭāntardhāne satīndriyeṇa sākaṃ sambandho nāsti tadbhāvād* (read: *tadabhāvād*) *ghaṭe nendriyajaṃ vijñānaṃ sampadyate.* "A cognition of a pot does not arise when the pot is covered with a cloth. When [the pot] is concealed by

the cloth, there is no relation (i.e., contact) between the sense [and the pot]. Because there is no [contact], a cognition which arises from the sense is not produced in respect to the pot."

[127] Jayarāśi probably reminds the Naiyāyika of his own objection to the Buddhist *kṣaṇikatvānumāna*: everything is momentary because it exists.

[128] Cf. § a.2b.

[129] The argument seems surprising: why should the cognition be present at the beginning and the end of the inferential process? One could well imagine an apprehension of smoke at the last moment before it vanishes; does this mean that one cannot infer fire from smoke? Or perhaps it is not the *hetu* (in this case *indriyārthasannikarṣajanyākāratā*), but the *dharmin* (i.e., the cognition itself) which has to be present throughout the inferential process. This second alternative fits better the literal formulation here, and it is corroborated by *TUS* p. 73.16-18: *api ca liṅgagrahaṇānantaraṃ vyāptismaraṇaṃ, tadanu parāmarśajñānaṃ, tato 'numeyapratipattiḥ. na caitāvantaṃ kālaṃ sāmagryavasthānam asti.* (In this context the *sāmagrī* has to be proved, it is not (yet) the *liṅga*.) This, however, does not solve the problem; the *dharmin* may usually be present when the inference is made, but I know of no text which makes it a necessary condition for all inferences.

I have no definite solution to this problem, but as a supposition I suggest that Jayarāśi's argument is based on the Nyāya analysis of the inferential process, especially the nature of *parāmarśa*; consider, for instance, the following description by Uddyotakara which clearly states that the *hetu* has to be present at the beginning and the end of the inferential process (*NV* 1.1.5 pp. 134.3-5, 140.2-3): *te ca dve pratyakṣe. liṅgaliṅgisambandhadarśanam ādyaṃ pratyakṣaṃ, liṅgadarśanaṃ dvitīyam. bubhutsāvato dvitīyāl liṅgadarśanāt saṃskārābhivyaktyuttarakālaṃ smṛtiḥ, smṛtyanantaraṃ ca punar liṅgadarśanam ayaṃ dhūma iti. tad idam antimaṃ pratyakṣaṃ pūrvābhyāṃ pratyakṣābhyāṃ smṛtyā cānugṛhyamānaṃ parāmarśarūpam anumānaṃ bhavati.*

"And the perceptions [by which inference is preceded] are two: the first perception is the apprehension of the relation between the [inferential] sign and that which is characterized by it. The second is the apprehension of the sign [again, without that which is characterized by it]. [Then] from the second apprehenson of the sign, after the awakening of the impressions [left by the first perception] a recollection [arises] for [a person] who has the desire to know [what can be inferred]. And immediately after the recollection, **the sign is seen again**: 'This is smoke.' This last perception, supported by the two previous perceptions and the recollection, is inference which has the nature of reflective cognition."

[130] This is clearly a paraphrase of one of the most famous fragments of Dignāga, which according to Frauwallner may have come from the *Hetumukha*, cf. "Dignāga, sein Werk und seine Entwicklung," p. 164, *Kl. Schr.*, p. 840; cf. also Randle, *Fragments from Dignāga*, p. 51f., to which we may add *PVSV* p. 2.22f., *ŚVV* p. 231.23-24, *NBhū* p. 254.11, *NMGBh* p. 18.1-2, etc. There are numerous variants to this fragment which need not be noted here. Frauwallner chose (for reasons which he does not explain) the following one: *sarva evāyam anumānānumeyavyavahāro buddhyārūḍhenaiva dharmadharmibhedena na bahiḥ sadasattvam apekṣate.* "All thinking/ speaking of inferences and inferred objects, by [being based on] a distinction between property and property-possessor which is just constructed by the mind, does not depend on [their] external existence or inexistence."

The Naiyāyikas, however, accepted the *dharma-dharmin* relation in inference as a real one (cf. the discussion of *anumeya* in *NV* 1.1.5 pp. 153.4f., especially pp. 154.11f.), and the question may arise why Jayarāśi imputes a Buddhist position to a Naiyāyika opponent. The answer to this question depends on the solution of the problem raised in the preceding note.

[131] Cf. § a.2b, cf. also *TUS* p. 71.7-8: ... *yathotpannaṃ vijñānaṃ svasaṃvedanaṃ na bhavati vijñānākārātiriktākārāntaravirahāt.* "The cognition does not apprehend by itself how it has arisen, because [it] has no other form over and above the form of cognition."

[132] Cf. *NVTṬ* 1.1.12 p. 199.16-17: *gandhopalabdhiḥ karaṇasādhyā kriyātvāc chidikriyāvad iti.* "Apprehension of smell is realized/brought about by an instrument, because it is an action, just like the action of cutting." Cf. also *PDhS* p. 168.1, *Vy* pp. 256.21, 393.3-4, *NKan* p. 88.7-8.

[133] Cf. n. 65.

[134] The special excellence in question seems to be *kārakatva*, the fact that the object becomes a causal factor in the production of a cognition. Or perhaps, by anticipation or as a smoother transition to the next chapter, the special excellence could be *jñātatva*, the fact that the object becomes known by the cognition. In this case Jayarāśi is referring to the Mīmāṃsā theory according to which a special excellence is produced in the object as soon as it is known. This change in the object is perceived, and the cognition is deduced from it by *arthāpatti*: unless there was a cognition the object could not be known (*jñātatvānyathānupapatti*); cf. *NR* on *ŚV śūnyavāda* 182, *ŚVV* pp. 276.12-15, 294.14f., and Bhatt, *Epistemology of Bhāṭṭa School*, pp. 51-54.

The same argument is more fully developed by Jayarāśi in *TUS* pp. 75.24-76.22: *ito 'py ātmā sukhādikāryādhikaraṇo 'vagantuṃ na pāryate. kiṃ tenātmanānupajātātiśayena tāpādi kāryāṃ kriyata āhosvid upajātātiśayenāpi, kiṃ vyatiriktopajātātiśayena, avyatiriktopajātātiśayena vā? tad yady anupajātātiśayenotpādyate tāpādi kāryaṃ, tadā sarvadā kuryād, anupajātabalasya kāryakāraṇābhyupagamān, na tāpādivikalaḥ syāt, samaṃ sukhādi kāryaṃ prasajyate. athāvyatiriktopajātātiśayenotpādyate tāpādi kāryaṃ, tadāvyatiriktopajātātiśaya iti kiṃ bhaṇitaṃ bhavati? ātmopajāyate. tataś ca smaraṇānumānapratyabhijñānānupapattiḥ. atha vyatiriktopajātātiśayena janyate tāpādi kāryaṃ, sa tenātmanā saha sambaddho vā, na vā. yadi na sambaddhaḥ, sa tasyātiśayaḥ katham? atha sambaddhaḥ, kiṃ janakatvenātha janyatvena tatsamavāyitvena vā? tad yadi janakatvena sambaddhas, tadātmā tenātiśayenotpadyata iti smaraṇānupapattiḥ. atha janyatvena, so 'pi tena katham utpādyate? kim anupajātātiśayena vyatiriktopajātātiśayena veti prāptā praśnaparamparā. atha tatsamavāyitvena, na, tasya sarvasādhāraṇatvāt, tadabhāvāc ca. athaikakāryajanakatvena sambaddhas, tad evedaṃ cintayitum ārabdhaṃ kim idaṃ janakatvaṃ nāmeti. kiṃ ca yad evānupajāte 'tiśaya ātmano rūpaṃ tad eva jāte 'pi, tat kathaṃ kāryaṃ kuryāt? atha pūrvarūpasyātadavasthyaṃ, susthitaṃ nityatvam! atha tādavasthyaṃ, tathāpi na karoti kāryam. evaṃ naiyāyikādimatenātmana upabhogasmaraṇādikaṃ na jāghaṭīti.*

"For the following [reason], too, it cannot be apprehended that the Self is the substratum of effects such as pleasure etc.: is the effect such as misery etc., produced by a Self in which a special excellence is not produced, or by [a Self] in which a special excellence is produced, [and if so, is it produced] by [a Self] in which the produced special excellence is something additional [to the Self], or by [a Self] in which the produced special excellence is not something additional?

In respect to these [alternatives], if the effect such as misery etc., is produced by [a Self] in which a special excellence is not produced, then it (i.e., the Self) would always produce [the effect], because [you] admit that something [eternal] in which a capacity is not produced is the cause of the effect; misery etc., would never be absent. Equally, [other contradictory] effects such as pleasure etc., would [also be produced].

If the effect, misery etc., is produced by [a Self] in which a special excellence is produced which is not something additional [to the Self], then what does it mean [to say that the Self] has a special excellence produced in it which is not something additional to it? [It means that] the Self is produced! And thus, recollection, inference, recognition, etc., are impossible [as they require a permanent Self].

If the effect, misery etc., is produced by [a Self] in which a special excellence is produced which is something additional [to the Self], [then] this [special excellence] is either connected with the Self or not. If it is not connected, how could it be **its** special excellence? If it is connected, is it by producing [the Self], or by being produced [by it], or by being inherent in it? In respect to these [alternatives], if it is connected [with the Self] by producing [it], then the Self is produced by this special excellence; consequently, recollection is impossible. If [it is connected with the Self] by being produced [by it], then how is this [special excellence], in its turn, produced by it? Is it [produced] by [a Self] in which a [further] special excellence is not produced, or by [a Self] in which a [further] special excellence is produced which is something additional [to it]? Thus, an [uninterrupted] succession of questions arises. If [the special excellence is connected with the Self] by inhering it, [then we say:]

no, because [inherence] is common to everything, and because it does not exist.

[Objection: The special excellence] is connected [with] the Self by the fact that [they both] produce one and the same effect.

[Reply:] This is exactly what we undertook to examine, [namely] what this fact of producing is. Besides, the nature of the Self, when a special excellence is not produced [in it], is exactly the same [when it] is produced; therefore, how could [it] produce the effect? If the previous nature does not last, the eternity [of the Self] is well established! If [it] does last, even so, [the Self] does not produce the effect. Thus, according to the system of the Naiyāyikas and others, experience, recollection, etc., are not possible for the Self."

Cf. also *TUS* pp. 121.16-122.3: *na ca nityasyānupajātavikārasya vijñānodayadānasāmarthyam asti. atha kriyate kim anupajātātiśayena vā, avyatiriktopajātātiśayena vā, vyatiriktopajātātiśayena vā? tad yady anupajātātiśayena kriyate, tadā sarvadā kuryād ekasmin vā kāle kuryāt taddehamātrānubandhena kālavilambanāyogāt. athāvyatiriktopajātātiśayena kriyate, tathāpi sanātanā varṇā, 'vyatiriktātiśayakaraṇapakṣe sa evopajāyate, phalāniṣpattikaraṇasvarūpānativṛtteḥ. atha vyatiriktopajātātiśayena kriyate, tasyātiśayaḥ katham? yo yasya kenāpi sambandhena na sambadhyate sa* <*na*> *tasyātiśayaḥ*. Cf. also n. 372.

[136] There is no doubt that by 'others' Jayarāśi means the Bhāṭṭa-Mīmāṃsakas. The opponents are called *śrutilālasa*, *mīmāṃsaka*, *śrotriya*, and *vedavid*, and a half-verse from the *ŚV* is quoted at the end of the chapter. The possibility that Jayarāśi referred to the Prābhākara-Mīmāṃsakas as well is easily discarded for they did not accept the definition of *pramāṇa* as agent of apprehension of an unapprehended object.

This definition of *pramāṇa* came only gradually to be accepted. Śabara, as far as I know, does not mention it anywhere. Kumārila's epistemology represents an intermediary stage: he explicitly says that the apprehension of an unapprehended object characterizes all *pramāṇas*, but he does not include this characteristic in his definition of *pramāṇa* (cf. ŚV 2.80). (Incidentally, the expression *anadhigatārthagantṛ* seems to appear nowhere in the ŚV.) For Pārthasārathimiśra it is already an integral part of the definition of *pramāṇa*.

The different stages in this historical development are clearly seen by comparing what each of the commentators has to say about *'arthe 'nupalabdhe'* in the *Autpattika-sūtra*. For Śabara, it means an object which is not apprehended by perception etc., i.e., the natural relation between word and object is the fundamental condition for the knowledge of *dharma* (characterized as *agnihotra* etc.) which is not apprehended by perception etc.; cf. *ŚBh* p. 24.5-6: *autpattikaḥ śabdasyārthena sambandhas tasyāgnihotrādilakṣaṇasya dharmasya nimittaṃ pratyakṣādibhir anavagatasya*. Kumārila, on the other hand, explains that these words were introduced into the *sūtra* in order to indicate that means of valid cognition are restricted to unapprehended objects; if an object was apprehended before, its re-apprehension must be a recollection; cf. ŚV 5.11ab: *sarvasya 'nupalabdhe 'rthe prāmāṇyaṃ smṛtir anyathā/*. Pārthasārathi defines a means of valid cognition as a cognition free from defective causes and sublation which apprehends an unapprehended object. All three qualifications, so he claims, are pointed out by the Sūtrakāra in the *Autpattika-sūtra*; cf. *ŚD* p. 71.10-12: *etac ca viśeṣaṇatrayam upādadānena sūtrakāreṇa kāraṇadoṣabādhakajñānarahitam agṛhītagrāhi jñānaṃ pramāṇam iti pramāṇalakṣaṇaṃ sūcitam*.

As to the reason why the Mīmāṃsakas accepted this definition of *pramāṇa*, some modern scholars offer quite a tautological answer: a means of knowledge must bring about something new, otherwise it is not a means of knowledge; therefore it has to apprehend an unapprehended object. G.P. Bhatt, to whom we owe the best study to date of the epistemology of the Bhāṭṭa school, goes as far as to affirm that "A knowledge which does not add something to our present stock of information, cannot be valid ... Thus, according to the Bhāṭṭa a valid knowledge is essentially useful and hence it must reveal something new" (*Epistemology of the Bhāṭṭa School*, p. 75). It seems to me that it was not for pragmatical reasons such as "we have to make fresh adjustments to the changing circumstances" (ibid.), that the Mīmāṃsakas attributed such an importance to the apprehension of an unapprehended object. It is enough to follow their awkward attempts to safeguard the validity of continuous cognitions (some relevant material is summarized by Bhatt, ibid., pp. 75f.), i.e., several successive cognitions of the same object, in order to understand that the Mīmāṃsakas were not worried about assembling new information all the time. By following the structure of their arguments, one can easily observe that the main, and perhaps only purpose of the qualification *anadhigatārthagantṛ* was to exclude recollection from the realm of the *pramāṇas*. And this point is common to the Bhāṭṭa- as well as the Prābhākara-Mīmāṃsakas, although the latter do not accept this qualification. We saw (in ŚV 5.11) that Kumārila takes the trouble to add the clarification *smṛtir anyathā* to the definition of *pramāṇa*; in the same manner Prabhākara emphasizes that his definition of *pramāṇa* does not apply to recollection: *pramāṇam anubhūtiḥ, sā smṛter anyā* (cf. *PP* p. 124.9-10 = Ch. ed. p. 42.15-16).

The Mīmāṃsakas' insistence on rejecting recollection from the realm of means of valid cognition is by no means unique among the Indian philosophical schools - the only exception being the Jainas (cf. Sanghavi, *Advanced Studies in Indian Logic and Metaphysics*, pp. 44-45), but nevertheless I feel that this point is more strongly emphasized by them than by other schools. The Naiyāyikas, for instance, who did not accord validity to recollection, abandoned this definition of *pramāṇa* because of the continuous cognitions (cf. Bhatt, ibid., p. 81).

It seems to me, therefore, that the Mīmāṃsā's insistence on this point comes from an issue which was of special concern for this school, namely, the distinction between Śruti and Smṛti. The Mīmāṃsakas probably felt that the admission of *smṛti* among the *pramāṇas* would upset the established relation and hierarchy of these two kinds of works, and would provide the Smṛti works with an authority independent of the Veda.

136 The arguments here repeat those advanced against Prabhākara's theory of error, cf. § c.

137 This maxim is the equivalent of 'to fall from the frying pan into the fire.' It does not appear in the collections of Jacob and Apte, but it is quoted and explained in the *Anekāntajayapatākā* (p. 56): (*sva.vyā.*) *so 'yaṃ gaḍupraveśe 'kṣitārakāvinirgamanyāyaḥ. prastutadoṣaparihāreṇādhikataradoṣāntarāpattir ity arthaḥ.* "This is the maxim of the going out of the pupil of the eye when the tumor enters. It means that by avoiding the defect in question another greater defect occurs."

Ignorant of the disease and medical treatment referred to in this maxim I am not totally certain what actually happens. The *Vivaraṇa* ad loc., offers the following explanation: *kasyacid akṣisamīpe tathāvidhabādhāvidhāyakaṃ gaḍūtpannam. tataś ca kenacid bhiṣajā tathāvidhauṣadhaprayogena tathopacaritaṃ yathākṣimadhye tat praviveśa. praviṣṭe ca tatrākṣiṇi tatkṣaṇād eva tadutpāṭitā kanīnikākṣitā-*

ri(ra?)kā bahir nirjagāmeti prastutadṛṣṭāntārthaḥ. "Near the eye of a certain person a tumor had arisen causing him pain accordingly. And therefore he was treated by a certain physician by means of the appropriate medicine in such a way that it (i.e., the tumor) entered [right in] the middle of the eye. And immediately after [it] had entered there, [i.e.] into the eye, the small one, [i.e.] the pupil of the eye, was uprooted by it. This is the meaning of the example in question."

138 These and two more examples of recollection appear also in *NBhū* 136.15-16. I could not trace their origin.

139 Śabara defines inference as follows (*ŚBh* p. 30.18-19): *anumānaṃ jñātasambandhasyaikadeśadarśanād ekadeśāntare 'sannikṛṣṭe 'rthe buddhiḥ*. "Inference is the cognition based on seeing one part with regard to the other part, [i.e.] the object which is not in contact [with the senses], for someone who knows the connection [between the two parts]."

According to this definition inference seems to be the recollection of an object which was previously perceived as connected with another object. The use of the word 'part' indicates that the two objects and the relation between them were considered as some sort of mental or actual whole; cf. Biardeau, *Théorie de la Connaissance*, p. 97: "C'est la relation elle-même qui est connue, qui donc a été perçue, et les termes n'en sont que des 'parties' - *ekadeśa* - ; l'inférence est donc en somme la reconstitution d'un tout primitivement perçu, grâce à la perception actuelle d'une partie seulement de ce tout: c'est un souvenir que la perception d'une partie aide à réveiller."

The decisive role played by memory in the inferential process is quite obvious, and it seems that inference does not provide any new knowledge, but only a recollection of something seen before. Moreover, even in cases when one infers something not seen before, for instance the movement of the sun from the fact that it has changed its place, Śabara employs the word 'remembering' (*smaraṇa*) where one would expect 'inferring,' cf. *ŚBh* p. 32.1-2: *yathā devadattasya gatipūrvikāṃ deśāntaraprāptim upalabhyāditye 'pi gatismaraṇam.*

Kumārila does not comment directly on the word *smaraṇa*, but he abolishes the distinction between *pratyakṣato dṛṣṭasambandhaḥ* and *sāmānyato dṛṣṭasambandhaḥ*, and maintains that all inferences are based on a perceived relation (cf. ŚV *anumāna* 138f.). Thus, it follows that all the different elements of inference, namely, the two terms, the relation between them, as well as the subject of inference (e.g., the mountain), were previously perceived; cf. ŚV *anumāna* 28:

na dharmamātraṃ siddhatvāt, tathā dharmī, tathobhayam/
vyastaṃ vāpi samastaṃ vā svātantryeṇānumīyate//.

What could be, therefore, the new knowledge which inference as a means of valid cognition must provide per definitionem?

Kumārila's answer is that the only thing that could at all be the object of inference (*anumeya*) is the property-possessor as qualified by a part of the connection as its property (ibid., 27ab: *ekadeśaviśiṣṭaś ca dharmy evātrānumīyate/*). This is, of course, a considerable modification of Śabara's definition. The most important difference is perhaps the addition of the property-possessor or the whole (*avayavin*). Thus, the two-term relation becomes a three-term relation. The third term, viz., the *dharmin*, was obviously not mentioned by Śabara, but according to Kumārila it is employed implicitly by Śabara because he talks of two parts, which Kumārila interprets as properties (ibid., 23cd): *upāttaś caikadeśābhyāṃ dharmy apy atraikadeśavān* (according to the ŚVV-recension: *dharmābhyām ekadeśavān*)//. He does not give any further information as to how the whole should be incorporated into Śabara's definition, and the issue is further complicated when one considers that he gives no less than four different interpretations of the compound *jñātasambandhasya* (cf. *NR* p. 251.23-25 on 24cd; the four interpretations are explained by Bhatt, op. cit., pp. 207-9). According to Umbeka (*ŚVV* p. 310.25) one has to read: *ekadeśiny ekadeśadarśanād, ekadeśāntare 'sannikṛṣṭe 'rthe buddhiḥ*. Pārthasārathimiśra, on the other hand, seems to consider the property-possessor as the object of inference, or the whole, to be referred to by the word *asannikṛṣṭe*, cf. *NR* p. 252.1: *pakṣadharmiṇo 'numeyatvam asannikṛṣṭagrahaṇena bhāṣye darśitam*.

Kumārila's theory deserves, no doubt, a more detailed exposé, but this would be useless for our purpose here, for it is already clear enough that there is a certain discrepancy between the theory in the *ŚV* and the one which is reflected in the *TUS*. Only when we look at the most general features a relation between the two texts can be established, for Jayarāśi quotes a verse which appears in the *ŚV*, and the problem of apprehension of an unapprehended object is one of the main topics of the *anumānavāda*. However, the details do not match. Among the six *vikalpas* raised by Jayarāśi, only one might be traced back to the *ŚV*, namely, the possession (*matup*, *matvartha*), i.e., that which is expressed by the suffix *-mant* (as in *parvato vahnimān*); and even that is not expressly the *siddhānta* opinion, but rather a presupposition of the qualification of the *dharmin* by the *dharma*, just as the word 'staff-bearer' presupposes a relation of possession between the person holding the staff and the staff (cf. *ŚV anumāna* 32cd-33).

It seems, therefore, quite certain that Jayarāśi does not refer to the *ŚV* here, and as he quotes elsewhere from the *Bṛhaṭṭīkā* (cf. *TUS* p. 116.9-10), we may assume that here, too, he refers to this lost text. The fact that the half-verse quoted at the end of this chapter appears in *ŚV*

4.234 does not invalidate this assumption, for we know that the *Bṛhaṭṭīkā* is a later and more extensive treatise which incorporates material from the ŚV, sometimes without any change. Furthermore, Frauwallner has already pointed out that Kumārila, in the *Bṛhaṭṭīkā*, had changed his theory of *vyāpti* under Dharmakīrti's influence (cf. "Kumārila's Bṛhaṭṭīkā," pp. 89-90 = Kl. Schr. pp. 334-35). The discussion in the *TUS* indicates that he has changed his theory of *anumeya* as well.

Unfortunately, nothing certain can be deduced from the laconic discussion in the *TUS*. However, as a supposition we may suggest the following: The object of inference in the *Bṛhaṭṭīkā* is not the property-possessor as qualified by a property, but the property itself, or in other words, it is not the mountain as qualified by the property 'fire,' but the universal 'fire'; and probably not just the universal 'fire' as such, but with some qualification such as to be dependent on the *liṅga* (*liṅgopasarjanatva*) and/or to exist at the same time as the operation of the *liṅga* (*liṅgavyāpārasamānakālāstitva*). Furthermore, after the inference, and before the practical conclusion 'There is fire on the mountain,' another means of valid cognition seems to intervene, namely, implication, or negative evidence (*arthāpatti*), by virtue of which the transition from the universal 'fire' to an individual fire is accomplished. No further information on this *arthāpatti* is provided here, but while considering the six types of *arthāpatti* Jayarāśi gives an example of *arthāpatti* based on inference, which could be just the one he has in mind here (*TUS* p. 109.23-24): *tathā, anumānapūrvikā - anumānād agnitvapratipattyanyathānupapattyāgnivyaktipratipattiḥ*. "In the same manner, [there is an implication] preceded by inference: [it consists in] the apprehension of the individual fire by the fact that the apprehension of the universal 'fire' by inference would be impossible otherwise." Cf. also *SVR* p. 262.23-24: *atha sāmānyasya vyaktiṃ vinānupapatteḥ pratīte tasminn anyathānupapat-*

tyā vyaktipratiter niyamena pravṛttir ity ucyate. "As the universal is not possible without an individual, when the [universal] has been apprehended one proceeds [into a] certain [direction] because of the cognition of the individual by the fact that [the universal] would not be possible otherwise." Cf. also *NBhū* p. 217.23f.

It seems reasonable that the sixth alternative (*agnivyaktipāratantryam*) points in the same direction. As for the expression *agnisvarūpa*, I do not think that Kumārila may have used it to denote anything other than the universal, and it is understandable in the context of the theory which claims that the universal and the individual have the same nature.

In epistemological questions which do not affect the validity of his theory of sacrifice it is typical for Kumārila to enumerate several possibilities which he considers equally acceptable. Thus, it is not impossible that all six *vikalpas* of Jayarāśi appeared in the *Bṛhaṭṭīkā*. Note, however, that Jayarāśi was acquainted with at least one commentary on this text (cf. *TUS* p. 116.1f.: *kumatimatānusāriṇo vadanti ...*) which may have been the source for some of the *vikalpas*.

Jayarāśi's criticism of Kumārila is quite simple and monotonous: Whatever the object of inference may be, either it was previously perceived as related to the inferential sign and thus its apprehension is that of an apprehended object, or it was not previously perceived and therefore cannot be inferred from the inferential sign.

This criticism seems closely connected with a famous Lokāyata verse, the purport of which seems to be that there is no concomitance between the object of inference and the *liṅga*, if the former is an individual, and if it is a universal, then what has to be proved is already proved (Jayarāśi gives different interpretations of it, cf. below). There are many variants to this fragment, which cannot be accounted for as different readings of the same verse. It seems that different Lokāyatikas have used it rather freely, especially the second half-verse. Mahendrakumar Jain (*NKC* p. 69, n. 5) assembled a number of quotations:

NKC p. 69.8-9, *NM* I p. 313.11-12 (Kashi p. 108.21-22):

viśeṣe 'nugamābhāvāt sāmānye siddhasādhanāt/
tadvato 'nupapannatvād anumānakathā kutaḥ//,

PP p. 206.1 = Ch. ed. p. 71.21:

viśeṣe 'nugamābhāvaḥ sāmānye siddhasādhyatā/,

PKM p. 177.16 (= Nirnayasagar ed. p. 45b), *TBV* p. 554.7:

viśeṣe 'nugamābhāvaḥ sāmānye siddhasādhanam/.

In both editions of the *PKM* the editors complete the verse with

nānumānaṃ pramāṇaṃ syān niścayābhāvatas tataḥ//,

but give no reference to their sources.

ŚD p. 115.12-13 (= Vidyavilasa Press ed. p. 63):

viśeṣe 'nugamābhāvaḥ sāmānye siddhasādhyatā/
anumānabhaṅgapaṅke 'smin nimagnā vādidantinaḥ//,

Bṛhadāraṇyakopaniṣadbhāṣyavārttika (Ānandāśrama ed.) p. 1401. v. 144:

viśeṣe 'nugamābhāvaḥ sāmānye siddhasādhyatā/
ityādidoṣaduṣṭatvān na ca no 'numitiḥ pramā//.

To these we may add *ŚVK* III p. 26.9-10 (= *ŚD*, but in reversed order), *PVṬ* p. 26.15 (= *PKM* and *TBV*) and *NMGBh* p. 63.1 (quotes the second *pāda* of the *NM*-version).

Mahendrakumar, who could use only the manuscript of the *TUS*, says that on folio 88 Jayarāśi quotes *viśeṣe 'nugamābhāvaḥ sāmānye siddhasādhanam*. Unfortunately, the microfilm in my possession does not contain folio 88. In any case, it does not appear in the printed edition. However, I was able to find the following quotations: *TUS* pp. 72.16, 82.17, 89.6: *sāmānye siddhasādhyatā*; *TUS* pp. 73.1, 82.12, 89.8: *viśeṣe 'nugamābhāvaḥ*. Of these passages, the most relevant to the present discussion are those contained in the section criticizing the Mīmāṃsā inference of the

Self, *TUS* pp. 82.7-83.7: *tathā mīmāṃsakamatenāpy ātmānumānaṃ na pravartate pramāṇāntarānavadhāritārthaviṣayatvābhyupagamāt pramāṇānām. niyataviṣayāṇi hi pramāṇāni pratipadyante - pratyakṣāvaseye nānumānaṃ pravartata, anumānāvaseye ca na pratyakṣaṃ pravartate. tataś cetaretaravyāvṛttiviśeṣaviṣayāṇi. tad ayuktaṃ* (read: *uktaṃ*) *"viśeṣe 'nugamābhāvaḥ." viśeṣo niyatapramāṇagrāhyo 'rthaḥ. tathābhūte 'rthe 'ṅgīkriyamāṇe 'numānasyānugamābhāvaḥ. anugamaḥ sambandhas, tadgrahaṇānupapattiḥ. arthe* (read: *atha*) *pratyakṣādyavadhārite 'py 'rthe 'numānaṃ pravartate; nanv evaṃ pratyakṣānumānasādhāraṇo 'rthaḥ prasaktaḥ. sādhāraṇatā samānatā. "sāmānye siddhasādhyatā" pratyakṣāvagatatvāt. anadhigatārthagantṛviśeṣaṇaṃ cāpārthakam. athavā sāmānye siddhe sādhanam ity anyo 'rthaḥ. sāmānyayor gamyagamakabhāvo 'bhyupagamyate mīmāṃsakena. na ca tat sāmānyaṃ vidyate. yathā ca na vidyate tathā prāg evoditam. tataś ca siddhasya sādhanaṃ vidyamānasya sādhanam. na cāgnitvam asti. tadabhāve kasyedaṃ jñāpakam? athavā siddhaṃ sādhanaṃ siddhasādhanam ity anyo 'rthaḥ. vidyamānaṃ sādhanam. na ca dhūmatvasāmānyam asti. tac ca vidyamānaṃ* (Sukhlal: *tat tv a-*; read: *tac cāvidyamānaṃ*) *sāmānyaṃ kathaṃ sāmānyaṃ* (read: *sāmānye*) *sādhanaṃ bhavitum arhati? athavā siddhasādhanaṃ jñātam anumānaṃ sādhanaṃ bhavati. na ca dhūmatvaṃ jñātaṃ svayamasattvāt, athavā grahaṇopāyābhāvāt, tasyānusyūtaṃ rūpam. na ca tad ātmany anusyūtam. nāpy ekasyāṃ vyaktāv, api tu bahvīṣu vyaktiṣu. na ca bahvyo vyaktaya upalabhyante. api tv ekaiva dhūmavyaktir upalabhate. na caikasyāṃ vyaktāv anugatātmatayā sāmānyasaṃvittir asti. na cākārāntarasāmānyam* (perhaps: *ākārāntaraṃ sāmānyasya*).

This passage is highly problematic; it seems to contain several lacunae and corruptions. Jayarāśi seems to have known both readings, *siddhasādhanam* and *siddhasādhyatā*, but I cannot explain the sudden switch from the one to the other (cf. the similar switch in *TUS* p. 72.20-21). I shall nevertheless offer a tentative translation of the passage to give the reader some idea about its content.

"In the same manner, according to the doctrine of the Mīmāṃsakas, too, the inference of the Self does not work, because [they] claim that means of valid cognition have for their objects things which are not determined by other means of valid cognition. For the means of valid cognition are considered as having their respective objects: inference does not operate on [an object] to be determined by perception, and perception does not operate on [an object] to be determined by inference. And thus, [means of valid cognition] have as objects special [objects] which are mutually exclusive. (Perhaps a lacuna here.) This has been said: 'In the case of a special [object of perception and inference respectively] there is no concomitance.' Special [object means] an object which can [only] be apprehended by [its] respective means of valid cognition. When such an object is adopted [as object of a means of valid cognition], inference lacks concomitance: concomitance is a relation; the apprehension of this [relation by inference] is impossible.

If [on the other hand] inference operates on an object even though it has been determined by perception etc., surely the object would be common to perception and inference. To be common [means] to be universal. 'In the case of commonness [of the object to perception and inference] what has to be proved is [already] proved,' because it has been [previously] apprehended by perception. And [thus] the qualification 'agent of apprehension of an unapprehended object' is not appropriate. (Probably a lacuna here in which Jayarāśi must have explained the words *viśeṣa* and *sāmānya* in a different meaning, namely, as particular and universal, and interpreted the verse according to these meanings.)

Or [the second part has] a different meaning: If the universal were established [inference would be] a means of proof. It is admitted by the Mīmāṃsaka[s] that the relation between what makes known and what has to be made known [obtains] between two universals. But the universal does not exist. And why it does not exist, has been explained above [in § a.]. And thus, proving what is established [means] proving [something] existing. But [the universal] 'fire' does not exist. When the [universal 'fire'] does not exist, what does this [means of proof] make known?

Or [the second part has] another meaning: *siddhasādhanam* [means] a means of proof which is [itself] established, [that is] an existing means of proof. But the universal 'smoke' does not exist. And how can this universal in as much as it does not exist be a means of proof for [another] universal?

Or a means of proof which is [itself] established [means that] inference (i.e., the inferential sign) becomes a means of proof [only] in as much as it is cognized. But [the universal] 'smoke' is not cognized, because it does not exist itself.

Or (probably a lacuna here) [even if the universal 'smoke' exists it cannot become a means of proof because it is not apprehended, and it is not apprehended] because there is no means of apprehending [it]. [For] the [universal] has a recurrent form. And this [form] is not recurrent in itself, nor in a single individual, but in many individuals. However, many individuals are not apprehended [at the time of inference], but only one individual smoke is apprehended. And in respect to a single individual there is no cognition of the universal as having a recurrent nature. And the universal does not have another form (i.e., a non-recurrent form by virtue of which it could be apprehended in a single individual)."

140 By 'nature of fire' (*pāvakasvarūpa*) Jayarāśi probably means fire as such, without any accidental properties,

i.e., not fire fed by grass (*tārṇa*), by cow-dung (*kārīṣa*), by leaves (*pārṇa*), by chaff (*tauṣa*), etc.

[141] The expression *liṅgājahadvṛtti* is not very common, but certainly not unique; cf. for instance Vy p. 564.5: *anumeyo hi liṅgaṃ na jahātīti*.

[142] On *matvartha* cf. ŚV *anumāna* 32cd-33, and n. 139. Cf. also ŚVV p. 307.20-24: *vyāpakaṃ gamyam iṣyata ity uktam. tad anupapannam. dharmidvayānavacchinnasya hi tasya gamyatvaṃ syāt, sādhyadharmāvacchinnasya vā. tatra dharmidvayānavacchinnapakṣe 'gnimātrasya sādhyatāyāṃ siddhasādhyatā. sādhyadharmāvacchinnapakṣe 'pi parvataviśiṣṭasya sādhyatāyāṃ hetor anugamābhāvaḥ. na hi yatra yatra dhūmas tatra tatra parvatāvacchinno 'gnir iti.*

"It has been said [in verse 4d] that the pervader is accepted as that which is to be made known [by inference]. [But] this is impossible. For either a [pervader] which is not delimited by both property-possessors (i.e., the *pakṣa* and *sapakṣa*) could be made known, or [a pervader] which is delimited by the property which has to be proved (i.e., being qualified by the *pakṣa*). In respect to these [alternatives], if the position [is opted for that a pervader] which is not delimited by the two property-possessors [is that which has to be made known, i.e.], if fire as such has to be proved, [then] what has to be proved is [already] proved. Similarly, if the position [is opted for that a pervader] delimited by the property which has to be proved [is that which has to be made known, i.e.], if [fire] qualified by the mountain has to be proved, [then] the reason lacks concomitance. For it is not the case that wherever there is smoke there is fire delimited by a mountain."

[143] The word *liṅga* may be used here in the sense of *anumā-*

na; this usage has already been noted by Steinkellner, cf. *PVin* II(2), Register (*liṅga*).

[144] This *vikalpa* seems strange, for universals are supposed to be eternal, and therefore it would be useless to infer their existence at a certain time. Could it be that universals were not considered eternal by Kumārila or one of his followers? One could argue that a theory which claims that the universal and the individual have the same nature implies something of that sort (cf. n. 27).

An object could be conceived as being partly individual and partly universal, or as having the nature of both. Thus, as universals were not hypostatized in such a high degree as in Nyāya-Vaiśeṣika, a Mīmāṃsaka could hold that when an object is produced or destroyed the universal part, the one which it has in common with other individuals of the same class, is produced or destroyed with it, though it continues to exist in, or better, as part of, other individuals of the same class. Cf. *ŚD* p. 207.12-208.2: *nanu anuvṛttā nityānutpattivināśadharmā ca jātir, viparītasvabhāvā ca vyaktiḥ, kathaṃ tayor aikyam? na hy ekam eva vastu anuvṛttaṃ vyāvṛttaṃ nityam anityam utpattivināśadharmam ataddharmakaṃ ca sambhavati, trailokyasaṅkaraprasaṅgāt. jātir apy evam anityatvādidharmā syād, vyaktir api nityatvādidharmā. naiṣa doṣo - nānākāraṃ hi tad vastu kenacid ākāreṇa nityatvādikaṃ, kenacic cānityatvādikaṃ bibhran na virotsyate. jātir api vyaktirūpeṇānityā, vyaktir api jātyātmanā nityeti nātra kācid aniṣṭāpattiḥ.*

"[Objection:] The universal is recurrent, eternal, and not subject to production and destruction, whereas the individual has the opposite nature. How could there be unity of these two? For one and the same thing cannot be recurrent and exclusive (or: non-recurrent), eternal and non-eternal, subject to production and destruction and not subject to them, for [otherwise] the three worlds would be mixed up. Not only would the universal have the properties of being non-eternal etc., in this manner (i.e., by assuming identity of the universal and the individual), [but] also the individual would have the properties of being eternal etc.

[Answer:] This is no fault. For in as much as this thing has many forms, it is bearing by a certain form [the properties] to be eternal etc., and by a certain [other form the properties of] being non-eternal etc.; [thus, our theory] is not contradictory at all. Not only is the universal, in the form of an individual, not eternal, [but] also the individual, with the nature of the universal, eternal. Thus, nothing unacceptable results in this [theory]."

[145] Cf. however *ŚVV* p. 314.16f.

[146] Śabara does not define verbal communication in general as a means of valid cognition, but only scripture (*ŚBh* p. 32.3): *śāstraṃ śabdavijñānād asannikṛṣṭe 'rthe vijñānam.* "Scripture is the cognition of an object not in contact [with the senses] from the cognition of words."

The Vedic words and sentences have no human author (*apauruṣeya*), that is, no author at all, and the relations between them and their objects are eternal (cf. *ŚBh* p. 42.16-19). Śabara considers the object of a word not as a universal but as a specific form (*ākṛti*); cf. *ŚBh* p. 40.13-14: *atha gaur ity asya śabdasya ko 'rthaḥ? sāsnādiviśiṣṭākṛtir iti brūmaḥ.* "When [one says] 'cow,' what is the object of this word? We say: It is the form qualified by a dewlap etc." (cf. also *MS* 1.3.33).

Note that *ākṛti* in early Mīmāṃsā writings was considered eternal, not being destroyed when its substrata are destroyed (cf. Frauwallner, "Sprachtheorie und Philosophie im Mahābhāṣyam des Patañjali," Anhang). However, in Kumārila's time this notion of *ākṛti* may have become obsolete because of the influence of the Nyāya (cf. *NS* 2.2.65 and

NBh ad loc., cf. also *NS* 2.2.63) which considered the *ākṛti* as the specific arrangement of the parts and the parts of the parts of existing things. Kumārila had, therefore, good reasons to modify the Mīmāṃsā theory, and he did that by identifying the form with the universal; cf. *ŚV ākṛti* 3ab: *jātim evākṛtiṃ prāhur vyaktir ākriyate yayā/*, cf. also ibid., 18cd.

Although the relations between words and objects are eternal and natural, they are also to some extent conventional, for the usage of a word has to be learnt; cf. *ŚBh* p. 36.17-18: *yāvatkṛtvaḥ śrutena 'iyaṃ sañjñā, ayaṃ sañjñi' ity avadhāritaṃ bhavati, tāvatkṛtvaḥ śrutād arthāvagamaḥ.* "The apprehension of the meaning by hearing arises after as many times [as needed] to determine by hearing 'This is the denomination, this is the denominated.'" This process can be observed with children watching and hearing their elders, cf. *ŚBh* p. 46.2-5: *vṛddhānāṃ svārthena vyavaharamānānām upaśṛṇvanto bālāḥ pratyakṣam arthaṃ pratipadyamānā dṛśyante. te 'pi vṛddhā yadā bālā āsaṃs, tadā 'nyebhyo vṛddhebhyas, te 'py anyebhya iti nāsty ādir iti.* "Children are observed to apprehend an object present before their eyes, while listening to [their] elders conversing among themselves and for their own sake (Frauwallner, however: '(die Wörter) für ihren Gegenstand gebrauchen'). These elders, too, when they were children, [learnt it] from other elders, and they, too, from others; thus, there is no beginning."

Jayarāśi's arguments against the validity of the apprehension of objects by words are basically the same as those against inference: if the relation between word and object has been apprehended before, then either the apprehension of the object at the present is not valid (as its apprehension is included in the apprehension of the relation), or one has to give up the qualification *anadhigatārthagantṛ*. If it has not been apprehended before, one cannot apprehend the object by a word.

[147] This objection is not clear to me, for it does not seem to add anything new to the alternatives presented above except the emphasis by *eva*. Perhaps the opponent means that although the meaning of the words has been apprehended before, the sentence as a whole conveys a new meaning. In that case Jayarāśi's answer would be that the apprehension of the sentence which the single words bring about is not valid either since the apprehension of the single word is not valid. On the Mīmāṃsā theory of the meaning of the sentence cf. Raja, *Indian Theories of Meaning*, pp. 151f., D'Sa, *Śabdaprāmāṇyam in Śabara and Kumārila*, pp. 166f.

[148] Cf. n. 139.

[149] On *arthāpatti* in general cf. Bhatt, *Epistemology of Bhāṭṭa School*, ch. 9; on this particular *arthāpatti*, namely, the apprehension of the individual as the locus of the universal based on the fact that otherwise the apprehension of the universal would be impossible, cf. n. 139.

[150] This half-verse corresponds to ŚV 4.234ab. However, I claimed above (n. 139) that it is more probable to assume that its source is the *Bṛhaṭṭīkā*. The fact that it appears in another work of Kumārila besides the ŚV is corroborated by the following quotation in the *PVṬ* (p. 94.17-22): *tad āha bhaṭṭaḥ* -

> *nityaṃ sadṛśa eveti yatra rūḍhā matir bhavet/*
> *sa iti pratyabhijñānaṃ bhrāntis tatrāvakalpate//*
> *iha nityaṃ sa eveti vijñānaṃ jāyate dṛḍham/*
> *tadastitvātirekāc ca prāmāṇyaṃ tasya yujyate//*
> *deśakālādibhedena tatrāsty avasaro mitaḥ/*
> *idānīntanam astitvaṃ na hi pūrvadhiyo(yā) gatam//*

As it stands, this quotation contains the verse ŚV *śabdanityatādhikaraṇa* 373, a modified version of ibid., v.

374, half a verse which appears nowhere in the ŚV (which is actually a modification of 4.233ab), and the half-verse 4. 234ab. It is therefore improbable that this quotation has the ŚV as its source. Note also that in the same context (p. 87) Karṇakagomin quotes eight verses from the *Bṛhaṭṭīkā*; cf. also *NMGBh* p. 10.18. For further quotations of *idānīntanam astitvam* ... cf. *TS* v. 452ab, *PKM* p. 339.14, *NKC* p. 698.9, *SVR* p. 675.19-20, *TBV* p. 319.17. Cf. also *NM* I p. 59.1-2.

[151] Recognition is considered as perception because it has positive and negative concomitance (*anvayavyatireka*) with the senses, just like in the case of other perceptions. The fact that it is necessarily preceded by recollection does not invalidate its nature of perception, because it is produced by a contact of the senses with the object; cf. ŚV 4.236f.; cf. also Bhatt, ibid., p. 84.

[152] The Buddhists, like the Mīmāṃsakas, define a means of valid cognition as agent of apprehension of an unapprehended object (*anadhigatārthagantṛ*). As far as I know, this definition was introduced for the first time by Dharmakīrti (for Dignāga's position cf. n. 156); cf. *PV pramāṇa* 7c and PVV ad loc., p. 8.6-11:
ajñātārthaprakāśo vā;
tad evam avisaṃvādanaṃ pramāṇalakṣaṇam uktam. idānīm anyad āha (ajñātetyādi). prakāśanaṃ prakāśo, 'jñātasyārthasya prakāśo jñānaṃ, tat pramāṇam. arthagrahaṇena dvicandrādijñānasya nirāsaḥ. ajñātagrahaṇena sāṃvṛtasyāvayavyādiviṣayasya pṛthaggṛhītānām eva rūpādīnam ekatvena vikalpanāt. smaraṇaṃ ca pūrvagṛhītārthavikalparūpatvān nādhikagrāhi. gṛhīte ca prāktanam eva pramāṇam. idānīṃ tu smaraṇam apravartakaṃ, tasyaiva sandehāt.

"Or [a means of valid cognition is] a light on an unapprehended object.

So far the definition of a means of valid cognition as [a cognition] which does not belie [its promise] has been explained. Now [Dharmakīrti] teaches another [definition: a light on an unapprehended object]. Light [means] illuminating (i.e., making known). The cognition which illuminates an unapprehended object is a means of valid cognition. By using [the word] 'object/thing' the [illusory] cognition of the double moon etc., is excluded [from the realm of the definition of means of valid cognition]. By using [the word] 'unapprehended,' [the cognition] relating to empirical reality, which has the whole etc., for [its] object [is excluded]. [It is excluded] because it conceptualizes as a unity the visible etc., which are already apprehended separately. As for recollection, it does not apprehend [anything] beyond [the previously apprehended object of perception] because it consists in a conceptualization of an object which has been apprehended before. And in respect to the [previously] apprehended [object], already the previous [cognition] is the means of valid cognition. At the present, on the other hand, recollection does not induce to act, because there is a doubt precisely in respect to it (i.e., as to whether the previously apprehended object still exists)."

The other commentators do not deviate from this interpretation in any significant way. However, they differ rather strongly in their interpretation of the relation between this definition and the one which qualifies a means of valid cognition as a cognition which does not belie its promise (*avisaṃvādi jñānam*, cf. § 3.2). The most faithful to Dharmakīrti's intention seems to be Prajñākaragupta's interpretation, according to which these two definitions are independent of each other. However, this interpretation, which seems to follow Dharmakīrti literally, is problematic, for if one takes the definition as an independent definition of *pramāṇa*, it would be too wide, since it would include false cognitions the objects of which appear for the first time (cf. *PVBh* p. 30.7-8: *nanu yady avisaṃvādanam antareṇājñātaprakāśanaṃ pramāṇaṃ, dvicandrādyākārasyāpi pramāṇatāprasaṅgaḥ*). In order to solve this problem Prajñākaragupta proposes two interpretations of the word *artha* (in the compound *ajñātārthaprakāśa*). According to the first, *artha* means something real, whereas the object of false cognitions is not real (ibid., p. 30.8: *arthagrahaṇād, asau (i.e., dvicandrādyākāro) hi nārthaḥ*). According to the second, *artha* means absolute reality (ibid., p. 30.19: *athavārthaśabdenātra paramārtha ucyate. ajñātārthaprakāśa iti paramārthaprakāśa ity arthaḥ*).

Dharmottara, who was probably faced with the same problem, opted for a different solution altogether. According to him the second definition (i.e., *ajñātārthaprakāśa*) is derived or deduced from the first (i.e., *avisaṃvādi jñānam*): a cognition which does not belie its promise is a cognition which **can** make you obtain its object. This is the reason why the result of a means of valid cognition is nothing but the apprehension of the object, and not its actual obtainment (*NBṬ* p. 19.1: *arthādhigatir eva pramāṇaphalam*; cf. also *DhPr* ad loc., and Stcherbatsky, *Buddhist Logic* II, p. 4, nn. 2 and 3). Consequently, the second cognition of an object is not *pramāṇa*, because the capacity to obtain the object is already produced by the first cognition, and it is not something which can be reproduced by the second cognition (cf. *NBṬ* p. 19.2-3: *arthādhigamāt samāptaṃ pramāṇavyāpāraḥ. ata eva cānadhigataviṣayaṃ pramāṇam*).

Finally, Manorathanandin points out that none of these definitions, taken separately, is satisfactory, and concludes that they depend on and complete one another (cf. *PVV* p. 8.19: *tasmād ubhayam api parasparāpekṣam eva lakṣaṇaṃ boddhavyam*).

As for the expression *anadhigatārthagantṛ*, it is used, as far as I know, neither by Dharmakīrti nor by Dignāga; it appears, however, in *PSṬ* (Derge ed.) 17a.5 quoted by Hattori, *Dignāga, On Perception*, p. 82, n. 1.24. For further references cf. Mimaki, *La Réfutation Bouddhique de la Permanence des Choses*, p. 284, n. 303.

[153] According to the Buddhists the particular (*svalakṣaṇa*) and the universal (*sāmānyalakṣaṇa*) are mutually exclusive and constitute the entire realm of objects of valid cognition (*prameya*); cf. *PS* pp. 176.6/177.7: *raṅ daṅ spyiḥi mtshan ñid dag las gṣan paḥi mtshan ñid gṣal bar bya ba gṣan ni med do.* (= *na hi svasāmānyalakṣaṇābhyām* **anyal lakṣaṇam** (!) *anyat prameyam asti*). "There is no other characteristic than the specific and the general (or: particular and universal) characteristic [which could serve] as a further object of valid cognition."

Even in the *Pramāṇasamuccaya*, his most elaborate treatise, Dignāga has little to say about *svalakṣaṇa*: it is real (the universal is not), it is apprehended by perception (the universal by inference), and it is not expressible by a word (the universal is nothing but a concept). This is more or less all. Considering this fact, Hayes ("Diṅnāga's Views on Reasoning," p. 244) suggested that Dignāga's view of the nature of the particular "does not deviate significantly from what might be called a commonsense view; a particular for him is essentially just a thing that is numerically different from other things."

It is not entirely clear to me whether Hayes means that this meaning of particular corresponds to our 'commonsense view,' or to the commonsense view of Dignāga and his contemporaries, or perhaps both. In any case, that Dignāga uses the word *svalakṣaṇa* in this meaning is still to be proved. At the present state of our knowledge it would be more reasonable to assume that Dignāga borrowed the term from the Abhidharma literature, the more so as he wrote a commentary on the AK. And this does not mean, of course, that he did not modify its meaning *en route*.

As a matter of fact, Vasubandhu (*AKBh* on I.10d) uses the term *svalakṣaṇaviṣaya*, as opposed to *sāmānyaviṣaya*, to designate the own special realm of a cognition which consists in one *āyatana*. The *pūrvapakṣin* argues that if a visual cognition has a complex object, such as an army, several colours, or a heap of diamonds, it would be *sāmānyaviṣaya*, a term which seems to mean here either a cognition the object of which consists of several things which have something in common, or perhaps (this seems to be Yaśomitra's interpretation) a cognition the object of which is general, non-specific (roughly synonym to *aniyataviṣaya*). In reply Vasubandhu explains that for the cognition to have its own realm does not mean to have a single thing as its object, but rather to be restricted to one *āyatana*; cf. *AKBh* p. 7.22-24: *nanu caivaṃ samastālambanatvāt sāmānyaviṣayāḥ pañca vijñānakāyāḥ prāpnuvanti, na svalakṣaṇaviṣayāḥ. āyatanasvalakṣaṇaṃ praty ete svalakṣaṇaviṣayā iṣyante, na dravyasvalakṣaṇam ity adoṣaḥ*.

From Yaśomitra's commentary ad loc., it becomes clear that the presupposition of the objection is that only the mental cognition (*manojñāna*) is *sāmānyalakṣaṇaviṣaya*, whereas the visual cognitions etc., are not; cf. AKV p. 36.24f., transl. de la Vallée Poussin p. 19, n. 2.

If Hayes is right that Dignāga uses *svalakṣaṇa* as a particular in the above mentioned meaning of 'commonsense view,' this would seem to be Dignāga's own invention, which resulted perhaps from applying the word used to designate the whole realm of operation of a certain kind of cognition to the constituent parts of this realm. Whatever the case may be, Hayes is right to point out that the term *svalakṣaṇa* changes its meaning with Dharmakīrti, and designates something which exists exactly one moment, which is absolutely different from everything else. It is this particular which Jayarāśi designates as *abhinnaikasvabhāva*.

In *PV pratyakṣa* 1-2 Dharmakīrti enumerates four criteria to differentiate the particular from the universal:

mānaṃ dvividhaṃ viṣayadvaividhyāt (1) *śaktyaśaktitaḥ/*
arthakriyāyāṃ keśādir nārtho 'narthādhimokṣataḥ//
(2) *sadṛśāsadṛśatvāc ca* (3) *viṣayāviṣayatvataḥ/*
śabdasya (4) *anyanimittānāṃ bhāve dhīsadasattvataḥ//*

Namely, (1) the particular is capable of an efficient action, the universal is not, (2) the particular is dissimilar to anything else, the universal is common, (3) the universal is the object of a word, the particular is not, (4) when all other causes except the object are present, the cognition of the universal arises, the cognition of the particular does not arise (this seems to be a roundabout way of saying that the universal does not produce its own cognition, and that the particular does).

154 Cf. the somewhat similar argument of Akalaṅka in *TAV* p. 56.6-7: *kṣaṇe kṣaṇe 'nyatvopapatter apūrvādhigamalakṣaṇam aviśiṣṭam*. "As [the object] arises as different/other at every moment, the definition [of means of valid cognition] as apprehension of a new [object] is not good."

155 For all Hīnayāna schools, with the exception of the Mahāsaṅghika, a series of cognition (*vijñānasantāna*) consists of one single cognition at each moment. For the Yogācāra, on the other hand, several cognitions which belong to the same series can co-exist at the same time, cf. Schmithausen, "Sautrāntika-Voraussetzungen in Viṃśatikā und Triṃśikā," pp. 113-14.

156 According to the first alternative the second cognition of the same object is not valid. This is the usual implication of *anadhigatārthagantṛ*, and needs no further

comment here. The second alternative, however, implies that the second cognition of the same object is indeed valid, but it does not involve any further means of valid cognition. This proposition in its turn may be interpreted in two ways:

(1) The second cognition of the same object does not involve a means of cognition different from the one by which the object was cognized at the first time. This means that one and the same object cannot be cognized by more than one means of cognition. This doctrine, known as *pramāṇavyavasthā*, is indeed held by the Buddhists, but has nothing to do with the principle of *anadhigatārthagantṛ*.

(2) The second cognition of the same object does not involve any further means of cognition besides those already accepted, in the Buddhist case perception and inference; for instance, a cognition of colour as non-eternal, cf. PS I 2c2-d1 (Hattori p. 24). This doctrine, which is called *dvitvāvadhāraṇa* by Jayarāśi, has nothing to do with the principle of *anadhigatārthagantṛ* either.

It is quite clear, therefore, that Jayarāśi mixes different philosophical topics which do not belong together. On the one hand, it is quite certain that Jayarāśi refers to the discussion concerning the number of means of valid cognition at the beginning of the *PS*. But Dignāga does not define the means of valid cognition as *anadhigatārthagantṛ*, though in the Vṛtti at least he seems to take it for granted (cf. PSVṛ pp. 176.26-27/177.26-27: *dper na dran pa daṅ ḥdod pa daṅ ṣe sdaṅ la sogs pa sṅar rtogs paḥi don la tshad ma gṣan ma yin pa bṣin no*. Hattori reconstructs *smṛticchādveṣādivat pūrvādhigataviṣayatvāt*; one would rather expect a locative *pūrvādhigatārthe* and *yathā ... tadvat*, cf. Jambuvijayaji's translation in *DANC*, *Bhoṭapariśiṣṭam*, p. 101.3).

Jayarāśi's interpretation of Dignāga is highly unnatural, and in my opinion not intellegible, unless we consider that he must have read the *PS* with a commentary, such as Jinendrabuddhi's, which twisted Dignāga's intention to conform it to Dharmakīrti's theory. In fact, while commenting on the above passage of Dignāga's, Jinendrabuddhi declares that a cognition which has for its object a previously apprehended thing is not a means of valid cognition (cf. *PSṬ* 20a 4: *gaṅ ltar rtogs zin paḥi don gyi yul can de tshad ma ma yin te dran pa la sogs pa bźin* ... = **yad adhigatārthaviṣayaṃ tan na pramāṇaṃ smṛtyādivat* ...). This change from 'no further means of valid cognition' to 'no means of valid cognition (at all)' does not impute perhaps something which Dignāga would not accept, but it certainly changes the perspective of our discussion, and Jayarāśi's *vikalpa* becomes understandable.

Although Jayarāśi interprets *anadhigatārthagantṛ* in this manner (namely, as *pramāṇāntarābhāva*), he nevertheless seems to be conscious of the fact that he deals with a completely different issue here. It has been noted above that he rarely bothers to explain the positions of his opponents, and is usually content to refer to them laconically in the form of *vikalpas*. However, the intention behind the position of an opponent appears sometimes at the end of the discussion in the form of an objection to be refuted in its turn. Thus, at the end of the discussion of *anadhigatārthagantṛ* according to the Mīmāṃsakas, the opponent objects that if the qualification is not accepted, recollection would become a means of valid cognition. In the same manner, here too one could say that the opponent shows his cards at the end of the discussion when saying that unless this qualification of *pramāṇa* is accepted, a different designation for perception and inference would not be possible. In other words, the opponent here does not defend his position in order to exclude recollection from the means of valid cognition, but to reject the theory of *pramāṇasamplava* (for an explanation of which cf. Stcherbatsky, *Bud. Log.* II, pp. 301f.), and to establish the difference between the *pramāṇas* according to the difference of their objects. And this position corresponds perfectly with Dignāga's.

It may be noted in passing that if it could be established that Jayarāśi must have known the *PSṬ*, Jinendrabuddhi's terminus ante quem may be drawn back by roughly two centuries.

[157] These arguments have already been raised more elaborately in the previous chapter, cf. § 2.1.

[158] The text is obviously corrupt. If Sukhlal's interpretation is accepted, one would have to translate: "Just as several cognitions of Devadatta which arise from the same blue [object] are designated as cognitions of Devadatta etc., because they have different causes and effects, [i.e.] because they have different agents and effects, in the same manner, here too [it is the same]."

[159] This quotation comes from PV *pramāṇa* 3: *pramāṇam avisaṃvādi jñānam, arthakriyāsthitiḥ/ avisaṃvādanam* ... "Means of valid cognition is a cognition which does not belie [its promise]. Not to belie [means] to stand firm in respect to an efficient action."

One should not take *avisaṃvādin* in the strong sense of 'true,' but only in a pragmatical sense, such as it is defined by Dharmakīrti. To designate the absolute correspondence with reality, Dharmakīrti uses the word *abhrānta*. Thus, he can affirm that although an inferential cognition is false, it is nevertheless a valid cognition (*bhrāntir api pramā*, cf. p. 176.2).

The brevity, or even ambiguity, of Dharmakīrti's proposition is probably the reason why the commentators fail to distinguish between two different questions, namely, what a valid cognition is, and how we know that a cognition is valid. Thus, Dharmottara (*NBṬ* pp. 17-19 on 1.1) comments mainly on the first, whereas Prajñākaragupta (*PVBh* p. 4. 3f.) comments mainly on the second. Manorathanandin (*PVV* p. 3.23f., cf. also 6.20-24), on the other hand, follows Kamalaśīla who deviates strongly from Dharmakīrti on this point. For the notion of *arthakriyā* clearly implies a theory of *parataḥ prāmāṇyam*, but Kamalaśīla (*TSP* p. 981.19-21., summarized by Kajiyama, *Introduction to Buddhist Philosophy*, p. 27, n. 19) maintains that the validity of certain cognitions comes from themselves.

No direct relationship can be established between any of these commentators and the different *vikalpas* raised by Jayarāśi. However, with the notable exception of *bādhārahitatva*, they could all be derived from the following passage in the *NBṬ* (pp. 17.1-18.2): *avisaṃvādakaṃ jñānaṃ samyagjñānam. loke ca pūrvam upadarśitam arthaṃ prāpayan saṃvādaka ucyate. tadvaj jñānam api svayaṃ pradarśitam arthaṃ prāpayat saṃvādakam ucyate. pradarśite cārthe pravartakatvam eva prāpakatvaṃ, nānyat. tathā hi - na jñānaṃ janayad arthaṃ prāpayaty, api tv arthe puruṣaṃ pravartayat prāpayaty artham. pravartakatvam api pravṛttiviṣayapradarśakatvam eva. na hi puruṣaṃ haṭhāt pravartayituṃ śaknoti vijñānam.*

"A valid cognition is a cognition which does not belie. For among the people [a person] who makes one obtain a previously indicated object is called 'one who does not belie [his promise].' In the same manner the cognition, too, is said to be not belying in as much as it makes one obtain the object indicated by itself (i.e., by the cognition). And to make obtain [means] only to induce to action towards the object indicated, nothing else. For the cognition does not make one obtain the object in as much as it produces it, but rather makes obtain the object in as much as it induces a person to act towards the object. To induce to action, in its turn, [means] only to indicate the object of action. For the cognition cannot induce a person to act by force."

Cf. also *NM* I p. 61.5f.

160 Vidyānanda's 'summary' of the following passage is of particular interest. It deviates so strongly from the text as we have it, that unless the direct relation could be established from the context, one would not be able to recognize that one text refers to the other. Such a strong deviation cannot be accounted for in terms of variant readings, lacunae, etc; it seems, therefore, that Vidyānanda brings Jayarāśi's arguments up to date, and paraphrases them in his own words. Apparently, in the century or so that separates Vidyānanda from Jayarāśi, Dharmakīrti's theory had become obsolete, and the dominating theory was the one developed, or accepted, by Śāntarakṣita and Kamalaśīla (cf. n. 159), according to which the validity of some cognitions, namely, those which recur frequently, is intrinsic. From Vidyānanda's presentation it even seems that in the final analysis the validity of other, non-repetitive cognitions could only be established by repetitive cognitions confirming their non-belying, and thus avoiding the charge of infinite regress. Cf. AS p. 40.12-21: *nāpy avisaṃvāditvena, tadavisaṃvādasyārthakriyāsthitilakṣaṇasyānavagatasya prāmāṇyavyavasthāhetutvāyogāt. tasyāvagatasya taddhetutve kutas tadavagamasya prāmāṇyam? saṃvādāntarād iti cen na, tadavagamasyāpi saṃvādāntarāt prāmāṇyanirṇaye 'navasthāprasaṅgāt. athārthakriyāsthitilakṣaṇāvisaṃvādajñānasyābhyāsadaśāyāṃ svataḥ prāmāṇyasiddher adoṣaḥ. ko 'yam abhyāso nāma? bhūyaḥ saṃvedane saṃvādānubhavanam iti cet tajjātīye 'tajjātīye vā. tatrātajjātīye na tāvad ekatra saṃvedane bhūyaḥ saṃvādānubhavanaṃ sambhavati kṣaṇikavādinaḥ. santānāpekṣayā sambhavatīti cen na, santānasyāvastutvād apekṣānupapatteḥ. vastutve vā tasyāpi kṣaṇikatvasiddheḥ kutas tadapekṣayā so 'bhyāsaḥ? santānasyākṣaṇikatve vā yat sat tat sarvaṃ kṣaṇikam iti na sidhyet. tajjātīye bhū-*

yaḥ saṃvādānubhavanam iti cen na, jātinirākaraṇavādinaḥ kvacit tajjātīyatvānupapatteḥ. anyāpohalakṣaṇayā jātyā kvacit tajjātīyatvam upapannam eveti cen na, anyāpohasyāvasturūpatvāt, tasya vasturūpatve vā jātitvavirodhāt svalakṣaṇasyāsādhāraṇasya vastutvopagamāt.

"Nor [is the validity of a cognition known] by the fact that it does not belie, because its non-belying, which consists in standing firm in respect to an efficient action, cannot be the reason for establishing the validity [of a cognition], in as much as it is [itself] not apprehended. If it is a reason for that (i.e., for establishing the validity) in as much as apprehended, wherefrom does its apprehension [obtain its] validity? If [you say:] from a further non-belying [namely, the one of its apprehension], [we answer:] no, because there would be an infinite regress, as the determination of the validity of the [second non-belying] apprehension, too, [would have to be established] from another non-belying. If [you say that] there is no fault, because the validity is established by [the cognition] itself in a situation of frequent repetition of the cognition of non-belying, which is characterized by standing firm in respect to an efficient action, [then we ask:] what is this frequent repetition? If [you say:] it is the immediate experience of non-belying once more in respect to a cognition, [then:] it is in respect to [a cognition] of the same kind or not.

Between these [alternatives], if it is in respect to [a cognition] which does not belong to the same kind, [then this is impossible, for] in respect to one single cognition, to begin with, an immediate experience of non-belying once more is impossible for someone who holds the doctrine of momentari[ness]. If [you say:] it is possible in dependence on the series (i.e., a repeated experience of non-belying is possible in respect to cognitions which are part of the same series as the original, non-belying cognition), [then we answer:] no, because the dependence is impossible, since the series is not real. [Only momentary things are real, and therefore the series as something which lasts for some time is not real.] Or if [the series] is real, [then] since its momentariness would be established too, how could this frequent repetition [be established] in dependence on it? Or if the series is not momentary [and nevertheless claimed to be real], [then your position, namely] 'Whatever is real is momentary' would not be established.

If [you say:] an immediate experience of non-belying once more [occurs] in respect to [a cognition] which belongs to the same kind, [we answer:] no; for someone who doesn't allow universals nothing can belong to the same kind. If [you say:] something can very well belong to the same kind by virtue of a universal which is characterized by the exclusion of [everything] else [which does not belong to the same kind], [we answer:] no, because the exclusion of [everything] else is not something real. Or if it is real [it would not be a universal], because there is a contradiction between [to be real and] to be universal. For [only] the particular, which is not common, is admitted [by you] as real."

[161] I suppose that the inferential cognition is sublated because its object, the universal, can be proved to be non-existent. Or perhaps Jayarāśi is referring to a well-known Lokāyata argument according to which inference is not a means of valid cognition, because every inference can be sublated by another inference; cf. for instance the Lokāyata *pūrvapakṣa* in *TS* v. 1458:

anumānavirodhasya viruddhānāṃ ca sādhane/
sarvatra sambhavāt kiṃ ca viruddhāvyabhicāriṇaḥ//

[162] The cognition of a feeling such as pleasure etc., cannot be produced by its object, i.e., the feeling, because according to the Buddhists pleasure etc., are not

something different from their cognition. If one claims that the cognition of a feeling is produced by its object, it follows that the cognition produces itself, which is absurd. On self-apprehension of *caittas* cf. *NB(T)* 1.10; cf. also *PV pratyakṣa* 251 = *PVin* I 22 quoted hereafter p. 228. 18f., and Stcherbatsky, *Bud. Log.* I, pp. 163-69, Vetter, *Erkenntnisprobleme bei Dharmakīrti*, pp. 76f.

[163] On *yogipratyakṣa* cf. *PS* I 6cd (Hattori's translation p. 27), *PV pratyakṣa* 281-89, *PVin* I 28f., Stcherbatsky, *Bud. Log.* I, p. 162, Kajiyama, op. cit., p. 53, n. 119, p. 54, n. 124, Steinkellner, "Yogische Erkenntnis als Problem im Buddhismus," Bühnemann, *Der allwissende Buddha*, pp. V-XV.

[164] Cf. p. 122.21f.; cf. also *PVV* p. 4.4-6: *ataś ca yato jñānād arthaṃ paricchedyāpi na pravartate, pravṛtto vā kutaścit pratibandhāder arthakriyāṃ nādhigacchati, tad api pramāṇam eva pramāṇayogyatālakṣaṇasyāvisaṃvādasya sattvāt.* "And [even] that cognition by which [a person] has determined the object and then nevertheless does not act, or [although] he acts [nevertheless] does not attain an efficient action because of some impediment etc., [this cognition] is indeed a means of valid cognition, because the non-belying which is defined as the capacity of a means of valid cognition exists."

[165] The first four alternatives were already dealt with in § 1.13a. However, most of the arguments employed here are different, for Jayarāśi uses the presuppositions of the Buddhist metaphysics. The fifth alternative is not clear to me. I did not come across it in any other text, and I do not see the necessity of taking into account all (?) causes of the cognition, where one could expect the object alone. Consequently the relationship between the last two *vikalpas*

is not clear to me either; it should be noted, however, that the introduction of a *vikalpa* with *atha*, and not with *vā*, is, at least stylistically speaking, highly unusual for Jayarāśi. Whether this implies a relation of implication between the two, I cannot say.

The meaning of 'necessary' for *dhruva* is not listed by MW, but obviously the listed meanings of firm, constant, eternal cannot be applied here. Cf. however *PW* s.v. 1.b) "feststehend, sicher, gewiss." Cf. *NB* II.36 and *NBṬ* ad loc., p. 131.10: *dhruvam avaśyaṃ bhavatīti dhruvabhāvī*. In the following sentences *dhruvabhāvin* and *avaśyambhāvin* are interchangeable (*ŚD* p. 307.10f.): *kiṃ ca kṛtakānāṃ bhāvānām avaśyambhāvī vināśas, tenāpi kṣaṇikatvaṃ ghaṭādīnām. tathā hi - 'yad yeṣāṃ dhruvabhāvī, na tatra teṣāṃ hetvantarāpekṣā. dhruvabhāvī ca kṛtakānāṃ vināśa' iti* ... Cf. also *PP* p. 369.10-22 (missing in the Ch. ed.), *TUS* p. 70.19-20: *anvayavyatirekayuktasya yasya pūrvakālabhāvitvaṃ tatkāraṇaṃ tad asti dhruvabhāvikāryadarśanāt*, ibid., p. 107.3-4: ... *svahetor eva dhruvabhāvivināśārhasyotpatteḥ*.

166 For this definition of universal cf. *PV pratyakṣa* 30ab: *arthānāṃ yac ca sāmānyam anyavyāvṛttilakṣaṇam/*. Jayarāśi is referring, of course, to the theory of *apoha*, for an explanation of which cf. Frauwallner, "Beiträge zur Apohalehre," also Hattori, "Anyāpoha and Pratibhā." Note also that the universal has already been refuted in § a.; the arguments here are more of a reminder.

167 This alternative probably refers to Dharmakīrti's theory, according to which a valid cognition the object of which is a universal actually apprehends the particular with the form of something else (*pararūpeṇa*); cf. nn. 170 and 173.

168 Cf. § a.2b.

[169] This is a quotation of *PVin* I p. 30.17-18: *'di dag gis don yoṅs su bcad nas 'jug pa na don bya ba la bslu ba med pa'i phyir ro*. To the Sanskrit fragments assembled by Vetter we may add *SVṬ* p. 22.1.

[170] Jayarāśi probably refers to *PVin* I p. 30.20-23: *tshad ma yin na ni 'di gñis kho nar 'dus pa'i phyir/*

tshad ma rnam gñis

kho na ste/

= (ibid., n. 3) *pramāṇasya sato 'traivāntarbhāvād dve eva pramāṇe*.

"Since [verbal communication, comparison, etc.] in as much as [they are] means of valid cognition, are included in [perception and inference], there are only two means of valid cognition."

Cf. also *PV pratyakṣa* 1ab: *mānaṃ dvividhaṃ viṣayadvaividhyāt .../*. "There are two kinds of means of valid cognition, because there are two kinds of objects."

Cf. as well *PS* I.2 (Sanskrit reconstruction by Hattori, op. cit., p. 237a):

pratyakṣam anumānaṃ ca pramāṇe

de (?) *gñis kho na ste, yasmāl*

lakṣaṇadvayam/

prameyam

"The means of valid cognition are perception and inference. They are only two, because the object of valid cognition [consists in only] two characteristics."

The similarity of formulation between Dharmakīrti's and Dignāga's statements may be deceiving. The basic principle upon which Dignāga constructed his theory of knowledge is the absolute distinction between perception and inference, according to their respective objects. Perception has for its object only the particular, and inference only the universal. But since inference has for its object something which does not exist, the question which immediately arises is: how could it be a means of valid cognition? As far as I know Dignāga does not answer this question. In *PS* II he proposes the triple-form criterion to distinguish between triform valid reasons (*trirūpaliṅga*) and non-valid reasons, but the basic supposition remains that inference has for its object a universal which does not exist.

Dharmakīrti had to complete and modify Dignāga's theory on this point. He had to find a further criterion to safeguard the validity of inference. This is probably the reason why he introduced the criterion of *arthakriyā* which was unknown to Dignāga (cf. Hattori, op. cit., p. 80, n. 1.14). However, since only an existing thing, i.e., a particular, can have an efficient action, a further modification of Dignāga's theory was inevitable: if the particular alone produces an efficient action, then inference, too, in order to be valid, must in the final analysis apprehend the particular. Consequently there is only one object of valid cognition for Dharmakīrti - the particular; cf. *PV pratyakṣa* 53d: *meyaṃ tu ekaṃ svalakṣaṇam//*.

However, as we saw above, Dharmakīrti does not renounce the duality of the object of valid cognition, but reinterprets it as a duality of aspects: perception apprehends the particular with its own form, and inference apprehends it with another form, or as having another form; cf. *PV pratyakṣa* 54cd: *tasya* (scil. *svalakṣaṇasya*) *svapararūpābhyāṃ gater meyadvayaṃ matam//*.

Cf. also *PVV* p. 118.8-11: *yady ekam eva prameyaṃ, tadācāryeṇa prameyadvaividhyaṃ yad uktaṃ 'na svasāmānyalakṣaṇābhyām anyat prameyam asti' iti tad virudhyata, ity āha - tasya svalakṣaṇasya pratyakṣataḥ svarūpeṇānumānataḥ pararūpeṇa sāmānyākāreṇa gater meyadvayaṃ mataṃ, na tu bhūtasāmānyasya sattvāt.*

"[Objection:] If there is only one object of valid cognition, then the duality of objects of valid cognition which was taught by the master [Dignāga], [when saying] 'There is no object of valid cognition other than the particular and the universal,' is contradicted. In order to [answer this question, Dharmakīrti] says: Two objects of valid cognition are maintained due to the apprehension of that, [i.e.] of the particular, with its own form by perception, with another form, [i.e.] with the form of the universal, by inference. [They are] not [maintained] because a real universal exists." Cf. also *PVBh* p. 212.29: *svalakṣaṇam eva paramārthataḥ prameyam*, and p. 213.15f.

As far as Jayarāśi's *vikalpas* are concerned, the second and the third correspond to the Buddhist position (*ākārabheda* fits with Dharmakīrti's position, and *viṣayabheda* with Dignāga's), but not the first (*vyaktibheda*). I suppose that the origin of this *vikalpa* is purely verbal, for the Buddhists sometimes use the word *vyakti* to denote not a specific individual, but a type of object, cf. for instance *NBṬ* p. 35.4-5: *saṅkhyāpradarśanadvāreṇa ca vyaktibhedo darśito bhavati*. (Stcherbatsky, *Bud. Log.* II, p. 12, translates *vyakti* here as 'variety.') It may also be noted that in later literature the word *vyakti* can designate any existing thing, cf. *NK* s.v.: *vyaktiḥ padārthamātram, yathā jātyādir api vyaktiḥ*. "*vyakti* [means] simply a thing; for instance, the universal etc., too, are *vyakti*."

Note also that the examination of the number of the means of valid cognition takes place in this chapter of the *TUS*, because their number was considered as a part of their definition; cf. *NBṬ* p. 36.3: *tato lakṣaṇakathanāṅgam eva saṅkhyābhedakathanam*.

171 Cf. § a.2b.

172 If there is a further form of perception and inference by which they could be differentiated, they lose the form of cognition, as one thing can only have one form.

[173] This *vikalpa* seems at first sight contradictory to the Buddhist *siddhānta*, but as noted above (n. 170), Dharmakīrti modified Dignāga's theory of inference and maintained that inference, too, apprehends the particular. This is clearly explained by Arcaṭa (*HBṬ* p. 4): *arthagrahaṇaṃ tu 'parokṣārthapratipatter' ity anumānasyāpi svalakṣaṇaviṣayaṃ prāmāṇyaṃ darśayitum. arthakriyāsamartho hy arthaḥ* (cf. *PVSV* p. 84.8: *arthakriyāyogyo 'rthaḥ*). *svalakṣaṇaṃ caivam-ātmakam. ata eva 'vastvadhiṣṭhānatvāt pramāṇavyavasthāyā' iti vakṣyati. anyathānumānāt tatra pravṛttir na syād artha-kriyārthinaḥ.*

"The use of the word thing/object, however, [in the sentence] 'because the apprehension of a thing/object which is not before the eyes [is based on inference]' (= *HB* 01) [serves the purpose] to show that the validity of inference, too, [is due to the fact that it] has the particular for its object. For a thing is [only] that which is capable of an efficient action. And [only] the particular has such a nature. This is precisely why [Dharmakīrti] says later on (*HB* I p. 35.12-14) 'because the establishment of the means of valid cognition is based on a real thing.' Otherwise, there would be no activity based on inference towards the [particular] for [a person] who desires an efficient action."

[174] The part of itself (*svāṃśa*) or the body of the cognition (*vijñānakāya*) is that part or aspect of the cognition which serves as the object of self-apprehension (*svasaṃvedana*); cf. Hattori, op. cit., pp. 100-3, nn. 1.60-61.

[175] According to Dharmakīrti one can apprehend by inference only general properties, and by perception only specific properties. Consequently, one can apprehend by inference that there is some fire, or fire as such (*agnimātra*), but not what sort of fire. This opinion is contested by the Mīmāṃsakas and the Sāṅkhyas who maintain that in certain

cases, when one infers something previously seen, this is possible; for example, having seen a particular fire, one may go away and infer that particular fire from its smoke, or having observed that two constellations of stars always appear together, one may infer one particular constellation from seeing the other. However, this possibility was not accepted by the Buddhists, for the danger it presents to the doctrine of two means of valid cognition according to two kinds of object is obvious; cf. *PV pratyakṣa* 77f., with *PVBh* and *PVV* ad loc.

176 The argument presupposes the Buddhist thesis that to exist, or in Dharmakīrti's jargon, to have an efficient action, is a property reserved to the particular. To say, therefore, that the universal exists, leads to the following inference: everything existing is particular; the universal exists; therefore the universal is particular.

177 For the reason why an eternal thing cannot produce its cognition cf. § a.2c.

178 To be an object, according to Dharmakīrti, means to produce the cognition and to be that which provides its form to the cognition. This definition which appears in the *PV*, as well as in the *PVin*, in the context of *mānasapratyakṣa*, has the purpose of defining an object which does not exist at the same time as its cognition; cf. *PV pratyakṣa* 247 = *PVin* I.20:

bhinnakālaṃ kathaṃ grāhyam iti ced grāhyatāṃ viduḥ/
hetutvam eva yuktijñā jñānākārārpaṇakṣamam//

"How could [an object which exists] at a different time [than its cognition] be apprehended [by the cognition]? The logicians know that to be apprehended [means] only [that] cause [of the cognition] which is capable of providing [its] form."

Cf. also *TSP* on v. 2033 p. 695.23: *svābhāsajñānajanakatvam evārthasya saṃvedyatvam.* "For an object, to be apprehended [means] to be the producer of the cognition in which it appears."

Other ways to express the same idea are to say that the cognition imitates (*anu-KṚ*), or grasps (*GRAH*) the form of the object. Prajñākaragupta and Manorathanandin illustrate this with the example of the child who 'grasps' the form of its father (*PVBh* p. 307.9: *putraḥ pitū rūpaṃ gṛhṇātīti yathā vyapadeśa iti*, *PVV* p. 175.16: *yathā pitṛrūpaṃ putreṇa gṛhītam iti kathyate*).

Dharmakīrti's definition repeats in fact the definition given by Dignāga in the *Ālambanaparīkṣā*, which itself repeats an old Abhidharma definition; cf. *ĀP* p. 158.11-12: *don gaṅ źig raṅ snaṅ ba'i rnam par rig pa bskyed pa de ni dmigs pa yin par rigs te* and *TrBh* p. 16.18: *bāhyo hy arthaḥ svābhāsavijñānajanakatvena vijñānasyālambanapratyaya iṣyate.* Cf. also Frauwallner, "Dignāga, sein Werk und seine Entwicklung," p. 130, Schmithausen, *Vibhramaviveka*, p.161.

The definition of object as *jñānākārārpaka* is closely related to the doctrine of *sākāravijñānavāda*, and consequently to the problem of *pramāṇa* and *pramāṇaphala*, but the problems involved cannot be discussed here; cf., however, *NBṬ* on I.20-21 and Hattori, op. cit., p. 98, n. 1.55. For further criticism of the definition of object cf. § d.7 and n. 232.

[179] This is a slightly defective quotation of *PVin* II(1) p. 24.6-7:

de ma yin la der 'dzin phyir/
'khrul kyaṅ 'brel phyir tshad ma ñid//

= (ibid., p. 25) *atasmiṃs tadgraho* (Tib.: *tadgrahāt?*) *bhrāntir api sambandhataḥ pramā//.*

Jayarāśi adds the word *artha* by taking into account the commentary (ibid., p. 24.8-10: *raṅ gi snaṅ ba don med pa la don du mṅon par źen nas 'jug pa'i phyir 'khrul pa yin yaṅ don daṅ 'brel pa de la mi 'khrul pa'i phyir tshad ma yin no.* = (ibid., p. 25) *svapratibhāse 'narthe 'rthādhyavasāyena pravartanād bhrāntir apy arthasambandhena (-sambaddhā?) tadavyabhicārāt pramāṇam.*

"Even though [the inferential cognition] is false, since it prompts to activity towards its own appearance, which is not a real object, by determining [it] as a real object, [it is nevertheless] a means of valid cognition because by being related to a real object it does not deviate from it."

[180] I am not sure how this argument should be understood. At least two interpretations seem possible:
(1) Jayarāśi deforms his opponent's position by taking it literally. Thus, he interprets the word 'object' in the proposition 'The cognition has for its object an unreal universal' as an internal object, i.e., the cognition's content; and if the universal appears in the cognition as an unreal thing, the cognition corresponds to reality.
(2) Jayarāśi may be referring to § 1.1ba, where he proves that there is no difference between the objects of valid and false cognitions.
The second alternative seems more reasonable to me.

[181] Cf. also *TUS* p. 93.18-19: *atha svāṃśaviṣayam anumānaṃ, tadā pratyakṣānumānayor bhedānupapattiḥ, pratīyamānajñānasya svalakṣaṇātmakatvāt.* "If inference has a part of itself as its object, then the difference between perception and inference is impossible, because the cognition [as something] which is being apprehended has the nature of a particular."

[182] From a structural point of view this passage is presented as analogous to the previous one; after examining the object of inference one proceeds to examine the object

of perception. But in fact the perspective changes completely. This is understandable, for by examining the object of inference as opposed to the object of perception, the latter is already indirectly examined, and it would have been a useless repetition to raise the same arguments again.

183 Since according to the Buddhists every cognition must apprehend itself, there is no apprehension of an object if at the same time there is no apprehension of the cognition. In other words, if there is no apprehension of an object, one cannot know that the object exists; in the same manner, if there is no apprehension of the cognition, one cannot know that the cognition exists. If one does not know that the cognition exists, one does not know that the object exists. Cf. *PVin* I p. 96.10-17:

dmigs pa mṅon sum ma yin na/
don mthoṅ rab tu 'grub mi 'gyur//55//

yul yod pas ni yul dmigs pa ma yin gyi/ 'on kyaṅ de'i dmigs pa yod pas so// de yaṅ tshad ma daṅ mi ldan pas yod pa'i rgyu mtshan can gyi tha sñad 'jug par mi 'gyur ro// de rab tu ma grub na don rab tu mi 'grub pa'i phyir thams cad nub par 'gyur ro// yod kyaṅ ma grub pa la yod pa'i tha sñad mi dmigs pa'i phyir ro// = (Sanskrit fragment from Steinkellner, "New Sanskrit-Fragments from *Pramāṇaviniścayaḥ*, First Chapter," p. 206)

apratyakṣopalambhasya nārthadṛṣṭiḥ prasidhyati//(55cd)
na hi viṣayasattayā viṣayopalambhaḥ. kiṃ tarhi (Tib. *kiṃ* **tu* is perhaps better) *tadupalambhasattayā. sā cāprāmāṇikī na sattānibandhanāṃs tadvyavahārān* (Tib. has no equivalent to *tad-*) *anuruṇaddhi. tadaprasiddhau viṣayasyāpy aprasiddhir iti sadvyavahārocchedaḥ* (Tib. **sarvocchedaḥ*) *syāt. na hi sad apy anupalabhyamānaṃ sad iti vyavahartuṃ śakyate.* (The last sentence is certainly not the Sanskrit original of Dharmakīrti, but merely a paraphrase by Bhāsarvajña.

According to the Tibetan translation one would expect something like *na hi saty apy asiddhe sadvyavahāra upalabhyate.*)
(The translation follows the Sanskrit.)

"Seeing of an object is not known to [a person] who has not perceived [his own] apprehension.

For the apprehension of the object is not due to the object's existence, but to the existence of its apprehension. And this [existence of its apprehension], in as much as it is not related to a means of valid cognition (i.e., in as much as we do not have a means of valid cognition for it), does not agree with thinking/speaking/acting with regard to it (i.e., the cognition) in as much as [thinking/speaking/acting are] conditioned by existence. When this [apprehension] is not known, the object, too, is not known. Thus, thinking/speaking/acting with regard to [something as] existing would be destroyed. For even if something exists, in as much as it is not apprehended it cannot be thought about/spoken about/acted upon as existing."

For further quotations of *PVin* I.55cd, in addition to those mentioned by Vetter, cf. *TUS* p. 86.9, *ŚVV* p. 246.22, *NM* I p. 84.13, *NKan* p. 220.8-9.

184 In order to determine the number of means of valid cognition, one has to have them all as the object of one and the same cognition. However, according to the Buddhists, a cognition is not apprehended by another cognition, but only by itself. Nor is there an *ātman* which could coordinate the different cognitions. Thus, one may perceive perception by perception, and inference by inference, but never both at the same time. Consequently, whatever the number of means of valid cognition may be, there is no way of knowing it. This is one of the most brilliant arguments in the *TUS*. Cf. also *PVV* p. 98.15f.

Cf. also *TUS* p. 93.22-25: *jñānayor api hetuphalabhāvāvadhāraṇaṃ na śakyate kartum. kāryajñānaṃ hi svasaṃvitparyavasitaṃ na jñānāntaram ātmasātkaroti. tadakaraṇe 'kena nirvartitaṃ mama svarūpam' ity etat kathaṃ vetti tadbhinnajñānasya piśācatulyatvāt.*

"The relation of cause and effect cannot be determined between two cognitions either. For the effect-cognition terminates in the apprehension of itself, it does not adopt another cognition [for its object]. Since [it] does not [adopt it], how [could] it know [the answer to the question] 'What accomplished my own form?', since the [cause-] cognition which is different from it is [as unknowable to it] as a ghost?" Cf. also *TUS* p. 88.24f.

Note that these arguments of Jayarāśi seem to have been directly borrowed by Vyomaśiva, cf. Vy p. 401.24-31: *nāpi svasaṃvidvādinaḥ kāryakāraṇabhāvagrahaṇam asti, kāraṇasaṃvidaḥ svātmany eva paryavasānāt. tathā kāryasaṃvido 'pīti na kāraṇajñānaṃ kāryasattām anubhavati, tatsattākāle tasyātītatvāt ... atha kāryakāraṇajñānābhyāṃ vāsanākrameṇāsti vikalpajñānaṃ kāryakāraṇabhāvagrāhakam iti cet, tasyāpy etadrūpasamāropatvābhyupagame 'pramāṇatvena kāryakāraṇabhāvasyāsiddhir eva.*

"Nor is the apprehension of the relation between cause and effect possible for someone who holds the doctrine of self-apprehension [of cognitions], for the cognition of the cause terminates in [the apprehension] of itself only. The same [holds true] for the cognition of the effect as well. Thus, the cognition of the cause does not experience the existence of the effect, because at the time of the existence of the [effect] it is already gone ...

[Objection:] The two cognitions of the cause and of the effect, by [leaving their] traces, [give rise to] a conceptual cognition which apprehends the relation between cause and effect.

[Reply:] Since this [conceptual cognition], too, is not a means of valid cognition, as [you] admit that it consists in a superimposition of that form (i.e., the form of a relation between cause and effect), the relation between cause and effect is not at all proved."

[185] This is the famous definition by Dharmakīrti as it appears in *PVin* I.4 and *NB* I.4. Note that the definition does not appear in the *PV*, and its absence is particularly significant in the context where it could be expected (i.e., *pratyakṣa* 1f. and 123f.). It seems, therefore, that while writing the *PV*, Dharmakīrti had not yet made up his mind to change Dignāga's definition by adding to it the word *abhrānta*. This is a further proof that the *PVin* was written after the *PV*, cf. Frauwallner, "Die Reihenfolge und Entstehung der Werke Dharmakīrtis," p. 147.

Cf. *PVin* I p. 40.2-5:

mṅon sum rtog bral ma 'khrul ba/

rab rib daṅ myur du bskor ba daṅ grur śugs pa'i 'khrugs pa la sogs pas 'khrul ba ma bskyed ciṅ rnam par rtog pa med pa'i śes pa ni mṅon sum mo//

= (ibid., n. 1) *pratyakṣaṃ kalpanāpoḍham abhrāntam. timirāśubhramaṇanauyānasaṅkṣobhādyanāhitavibhramam avikalpakaṃ jñānaṃ pratyakṣam.*

"Perception is free from conceptual construction and nonerroneous.

Perception is non-conceptual cognition which is not affected by error due to *timira* [sickness], to the quick whirling around [of a torch which produces the illusion of a circle of light], to agitation [of the three humours of the body, i.e., *vāta*, *pitta*, and *śleṣman*, caused] by travelling in a boat [which causes the illusion of moving trees], etc."

Cf. also *NBṬ* I.4 p. 40.6-8: *tatra pratyakṣam anūdya kalpanāpoḍhatvam abhrāntatvaṃ ca vidhīyate. yat tat bhava-*

tām asmākaṃ cārtheṣu sākṣātkāri jñānaṃ prasiddhaṃ tat kalpanāpoḍhābhrāntatvayuktaṃ draṣṭavyam.

"Regarding these [two means of valid cognition], when mentioning perception again [Dharmakīrti] affirms that [it] is free from conceptual construction and nonerroneous. The direct cognition with regard to the objects, which is well known to you and to us, has to be considered as connected with [the properties] being free from conceptual construction and being nonerroneous."

In respect to this passage, Stcherbatsky, *Bud. Log.* II, p. 15, n. 1, makes a rather disconcerting remark: "As e.g., in the sentence 'sound is impermanent' impermanence is a characteristic (*lakṣaṇa*) of the sound, but not its essence (*svarūpa*). These remarks are directed against Vinītadeva who has interpreted the sūtra as containing a definition and has even reversed the order of subject and predicate by stating that 'whatsoever is non-constructive and non-illusive is direct knowledge' (p. 39.12). The same is done by Kamalaśīla, *op. cit.*, p. 366.25, who maintains that, although *pratyakṣa* is here the *lakṣya*, it is also the predicate (*vidhīyate*). Cp. Ṭipp., p. 17-18."

It seems in fact that Vinītadeva has interpreted the *sūtra* as a definition. But if so, he was not criticized by Dharmottara, for Dharmottara, too, interprets it as a definition. This is quite clear not only from the *NBṬṬ* (ad loc., p. 17.3-4) and the *DhPr* (ad loc., p. 41.11f.), but also from the *Ṭīkā* itself on I.6 (p. 54.3-5): *kalpanāpoḍhatvābhrāntatve parasparāpekṣe pratyakṣalakṣaṇaṃ, na pratyekam iti darśayituṃ tayā rahitaṃ yad abhrāntaṃ tat pratyakṣam iti lakṣaṇayoḥ parasparāpekṣayoḥ pratyakṣaviṣayatvaṃ darśitam iti.*

Stcherbatsky himself translates this passage as follows (ibid., p. 24): "... because absence of construction and absence of illusion constitute the definition of perception taken together and not separately. In order to point out this, it is said that knowledge which is free from construction, if at the same time it does not produce an illusion, is perceptive knowledge. [Doesn't that correspond to Vinītadeva who "has even reversed the order of subject and predicate"?] Thus it is shown that both these characteristics combined with one another determine the essence of perception." But then cf. p. 15 again: "(It is not a definition of its essence. What its essence is) you and I very well know (in general)." Note, however, that with 'essence' he translates two different words: *svarūpa* (p. 15) and *viṣaya* (p. 24).

On the interpretation of *NBṬ* ad I.4 the *DhPr* and the *NBṬṬ* are unanimous: First the *Ṭīkā* criticizes an interpretation of the *sūtra* according to which the *sūtra* contains a relation between a technical term and that which is designated by it (*sañjñāsañjñisambandha*); perception is a technical term, and absence of conceptual construction and error are designated by it. This interpretation is rejected by Dharmottara because he considers that the purpose of the *sūtra* is to reject divergent opinions (*vipratipattinirākaraṇa*). This would not be possible if one interprets the *sūtra* as containing *sañjñāsañjñisambandha*, for by saying 'You call x *pratyakṣa*, I call y *pratyakṣa*' the opponent is not likely made to change his opinion on what *pratyakṣa* is. At the most he would concede that different things can be designated by *pratyakṣa*. Second, (and on this point too the commentaries are unanimous) Dharmottara rejects an opinion according to which the absence of conceptual construction and nonerroneousness are repeated, and perception is affirmed. Cf. *DhPr* p. 41.11-15: *evaṃ cānuvādavidhikrameṇa yad anyad anena vyākhyātaṃ "pratyakṣam iti sañjñā kalpanāpoḍhatvādi sañjñy eva. tena sañjñāsañjñisambandhaḥ pratipādyata" iti tad vipratipattinirākaraṇe prastute 'prastutam. tato 'pavyākhyānam iti prakāśayati. yad apy apareṇa vyākhyātaṃ "pradeśāntaraprasiddhayoḥ kalpanāpoḍhatvābhrāntatvayor anu-*

vādena pratyakṣatvaṃ vidhīyata" iti tad api na caturasram iti pratipādayati.

Cf. also *NBṬṬ* pp. 17.3-5, 12-13: *pratyakṣam anūdyety lakṣyanirdeśaḥ. kalpanāpoḍhatvam abhrāntatvaṃ ca vidhīyata iti lakṣaṇanirdeśaḥ. anena lakṣyalakṣaṇabhāvaṃ darśayatā vinītadevavyākhyānaṃ sañjñāsañjñisambandharūpaṃ pratyuktam ... yas tv anayoḥ pradeśāntaraprasiddhayor anuvādaṃ kṛtvā pratyakṣatvaṃ vidadhāti tenāpy atra lakṣyalakṣaṇabhāvo viparītam ākhyātaṃ (ākhyāto?) bhaṅgyā ...*

This second opinion is rejected because of the following rule (*nyāya*): When the relation between what is being defined and the defining property is not known or established, one repeats what has to be defined and affirms the defining property. Only when the relation is well known, one can repeat the defining property and affirm what is defined. Cf. *DhPr* p. 41.15-16: *yataḥ prasiddhe lakṣyalakṣaṇabhāve lakṣaṇānuvādena lakṣyaṃ vidheyam. aprasiddhe tu lakṣaṇavākyena lakṣaṇam eva vidheyaṃ, na lakṣyam iti nyāya iti.* Cf. also *NBṬṬ* pp. 17.13-18.2.

There is a strong resemblance between the two commentaries (which is probably due to the fact that they both refer to the *Pramāṇaviniścayaṭīkā* of Dharmottara, cf. *DhPr* p. 41.17 and *NBṬṬ* p. 18.2), but the *NBṬṬ* provides us with the additional information that the opponent is Vinītadeva. This identification, however, is problematic, for the text, at least as it reached us in Tibetan translation, agrees with Dharmottara's interpretation and explicitly states that *pratyakṣa* is *lakṣya*, and *kalpanāpoḍha* and *abhrānta* are *lakṣaṇa*; cf. *NBṬ(V)* p. 39.10-11: *mṅon sum śes bya bas ni mtshad ñid kyi gźi bstan to/ rtog pa daṅ brel śiṅ ma 'khrul ba'o śes bya bas ni tshad ñid bstan te/.* It seems, therefore, that either the author of the *NBṬṬ* was mistaken in his identification of the opponent as Vinītadeva, or, what seems more probable to me, Vinītadeva's original text was changed by someone in order to harmonize it with Dharmottara's.

Note that Jayarāśi's criticism of *kalpanā* was partly translated by Jayatilleke, op. cit., p. 85.

[186] Jayarāśi probably refers to Dignāga's definition of *kalpanā* in PS(V) I.3d (Sanskrit reconstruction by Hattori, op. cit., p. 237b):

atha keyaṃ kalpanā nāma/

nāmajātyādiyojanā//3//

yadṛcchāśabdeṣu nāmnā viśiṣṭo 'rtha ucyate ḍittha iti/ jātiśabdeṣu jātyā gaur iti/ guṇaśabdeṣu guṇena śukla iti/ kriyāśabdeṣu kriyayā pācaka iti/ dravyaśabdeṣu dravyeṇa daṇḍī viṣāṇīti.

"If [it is asked] what this [thing] called conceptual construction is [I answer]:

> [Conceptual construction is] the connection with a name, a universal, etc.

In the case of arbitrary words, a thing is expressed as distinguished (or: qualified) by a name, [for instance] 'Ḍittha.' In the case of genus-words, [a thing is expressed as distinguished] by a genus, [for instance] 'cow.' In the case of quality-words, [a thing is expressed as distinguished] by a quality, [for instance] 'white.' In the case of action-words, [a thing is established as distinguished] by an action, [for instance] 'a cook.' In the case of substance-words, [a thing is expressed as distinguished] by a substance, [for instance] 'a staff-bearer,' 'a horn-bearer.'"

It is quite clear that the classification into universal, quality, action, etc., is a classification of words. These are categories of language which do not denote things in reality; and, therefore, a conceptual cognition cannot be produced by a real universal etc., or be connected to it with a real relation. Thus, it seems at first sight that

Jayarāśi falsifies Dignāga's position in interpreting the compound (which he may have formed himself) as if the conceptual cognition is produced by qualifications such as quality, action, etc., instead of being produced with such qualifications. Although one could hesitate as to which of the two interpretations Jayarāśi has in mind when the *vikalpa* is raised for the first time (p. 182.5), the refutation (l. 12f.) leaves no doubt that Jayarāśi's expression must be understood according to the first interpretation, all the more so as the *vikalpas* regarding the content of the cognition (*saviṣaya*, *nirviṣaya*) are raised only later on (p. 184.3-4). Do we have to assume a simple sophistry on Jayarāśi's part? Such an assumption, I think, is highly improbable. We saw in the analysis of *anadhigatārthagantṛ* (cf. § 3.1) that Jayarāśi refers to the *PS* while taking into account later interpretations of this text. We could have a similar case here. As a matter of fact, some Buddhist commentators interpreted Dignāga's theory of conceptual construction as if conceptual construction were related to a real universal etc. It is probably these commentators that the present *vikalpa* addresses. Unfortunately, we know neither their names nor their works. Their interpretation, however, appears as a short *pūrvapakṣa* in the *TS(P)*, and the elaborate pains which Śāntarakṣita and Kamalaśīla take to refute them indicates that their interpretation of Dignāga carried a considerable weight at the time.

Cf. *TSP* on v. 1218 p. 451.9-10: *nanu cānye 'pi na kevalam abhilāpinīṃ pratītiṃ kalpanāṃ varṇayanti, kiṃ tu jātiguṇakriyādisambandhayogyām api, sā kasmān na gṛhyeta?*

"[Objection]: Others, however, are of the opinion that the conceptual construction is not only a cognition characterized by a word, but also [a cognition] which is capable of connecting a [real] universal, a quality, an action, etc. [with the perceived object]. Why should this [kind of conceptual construction] not be included [in the definition of conceptual construction]?"

I have presented elsewhere the position of the 'others' and argued that it was based on a misunderstanding of Dignāga's text due to Dharmakīrti's influence on the one hand, and to a confusion between attribute and predicate in the *Vṛtti* on the other hand, cf. Franco, "On the interpretation of *PS*(V) I,3d."

[187] The compound *saviṣaya* (unlike *tadviṣaya*) does not imply an identity between the object which produces the cognition and the object which appears in it, but Jayarāśi seems to take it for granted here, and does not take into consideration that the external and internal objects of a cognition can be different.

The expression *arthasāmarthyasamudbhavatva* reminds strongly of *PVin* I.4d, cf. *PVin* I p. 40.9-13:

dbaṅ po'i śes pa la ni de srid pa ma yin te/
don gyi mthu yis ni/
yaṅ dag skye ba yin phyir ro//4//

gaṅ gi phyir de don gyi nus pa las skyes pa na de'i raṅ bźin kho na'i rjes su byed pa'i phyir ro//

= (ibid., n. 1) *indriyajñāne sā* (scil. *kalpanā*) *nāsti*
arthasya sāmarthyena samudbhavāt//

tad dhy arthasya sāmarthyenotpadyamānaṃ tadrūpam evānukuryāt.

(I translate from the Sanskrit.)

"There is no [conceptual construction] in sensorial cognition,

because [it] is produced by the capacity of the object.

For this [sensorial cognition], being produced by the capacity of the object, has to imitate exactly/only the form of that [object]."

Thus, for Dharmakīrti, too, the production by an object implies necessarily having the form of that object.

But for him this rule is valid for sensorial cognition alone, whereas Jayarāśi seems to generalize it. Cf. also § 4.1a.

[188] The argument presupposes the Buddhist doctrine that cognitions are differentiated according to their objects (cf. *mānaṃ dvividhaṃ meyadvaividhyāt*). Thus, the following equation is obtained: conceptual construction = cognition without an object = simply a cognition = every cognition.

[189] Recollection (*smṛti*) is not used by the Buddhists as a defining property of *kalpanā*, but it plays an important role in the context of *pratyakṣābhāsa*. Not only does it constitute itself one type of *pratyakṣābhāsa*, but it is also a necessary factor for the production of all other *pratyakṣābhāsas*, with the possible exception of the *taimirajñāna*. For instance, the water which appears in an illusory cognition arises from the traces left by past experience.

The three *vikalpas*, *smṛtyutpādaka*, *smṛtirūpa* and *smṛtyutpādya*, could be understood as an analysis of one expression. Being closely related, they perhaps refer to the expression *smārta* used by Dignāga in his list of *pratyakṣābhāsa* (*PS* I.8a). Indeed, the word *smārta*, 'that which has a relation to recollection,' is ambiguous enough to allow these three interpretations.

Dharmakīrti reduces the semantical field of *smārta* to *smaraṇātmika* (*PV pratyakṣa* 291), and Manorathanandin glosses it simply with *smṛti* (*PVV* p. 186.14). However, Jayarāśi does not do injustice to Dharmakīrti by raising the other two *vikalpas*. They are both necessary, for instance, in the inferential process: an inferential cognition cannot arise without a recollection of the *vyāpti* (*smṛtyutpādya*); and the recollection of the *vyāpti*, in its turn, cannot arise without the particular being conceptualized as an inferential sign (*smṛtyutpādaka*).

smṛti is not thematic as such in the Buddhist works, probably because nobody objected to its being considered as a conceptual construction. The reason why it is a conceptual construction is quite clear: it is not produced by its object; cf. also *PVV* p. 8.9-11, quoted above n. 152.

190 This is a quotation of *PVin* I.11cd (p. 48):

gaṅ źig yod la gaṅ mthoṅ ba/
de mthoṅ ba las de yi sgra//11//

(Sanskrit reconstruction ibid., n. 1)

Both Abhayadevasūri (*TBV* p. 523.13-14) und Umbeka (*ŚVV* p. 150.16) who quote this sentence refer to it as a *nyāya*. It is possible, therefore, that Dharmakīrti is in fact quoting from some other source. In any case, there is nothing particularly Buddhist about it.

191 Cf. p. 126.14f.

192 For only the object can differentiate the conceptual from a non-conceptual cognition.

193 I am not quite sure what the double nature is, and whether it refers to the cause or to the effect. I take it as referring to the cause, and understand the double nature as *bodhasvabhāva* and *smṛtisvabhāva*.

Another reason why the opponent's mind is confused is that his statement amounts in fact to the previous *vikalpa* (*smaraṇākāra* = *smṛtirūpa*), which has already been refuted.

Jayarāśi's arguments in both *vikalpas* are based on the fact that perceptual and mnemonic cognitions must sometimes succeed each other.

[194] The next two *vikalpas*, viz., *abhilāpasaṃsargapratibhāsā pratītiḥ* and *abhilāpavatī pratītiḥ*, could refer to *PVin* I.4, cf. *PVin* I p. 40.5-8:

rtog pa de yaṅ gaṅ že na

rtog pa mṅon par brjod can gyi/

śes pa

rtog pa ni brjod pa daṅ 'drer ruṅ ba snaṅ ba'i śes pa ste/

= (ibid., n. 1) *kā punar sā kalpanā*

abhilāpinī/

pratītiḥ kalpanā

abhilāpasaṃsargayogyapratibhāsā pratītiḥ kalpanā.

"What then is this conceptual construction?

Conceptual construction is a cognition characterized by a word.

Conceptual construction is a cognition whose appearance is capable of blending with a word."

Cf. also *NB* I.5: *abhilāpasaṃsargayogyapratibhāsā pratītiḥ kalpanā*; *TS* v. 1213: ... *abhilāpinī/ pratītiḥ kalpanā* ...; *PV pratyakṣa* 123d: *vikalpo nāma saṃśrayaḥ//*.

Dharmakīrti modifies Dignāga's definition of *kalpanā* by introducing the word *yogya*. By this he is able to overcome Śaṅkarasvāmin's criticism of Dignāga, namely, that children are capable of conceptual construction even before they learn the appropriate words (cf. *PV pratyakṣa* 141-44 and *PVV* ad loc.). This is however an exception. Normally conceptual constructions are not only potentially, but actually related to words.

The difference between the two *vikalpas* raised by Jayarāśi does not seem to be very important. According to the first, conceptual construction is a cognition in which a relation (of the object) to a word appears, whereas according to the second, it consists in the appearance of the word itself. The difference is probably based on such statements as for example *PV pratyakṣa* 173ab: *tasmāj jātyāditadyogā nārthe .../.* "The universal [quality, action] etc., and their relation [to a real thing] do not [exist] in the thing [itself]."

Cf. also *PVV* p. 153.14: *tad evaṃ jātyādikalpanā tatsambandhakalpanā ca nāstīty uktam.* "Thus, it has been explained that the conceptual construction of the universal [quality, action] etc., and the conceptual construction of their relation [to the object] do not exist [outside the cognition]."

As far as I understand Dharmakīrti, the conceptualization of a universal etc., and the conceptualization of a relation between an object and a universal etc., do not constitute different kinds of conceptual construction. The conceptualization of a universal may be possible, of course, even without conceptualizing its relation to a particular object. However, both Dignāga's and Dharmakīrti's definitions of *kalpanā* emphasize the relation to an object, probably because in the context of *pramāṇa* pure conceptualization is not thematic. It goes without saying that the universal itself also appears, when the relation with a universal appears in a cognition.

196 Cf. n. 178.

197 There is no doubt that Jayarāśi alludes to the definition of perception quoted in § 4.1. Strangely enough he replaces the word *abhrānta* systematically with *avyabhicārin*, cf. § 4.2 and n. 255.

198 Cf. n. 194, also *NKC* pp. 47.18-48.1: *...pratibhāsasyābhilāpavattvānupapatteḥ. tad dhi tatsvabhāvatvāt taddhetutvād vā syāt. na tāvad tatsvabhāvatvāc, cetanācetanayor viruddhadharmādhyāsatas tādātmyāsambhavāt. yayor viruddhadharmādhyāso na tayos tādātmyaṃ yathā jalānalayor, viruddhadharmādhyāsaś ca cetanācetanarūpatayā śabdajñānayor iti. atas tatsvabhāvaśūnyatayā pratyakṣasyāvikalpakatvasādhane*

siddhasādhanam. nāpi taddhetutvāt, tad dhi tajjanyatvaṃ tajjanakatvam ubhayaṃ vā. tajjanyatvena tadvattve, śrotrajñānasyāvikalpakatvaṃ na syāt, tasyābhilāpaprabhavatayā tadvattvaprasaṅgāt. tajjanakatvāt tadvattve, prakṛtipratyayādipratyakṣasya savikalpakatvaṃ syāt. ubhayapakṣe 'py ubhayadoṣānuṣaṅga, ekatrobhayarūpatāvirodhaś ca.

"For an appearance (i.e., the objective appearance of a cognition) cannot be characterized by a word. For [it could be so] either because it has the nature of a [word], or because of causality with a [word]. First of all, [it can] not [be characterized by a word] because [it] has the nature of a [word], for, as one attributes contradictory properties to conscious and unconscious [entities], it is impossible that [appearance and word] have the same nature. Two [things] to which one attributes contradictory properties do not have the same nature, just like water and fire. And one attributes contradictory properties to word and cognition in as much as [they] have a conscious and an unconscious nature. Therefore, if [you] prove that perception is free from conceptual construction because [it] is devoid of the nature of a [word], [you] prove what is [already] proved.

Nor [is a cognition characterized by a word] because of causality with a [word]. For this [means] either that it is produced by a [word], or that it produces a [word], or both. If it is characterized by a [word] because it is produced by a [word], auditory cognition would not be nonconceptual, because in as much as it has a word as its source, it would be characterized by a [word]. If [a cognition] is characterized by a [word] because it produces a [word], [then] the perception of the elementary form [of a word], [its] affix, etc., would be conceptual. And if one holds both (i.e., that it is produced by a word and produces a word), both faults result, and [also] a contradiction which consists in the fact that one thing would have both natures."

199 Jayarāśi seems to play on the ambiguity of the word *śabda-* or *abhilāpajñāna*, which can designate the apprehension of a word taken phonetically or semantically.

200 Jayarāśi does not explain why the determination of words becomes impossible. I suppose he means that if the cognitions of words are nothing but conceptual constructions, the convention (*saṅketa*) that a particular series of sounds should be used to designate a particular class of objects is impossible. Cf. *PV pratyakṣa* 171-72, on *śabdavyavasthā* cf. *PVin* II(2) p. 72.

201 For Dharmakīrti, indistinct cognition and conceptual cognition are of the same extension: every indistinct cognition is conceptual, and every conceptual cognition is indistinct (cf. *PVBh* p. 326.23: *spaṣṭābhātvād evāvikalpakam*; *PVV* p.184.13: *avikalpakatvāc ca spaṣṭam*.) The indistinctness of a cognition is apprehended directly by *svasaṃvedana*, and it is used as a criterion for a conceptual construction. We know that a cognition is a conceptual construction because it is indistinct, and we know that it is free from conceptual construction because it is vivid (*spaṣṭa*, *sphuṭa*, *viśada*).

The notions of vividness and indistinctness play an important role in the context of *yogipratyakṣa*. Unlike in the case of perception, the fact that it is free from conceptual construction cannot be deduced from the fact that it is produced by its object (the particular), because the yogi apprehends past and future objects (cf. *PVBh* p. 326.24-26: *atītānāgataviṣayasyāvidyamānaviṣayasya ca kathaṃ bhāvanāmātrād avikalpakatā. bhāvanāpy evambhūtakāryasamarthaiveti darśayaty avidyamānaviṣaye 'pi*.

"How [is it possible that a cognition] which has a past or future [thing] for its object and [a cognition] which has an inexisting [thing] for its object are free from conceptual construction, just because [they arise from] intensive meditative practice? Intensive meditative practice, too, [just as sense perception etc.] is capable of such an effect (i.e., of producing a cognition free from conceptual construction). [Dharmakīrti] shows this [in verse 283] even in respect to [a cognition] which has an inexistent [thing] for its object."

Note that on this point Dharmakīrti deviates from Dignāga. For Dignāga, the cognition of the yogi which is free from conceptual construction is necessarily true, whereas for Dharmakīrti it may very well be false.

[202] Note that the last two *vikalpas* are discussed in reversed order.

[203] This *vikalpa* is obviously absurd, but not unexplainable. One of the *pratyakṣābhāsas* enumerated by Dignāga (cf. PS I.8b) is the *taimira(-jñāna!)*. Dharmakīrti (PV *pratyakṣa* 293f.) explains it as an exception (*apavāda*) to the rule that all *pratyakṣābhāsas* consist in conceptual construction. This interpretation is unfaithful to Dignāga, because it invalidates his definition of perception. Indeed, Dharmakīrti saw the problem, and this is probably the reason why he later on modified the definition of perception and added the word *abhrānta* to it. As a result, all the commentators after Dharmakīrti had to explain why Dignāga did not mention the word *abhrānta* in his definition.

One such attempt (equally unfaithful to Dignāga) was to say that the word *abhrānta* is not mentioned because even false cognitions such as that of a yellow conch-shell are perception, for in as much as they produce an efficient action (note that the concept of *arthakriyā* does not appear anywhere in Dignāga's writings) they do not belie their promise (*avisaṃvādaka*). Thus, according to them, for Dignāga perception is defined as *kalpanāpoḍha* and *avisaṃvādaka* (not as *abhrānta*). But of course Dignāga does not mention the word *avisaṃvādaka* either. This word, they claimed, is contained implicitly in the definition of perception on account of Dignāga's enumeration of *pratyakṣābhāsa*, for the word *taimira* is to be understood in the following manner: *taimira* means *visaṃvādaka* as it is derived from the word *timira* not in the usual sense of an eye-sickness, but in the sense of nescience (*ajñāna*, literally non-cognition!). Cf. *TSP* p. 483.11-13: *sataimiram iti tu timiraśabdo 'yam ajñānaparyāyaḥ. "timiraghnaṃ ca mandānām" iti yathā timire bhavaṃ taimiraṃ, visaṃvādakam ity arthaḥ.* (The position of these commentators is summarized by Hattori, op. cit., p. 97, n. 1.53. Note, however, that *PVBh* pp. 252.29-253.2 does not deal with them. Cf. also Franco, "Once again on Dharmakīrti's Deviation from Dignāga on *pratyakṣābhāsa*.")

I think that it is probable that in interpreting *aspaṣṭatā* as *avijñānātmaka*, Jayarāśi is referring to the interpretation of *timira* as *ajñāna*. Even though in the passage quoted above *taimira* means neither *kalpanā* nor *aspaṣṭatā* in Dharmakīrti's sense of the word, the reason why Jayarāśi associates them is quite clear, for primarily *timira* means obscurity (indeed, this is how Hattori, p. 28, mistranslates *taimira*), darkness, and the *timira* sickness gets its name from the fact that it causes the crystalline lens to become opaque. Note also that for Dharmakīrti the "obscure" cognition (*taimirajñāna*) is vivid (*spaṣṭa*).

[204] It may be reminded that the universal cannot produce its own cognition, since it is unreal.

[205] Cf. n. 162.

[206] Cf. p. 250.16f.

[207] This is a quotation of *PVin* I.32ab = *PV pratyakṣa* 283ab. Cf. *PVin* I p. 74.21-29:
bsgoms pa'i stobs kyis gsal bar snaṅ ba yin du zin kyaṅ rtog pa med par ji ltar 'gyur źe na/ gaṅ gi phyir

rnam rtog rjes su 'brel pa la/
don gsal snaṅ ba yod ma yin/

rnam par bslad pa'i blo yaṅ ruṅ ste brjod pa daṅ 'dres pa'i śes pa thams cad la ni don gsal ba ñid ldog pa'i phyir ro// des na rnam par rtog pa can 'di ni gsal bar snaṅ bar 'os pa ma yin no//
"Even if [a cognition] appears vivid by the strength of intensive meditative practice, how [can it be] free from conceptual construction. Because

there is no appearance of a vivid object in [a cognition] which is related to conceptual construction.

Even a cognition which is corrupted [by passion, fear, etc., in as much as it has a vivid object, is free from conceptual construction], because the fact of having a vivid object does not occur in any cognition which consists in a relation [of the object] to a word. This is why this [cognition, if it were] conceptual, could not appear as vivid."

[208] The body of cognition (*vijñānakāya*) is the object of self-apprehension (*svasaṃvedana*), cf. n. 174.

[209] Just as a conceptual cognition, an erroneous cognition, too, is perception in respect to itself. The apprehension of the double moon may be false, but the consciousness of the fact that the two moons are being apprehended is always true; cf. for instance *PVBh* pp. 252.31-253.2.

[210] This *vikalpa* presents a problem similar to the one on p. 190.7f. I can see at least two possibilities to interpret it. It could refer to some Buddhist commentators who

perhaps expressed themselves somewhat sloppily, saying that conceptual constructions are not real while meaning that their objects have no counterpart in reality. Or, and this seems more probable to me, it refers to some illusionistic theory, which denied the existence of the cognition through the inexistence of its object. The illusionist accepts the realist's claim that cognition is not possible without an object, but draws from it the opposite conclusion: since the object does not exist and the cognition cannot exist without it, it follows that the cognition, too, does not exist.

This procedure is quite common in Buddhist as well as Vedānta texts, cf. Vetter, "Die Gauḍapādīya-kārikās," p. 99; cf. also Schmithausen, *Nirvāṇa-Abschnitt*, p. 137-142, n. 101, especially A2 and C1.

Even if this *vikalpa* seems strange, it is highly improbable that Jayarāśi invented it. This is corroborated by the fact that *TS*(*P*) v. 1217 refutes the same opinion. Cf. *TSP* p. 450.21-23: *yadi cāsyāḥ kalpanāyā asattvaṃ syāt, tadā sā śabdārthavyavasthā īdṛśy api bhrāntāpi na sambhavet.* "And if this, [i.e.] the conceptual construction, did not exist, then this, [i.e.] the fixed relation between word and object, would not be possible even as such, [i.e.] even as false."

211 This *vikalpa* repeats in fact the definition of *svārthānumāna*, cf. *PVin* II(1) p. 22.24-25:

raṅ don ni/
tshul gsum rtags las don mthoṅ yin/

= (ibid., p. 23) *svārthaṃ trirūpāl liṅgato 'rthadṛk/* "[Inference] for oneself is the cognition of the [inferred] object through an [inferential] sign which has the three forms."

Dharmakīrti is quoting here Dignāga's definition from *PS* II.1ab, transl. Hayes, "Diṅnāga's Views on Reasoning," p. 247 (2.1.1). Cf. also *NB* II.3: *tatra svārthaṃ trirūpāl liṅgād yad anumeye jñānaṃ tad anumānam*. *NBṬ* p. 90.4: *trirūpāl liṅgād yad utpannam anumeyālambanaṃ jñānaṃ tat svārtham anumānam iti*. *TS* v. 1361cd: *svārthaṃ trirūpato liṅgād anumeyārthadarśanam//*

[212] Before the logical mark is apprehended as such, i.e., before it is conceptualized as a logical mark, it has to be apprehended by perception. This perception would be a conceptual construction.

[213] A recollection of the concomitance (*vyāptismaraṇa*) must occur between the apprehension of the sign and that of the inferred object.

[214] Cf. *TBV* p. 501.31f.

[215] Sanghavi and Parikh analyze the text differently. According to their division of the text, this question starts a new section (§ 2) which runs parallel to p. 34.12 (§ 1; all page numbers in this note refer to their edition). Their interpretation is probably due to the similarity in formulation between p. 34.13 (*athāspaṣṭākārā pratītiḥ kalpanā, aspaṣṭatā kā?*) and p. 35.24 (*pratyakṣajñānasya ca spaṣṭatā kā?*). Under closer examination, however, the analogy breaks down. It seems to me that the discussion here is logically subordinated to p. 35.20 (*atha yan nirvikalpakam* ...), which in its turn is subordinated to p. 35.11 (*atha trirūpāl* ...). If the editors' interpretation is accepted, it would be difficult to explain why the three *vikalpas* on pp. 35.8, 35.9 and 35.11 are raised in the middle of a discussion of *spaṣṭa* and *aspaṣṭa*.

My understanding of the passage is as follows: The opponent on p. 35.20 tries to avoid the difficulties raised on p. 35.11 by arguing that the concepts of 'free from conceptual construction' and 'vivid,' have the same extension. Inference is not vivid, therefore it is not free from conceptual construction. Jayarāśi's objection to this last move is twofold: First, he points out that the opponent has already failed to provide a satisfactory definition for indistinctness (cf. p. 34.13f.). Second (= Sanghavi and Parikh's new section), he proceeds to refute the definition of vividness.

[216] Cf. *PVin* I p. 96.10-17, quoted above n. 183.

[217] Cf. *NB* III.75: *parasparaparihārasthitalakṣaṇatayā vā bhāvābhāvavat.*

[218] The argument can only be valid under the assumption on p. 194.12f. according to which vividness is due to the production by the particular which appears in the cognition. Thus, if the cognition is vivid and appears in itself, it has to be produced by itself.

[219] Cf. *TUS* p. 86.10-17: *api ca yat tad dahanagrahaṇaṃ tatra kim avabhāti? kim artho, jñānam, ubhayaṃ vā? yady arthaḥ pratibhāti, tad ayuktam, asaṃviditāyāṃ saṃvittau tatsaṃvittyayogāt. atha jñānaṃ,* (probably a lacuna here) [*na*] *tarhi dahanadhūmayoḥ sambandho 'vagatas, tatsaṃvittipūrvakatvāt sambandhabuddheḥ. athobhayaṃ pratibhāti, tad ayuktam, ekopalambhasyā(sya) dvitiyākāraparihārasthitidharmatvāt. na ca dahanajñāne jñānārthākārau pratīyeta, api tu dahanasyaiva pratibhāsanāt.*

"Besides, what appears in this apprehension of fire? Is it the object, the cognition, or both? If the object appears, [then] this is not correct, because its cognition is impossible when the cognition is not [itself] cognized. If it is the cognition ... [then the object, namely, fire, is not apprehended, and] consequently the relation between fire and smoke [upon which your inference is based] is not apprehended, because the cognition of [their] relation is preceded by their cognition. If both appear, [then] this is not correct, because the apprehension of one thing necessarily stands by the exclusion of any other forms. And both the forms of cognition and object are not apprehended in the cognition of fire, but [the form] only of fire, because [it alone] appears [in the cognition]."

220 For the *svabhāvahetu* and *kāryahetu* cf. especially *PVin* II(2) pp. 81f. and 101f., as well as Steinkellner's notes thereupon.

221 The *kāryahetu* is employed when the inferential mark and the inferred object are different things, the *svabhāvahetu* when they are the same thing. It is clear, therefore, that the word *kārya* in the compound *tatkāryatādātmya* cannot refer to the inferential mark. I assume it refers to the result of the inference, i.e., the inferred object.

222 Cf. the discussion against the Naiyāyikas § 1.4, especially § 1.42.

223 The word *artha* in *parasantānajñānārthakalpam* is not clear to me. The argument would have been clearer without it. Perhaps 'equal to the cognition in another series and its object'? Whatever the case may be, *artha* seems to refer here to the content of the cognition. It is possible that there is a lacuna in the manuscript just before this word, and that we have here only the end of a more detailed argument.

224 *tatkāryajñānasya* could perhaps be construed with *svasaṃvedyam* instead of *bhinnatvāt*. The meaning is not affected anyhow.

225 I interpret the word *prasiddhi* as cognition, i.e., as a synonym of *jñāna*, *pratīti*, etc. The usage of the word in this sense is not very common, but cf. for instance *Vy* p. 393.14 (on *PDhS* p. 168.3f. = *Vy* ed. p. 360.4-5: *śabdādiṣu prasiddhyā ca prasādhako [ko] 'numīyate*): *śabdādiṣu viṣayeṣu prasiddhir vijñānaṃ tayā prasādhakaḥ samavāyikāraṇam ātmānumīyate*.

226 Jayarāśi is turning Dharmakīrti's own words against him: *abhāvasāmarthyena samudbhavāt* is a slightly manipulated version of *PVin* I.4d: *arthasya sāmarthyena samudbhavāt*. Cf. n. 187 and the Buddhist fragment in § 4.1a.

227 In order to avoid the conjecture one could translate: "But it is not determined [neither as conceptual nor as non-conceptual] by being [determined] only [as] cognition." I did not adopt this interpretation because the text would be a bit too elliptical, and the adversative *api tu* would become awkward.

228 Since 'object' is defined by Dharmakīrti as that which produces the cognition and that which provides its form to the cognition, a mere absence, too, would have to fulfill these two conditions in order to become an object of cognition. Since it cannot do that the cognition is without an object.

229 At this point all the *vikalpas* enumerated as possible interpretations of *kalpanā* (§ 4.1) are already examined and rejected. Jayarāśi proceeds now to examine the word *kalpanā* as well as *kalpanāpoḍha* in various other Buddhist statements. Those quotations which I was able to identify come from *PVin* I and II.

230 This fragment strongly resembles *PVin* I.4d quoted above in n. 187. The only difference is that the proposi-

tion is presented here as a formal inference by the addition of an example.

[231] Jayarāśi uses similar arguments in § 4.17, cf. as well § 4.1(10)a2.

[232] The microfilm is absolutely illegible here. Sanghavi's edition (p. 38.5) reads *tatrāpi[pratīyamānārthasamudbhava?]sya* ... If this conjecture is accepted, the translation would run "Because the production by the perceived object has the purpose of refuting the external object."

This conjecture seems physically impossible (the unreadable part could contain at most seven or eight *akṣaras*), but as far as the content goes, it is quite reasonable. Dharmakīrti's refutation of the external object occurs in the context of the discussion of *pramāṇa* and *pramāṇaphala*, and it constitutes in fact one of the proofs which deny this distinction. Nothing can fulfill both conditions required by the definition of object (to produce the cognition and to provide the form to the cognition). The atoms may fulfill the first but not the second, the whole (*avayavin*) may fulfill the second but not the first. Thus, there is no object and consequently no contact between sense and object which could be considered as *pramāṇa* (cf. *PVin* I pp. 84.1-86.10). Since there are no sense data independent of cognitions, nobody knows whether there are objects outside the cognitions. One could assume this, of course, but the assumption is superfluous. Further, if the object were a necessary causal factor of a cognition, wrong cognitions which are not produced by their object would not be possible. Cf. *PVin* I.44 = *PV pratyakṣa* 353:

yathākathañcit tasyārtharūpaṃ muktvāvabhāsinaḥ/
arthagrahaḥ katham? satyaṃ na jāne 'ham apīdṛśam//

"How is the apprehension of an object [possible] for a [cognition] which appears somehow or other without the form of an object? True. I don't know either how [it is possible]." Cf. also *PVBh* ad loc., p. 395.17-22.

On Dharmakīrti's combination of the Sautrāntikas' 'one-layered series of cognition' (einschichtiger Erkenntnisstrom) with Yogācāra-Idealism cf. Schmithausen, "Sautrāntika-Voraussetzungen," pp. 127-29.

233 In the production of a cognition the Buddhists consider the previous cognition in the same series as *upādānakāraṇa* (= *samanantarapratyaya*) and the object, the senses, etc., as *nimittakāraṇa*, cf. Vetter, *Erkenntnisprobleme*, pp. 20-21. The object such as the visible etc., is *upādānakāraṇa* in respect to the visible which arises next in the same series.

234 Cf. *TUS* pp. 86.22-87.3: *atha tajjananasvabhāvo, na tarhi dahanād dhūmasyotpattir, dahanasya dahanajñānotpādakasvābhāvyena dhūmotpādakatvāyogāt. atha tenaiva svabhāvena dhūmam utpādayati, prāptā vijñānasyāpi dhūmarūpatā, dhūmasya vā vijñānarūpatā, abhinnātmotpādyate bhedakaṃ ca na bījam asti. atha svabhāvāntareṇa janayati, [na] ekasya svabhāvadvayābhāvāt - svabhāvadvaye ca* (read: *vā*) *ekatānupapannā. tataś ca dahanena dhūmotpādanaṃ kriyate na tadā svajñānam utpādayati.*

"If [fire] whose nature is to produce the [cognition of fire produces the cognition of fire], then smoke does not arise from fire, because fire, by having the nature of that which produces the cognition of fire, cannot be that which produces smoke.

If it produces smoke with exactly the same nature [with which it produces the cognition of fire], [then] the cognition, too, would have the nature of smoke, or smoke would have the nature of cognition. [Fire] is produced as something whose nature is unique/undivided, and there is no cause which differentiates [different aspects within the nature of fire].

If [fire] produces [the cognition/smoke] with another nature, [we answer: no,] because [one thing] does not have a double nature. Or if it had a double nature, its unity would become impossible. And thus, [if] smoke is produced by fire, then [fire] does not produce its own cognition."

235 The statement *sarvam avijñānātmakaṃ jagat syāt* is certainly formulated in analogy to the Yogācāra thesis according to which the whole world is nothing but cognition, although a bit strange in the context of the present *vikalpa* where the existence of the external object is accepted.

236 This is probably a free rendering of *PVin* I p. 60.1-4: *raṅ gi yul gyi de ma thag pa'i skad cig ma lhan cig byed pa can gyi dbaṅ po'i rnam par śes pa mtshuṅs pa de ma thag pa'i rkyen gyis bskyed pa'i yid kyaṅ mṅon sum yin no//*. Cf. also *NB* I.9: *svaviṣayānantaraviṣayasahakāriṇendriyajñānena samanantarapratyayena janitaṃ tan manovijñānam*.

I translated *anantara* as 'not different' in order to comply with Jayarāśi's intention. It is clear from the context that he interprets it that way. I am not sure whether this interpretation is linguistically correct, but this is the way the Buddhists themselves understood it. Cf. *NBṬ* p. 58.1-2: *anantaro - na vidyate 'ntaram asyeti. antaraṃ ca vyavadhānaṃ viśeṣaś cocyate.* "*anantara* means that for which there is no difference, and difference means difference [in time or space] as well as a distinguishing [property]." Dharmottara's intention is further clarified in the next sentence where as a result of the negation of both differences the object of *manojñāna* is said to be of the same kind (*samānajātiya*) as the previous one and existing in the next moment (*tataś cāntare pratiṣiddhe samānajā-

tīyo dvitīyakṣaṇabhāvy upādeyakṣaṇaḥ ...). Jayarāśi is aware of both interpretations, for on p. 204.18 he interprets *anantara* in the usual meaning of 'that which immediately follows.'

It is not entirely clear to me on what the argument bears. For as far as I understand him, Jayarāśi refers to the object of sense cognition and to the object of mental cognition as one and the same thing which the different names do not change. Note, however, that the compound *svaviṣayānantaraviṣaya* was introduced into the definition precisely in order to avoid the charge of apprehension of an apprehended object, i.e., to provide the mental perception with an object different from the object of sense perception. Cf. *NBṬ* p. 61.1-2: *yadā cendriyajñānaviṣayād anyo viṣayo manovijñānasya tadā gṛhītagrahaṇād āsañjito 'prāmāṇyadoṣo nirastaḥ.* "And since the mental cognition has an object different from the object of sense cognition the fault of non-validity which has been attached [to it] because of the apprehension of an apprehended [object] is dispelled."

However, Jayarāśi's statement is not without basis in the Buddhist writings. It is clear from Dharmakīrti's and Dharmottara's polemical statements that other logicians rejected mental perception as a means of valid cognition because it apprehends an apprehended object, that is, because it apprehends the object of sense perception. Furthermore, even in Dharmakīrti's writings one can find the same. Immediately after the definition in the *PVin* I quoted above he says (p. 60.4-5): *de ñid kyi phyir dbaṅ po med par mthoṅ ba ma yin źiṅ/ yul gźan pa ñid kyaṅ ma yin no//.* "Therefore, [mental perception] is not seeing without the senses and does not have an object different [from the object of sense perception]."

This statement of Dharmakīrti is a bit perplexing, and Vetter notes (p. 104, n. 32) that "Im Sinne von *PV* III, 243c würde man keine oder zwei Negationen erwarten: 'und

Verschiedenheit des Objekts' oder 'noch keine Verschiedenheit des Objekts'. Es ist aber auch möglich, dass hier diese Seite der Argumentation noch nicht berührt wird, und dass sie erst nach Vers 20 zum ersten Mal erwähnt wird." This, however, does not solve the problem, for even granting that Dharmakīrti elaborates on the subject after verse 20 this does not explain why he should say the opposite before. For lack of any better explanation I think we should follow Dharmottara in his interpretation which explains the non-difference as a qualitative non-difference, i.e., both objects are of the same kind (*samānajātīya*).

[237] An example which lacks the reason (*sādhanavikala*) is one of the three kinds of false examples (*dṛṣṭāntābhāsa*). The other two are the examples without the *sādhya* and without both, cf. *NB* III.124: *yathā nityaḥ śabdo 'mūrttatvāt, karmavat paramāṇuvad ghaṭavad iti. ete dṛṣṭāntābhāsāḥ sādhyasādhanadharmobhayavikalāḥ*.

[238] If the example wouldn't be devoid of the reason, one could infer: the visible etc., is free from conceptual construction, because it is produced by the capacity of an object, which appeared in the form of a visible etc. This inference is disproved by the immediately preceding discussion where Jayarāśi argued that if a visible produces a cognition, it cannot produce another visible. Note that the whole argument is only valid in the context where the object which produces the cognition is considered as identical with the object which appears in the cognition (p. 202.16). This is the reason why the argument is raised here, before the second *vikalpa* is taken up, and not at the end of the discussion.

[239] This refers back to p. 202.15 (*arthamātrodbhavatva*).

[240] I was unable to identify this quotation. I followed Sanghavi and Parikh in translating up to p. 206.9 as a quotation; but perhaps the fragment extends only up to the *iti* on p. 206.7. The word *kila* is not quite clear to me in this context. It is often used to denote a somewhat ironical disagreement with one's opponent's statement (roughly: 'supposedly'). It is possible, therefore, that Jayarāśi paraphrases the Buddhist statement before affirming that it is not correct. On the other hand it is natural to connect *yad apy anyad uktam* with *tad api na yuktam*. Unable to decide between the two alternatives I simply followed my predecessors.

Dharmakīrti defines non-apprehension (*anupalabdhi*) as another apprehension, cf. *HB* I p. 71.21-22: *tasmād anyopalabdhir anupalabdhir, vivakṣitopalabdher anyatvād abhakṣyāsparśanīyavat paryudāsavṛttyā*. "Therefore, non-apprehension is a different apprehension, because [it] is different from the intended apprehension, in as much as it consists in excluding negation, just as [talking of specific things as] not to be eaten, not to be touched [means that something else can be eaten etc.]."

Non-apprehension is always considered as excluding negation (*paryudāsa-* as opposed to *prasajyapratiṣedha*), i.e., the affirmation of one thing through the negation of another. Thus, 'The pot is not perceived' means 'The ground is perceived.'

On the basis of the perception of one of two things, the following consideration arises: if two things which equally fulfill the conditions for perception (*upalabdhilakṣaṇaprāpta*) were present here, both of them would have to appear in the cognition. Since only one of them (the ground) appears, the other (the pot) must be absent. It is probably in this sense that the fragment has to be understood. A somewhat similar formulation occurs in *HB* I p. 83.9-10: *tad evam ekasyopalambhāt tasya tadanyātmano vyava-*

cchedaḥ ... "Thus, from the apprehension of one [thing] this [other thing] which is different from it is excluded/ negated."

On Dharmakīrti's theory of *anupalabdhi* cf. especially *HB* § c., and Steinkellner's notes thereupon.

241 *pratyakṣasādhana evendriyadhiyaḥ kalpanāvirahaḥ* is a new Sanskrit fragment for *PVin* I p. 50.12-13: *yaṅ na dbaṅ po'i blo rtog pa daṅ bral bar sgrub par byed pa ni mṅon sum ñid de/*. Cf. also *PV pratyakṣa* 123ab: *pratyakṣaṃ kalpanāpoḍhaṃ pratyakṣeṇaiva sidhyati/*. "Perception is free from conceptual construction; this is established by perception itself."

The proof intended here is that a colour cognition arises even when all thinking stops, cf. *PVin* I.13 = *PV pratyakṣa* 124:

saṃhṛtya sarvataś cintāṃ stimitenāntarātmanā/
sthito 'pi cakṣuṣā rūpam īkṣate sākṣajā matiḥ//

"Even when [a person] withdraws [his] thinking from everything [and] remains with [his] inner self motionless, he perceives something visible with [his] eye. This cognition [of something visible] arises from the sense [without thinking, and therefore it cannot be conceptual]."

The particle *eva* in the first two quotations from Dharmakīrti should not be understood as an exclusion, 'only by perception,' but simply as an emphasis, 'by perception itself.' Dharmakīrti considers other proofs as superfluous (ibid., p. 50.19-20: ... *'di la sgrub par byed pa gźan gyis ci źig bya*), but certainly not as objectionable, for he formulates himself another proof in the immediately preceding discussion; cf. also *TSP* p. 461.17: *evaṃ pratyakṣato dhiyaḥ kalpanāviraham pratipādya, sāmpratam anumānato pratipādayati*.

[242] Sanghavi and Parikh consider *kathaṃ syur vividhākārās tadekasya vastunaḥ* as the quotation of a half-verse. Note, however, that there are only 15 syllables, and that there is nothing external to the proposition (*iti, yad uktam*, etc.) to indicate that it is a quotation. Perhaps the reason which compelled them to take it as a quotation is the *tad* in *tadekasya*.

In any case, one is strongly reminded of *PVin* I.49 = PV *pratyakṣa* 358:

anyathaikasya bhāvasya nānārūpāvabhāsinaḥ/
satyāḥ (satyaṃ) kathaṃ syur ākārās tadekatvasya hānitaḥ//

"Otherwise (i.e., if the cognition had parts such as apprehender, apprehended object and self-apprehension) how could the forms, which appear as many different forms of one single thing,
be real, for the unity of this [thing, i.e., the cognition] would be destroyed."

Cf. also § 4.25a.

[243] The Buddhist argument is not raised against the cognition of the word 'cow,' but rather against the conceptual perception (*savikalpakapratyakṣa*) 'cow.' The Naiyāyikas of the Ācārya school do not admit the *savikalpakapratyakṣa* as a cognition based on a word (*śābda*), although they accept (in some cases?) that it depends on the recollection of the word. Cf. *NM* I p. 210.7-8: *na gaur ityādijñānam indriyārthasannikarṣotpannam apīdaṃ śābdam iti vaktuṃ yuktam. na cātra śabdāvacchinnārthaḥ prakāśate* ... "And it is not correct to say about the cognition 'cow' etc., that it is a verbal cognition, although it arises from the contact between sense and object. For an object qualified by a word does not appear in it ..."

Cf. also *NBhū* pp. 180.25-181.1: *yad api na hy arthe śabdāḥ santītyādi tad api viśeṣaṇaviśeṣyayor ekajñānālambanatvapratiṣedhenaiva nirastam. na cāyaṃ gaur iti jñāne śabdaḥ pratibhāti, kiṃ tarhi? sāsnādimān arthaḥ, śuklo 'yaṃ pīno viṣāṇī gacchatītyādi sāmānādhikaraṇyapratīteḥ.*

"As for [Dharmakīrti's objection in *PVin* I p. 40.13-14, viz., that] 'Words do not exist in the object,' etc., this [objection], too, is refuted already by [our] denial that the qualifying [word] and the qualified [thing] are the object of the same cognition. For the word ['cow'] does not appear in the cognition 'This is a cow.' What then? A thing which has a dewlap etc., [and it appears that way] because of the cognition that [several perceptible factors] have a common locus [in the form:] 'This white, plump, horned [thing] goes,' etc."

The recollection of the word may play an important role in enriching the content of the cognition, but the word itself is not admitted as the object of cognition. Cf. *NBhū* p. 182.10-12: *na hi cakṣurādijñānaviṣayatvaṃ śabdasyābhyupagamyate, kiṃ tu saṅketānubhavasahakāriṇā tatsmṛtisahakāriṇā vā cakṣurādinā svasminn eva viṣaye gaur ityādijñānam utpadyate.* "For it is not admitted that the word is the object of an eye-cognition etc., but [only that] the eye etc., assisted by the experience of the convention [that this word denotes that object], or by the recollection of the [word], produces the cognition 'cow' etc., in respect to its **own** object (i.e., the visible cow etc.)."

In opposition to the Ācārya school the Vyākhyātṛ school did not accept any conceptual cognition as perception, cf. Schmithausen, *Vibhramaviveka*, pp. 181-82, 255.

[244] The following two verses are *PVin* I.5-6 (quoted inversely). I quote only the Sanskrit fragment from Steinkellner, "New Sanskrit-Fragments," p. 201: *PVin* I pp. 40.20-42.30 = *NBhū* p. 179.2-17:

nāpi tadbalenodīyamānaṃ vijñānam arthāntaram anusartuṃ yuktaṃ, rasādi<*vi*, so tib.>*jñānavat. sato 'pi tadātmanendriyāntarajñānotpattāv asāmarthyād atiprasaṅgāc ca. vikal-*

pakaṃ tu manovijñānam, arthasannidhānānapekṣaṃ vikalpavāsanotthāpitam aniyatendriyārthagrāhi kutaścid anubhavasambandhāt saha pṛthag vā gṛhṇīyāt. api ca

arthopayoge 'pi punaḥ smārtaṃ śabdānuyojanam/
akṣadhīr yady apekṣeta so 'rtho vyavahito bhavet//5//

na hi saṅketakālabhāvinam abhilāpasāmānyam asmaratas tadyojanā sambhavati, śabdāntaravat. na cārthābhipātakṛte 'saty āntare vikāre śabdaviśeṣe smṛtir yuktā, tasyātatkṛtatve tannāmā(NBhū: nāma)grahaṇaprasaṅgāt. tatsmṛtyā vyavadhānān nārthopayogo 'nantaravyāpāraphalaḥ syāt, tataś ca

yaḥ prāg ajanako buddher upayogāviśeṣataḥ/
sa paścād api

syāt. ātmābhedena sāmarthyāviśeṣān naikasyaikatra kriyākriye sambhavataḥ.

tena syād arthāpāye 'pi netradhīḥ//6//

arthasya sākṣād buddhāv anupayogāt smṛtiprabodhe copayuktatvān nāsyānupakāriṇo buddhir bhāvam apekṣeta. arthābhipātakṛte ca buddhijanmany abhilāpasmṛtyantarābhāvāt.

"Nor can the cognition which is produced by the capacity of that [object] correspond to another object, just as the cognition of flavour etc. [being produced by flavour, cannot correspond to a visible etc.], because, although it exists, it (i.e. the word) is not capable to produce a cognition by [means of] another sense [like the eye etc.] with that nature (i.e., the nature of a word), and because this would lead too far. A conceptual [cognition], however, is a mental cognition: In as much as it has arisen by traces [left] by [previous] conceptualizations, independently of the presence of an object, it apprehends an object which is not restricted to a [certain] sense; [this mental cognition] can apprehend [its object] either together [with a present object of sensory cognition] due to some relation with [immediate] experience, or separately [without any relation to a present object]. Furthermore,

> even if [one admits] the capacity of the object [to produce this conceptual cognition], nevertheless if sensory cognition would depend on the remembered relation [of the object] with a word [as well], this object (i.e., the object of the sensory cognition) would be separated [in time from its result]. (5)

For relating [the object] with that [word] is impossible for someone who does not recollect the universal which [consists in] a word/concept [and] which is impressed at the time of the convention [that this word denotes a certain object], just as [it is not possible to relate to that object] another word [which does not designate it]. And when there is no inner modification caused by the presence of the object, the recollection of a specific word is not possible, because when this [inner modification] is not caused by that [presence of the object], there can be no apprehension of its name. The [causal] capacity of the object would not result in an immediately following activity, because [it] is separated [from its result] by the recollection [of the word]. And therefore:

> That which did not produce the cognition before, would [not produce it] afterwards either, because there is no difference in [its causal] efficiency.

Since there is no difference in the capacity [of the object], in as much as [its] nature remains the same, [both] action and non-action of one [thing] in respect to another [thing] are impossible.

> Thus there would be a visual cognition even when the object has [already] disappeared. (6)

Since the object is not capable to [produce this conceptual] cognition directly, and since it is capable to cause the awaking of the recollection, the [conceptual] cognition cannot depend [in its production] on the presence of the [object] which does not participate [in it]. And because the recollection of a word does not come in between when the cognition arises due to the presence of an object [perception is established as free from conceptual construction = ibid., p. 42.30-31: ... *mṅon sum rtog pa med par grub pa yin no//*].

For the slight disagreements with the Tibetan translation cf. Steinkellner, ibid., nn. 14-16. Cf. also *NM* I p. 237.7f and *ŚVV* p. 178.13-18.

245 Cf. the previous note.

246 According to the arguments in the following passage all perceptions are conceptual. Jayarāśi propounds here a position which is even more extreme than that of the Naiyāyikas, for even they admit that the first cognition of an object is not conceptual. However, it is quite clear from the following discussion (cf. especially the parody of *NB* I.9 on p. 212.15-17) that Jayarāśi does not take this position seriously, but simply uses it as an analogy in order to point out that the Buddhists are guilty of the same inconsistencies and arbitrariness of which they accuse their opponents.

I do not think that Jayarāśi thought up the position he maintains here. As a matter of fact it bears a strong resemblence to that of Bhartṛhari, cf. *VP* 1.123:

na so 'sti pratyayo loke yaḥ śabdānugamād ṛte/
anuviddham iva jñānaṃ sarvaṃ śabdena bhāsate//

"There is no cognition in the world which is not accompanied by a word.
Every cognition appears, as it were, as permeated by a word."

Cf. also the discussion of this verse in *NM* I p. 209.7f. and *NBhū* pp. 580.27f. Cf. also Biardeau, *Théorie de la Connaissance*, pp. 311f., especially pp. 317-19, Iyer, *Bhartṛhari*, pp. 100f. Cf. also *DhPr* p. 35.21: *savikalpakam eva pratyakṣam iti vaiyākaraṇabārhaspatyādinām.*

[247] I felt obliged to interpret *-nayanālokavijñāna* as a *dvandva* compound. One could perhaps interpret *āloka* as *ālocana*, and thus translate 'visual perceptual cognitions,' but in this case the mode of expression would be highly redundant. Besides, I am not at all sure whether *ālokajñāna* can be interpreted as *ālocanajñāna*; as far as my reading goes, I never saw it used that way. If, on the other hand, *āloka* is taken in its usual meaning, one may interpret *ālokajñāna* as 'light-cognition,' i.e., as visual cognition. In this case, however, *nayana-* is absolutely redundant. I see, therefore, no other way but to take the compound as a *dvandva*. This interpretation is also corroborated by the parallel passages in the *TUS* p. 71.15, 74.26, 85.15, etc. But then we have to conclude that a blue object produces not only its cognition, but also the light, the eye, etc. This conclusion is quite strange, but it fits perfectly the Buddhist theory presupposed by Jayarāśi in his arguments against the series of cognitions (*vijñānasantāna*), cf. § e. According to this theory, every element is material cause (*upādānakāraṇa*) of the element similar to it, and efficient cause (*nimittakāraṇa*) of all other causes of the cognition in the next moment. Thus, the cognition, too, is the material cause of the cognition in the next moment, and the efficient cause of the object, the light, etc., in the next moment. This amounts, of course, to the affirmation that the cognition produces the object at the next moment! Cf. for instance p. 258.11-12: *ekasvabhāvād api vijñānād anekaṃ nayanālokādikāryam utpadyate.* "Several effects, the eye, the light, etc., are produced from a cognition although it has a unique character."

This theory may be represented as follows:

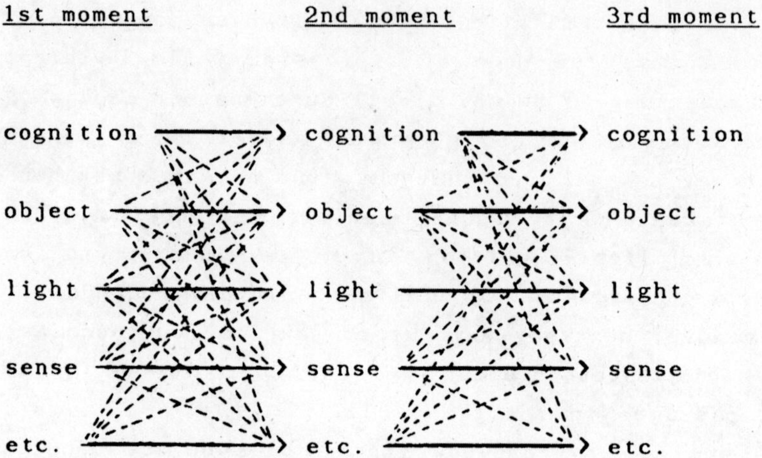

——> stands for the relation between material cause and its effect,

----> stands for the relation between efficient cause and its effect.

I did not come across this theory in the Buddhist writings, but it could be developed from Dharmakīrti's statements on causality, cf. for instance *HB* § b.122153(1), where certain co-producers are said to bring about changes (keenness etc.) in the sense, or water, earth, etc., to modify the seed (before the sprout is produced!), in as much as they co-produce the sense and the seed at the next moment.

[248] Cf. § d.7, cf. also *TUS* p. 87.8-18: *ito 'pi dahanadhūmayor hetuphalabhāvānupapattiḥ. yathāvicalitadahanasvarūpasya pūrvāparānekakāryāvirbhāvakatvaṃ na pratipadyate bhavadbhis tathānāyattavikārasya yugapadutpannānekakāryāvirbhāvakatvam api na pratyetavyam. athābhyupagamyate yugapadanekakāryotpādakatvaṃ yugapadanekakāryotpādanaśaktiyuktasyotpatteḥ. yady evaṃ, kramabhāvyanekakāryāvirbhāvakatva-*

syotpatter (read with ms: *-kasyotpatter*) *ayugapadekaṃ kāryaṃ vidadhyāt. vidadhāty eveti ced, idam āpekṣikaṃ* (read with ms: *idam evākṣaṇikatvaṃ*) *yat kramabhāvyanekakāryajanakātmakaṃ svarūpam. etadabhyupagame 'bhyupetahānam āpadyate. athāvicalitarūpeṇa pūrvāparakāryaṃ na janyate, tadā yugapad api na kuryād anāyattavikāraḥ. tataś ca na dahanād dhūmasyotpattiḥ.*

"For the following [reason], too, the relation of cause and effect between fire and smoke is impossible: just as you do not accept that something whose nature of fire is steady manifests (i.e., produces) several effects one after the other, in the same manner, [you] should not accept as well that something in which a modification does not occur manifests several effects which arise at the same time.

[Objection:] The fact that something produces several effects at the same time is admitted, because it arises connected to the capacity of producing several effects at the same time.

[Reply:] If so, [then] because [fire] arises as something which manifests several effects one after the other, it should produce an effect which is neither one nor [arises] at once. If [you claim that] it does produce [such an effect], [it] is certainly not momentary, for it is something whose nature is to produce several effects one after the other. When this is admitted, [you] would give up [your] position. [Therefore] if something whose nature is steady does not produce [several] effects one after the other, then something in which a modification does not occur would not produce [several effects] at the same time either. And thus, smoke does not arise from fire [in as much as fire produces its own cognition]."

249 Cf. n. 236. Note that Jayarāśi interprets here *anantara* as 'that which immediately follows,' and not, as on p. 204.18, as 'that which is not different.'

[250] *nirviṣayatvābhāva* refers back to *arthenājanitatvāt* p. 208.20.

[251] Cf. p. 210.2.

[252] Cf. p. 174.2-5.

[253] Cf. for instance *PVSV* p. 17.1-2: *evaṃ ca svabhāvaṃ parityajya kathaṃ bhāvo bhavet.*

[254] Cf. p. 226.15-21.

[255] It is quite clear that Jayarāśi uses the word *avyabhicārin* with reference to Dharmakīrti's definition of perception quoted in § 4.1. However, I do not know why he uses this word instead of *abhrānta* (cf. already p. 188.11). One reason for that could be the lack of unanimity among the Buddhist logicians about the meaning of the word *abhrānta*.

The problem, as I see it, arises from Dharmakīrti's modification of Dignāga's definition of perception. Dharmakīrti claimed that there are errors free from conceptual construction, for instance *taimirajñāna*, and therefore added the word *abhrānta* in order to exclude them from the definition. By adding this word, Dharmakīrti transgressed one of the basic rules of correct definition, namely, that every word in a definition must have a purpose; in other words: any superfluous word invalidates the whole definition. Since both Dignāga and Dharmakīrti regarded inference as a somewhat false means of knowledge (*bhrānta*), the addition of the word *abhrānta* to the definition of perception rendered the word *kalpanāpoḍha* superfluous: inference is *bhrānta*, and therefore nothing is excluded from the definition by the word *kalpanāpoḍha*.

I do not know whether Dharmakīrti himself was already aware of this problem. In any case, every logician after

Dharmakīrti had to struggle with it. Some, like Vinītadeva and Kamalaśīla (cf. *NBṬ(V)* ad I.3, *TSP* p. 479.21) explained *abhrānta* as *avisaṃvādaka*, justifying their interpretation by claiming that otherwise the definition would not be acceptable from the Yogācāra point of view which denies the existence of the external object. Dharmottara objected to Vinītadeva's interpretation by pointing out that *avisaṃvādaka* is the general definition of a means of valid cognition, and thus part of the definition would be rendered redundant: perception which as a means of valid cognition does not belie its promise is free from conceptual construction and does not belie (cf. *NBṬ* p. 47.5: *pratyakṣākhyaṃ yad avisaṃvādakaṃ jñānaṃ tat kalpanāpoḍham avisaṃvādakaṃ ceti*). According to Dharmottara each one of the two words is enough to differentiate perception from inference, and both are used to reject diverging opinions (*vipratipatti*). The word *abhrānta* is directed against those who think that the illusion of moving trees is perception because it is not conceptual and the trees can be reached. Which opinion is rejected by the word *kalpanāpoḍha* he does not say, but Durveka (*DhPr* p. 46.23f.) explains it as directed against those who accept *savikalpakapratyakṣa*. Prajñākaragupta (*PVBh* p. 334.24-26) on the other hand claims that only the word *kalpanāpoḍha* is used to reject the opinion of others (again *savikalpakapratyakṣa*), whereas the word *abhrānta* is used to define perception. Still others argued that the word *abhrānta* does not exclude the *taimirajñāna*, which they considered as conceptual, but the *svapnāntikajñāna* (cf. *TS(P)* v. 1312-3, on the difference between *svapna* and *svapnāntika* cf. *TSP* p. 103.21-22). And finally there were those who suggested to drop the word *abhrānta* altogether, and to revert to the old definition of Dignāga (cf. *TS(P)* v. 1323, the same suggestion appears in *PVBh* pp. 352.30-353.2, but supported by different reasons).

An echo to this embarrassing situation may be found in the famous verse of Jayanta which mocks Dharmakīrti - desirous of making a correct definition, but unable to put two words together (*NM* I p. 259.1-4):

iti sunipuṇabuddhir lakṣaṇaṃ vaktukāmaḥ
padayugalam apīdaṃ nirmame nānavadyam/
bhavatu, matimahimnaś ceṣṭitaṃ dṛṣṭam etad
jagad abhibhavadhīraṃ dhīmato dharmakīrteḥ//

As far as Jayarāśi's arguments are concerned, he uses the word *avyabhicārin* as 'absolutely nonerroneous,' i.e., as in Dharmottara and Prajñākaragupta's interpretation of the word *abhrānta*, which is, I think, the most faithful to Dharmakīrti. The arguments on the whole repeat those in § 1.1b, although some changes are necessary since the opponent there is a Naiyāyika and here a Buddhist. Thus, the argument based on *jñānāyaugapadya* (p. 114.7) could not be introduced here without complicating matters unnecessarily; in the same manner, the arguments based on *svasaṃvedana* could not be applied to the Naiyāyika. In spite of these differences the frame of the discussion remains very much the same. Perhaps one reason why Jayarāśi uses *avyabhicārin* instead of *abhrānta* is to point out that by employing this word Dharmakīrti does not mean anything different from what the Naiyāyikas mean while using *avyabhicārin*, and if so, the arguments raised by Dignāga against the word *avyabhicārin* (cf. *PS* I section 3, Hattori's translation p. 36 and n. 7 thereupon) may be used against Dharmakīrti and his followers.

[256] Cf. p. 116.10-11.

[257] Cf. p. 112.14f. (§ 1.1b).

[258] Cf. p. 120.15f.

[259] Here again, the expression *yadi nāma* is not clear to me. According to Sanghavi and Parikh's punctuation it has

to be construed with *bādhyate*, but I cannot figure out in which meaning. If the meaning is 'although,' it is probably better to construe it with *pratīyate*.

[260] On Dharmakīrti's definition of object cf. n. 178.

[261] On *svāṃśa* cf. n. 174.

[262] Cognitions of feelings etc., are nothing but the feelings themselves; thus, they are cognitions which have themselves as their objects, but they are not called 'a cognition of water.'

[263] Cf. *TUS* p. 93.12-14: *atha nirviṣayam ānumānikaṃ jñānaṃ, tad ayuktaṃ, svāṃśaviṣayatvāt. na hi bhavatāṃ pakṣe nirālambanaṃ kiñcid vijñānam asty, ātmāvagāhakatvenotpatteḥ.* "If inferential cognition is without an object, this is not correct, because [it] has a part of itself as object. For according to your position there is no cognition whatsoever without an object, because [every cognition] arises as apprehending itself."

Cf. also *TUS* p. 95.13-14: *na hi bhavatāṃ pakṣe nirālambanajñānam asti svāṃśaparyavasitatvāt*; *ŚVV* p. 195.12-13: *bāhyārthābhāve pramāṇatadābhāsavyavasthā na syāt, svāṃśālambanasyaiva sarvatra vidyamānatvāt.* "If the external object does not exist, there would be no determination of means of valid cognition and their [false] appearances, because the object which [consists in] a part of [the cognition] itself is present in every [cognition]." Cf. also ibid., p. 222.15-16: *bauddhapakṣa eva tu sarveṣāṃ svāṃśālambanatvena tulyatvāt svapnādau nirālambanāsadālambanaśabdayoḥ sapramāṇakaḥ prayogo na prāpnotīti.*

[264] The arguments here repeat in more detail those already used in § 1.142. The whole passage seems quite tedious.

Jayarāśi seems to enjoy leading his opponent by the nose through a labyrinth of *vikalpas*, a great deal of which seems gratuitous, and when one finally reaches the crucial one (p. 222.11), Jayarāśi twists the opponent's words (by taking them literally!) in such a way that we have to go through the same *vikalpas* all over again. The only argument of any consequence is not raised until p. 224.16.

265 The presupposition for this argument becomes clear only in the next passage: the material cause has no parts. This is generally true for every atomic entity as accepted by the Sautrāntikas. As far as the cognition is concerned, Dharmakīrti explicitly states that any division within a cognition such as into apprehended and apprehending part is illusory. The basic idea in this passage is that a cognition cannot be partly imitated, since it has no parts. Thus, all cognitions within the same series, i.e., all cognitions which are in a causal relationship to each other, and therefore imitate each other, would have to be of the same kind; either all are true, or all are false, since the result is supposed to imitate its immediately preceding cause (*samanantarapratyaya*). On Dharmakīrti's denial of parts in a cognition (which is a blatant critique of Dignāga even though the latter's name is not mentioned) cf. *PVin* I.45 = *PV pratyakṣa* 354:

avibhāgo 'pi buddhyātmā viparyāsitadarśanaiḥ/
grāhyagrāhakasaṃvittibhedavān iva lakṣyate//

"Although the nature of cognition has no parts, [nevertheless] it is characterized by [people] who see [it] wrongly as if it had an apprehended [part], an apprehending [part], and a [self-]apprehending part."

Cf. also *PVin* I.49 quoted in n. 242.

266 Cf. § 4.1e.

[267] The arguments in this passage are basically the same as in the previous one (p. 224.19f.). Note, however, that the topic changes. We are not dealing with erroneous and nonerroneous cognitions, but with cognitions as such.

[268] Cf. *TUS* pp. 87.24-88.4: *ito 'pi dahanasya dhūmāvirbhāvakatvaṃ na jāghaṭīti. kiṃ nimittabhūtena dhūmotpādanaṃ kriyate, kiṃ vopādānabhūtena? tad yadi nimittabhūtenotpādyate, tadā dhūmarūpatā na prāpnoty upādānaṃ vinā. athopādānabhūtenotpādanaṃ kriyate, nanv asamānajātīyaṃ katham upādānakāraṇaṃ bhavet? abhyupagame vā dehendriyasaṅghātād eva garbhādau vijñānaṃ bhaviṣyaty alaṃ paralokavijñānakalpanayā.*

"For the following [reason], too, fire cannot manifest smoke: is smoke produced by [fire] as efficient [cause], or as material [cause]? In respect to these [alternatives], if [smoke] is produced by [fire] as efficient [cause], then [this is not correct, because smoke] does not obtain the nature of smoke without a material [cause]. If [smoke] is produced by [fire] as material [cause], how could [something] which is not of the same kind [as smoke] be [its] material cause? Or, if [this] is admitted, the [first] cognition in a foetus etc., could arise from the combination of body and senses alone. [Thus] the assumption of a cognition in another world (i.e., a previous life) [as the material cause of the first cognition in the next life] is superfluous."

Cf. also § d.8.

[269] Cf. p. 204.16.

[270] The use of the word *ātman* is somewhat strange in this context where the opponent is a Buddhist. Jayarāśi is right, I believe, in equating *paralokin* and *ātman* in as much as the original intention of the *Bṛhaspatisūtra* is

concerned; for the Buddhists, however, *paralokin* as well as *ātman* can only refer to a cognition or a series of cognitions.

271 *paralokino 'bhāvāt paralokābhāvaḥ* is a quotation of a *bṛhaspatisūtra* (A 11 in Namai's enumeration). The *sūtra* is also quoted e.g., *TSP* p. 633.20-21, *SVR* p. 1109.17, *TBV* pp. 71.29, 91.33, 731.37-38, *NKC* pp. 343.16-17, 345.16-17.

I have translated *paraloka* as 'other world' because this is probably the original meaning of the expression in the *sūtra*, which was written in a strong anti-ritualistic vein. However, in Jayarāśi's time *paraloka* means simply other existences or rebirth, and does not exclude rebirth in this world. Cf. e.g., *NM* II p. 358.16-17, cf. also Preisendanz, *Nayatattvāloka*, n. 27.

272 This seems to be a variant of *PVin* I.22 = *PV pratyakṣa* 251:

de daṅ de min raṅ bźin can/
de de min dṅos rgyu las skyes/
des śes tha dad med rgyus bskyed/
bde sogs ci phyir śes ma yin//

tadatadrūpiṇo bhāvās tadatadrūpahetujāḥ/
tat sukhādi kim ajñānaṃ vijñānābhinnahetujam//

The only difference between this verse and the one quoted by Jayarāśi is that Jayarāśi has *rūpādi* instead of *sukhādi*. It is interesting to note that the verse is quoted with the same variant *PVBh* p. 313.11-12, but as a *pūrvapakṣa* (it is introduced with *anenaitad api nirastam*). Mahendrakumar Jain who refers to this passage (*SVṬ*, English introduction, p. 42) suggests that it was Jayarāśi who modified the verse, and that in fact Prajñākaragupta is replying to Jayarāśi. This suggestion, however, does not seem very likely, for the *pūrvapakṣa* in the *PVBh* seems to be a Mīmāṃsaka (note the use of *arthāpatti* in the discussion). I think it is more probable to assume that Jayarāśi quotes a variant of *PVin* I.22, a variant which was also known to Prajñākaragupta and rejected by him. In any case, I fail to discover any reference to the *TUS* in the *PVBh* (cf. also pp. 10-11 above).

The same verse is also quoted in *NM* I p. 195.8-9, *NKC* p. 126.18-19, *ŚVK* I p. 239.12-13, *AS* p. 78.13-14, *SVR* p. 174.9-10, *Vy* p. 627.18-19, which all read *sukhādi* (for some more references which I was unable to check cf. *NKC* p. 126, n. 1); thus, the variant *rūpādi* is surely to be discarded (unless, of course, we do not deal at all with a quotation from the *PVin* or *PV*). However, Dharmakīrti's position is not misrepresented by the reading *rūpādi*, cf. for instance *PVin* I.55ab: *sahopalambhaniyamād abhedo nīlataddhiyoḥ/*. "Because [they] are necessarily apprehended together, there is no difference between a blue [object] and its cognition."

[273] Cf. n. 265.

[274] The following arguments are probably inspired by the Buddhist critique of the universal and the whole (*avayavin*). One of Jayarāśi's favourite techniques is to take a Buddhist argument, originally formulated against the Naiyāyikas or the Mīmāṃsakas, and to apply it against the Buddhists themselves. In the present case he seems to draw an analogy between the residence of the universal in the individual and the whole in its part on the one hand, and the production of cognition on the other hand; an analogy which is based on the fact that the universal and the whole (for the Naiyāyikas) and the cognition (for the Buddhists) have no parts. If the entire universal or whole, argues the Buddhist, resides in an individual or a part (if they are 'exhausted' in them), then they cannot reside in another individual of the same class or in other parts. If, on the

other hand, only part of the universal or part of the whole resides in one individual or part, then the universal and the whole have parts, and thus they lose their unity.

Such arguments were raised very early by the Buddhist logicians and appear already as a *pūrvapakṣa* in the *Nyāya-sūtra*, cf. *NS* 4.2.6-8: *vṛttyanupapatter api* (variant: *api tarhi*) *na saṃśayaḥ. kṛtsnaikadeśāvṛttitvād avayavānām avayavyabhāvaḥ. teṣu cāvṛtter avayavyabhāvaḥ.* "There is no doubt [that the whole does not exist] as well because the residence is impossible. Because the parts reside neither in the entire [whole] nor in a part [of the whole], there is no whole (i.e., no part can reside in the entire whole because the whole is bigger than a part, nor can it reside in a part of the whole because the whole has no parts). And because [the whole] does not reside in the [parts] there is no whole (i.e., the entire whole cannot reside in a part because it would be absent in the other parts, and it cannot reside partly in a part because it has no parts)."

Cf. also *AKBh* on III.100ab, p. 189.19f., de la Vallée Poussin's translation chapter 3, pp. 212f.

It seems that this argument was first raised against the whole and then applied by analogy to the universal, cf. for instance *NV* 2.2.64 p. 668.19-21: *yady anekānuvṛtti gotvaṃ tat kiṃ pratipiṇḍaṃ parisamāptyā vartata athaikadeśeneti? kiṃ cātaḥ? yadi pratipiṇḍaṃ parisamāptyā vartate, piṇḍavad asādhāraṇatvān na sāmānyaṃ bhavitum arhati. athaikadeśena vartate tathāpi naikam anekatra vartate, kiṃ tv anekam anekatreti.*

"If [the universal] 'cow' is recurrent in several [cows], then does it reside entirely or partly in a [given] individual [cow]? And what are the consequences? If it resides entirely in a [given] individual, then it cannot be a universal because it is not common, just like the individual. If it resides partly [in one individual and partly in others], even then it is not one which resides in many, but many [which reside] in many. [Thus, a unique universal which resides in many individuals is impossible.]"

In very much the same manner Jayarāśi argues that if a cognition is produced completely by its object, it cannot be produced by other causal factors; if it is partly produced by the object, it would have parts and loose its unity. Put in this way, the argument is formulated from the point of view of the effect, but it can also be formulated from the point of view of the cause (cf. § 4.25c): If the causal efficiency of an object is exhausted in producing its cognition, it cannot produce the object in the next moment. Nor can it produce the cognition with only a part of itself, because it has no parts (it may be reminded that for Dharmakīrti things are nothing but their causal efficiency).

Dharmakīrti's theory of the production of cognition is clearly illustrated by the following scheme taken from *HB* II p. 127, n. 38:

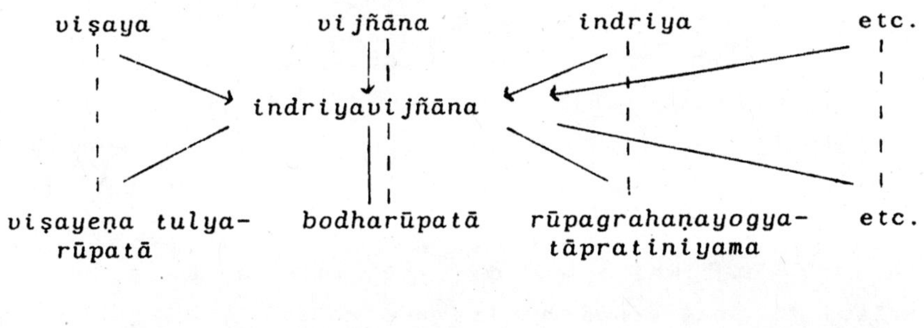

Arrows represent causal relation, lines qualifications through properties, broken lines attribution of characteristic properties to the corresponding cause in the causal complex.

On *vṛttivikalpadoṣa* cf. also n. 276.

Jayarāśi's direct answer to the Buddhist critique appears in *TUS* p. 94.1-15: *yāpi yuktir apadiṣṭā vijñānamātrasthitāv avayavinirākaraṇaparā vṛttyanupapattyādirūpā "na kilāvayavy ekadeśena vartate, nāpi sarvātmanā. ekadeśavṛttyabhyupagame hy avayavino bhedaprasaṅgaḥ. atha sarvātmanā vartate, tarhy anyatrāvṛttiprasaṅga" ityādikā, sāpi na yuktiyuktā. katham? kim ekadeśaśabdenāvayavy abhidhīyate, 'vayavo vā? yady avayavy abhidhīyate, tadaikadeśenaiva sarvatra vartata iti brūmaḥ svakāraṇān niyamitasya tathābhūtasyotpatteḥ. athāvayavo 'bhidhīyate tadekadeśaśabdena, tadā naikadeśenāvayavī vartate, 'vaya[va]syāvayave vṛttyayogāt. bhavatu vāvayaveṣu vṛtter abhāvo 'vayavinas, tathāpy asattvaṃ na sidhyati, taddehopalambhasya tadastitvavidhānaparatvāt. yathā "anudakaḥ kamaṇḍalur" ity ukte saty udakakamaṇḍalusambandhābhāvaḥ pratiyate, na tu kamaṇḍalor abhāvas, tadudakasya vā.*

"As for the reasoning which has been pointed out for the purpose of the refutation of the whole in order to establish [that there is] nothing but cognition [and] which consists in [showing] the impossibility of the residence etc. [namely] - 'The whole does not reside partly [in the parts], nor entirely. [For] if it is admitted that [it] resides partly [in the parts], the whole would be split. If it resides entirely, then it could not reside in other [parts],' etc. - this [reasoning], too, is unreasonable. Why? Is it a whole which is referred to by the word 'partly,' or is it a part? If a whole is referred to, then we say that it resides only partly in every [part], for such a thing (i.e., which resides only partly in every part) arises as determined by its own cause. If a part is referred to by the word 'partly,' then the whole does not reside partly [in the parts], because there is no residence of a part in a part. Or let [us assume a residence of a part in a part and claim that] the whole does not exist because [a part] resides in the parts; even so, this does not prove [its] inexistence, because the apprehension of the body of the [whole] (i.e., the whole as such) amounts to an affirmation of its existence. For instance, when one says that the pot is without water, the absence of relation between the pot and water is apprehended, but not the inexistence of the pot or that water."

[275] Some of the Vaiśeṣika qualities (*guṇa*) are supposed to inhere more than one substance (*anekavṛtti*); conjunction and disjunction, for instance, inhere always two substances. Numbers, except for the number one, also reside in more than one substance, for they are supposed to inhere as many substances as they denote. On the relation between qualities and universals in Vaiśeṣika metaphysics cf. Halbfass, "The Vaiśeṣika concept of *guṇa* and the problem of universals."

[276] The *vṛttivikalpadoṣa* (cf. n. 274) constitutes one of the most important parts of the Buddhist critique of the universal, the whole, etc. (according to Jayanta, it is fear of the *vṛttivikalpa* which led the Bhāṭṭa-Mīmāṃsakas to disavow the relation of *samavāya*, cf. *NM* II p. 33.12-18). There is a tremendous amount of material on this subject which could not possibly be discussed here (some of it is summarized in Sinha, *Indian Psychology* I, ch. 10, Mookerjee, *Buddhist Philosophy of Universal Flux*, ch. 6, Shastri, *Philosophy of Nyāya-Vaiśeṣika*, ch. 9, Dravid, *The Problem of Universals in Indian Philosophy*, ch. 4-5, cf. in addition *NBhū* pp. 104.16f., 267.2f., *TS(P)* v. 797f., *Vy* p. 458.17f., *AS* p. 214.10f.).

Instead, I shall quote only the passage from the *PVSV* which became the standard argumentation and which is repeatedly quoted and referred to in almost all later discussions (pp. 76.25-77.15, 78.13-14):

api cāyaṃ sāmānyam arthāntaraṃ kalpayan svāśrayamātragataṃ vā kalpayet, sarvagataṃ vākāśādivat. tatra yadi svāśrayamātragataṃ ghaṭatvādiśūnyeṣu pradeśeṣu ghaṭādyutpattau kathaṃ teṣu bhinnadeśadravyavartinaḥ sāmānyasya sambhavaḥ? yasmāt tat pūrvadravyād utpitsu dravyaṃ

na yāti

niṣkriyatvopagamāt. na hy anyadravyavṛtter bhāvasya tato 'vicalato bhinnadeśena bhāvena tadubhayāntarālāvyāpino yogo yuktaḥ. prāk sa

na ca tatrāsīd asti paścān

na ca tatrotpanno na kutaścid āyāta iti ka imaṃ vyāghātabhāram udvoḍhuṃ samartho 'nyatra jāḍyāt. api ca

na cāṃśavat/

jahāti pūrvaṃ nādhāram

utpitsudeśād bhinnadeśaṃ, tayoś ca vartata ity

aho vyasanasantatiḥ//152//

...

vyaktaivaikatra sā vyaktyābhedat sarvatragā yadi/

jātir dṛśyeta sarvatra (155abc)

"Besides, in as much as one assumes the universal [to be] something different [from the individual], one has to assume that it is present either in its substrata alone (i.e., only in the individuals of its class), or everywhere, like ether etc. In respect to these [alternatives], if it is present in its substrata alone, [then] when a pot and other [substances] are produced in places where there are no [universals like] 'pot' etc., how could the universals, which reside in substances [which are found] in other places, appear in them (i.e., in the newly produced substances)? For it

does not go

away from the previous substance to the substance which is about to arise, as [you] admit that [the universal] is devoid of movement. For it is impossible that a thing which resides in another substance [and] which does not move from that [other thing] comes in contact with a [third] thing which [is found] in a different place without pervading the space between these two [things]. And before, it

was not there, it [is] there afterwards.
But it has not arisen there, nor has it come from somewhere. Thus, who is able to carry this load of contradiction unless it is out of sheer stupidity? Furthermore:

And it has no parts, it does not leave the previous substratum
Which [exists] in a place different from the place of the new [substratum], and [nevertheless you say that] it resides in both.
Ah, what a series of predicaments!*

...

If the [universal] is present everywhere, [then] since it is not differentiated by being manifested, the universal should be seen everywhere, when it is only manifested in one place."

*Note that Randle (*Fragments*, p. 59) and Vidyabhusana (*History of Indian Logic*, pp. 273-74) attribute this verse to Dignāga on the basis of Dharmabhūṣaṇa's testimony.

277 Cf. *TUS* p. 94.14-15 quoted in n. 274.

278 *ghaṭasāmānyam* is a *samāhāradvandva*-compound, which is quite rare in the philosophical literature (except for natural couples such as 'day and night,' 'hand and foot'). According to Renou (*Grammaire*, § 86.B) "les textes bouddhiques semblent en général étendre la catégorie," and it is quite clear that Jayarāśi uses it here under the influence of the Buddhist fragments quoted in §§ d.2 and d.3.

279 I was unable to identify this fragment. The argument, however, is well known, cf. for instance *NM* II p. 7.2-8: *ataś ca na vyaktivyatiriktaṃ sāmānyaṃ bhedenānupalambhāt. tathā hi kuvalayāmalakabilvādīni karatalavartīni pṛthag avalokyante, na jātivyaktī iti na tayor bhedaḥ. deśabhedasya cāgrahaṇād - yat khalu yato 'tiriktaṃ tat tadadhiṣṭhi-*

tadeśavyatiriktadeśādhiṣṭhānam avadhāryate ghaṭād iva paṭo, na caivaṃ jātivyaktī iti na tayor bhedaḥ.

"And for the following [reasons] there is no universal beyond the individual: [first] because [the universal] is not apprehended as different [from the individual]. For a blue water-lily, a myrobalan seed, a wood apple, etc., placed on the palm of the hand, are seen separately, [but] not the universal and the individual; thus, there is no difference between them. And [second] because a difference in place is not apprehended. Indeed, [when] A is different from B, it is determined as occupying a place which is different from the place occupied by B, just as a cloth [occupies a place which is different] from [the place occupied by] a pot. But this is not the case with the universal and the individual; therefore there is no difference between them."

AS p. 213.16-17: *kāryakāraṇayor guṇaguṇinoḥ sāmānyatadvatos tādātmyam abhinnadeśatvāt. yayor atādātmyaṃ na tayor abhinnadeśatvaṃ, yathā sahyavindhyayoḥ.* "Cause and effect, quality and qualified, universal and individual are identical, because [they] occupy the same place. When two things are not identical, they do not occupy the same place, like [the mountain chains] Sahya and Vindhya."

Vy p. 458.25-26: *ito 'py asattvaṃ deśabhedenānupalabdhes tadagrahe tadbuddhyabhāvāc ceti.* "For the following [reasons], too, [numbers etc.] do not exist: because [they] are not apprehended with a difference in place [from colour etc.] and because there is no cognition of them (i.e., numbers etc.) when they (i.e., colour etc.) are not apprehended."

Cf. also *NBhū* p. 105.3-5.

280 Cf. *NM* II p. 35.7-8:

pratītibhedād bhedo 'sti deśabhedas tu neṣyate/
tenātra kalpyate vṛttiḥ samavāyaḥ sa ucyate//

"[We know that] there is a difference [between the parts and the whole] since there is a difference in [their] cognition, but a difference in place is not admitted. This is why a residence is assumed there, [and] this [residence] is called inherence."

Cf. also AS p. 213.8-9: *kriyātadvator avayavāvayavinor guṇaguṇinor viśeṣatadvatoḥ sāmānyatadvator abhāvatadviśeṣyayoś cānyataiva bhinnapratibhāsatvāt sahyavindhyavat.* "Movement and the [substance] possessing it, parts and whole, quality and qualified, distinguishing property and the [substratum] possessing it, universal and [individual] possessing it, absence and what is qualified by it are indeed different, because [they] have a different appearance, just like [the mountain chains] Sahya and Vindhya."

Cf. also § a.2b.

281 In other words, Jayarāśi accuses the opponent of a confusion between 'different' and 'separate' (a confusion which is not uncommon in Indian philosophy). Certain qualities such as colour and smell may always appear together, but they are not the same thing. The same argument is used Vy p. 46.15: *deśabhedenāgrahaṇād iti rūpādibhir vyabhicāraḥ.* "[The reason] 'because [they] are not apprehended with a difference in place' deviates, because of colour etc. (i.e., because colour, flavour, smell, etc., are not apprehended with a difference in place, but are nevertheless different)."

On the inference of coincidence of *rūpa* and *rasa* cf. PV *svārthānumāna* 9 (Mookerjee and Nagasaki's translation p. 36).

282 I was unable to identify this fragment, which seems to be closely related to the one in § d.3. In *NM* II p. 7.10 and Vy p. 458.26 as well both arguments appear one after the other, and in the same order as in the *TUS*. This is

hardly surprising, for when two things occupy the same place, then, when one does not apprehend the one, one does not apprehend the other (provided that they are both apprehended by the same sense, as is the case with the parts and the whole, the universal and the individual, etc.). Cf. n. 279.

Cf. *NV* 1.1.14 p. 206.9-11: *na nāsti tadagrahe tadbuddhyabhāvāt. yad yasmād anarthāntaraṃ bhavati tadagrahe tasyāgraho dṛṣṭas, tad yathā yūṣasya paṅkteś ca. yac ca yato 'rthāntaraṃ bhavati, tadagrahe tasya graho dṛṣṭas, tad yathā rūpādyagrahe bālagraha* (Thakur's ed. p. 420.3: *rasagraha*) *iti*.

"It is not [true] that there is no [proof for the identity of the pot and its qualities], because when the [qualities] are not apprehended there is no cognition of the [pot]. When A is identical with B, one observes that it is not apprehended when B is not apprehended. For instance, a soup or a row [are not apprehended, when their ingredients or constituents are not apprehended]. And when A is different from B, one observes that it is apprehended [even] when B is not apprehended. For instance, perfume (or according to the variant: flavour) is apprehended [even] when something visible etc., are not apprehended."

ŚVV p. 158.11-15: ... *yato na rūparasādivyatiriktam anyaṃ dharmiṇam upalambhāmahe rūpādīnām agrahaṇe tasyāpratibhāsanāt. yathā vṛkṣāgrahaṇe vanam ity apratibhāsanān na vṛkṣavyatirekeṇa vanaṃ nāmānyat syād, ekadeśasthitāṃs tu vṛkṣān ālocya vanam iti pratyaya utpadyate, tathaikadeśāvasthitān rūpādīn ālocya gaur ayaṃ ghaṭo 'yam iti vā pratyaya utpadyate.*

"... For we do not apprehend a property-possessor as different [and] as something beyond [the properties] visible, flavour, etc., because the [property-possessor] does not appear when the visible etc., are not apprehended. For instance, there cannot be something different called forest over and above the trees because [the cognition] 'forest' does not appear when the trees are not apprehended, but the cognition 'forest' arises when one sees trees occupying the same place. Similarly, when one sees [properties] such as the visible etc., occupying the same place, the cognition 'This is a cow' or 'This is a pot' arises."

NBhū p. 126.6: *itas tarhi nāvayavī pṛthag asty, avayavāgrahe tadagrahād iti.* "For the following [reason] the whole does not exist as distinct [from the parts]: because it is not apprehended when the parts are not apprehended."

NM II p. 7.10-15: *ataś caivaṃ tadagrahe tadbuddhyabhāvāt. yad dhi yato vyatiriktaṃ tat tasminn agṛhyamāṇe 'pi gṛhyate ghaṭād iva paṭaḥ. na ca vyaktāv anupalabhyamānāyāṃ jātir upalabhyate. tasmān na tato 'sau bhidyate. tadvṛttitvāt sāmānyasya tadagrahe tadanupalabdhir iti cen na vṛttyanupapatteḥ* (cf. also p. 513.12-14).

"And for the following [reason, too,] this is so (i.e., the universal is not different from the individual): because there is no cognition of the [universal] when the [individual] is not apprehended. If A is different from B, it is apprehended even when B is not apprehended, just like a cloth [which is different] from a pot [is apprehended even without the apprehension of a pot]. But the universal is not apprehended when the individual is not apprehended; therefore it does not differ from it.

[Objection:] Because the universal resides in the [individual], it is not perceived when the [individual] is not apprehended.

[Answer:] No, because the residence [itself] is impossible."

Cf. also *PP* p. 68.4-9 (= Ch. ed. p. 18.14-21): *avayavebhyaś cāvayavī vyatiricyamāno 'vyatiricyamāno vā na pramāṇena saṅgacchate. vyatirikto hi tadagrahe 'pi grahaṇaṃ kadācid anubhavet. na khalu bhinnayoḥ sahopalambhaniyamo ghaṭapaṭayor* (Ch. ed.: *ghaṭayor*) *iva. tadvad avayavy api bhidyamāno nāvayavair eva sahopalabhyeta. kasyāñcid api daśāyām ananubhūyamāneṣu apy avayaveṣu anubhūyeta. na cāvayavinam avayavānubhavam antareṇa kecid upalabhante. avyatiricyamānas tu nāsty eveti vacanabhaṅgimātreṇoktaṃ bhavati.*

"And whether the whole is something beyond the parts or not, it [can]not be known by a means of valid cognition. For in as much as it is something beyond [the parts] it should sometimes attain apprehension even when they (i.e., the parts) are not apprehended. Indeed, there is no necessity for two different [things] to be [always] apprehended together, just as a pot and a cloth [are not always apprehended together]. In the same manner the whole, too, in as much as it is different [from the parts] should not be apprehended only with the parts; under certain conditions it should be experienced even when the parts are not experienced. But nobody apprehends the whole without an experience of the parts. If, on the other hand, [the whole] is not something beyond [the parts], then this is nothing but a roundabout way of saying that it does not exist."

For further material regarding this argument which was probably first used to refute a substance different from its qualities, cf. Preisendanz, *Nyāyatattvāloka*, n. 18.

In spite of these parallel passages, the position of the *pūrvapakṣin* is not easy to reconstruct. Jayarāśi's arguments clearly raise the problem of inferences with empty subject terms (for a brief sketch of this problem cf. Ruegg, "On Ratnakīrti," pp. 300-5), but is the *pūrvapakṣin* aware of the problem? And if so, how does he try to solve it? My guess (and it is no more than a guess) is that the *pūrvapakṣin* tried to avoid the problem by employing propositions of identity instead of negations. That is, instead of saying 'A does not exist' he says 'A is nothing but B.' The implication of inexistence becomes clear, even though it does not have to be stated explicitly. If one says that there is no whole beyond the parts (or no universal beyond the individuals), it means that the whole (or the universal), at least as the Naiyāyikas understood it, does not exist. The inference would not use empty subject terms, for both words (the parts and the whole) would refer to the same thing, namely, the parts, taken together or separately. If this is indeed the opponent's intention, then Jayarāśi's *vikalpas* ('Is it the whole or the parts which become the subject of inference?') are understandable. If the whole is the subject of inference, the Buddhist is using an empty subject term. If the parts are the subject of inference, the proposition which has to be demonstrated is either contradictory or tautological. Jayarāśi's arguments in the second *vikalpa* seem sophistical at first sight, but in fact they raise a serious philosophical problem towards the solution of which Western philosophers are still fighting their way (cf. Frege's 'The morning star is the evening star').

Siderits has argued recently that Dharmakīrti and the Prābhākara-Mīmāṃsakas were on the threshold of developing a distinction between sense and reference, cf. "The sense-reference distinction in Indian philosophy of language," pp. 90f.

283 It may be reminded that the first of the three conditions for a valid inferential sign is its existence in the subject of inference (*pakṣe sattvam*). When the subject is absent, one is left with the *sādhya* as the result of the inference, but since the *sādhya* was already known, the inference would not add anything to our knowledge.

284 The text is obviously corrupt. Sanghavi and Parikh, though silent on this point, seem to have reconstructed the text on the basis of the parallel passage *TUS* p. 103.3-6: *atha jñānasyaivāvyatirekapratipādanaṃ kriyate, tat kiṃ svasmāt svarūpād avyatiriktam, āhosvit pararūpād avyatiriktam?*

tad yadi svasmāt svarūpād avyatiriktaṃ jñānaṃ, tadāvivādena sambodhayitavyāḥ.

[285] Cf. *TUS* pp. 102.19-103.22: *api ca kasyātra pakṣīkaraṇam? kiṃ vijñānasya, utārthasya? tad yadi jñānaṃ pakṣayasi, tasya kiṃ sādhyate, 'bhāvo 'vyatireko vā? tad yady abhāvaḥ, sa kiṃ jñānasya, utārthasyeti? yadi jñānasya, tadābhyupetahānaṃ, hetoś ca pakṣadharmatā na labhyate. athārthasya, tadāsambaddhatvaṃ, jñānaṃ pakṣayasy, artho nāstīti vyāhatam apadiśyate, sahopalambhasya ca vyadhikaraṇatvam.*

athāvyatirekaḥ sādhyate, sa kiṃ jñānasya, āhosvid arthasya? tad yady arthasya, tadāsambaddhābhidhātṛtvam. jñānaṃ pakṣayasy, arthasya cāvyatirekapratipādanaṃ karosīti vyāhatam apadiśyate, 'rthāvyatireko hy arthadharmaḥ.

atha jñānasyaivāvyatirekapratipādanaṃ kriyate, tat kiṃ svasmāt svarūpād avyatiriktam, āhosvit pararūpād avyatiriktam? tad yadi svasmāt svarūpād avyatiriktaṃ jñānaṃ, tadāvivādena sambodhayitavyāḥ. atha parasmād avyatirekapratipādanaṃ kriyate, sa parātmā tāttviko 'tāttviko vā. tad yady atāttvikas, tato 'vyatiriktaṃ jñānam apy atāttvikaṃ bhavet.

atha tāttvikaḥ, so 'py avadhāritadeho vā, anavadhāritadeho vā. tad yady avadhāritadehaḥ, sa kiṃ bhinnākāratayāvagato, 'bhinnākāratayā vā? yadi bhinnākāratayāvadhāritas, tadā bhinnākārāvagāhakavijñānadūṣitapakṣatvena sahopalambhahetor asiddhatā kālātyayāpadiṣṭatā vā. athābhinnasvabhāvatayāvadhārito, na tarhi parātmā, parātmā cābhinnasvabhāvatayāvadhārita iti ca vyāghātaḥ.
kiṃ cābhinnasvabhāvatayā yadi prāg evāvagāhitas, tadā kiṃ tatra sahopalambhasādhanena prayojanam? niṣpāditakriye karmaṇi sādhanaṃ sā[dha]nanyāyam atipatati.
athānavadhāritadehaḥ, sa parātmāstīti kathaṃ jāniṣe? na cāvadhāritānavadhāritākārayor ekatvaṃ bahuvido vadanti. anavadhāritākāraikatve ca jñānasyāpy asaṃvedanaṃ prasaktam.
"Further, what is made the subject of the inference here (i.e., in the inference which aims to refute the reality of the external object, namely, 'The object and the cognition

are one because they are apprehended together')? Is it the cognition or the object? If you make the cognition the subject of [your] inference, [then] what has to be proved for it (i.e., the subject), inexistence or non-difference? In respect to these [alternatives], if it is inexistence, is it [inexistence] of the cognition or of the object? If it is [inexistence] of the cognition, [your] position is abandoned, and the reason (i.e., the simultaneous cognition) would not be a property of the subject of inference.

If it is [inexistence] of the object, then [this] is incoherent: [on the one hand] you make the cognition the subject of inference, [and on the other hand you want to prove that] the object does not exist. Thus, something confused is pointed out [by you] and [the reason] 'simultaneous apprehension' has a different locus [from the locus of the property to be proved].

If non-difference [has to] be proved, [then] is it [non-difference] of the cognition or of the object? In respect to these [alternatives], if it is [the non-difference] of the object, then [you] talk incoherently: [on the one hand] you make the cognition the subject of [your] inference, and [on the other hand] you [try to] prove that the object is not different. Thus, something confused is pointed out [by you], for the non-difference of the object is a property of the object.

If [you] prove that the cognition itself is not different, [then] is it not different from its own form or from another form? In respect to these [alternatives], if the cognition is not different from its own form, then [you] should be informed that there is no quarrel [about it]! If [you] prove that [the cognition] is not different from another [form], [then] this other nature is either real or unreal. In respect to these [alternatives], if it is not real, [then] the cognition which is not different from it would also be unreal.

If [the other nature] is real, [then] this [other nature] as well has either a determined body (i.e., nature) or an undetermined body. In respect to these [alternatives], if it has a determined body, [then] is it apprehended as having a different form [than the cognition], or as having a non-different form? If it is determined as having a different form, then because the subject of the inference is shown to be faulty by the cognition which apprehends the different form, the reason, [namely] the simultaneous apprehension, is either not established, or it is pointed out after the proper time has passed.*

If [the other nature] is determined as having a non-different nature, then it is not a different nature. There is a contradiction between [being] a different nature and [being] determined as having a non-different nature.

Besides, if [the other nature] is already previously apprehended as having a non-different nature, what purpose [is served] by the proof that [it] is apprehended together [with the cognition]? To accomplish something which is [already] accomplished is beyond the right manner of accomplishing [anything].

If [the other form] has a body which is not determined, [then] how do you know that this other nature exists? And learned people do not say that there is a unity between something that has a determined form and something which has an undetermined form. And if [the cognition] is one with something whose form is undetermined, the cognition, too, would not be apprehended."

*For different interpretations of *kālātyayāpadiṣṭa* cf. for instance Preisendanz, *Nyāyatattvāloka*, n. 88. Jayarāśi seems to use the term as it appears in later literature, cf. *NM* II p. 634.7-9: *hetoḥ prayogakālaḥ pratyakṣāgamānupahatapakṣaparigrahasamaya eva. tam atītya prayujyamānaḥ pratyakṣāgamabādhite viṣaye vartamānaḥ kālātyayāpadiṣṭo bhavati.* "The time of employment of a reason is the occasion when one takes a position which is not 'damaged' by perception or sacred writings. [A reason] which is employed while transgressing that [time], i.e., which is referring to an object sublated by perception or sacred writings, becomes [a reason which is] pointed out after the [proper] time has passed."

Cf. also *NSāra* p. 310.1/*NBhū* 310.6: *pramāṇabādhite pakṣe vartamāno hetuḥ kālātyayāpadiṣṭaḥ*. It seems that the *TUS* is the earliest source among those which have come down to us which uses the term in this meaning.

On the *asiddhahetu* cf. for example Preisendanz, op. cit., n. 12.

[286] The strategy of the opponent changes: instead of claiming that the universal/whole is not different from the individuals/parts, he now claims that the universal/whole simply does not exist. Notwithstanding, Jayarāśi still raises the same *vikalpas* as on p. 236.13-14, but in this context the second *vikalpa* seems pointless, for nobody claims that the parts or the individuals do not exist. A friend of mine suggested that the Buddhist may have been trying to avoid the use of empty subject terms by having recourse to *viśeṣapratiṣedha*. Instead of saying 'The whole does not exist,' the Buddhist could claim that the parts **of the whole** do not exist, just as the horns **of the rabbit** do not exist, cf. *NV* 3.1.1 p. 708.4-5, *Vy* pp. 159.28, 322.30f., *NVTṬ* 3.2.14 p. 836.25, 3.2.55 p. 895.18.

Another interpretation, which is hinted at by Sanghavi and Parikh's punctuation, but which I fail to understand, would be to assume that the parts form the *pakṣa*, whereas the whole appears in the *pratijñā*, cf. the next note.

[287] Taking into account the punctuation proposed by Sanghavi and Parikh, one would have to translate this sentence as follows:

"[Objection:] The parts as well as the substrata are made the subject of the inference (*pakṣa*), 'The pot as well as the universal does not exist' is the thesis (*pratijñā*).

[Answer:] There is no relation between the reason 'because there is no apprehension of the [whole or the universal] when these (i.e., the parts or the individuals) are not apprehended' and the inexistence of the [whole or the universal]."

The reason for my reluctance to accept this interpretation is that in this case the *pakṣa* would not be a part of the *pratijñā*. I am not claiming, of course, that the Buddhists couldn't possibly develop such a theory, but so far I have found no evidence for it. Therefore I consider *ghaṭasāmānyaṃ nāstīti pratijñā* as an interpolation, that is, somebody added it as an explanation to *avayavādhikaraṇasya pakṣīkaraṇam*. Later the ms was copied with the note as if it were a part of the text.

In any case, the *pūrvapakṣa* cannot be fully understood before the fragment and its context are identified. On top of that, the manuscript has probably two lacunae in this passage.

[288] Cf. *NB* III.31: *sa* (scil. *svabhāvapratibandha*) *ca dviprakāraḥ sarvasya, tādātmyalakṣaṇas tadutpattilakṣaṇaś cety uktam.*

[289] This sentence is probably formulated in opposition to *PVin* I.55ab, quoted n. 272.

[290] Cf. Vy p. 46.17-19: *evaṃ tadagrahe tadbuddhyabhāvāc cety ayam api viruddhaḥ. tathā hi teṣām avayavānām agrahe tasminn avayavini buddhyabhāva ity ayam artho 'vayavagrahe 'vayavini buddhir ity avayavinaḥ sattvam.*

"Thus, the [reason] 'because there is no cognition of the [whole] when the [parts] are not apprehended' is also contradictory. For [to say that] there is no cognition of this, [i.e.] the whole, when they, [i.e.] the parts, are not apprehended means that there is a cognition of the whole when the parts are apprehended. Therefore the whole exists."

[291] A contradictory inferential sign, *viruddha(-hetu)*, means here a sign which is absent in the *sapakṣa* and present in the *vipakṣa*; cf. *PDhS* p. 578.4f., *NB* III.84-85.

[291] I was unable to identify this quotation. The argument is directed against one of the Nyāya proofs of the universal: when one sees an individual of a certain class for the first time, one is not aware of the universal which resides in it, but when one sees a second individual of the same class, one immediately relates it to the first. Therefore, there must be something responsible for the notion of commonness or similarity among different individuals, namely, the universal. Cf. *ŚVV* p. 150.7-8: *nanu prathamavyaktisandarśane sati jātyavagamo nāsti, tat katham lakṣyāntaropalabdhau sa evāyam iti pratyabhijñā pratyayaḥ?* Vy p. 686.30-687.1: *tathā caikapiṇḍopalambhakāle nānugataṃ sāmānyaṃ pratibhāti. dvitīyapiṇḍopalambhakāle 'pi prathamapiṇḍasyāgrahaṇād anugatajñānābhāva eva.*

A word is due perhaps to the expression *upalabdhilakṣaṇaprāpti*. Dharmakīrti distinguishes between two kinds of non-perception: non-perception of perceptible things - *upalabdhilakṣaṇaprāpta* or, shortly, *dṛśya* - and of imperceptible things. Of these two only the first may be used as an inferential sign (cf. Steinkellner, *PVin* II(2) p. 46, n. 120). If a pot does not exist in a certain place, one may infer its inexistence at that place, for if it would have been there it would have been perceived (cf. *PVSV* p. 2.16-18: *pradeśaviśeṣe kvacin na ghaṭa upalabdhilakṣaṇaprāpta-*

syānupalabdheḥ. yadi syād upalabhyasattva eva syān nānyathā).

This kind of reasoning is obviously useless when we deal with non-perceptible entities. To infer that there are no demons here because they are not perceived is a false inference, for demons are not perceived even when they are present. For this reason Dharmakīrti did not allow the use of non-perception of imperceptible things as an inferential sign. For there is no way we can either prove or disprove the existence of such entities. If something is never perceived, we can treat it for all practical purposes as non-existent (*asadvyavahāraviṣaya*, *sadvyavahārapratiṣedha*, *sajjñānaśabdavyavahārapratiṣedha*, etc.), but its real inexistence always remains doubtful (cf. *PVSV* p. 5.2-6, *PVin* II(1) pp. 66.33-68.6; cf. also *PVSV* p. 4.5-15, *PVin* II(2) pp. 79-81 and Steinkellner's notes thereupon). (The historical development of this doctrine still remains to be studied. Note, however, that in a nut shell it appears already in several passages of the *NV*, for instance 3.1.35 p. 764. 12: *yat khalūpalabdhilakṣaṇaprāptaṃ nopalabhyate tan nāsti yathā ghaṭādi*.)

Bearing Dharmakīrti's theory in mind the above fragment becomes problematic, for by using the non-perception of a perceptible thing as a sign, the Buddhist would presuppose that the universal is an existing and perceptible entity, and would only deny its presence in a particular place. Since this is obviously absurd, we are probably not dealing with a regular inference here, but rather with a *prasaṅgasādhana* (an assumption corroborated by *PVBh* pp. 481.17f., 482.19f., *NBhū* p. 232.14).

According to Mookerjee, who equates *prasaṅgasādhana* with *prasaṅgānumāna*, *prasaṅgasādhana* should fulfill three conditions (*Buddhist Philosophy of Universal Flux*, pp. 402-3):

(1) The *hetu* should be false, i.e., it should be accepted only by the opponent;
(2) the *sādhya* is false and is forced on the opponent;
(3) the implication of the argument is the truth of the contradictory position.

Although all these conditions may occur in a *prasaṅgasādhana*, not all of them seem to be necessary. The third is violated in cases of *prasajyapratiṣedha* (cf. *Prasannapadā* p. 7.29f., and Mookerjee's own comments thereupon, ibid., p. 404). The second is not appropriate in cases like the present one - the *sādhya* '*nāsti*' is certainly acceptable for the Buddhist when it applies to the universal.

Mookerjee's analysis seems to be a generalization of the *prasaṅgasādhana* in *TSP* p. 535.5f. (GOS ed. p. 437, quoted by Mookerjee, op. cit., p. 405) where Kamalaśīla argues that the Vedas were meaningless, because they are authorless. But this particular case cannot be used as a model for all *prasaṅgasādhanas*. As far as I can see, what characterizes *prasaṅgasādhana* is that one or more elements of the inference are accepted by the opponent alone (*parābhyupagata, parābhiprāya*). Its main function was to negate the existence of entities accepted by the opponent alone (e.g., the universal, the substance, etc.) without committing the fallacy (*hetvābhāsa*) of *āśrayāsiddhi* (cf. for instance *PVBh* p. 481.20: *prasaṅgasādhanam idaṃ, nāśrayāsiddhatā tataḥ ...*; *TSP* p. 64.16-17: *prasaṅgasādhanaṃ cedaṃ, tenāśrayāsiddhatā hetor nāśaṅkanīyā*; *NBhū* p. 232.14: *nanu ca prasaṅgasādhanam idam uktaṃ, tenāśrayāsiddhatvādidoṣo nāsti*.

Note that not all *prasaṅga*-arguments are *prasaṅgasādhana*. A normal *prasaṅga*-argument can be transformed into an inference without raising problems such as *āśrayāsiddhatā* by a simple negation of the reason: 'not X because of *prasaṅga* of Y' can be expressed by 'not X because not Y.'

Mookerjee further points out that Dharmakīrti did not allow the use of *prasaṅgasādhana*, because a valid reason should be accepted by both the *vādin* and the *prativādin* (op. cit., p. 403, cf. e.g. *NB* III.59). If this is indeed Dharmakīrti's intention (for it is possible that *prasaṅgasādhana* was not considered as *anumāna*), then his opinion did not prevail, for, as mentioned above, later Buddhist logicians like Śāntarakṣita, Kamalaśīla and Prajñākaragupta certainly used this way of reasoning. It is interesting in this context to note that according to Durvekamiśra *NB* II.36 involves a *prasaṅgasādhana* (cf. *DhPr* p. 133.11-12: *ata eva mūle 'piśabdaḥ prasaṅgasādhanatvaprasaṅgārtho lakṣyate*; cf. also *NBṬ* p. 132.1-2).

293 Cf. *NB* II.13-14: *upalabdhilakṣaṇaprāptir upalambhapratyayāntarasākalyaṃ svabhāvaviśeṣaś ca.. yaḥ svabhāvaḥ satsv anyeṣūpalambhapratyayeṣu san pratyakṣa eva bhavati sa svabhāvaviśeṣaḥ.* "The fulfillment of conditions of perception [consists in] the completeness of [all] the other causes of perception and a special nature. Special nature [means] that nature which is perceived in as much as it is present when [all] the other conditions of perception are present."

Cf. also *VN* p. 20.2-3: *tatropalabdhilakṣaṇaprāptiḥ svabhāvaviśeṣaḥ kāraṇāntarasākalyaṃ ca. svabhāvaviśeṣo yan na trividhena viprakarṣeṇa viprakṛṣṭam."*... Special nature [means] not to be remote by one of the three ways of remoteness (i.e., by time, space and nature, cf. VA ad loc., p. 20.15-16, *NBṬ* p. 104.7)."

294 Cf. *TUS* p. 94.17-25: *athāvayavina upalabdhir eva nāsti, sā kiṃ dṛśyānupalabdhir āhosvid adṛśyānupalabdhiḥ? yadi dṛśyānupalabdhiḥ, sā nopapadyate. dṛśyaśabdena kim apadiśyate? upalabdhilakṣaṇaprāpto 'rtho 'bhidhīyate. upalabdhilakṣaṇaprāptiś ca pratyayāntarasākalyaṃ svabhāvaviśeṣaś ca. etac ced vidyate, katham anupalambhaḥ? upalabdhikārakasākalye saty upalabdhyā bhavitavyaṃ, nānupalabdhyā tatsvabhāvanibandhanatvāt tadupalabdheḥ. upalabdhilakṣaṇa-*

prāptasya yady anupalambho, 'nupalabdhilakṣaṇaprāptasya tarhy upalambhaḥ syād, aniṣṭaṃ caitat.

"If the whole is not apprehended, [then] is it non-apprehension of something perceptible or non-apprehension of something imperceptible? If it is non-apprehension of something perceptible, this is impossible. What is designated by the word 'perceptible'? Something which fulfills the conditions of perception is designated. And to fulfill the conditions of perception [means] the completeness of [all] other causes and [having] a special nature. If both [conditions] are found, how is non-apprehension [possible]? When the causal factors for an apprehension are complete, an apprehension must take place, not a non-apprehension, because the apprehension of something depends on the nature of that [thing]. If something which fulfills the conditions of perception is not apprehended, then something which does not fulfill the conditions of perception would be apprehended, and this is not acceptable."

[295] At this point the *pūrvapakṣa* deviates from Dharmakīrti's theory, and there is perhaps no real opponent behind this statement.

The *pūrvapakṣa* seems to imply that there are no imperceptible entities, and that if the universal is not perceived when all the other causes for perception are present, one has to conclude that the universal does not exist; one should not conclude that it exists, but has an imperceptible nature. To this Jayarāśi replies that in this case the formulation of the inference cannot be correct, for only imperceptible things cannot be apprehended and non-apprehension of something which fulfills the conditions of perception is impossible.

[296] In other words, if the presence of all other causes constitutes the fulfillment of the conditions of perception (without taking into account the object itself), then perception should take place whether the object is present or not.

[297] The conclusion seems to bear on the discussion as a whole, and not just on the last *vikalpa*. The mode of expression is highly laconic, and a lacuna in the middle of the sentence is not inconceivable; nevertheless the argument may be reconstructed as follows: According to Dharmakīrti only the non-apprehension of a visible thing can be used as a valid inferential sign. However, among the conditions of perception we find the 'special nature,' which Dharmakīrti further explains as not being remote in space, time and nature (cf. n. 293). This definition entails that there can never be a perception of an object which does not fulfill the conditions of perception. Therefore, the reason 'non-perception of that which fulfills the conditions of perception' is self-contradictory in as much as all the other causes of perception (such as light etc.) are present. To take an example: The pot which I saw yesterday, or the one which is now in the other room, does not fulfill the conditions of perception, because the one is remote by time, the other by space. Thus, I cannot use their non-perception as a valid inferential sign. This seems to be the conclusion reached at by Jayarāśi: there is no non-perception of something which fulfills the conditions of perception, only of something which does not fulfill these conditions.

It may be objected that Dharmakīrti talks about something which is in principle not accessible in space and time when using the expression *upalabdhilakṣaṇaprāpta* (Śāntarakṣita gives the examples of Mount Meru and Rāma), but I do not see how this would change the validity of the inference, for unlike in the case of a demon where the inference of its absence is doubtful, since it is not perceived even when it is present, in the case of Rāma one can very well infer that he is not here, since he is not perceived. Thus, Jayarāśi seems to point out a serious deficiency in Dharmakīrti's theory of non-apprehension as an inferential sign.

[298] I was unable to identify this quotation. A similar argument appears in *TS* v. 1219:

jātyādīnām adṛṣṭatvāt tadyogāpratibhāsanāt/
kṣīrodakavac cārthe ghaṭanā ghaṭate katham//

"Since the universal [the substance] etc., are never seen [separately of the individuals, parts, etc.], for their connection [to the individuals, parts, etc.] never appears [in a cognition],
just like [mixed] milk and water [are not seen separately of each other, and just like their connection does not appear in a cognition], how could [their] connection to a thing (i.e., an individual, part, etc.) be possible?"

Cf. also *TSP* p. 451.14-15: *yathā kṣīrodakāder miśrībhūtasya vivekenāpratibhāsanān na ghaṭanā śakyate kartuṃ, tadvaj jātyādīnāṃ sattve 'pi vivekenāśrayād apratibhāsanān na śakyate tadāśrayena sahety arthaḥ.* "This is the meaning: Just as milk, water, etc., mixed together, cannot effect a connection [among themselves], because [they] do not appear as distinguished [from one another], in the same manner, even if the universal etc., existed, [they] could not [effect a connection] with their substratum because [they] do not appear [in the cognition] as distinguished from the substratum."

Cf. also *PVin* I p. 44.12-14 and Steinkellner, "New Sanskrit-Fragments," p. 202. On the context of this verse in the *TS* cf. Franco, "On the Interpretation of *PS(V)* I,3d."

The example of water and milk usually stands for a homogeneous blend. According to the Indian belief, the flamingo is capable of drinking the milk alone, cf. Frauwallner, *Philosophie des Buddhismus*, p. 335.

[299] Cf. *Vy* p. 682.20-22: *yathā hi svalakṣaṇaṃ vyāvṛttarūpatayā pratibhāsanād asty evam anugatasvarūpatayā pratibhāsanāt sāmānyam apy asti.* "Just as the particular exists because it appears [in a cognition] as having a distinctive nature, in the same manner the universal, too, exists because it appears as having a recurrent nature."

[300] Cf. *TUS* p. 92.11f.

[301] This is a quotation of *PVin* I.16 = *PV pratyakṣa* 126:

gcig tu mthoṅ ba'i khyad par ni/
gźan 'ga' źig tu ma mthoṅ phyir/
de las spyi gźan tha dad ni/
yod min tha dad blo med phyir//

=

ekatra dṛṣṭo bhedo hi kvacin nānyatra dṛśyate/
na tasmād bhinnam asty anyat sāmānyaṃ buddhya-bhedataḥ//

The interpretation of this verse is problematic. Vetter (*PVin* I, p. 104, n. 30) notes that "Dh[armottara] (91 b1) versucht, das *phyir*, das offensichtlich das Sanskrit *hi* wiedergibt, so zu deuten, dass die zweite Vershälfte die Begründung für die erste gibt. Um zumindest einen Widerspruch mit dieser Auffassung zu vermeiden, ist es angebracht, das *tasmāt* von *PV* III.126cd nur zu *bhinnam* zu ziehen und die Möglichkeit, dass es eine Begründung der zweiten Vershälfte durch die erste anzeigt, nicht weiter in Betracht zu ziehen."

I am afraid that in spite of this clarifying remark, I still don't know how Vetter wants us to understand the verse. As far as I can see, none of the two half-verses can

be understood as a reason for the other, but they are rather meant as reasons for a third proposition, and thus the logical connection between them is a conjunction. It is clear from the context of both *PVin* and *PV* (as well as from PVV and *PVBh* ad loc.) that the subject matter is not a refutation of the universal, but rather a refutation of the opinion that conceptual construction (the object of which is the universal) is sense perception, or, in other words, the proof that the universal is not the object of perception. The above quoted verse provides the reasons for this proposition: on the one hand, the individual which is the object of sense perception cannot be the object of conceptual construction, because it does not occur repeatedly/is not pervading (*anuyāyin*, 'durchgängig'); on the other hand, there is no further object such as the universal which could be the object of sense cognition, because it does not exist, and it does not exist because its cognition is not different from that of the individual. Therefore, as only the particular can be its object, perception is free from conceptual construction.
Cf. also the parallel discussion in *TS* v. 739f. and *TSP* ad loc.

302 Jayarāśi probably refers to *PVin* I p. 56.21-24: *gaṅ las sgra 'jug par 'gyur ba gsal ba'i bdag ñid rnams las tha dad pa'i rjes su 'gro ba'i don ni ma mthoṅ ba'i phyir ro// don tha dad pa ñid la ni blo tha dad pa mthoṅ ste/ 'byuṅ po daṅ mgul chiṅs bźin no//*

"[The universal is not the object of sense cognition] because a pervading object, which [could] be the object of a word [and] which is different from the [particulars] whose nature can be cognized, is never seen. One sees that when there is a difference of objects, the cognitions are different, just like [in the case of] demons and necklace (i.e., just like several demons who wear the same necklace (?), cf. Vetter's n. 31)."

[303] I was unable to identify this quotation; cf., however, *PVin* I p. 42.23-24, quoted in n. 244, *TS(P)* v. 809-10, *NKC* p. 8.2f., *ŚD* p. 306.8f.

'Gradually' and 'at once' are the only possible ways of being causally efficient. An eternal entity cannot be gradually efficient, for it is by definition devoid of change. Thus, it can be efficient either always or never. Since the first possibility is contradicted by experience, it is never efficient, and since existence is defined as causal efficiency, it does not exist.

Obviously, this kind of argument is not restricted to the refutation of the universal and can be applied to any eternal entity. Vasubandhu, for example, uses it in order to refute God as the creator of the world (cf. *AKBh* p. 101.25f. on II.64d, cf. also *TS(P)* v. 394, *NM* II p. 301. 1f.

Jayarāśi probably considered these arguments quite convincing, for he uses very similar ones while refuting the universal (§ a.2c). The only important objection he raises is against the equation of existence and causal efficiency, for, so he argues, things may exist without being causally efficient (p. 252.4; cf. also p. 124.21). But in as much as one considers an eternal entity as causally efficient, he seems to find no fault with this argument. His main purpose in this passage is to show that the Buddhist who employs the argument is himself guilty of the same inconsistencies of which he accuses his opponent. This is also the upshot of the argument in *TUS* p. 87.8-18, quoted above in n. 248.

Although Jayarāśi does not raise the problem again, it is clear that the inference contains an empty subject term and has to be considered as a *prasaṅgasādhana*, cf. *TSP* p. 182.3-21. On *prasaṅgasādhana* cf. n. 292.

[304] Cf. p. 164.13; cf. also *TUS* p. 105.1-24: *yad apy uktam* - "*avayavinirākaraṇe kṣaṇikatvam. yadi hi kilākṣaṇiko bha-*

vati bhāvas, tadā bhavaty a[vayavā](?)vayavibhāvas, tadabhāve tatsva(tasyā ')bhāvāt. atha katham tasyābhāvaḥ? sthāyino 'rthakriyākaraṇāt. tad eva katham? kathyate - kiṃ yena svabhāvenādyām arthakriyāṃ karoti kiṃ tenaiva svabhāvenottarāṇy api kāryāṇi karoty, atha samāsāditasvabhāvāntaraḥ karoti? yadi tenaiva karoti, tadaikakālayogitvaṃ sarvakāryāṇāṃ prasajyate, kramakaraṇaṃ hīyate tasya. na hy ekasvabhāvāyatto vastūnāṃ kālavikalpo nāma. vikalpe vaikasvabhāvāyattatām atikrāmanti. atha svabhāvāntarāpattau janayati, svabhāvāntarāpattiś ca pūrvākāraparihāranāntarīyakarūpā. tadaparityāge nākārāntarānupraveśo 'sty, ākārayor ekatvāyogāt. atha pūrvākāraparihāras, tadaitad eva kṣaṇikatvaṃ yat pūrvāparakāryakāraṇam," -

tad etad ayuktam. yadi krameṇa kāryaṃ na karoti yugapad api kathaṃ karoti? ekaṃ nīlasvalakṣaṇam anekaṃ vijñānanīlādikaṃ kāryaṃ karotīti vaḥ siddhāntaḥ. tad anekaṃ kāryaṃ kim a(kim eke)nākāreṇa karoty, ākārabhedena vā? tad yady ekena karoti, tadāyātā sarvakāryāṇām ekākārarūpataikatvam, ekasya cānekatvam āpadyate. athākārabhedenānekakāryaṃ janayaty, ākārabhedāt tadekatvaṃ vyāvartate, tadvyāvṛttau naikam anekaṃ kāryaṃ karoti.

athetthambhūtaṃ svahetubhyas (interpolation?) *tadudgataṃ yad anekayugapatkāryakaraṇātmakam. yady evaṃ mamāpi kramabhāvyanekakāryakaraṇātmakaṃ samudbhūtaṃ svahetubhyaḥ.*

"What has been said as well: 'When the whole is refuted, momentariness [is established]. For if supposedly there would be something which is not momentary, there would be [something which is] a whole, because if there is no[thing non-momentary] there is no [whole]. (?)

Why does the [whole] not exist? Because something which lasts does not cause an efficient action. Why is that? [I] explain: Is the nature with which [the whole] causes the first efficient action exactly the one with which it produces the posterior effects as well, or does [it] produce [the posterior effects] as something which has acquired a different nature? If it produces with exactly the same [nature], then all effects would be connected to the same time; it [would] not produce gradually. For the difference in time among [different] things does certainly not depend on a single nature. Or if there is a difference [in time], [the different things] are beyond dependence on a single nature.

Or [the whole] produces [the posterior effects] after the change to a different nature, and change to a different nature is of such a nature that it is not [possible] without abandoning the previous form. [For] if [the whole] does not abandon the [previous form], it does not enter into another form, because two forms cannot be identical. If it abandons the previous form, then this [means its] momentariness which is the cause for previous and posterior effects.'

this is not correct. If something does not produce an effect gradually, how could it produce at once? Your established doctrine is that one particular blue [object] produces several effects such as the cognition, the blue [object at the next moment], etc. Does it produce the several effects with one form or with different forms? In respect to these [alternatives], if it produces with one [form], then it follows that all the effects would have one form, [that is] would be one [thing]; and one [thing] would be many (i.e., it would be a cognition, a blue object, etc.).

If [it] produces several effects with different forms, [then] because of the difference of forms, its unity ceases. When the [unity] has ceased, it is not one [thing] which produces several effects [but many].

[Objection:] It has arisen from its own causes as having the nature of producing several effects at the same time.

[Reply:] If so, according to me as well, something has arisen from its own causes as having the nature of producing several effects gradually."

[305] Cf. *TUS* p. 97.20-26: *atha tad eva dravyam upajātakriyaṃ calaty anupajātakriyaṃ ca na calati. satyam. tad eva calati, tad eva na calati. natv(nv) avayavino bhedaḥ prasajyate. na prasaṅgaś calanasya tato 'nyathā(nyatvāt). calācalavyapadeśaś cānyopādhikṛtaḥ. yathā bhavatpakṣe jñānaṃ kāryaṃ kāraṇaṃ ca vyapadiśyate - svakāryāpekṣayā kāraṇaṃ, svakāraṇāpekṣayā kāryaṃ - na ca tasya bhedo 'sti, tathāvayavicalācalatvena na bhedo dṛśyate.*

"[Objection:] One and the same substance does move when movement is originated in it, and does not move when movement is not originated in it.

[Reply:] True, one and the same [substance] moves and does not move.

[Objection:] The whole (i.e., the substance) would be different [when it moves and when it does not move].

[Reply:] It would not be, because [the movement] is different from it. For the designation [of a substance] as moving and not moving is [only] effected by additional qualifications which are different [from the substance and do not change its nature]. Just as according to your position a cognition is designated as effect and as cause, as cause in respect to its effect, and as effect in respect to its cause, and is [nevertheless] not different [when designated as cause and as effect], in the same manner a difference [in the whole] due to the fact that it both moves and does not move is not observed."

[306] If I understand the argument correctly, the opponent tries to avoid the charge of opposite attributes in the same individual by assuming that the causal relationship is reflexive. As a rule, when A produces B and B produces C,

the relations AB and BC are different. If, however, we replace A, B and C with three A's, the relation remains the same, for A always stands in the same relation to itself. In other words, A produces itself (A) in the next moment, and A at the second moment produces A in the third moment. Thus, A in the first moment produces itself = A in the second moment, which is equally its own (A's) cause for the third moment.

If this is indeed what is meant, the argument seems perfectly absurd, and one is tempted to assume that Jayarāśi is just toying with logical (or in fact illogical) possibilities which have no real opponent behind them. On the other hand, if there is no real opponent, the whole discussion would be a waste of time (note that a similar opinion is rejected in *MMK* 7.8, cf. also 7.13). In any case, we cannot argue that what seems absurd to us was not seriously accepted by somebody else. In this connection one is reminded of the Sarvāstivāda theory of causation according to which an entity is efficient before it is produced. However, the Sarvāstivādins did not accept reflexive causation, but rather, among other kinds, reciprocal causation (i.e., not A produces itself, but rather A produces B and B produces A). It seems that it is precisely in order to avoid reflexive relationships that they postulated the four *anulakṣaṇas*: *utpādotpāda*, *sthitisthiti*, *jarājarā*, and *anityatānityatā* (cf. *AKBh* pp. 75.20f. ad *AK* II.45cd).

Since the quotation and its context are not identified as yet, nothing certain can be said about the causal theory referred to by Jayarāśi, but as a working hypothesis I would suggest that the opponent (if indeed it is not an imaginary one), while saying that something produces itself and its own cause, probably does not have in mind an absolute identity between cause and effect, but rather what may be called a categorical identity, namely, that each *dharma* produces a *dharma* of the same kind, e.g., a visible produces a visible etc.

[307] It may be reminded that the concept of *arthakriyā* was already criticized on pp. 122.18-126.12. Note, however, that there it is used as an epistemological concept and here as an ontological one. For an analysis of these two realms of reference cf. Nagatomi, "Arthakriyā."

[308] Jayarāśi reminds the opponent of his own theory, for the Buddhist as well claims that the cognition of the universal is not produced by the universal.

[309] On the Buddhist definition of object cf. n. 178. Cf. also *TUS* pp. 84.24-85.16: *api ca dahanākāratā dahanavijñānāt kiṃ bhinnā, abhinnā vā? yadi bhinnā, sā kiṃ tāttviky āhosvid atāttvikī? tad yadi tāttvikī, tadgatiḥ katham? na svasaṃvedyatvena nāpi janakatvākārārpakatvena. svasaṃvedyā na bhavati vijñānakārya(kāya)vyatirekāt. nāpi janakatvākārārpakatvena gṛhyate. artho hy ākāram arpayati na viṣayākāratā. tadākārārpakatve vā prāptākāraparamparā. athātāttvikī viṣayākāratā, sātāttvikatvenāsaṃviditadehā, kathaṃ pratikarmaniyāmikā bhavati? athāvyatiriktā, sā kiṃ tāttviky āhosvid atāttvikī? yadi tāttvikī, sā kiṃ jaḍātmikāhosvic citsvabhāvā? tad yadi jaḍātmikā, tadā jñānāvyatirekitvaṃ na sambhavati cidacitor ekatvāyogād anyonyaparihārasthitidharmatvena. atha cidātmikā, tadā paribhāṣamātraṃ bhidyate - jñānaṃ viṣayākāra iti. athātāttvikī, tadā jñānasyāpy atāttvikatvam. na ca jñānavyatiriktā viṣayākāratā nāsty* (read: *asty*), *api tu jñānasvarūpam eva viṣayākāratātmakam apadiśyate. tac ca nayanārthālokasādhāraṇa* (read: *-sādhāraṇam*) *utpādyatvena, samaṃ saṃvedanaṃ prasaktaṃ sarvakārakāṇām.*

"Besides, is the fact of having the form of fire [for a cognition of fire] different from the cognition of fire or non-different? If it is different, is it real or unreal? In respect to these [alternatives], if it is real, how is its apprehension [brought about]? Not by being apprehended by itself, nor by producing [the cognition] and being that which provides [its] form [to the cognition]. It is not apprehended by itself, because it is different from the body (i.e., nature) of cognition. Nor is it apprehended by producing [the cognition] and being that which provides [its] form [to the cognition]. For the object provides [its] form, not the fact of having the form of the object. Or if it (i.e., the fact of having the form of the object) provides [its] form, there would be an [uninterrupted] succession of forms.

If the fact of having the form of the object is not real, [then] by being unreal it has an unapprehended body; how could it be the restricting factor [of every cognition] according to [its] object?

If [the fact of having the form of fire] is not different [from the cognition of fire], is this [fact] real or unreal? If it is real, does it have an unconscious or conscious nature?

In respect to these [alternatives], if it has an unconscious nature, then it cannot be non-different from the cognition, because something conscious and something unconscious cannot be one, as they have properties which stand by mutual exclusion.

If it has a conscious nature, then only the terminology is differentiated [for one thing, namely], 'cognition' [and] 'the form of object.'

If it is not real, then the cognition, too, would not be real.

And the fact of having the form of the object is not over and above the cognition [itself]. On the contrary, the own nature of the cognition itself is designated as having the nature of having the form of the object. And this [nature of cognition] is common to the eye, the object and the light by being produced [by all of them]. [Therefore not only the object would be apprehended, but] all causal factors would be apprehended together."

[310] Just as the object has to provide its form to the cognition in order to be apprehended by it, this form, too, in order to be apprehended, has to provide another form, and so on ad infinitum.

[311] This is a quotation of *PVin* I.34 (cf. Steinkellner, "New Sanskrit-Fragments," p. 204). The quotation is slightly defective: Jayarāśi reads *arthādhigateḥ* instead of *prameyādhigateḥ*, and the half-verse has accordingly only 15 syllables. Note that I.34ab appears as *PV pratyakṣa* 305ab.

Cf. also *TUS* p. 85.18-20: *ādarśamaṇḍalaṃ mukharūpatāṃ svīkaroti na cādarśarūpatāṃ parityajati. tathā jñānam api viṣayarūpatāṃ svīkurvan na vijñānarūpatāṃ tyajati.* "The mirror adopts having the form of the face, but it does not abandon having the form of a mirror. Similarly, in adopting having the form of an object, the cognition as well does not abandon having the form of a cognition."

[312] On *vṛttivikalpadoṣa* cf. nn. 274 and 276.

[313] This seems contradictory to the Buddhist position. In case there is an opponent behind this position, I have been unable to identify him. Could it be derived from the Buddhist siddhānta "*na kiñcid ekam ekasmān, nāpy ekasmād anekam*" (cf. Stcherbatsky, *Bud. Log.* I, p. 127, n. 7; cf. also ***NM*** II pp. 318.11f.)? For if many things do not arise from one thing, does this imply that one thing arises from one thing?

Cf. also *TUS* p. 87.19-23: *athaikam eva tena jvalanena janyate, kiṃ tad ekaṃ vijñānaṃ dhūmo vā? tad yadi vijñānam eva janyate, na tarhi dhūmaṃ dṛṣṭvāgniṃ (agniḥ) pratīya[te ']tadvyāpāralabdhajanmavattvāt. atha dhūma evotpādyate, tadā tadvijñānaṃ vinā kena hetuphalabhāvo 'vagamyate?*

"If only one [effect] is produced by this fire, is this one [effect] a cognition or smoke? In respect to these [alternatives], if only a cognition is produced, fire [would] not be apprehended by seeing smoke, because [smoke] does not obtain birth by the activity of that [fire]. If only smoke is produced [by fire], then, without the cognition of [fire], by whom (or: by what [means of valid cognition]) [would] the relation of cause and effect [between fire and smoke] be apprehended?"

Cf. also *TUS* p. 86.22-26.

314 *kevalam* is not made redundant by *eva*; *kevalam* should be construed with *utpādyate* as qualifying the mode of action, whereas *eva* restricts the result of the action.

315 Cf. § 4.25a and n. 268.

316 Cf. *NB* I.9 quoted above n. 236.

317 The following passage stands in no obvious connection with what follows. It seems to have been meant as a further substantiation of the claim made at the beginning of § d.8, namely, that the Buddhists are inconsistent in criticizing the Naiyāyikas with the *vṛttivikalpadoṣa*. In the previous passage Jayarāśi argues that the visible object is common to several effects; now he argues that the cognition is common to several causes. And just as the visible and the cognition are common to their effects and causes, so is the universal to the individuals of one class.

318 It is difficult to determine what kind of causal theory Jayarāśi had in mind in this passage. I suppose he could be referring to some Abhidharmic theory, especially as he quotes from what seems to be an Abhidharma source, cf. n. 321.

[319] Cf. *TUS* p. 77.21-24: *atha kāraṇānyatvena bhedaparikalpanā, tad ayuktaṃ, bhinnād api kāraṇād abhinnaṃ kāryaṃ dṛṣṭam. mṛtpiṇḍadaṇḍādy anekaṃ kāraṇam akhaṇḍitaṃ kāryaṃ janayati. tathaikenāpi kāraṇenānekaṃ kāryaṃ janyamānaṃ dṛṣṭaṃ ghaṭādi.*

"If [you] assume a difference [in the effect] because of difference in the cause, [then] this is not correct. One observes that an undifferentiated effect [arises] even from different causes. Several causes, a lump of clay, a [potter's] stick, etc., produce an effect [namely, a pot] which has no parts. Similarly, several effects, a pot [a cognition] etc., are seen to be produced even by a single cause."

[320] Cf. *PVSV* p. 23.18-21: *katham tarhīdānīṃ bhinnāt sahakāriṇaḥ kāryotpattir yathā cakṣūrūpāder vijñānasya. na vai kiñcid ekaṃ janakaṃ tatsvabhāvam. kiṃ tu sāmagrī janikā tatsvabhāvā. saivānumīyate.*

"Consequently, how is it [possible] now that an effect arises from different co-producers, for instance the cognition from the eye, the visible, etc.? Indeed, not even one causal factor has the nature of the [effect], but the causal complex which produces [the cognition] has that nature. [And] that [causal complex] alone is inferred."

Cf. also *PVin* II(1) pp. 92.12f.

[321] I was unable to identify this quotation; cf., however, AK II.64a: *caturbhiś cittacaittā hi*. Cf. also *PS* I (section 2) p. 187.31, translation p. 33, and n. 2.11; *TSP* p. 108. 18. For an explanation of the four kinds of causes cf. Stcherbatsky, *Bud. Log.* I, pp. 138-39.

[322] The same criteria are rejected by Vyomaśiva (*Vy* p. 20(ṅ).4-8), using different arguments: *na ca vilakṣaṇād api kāraṇād vilakṣaṇakāryasyotpattidarśanād bodharūpateti pramāṇam asti. ata evāsya jñānasya jñānāntarahetutve na pūrva-*

kālabhāvitvaṃ samānajātīyatvam ekasantānatvaṃ vā [*na*] *hetur, vyabhicārāt. tathā hi pūrvakālabhāvitvaṃ tatsamāna*<*kāla*>*kṣaṇaiḥ samānajātīyatvaṃ ca santānāntarajñānair vyabhicārīti, teṣāṃ hi pūrvakālabhāvitvena* (probably a lacuna here) *samānajātīyatve 'pi na vivakṣitajñānahetutvam iti. ekasantānatvaṃ cātyantājñānena vyabhicārīti.*

"But there is no proof that the fact of having the form of cognition [is due to the fact of being produced by the previous cognition], because it is observed that an effect of one kind is produced by a cause of a different kind as well. Precisely for this [reason], neither the fact of existing at an earlier time, nor the fact of being of the same kind, nor the fact of belonging to the same series [of cognition] is the reason for the fact that one cognition is the cause of another cognition, because [all three reasons] deviate. For the fact of existing at an earlier time deviates because of moments simultaneous with it, and the fact of belonging to the same kind [deviates] because of cognitions belonging to a different series [of cognitions], since the [moments simultaneous with the preceding cognition] <cannot be the cause of the intended cognition?> by the fact of existing at an earlier time <and the cognitions belonging to another series of cognitions?> cannot be [considered] the cause of the intended cognition, although [they] are of the same kind. And the fact of belonging to the same series deviates because of [moments in the same series] which are completely devoid of cognition [as in deep sleep etc.]."

[323] The determination of causal relations by temporal relations, namely, that the cause is that which precedes the effect, is criticized by Jayarāśi in *TUS* pp. 70.14-71.6: *anyac ca, tantūnāṃ kāryaṃ vastraṃ kiṃ pūrvāparakālabhāvitvena, āho pūrvāparagrahaṇena? tad yadi pūrvāparakālabhāvitvena, tadā niyatakāraṇakāryatvaṃ na labhyate 'mbara-*

phalasya, tatsamānakālīnānekakāryotpādakānāṃ tatpūrv[āparakāl]abhāvitvāviśeṣāt. athānvayavyatirekayuktasya yasya pūrvakālabhāvitvaṃ tat kāraṇam. tad asti dhruvabhāvikāryadarśanāt. anvayavyatirekaśabdena kim abhidhīyate? kiṃ kāraṇam anyad vā? tad yadi kāraṇaṃ, tadā na kiñcid bādhyate kāraṇātmatayā tat kāraṇām. athānyat tan, na jānīmaḥ kiṃ tad iti. na ca pūrvāparabhāvaḥ siddho 'tra jñānam antareṇa. jñānaṃ vinā na jāne kiṃ sahotpannau, pūrvāpara[bhāvo]<kālo>tpannau vānutpannau vā? atha pūrvāparagrahaṇakrameṇa pūrvāparotpādatadabhāvavyavastheti cet, tad etad api [grahaṇe 'pi] tulyam. satī sattā saṃvedyate nāsatī. sahotpannayor api krameṇa grahaṇaṃ dṛṣṭaṃ goviṣāṇayor, anutpannayoś ca gotvāstitvayoḥ. tathā paṭagrahaṇānantaraṃ tantūnāṃ grahaṇaṃ dṛṣṭam. tathaikam eva grahaṇaṃ dṛṣṭam. na ca tayor bhedo 'sti, na ca tayor hetuphalabhāvaḥ. yathā ca bhedo nāsti tathā prāg eva prapañcitam. evaṃ saṃvedanam api saṃvedyān na bhidyate sadākāratayā, na ca tayor ākārāntaram asty, ekaṃ hi vastu.

"And [there is] another [reason why the relation of cause and effect cannot be determined]: the cloth is [considered as] the effect of the threads - is [this] due to the existence [of the threads] before and [of the cloth] afterwards, or due to the apprehension [of the threads] before and [of the cloth] afterwards? In respect to these [alternatives], if it is due to existence [respectively] before and afterwards, then the result, [namely] the cloth, cannot be an effect which has a determined cause, because the producing factors of many effects which exist at the same time as the [cloth] are equally existing before the [cloth].

[Objection:] The cause is that which exists before [the effect] and is connected [to the effect] by positive and negative concomitance. There is [such a cause], because one observes the effect as arising necessarily [when this cause was present](?).

[Reply:] What is designated by the words 'positive and negative concomitance'? Is it a cause or something else? If it is a cause, then nothing is sublated, [your statement is tautological, for it amounts to the affirmation that] something is a cause by having the nature of a cause. If it is something else, we do not know what this [something else] is. And [moreover] previous and posterior existence is not established in this [case] without a cognition. Without a cognition I do not know whether [the threads and the cloth] have arisen together, one after the other, or not at all.

[Objection:] The determination whether [two things] arise one after the other or not is due to the sequence of previous and posterior apprehensions.

[Reply:] This [argument] as well is similar [to the first one in as much as the same difficulties as raised above apply to it]. Existence is perceived when it exists, not when it does not [yet] exist (i.e., by apprehending something as existing, we do not apprehend when it came into existence). It is observed that two horns of a cow are apprehended one after the other even though they have arisen together; and [similarly the universals] 'cow' and existence which [being eternal] are not produced [are apprehended one after the other]. In the same manner it is observed that the threads are apprehended immediately after the cloth is apprehended, and also only one apprehension [of both threads and cloth] is observed. But there is neither difference between the two, nor a relation of cause and effect between them. And why there is no difference has been explained in detail already above.

Thus the apprehension, too, does not differ from the [object] to be apprehended in as much as [they both] have the form of something existing. And they do not have [any] other form [to differentiate them], for a real thing is unique."

[324] Cf. *AKBh* p. 92.4 on *AK* II.55: *sarvam evāsaṃskṛtam adravyam iti sautrāntikāḥ.*

[325] Cf. § a.2b, p. 140.19-21 and *TUS* p. 120.22f.

[326] Cf. the previous note.

[327] Cf. § d.7 and n. 306.

[328] The compound *svajanabhujaṅgamādi* is not entirely clear to me; perhaps Jayarāśi means the eight classes of beings known as *graha*, which include *deva*, *asura*, *gandharva*, *yakṣa*, *pitṛ*, *bhujaṅgama*, *rākṣasa* and *piśāca* (cf. *Suśruta*, *Uttaratantra* 60.7). If this is the case, then *svajana* should be interpreted as *pitṛ*.

[329] On the omniscience of the Buddha cf. Bühnemann, *Der allwissende Buddha*; Steinkellner, "Yogische Erkenntnis als Problem im Buddhismus."

[330] It seems to me that Jayarāśi's arguments in this passage are inspired by Vasubandhu's refutation of the atom (cf. *Viṃś* 12). Just as the atom is not supposed to occupy more than one point in space, the cognition (and for that matter any momentary entity) should not last for more than one point in time. And just as an aggregate of seven such atoms occupies only one point in space, the production and destruction of a cognition should occupy the same point in time.

Jayarāśi's argument is repeated almost verbatim *Vy* p. 401.18-21: *na ca kṣaṇikatve sati kāryakāraṇabhāvo ghaṭate. tathā ca yadaiva kāryasyotpādas tadaiva kāraṇasya vināśaḥ, sa cotpādān na bhidyata ity abhyupagame sahotpannayor na syāt kāryakāraṇabhāvaḥ savyetaragoviṣāṇayor iva.*

"And if there is momentariness, the relation of cause and effect is impossible. For if [you] admit that the cause is destroyed precisely when the effect is produced and [that] the [destruction] does not differ [in time] from the production, [then] since the two arise at the same time there would be no relation of cause and effect [between them], just as between the left and the right horn of a cow."

Cf. also Vy p. 543.6-8: *kṣaṇikatve sati yadaiva kāryotpādas tadaiva kāraṇasya vināśaḥ. sa cotpatter nārthāntaram iti sahotpannayor na kāryakāraṇabhāva iti.*

331 I was unable to identify this quotation; cf. however *TS* v. 1896:

tasmāt tatrādivijñānaṃ svopādānabalodbhavam/
vijñānatvādihetubhya idānīntanacittavat//

"Therefore, the first cognition in the [foetus] (cf. v. 1880) arises from the capacity of its material cause [which is the last cognition in a previous life],
because [it] is a cognition etc., just like the present cognition."

Note that the Lokāyata position against which the above verse is directed is somewhat different from Jayarāśi's. For the opponent in the *TS* seems - at least as an alternative - to admit that the material cause of a cognition has to be a cognition (cf. v. 1893), but claims that the first cognition in this life has a cognition of the parents as its material cause. Jayarāśi does not seem to be acquainted with this position; in any case, he does not take it into consideration and argues, just as is argued in the *Bṛhaspatisūtra*, that the cognition arises from the material elements alone.

Note also that there is a difference between the inference quoted by Jayarāśi and the one in *TS* v. 1896 as to the question when the first cognition in this life occurs.

According to the quotation in the *TUS* it occurs only after birth, whereas according to the Buddhist position maintained in the *TS* it occurs already in the embryonic stage. The Lokāyata *pūrvapakṣa* in *TS* v. 1864-66 which is in fact a quotation of *ŚV ātmavāda* 65-67 denies the possibility of cognition before birth, but Śāntarakṣita does not deal with the point in his refutation.

[332] Cf. §§ e.3-4.

[333] Jayarāśi may be referring to the Abhidharmic *sabhāgahetu*, cf. AK(*Bh*) II.52, but there things do not arise exclusively from similar causes.

[334] Cf. § 4.25 and n. 268; cf. also *TUS* p. 88.5-20: *atha samānajātīyena vijñānena vinā na vijñānasyodgatir iti ced, evaṃ tarhi dhūmasyāpy asamānajātīyād dahanāt katham utpattiḥ? atha rūparūpatayā vahneḥ samānajātīyatvam, evaṃ dehāder api samānajātīyatvaṃ svalakṣaṇarūpatayā. idam eva cetasi samāropyoktaṃ śarīrād eveti* [*bṛhaspatiḥ*] (perhaps an interpolation). *atha jñānarūpatayā na samānajātīyatvaṃ dehasya, dahanasyāpi dhūmarūpatayāsamānajātīyatvam. niyatakāraṇajanyākāratayā niyatadeśakālasvabhāvatayā ca sarve bhāvā anyonyavyāvṛttatanavaḥ. na ca teṣām anyonyākārānugamo 'sti, nāpy ekajātyanugamaḥ. tad uktaṃ -*

sarve bhāvāḥ svabhāvena svasvabhāvavyavasthiteḥ/
svabhāvaparabhāvābhyāṃ yasmād vyāvṛttibhāginaḥ//

tataś ca bhinnajātīyāt sarvaṃ jāyamānaṃ dṛṣṭaṃ, na samānajātīyād bhavat kiñcid dṛṣṭapūrvam. evaṃ ca bhinnajātīyaṃ dehādikaṃ garbhādau vijñānam utpādayiṣyati. tataś ca na paralokaḥ prasidhyati.

"If a cognition is not produced without a cognition which belongs to the same kind, then how could there be production of smoke by fire which does not belong to the same kind [as smoke]? If the fact that fire is of the same kind [as smoke] is due to the fact that [they both] have the nature of a visible, [then] in the same manner the body etc., too, are of the same kind [as the cognition] by the fact that [they] have the nature of a particular. Having precisely this in mind, [Bṛhaspati] said: '[Consciousness arises] from the body alone.' If, by [taking into consideration] having the nature of a cognition, the body is not of the same kind [as the cognition], [then] by [taking into consideration] having the nature of smoke, fire, too, is not of the same kind [as smoke]. All things have mutually exclusive natures because [they] have forms produced by respectively different causes and because [they] have respective places, times and natures. And their respective forms do not pervade [all the others], nor is there a pervasion by a single universal. This has been said:

> 'Since all things, for [they] subsist by their own nature, are distinct by their nature from similar natures and other natures [different universals are assumed, which depend on whatever the things are distinguished from].' (*PV svārthānumāna* 40 = *PVin* II.29)

And thus, every thing is observed to arise from [causes] which do not belong to the same kind. Something which arises from [causes] belonging to the same kind has not been observed before. And consequently, the body etc., being of a different kind, should [be able to] produce a cognition in a foetus etc. And thus the other world (in this case a previous life) is not established."

Jayarāśi's arguments are reemployed by Vyomaśiva *Vy* pp. 400.30-401.7: *na ca santānasadbhāve pramāṇam asti, buddher buddhyantarakāryatve pramāṇābhāvāt. athāsti bodharūpateti cet, tathā hi bodharūpaṃ kāryaṃ bodhād eva bhavati, yathā śuklāc chuklam ityādi. nanv evaṃ tarhi dhūmasyāgnijanyatvaṃ na syāt, samānajātīyasya dhūmakṣaṇasya bhāvāt. atha vilakṣaṇād apy agnikṣaṇād dhūmasyotpattir iṣyeta, bodhasyāpi vilakṣaṇāc charīrāder utpattir bhaviṣyatīti na bodhāntarasadbhāve pramāṇam asti. atha kiñcitsādṛśyatayā-*

gnir dhūmasya kāraṇaṃ, tadā jñānotpattau śarīrādāv api samānam.

"And there is no proof for the existence of the series [of cognitions], because there is no proof that a cognition is the result of another cognition.

[Objection:] There is [a proof which consists in] the fact of having the nature of cognition. For an effect which has the nature of cognition arises only from a cognition, just as [an effect which has the nature of] something white arises from something white [alone], etc.

[Reply:] If so, then smoke would not be produced by fire, because there is a moment of smoke which belongs to the same kind [and which would have to be considered as its cause]. If it were admitted that smoke arises from a moment of fire although [fire] is not of the same kind [as smoke], the cognition, too, could arise from a body etc., which are not of the same kind [as the cognition]. Thus, there is no proof for [its production by and therefore] the existence of another cognition. If fire is the cause of smoke by the fact that it is somewhat similar to it, then this is the same for the body etc., too, with regard to the production of cognition (i.e., there is some similarity between the body etc., and the cognition)."

[336] Cf. Vy p. 401.8-10: *atyantasamānajātīyaṃ ca samanantarakāraṇam ity abhyupagamyamāne rūpajñānād eva rūpajñānaṃ rasajñānād eva rasajñānaṃ sukhād eva sukhaṃ duḥkhād eva duḥkham iti santānānantyaṃ* (perhaps: *santāno 'nanyaḥ*; Ms: *santānāntya*) *syāt.*

"And if it is admitted that the immediately preceding cause is absolutely similar [to its effect], [it would follow that] a cognition of a visible [would arise] only from a cognition of a visible, a cognition of flavour only from a cognition of flavour, pleasure only from pleasure, sorrow only from sorrow. Thus, the series [of cognitions] would not [contain] different [elements]."

[336] For inference is impossible without a recollection of the *vyāpti*.

[337] This is a quotation of the first half of *MS* 1.1.4; the whole *sūtra* reads as follows: *satsamprayoge puruṣasyendriyāṇāṃ buddhijanma tat pratyakṣam animittaṃ vidyamānopalambhanatvāt*. "Perception is the arising of a cognition when the senses of a person are in contact with an existing [object]; it is not a means [for the apprehension of *dharma*] because it apprehends a present [object]."

I translated the *sūtra* according to what I think was its original meaning. Note, however, that Śabara interprets *satsamprayoga* as a *karmadhāraya*-compound, and that he construes, following the Vṛttikāra (cf. *ŚBh* p. 26.3-4), *puruṣasya* with *buddhi* (*ŚBh* p. 22.13-14): *satīndriyārthasambandhe yā puruṣasya buddhir jāyate, tat pratyakṣam*. According to this interpretation which is also accepted by Jha and Frauwallner one would have to translate: "Perception is the arising of cognition of a person when there is a contact of the senses [with an object] ..." For the use of *nimitta* as 'instrument' or 'means' cf. *Bhagavadgītā* 11.33.

[338] Two of the three interpretations of the *sūtra*, namely, as a definition of perception and as a repetition of the definition of perception, are well known from the *ŚV*; as for the third interpretation, namely, as an enumeration of the causes of perception, it does not seem to be mentioned in any of the Mīmāṃsā texts known to me, but it appears as a *pūrvapakṣa* in Dignāga's *PS*.

The opinion according to which the *sūtra* contains a definition of perception is attributed by Pārthasārathi to the early (pre-Śabara) Mīmāṃsā commentator Bhavadāsa. The latter divided the *sūtra* in two parts, the first of which starts with *satsamprayoga* and ends with *pratyakṣam*; the purpose of this part is to define perception. The purpose of the second part, from *animittam* onwards, is to state that perception is not a means for the apprehension of *dharma*. Cf. *NR* p. 97.3-4 (introduction to ŚV 4.1): *bhavadāsenaitat sūtraṃ dvidhā kṛtvā satsamprayoga ityevamādi tat pratyakṣam ityevamantaṃ pratyakṣalakṣaṇaparam. animittam ityādi ca tasya dharmaṃ praty animittatvaparaṃ vyākhyātam.* Cf. also ŚVV p. 121.9-11 and ŚVK I p. 204.10-11.

Kumārila rejects this interpretation of the *sūtra* arguing that a definition would be inappropriate in this context, for one would not be able to establish a connection with the preceding *sūtra* (*nimittasūtra*). The purpose of the *MS* is to investigate *dharma*, and there is no reason to undertake a definition or investigation of perception which does not contribute to the apprehension of *dharma*. If Jaimini wanted to define the means of valid cognition, he would have defined inference etc., as well. Besides, if the *sūtra* can be read as one sentence, it is not right to split it into two. Furthermore, as a definition it would be too wide, because it does not exclude false cognitions which arise when the senses are in contact with an object (cf. ŚV 4.1f.). However, all these objections can be avoided by re-interpreting the word *samprayoga*: the prefix *sam* may be understood as *samyak* (correct), and *prayoga* as activity, functioning (i.e., perception is a cognition of a person when the senses are functioning correctly). Interpreted in this manner, the *sūtra* can be understood as a repetition of the definition of perception; cf. ŚV 4.39cd: *evaṃ saty anuvādatvaṃ lakṣaṇasyāpi sambhavet.*

The interpretation of the *sūtra* as an enumeration of the causes of perception seems to have been introduced by the Vṛttikāra of Dignāga (who is certainly not the same person as the Vṛttikāra in the *ŚBh*) whom Frauwallner identifies with Bhavadāsa (*Materialien zur ältesten Erkenntnislehre der Karmamīmāṃsā*, pp. 98ff.).

As is well known, in earlier times the word perception (*pratyakṣa*) referred to a cognition. Later on, when the word *pramāṇa* was analyzed as *pramīyate 'nena* ("that by which [the object] is rightly cognized"), the concept of means of valid cognition was applied to perception, the meaning of which was transformed accordingly. (The same development is clearly seen in Nyāya; *NS* 1.1.4 defines perception as cognition, whereas Vātsyāyana interprets it as a means of cognition.) The means of valid cognition according to the Vṛttikāra is the totality of causes or the causal complex (*kārakasāmagrī, -samudāya, -saṅghāta*), cf. PS(V) I (section 6) 5cd-6a(1) p. 231.9-16:

blo yi rgyu yi tshogs pa dag/
brjod las ḥgrol baḥi tshad ma gaṅ//
gaṅ las

ḥgrel pa byed pa ni ḥbras bu don gṣan du smra ba la blo skye ba las gṣan ḥbras bu ma mthoṅ nas gaṅ las blo ḥbyuṅ ba de mṅon sum mo ṣes zer ba der yaṅ, gaṅ mṅon sum ñid du bstan par bya ba ji skad bśad paḥi bdag daṅ phrad pa la sogs pa ḥdu byed daṅ bcas pa la sogs pa las gṣan bloḥi rgyu yod pa ni ma yin no.

"What else could be the means of valid cognition except the totality of causes of cognition mentioned [by the Vṛttikāra], from which [the cognition arises]? The Vṛttikāra says that the result is something different [from the cause] and maintains that, because one does not observe a result different from the arising of cognition, perception is that from which the cognition arises. In respect to this, there is no cause for the cognition different from the contact of the Soul etc., together with the impressions, as mentioned, which could be taught as perception."

It is quite obvious that the Vṛttikāra construed the *sūtra* in a very ingenious way which neither Hattori nor

Frauwallner seem to have realized. In order to accomodate his theory into the *sūtra* he has probably construed *satsamprayoge* not only with *indriyāṇām*, but also with *puruṣasya*. The word *puruṣa* is therefore interpreted not as 'person,' but as 'Soul,' and thus it also includes the properties or qualities of the Soul, such as the impressions which are explained as *dharma* and *adharma*. According to this interpretation we would have to translate the *sūtra* as follows: "Perception is [the means of valid cognition whose result is] the arising of cognition when there is a contact of the senses [and] the Soul [together with its properties] with an existing [object]." Problematic remains the question how (if at all) the contact of the Soul and the senses with the *manas* was incorporated into the *sūtra*.

It should be noted that although enumeration of causes and definition are dealt with by Jayarāśi as two independent *vikalpas*, for Bhavadāsa (or whoever the opponent is) it is one and the same thing, as for him the definition of perception consists in the enumeration of the causes of perception.

339 Cf. §§ 1.11-1.14.

340 The distinction between *vijñāna* and *avabodha* is not clear to me; cf., however, the last section in this chapter where the opponent tries to establish the existence of cognition (*buddhi*) by the fact that otherwise apprehension (*avabodha*) would be impossible.

341 Since the senses (which are not to be confounded with their perceptible bases such as the eye-ball etc.) are imperceptible, their coming into contact with their objects is imperceptible, too. The problem of production by contact between the senses and the object is discussed in more detail in § 1.4; cf. also *NM* I p. 261.9f.

[342] On the problem of *prāpyakāritva* cf. Preisendanz, *Nayatattvāloka*, nn. 146, 147, 155, 159, 185, 189, 191.

Kumārila does not have a strong opinion on the subject. If the Buddhists will be able to prove that all perceptions are produced without a contact, this will not affect the Mīmāṃsā position, for the word *samprayoga* in the *sūtra* can be understood as activity as well. In the meantime Kumārila prefers to rely on the Sāṅkhya position, and as long as this theory is not refuted it should be admitted that the eye and the ear, too, come in contact with their objects (cf. *ŚV* 4.40-44). The only point which Kumārila finds unacceptable in the Sāṅkhya theory is that the auditory sense goes out to meet its object. According to him the contact occurs in the ear itself (cf. ibid., 51cd).

[343] Cf. *ŚV* 4.24cd: *sarvathā lokasiddhatvād dharmo 'yaṃ tāvad iṣyate//*. "This property [of being produced by contact with the senses] is accepted meanwhile because it is known among the people by all means."

Cf. *ŚVV*, *NR* and *ŚVK* ad loc., as well as *ŚVV* p. 124.16-17: *tena nātra lakṣaṇam uddiśya lakṣyaṃ vidhīyate, kiṃ tu lokaprasiddhasya pratyakṣasya satsamprayogajatvena vidyamānopalambhanatvād dharmaṃ praty aprāmāṇyam iti.* "Therefore, one does not affirm here [in this *sūtra*] the definiendum (i.e., perception) after pointing out the definition, but [one affirms that] perception, which is well known among the people, is not a means of valid cognition in respect to *dharma*, because it apprehends a present [object], since it arises from a real contact."

Cf. also *NM* I p. 263.10-11: ... *api tu lokaprasiddhapratyakṣānuvādena dharmaṃ praty animittatvam eva vidhīyate.*

[344] Cf. the discussion of *anuvāda* and *prasiddha* in respect to *dharma* in *ŚVV* p. 30.2f.

[345] I was unable to identify this quotation; similar formulations, however, occur often enough. In fact, this sentence is nothing but a slightly different formulation of the second half of the *sūtra* (cf. n. 337) in which the production by contact becomes the reason for the fact that perception is not a means of apprehension of *dharma*. It should be noted, however, that the quotation, as it stands, differs slightly from the usual Mīmāṃsā interpretation, for the production by contact is usually understood as a reason not for the fact that perception is not a means in respect to *dharma*, but for the fact that it apprehends a present object; cf. ŚVV p. 124.16-17 (quoted above, n. 343), *ŚD* p. 29.8-9: *ucyate - pratyakṣaṃ tāvat saṃyuktaviṣayatvena vidyamānopalambhanatvād bhaviṣyati dharme na samartham*; ibid., p. 51.1-2: *pratyakṣaṃ tāvad indriyārthasamprayogajanyatvena vidyamānopalambhanatvād bhaviṣyati dharme na nimittam*. *NM* I p. 263.17-18: *yadi vidyamānopalambhanatvam asiddham iti paro brūyāt, sa vaktavyo - vidyamānopalambhanaṃ pratyakṣaṃ satsamprayogajatvād iti*.

Pārthasārathi even adds a third inference which completes the circle, cf. *NR* p. 100.23-24: *tad ete trayaḥ prayogāḥ - pratyakṣam animittaṃ vidyamānopalambhanatvād, vidyamānopalambhanatvaṃ ca satsamprayogajatvāt, satsamprayogajatvaṃ ca pratyakṣatvād iti*.

[346] While saying that perception is not a means for the apprehension of *dharma*, the *Sūtra* as well as the *Bhāṣya* certainly meant perception in general. However, Kumārila interpreted the *sūtra* as referring to *yogipratyakṣa* alone, for it would have been too obvious to state that normal perception cannot apprehend *dharma*. Cf. ŚV 4.21cd: *asmadādau prasiddhatvād yogyartham abhidhīyate//*. "Because in respect to people like us it is well known [that perception is not a means for the apprehension of *dharma*], [this] is said while intending the yogi."

When raising his *vikalpas*, Jayarāśi certainly has in mind Kumārila's interpretation of the *sūtra*. Perception in which something other than *dharma* appears refers to normal perception, whereas perception in which *dharma* appears refers to the perception of a yogi. The third *vikalpa*, namely, perception which does not arise, looks strange at first sight, but becomes understandable when one considers that according to the Mīmāṃsakas there is no such thing as *yogipratyakṣa*. This, obviously, could render the inference false, because the *hetu* is charged with *āśrayāsiddhatā*. The Mīmāṃsaka would answer in this case that this is not a normal inference, but a *prasaṅgasādhana* (cf. *NM* I p. 266.4f.).

Besides the above mentioned fallacy the Mīmāṃsakas were also charged with the absence of an example/similar instances (*dṛṣṭānta*, *sapakṣa*). The inference (i.e., perception is not a means for the apprehension of *dharma* because it apprehends a present object) cannot have perception itself as an example, because in this case *pakṣa* and *sapakṣa/dṛṣṭānta* would be one. Nor can it have anything else as an example, because the *hetu* resides nowhere else. To comply with this objection, the Mīmāṃsakas claimed that *yogipratyakṣa* is used as the subject of inference (*pakṣa*) and normal perception as its example/similar instance. Cf. *ŚVK* I p. 212.9-11: *pratyakṣaviśeṣaṃ pakṣīkṛtya pratyakṣāntaraṃ sapakṣīkriyata iti na pakṣasapakṣayor ekatā, nāpi siddhasādhyateti*; *NR* p. 101.12-13: *asmiṃś ca pratyakṣaviśeṣe pakṣīkṛte 'smadādipratyakṣaṃ dṛṣṭāntaḥ*.

[347] Cf. *NM* I p. 264.9-13: *katarasya pratyakṣasya dharmaṃ praty animittatvaṃ pratipādyate? kim asmadādipratyakṣasya yogipratyakṣasya vā? tatra asmadādipratyakṣasya tathātve sarveṣām avivāda eveti kiṃ tatreyatā śrameṇa? yogipratyakṣasya tu bhavatām asiddhatvāt kasya dharmaṃ praty animittatvapratipādanam?*

"Which of the two [kinds of] perception do you proclaim as not being a means in respect to *dharma*? Is it the perception of people like us, or is it the perception of the yogi? In respect to these [alternatives], if perception of people like us is such, [then] nobody is of a different opinion! What [is the use of] so much effort about it? On the other hand, since you do not admit the perception of the yogi, what is it that you proclaim as not being a means in respect to *dharma*?"

[348] Cf. §§ 1.41, 5.12.

[349] I was unable to identify this quotation.

[350] Cf. *TUS* p. 119.9-20: *athavā codanājanitavijñānasya nirviṣayatvam eva bhrāntatvaṃ codanājanitavijñānasamānakālīnakartavyatārūpārthasyāsambhavāt. sambhave vā codanāvacaso vaikalyaṃ, vitānakriyāvilopaḥ. atha na vidyate kartavyatārūpo 'rthaḥ, kathaṃ codanāvacanodbhūtaṃ vijñānaṃ na mithyā? anyathā keśoṇḍukasaṃvido mithyātvaṃ na bhavet. atha tasyā[ḥ] pratīyamānārthāsambhavena mithyātvaṃ, tad ihāpi tad evāstu. atha codanājanitavijñānārthasya punaḥ sadbhāvo bhavati tena tasya yathārthatvaṃ, na tu keśoṇḍukavijñān<ārth>asya kadācid api sadbhāvo 'sti. so 'yaṃ viṣabhakṣaṇena paraṃ pratyāyayati tapasvi. codanārthasya paścād bhavanaṃ tadvijñānānupayogi tasmin kāle jñānasyāstamitatvād, vijñānakāle cārthasya(syā)sambhavāt.*

"Or the cognition produced by Vedic injunction is false in as much as it lacks an object, because the object which has the nature of duty cannot exist at the same time as the cognition which is produced by Vedic injunction. Or if [it] can [exist at the same time], the Vedic injunction is incompetent [in as much as it teaches something already done], and sacrificial actions [should be] annulled. If the object which has the nature of duty does not exist, how could the cognition which arises from the Vedic injunction not be false? Otherwise, the cognition of the hair-net would not be false. If it is false because the perceived object does not exist, then here, too, it would be exactly the same (i.e., the inexistence of the object of Vedic injunction would be the reason for its falsity).

[Objection:] The object of the cognition which is produced by Vedic injunction [has existed some time before and now] exists again [after the performance of duty]. This is why its [cognition] is true, but the object of the cognition of the hair-net never exists.

[Reply:] This is [just like the maxim of] the ascetic who proves the absolute truth by drinking poison. The arising of the object of Vedic injunction at a later time does not assist the cognition of this [object], because at the time [when the object arises] the cognition is [already] destroyed, and at the time of the cognition, the object does not [yet] exist."

351 Literally: the fact that something has to be done.

352 For Kumārila non-existence is a fact just like existence; negative statements which are found to be valid indicate the reality of the non-existence. If there were no negative facts which correspond to our negative statements, the latter would always be false; cf. Bhatt, *Epistemology of the Bhāṭṭa School*, pp. 342f., cf. also § 4.1(11).

353 Cf. *MS* 1.1.4 quoted in n. 337.

354 The Bhāṭṭa-Mīmāṃsakas do not admit self-apprehension; cf. ŚV *śūnyavāda* 185cd: *na cātmānubhavo 'sty asyety ātmano na prakāśakam//*. "The [cognition] does not experience itself, thus [it] does not illuminate itself."

[356] This was the early position of Mīmāṃsā as represented by the Vṛttikāra, cf. *ŚBh* p. 28.20-30.2: *utpadyamānaivāsau jñāyate jñāpayati cārthāntaraṃ pradīpavad iti yady ucyeta, tan na. na hy ajñāte 'rthe kaścid buddhim upalabhate, jñāte tv anumānād avagacchati.* "If it is said that as soon as it arises the [cognition] is cognized [by itself] and makes known other objects just like a lamp, then this is not [correct]. For nobody apprehends a cognition when the object is not [yet] cognized, but when [the object] is cognized one apprehends [the cognition] through inference."

Cf. also *NR* and *ŚVK* on *śūnyavāda* 232, and *NM* I p. 44.3-4.

The Buddhist *pūrvapakṣa* in *ŚD* gives the following reasons why there is no inferential sign for the cognition (pp. 86.8-87.6): *anumānam iti cen, na liṅgābhāvāt. na tāvad artho liṅgaṃ, vināpi tena suṣuptyādyavasthāyām arthasadbhāvābhyupagamāt. arthavyavahāro liṅgaṃ - sa hi kādācitkaṃ kāraṇaṃ kalpayatīti ced, evaṃ tu prāg vyavahārāj jñānapratibhāso na syāt. avyavaharann api ghaṭaṃ paśyan jāne 'haṃ ghaṭam iti jñānam anusandhatta iti pratītisākṣikam. arthadharmo jñānajanmā liṅgam iti cen, na tadsadbhāve pramāṇābhāvāt. atītānāgatayoś cārthayor dharmāsambhavād atītādyanumāne jñānasiddhir na syāt. tasmād avaśyaṃ vijñānaṃ pratyakṣam eṣitavyam.*

"If [you say that] inference [is the means for the apprehension of cognition], [then this is] not [correct], because there is no [inferential] sign. The object, to begin with, is not the [inferential] sign, because [you] admit that the object exists even without the [cognition], [as] in a state of deep sleep etc. (Unlike the Vedāntins, the Mīmāṃsakas do not admit pleasure and its cognition in a state of deep sleep; the recollection of the good feeling which accompanies deep sleep is due only to the absence of the recollection of any suffering in that state, cf. *ŚD* p. 258.5f.)

[Objection:] The activity towards the object is the [inferential] sign, for the activity makes [you] assume [its] incidental cause.

[Reply:] But so there would be no appearance of cognition before the activity. Even without acting, [a person] who sees a pot ascertains the cognition [when thinking] 'I cognize a pot'; thus, there is a witness for the cognition [namely, this ascertainment, even without activity].

[Objection:] A property of the object produced by the cognition is the [inferential] sign.

[Reply:] No, because there is no proof for the existence [of such a property]. And because the property [of being produced by the cognition] is impossible for past and future objects, there would be no proof for [the existence of] cognition in the case of an inference of a past [object] etc. Therefore, it has necessarily to be admitted that the cognition is directly perceived."

[366] According to Kumārila cognitions are apprehended by implication, cf. ŚV śūnyavāda 190cd: *arthāpattyāvabudhyante vijñānāni punaḥ punaḥ//*. The *arthāpatti* is based on the fact that otherwise (i.e., if the cognition did not exist) the existence of the object would not be seen, cf. ibid., 182:

nānyathā hy arthasadbhāvo dṛṣṭaḥ sann upapadyate/
jñānaṃ cen nety ataḥ paścāt pramāṇam upajāyate//

Later commentators like Umbeka hypostatized a special property 'to be known' (*jñātatva, vedyatva*) or 'to be manifested' (*prākaṭya*) which is produced in the object the moment of its cognition. This property is perceived in its turn and is used for the following implication: the cognition has arisen, for otherwise the fact that the object has been cognized would be impossible (*arthasya jñātatvānyathānupapattiḥ*).

In the *ŚD* Pārthasārathi still considers this theory acceptable (though it is not the only acceptable one), but he rejects it in the *NR*. His reason, however, was not that he objected to the production of an objective property by the cognitive process, but that such a property could hardly be apprehended in the case of mediate objects such as the objects of inference etc. His proof of cognition is explained as follows: A relation of obtainment between the cognizer and the object is produced by the act of cognition. This relation is apprehended by mental perception, and it leads to the assumption of the cognition which is not done automatically, but only when there is a desire to know the cognition (cf. *NR* p. 228.3f.).

It is striking, however, that none of the different interpretations of *jñātatā* is known to Jayarāśi, who certainly does not follow here the commentatorial tradition of the *ŚV*.

[357] This seems to be the opinion of certain Mīmāṃsakas who are referred to (and rejected) in *NR* p. 227.24-27 (on *śūnyavāda* 182): *tatra kecid āhuḥ - sarvathā tāvad asti jñānam. tathā hi vidyamāna eva hi* (read: *api*) *ghaṭaḥ kasyacid eva vyavahārayogyatām āpadyate na sarveṣāṃ, nāpi sarvadā, tad avaśyaṃ yo yadā tena vyavaharati tasya tad*(read: *tadā*)*vyavahārānuguṇaḥ kaścid atiśayaḥ sañjāta iti kalpanīyaṃ, sa jñānam iti.*

"In this [connection] some [Mīmāṃsakas] say: 'The cognition exists by all means. For although the pot exists [equally for all people] it becomes suitable for the activity of a certain [person] only, not for all [people], nor all the time. Therefore, it has necessarily to be assumed that when a [person] is busy with this [pot], then a certain additional property has arisen for him which is suitable to [his] activity. This [additional property] is the cognition.'"

Pārthasārathi accepts this only as a secondary proof of cognition, because one apprehends the cognition even before the activity towards the object (*NR* p. 227.27-29).

358 Cf. also § 1.42.

359 The closest formulation to this position which I was able to find appears in *ŚVV* on *śūnyavāda* 232. The opponent asks why the cognition should not be apprehended as soon as it arises as there is nothing to obstruct (*pratibandha*) its apprehension. (v. 231; this refers to the objection in *ŚBh* p. 30.3-5.) Kumārila agrees that there is no obstructing factor, but claims that there is no apprehension because there is no *liṅga*. Both Pārthasārathi and Sucaritamiśra (*NR* and *ŚVK* ad loc.) interpret the *liṅga* as *jñātatva*. Umbeka, however, provides a different interpretation which comes close to Jayarāśi's *vikalpa* (p. 294.15-17): *arthagrahaṇaṃ hi liṅgabhūtam anyathānupapadyamānaṃ vā buddher grāhakaṃ pramāṇam upajanayati. tac cottarakālam arthagrahaṇād utpadyate, na pūrvaṃ, nāpy arthagrahaṇasamakālam.* "For the apprehension of the object which functions as inferential sign or which otherwise (i.e., without the existence of a cognition) would be impossible, gives rise to a means of valid cognition which apprehends the cognition. And this [means of valid cognition] arises after the apprehension of the object, neither before, nor at the same time as the apprehension of the object."

Note, however, that Jayarāśi's opponent seems to distinguish between different types of apprehensions or cognitions (for him, *avabodha* and *buddhi* are probably not synonyms, for otherwise there is no point for Jayarāśi to claim that they are). This does not seem to be the case with Umbeka, although he uses two different expressions (*grahaṇa* and *buddhi*).

In this connection it is interesting to point out that according to Umbeka Kumārila was arguing also against some ancient Naiyāyikas (*vṛddhanaiyāyika*) who claimed that the cognition was cognized at the same time as the object (ŚVV p. 294.18-20): *ta evam āhur - utpadyamānaiva sārtham avagamayaty ātmamanaḥsaṃyogajena pratyakṣeṇa svayaṃ ca sukhādivad avagamyata iti.* "They (i.e., the ancient Naiyāyikas) say: 'As soon as it arises the [cognition] makes known the object and is itself apprehended by perception which arises from a contact between the Self and the mind, just like pleasure etc.'"

It seems, therefore, that these Naiyāyikas did not yet accept the principle of strict *jñānāyaugapadya*, but the question remains open how the cognition of the cognition can arise without the cognition being there at the previous moment. Perhaps these Naiyāyikas still operated with the seemingly archaic notion that an object and its cognition exist at the same time.

360 This is Vindhyavāsin's definition of perception, cf. *TBV* p. 533.2: *śrotrādivṛttir avikalpiketi vindhyavāsipratyakṣalakṣaṇam* ... . Cf. also *NM* I p. 259.6-7: *śrotrādivṛttir aparair avikalpiketi pratyakṣalakṣaṇam avarṇi*. *PM* p. 28.4 (on 1.29): *śrotrādivṛttir avikalpikā pratyakṣam iti vṛddhasāṅkhyāḥ*.

As is well known Vindhyavāsin's definition consists in a modification of Vārṣagaṇya's definition of *pratyakṣa* as it appears in the *Ṣaṣṭitantra*: *śrotrādivṛttiś ca (pratyakṣaṃ pramāṇam)*. For a hypothetical reconstruction of parts of the *Ṣaṣṭitantra* cf. Frauwallner, "Erkenntnislehre des klassischen Sāṃkhya-Systems."

Vārṣagaṇya paraphrased his definition as follows (ibid., p. 98 = Kl. Schr. p. 263): *śrotratvakcakṣurjihvāghrāṇānāṃ manasādhiṣṭhitā vṛttiḥ śabdasparśarūparasagandheṣu yathākramaṃ grahaṇe vartamānā pramāṇaṃ pratyakṣam.* "The functioning of [the senses] hearing, touching, seeing, tasting and smelling which is governed by the mind [and] which is engaged in the apprehension of sound, touch, colour, flavour and smell respectively, is a means of valid cognition, [namely] perception."

According to Jinendrabuddhi's commentary on the *PS* it seems that while criticizing the Sāṅkhya position Dignāga had used the *Ṣaṣṭitantra* together with two commentaries thereon. Regarding the theory of perception, these two commentaries had conflicting interpretations of the words *manasādhiṣṭhitā vṛttiḥ*. According to the one, which probably represents the older interpretation, the senses and the mind come in contact with the external objects at the same time. According to the other commentary, which is probably Vindhyavāsin's, only the senses come in contact with the external objects, whereas the mind apprehends the functioning of the senses afterwards, for it would be pointless that two senses would function in respect to the same object. Furthermore, if the mind could apprehend the external objects directly, the senses would be superfluous, and there would be no deaf or blind people. Cf. also *YD* p. 110.11-19.

The opponent may claim that the senses are not superfluous because the mind is assisted by them, and therefore cannot apprehend the objects without them, just as a lamp enables the eye to see (Frauwallner, ibid., p. 107 = Kl. Schr. p. 246). But even so, a difficulty remains: the functioning of the senses is not conscious (*acetana, apratyaya*), and therefore cannot be a means of valid cognition as the definition requires. According to Vindhyavāsin's theory, on the other hand, the functioning of the senses consists only in assuming the form of the object, and the thus determined object is determined again by the mind. Thus, the determination of the object by the senses and the determination of the object by the mind are fused in the mind, and in this manner the functioning of the senses becomes conscious, for it takes over the consciousness of the Soul which is mirrored in the mind (ibid., p. 107 = Kl. Schr. pp. 246-47). (Note that for Vindhyavāsin there is only one internal organ, cf. Frauwallner, *Geschichte* I, pp. 401-2) Further, while commenting on the words *grahaṇe vartamānaḥ* (cf. above) Vindhyavāsin says that they are employed in order to exclude conceptual construction from the realm of the definition of perception. And this, of course, is the reason why he added to the definition the word *avikalpikā* (cf. "Erkenntnislehre," pp. 113-14 = Kl. Schr. pp. 252-53). On Vindhyavāsin's innovations within the Sāṅkhya system cf. Frauwallner, op. cit., pp. 401-6, 410, Chakravarti, *Origin and Development of the Sāṃkhya System of Thought*, pp. 142-55.

361 Jayarāśi does not provide any further details on the nature of the transformation; however, it is quite certain that at the time of the *TUS* the doctrine of transformation in terms of a new arrangement of the parts (*sanniveśa*) was interpreted and explained as a *dharma-dharmin* relation. Transformation is, therefore, the disappearance of one property and the appearance of another, cf. *AKBh* p. 159. 21f. on AK III.50a, *YD* pp. 49.10-11, 75.6-7, *YBh* 3.13, Frauwallner, *Geschichte* I, pp. 389-90, Chakravarti, op. cit., pp. 258f. Unlike in other systems, the *dharma-dharmin* relation in the Sāṅkhya-Yoga system is a causal and relative relation. For not only a property pre-exists in its cause, the property-possessor, but also a property - in respect to a previous stage of development - may be regarded as a property-possessor in respect to a posterior stage of development, cf. Chakravarti, op. cit., pp. 198-208.

362 Cf. *YD* p. 103.26: *viṣayākārapariṇāmātmikā vṛttiḥ* ... .

363 The sentence which is quoted next contains in fact only examples of errors; it should be borne in mind,

though, that Sāṅkhya commentators subsume doubt under error, for instance *GBh* p. 58.4-5: *tatra saṃśayo 'jñānaṃ viparyayaḥ*. *MV* p. 46.27: *saṃśayabuddhir viparyayaḥ sthāṇur ayaṃ puruṣo veti*. Cf. also *TV* p. 12.24f. and *RM* p. 12.6 on *YBh* 1.8.

364 These are the five kinds of error referred to in *SK* 47-48, and the sentence quoted by Jayarāśi is also quoted by all commentaries thereon: *GBh* p. 58.27-28, *YD* p. 127.23, *MV* p. 47.14, SV(1) p. 62.2, *STK* p. 279.4-5, *JM* p. 103.21-22 (SV(2) is missing for these *kārikās*). Unfortunately none of them identifies its origin. Frauwallner (*Geschichte* I, pp. 326f.) discusses these terms in the context of the *Ṣaṣṭitantra*, but the archaic flavour they carry indicates an even earlier origin. Whatever the case may be, in the classical period the five errors were considered as one of the four groups of elements which are relevant to salvation, the other three being the 28 kinds of incapacity (*aśakti*), the 9 kinds of satisfaction (*tuṣṭi*) and the 8 kinds of perfection (*siddhi*). Each of the five kinds of error was further differentiated into several sub-classes: *tamas* and *moha* are eightfold, *mahāmoha* is tenfold, *tāmisra* and *andhatāmisra* are eighteenfold (cf. *SK* 48).

As can be expected, the different commentaries do not always agree upon what all these kinds of error actually consist of, but differences are only minor. I follow the exposé of the *YD* which is the most detailed:

1) The eight kinds of *tamas* consist of the illusion of taking the eight *prakṛtis* (i.e., *pradhāna*, *buddhi*, *ahaṅkāra* and the five *tanmātras*) which are inferior (to the Self) as superior (cf. p. 128.28-29, cf. also p. 130.21-22).

2) The eight kinds of *moha* consist of taking oneself as the possessor of the eight kinds of divine power (*aiśvarya*), like becoming as small as an atom etc. (*aṇimādi*), which are actually different conditions of the *buddhi* (p. 128.31, but cf. also p. 127.25f.).

3) The ten kinds of *mahāmoha* consist of conceiving as 'mine' the ten members of the household, namely, mother, father, brother, sister, wife, son, daughter, guru, friend and servant. Or, as other commentators maintain (this is probably a reference to the *GBh*, p. 59.23-26, which is followed by all other commentaries in this respect), these ten kinds of error refer to the ten kinds of objects (five human and five divine - *dṛṣṭānuśravika*) (p. 128.33-34). The human objects are sound, touch, colour, flavour and smell which are properties of the five material elements and are characterized by pleasure, pain and confusion. The divine objects are the above five in the form of the *tanmātras* and are characterized by pleasure alone (cf. also *GBh* on SK 38). These objects are perceptible only for the gods and we know of them only through the sacred writings.

4) The eighteen kinds of *tāmisra* consist of the anger (*āveśa* = *krodha*) of someone who is kept back from the above mentioned eight divine powers and either the tenfold household or the ten objects (p. 128.36).

5) The eighteen kinds of *andhatāmisra* consist of the despair (*viṣāda*) of someone who is parting from the eight divine powers and the ten members of the household. It is also described as the despair one experiences after death (*maraṇaviṣāda*, pp. 128.15, 138.32-139.4).

The *YBh*, on the other hand, identifies the above five kinds of error with the five defilements (*kleśa*) (certainly under Buddhist influence, cf. de la Vallée Poussin, "Le Bouddhisme et le Yoga de Patañjali," esp. p. 233). Cf. *YBh* 1.8 p. 13.4-6: *seyaṃ pañcāparvā bhavaty avidyā, avidyāsmitārāgadveṣābhiniveśāḥ kleśā ity eta eva svasañjñābhis tamo moho mahāmohas tāmisro 'ndhatāmisra iti*. "This [false functioning] (cf. *YBhV* p. 35.12: *viparyayavṛttiḥ*) is ignorance [in general] which has five parts [which are enumerated in YS 2.3]: 'The defilements are ignorance, [the wrong notion of] 'I am,' desire, hatred and attachment.' These very same [defilements are designated] by their technical terms as obscurity, delusion, great delusion, darkness and blind darkness." Cf. also *JM* p. 103.22-24 as regards the equation of the five kinds of error with the five defilements; in his explanation the author follows, however, the *YD* etc., taking the examples from the *GBh* tradition.

According to Vācaspatimiśra (*STK* on 47) there are two possible explanations why feelings and desires are considered as errors: either they are the cause of the origin of errors and thus have the nature of error, or they are the result of errors, i.e., they arise because of a wrong determination of reality. This second interpretation is attributed to Vārṣagaṇya (ibid., p. 279.7-8): *ata eva pañcaparvāvidyety āha bhagavān vārṣagaṇyaḥ*. This formulation strongly reminds of the one in the *YBh* and it is probable that Vyāsa followed Vārṣagaṇya, and possibly Vindhyavāsin, on this point, as he does in many other cases, cf. Frauwallner, *Geschichte* I, pp. 410f.

365 Cf. *SVT* p. 85.17-18: *taimirike tadvṛttir yadi pratyakṣaṃ, tadābhāsavilopaḥ. yathārthajñānahetur iti cen, na tathāviśeṣaṇābhāvāt*. "If the functioning of the [senses] of a person who suffers from *timira* sickness is perception, there would be no false [sensory cognitions]. [Objection: Only the functioning which is] the cause of true cognition [is perception]. [Reply:] No, because [your definition] does not have such a qualification."

For further parallel passages cf. Mahendrakumar's n. 14 ad loc.

366 Cf. §§ 1.11-1.14.

367 Cf *YD* p. 103.26 (on *SK* 28): ... *viṣayākārapariṇāmātmikā vṛttir vṛttimato 'nanyā satī sambhavaty eva*. "[The Sāṅkhya elders (*sāṅkhyavṛddha*) say:] ... the functioning whose

nature is a transformation into the form of an object [and] which is not different from [the sense] which functions is possible."

[368] This argument, as in fact the whole remainder of this chapter, is based on the Sāṅkhya theory of causality (*satkāryavāda*). The details of this theory need hardly be described here; for a brief historical sketch cf. Frauwallner, *Geschichte* I, pp. 385-91. Two characteristic features of this theory should be borne in mind while reading this chapter:

1) The effect exists always in its cause (not only before it is 'produced,' but also after it is 'destroyed').

2) The effect is not different from its cause.

For further parallel passages on identity and difference of senses and functioning cf. *NKC* p. 41.4f., *PKM* p. 19.5f., SVR p. 73.4f., Vy p. 523.12f.

Jayarāśi's argument may have been inspired by *NV* 3.1.34 p. 762.10-14: *yugapadanekavijñānaprasaṅgāc ca. yadi ca vṛttir vṛttimato nānyā bhavati vṛttimato 'vasthānād vṛttīnām avasthānam iti yugapadanekavijñānaprasaṅgaḥ. vṛttyanekatve caikam indriyam anekaṃ prāpnoti vṛttibhyo 'nanyatvāt. atha mā bhūd indriyabheda iti, vṛttīnāṃ tarhy ekatvaṃ prāpnoti vṛttivṛttimator ananyatvāt. atha mā bhūd ayaṃ doṣa ity ubhayaṃ neṣyate, bhedas tarhi vṛttivṛttimator iti. na cānyā gatir asti.*

"And there would be several cognitions at the same time. For if the functioning is not different from that which functions, [then] the continuity of the functions [follows] from the continuity of [the sense] which functions; thus, there would be several cognitions at the same time. And if the functions are more than one, one sense would become more than one, because it is not different from the functions. If [you maintain that] the sense should not be split, then the functions would be one, because the functions and [the sense] which functions are not different. If [you maintain that] this fault does not arise, [that is] both [alternatives] are not acceptable [to you], then [you should admit that] there is a difference between a functioning and [the sense] which functions. For there is no other way."

369 Cf. *AKBh* p. 301.1-3 (on V.27c): *vārṣagaṇyavādaś caivaṃ dyotito bhavati "yad asty asty eva tad, yan nāsti nāsty eva tat. asato nāsti sambhavaḥ, sato nāsti vināśa" iti.* "And Vārṣagaṇya's theory is thus expressed [by you, namely]: 'Whatever exists, exists; whatever does not exist, does not exist. There is no production of what does not exist, there is no destruction of what exists.'"

Cf.also *YBh* 4.12 p. 186.1: *nāsty asataḥ sambhavo, na cāsti sato vināśa iti.* "There is no production of what does not exist, nor is there destruction of what exists." For further references cf. de la Vallée Poussin, *L'Abhidharmakośa de Vasubandhu*, Vol. V, p. 64, and *Additions*.

Note that the theory of *satkāryavāda* seems to have been introduced rather late into Sāṅkhya. It does not appear in the Upaniṣadic form of Sāṅkhya, nor in the Mokṣadharma, nor in the Carakasaṃhitā, nor in the Buddhacarita. It is possible, therefore, that it was introduced by Vārṣagaṇya himself, cf. Johnston, *Early Sāṃkhya*, pp. 66-67, 88; Liebenthal, *Satkārya in der Darstellung seiner buddhistischen Gegner*, pp. 43f., 150 (conclusion).

370 Cf. Frauwallner, *Geschichte* I, p. 352.

371 Cf. n. 361.

372 Perhaps Jayarāśi is following here *NV* 3.1.33 p. 761.15-21: *yadi vṛttyavyatirekīndriyaṃ yathā vṛtter utpādavināśāv evam indriyasyāpi prāpnutaḥ. vṛtter vyaktir notpattir iti ced - atha manyase na mayā vṛtter utpattir abhyupa-*

gamyate 'pi tu vyaktir, na nirodho vināśo 'pi tu tirobhāva iti. notpattiviśeṣatvād - vyaktir utpatter viśeṣaḥ. katham iti nānupajātaviśeṣasya vyaktir iti. athānupajātaviśeṣaṃ vyajyata iti manyase, nityaṃ vyaktiḥ syāt. etena vināśo vyākhyātas tirobhāva iti vidyamānaṃ na kiñcin niruddhaṃ, na hy anivṛttaviśeṣasyāgrahaṇaṃ bhavati. na ca sarvanityavādinā grahaṇāgrahaṇe yukte - viśeṣasyānupajananān na grahaṇaṃ, viśeṣasyānupacayān (read: *-ānapacayān*) *nāgrahaṇam iti.*

"[And] if the sense is not different from the functioning, [then] just as the functioning arises and perishes, in the same manner the sense, too, would [arise and perish].

[Objection:] The functioning undergoes a manifestation, not production. - You [may] think: I do not admit production of the functioning, but [only] a manifestation, [and I do] not [admit] extinction, [i.e.] destruction, but [only] disappearance.

[To this we answer:] No! Because [it] is a special kind of production. - Manifestation is a special kind of production. How is that? There is no manifestation of something without a special property being produced in it. If you think that something is manifested without a special property being produced in it, [then] the manifestation would be eternal. By this destruction [too] is explained [by you] as disappearance (i.e., something does not cease to exist, but only disappears, and without a special property perishing in it). Therefore nothing existing [would become] extinct; for [only] something in which a special property perished is not apprehended [anymore]. And for someone who claims that everything is eternal both apprehension and non-apprehension are impossible: there is no apprehension because a special property is not produced, [and] there is no non-apprehension because a special property has not declined."

373 It seems that the increase of a part takes place in the buddhi, and not in the object. Cf. Vy p. 521.19-26:

viviktadṛkpariṇatau buddhau bhogo 'sya kathyate/

pratibimbodayaḥ svacche yathā candramaso 'mbhasi//

iti. viviktadṛg viṣayākārapariṇatendriyākārapariṇatir yasyāḥ sā tathoktā tasyāṃ buddhau satyām ātmano bhogaḥ kathyate. kiṃrūpaḥ? pratibimbodayo, na vāstavaḥ. yathā candramasaḥ pratibimbanaṃ svacche na kaluṣātmake 'mbhasīty udāharaṇam. yathā hi candramasaḥ pratibimbanam ambhasy evaṃ viśiṣṭapariṇāmopacitāyāṃ buddhāv ātmana iti. vāstave hi bhoge puruṣasya pūrvasvarūpanivṛttau svarūpāntarāpattir vikāraḥ syāt.

"'When the *buddhi* is transformed into a distinct cognition it is said that there is an experience for the [Self],

just as a reflection of the moon arises in clear water.'

The [*buddhi*], whose transformation into the form of a sense which has become transformed into the form of an object is a distinct cognition, is thus called (i.e. transformed into a distinct cognition). When this *buddhi* is present it is said that there is an experience for the Self. Of what form [is this experience]? [It consists in] the arising of a reflection, it is not real. Just as the reflection of the moon [arises] in clear [water], not in muddy water; this is the example. For just like the moon is reflected in water, so the Self [is reflected] in the *buddhi* when increased by a certain transformation. For if real experience [were to take place], the *puruṣa* would undergo a transformation which consists in obtaining a new nature after the previous nature has ceased [to exist]."

Cf. also *YD* p. 48.8-11 (read: *apagataviśeṣa* instead of *apagataviśeṣāviśeṣa*, and *lakṣaṇāpacayāḥ* instead of *lakṣaṇopacayāḥ*).

Although it is not said explicitly, it is clear that the increase refers to the increase in *sattva*; when *sattva* dominates the *buddhi*, it becomes luminous and light (*laghu*, SK 13). Note also that the above quoted verse is attributed by Guṇaratna (*TRD* p. 151.5) to Āsuri, but this could hardly be taken as a reliable testimony; the verse is probably to be attributed to Vārṣagaṇya.

Cf. also *YD* pp. 35.9-10 (*sattvodreka*) and 81.13-14, 94.10-11.

[374] This probably refers to the passage from the unmanifested (*avyakta*) to the manifested. In the primordial matter the three *guṇas* stop every activity of transformation (*nivṛttapariṇāmavyāpāra*) and loose all particular properties (*apagataviśeṣa*), and thus obtain the highest stage of non-distinction. At this stage, they are neither existing nor inexisting (*niḥsadasat*). At the beginning of the cosmic process the balance is disturbed (*vaiṣamya*) and the activity of transformation begins (*upajātapariṇāmavyāpāra*). Because of the commitment or obligation of the primordial matter to the *puruṣa* they take up the activity of transformation and as a first result of this process, the *guṇas* obtain the characteristic of being only (*sanmātralakṣaṇa*). After this they increase (*pracaya*) and obtain specific configurations that constitute the manifest. Cf. *YD* p. 48.8-11 (cf. also p. 27.5-8) and Frauwallner, Geschichte I, p. 353.

Whether with *svalakṣaṇa* Jayarāśi refers to *sanmātralakṣaṇa* is not evident, but possible. Another interpretation could be that he refers to the specific characteristics or properties of the *guṇas*. SK 13 mentions luminosity and lightness for *sattva*, mobility and strength for *rajas*, and heaviness and obstructiveness for *tamas*. It is not clear from the *TUS* whether the change occurs in the object or in the cognition. In principle the same argument could apply to both of them.

[375] This probably refers to the special arrangement (*vyūha*, *sanniveśa*) of the *guṇas*. The difference in the arrangement of the *guṇas* is responsible for the different configurations (*saṃsthāna*) of things, and the configurations are responsible for their manifestation (cf. *YD* p. 60.8-9). For different interpretations of the concept of *saṃsthāna* cf. *PS* I section 5, Hattori's translation p. 53f. Here, too, it is not clear to me whether Jayarāśi means the configuration of the object or of the cognition.

[376] The last three *vikalpas* consider the conditions of perception from three different points of view: the first (*avayavopacaya*) attributes the possibility of perception to an increase in one of the *guṇas*, namely, *sattva*; the change is quantitive and probably occurs in the *buddhi*. In the second *vikalpa* (*svalakṣaṇapuṣṭi*) the change of the *guṇas* is qualitive and perhaps occurs in the object. The third *vikalpa* (*saṃsthānotkarṣa*) attributes the possibility of perception to a special arrangement of the three *guṇas*, and here, too, probably in the object; the change may be understood both qualitatively and quantitatively.

[377] To be tied down by causal factors as place and time must have appeared as a reason for non-perception in the context of the proof of *prakṛti* by *vaiśvarūpya* (cf. n. 382) in the *Ṣaṣṭitantra*, cf. *NĀA* p. 11.26-27: *sarvaṃ sarvātmakam. yady evaṃ kasmāt sarvam ekatra nopalabhyate sarvatra caikam ity ucyate - deśakālākāranimittāvabandhāt tu na samānakālam ātmābhivyaktiḥ*. "Everything has the nature of everything. If so, why is everything not apprehended at one [place and time] and [why is] one [thing not apprehended] everywhere [and always]? It is said: [Because the universal pervades, everything has the nature of everything (cf. p. 320.3)] but because [things] are tied down by the conditions place, time and form the manifestation of the nature

[of all things] does not happen at the same time." Cf. also Wezler, "Studien zum Dvādaśāranayacakra. I. Der Sarvasarvātmakatvavāda."

Cf. also *YBh* 3.14 p. 134.3-4: *deśakālākāranimittāpabandhān na khalu samānakālam ātmanām abhivyaktir iti*. The commentators differ on the meaning of the word *apabandha* (which does not appear in the *MW* and *PW*); Vācaspati (*TV* p. 134.22) glosses it with *apagama* (going away, absence), the Vivaraṇakāra (p. 258.12) with *avabandha* (tying down) and Vijñānabhikṣu (*YV* p. 311.4) with *pratibandha* (obstruction). I adopted the Vivaraṇa's interpretation which is corroborated by Siṃhasūri. Cf. also *NMGBh* p. 204.16 (*-anubandha*) and p. 206.10 (*-apabandha*, a quotation from the Vṛkṣāyurveda).

378 Again the similarity of argument to the *NV* is striking; cf. *NV* 3.1.33 pp. 761.21-762.7: *nityaṃ vyāpakaṃ cendriyam abhyupagacchataḥ kāraṇārtho hīyate - kāraṇaṃ nāma yasyānantaraṃ yad bhavati, kāraṇaṃ ca nityaṃ kāryaṃ ca nityam iti kasyānantaraṃ, kāryakāraṇabhāvaś ca kathaṃ tayor nityatvāt?* "For someone who accepts the senses as eternal and pervading [the word] cause makes no sense. A cause is called that upon which [the effect] immediately follows. [And if you claim that] both cause and effect are eternal, [which] follows upon which? And how could there be a relation of cause and effect [between them] since they are both eternal?"

379 These are four of the seven relations which are used by Vārṣagaṇya for proving *puruṣa* and *prakṛti*, cf. *Ṣaṣṭitantra*, Frauwallner's reconstruction p. 123 = Kl. Schr. p. 262:

sambandhād ekasmāt pratyakṣāc cheṣasiddhir anumānam.

'brel pa rnams kyi don rnams kyi 'brel pa ni rnam pa bdun ñid de/ nor daṅ bdag po'i dṅos pos daṅ/ rgyal po daṅ bran bźin daṅ/ gtso bo daṅ skyes bu bźin te/ raṅ bźin daṅ rnam

'gyur gyi dṅos pos ni/ źo daṅ 'o ma bźin daṅ/ gtso bo daṅ chen po la sogs pa bźin no// 'bras bu daṅ rgyu'i dṅos pos ni/ śiṅ rta daṅ yan lag bźin daṅ/ sñiṅ stobs la sogs pa bźin te/ rgyu mtshan daṅ rgyu mtshan can gyi dṅos pos ni/ rdza mkhan daṅ bum pa bźin daṅ/ skyes bu daṅ gtso bo'i 'jug pa bźin no// tsam po daṅ tsam po can gyi dṅos pos daṅ/ yal ga la sogs pa daṅ śiṅ bźin daṅ/ sgra la sogs pa daṅ 'byuṅ ba chen po bźin no// lhan cig spyod pa'i dṅos pos ni/ ṅur ba lta bu daṅ/ sñiṅ stobs la sogs pa bźin no// gnod bya gnod byed kyi dṅos pos ni/ sbrul daṅ sbre mo bźin daṅ/ yan lag daṅ yan lag can du gyur pa'i sñiṅ stobs la sogs pa bźin no//

"Inference is a proof of the rest from one [part], which is visible, through a relation.

The relation among related things is sevenfold

1) by a relation between belongings and owner (*svasvāmibhāva*), as between a king and a servant, or between the primordial matter and the Self;

2) by a relation between original substance and its derivative (*prakṛtivikārabhāva*), as between milk and curds, or between the primordial matter and the great [principle] etc. (*mahadādi*);

3) by a relation between effect and cause (*kāryakāraṇabhāva*), as between a chariot and [its] parts, or between the [*guṇas*] *sattva* etc. [and their result];

4) by a relation between efficient cause and its effect (*nimittanaimittikabhāva*), as between a potter and a pot, or between the Self and the activity of the primordial matter;

5) by a relation between portion and total (*mātrāmātrikabhāva*), as between a branch etc., and a tree, or between sound etc., and the [five] material elements;

6) by a relation between companions (*sahacāribhāva*), as between the Cakravāka ducks, or between *sattva* etc. (i.e., *sattva* and the other *guṇas*).

7) Through a relation between obstructed and obstructing (*vandhyaghātakabhāva*), as between a serpent and an ichneumon, or between *sattva* etc., in as much as [they] are subordinate and principal (*aṅgāṅgibhūta*)."

Cf. also *JM* p. 71.4-10 (on *SK* 5): *sambandhāś ca sapta - tatra svasvāmibhāvasambandho yathā rājapuruṣayoḥ. kadācit puruṣeṇa rājā rājñā vā puruṣaḥ. evaṃ prakṛtivikārasambandho yathā yavasaktvoḥ. kāryakāraṇasambandho yathā dhenuvatsayoḥ. pātrapātrikasambandho yathā pariv[rṭ]<rāṭ>triviṣṭabdhayoḥ. sāhacaryasambandho yathā cakravākayoḥ. pratidvandvisambandho yathā śītoṣṇayoḥ. tatraikasya bhāve 'nyābhāvaḥ pratīyate. nimittanaimittikasambandho yathā bhojyabhojakayor iti.*

"And the relations are seven:

1)The relation between owner and belonging, as between a king and [his] servant. Sometimes the king [is inferred] from the servant, or [sometimes] the servant from the king.

2) The relation between original substance and derivative, as between barley and groats [made of barley meal].

3) The relation between cause and effect, as between a cow and a calf.

4) The relation between a worthy man and his characteristics (?), as between an ascetic and the three staves.

5) The relation of companionship, as between two Cakravāka ducks.

6) The relation of opposites, as between cold and hot. In this [case, unlike to the previous relations] when one [of the relata] is present, one apprehends that the other is absent.

7) The relation between efficient cause and its effect, as between enjoyer and enjoyed."

The only important difference between the above two passages is the replacement of the relation between portion and total (*mātrāmātrikabhāva*) by the relation *pātrapātrikasambandha*. This new relation, however, which is not entirely clear to me, probably owes its birth not to any philosophical development, but to a simple misreading of *m* as *p*. The example of the ascetic was construed accordingly.

Cf. also SV(2) p. 10.14-15: *liṅgaliṅgisambandhas tu svasvāmiprakṛtivikārakāryakāraṇamātrā<mā>trikaprati[patti]-<dvandvi>sahacaranimittanaimittika[pra]bhāvair iti.*

Vācaspatimiśra quotes a verse in which seven kinds of inference recognized by the Sāṅkhyas are mentioned (*NVTṬ* 1.1.5 p. 138.24-25):

mātrānimittasaṃyogivirodhisahacāribhiḥ/
svasvāmivadhyaghātādyaiḥ sāṅkhyānāṃ saptadhānumā//

Here again we see some variations in terminology: *prakṛti-vikārabhāva* and *kāryakāraṇabhāva* are absent and instead *saṃyogin* and *nirodhin* appear. Unfortunately Vācaspati does not illustrate these relations, and nothing certain can be said about these new terms, except that they must be in some way related to VS 9.18 (*Upaskāra* 9.2.1), as is obvious from the context.

Note that one of the terms employed by Jayarāśi, namely, *upakāryopakārakabhāva*, appears in none of the other sources. Nor is it clear to me why Jayarāśi mentions only four relations (as the number seven seems to have been well established) and why exactly these four. One could expect him to mention only those relations which can be used for proving *prakṛti* or the three *guṇas* and to ignore those which were meant to be used for the proof of the *puruṣa*, but at least in one case, that of *nimittanaimittikabhāva*, such a hypothesis would go against the examples of the *Ṣaṣṭitantra*.

380 This verse is often quoted, and attributed to Vārṣagaṇya and the *Ṣaṣṭitantra*. Frauwallner ("Erkenntnislehre," p. 138 = Kl. Schr. p. 277) mentions *PS* V.42 (Hattori's ed. p. 143.3-6, cf. also *DANC Bhoṭapariśiṣṭam* p. 134, n 8), *YBh* 4.13 p. 187.13-14 and *NĀA* p. 63.25-26; to these we may add

further commentaries on *YS* 4.13 (*YP*, *YSV*, *MP*) as well as *NBhū* p. 192.14-15, *PVBh* p. 480.7, *JM* p. 113.11-12 on SK 60, *SVṬ* pp. 89.12-13, 260.25-26 and *NKC* p. 628.12-13 (further references ibid., n. 6). Woods translates this verse very nicely (*The Yoga-System of Patañjali*, p. 317):

"The aspects from their utmost height
Come not within the range of sight.
But all within the range of sight
A phantom seems and empty quite."

It is indeed strange that a Sāṅkhya teacher should claim that the empirical world is like an illusion. According to Frauwallner (ibid.) Vārṣagaṇya is twisting in this verse his opponents' words (probably Madhyamaka or perhaps Yogācāra) and adopting them to establish the Sāṅkhya theory against their polemics. Unfortunately Frauwallner remains vague as to the precise meaning of this verse. It should be noted that although the opponents of Sāṅkhya, for instance Bhāsarvajña, interpret this verse as if it affirmed that the phenomenal world is an illusion, this was probably not Vārṣagaṇya's intention, and certainly not the established interpretation within the school. The *YBhV* emphasizes that the phenomenal world is like an illusion, but not an illusion itself (p. 338.19-20: *tan māyeva, na tu māyaiva*). It is said to be like an illusion not because it is not real, but because it is worthless (*asāratvāt*). Vācaspatimiśra also emphasizes that to be like an illusion does not mean to be an illusion (*TV* p. 188.11: *māyeva, na tu māyā*) and explains that the phenomenal world is like an illusion in as much as it is evanescent (*sutucchakaṃ vināśi*), that is, it changes every moment (*pratikṣaṇam anyathā*).

Jayarāśi's argument does not bear on the second half of the verse where the comparison to an illusion appears (what matters to him is that the *guṇas* cannot be perceived), and thus we cannot be sure as to how he understood the comparison. However, in the context of this *vikalpa* it is assumed that the earth etc., are not real.

[381] Cf. *SK* 17c: *puruṣo 'sti bhoktṛbhāvāt*.

[382] These are the five reasons which are used for proving *prakṛti* or *pradhāna*; they appear in the *Ṣaṣṭitantra*, cf. Frauwallner's reconstruction p. 125 = Kl. Schr. p. 264. (Unfortunately, only the first of these reasons is reconstructed.) These five reasons are repeated in *SK* 15, and the commentaries thereon give different interpretations of them, which cannot be discussed here in detail. Most of the important material was collected by Muni Jambuvijayaji in his notes on *NĀA* p. 314.7f. In presenting the inferences I follow the *YD*:

1) The primordial matter exists because whatever pervades exists, for instance clay in pots etc. (as their universal). Sound etc., are pervaded by pleasure, pain, and illusion (*sukha*, *duḥkha*, *moha*); therefore pleasure etc., exist. Pleasure etc., when their particular properties are destroyed, are the unmanifested. Therefore the unmanifested (primordial matter) exists (cf. p. 64.19f.).

2) The primordial matter exists because every activity is due to a capacity, for instance the potter has a capacity for his activity of making pots. The manifested world, because it is a result, presupposes an activity which presupposes capacity. This capacity is the unmanifested; therefore the unmanifested exists (p. 65.7f.).

3) The primordial matter exists because whatever is limited arises from an existing source, for instance the sprout from the roots etc. (cf. also p. 131.17). The *mahat*, the *ahaṅkāra*, the senses, the *tanmātras*, etc., are limited (since they are delimited by numbers; one talks of eleven senses, five *tanmātras*, etc.). Therefore, they have an existing source, namely, the unmanifested (p. 63.30f.).

4) The primordial matter exists because what is omniform lacks - in the final analysis - distinction. Omniformity is explained as a differentiated subsistence (*viśiṣṭam avasthānam*), and to lack distinction means a state

in which all particularities have disappeared. Because all particular conditions presuppose a universal, all the different things of this world must go back to one undifferentiated entity, namely, the unmanifested (p. 68.15f.). The text of the example in the *YD* (l. 15) is corrupt, but the example is preserved in *NĀA* p. 320.2-4, *YBh* 3.14 p. 133. 8f., SV(1) p. 29.9-11, *MV* p. 20.16-18 and *NMGBh* p. 204.12-18: Water and earth take every form of flavour etc., in the different plants (which consume them) due to transformation. Similarly, plants take every form of flavour etc., in the different animals, and equally animals are consumed in their turn by plants, plants by plants, animals by animals, etc. Thus, because the universals 'flavour' etc., subsist everything has the form or nature of everything (cf. also *YBhV* p. 257.18f.).

5) The primordial matter exists because of the distinction between cause and effect. The distinction between cause and effect is preceded by a subsisting being (*avasthitabhāva*) which puts them into the relation of cause and effect, for instance sitting and a chair, traveling and a vehicle. The manifested world contains the distinction between cause and effect; therefore it is preceded by a subsisting being. This is the unmanifested (p. 66.24f.). This last example seems to indicate that although the author of the *YD* follows the SK and uses the terms *kārya* and *kāraṇa*, he actually thinks of *upakārya* and *upakāraka* (= *upakaraṇa*) as is the case in the *TUS*; cf. also *NĀA* p. 319. 5-6: *ekakartṛkā bhedāḥ parasparopakārakopakāryatvāc chayanādivat* (= *Ṣaṣṭitantra*).

[383] This is a quotation from the *Bṛhaspatisūtra*, cf. n. 271.

Appendix

Bhāsarvajña and Jayarāśi: The Refutation of Scepticism in the *Nyāyabhūṣaṇa*[1]

To judge by Western publications on the subject, the historical development of Indian epistemology in its most creative period, roughly between the second and the twelfth century A.D., was to a large extent the outcome of the ongoing controversy between two formidable protagonists, the Naiyāyikas and the Buddhists. Although there is much truth in this picture in the sense that these two schools occupied the central and most prominent positions at that time, it is also obvious that this conflict, important as it may be, cannot exhaust the complexity of the philosophical scene. The Jainas, the Prābhākara-Mīmāṃsakas, the Lokāyatikas, to mention only three of the most conspicuous examples, still await their integraton into a broader and more comprehensive understanding of the plurality of forces and currents which shaped, transformed and reshaped all these remarkable theories of knowledge.

This general observation is especially true in the case of Jayarāśi Bhaṭṭa, whose *Tattvopaplavasiṃha* (hereafter *TUS*) is the only Lokāyata text which has been discovered so far, and as such it must attract our attention and curiosity, especially as it is the only text where full-fledged scepticism is propounded. I believe it is no longer true that specialists are unaware of its existence, but nevertheless it is still largely ignored. Sometimes, even when the book is mentioned or referred to, one has the feeling that many scholars do not have a clear picture about its content, and treat this important work as a mere curiosity, a bizarre off-shoot outside the main stream of Indian philosophy. Consequently, the relevance of Jayarāśi's thought for the understanding of various non-Lokāyata philosophers has been hitherto completely ignored.

In this respect, the importance of the *TUS* is twofold. On the one hand it contains important and valuable insights into the different philosophical systems which are mercilessly criticized in it. In a recent study[2] I took some trouble to show that the *TUS*, albeit unique, belongs nevertheless to the main stream of the *pramāṇa* literature, and that the problems discussed in it are absolutely pertinent and essential to all philosophical schools of its time. To be more specific, we can mention among the works analyzed and criticized in it Vārṣagaṇya's *Ṣaṣṭitantra* and Vindhyavāsin's commentary thereon, Kumārila's *Bṛhaṭṭīkā*, Uddyotakara's *Nyāyavārttika* and some unknown commentaries on it (most probably Adhyayanapāda's *Ruciṭīkā*), Dharmakīrti's *Pramāṇaviniścaya*, etc. On the other hand the *TUS* has been often enough referred to and criticized by Buddhist, Hindu and Jaina philosophers between the 9th and the 15th century. The identification of the relevant passages in the later philosophical works is necessary not only in order to evaluate Jayarāśi's place and role in the historical development of Indian philosophy, but is also an imperative for better understanding of these later works themselves. Some preliminary work was already undertaken in the above mentioned study, in which I collected and translated quite a few passages which refer directly to the *TUS*. In the present paper I would like to pursue this line of work, and study in some detail Bhāsarvajña's response to the sceptical challenge laid down by Jayarāśi.

Bhāsarvajña never mentions, to the best of my knowledge, either Jayarāśi's name, or the title of his work[3] (cf., however, *NBhū* p. 24.13: *tattvopaplavasiddher iti cet*); notwithstanding that, the *Nyāyabhūṣaṇa* contains one of the earliest, most serious and detailed discussions of the *TUS*. A quick glance at the following comparison between the two texts should be enough to reveal not only that Bhāsarvajña knew Jayarāśi, but also that he reproduces some of his arguments in a most detailed and accurate manner.

NBhū pp. 23.21-24.6:	*TUS* pp. 132.19-136.5:
nanu ca saṃśaya eva nāsti kutas tatrāntarbhāvaś cintyate? tathā hi tasmin saṃśayajñāne kiṃ pratibhāti? dharmī dharmo vā?	*... tad yadi [sandehajñāne kiñcit] pratibhāti, sa kiṃ dharmī dharmo vā?*
yadi dharmī, sa tāttviko 'tāttviko vā. yadi tāttvikaḥ kathaṃ tadbuddheḥ sandeharūpatā? tāttvikārthagṛhitirūpatvāt karatal<āmalak?>ādinirṇayavat.	*tad yadi dharmī pratibhāti, sa tāttviko 'tāttviko vā. yadi tāttviko, nāpaneyatā tadviṣayavijñānasya.*
athātāttvikas, tathāpy atāttvikārthaviṣayatvāt keśādijñānavad bhrāntir eva, na sandehaḥ.	*athātāttvikas, tadāvyabhicāripadenāpanitatvān na vyavasāyātmakapadam upādeyam.*
atha dharmaḥ, sthāṇutvalakṣaṇaḥ, puruṣatvalakṣaṇa, ubhayaṃ vā.	*atha dharmaḥ pratibhāti, sa sthāṇutvalakṣaṇaḥ, puruṣatvalakṣaṇa, ubhayaṃ vā.*
yadi sthāṇutvalakṣaṇas tatas tāttvikātāttvikayoḥ pūrvavad doṣaḥ.	*tad yadi sthāṇutvalakṣaṇo dharmaḥ pratibhāti sa tāttviko 'tāttviko vā. yadi tāttvikaḥ, kathaṃ tadbuddheḥ sandeharūpatā? tāttvikārthagṛhitirūpatvena satyodakasaṃvedanavat. athātāttvikas, tadāvyabhicāripadenāpoditatvān na vyavasāyātmakapadam upādeyam.*
atha puruṣatvalakṣaṇas, tatrāpi pūrvavad eva doṣaḥ.	*atha puruṣatvalakṣaṇo dharmaḥ pratibhāty, asāv api tāttviko 'tāttviko vā. yadi tāttvikaḥ, kathaṃ tadbuddheḥ sandeharūpatā? athātāttvikas, tadāvyabhicāripadenāpoditatvād vyavasāyātmakapadaṃ na sādhīyaḥ.*
athobhayaṃ tathāpy ubhayasya tāttvikātāttvika<tva>yoḥ sa eva doṣaḥ.	*athobhayaṃ pratibhāti, tadobhayos tāttvikatvam atāttvikatvaṃ vā...*

athaikasya tāttvikatvam anyasyātāttvikatvaṃ, tathāpi tadviṣayaṃ jñānaṃ tad eva bhrāntaṃ tad eva cābhrāntam iti prāptam.	*... athaikasya tāttvikatvam anyasyātāttvikatvaṃ, tadā tad eva jñānaṃ vyabhicāri tad evāvyabhicāri...*
atha sandigdho 'rtho 'vabhāti sandehajñāne, sa sandigdho 'rtho vidyate <vā?> na vā...	*atha sandigdhārthākārapratibhāsi sandehajñānam iti cet, sa sandigdho 'rtho vidyate vā na vā...*

Since the *NBhū* has not yet been translated,[4] it seems worthwhile for our purpose here to translate the passages in which Bhāsarvajña summarizes and criticizes Jayarāśi to allow the non-specialist to follow the discussion and the specialist to check my understanding of it (*NBhū* pp. 23.21-24.22):[5]

[PŪRVAPAKṢA]

"Doubt itself does not exist, how could one conceive that [deliberation and indecision] are included in it? For what does appear in a doubtful cognition? A property-possessor or a property?[6] If it is a property-possessor, is it real or unreal? If it is real, how could its cognition have the nature of doubt? For it has the nature of an apprehension of a real thing, just like the determination of the palm of the hand (perhaps: of a myrobalan lying in the palm of the hand) etc. If [the property-possessor] is unreal, even so, since [the cognition] has an unreal thing for its object, it is not a doubt but an error, just like the cognition of hair etc., [which arises from *timira*-sickness].

If a property [appears in a doubtful cognition], is it characterized as being a trunk, is it characterized as being a man, or as both? If it is characterized as being a trunk, then, whether real or unreal, the [same] fault as above [obtains]. If [a property] characterized as being a man [appears], in this [case] too the [same] fault just as above [occurs]. If both [properties appear], even so, if both are real or unreal, precisely the same fault [occurs]. If one property is real and the other unreal, even so [it is not a doubtful cognition, rather] the cognition which has that (i.e., one real property and one unreal) for its object would be both erroneous and nonerroneous.

If a doubtful object appears in a doubtful cognition, then does this doubtful object exist or not? The poor doubt has indeed fallen into the abyss of these *vikalpas* and similar ones. [Therefore, doubt] cannot reveal itself as being different from valid cognition or error.

[UTTARAPAKṢA]

This [person] who is refuting doubt in the manner of the cow dung and the milky preparation[7] is disregarded even by uneducated[8] people. Indeed, all living beings can apprehend doubt by themselves as having the nature of undetermined cognition. It must have a property-possessor for its object, or a property. It consists of one cognition or of more than one.[9] It must have for its object a real or an unreal thing. - Are these *vikalpas* capable of hurting even the tip of one of its (i.e., the doubt's) hair? For if one denies a distinction established by perception, one would (or: could) deny the distinction between pleasure and pain. If [you claim] that this is accepted (i.e., if you do deny the distinction), [then we ask:] on which grounds? If [you reply:] because the annihilation of principles is established, [then we ask:] how is this establishing established in its turn? If it is because there are no means of valid cognition, [then] how is the absence of the means of valid cognition established in its turn? [If you reply:] Because [the means of valid cognition] lack a [correct] definition, there too, if a proof is stated for the establishing of the absence of [correct] definitions, then precisely this proof is a principle. Consequently, how [can] the annihilation of principles be established?

If [this proof] is not stated, even so, because there is no proof, [the annihilation of principles] is not established. If [the annihilation of principles] is established by mere talk, all doctrines would be established.

Moreover, since the absence of definition is also a means of valid cognition, in as much as it makes known the absence of means of valid cognition, how could it be established that all means of valid cognition are absent? [If you say:] 'we only question [the doctrine of] others; [we] do not establish anything [for ourselves],' then this is not correct, because unless the nature/own form of the [doctrine of] others is determined, [their] questioning is impossible. [Furthermore,] because all means of valid cognition are rejected, the world is not established, nor its everyday practice, nor can this [everyday practice] be delightful in as much as it is not deliberated upon. Therefore, all [the above said] is a mere prattle [and] nonsensical."

The arguments are quite amusing, and for a moment it seems as if the sceptic and the dogmatic philosopher are trading places. For usually it is the former who wants to raise doubt in respect to every possible thing, and the latter who tries to secure certain cognitions beyond any doubt. This apparent paradox is soon dispelled if we take a closer look at the context. Although the discussion may use general terms, it is clear that both protagonists have a specific conceptual framework in mind, namely, that of the word *vyavasāyātmaka* in the definition of perception in *NS* 1.1.4. And the purpose of this word in the definition is not to reject any doubt, but only a special sort of doubtful cognition which arises from a contact between sense and object.[10] Bhāsarvajña is fully aware of Jayarāśi's intention, for in a different context he does attribute to him the opinion that he wants to point out doubt everywhere (p. 34.22: *na mayā pramāṇaṃ kvacid ucyate sarvatra sandehamātrapradarśanād iti cet*). Moreover, Bhāsarvajña seems not to be able to detect any faults in the arguments themselves, that is, he does not (or cannot) positively show what is wrong in them; instead he points out that they are as nonsensical as if one were trying to prove that cow dung is a milky substance because it has its origin in a cow. Jayarāśi's arguments lack any power of persuasiveness and can do the doubt no harm (they cannot even hurt the tip of one of its hair), because they are in contradiction to the direct awareness of all people (and even all animals? Bhāsarvajña says 'all living beings') of doubt as an undetermined cognition. But Bhāsarvajña knows what Jayarāśi would reply: We cannot trust even direct perception, because all principles are annihilated. At this point, Bhāsarvajña changes his strategy and uses what one may call 'attack is the best defence,' or 'play the ball into the opponent's field.' And this too indicates that he can find nothing wrong in Jayarāśi's arguments. Instead of attempting some explanation of how doubt could arise from contact between sense and object, and what its content could possibly be, he turns the discussion into an examination of Jayarāśi's position and raises the well known argument of self-refutation. Isn't the annihilation of principles itself a principle? And if it is not a principle, how could it be established? One cannot fail to notice that Bhāsarvajña is, at least to some extent, begging the question when he presents Jayarāśi's position (p. 24.13) as *tattvopaplavasiddher iti cet*. For nowhere in the *TUS* does Jayarāśi say that the annihilation of principles is established. Nor is he likely to make such a claim. However, this distortion of the opponent's position does not seem to be a conscious misrepresentation (something which is by no means not unheard of in this kind of texts) on Bhāsarvajña's part. Be it as it may, the annihilation of principles is further explained as being based on the absence of *pramāṇas*, which is based, in its turn, on the absence of (correct) definition. So far, Bhāsarvajña follows faithfully the first lines of the *TUS*.[11] The next reason (i.e., *atha paraparyanuyoga eva kriyate 'smābhir na kasyacit siddhir iti*), however, is a bit surprising, because it does not have a counterpart in the *TUS*. It obviously refers to the famous Lokāyata fragment which reads *sarvatra paraparyanuyogaparāṇy eva bṛhaspateḥ sūtrāṇi*.[12] "Everywhere (i.e., throughout the text) the *sūtras* of Bṛhaspati have as their sole purpose the questioning of the [opinions of] others."

It is interesting to note that Bhāsarvajña's association of the above fragment with Jayarāśi is corroborated by the Jaina philosophers Vidyānanda and Anantavīrya,[13] and on the basis of these three testimonies taken together I would like to attribute the above fragment to Jayarāśi, perhaps in one of his lost works such as the *Lakṣaṇasāra*.[14]

Bhāsarvajña concludes the discussion with a reference to the last lines of the *TUS*, which promise the reader that everyday practice may be delightful when the principles are annihilated in as much as it no longer has to be deliberated (*avicāritaramaṇīya*).[15] The history of the expression *avicāritaramaṇīya* remains to be studied. So far I was able to distinguish at least two realms of reference: Sometimes, as above, it designates a Lokāyata ideal,[16] and should probably be connected with the traditional Lokāyata call to live happily in this world (*yāvaj jīvet sukhaṃ jīvet*). I do not think that Jayarāśi has coined the term, but rather that he used it to point out a certain continuity between the annihilation of principles and the older Lokāyata doctrines. This must have been also the purpose of the above mentioned fragment, namely, to show the agreement between the *TUS* and the *Bṛhaspatisūtra*, which formed the basic textbook of the Lokāyata school. Everything in the *Bṛhaspatisūtra* which disagrees with the annihilation of principles has to be interpreted away as a *pūrvapakṣa* opinion which appears in the sūtras only to be questioned and rejected. A second realm of reference, which I am not quite sure how to connect with the first, appears in non-Lokāyata texts, and unlike the references given above, it does not even appear in contexts which have anything to do with the Lokāyata. In such cases it is simply used pejoratively to tell the opponent he did not think enough on what he said.[17]

Interesting as it is, the discussion on doubtful cognitions is nothing but an aside. The main controversy about Jayarāśi's scepticism does not begin until some ten pages later, and in a different context altogether. After discussing several theories of error (*akhyāti*, *asatkhyāti*, etc.)

and concluding that *viparītakhyāti* is the one to be preferred, Bhāsarvajña reproduces the opinion of certain people (*eke*) who claim that there is no error, and here too the following comparison should reveal that he must have had Jayarāśi in mind (for further parallel passages cf. p. 302, n. 11 above):

NBhū pp. 33.8-34.14:	*TUS* pp. 72.4ff.
etena yad āhur eke satyodakam asatyodakaṃ cety udakaprapañco 'yaṃ madhurodakādivat. tatra yathā satyodakabuddhau nāsatyodakaṃ pratibhāty anudakaṃ vā, evam asatyodakajñāne 'pi na satyodakaṃ pratibhāty anudakaṃ veti. svaviṣaye paryavasāyino hi buddhayaḥ...	*... yady evam udakaprapañco 'yaṃ dīrghodakaṃ madhurodakam iti yathā... satyodakajñāne satyodakam avabhāti nāsatyodakam anudakaṃ vā. tathāsatyodakajñāne 'satyodakaṃ pratibhāti na satyodakam anudakaṃ vā. svaviṣayaparyavasāyinyo hi buddhayaḥ.* (p. 116.10-19)
api cābhrāntatvasya liṅgaṃ kim aduṣṭakārakotpādyatvam uta bādhānutpādaḥ kiṃ vā pravṛttisāmarthyam iti	*tac cāvyabhicāritvam ... kim aduṣṭakārakasandohotpādyatvenāhosvid bādhārahitatvena pravṛttisāmarthyenānyathā vā? ...*
na tāvad aduṣṭakārakotpādyatvaṃ, nayanādṛṣṭādikāraṇānām atīndriyatvenāduṣṭatvasyāniścayāt...	*kāraṇānām aduṣṭatā kenāvagamyate? na pratyakṣeṇa nayanakuśalāder atīndriyatvāt...*
na ca tadudbhūtaviśiṣṭajñānād eva kārakāduṣṭatvasiddhir itaretarāśrayatvadoṣeṇobhayor asiddher iti.	*nanu idam eva jñānaṃ liṅgaṃ taduttham tasya viśiṣṭatāṃ gamayati. yady evam itaretarāśrayatvaṃ duruttaram āpanipadyate.* (p. 72.4-15)
nāpi bādhānutpādas tasya liṅgaṃ, bādhānutpādasya puruṣāpravṛttideśāntara-	*... pratipattur bādhakajñānānutpāde 'pi deśāntaragamanamaraṇādinā maṇimarīcyādivipar-*

gamanamaraṇādinimittād api sambhavāt...	*yayajñānadarśanāt.* (p. 76.1-3)
api ca sarvapuruṣabādhānutpatter asarvavidāvagantum aśakyatvāt...	*tad yadi sarvapuruṣāpekṣayā... tadviraho 'py ... <sa>rvajñāḥ syuḥ.* (p. 74.18-19; the manuscript is defective.)
nāpi pravṛttisāmarthyam. pravṛttisāmarthyaṃ hy arthaprāptyanarthaparihāralakṣaṇam. tac ced anavagataṃ, katham asiddhaṃ gamakaṃ bhavet? athāvagataṃ, tadavagater avyabhicāritvaṃ katham avagamyata ity aparihāryā purvoktavikalpaparamparā syād iti.	*pravṛttisāmarthyaṃ phalenābhisambandhaḥ... tat kim avagatam anavagataṃ vā? yadi nāvagataṃ, tad astiti kathaṃ vetsi? athāvagataṃ, tadavagater avyabhicāritā katham avagamyata iti pūrvoktam anusartavyam.* (p. 76.12-20)
api ca candrādipratibhāsasyābhrāntatvaṃ na sidhyec, candrādyarthasya prāptyasambhavāt.	*yan na prāpayati tad vyabhicāri tarhi mumūrṣupadārthotpāditaṃ jñānaṃ candrārkagrahanakṣatratārakādisaṃvedanaṃ ca vyabhicāri prāpnoti.* (78.12-15)
na codakārthasyāpi pratibhātasya prāptiḥ sambhavati, tasya vāyvādibhiḥ prāṇiviśeṣaiś cāvayavakriyotpādanadvāreṇa pratikṣaṇaṃ vināśyamānatvāt.	*pratibhātodakasyāvasthānaṃ nopapadyate, jhaṣamahiṣaparivartanābhighātopajātāvayavakriyānyāyena pratyastamayasambhavāt.*
tajjātīyārthaprāptes tu anekāntikatvān na gamakam.	*atha tajjātiyodakaprāptyā, evaṃ tarhy asatyodakajñāne 'pi jāte kvacit toyam āsādayanti pumāṃsas tad apy avitathaṃ syāt.* (p. 78.2-7)

tadvaṃśajārthaprāptir gamiketi cen, na, antyāvayavinām ajanakatvena tadvaṃśajārthāsambhavāt.

atha tadvaṃśajajalaprāptyāvyabhicāritā jñāyate tad ayuktam antyāvayavidravyāṇāṃ janakatvavyatirekāt. (p. 96.12-14)

NBhū pp. 33.8-38.17[6]:

"Certain [people] have said: '[What is called] 'real water' and 'unreal water' is only a variety of water, just like sweet water etc. Thus, just as unreal water, or something which is not water [at all], does not appear in a cognition of real water, in the same manner real water, or something which is not water, does not appear in a cognition of unreal water. For cognitions terminate in (i.e., convey no other information than) their own objects. Therefore, there is no [inner object] which is different [from the external object].'[18] This, too, has been refuted by the [above proof of *viparītakhyāti*]. For there is no such thing called unreal water. [And] even if it exists, if it is determined as unreal water, then [its] cognition would not be erroneous. But when [this unreal water] is determined as having the form of water which is capable of being drunk etc., then how could the cognition be nonerroneous? For it is well known among all people and in all sciences that the determination of a wrong/opposite object is false. And this [person] who proceeds in contradiction with this (i.e., what is well known among all people and in all sciences) is neither a [serious] enquirer, nor familiar with the ways of the world. Thus, he can very well be neglected.

[PŪRVAPAKṢA]

But how is the erroneousness of a cognition apprehended? Not by perception, because [if it were so] there would be no activity on the part of the mistaken cognizer [who is motivated] by the wish to obtain the object of the [erroneous cognition]. Nor is the [erroneousness] perceived [directly] at the time when the sublation arises, because at that time the erroneous cognition belongs already to the past. And something which belongs to the past is not apprehended by perception of [normal people] like us. And thus, since no concomitance is well known between that [erroneousness] which is absolutely imperceptible and the arising of sublation, or [for that matter] any other inferential sign, inference also [just as perception] does not function (i.e., cannot make known the erroneousness). For nowhere is a concomitance between [these two] apprehended, [not] even [a concomitance apprehended] on the basis of a common factor such as [the concomitance] between result and agent (i.e., every result has an agent of production)[19] etc. Further, if the concomitance in every [inference] is apprehended by [another] inference, there would be an infinite regress. By this [same reasoning] the apprehension of nonerroneousness too is contradicted.

Moreover, is the inferential sign of nonerroneousness (1) the fact that [the cognition] is produced by faultless causal factors, (2) the non-arising of sublation, or (3) the efficiency of the activity?

(1) First, it is not the fact that [the cognition] is produced by faultless causal factors, because, in as much as causes like the eye, *adṛṣṭa*, etc., are beyond [the apprehension of] the senses, their faultlessness cannot be determined. For an inferential sign which is itself unknown does not make known [anything] connected to it. Nor is the faultlessness of the causal factors established by the cognition itself, which is qualified [as valid], and which arises from them. For both [the validity of the cognition and the faultlessness of the causal factors] are not established because of the fallacy of mutual dependence.

(2) Nor is the non-arising of sublation [suitable as] an inferential sign for the [nonerroneousness of a cognition], because the non-arising of sublation is possible from causes [other than nonerroneousness] such as the fact that the [cognizing] person does not act [in view of obtaining the object], goes to another place, or dies [before he reaches the object], etc.

Further, (a lacuna?) [by the non-arising of sublation you may mean that it does not arise for all people or that it does not arise for the perceiver alone. The first alternative is impracticable,] because a person who is not omniscient cannot know that a sublation does not arise for all people. As for the non-arising of sublation for the cognizer [alone], it is not conclusive, because one observes that even several people [may] be mistaken for a period of time. And someone who is not omniscient cannot know whether a sublation will never arise. Therefore, the non-arising of sublation is also not an inferential sign [for nonerroneousness].

(3) Nor is the efficiency of the activity [such an inferential sign]. For the efficiency of the activity is characterized by obtaining a useful object and getting rid of/avoiding an unuseful one. But if this [efficiency of activity] is not apprehended, how could something [which is itself] unproved make known [anything]? If it is apprehended, how does one know that its apprehension is not erroneous? Thus, the [infinite] succession of the *vikalpas* stated above would be unavoidable.

Moreover, the nonerroneousness of [cognitions] in which [objects like] the moon etc., appear could not be established, because one cannot obtain an object such as the moon etc. And even an object such as water which appeared [in the cognition] cannot be obtained, because the [water] is being destroyed at every moment through the production of action in its parts by wind etc., and by certain living beings, [such as fish, buffalos] etc. As for obtaining an object which belongs to the [same] universal as the [object which appeared in the cognition], it does not make known [the nonerroneousness of the cognition], because this is not conclusive.

[Objection:] Obtaining an object which arises in the [same] series as the [object which appeared in the cognition] makes known [the nonerroneousness of the cognition].

[Reply:] No, because an object which arises in that [same] series is impossible, for final wholes do not produce [any further wholes].[20] And when this is not established, there is no inferential sign[21] whatsoever [which takes the form:] 'This object has arisen in the [same] series as the [perceived object].' By such adverse arguments and others an inferential sign for nonerroneousness is refuted. Therefore, [nonerroneousness] is not apprehended by an inferential sign either.

[UTTARAPAKṢA]

To the above [arguments we] reply: If there is no determination of erroneousness etc., how [would] the everyday practice[22] both among the people and in the sciences [having the form] 'I have apprehended rightly,' 'you have understood [it] wrongly,' and so on [be possible]? This practice is impossible without the determination of the object as it really is.

[Objection:] This everyday practice is preceded by false determination.

[Reply:] If the falsity of the determination is not apprehended, how do you know that this practice is preceded by false determination? And whatever you claim to be the means of apprehension [of falsity] in that [statement of yours which affirms that everyday practice is preceded by false determination], by precisely that [means] there is a determination of erroneousness in other cases as well. And from its opposite, there is also a determination of nonerroneousness. Thus, how could [you say that] in all cases there is no determination of erroneousness, etc.?

[Objection:] In no case do I proclaim a means of valid cognition, for in all cases I only point out that there is a doubt.

[Reply:] But even doubt arises when two [alternatives] are seen.[23] Thus the determination of erroneousness etc., has to be admitted in some cases, just as [the properties] 'being a trunk,' 'being a person,' etc., [even if they are not determined in the present case of doubt, they must have been determined sometime in the past in respect to something in order to make the present doubt possible]. And if these (i.e., nonerroneousness etc.) are [therefore at least once] established, you as well must necessarily think about the means of valid cognition which is well established as [the necessary] condition for that [determination]. For the chief purpose of enquiring people is to think about the causes of well known practices. Nor is it possible to point out a doubt without a means of valid cognition. How is a means of valid cognition not proclaimed [at least] in some cases?

[Objection:] The doubt is created for someone else by [raising] several *vikalpas*, but it is not pointed out [in the sense that it presupposes a means of valid cognition].

[Reply:] No, because if there is no determination of the several *vikalpas* as [appropriate for] raising a doubt [in the mind of somebody else], [they] could not be employed [for that purpose]. For if the capacity of a certain cause is not determined, it cannot be employed towards a special effect, for [otherwise] anything whatsoever [could] be employed.

[Objection:] It is observed that threads etc., are employed towards a special effect even when there is a doubt [whether one will succeed to produce the cloth etc.].

[Reply:] No, because the threads etc., too are determined as capable[24] of producing an effect such as a cloth etc., and because it is determined that an effect such as the cloth is not produced when the threads etc., are absent, the restricted employment [of only threads etc., towards the production of a special effect such as the cloth, and not of anything whatsoever] is correct. But according to you there is no determination in respect to anything. Consequently, there would either be no activity, or [if there is an activity] the activity would not be fixed [in the sense that certain causes are employed towards certain effects]. Therefore, in order to avoid [the charge] that you prattle incoherently you must proclaim a means of valid cognition in some cases. And [as long as] this [means of valid cognition] is not determined it cannot be proclaimed, but its determination is impossible, because [according to

you] there is no determination of a difference between erroneous and nonerroneous [cognitions]. Therefore, there is [after all] a determination of erroneousness etc.
[Objection:] But from which means of valid cognition could this [determination arise]?
[Reply:] Both of us should attend to this [problem together]. In respect to this [I propose the following:] one has to admit that immediately after the arising of a cognition there is a non-conceptual cognition which apprehends the cognition [which has arisen a moment before] as qualified by erroneousness etc. For otherwise everyday practice concerning erroneous and nonerroneous [cognitions] would have no basis. And it would not follow that a mistaken [cognizer] would [therefore] not act [towards the object], because the [cognition] which apprehends the erroneousness of the [previous one] is not [always] distinct, just as the apprehension of thorns [or other obstacles on the way is not distinct] for a running [person]. For it is observed that the distinct cognition, [and it does not matter here] whether it has the nature of recollection or of a direct experience, is a condition for escape from an undesired object. [And] a recollection is observed to be distinct because of some special cause, even when the [former] apprehension [of the now recollected object] was not distinct. For instance, when one apprehends an individual cow for the first time, there is an indistinct apprehension of the recurrent nature of [the universal] 'cow' and of its distinct nature (i.e., distinct from the individual); later on, by seeing similar and dissimilar individuals a clear recollection [of the universal 'cow'] arises: 'I saw something similar to that,' 'I saw something dissimilar to that,' 'This is similar to that,' '[This] is dissimilar to that.' Thus, after the indistinct apprehension of erroneousness and nonerroneousness, because of sublating and confirming [cognitions respectively] a clear recollection arises: 'This is a false [cognition],' or 'This is a valid cognition.' Or [if the above is not acceptable, one can also maintain that] the two (i.e., falsity and validity) are directly perceived

[for the first time] immediately after the arising of the sublating or confirming cognitions.

[Objection:] At that time the two cannot be perceived [for the cognition qualified by validity or falsity has long been destroyed].

[Reply:] No, because the mind has [objects in] the three times as its object. For otherwise even the yogis would not [be able to] apprehend past and future objects.

[Objection:] The yogis may have a perception of past etc., [objects] by the capacity of merit (*dharma*) which arises from [practicing] yoga.

[Reply:] Why couldn't it be [the same] for [simple people] like us as well, [namely, that we perceive] some [past or future] objects by the capacity of previously acquired *adṛṣṭa* [when] accompanied by special conditions? For the capacity of *adṛṣṭa* can be inferred from its effect, [namely, the apprehension of past and future objects].

Or erroneousness etc., are determined by an inferential sign, [namely,] the arising of sublation etc. (etc. = nonerroneousness is inferred by confirmation (*saṃvāda*)).

[Objection:] Then by what [means of valid cognition] is the [universal] concomitance [between erroneousness and arising of sublation etc.] apprehended? Surely, [if it is apprehended] by another inference, and the [concomitance of the second inference] by [still] another inference, an infinite regress follows.[26]

[Reply:] What is wrong with that? [This infinite regress] is very well maintained [by us], since *saṃsāra* has no beginning. Just as the recollection of taking food etc., [from the previous life] for the first time [in this life when hunger occurs],[26] the recollection of the concomitance too arises from traces [left] from another [previous] birth/life which are accompanied by *adṛṣṭa*.

[Objection:] Being exhausted by/absorbed in proving an [infinite] succession of examples [you will] not establish the probandum under discussion. (Or: Having decayed into a proof of a succession of examples [your argument] does not establish the probandum under discussion.)

[Reply:] No! Because the example is already established before. For no one apprehends the relation between fire and smoke in the kitchen etc., at the time when the inference of fire [on the mountain is effected].
[Objection: You may be satisfied with your own presumed knowledge, but] the example must necessarily be proved at the time of inference for another person.
[Reply:] If this other [person] is of a different opinion about the example in all [cases], then [we conclude that] for him there would be no determination of erroneous and nonerroneous [cognitions] based on that [example]. When this [determination] is absent, everyday practice [which recognizes] something as that (i.e., as erroneous or nonerroneous) [and] which is well known among the people and in the sciences [would] stop. For the [person] who denies even the apprehension of the concomitance between [fire and] smoke etc., is refuted only by the contradiction to everyday practice of the people, not in any other way. And this contradiction (i.e., to the everyday practice of the people) is the same here too (i.e., in the case of the denial of the determination of erroneous and nonerroneous cognitions). Therefore, for the other [person] too, [there must be] a well known example in respect to certain [things], [and] by the force of that [example] another [example] is also established.

Or [one can prove the validity etc., in another way by assuming that] at the beginning a certain [omniscient person], who perceived everything directly, taught the universal concomitance to some non-omniscient people: 'The cognition for which a sublation arises is erroneous,' 'The cognition, however, for which another corroborating cognition arises is nonerroneous'; having apprehended this concomitance from the teaching of [this] reliable person, they, however, taught it to others, they too to others, and they too to others, [and] so [on] till [it reached people] like us, just like the concomitance of the ordeal by balance etc.[27] The apprehension of the concomitance between cause and effect by means of perception and inference is also to be established by this very same reasoning.

As for what has been said [namely] 'The production by faultless causal complex is not the [inferential] sign for nonerroneousness,' [we] indeed accept that. But the non-arising of sublation must be admitted as making known [the nonerroneousness] in some cases where even enquiring people cannot imagine the non-arising of sublation otherwise, [that is] without the object which appeared [in the cognition] being true, for instance, in the case of the cognition of the moon's being one by a cognizer endowed with special qualifications of place, time, state, etc.

As for the [following objection, namely,] 'The false cognition arises from the capacity of its cause in such a way that it obstructs (or: prevents) the arising of the sublating cognition. The perishing of this [false cognition] as well is exactly so (i.e., it also obstructs the arising of sublation), just like the true cognition which is accepted by the opponent,' this is also not correct. For the opponent (i.e., we, the Naiyāyikas) does not admit that a valid cognition obstructs the arising of a sublating cognition [and, therefore, the analogy does not hold good].[28] Then what [do we accept]? [We accept that validity consists] either [in] the fact that the object as it appeared [in the cognition] is not contrary [to reality], or [that it consists in the fact that] falsity does not arise, [it does not consist in the fact that the cognition obstructs the arising of sublation]. For one cannot obstruct the arising of something, [be it] accomplished or not [yet] accomplished. Rather we maintain that the cause can be obstructed. The cause which does not produce its effect when something [else] is present, even though the co-producers are present, but does produce [the effect] when that [thing] is absent, that [cause] is said to be obstructed by that [thing]. For instance, [qualities like] heaviness etc., [are obstructed to produce their effects like falling down etc., of the substance they inhere] by conjunction etc.[29] But in respect to the production of sublation, what is obstructed by what? And [if] one thing obstructs another, [then] its perishing does not as well obstruct the other. For it is not as well the perishing of conjunction etc., which obstructs heaviness etc., rather [its perishing] assists [heaviness in bringing about falling down].[30] Therefore, it is impossible [to maintain that] the perishing of that [false cognition] as well is exactly so (i.e., obstructs the arising of sublation). For it is well known among the people and in the sciences that the cognition 'This is a conch shell, not silver,'[31] sublates the previously arisen cognition 'This is silver.'

Its rejection by several *vikalpas*, such as 'Is the object sublated, or the cognition?', necessitates the maxim of the cow dung as a milky preparation.[32] And thus, the deliberation 'What is the sublation of the cognition? Is it characterized by the removal of the object or by the removal of the fruit?'[33] etc., as well is of no use in respect to anything. Useful [however] is to make known the following concomitance: 'Sublation arises only for an erroneous cognition, not for a true cognition,' and nothing else. Therefore, nonerroneousness is made known in some cases by non-arising of sublation, in some [other] cases again by an efficiency of activity, e.g., by obtaining an object such as water etc., [the nonerroneousness] of the cognition of water etc., which has arisen previously [is made known].
[Objection:] It is impossible to obtain the object which appeared [in the cognition]; we have explained that [above, *NBhū* p. 34.7-10].
[Reply:] No! For it is possible to obtain certain objects such as stones etc., which appeared [in the cognition]. As for objects such as water etc., even though they are destroyed, the obtaining of the [object] which arises in the [same] series as the [object which appeared in the previous cognition] makes known [the validity of the cognition of water etc., which has previously arisen].
[Objection:] But what is this series?
[Reply:] The immediate arising of something similar to the [destroyed object]; it is the cause of the mundane, non-belying cognition 'This is exactly that.' For [a person] who acts after determining an object by error obvious-

ly does not obtain even an object which arises in the [same] series as the [object which appeared in the cognition]. Therefore, by obtaining an object which appeared [in the cognition], and by obtaining an object which arises in the [same] series as the [object which appeared in the cognition], the nonerroneousness of the previous cognition is known. In the same manner [we] explain [the obtaining of an object which exists] at the [same] place [as the place] of the [object which appeared in the cognition] (i.e., even if the place is destroyed, one obtains an object at the place which belongs to the same series as the place of the object which appeared in the cognition).[34]

[Objection:] When this [water which appeared in a past cognition] is not determined, how could you determine that [something] arises in the [same] series as the [undetermined water]?

[Reply:] No, [it is not correct that it is not determined] for it is determined by the fact that there is no disagreement. For if the object which appeared [in the previous cognition] does not exist [at all], or if it is different [in a significant mannner from the obtained object], [then] it is not [possible that] the cognizer who after the activity [to obtain the object] determines that object as 'This is exactly that [which appeared in the cognition],' is not contradicted, even if he speaks/deals with many people. Therefore, it is determined by agreement that [the obtained object] is exactly as the object which appeared [in the cognition].[35] But a person who, although he does not act [to obtain the object], apprehends the particular properties of the object which appeared [in the cognition], apprehends [also] the nonerroneousness of the previous cognition [even if] he does not move from his place, in as much as he determines the true nature of the object by these particular properties, or by the conformity with the statements of other people. And thus, it is not correct[36] [to say] that the nonerroneousness of the cognitions of the moon etc., is not established [because the moon etc., cannot be obtained]. For [their nonerroneousness] is not determined by the efficiency of the activity alone, for just as fire etc., nonerroneousness as well can be inferred by several inferential signs alternately, and can be apprehended by another means of valid cognition.

Others, however, are of the opinion that by 'efficiency of activity' the conformity with other means of valid cognition is intended [and not the obtainment of the object]. And this [conformity] arises either from the apprehension of the particular properties of the object which appeared [in the cognition], whether destroyed [in the meantime] or not, or from the statements of many people brought together (or: from the statements of many respected persons). Thus, there is no fault whatsoever in admitting that in all cases which are object to a doubt the determination of nonerroneousness is due to the efficiency of activity alone. [Thus, one can avoid the problems which arise from 'obtaining the object,' 'absence of sublation,' etc.]

As for the charge of infinite regress [namely] 'How is the nonerroneousness of the apprehension of the [efficiency of activity] known?' etc., it is not possible, because it is sublated by the everyday practice of the people which is preceded by determination. For it is observed that people who act do not have any desire [to pursue the matter any further] after the second or third apprehension of the special [properties] (i.e., validity etc.). Or [another reply to this charge is that] the infinite regress has already been refuted above [*NBhū* p. 36.3f., by pointing out that *saṃsāra* has no beginning]. Therefore, intrinsic validity too need not be maintained out of fear of infinite regress."

Bhāsarvajña's handling of the sceptical problems posed by Jayarāśi is extraordinarily rich and suggestive. One feels as if he were sharing his thoughts with the reader, rather than presenting ready made fixed solutions. He certainly realizes how powerful Jayarāśi's arguments are, and seems to go into great trouble to find some way out of this devastating critique of the very possibility of knowledge, for which purpose he is willing to accept new, for a Naiyāika highly unorthodox, and even surprising, theories of validity.[37] His first suggestion (p. 35.14f.), namely, that falsity and validity are directly apprehended as qualifications of cognitions as soon as the cognition arises, comes dangerously close to giving up the traditional Nyāya theory of *parataḥ prāmāṇya*, and adopting something similar to the Sāṃkhya theory according to which both validity and falsity are inherent to the cognition. In the second suggestion (p. 35.23f.), namely, that validity and falsity are directly perceived at the time when the corroborating or sublating cognition arises, that is, after the cognition has disappeared, he is willing to accept direct perception of past and future objects (a privilege usually reserved for the yogis) even by simple people like you and me.[38] How this could be possibly done, he does not really know and has recourse to the 'black box' of *adṛṣṭa*. In a third alternative (p. 36.1f) he suggests that validity and falsity can be inferred. But there too he is forced to an unusual proposition: in order to establish the *vyāpti* he is willing to go as far as to accept the charge of infinite regress. Every inference depends on a previous one, but one needs no beginning, because *saṃsāra* has no beginning. But does this solve the problem? Nice as it is to grant everyone of us an infinite experience, how can one establish a universal concomitance with something which has never been perceived? Isn't it comparable to a blind person who is basing his knowledge, say of colours, on an infinite succession of other blind persons? Here Bhāsarvajña comes close to admit that he does not have an answer to full-fledged scepticism. The only refutation of a complete sceptic, who will not even admit the universal concomitance between fire and smoke, is everyday practice (*vyavahāra*), there is no other way (p. 36.10-11).[39] But how could everyday practice refute scepticism? And is it so obvious that it needs no further explanation?

I must admit that I am not at all sure how to interpret the argument. Do we have here an Indian counterpart to the famous claim that scepticism is psychologically impossible, and that the sceptic betrays himself by his own actions? If this is the case, we may interpret the disjunction on p. 35.10, namely, if nothing is determined either there would be no activity or activity would be random, as a two-tiered *prasaṅga*, that is, not that either one of the two must take place, but rather that the first alternative necessarily follows, and the second represents only a further hypothetical state of affairs. In other words, since you, the sceptic, do not allow a determination in respect to anything, you will not be able to act; and even if we assume only for the sake of argument that you may somehow act, your activity would be at random. It seems to me, however, that such an interpretation brings too much into the disjunction.[40] Further, the above argument does not seem to have enjoyed in India the popularity it had, and still has, in the West. Why this is so, I cannot say. Perhaps because the distinction between the two levels of truth was widely spread and legitimized; perhaps because the dominant religions and philosophies (including the Nyāya, cf. *NS* 1.1.2) considered that ignorance, error or illusion are at the very root of human existence. In any case, knowledge and action, or what one may call the intellectual and vital principles, were often considered not only independent, but also incompatible. This disconnection between knowledge and action has even found its way into a popular maxim: *lokavyavahāraṃ prati sadṛśau bālapaṇḍitau* - "In respect to everyday practice of the people, the learned and the ignorant are similar" - which means that the wise knows better, but nevertheless acts like a fool, as if knowledge had no bearing on everyday practice. For instance, the Buddhist saint knows that external objects do not exist, but nevertheless undertakes such actions as bathing.[41] However, it is not so much because of these and other generalities that I am perplexed by the argument of *vyavahāra*, but rather because I find it difficult, at least at first sight, to reconcile it with other passages in the *NBhū*, where everyday practice is said to be independent from the determination of validity. For instance p. 43.2-4: *pravṛttir api puruṣasyābhilāṣādipūrvikārthaprāptyanarthaparihārānuṣṭhānalakṣaṇā bhavanti prāyeṇa pramāṇatadābhāsavivekaniścayaṃ nāpekṣate.* "As for the activity, in as much as it is preceded by the desire etc., of men [and] is characterized as an undertaking to obtain a useful object and to avoid an unuseful one, mostly (or: as a rule) it does not depend on the determination of the distinction between means of valid cognition and pseudo means of valid cognition." Similarly p. 208.1-2: *vyavahāriṇām api vyavahāraḥ kaścin mithyārthaḥ kaścit tattvārtha iti katham aparīkṣitena vyavahāreṇa prāmāṇyaṃ vyavasthāpyate?* "As for the everyday practice of the people, some of it has a false object and some of it has a real object. Thus, how could validity be established by unexamined everyday practice?" The above quotation recapitulates in fact the detailed refutation of *PV*, *pramāṇasiddhi* 5 (*prāmāṇyaṃ vyavahāreṇa*) and Prajñākaragupta's commentary thereon, and it gives a clear picture of the shaky foundations of the *vyavahāra* argument, of which Bhāsarvajña was fully aware (*NBhū* p. 202.2-27):

"On the above [we] reply: First, in as much as [your statement] 'Validity [is established] by everyday practice' is concerned, [we ask:] is everyday practice a means of valid cognition or not? If it is not a means of valid cognition, how [could] validity be established by it? For nothing is established by something which is not a means of valid cognition, because this is absurd. Consequently the validity of all sciences [even the bogus ones] would be established, and lasting objects etc., would be established as well [contrary to your theory of momentariness], because mere everyday practice is possible in respect to everything (i.e., even in respect to the most fantastic objects).

If validity is established by everyday practice which is a means of valid cognition, this is not correct, because you do not admit any other means of valid cognition over and above the two means of valid cognition (i.e., perception and inference). Even if [you claim that] everyday practice is included in these [two], then since it is criticized by this very same criticism (or: since it is refuted by the refutation of these two), validity is not established by it.

If validity is established by unexamined everyday practice, even so, as has been explained [above, *NBhū* p. 202.3], this is absurd, for mere everyday practice is the same in respect to everything.

[Objection:] A means of valid cognition is established by everyday practice upon which everybody agrees.

[Reply:] No, because everyday practice upon which everybody agrees is impossible [to know] and because a difference of opinion is possible everywhere.

[Objection:] What[ever] is thought/spoken of/treated as[22] being valid even by [people] who have no idea of sciences, that is a means of valid cognition.

[Reply:] Then the Vedas etc., would indeed be means of valid cognition, for it is well known to everybody that they are thought/spoken of/treated as being valid.

[Objection:] The validity of cognitions of directly perceived objects alone [is established] by everyday practice, not of the cognitions of [imperceptible] objects of the Vedas etc.

[Reply:] Are you taking refuge now in the Lokāyata?[42] Accordingly, we shall state a refutation of the [Lokāyata] as well [p. 213ff.]. And [furthermore], the cognitions of the Buddha etc., would not be valid.

[Objection:] On account of what means the people busy in everyday practice treat as valid the cognitions, [which lead] to obtaining and rejecting of [objects] which bring about pleasure and pain [respectively] which are well known among the people (i.e., not those which bring about pleasure and pain after death), if that [means] is apprehended elsewhere as well, then this, too, is a means of valid cognition (i.e., there is some factor conducive to the treatment as valid not only in respect to directly perceived objects, and thus the cognitions of the Buddha can be treated as valid).

[Reply:] And so, the people busy in everyday practice treat as being valid only that which is apprehended to be neither doubtful nor erroneous, for one observes that when the opposite is apprehended, however (contaminated construction?), one treats [something] as not being valid. Therefore, elsewhere as well validity is to be determined only by the apprehension that [something] is free from doubt and error, and not in dependence on efficient action, nor by connection with the object to be obtained, or prompting [the cognizer] to activity.[43] For in respect to cognitions of vanishing or negligible objects, although valid, efficient action, [prompting to action] etc., are impossible, [and] because efficient action etc., are possible in the case of mnemonic, doubtful and erroneous cognitions as well. This has been explained [above]. And how [something] is apprehended by a means of valid cognition to be free from doubt and error, has been explained above in the examination of the general definition of the means of valid cognition [p. 11ff.]."

How can we reconcile the above passage with the claim that contradiction with everyday practice refutes scepticism? The easiest way would be to claim that Bhāsarvajña argues from the Buddhist presuppositions. And this is, no doubt, partly true, but would not solve the problem, for the claim that everyday practice as such cannot establish something as a means of valid cognition seems to be Bhāsarvajña's own opinion in this passage. And if so, he seems to contradict what he said on p. 36.10-11, namely, that the contradiction to *vyavahāra* refutes anyone who will not accept even the universal concomitance between fire and smoke.

I can suggest no definitive conclusion to what exactly Bhāsarvajña meant while arguing with the concept of *vyavahāra*. Perhaps he meant that everyday practice is never enough to establish validity or falsity in any specific case, but the fact that the distinction between validity and falsity appears at all in everyday practice proves that the distinction must be valid in some cases, even if one cannot point out and say which cases. In other words, one may always be wrong about this or that case, but not about the distinction as such, namely, that there is a difference between valid and false cognitions. Further, the fact that the distinction has arisen in people's minds indicates that at some point someone was able to tell the difference between the two, even if we have to assume that he must have been omniscient in order to make such an extraordinary distinction. (This amounts to the claim that the validity of all the means of valid cognition is derived from *āptavacana*; cf. *NBhū* p. 36.13f.) Therefore, the distinction as such between validity and falsity is right, and thus we have at least one determination which is established; and whatever the means for that determination may be, the very same means may be applied elsewhere as well and reopen the way to knowledge. It is easy to see how Bhāsarvajña could be compared with Descartes at this point. Both philosophers would seem to agree that if we succeed in obtaining certainty in respect to one single proposition or cognition, that would be enough not only to refute scepticism definitively, but also to provide a criterion which is apparent from that very cognition and which may be used to secure the truthfulness of other propositions as well. In Descartes' case it was, as is well known, the *cogito*, and the criterion derived from it was clearness and distinctness of ideas. In Bhāsarvajña's case it was the distinction itself between validity and falsity; as for the criterion derived from it, he does not seem to give a definitive answer, unless it is the "apprehension of something as free from doubt and error."

To conclude, it seems probable that Bhāsarvajña was fully aware of the shortcomings and weaknesses of the *vyavahāra* argument,[44] but perhaps could think of nothing better. On the whole, his reaction towards scepticism is not uncommon even today. He was basically convinced that

Jayarāśi must be wrong, and that knowledge must be possible somehow, but how exactly he did not know. He attempted several solutions, none of which, he must have known, is unproblematic, but this did not shake his conviction that some solution must be possible. Thus, he invites the sceptic to abandon his position, which he considers to be self-defeating, and employ his time and wits to help the Naiyāyika to examine the question and develop a better theory.[45] In a way, this is exactly what Jayarāśi does. For, as we saw, his arguments against the criterion of truth pointed out serious flaws in the older Nyāya criterion of truth and stimulated Bhāsarvajña to rethink the whole issue and to suggest some new and unorthodox theories. In this respect, Jayarāśi had a positive role to play and has become, perhaps in spite of himself, an important driving force in the historical development of Indian philosophy.

Notes

[1] The following reproduces a paper published under the same title in *Berliner Indologische Studien*, Band 3, 1987, pp. 23-49. No significant changes have been introduced here except that, whenever possible, references to the *Tattvopaplavasiṃha* refer to the present edition. The abbreviations are the same as those on pp. 587ff., except *TŚVA*: *Tattvārthaślokavārttikālaṅkāra* of Vidyānanda. Ed. Vardhamāna Pārśvanātha. Śrī Ācārya Kuṃthusāgara Granthamālā No. 41. 1949.

I would like to thank again Dr. K. Preisendanz who read the paper and discussed it with me, defending the Nyāya position against my slightly biased sceptical point of view. Special thanks are also due to Prof. A. Wezler for some very useful suggestions. My stay in Germany during which this paper was written was made possible by a fellowship of the A. von Humboldt-Stiftung.

John Taber has kindly drawn my attention to the discussion in *NVTṬ* (Thakur ed. pp. 29-30), where Vācaspati admits some similar ideas to those professed by Bhāsarvajña, namely, the acceptance of *svataḥ prāmāṇya* in certain cases and the charge of infinite regress. This passage is also discussed in some detail by Matilal, *Perception*, Oxford 1986, pp. 160ff. Unfortunately, however, Matilal's presentation is not always reliable. On the one hand, Vācaspati's statements are hopelessly intermingled with those of Udayana, Gaṅgeśa and Vardhamāna (e.g., pp. 170-171), and the latter are heavily and ahistorically relied upon for the interpretation of the former. On the other hand, Matilal fails to recognize Vācaspati's direct or indirect indebtedness to Kamalaśīla (*TSP* on 2945).

It seems that the Nyāya theory of validity was in a state of flux during the 9th and 10th century, and that the common perception of Nyāya as committed to a strict *parataḥ prāmāṇya* doctrine is based not on the classical Nyāya texts, but rather on Navya Nyāya hermeneutics and on the late doxographical work *SDS*. At the present I cannot say whether *NBhū* and *NVTṬ* represent a break in the established Nyāya tradition or whether the *svataḥ prāmāṇya* doctrine was only consolidated later on as the official Nyāya position.

[2] *Perception, Knowledge and Disbelief*. Alt- und Neu-Indische Studien 35, Stuttgart 1987.

[3] This is hardly surprising. As a rule Bhāsarvajña does not refer to his opponents by their proper names, but only in general terms; either simply by expressions like 'others' (*anye, apare, eke,* etc.), or according to school (Bauddha, Mīmāṃsaka, etc.), or according to doctrine (*anātmavādin, advaitavādin,* etc.).
The Lokāyatikas are referred to by several names: Cārvāka pp. 203.9, 228.5; *bhūtacaitanyavādin* p. 500.4; Lokāyata p. 202.17; Laukāyatika pp. 213.18, 330.25; *suragurumata* p. 218.16. Note, however, that none of these appellations refers to Jayarāśi; they all refer to the materialistic Lokāyata.

[4] For a detailed and reliable paraphrase of these passages cf. L.V Joshi, *A Critical Study of the Pratyakṣa Pariccheda of Bhāsarvajña's Nyāyabhūṣaṇa*, Research Work Publication Series 22, Ahmedabad 1986, pp. 199-203. Unfortunately, and unlike in the discussion of validity (pp. 133ff.), he fails to establish the connection between the two texts (in spite of the quotations on p. 202, nn. 78-79), and consequently misinterprets the parallel passages from the *PKM* p. 47.10f. quoted p. 200, n. 74. For further parallel passages cf. *SVR* p. 143.25f.; *TBV* p. 551.17f.

[5] In order to save space I refrain from reproducing the Sanskrit text in full (most of the *pūrvapakṣa* part is quoted in the comparison above).

[6] Take for instance the stock example 'Is this a man or a trunk?'; one could say either that something appears only with its general properties, in which case a property-possessor appears, or that a general property such as being upright (*ūrdhvatva*) appears, in which case a property appears.

[7] Cf. Col. G.A. Jacob, *Laukikanyāyāñjaliḥ, A Handful of Popular Maxims*, repr. Delhi 1983, Part I, p. 25: "*gomayapāyasīyaḥ*. The maxim of *cowdung as a milky preparation*. Some stupid person is supposed to argue that cowdung is

made of milk, because it comes from the cow; hence it is used to denote an utterly absurd argument or statement."

[8] Read (p. 24.8) *prākṛta-* instead of *prakṛta-*.

[9] Note that this alternative does not appear in the *TUS*; it appears, however, in *Vy* p. 537.15-18, cf. p. 380, n. 121 above.

[10] Cf. *NBh* on 1.1.4, p. 121.2-4.

[11] Cf. p. 68.17f. above: *sallakṣaṇanibandhanaṃ mānavyavasthānam...*

[12] The best collection to date of Lokāyata fragments may be found in M. Namai, "A survey of Bārhaspatya philosophy." For this fragment (F5) cf. p. 44.

[13] Cf. *SVṬ* p. 277.19f., *PrP* p. 62.12f., *TŚVA* p. 609.3f.

[14] Cf. p. 381, n. 123 above.

[15] Cf. *NBhū* p. 24.20-21: *sarvapramāṇānabhyupagamān na lokaḥ siddho na tadvyavahāro na tasyāvicāritasya ramaṇīyatvam iti* with *TUS* p. 125.11-12: *tad evam upapluteṣv eva tattveṣv avicāritaramaṇīyāḥ sarve vyavahārā ghaṭanta iti.* (cf. p. 44 above.)

[16] Cf. the previous note and the very similar formulations in *NM* I p. 317.10, *ĀḌ* p. 60.17 quoted above p. 49, n. 23.

[17] Cf. for instance *PP* p. 371.1, *TSP* I p. 15.8, *VP* III.1 p. 228.11. My guess is that the original meaning of the term referred to notions which proved useful in everyday life, perhaps somewhat similar to what British philosophers take to be common sense, but which become problematic when philosophically analyzed.

[18] For an interpretation of these puzzling statements cf. my "Studies in *TUS* II," pp. 127ff.

[19] The common factor consists in being a result, and as in other cases one observes that a result has a perceptible agent, one concludes that e.g., sensory cognition as a result has also an agent, albeit imperceptible, namely, the sense. Jayarāśi argues against this point on p. 142.3f. above.

[20] So far I have failed to find in Nyāya texts a clear answer to the question whether water was considered as a final whole, and if so, under which conditions. Since Jayarāśi raises the argument in respect to water, and especially since Bhāsarvajña does not reply directly to this argument (cf. below) by saying that water does not form final wholes, I tend to conclude that, strange as it may seem to us, water was indeed considered as being able to form final wholes; cf. also pp. 312-313 above.

[21] *anumāna* is used here in the sense of *liṅga*; the complete inference would be: The cognition of object x is not erroneous, because it leads to the obtainment of object y which has arisen in the same series as object x.

[22] On the threefold meaning of *vyavahāra* cf. *HB* II, p. 156, n. 3.

[23] Read (p. 34.23) *ubhayadarśane* instead of *ubhayādarśane*; the conjecture is confirmed by Joshi, *op. cit.*, p. 141, n. 55.

[24] Perhaps (p. 35.8) *-yogyatayā* instead of *-yogyatāyā(ḥ)*.

[25] Perhaps (p. 36.3) *syūtā* instead of *bhūtā*.

[26] Cf. *NS* 3.1.20: *pretyāhārābhyāsakṛtāt stanyābhilāṣāt*. Bhāsarvajña comments on this *sūtra* on p. 546.30f.

[27] The procedure of ordeal by balance is described in Kane, *History of Dharmaśāstra*, vol. III, pp. 369-70. The suspect is weighed twice. If at the second time, after invoking the balance etc., he is found lighter, he is innocent. If he weighs the same or more, he is guilty. According to Joshi, however (*op. cit.*, p. 147), if he weighs more, he is guilty, otherwise he is innocent (which does not seem much of an ordeal). For a detailed description of ordeals in Hindu law cf. R.W. Lariviere's introduction to *The Divyatattva of Raghunandana Bhaṭṭācārya*, Delhi 1981.

[28] It seems to me that Bhāsarvajña misunderstands Jayarāśi on this point, for the opponent (*TUS* p. 76.3-7 above) is not a Naiyāyika, but a Mīmāṃsaka (cf. the quotation from the *Vṛttikāragrantha* on the very next line). However, Bhāsarvajña's mistake is understandable for the Mīmāṃsā position appears within the context of the examination of *NS* 1.1.4. Note also that the reading (p. 76.6 above, cf. *NBhū* p. 37.1f) *taddhvaṃso 'pi* is not absolutely certain. The manuscript of the *TUS* reads *tadvaśo 'pi*. But as far as I can judge, the *NBhū* gives the better reading and I have amended the *TUS* accordingly.

[29] Cf. VS 5.1.7: *saṃyogābhāve gurutvāt patanam*. Cf. also *id.* 5.2.3.

[30] A different interpretation of the same argument would be that the absence of conjunction is nothing but a coproducer for momentum which, in its turn, prevents the falling down of an object. Cf. VS 5.1.17-18: *nodanād ādyam iṣoḥ karma karmakāritāc ca saṃskārād uttaraṃ tathottaram uttaraṃ ca. saṃskārābhāve gurutvāt patanam*.

[31] Read (with the manuscript as reported by Joshi, *op. cit.*, p. 150, n. 64): *na rajatam* instead of *rajatam*.

[32] Cf. n. 7 above.

[33] These *vikalpas* do not appear in the *pūrvapakṣa* part, but cf. above p. 122.7f.: *atha jñānaṃ bādhyate, tasyāpi bādhā kā? kiṃ svarūpavyāvṛttirūpā, svarūpāpahnavarūpā vā, viṣayāpahāralakṣaṇā vā?*

[34] This argument too does not appear in the *pūrvapakṣa*; cf., however, above p. 78.15-16: ... *na ca taddeśakālasaṃlagnodakaprāpakatvam asti, deśasyāpy udakavad vināśasaṃbhavāt.*

[35] Note that in all the above Bhāsarvajña did not reply to the actual argument of Jayarāśi, namely, that final wholes do not produce further wholes.

[36] Read (p. 38.7) *ity ayuktam*, or perhaps better *ity uktam ayuktam*, instead of *ity uktam*.

[37] I cannot undertake here a discussion of Bhāsarvajña's specific arguments against Jayarāśi (my interpretation of them should be clear from the translation, and that they cannot refute the sceptical position is rather obvious); in what follows I shall restrict myself to Bhāsarvajña's positive suggestions.

[38] This may be considered as a forerunner of what came to be called later on *jñānalakṣaṇam alaukikapratyakṣam*, cf. Shastri, *Philosophy of Nyāya-Vaiśeṣika*, pp. 462ff., especially p. 469.

[39] For a different interpretation of the argument cf. Joshi, *op. cit.*, p. 146: "and not in any other way (= no other argument is necessary)."

[40] The usual expression of such a two-tiered *prasaṅga* repeats the opposite of the first alternative (often with an abstract suffix added) in the locative; in our case I would expect something like *pravṛttau vā* (or *pravṛttitve vā*) *avyavasthitapravṛttiḥ prasaktā*.

[41] The example is taken from *Vy* p. 526.26-28.

[42] Bhāsarvajña probably refers to the materialistic Lokāyata, not to Jayarāśi.

[43] Cf. *NBṬ* on 1.1, pp. 17-18.

[44] Cf. also *NBhū* p. 218.5-7: *agnibhāvo 'gnitvaṃ na gardabhādibhāva ity etad eva kuto niścitam? lokaprasiddhita iti cet, saiva prasiddhiḥ katamapramāṇamūleti vicārayituṃ prārabdhā, loke ca kṛṣṇākāśādiprasiddhivan mithyāprasiddhir api dṛṣṭā.* "How do [you] determine that [the universal] 'fire' has the nature of fire and not the nature of an ass etc.? - Because it is well known among the people. - But this is precisely what [we] undertook to examine, [namely,] which means of valid cognition is at the basis of common knowledge. And [moreover] mistaken common knowledge as well

is observed in the world, for instance the common knowledge that ether is black, etc."

[46] Cf. *NBhū* p. 35.13-14: sa [*bhrāntatvābhrāntatvaniścayaḥ*] *kutaḥ pramāṇād iti cen, nanu paryālocanīyam etad āvayor api.*

Abbreviations and Bibliography

1. Primary Sources

AKBh — *Abhidharmakośabhāṣyam* of Vasubandhu. Ed. by P. Pradhan. Tibetan Sanskrit Works Series VIII. 2nd ed., Patna 1975

AKV — *Abhidharmakośavyākhyā* (*Sphuṭārthā*) of Yaśomitra. Ed. by Dwarikadas Shastri. Bauddha Bharati Series 5-6. 2nd ed., Varanasi 1981

Anekāntajayapatākā — of Haribhadra Sūri, with *Vṛtti* and Muṇicandra Sūri's *Vivaraṇa*. Ed. by H. Kapadia. GOS 88, 105. Baroda 1940, 1947

Aṣṭādhyāyī — of Pāṇini in Böhtlingk, *Pāṇini's Grammatik*. 2nd ed., Leipzig 1887

AS — *Aṣṭasahasrī* of Vidyānanda. Ed. by Vaṃśīdhara. Bombay 1915

ĀḌ — *Āgamaḍambara otherwise called Ṣaṇmatanāṭaka of Jayanta Bhaṭṭa*. Ed. by V. Raghavan & A. Thakur. Mithila Institute Series Ancient Text No. 7. Darbhanga 1964

ĀP — *Ālambanaparīkṣā* of Dignāga. Ed. by E. Frauwallner in "Dignāga, sein Werk und seine Entwicklung."

ĀM — *Āptamīmāṃsā* of Samantabhadra. Ed. by Gajadharalal. Kashi 1914

Uṇādisūtra — *The Uṇādisūtras in Various Recensions*. Part I. Ed. by T. Chintamani. Madras University Sanskrit Series No. 7. Part 1,4. Madras 1933

Upaskāra	*Vaiśeṣikasūtropaskāra* of Śaṅkara Miśra. Ed. by Narayana Mishra. KSS 195. 2nd ed., Varanasi 1969
Kus	*Nyāyakusumañjali* of Udayana. Ed. by M. Goswami. Mithila Institute Series Ancient Text No. 23. Darbhanga 1972
Kṣīrataraṅginī	Kṣīrasvāmins *Kommentar zu Pāṇinis Dhātupāṭha*. Hrsg. von B. Liebich. Breslau 1930
GBh	*Gauḍapādabhāṣya* in *Les Strophes de Sāṃkhya avec le Commentaire de Gauḍapāda*, par A.-M. Esnoul. Paris 1964
CS	*Carakasaṃhitā* of Agniveśa with the *Āyurvedadīpikā* of Cakrapāṇidatta. Ed. by G. Pandeya. KSS 194. 2nd ed., Varanasi 1983
Jaina Lakṣaṇāvalī	An authentic and descriptive dictionary of Jaina philosophical terms. Ed. by Balchandra Siddhantashastri. Vir Sewa Mandir Series 15. Delhi 1972, 1973, 1979
JM	*Jayamaṅgalā* of Śrī Śaṅkara. Ed. by S. Vangiya in *Sāṃkhyakārikā* of Īśvarakṛṣṇa with the *Māṭharavṛtti* and the *Jayamaṅgalā*. CSS 56. 2nd ed., Varanasi 1970
TAV	*Tattvārthavārttika* of Akalaṅkadeva. Ed. by Mahendrakumar Jain. Jñānapīṭha Mūrtidevī Jaina Granthamālā No. 10. 2nd ed., Delhi 1982
TUS	*Tattvopaplavasiṃha of Jayarāśi Bhaṭṭa*. Ed. by S. Sanghavi and R. Parikh. GOS 87, Baroda 1940
TBV	*Tattvabodhavidhāyinī* of Abhayadevasūri in *Sammatitarkaprakaraṇa* of

Siddhasena. Ed. by S. Sanghavi and B. Doshi. 5 Vols., Ahmedabad 1921-31

TR — *Tarkarahasya*. Ed. by Paramanandan Shastri. Tibetan Sanskrit Works Series No. XX. Patna 1979

TRD — *Tarkarahasyadīpikā* in *Ṣaḍdarśanasamuccaya of Haribhadra Sūri, with the Commentaries of Tarkarahasyadīpikā of Guṇaratna Sūri and Laghuvṛtti of Somatilaka Sūri and an Avacūrṇi*. Ed. by Mahendrakumar Jain. Jñānapīṭha Mūrtidevī Grantha-mālā No. 36. 2nd ed., Delhi 1981

TrBh — *Triṃśikāvijñaptibhāṣya* of Sthiramati. Ed. by S. Lévi in *Vijñaptimātratāsiddhi*. Paris 1925

TV — *Tattvavaiśāradī* of Vācaspati Miśra in *Pātañjalayogasūtrāṇi*. Ed. by Ganapat Rao Natu. ASS 47. 4th ed., Poona 1978

TS(P) — *Tattvasaṅgraha of Ācārya Shāntarakṣita with the Commentary Pañjikā of Shrī Kamalashīla*. Ed. by Dwarikadas Shastri. Bauddha Bharati Series 1-2. Varanasi 1968

DANC — *Dvādaśāraṃ Nayacakram* of Mallavādin with *Nyāyāgamānusāriṇī* of Siṃhasūri. Ed. by Muni Jambuvijayaji. Śrī Ātmānand Jain Granthamālā No. 92, 94. Bhavnagar 1966, 1976

DhPr — *Dharmottarapradīpa* of Durvekamiśra. Ed. by D. Malvania. Tibetan Sanskrit Works Series No. II. 2nd ed., Patna 1971

NĀA — *Nyāyāgamānusāriṇī* in *DANC*

NK	*Nyāyakośa* by B. Jhalakikar. Bombay Sanskrit and Prakrit Series XLIX. Revised by Abhyankar. 4th ed., Poona 1978
NKan	*Nyāyakandalī* in *PDhS*
NKC	*Nyāyakumudacandra* of Prabhācandra. Ed. by Mahendrakumar Jain. Māṇikacandradigambarajainagranthamālā 38-39. Bombay 1938, 1941
NB(Ṭ)	*Nyāyabindu* of Dharmakīrti and *Nyāyabinduṭīkā* of Dharmottara in *DhPr*
NBṬ(V)	*Nyāyabinduṭīkā* of Vinītadeva. Ed. by L. de la Vallée Poussin. Bibl. Ind. 171, Calcutta 1908-13
NBṬṬ	*Nyāyabinduṭīkāṭippaṇī*. Ed. by Th. Stcherbatsky. Bibl. Buddh. 11. St. Petersburg 1909
NBh	*Nyāyabhāṣya* of Vātsyāyana in *NS*
NBhū	*Nyāyabhūṣaṇa* of Bhāsarvajña in *NSāra*
NM	*Nyāyamañjarī of Jayantabhaṭṭa*. Ed. by K.S. Varadacharya. Oriental Research Institute Series No. 116, 139. Mysore 1969, 1983
NM(Kashi)	*Nyāyamañjarī of Jayanta Bhaṭṭa*. Ed. by S.N. Shukla and M. Adya. KSS 106. 2nd ed., Varanasi 1971, 1969
NMuk	*Nyāyamuktāvalī* in *Nyāyasāra of Bhāsarvajña with the Commentaries Nyāyamuktāvalī of Aparārkadeva and Nyāyakalānidhi of Ānandānubhavācārya*. Ed. by V. and S. Subrahmanya Shastri. Madras Government Oriental Series No. CLXVII. Madras 1961
NMGBh	*Nyāyamañjarīgranthibhaṅga* of Cakradhara. Ed. by N. Shah. LD Series No. 35. Ahmedabad 1972

NR — *Nyāyaratnākara* in *ŚV*

NV — *Nyāyavārttika* in *NS*

NVTṬ — *Nyāyavārttikatātparyaṭīkā* in *NS*

NS — *Nyāyasūtra* in *Nyāyadarśanam with Vātsyāyana's Bhāṣya, Uddyotakara's Vārttika, Vācaspati Miśra's Tātparyaṭīkā and Viśvanātha's Vṛtti*. Ed. by Taranatha Nyayatarkatirtha and Amarendramohan Tarkatirtha. Calcutta Sanskrit Series 18, 29. Calcutta 1936, 1944

NS(Thakur) — *Nyāyadarśana of Gautama with the Bhāṣya of Vātsyāyana, the Vārttika of Uddyotakara, the Tātparyaṭīkā of Vācaspati and the Pariśuddhi of Udayana*. Ed. by A. Thakur. Mithila Institute Series No. 20. Darbhanga 1967

NSāra — *Nyāyasāra* of Bhāsarvajña with Autocommentary *Nyāyabhūṣaṇa*. Ed. by Yogindrananda. Varanasi 1968

Pañcapādikā — of Padmapādācārya with two commentaries and *Pañcapādikāvivaraṇa* with two commentaries. Ed. by Shrirama Shastri and Krishnamurti Shastri. Madras Goverment Oriental Series No. CLV. Madras 1958

PKM — *Prameyakamalamārtaṇḍa* of Prabhācandra. Ed. by Mahendrakumar Jain. 2nd ed., Bombay 1941

PDhS — *Padārthadharmasaṅgraha (Praśastapādabhāṣya)* of Praśastapāda with the commentary *Nyāyakandalī* of Śrīdhara. Ed. by D.J. Sharma. Gaṅganātha-Jhā-Granthamālā No. I. 2nd ed., Varanasi 1977

PP — *Prakaraṇapañcikā* of Śālikanātha Miśra with the *Nyāyasiddhi* of Jaipuri Nārāyaṇa Bhaṭṭa. Ed. by A. Subrahmanya Shastri. Benares Hindu University Darshana Series No. 4. Benares 1961

PP (Ch. ed.) — *Prakaraṇapañcikā*. Ed. by Mukunda Shastri. CSS 61. Benares 1903-4

PM — *Hemacandra's Pramāṇa-Mīmāṃsā*. Text and transl. by S. Mookerjee and N. Tatia. Prachya Bharati Series 11. Varanasi 1970

Prasannapadā — of Candrakīrti in *MMK*

PrP — *Pramāṇaparīkṣā* of Vidyānanda. Ed. by Gajadharalal. Kashi 1914

PV — *Pramāṇavārttika of Dharmakīrti with the Commentary Vṛtti of Manorathanandin*. Ed. by Dwarikadas Shastri. Bauddha Bharati Series No. 3. Varanasi 1968

PVin I — *Dharmakīrti's Pramāṇaviniścayaḥ*. 1. Kapitel: Pratyakṣam. Hrsg. und übers. von T. Vetter. Wien 1966

PVin II(1) — *Dharmakīrti's Pramāṇaviniścayaḥ*. 2. Kapitel: Svārthānumānam. Tib. Text und Sanskrittexte von E. Steinkellner. Wien 1973

PVin II(2) — *Dharmakīrti's Pramāṇaviniścayaḥ*. 2. Kapitel: Svārthānumānam. Übers. von E. Steinkellner. Wien 1979

PVṬ — *Pramāṇavārttikaṭīkā* of Karṇakagomin. Ed. by R. Sankrityayana. Allahabad 1943

PVBh — *Pramāṇavārttikabhāṣyam or Vārttikālaṅkāraḥ of Prajñākaragupta*. Ed. by R. Sankrityayana. Patna 1953

PVV	*Pramāṇavārttikavṛtti* in PV
PVSV	*Pramāṇavārttikasvopajñavṛtti* in R. Gnoli, *The Pramāṇavārttikam of Dharmakīrti*. SOR No. XXIII. Roma 1960
PS(V)	*Pramāṇasamuccaya(vṛtti)* of Dignāga. Chapter I in M. Hattori, *Dignāga, On Perception*. Chapter V in M. Hattori, *The Pramāṇasamuccayavṛtti of Dignāga with Jinendrabuddhi's Commentary*. Memoirs of the Faculty of Letters, Kyoto University, No. 21, 1982
PSṬ	*Pramāṇasamuccayaṭīkā (Viśālāmalavatī)* of Jinendrabuddhi. TTP No. 5766
Bṛhatī	of Prabhākara Miśra with the *Ṛjuvimalā* of Śālikanātha. Ed. by Chinnaswami Shastri. CSS 391. Benares 1929
Bhagavadgītā	Ed. by Wasudev Laxman. 2nd. ed., Delhi 1978
MP	*Maṇiprabhā* of Rāmānanda in *YS*
MMK	*Mūlamadhyamakakārikā* of Nāgārjuna in *Madhyamakaśāstra of Nāgārjuna with the Commentary: Prasannapadā by Candrakīrti*. Ed. by P.L. Vaidya. Buddhist Sanskrit Texts No. 10. Darbhanga 1960
MV	*Māṭharavṛtti*, ed. by V.P. Sharma, cf. *JM*
MS	*Mīmāṃsāsūtra* 1.1.1-5 in E. Frauwallner, *Materialien zur ältesten Erkenntnislehre der Karmamīmāṃsā*. Wien 1968; otherwise in *Mīmāṃsādarśanam*. Ed. by Abhyankar et al. ASS 97. 2nd ed., Poona 1970
YD	*Yuktidīpikā*. Ed. by R.C. Pandeya. Delhi 1967

YP	*Yogapradīpikā* of Bhāvāgaṇeśa in *YS*
YBh	*Yogabhāṣya* in *TV*
YBhV	*Pātañjalayogasūtrabhāṣyavivaraṇam of Śaṅkara-Bhagavatpāda*. Ed. by Rama Shastri and Krishnamurti Shastri. Madras Government Oriental Series No. XCLV. Madras 1952
YV	*Yogavārttika* of Vijñānabhikṣu in *Pātañjalayogadarśanam*. Ed. by Narayanamishra. 2nd ed., Varanasi 1982
YS	*Yogasūtram with Rājamārtaṇḍa by Bhojarāja, Pradīpikā by Bhāvāgaṇeśa, Vṛtti by Nāgoji Bhaṭṭa, Maṇiprabhā by Rāmānandayati, Chandrikā by Anantadeva and Yogasudhākara by Sadāśivendra*. Ed. by Dundhiraj Shastri. KSS 83. 2nd ed., Varanasi 1982
YSV	*Yogasūtravṛtti* of Nāgoji Bhaṭṭa in YS
RM	*Rājamārtaṇḍa* of Bhojarāja in *YS*
Lokatattvanirṇaya	of Haribhadra Sūri. Ed. and transl. into Italian by L. Suali. GSAIF No. 18, 1905, 263-319
VA	*Vipañcitārthavyākhyā* of Śāntarakṣita in *VN*
Viṃś	*Viṃśatikā* of Vasubandhu cf. *TrBh*
VN	*Vādanyāya* of Dharmakīrti with the *Vipañcitārthavyākhyā* of Śāntarakṣita and *Sambandhaparīkṣā* of Prabhācandra. Ed. by Dwarikadas Shastri. Bauddha Bharati Series No. 8. Varanasi 1972
VP	*Vākyapadīya* of Bhartṛhari. *Brahmakāṇḍa* cf. Biardeau; Kāṇḍa III with the Commentary of Helārāja. Ed. by K.A.S. Iyer. Deccan College Mono-

graph Series No. 21. Part 1. Poona 1963. Part 2. Poona 1973

Vy — *Vyomavatī* of Vyomaśiva in *Praśastapādabhāṣyam*. Ed. by G. Kaviraj. CSS 61. Benares 1930

Vy(Ms) — Manuscript of the *Vyomavatī*, belonging to the University of Mysore Oriental Research Institute. Ms.-No. C 1575

VV — *Vigrahavyāvartanī* of Nāgārjuna in K. Bhattacharya, E.H. Johnston and A. Kunst, *The Dialectical Method of Nāgārjuna*. Delhi 1978

VS — *Vaiśeṣikasūtra of Kaṇāda with the Commentary of Candrānanda*. Ed. by Jambuvijayaji. GOS 136. Baroda 1961

VSVṛ — *Vaiśeṣikasūtravṛtti* of Candrānanda in VS

VSVyākhyā — *Vaiśeṣikasūtravyākhyā* in *Vaiśeṣikadarśana of Kaṇāda with an anonymous Commentary*. Ed. by A. Thakur. Mithila Institute Series Modern Text No. 5. Darbhanga 1957

ŚD — *Śāstradīpikā* of Pārthasārathi Miśra. Ed. by Kishordas Svami. Varanasi 1977

ŚBh — *Śābarabhāṣya* cf. MS

ŚV — *Ślokavārttika of Śrī Kumārila Bhaṭṭa with the Commentary Nyāyaratnākara of Śrī Pārthasārathi Miśra*. Ed. by Dwarikadas Shastri. Prachyabharati Series No. 10. Varanasi 1978

ŚVK — *Kāśikā* in *Mīmāṃsāślokavārttika of Kumārila Bhaṭṭa with the Commentary Kāśikā of* Sucaritamiśra. Ed. by Shambashiva Shastri and Ramasvami

	Shastri. Trivandrum Sanskrit Series No. XC, XCIX, CL. Trivandrum 1926, 1929, 1943
ŚVV	*Ślokavārttikavyākhyā* (*Tātparyaṭīkā*) *of Bhaṭṭombeka*. Ed. by Ramanatha Shastri. Madras University Sanskrit Series No. 13. Madras 1940
Siddhitraya	of Yāmuna. Ed. by Ramamishra Shastri. CSS 10. Varanasi 1900
Suśruta	*Suśrutasaṃhitā of Suśruta with the Nibandhasaṅgraha Commentary of Śrī Ḍalhaṇāchārya*. Ed. by Jadavji Trikamji and Narayan Ram. Jaikrishnadas Ayurveda Series No. 34. 4th ed., Varanasi 1980
SK	*Sāṅkhyakārikā* in GBh
STK	*Sāṅkhyatattvakaumudī* of Vācaspati Miśra. Ed. by Ramashankar Bhattacarya. Delhi 1967
SDDP	*Sāmānyadūṣaṇadikprasāritā* of Aśoka in Haraprasad Shastri, *Six Buddhist Nyāya Tracts*. Bibl. Ind. 185. Calcutta 1910
SDDP(Thakur)	in *Aśokanibandhau*. Ed. by A. Thakur. Tibetan Sanskrit Works Series No.XV. Patna 1974
SDS	*Sarvadarśanasaṅgraha of Sāyaṇa-Mādhava*. Ed. by Abhyankar. Government Oriental Series A, No. 1. 3rd ed., Poona 1978
SV(1)	*Sāṃkhya-Saptati-Vṛtti* (V1). Ed. by E. Salomon. Ahmedabad 1973
SV(2)	*Sāṃkhya-Vṛtti* (V2). Ed. by E. Salomon. Ahmedabad 1973
SVṬ	*Siddhiviniścayaṭīkā* of Anantavīrya. Ed. by Mahendrakumar Jain. Jñānapī-

ṭha Mūrtidevī Jaina Granthamālā No. 22-23. Varanasi 1959

SVM — *Syādvādamañjarī* of Mallişeṇa Sūri. Ed. by Jagadishacandra Jain. 4th ed., Ahmedabad 1979

SVR — *Syādvādaratnākara* of Vādideva Sūri. Ed. by M. Osval. Ārhatamataprabhākara No. 4. Poona 1926-30

HB — *Dharmakīrti's Hetubinduḥ*. Teil I. Tib. Text und rekonstruierter Sanskrit-Text von E. Steinkellner. Wien 1967
Teil II. Übers. und Anm. von E. Steinkellner. Wien 1967

HBṬ — *Hetubinduṭīkā* of Arcaṭa. Ed. by S. Sanghavi and Jinavijayaji. GOS CXIII. Baroda 1949

2. Secondary Sources

Bhatt, G.: *Epistemology of the Bhāṭṭa School of Pūrva Mīmāṃsā*. Chowkhamba Sanskrit Studies No. XVII. Varanasi 1962

Biardeau, M.: "La définition dans la pensée indienne." *JA* CCXLV 1957, 371-84

" *Théorie de la Connaissance et Philosophie de la Parole dans le brahmanisme classique*. Paris, La Haye 1964

" *Vākyapadīya Brahmakāṇḍa avec la Vṛtti de Harivṛṣabha* (Transl.). Publications de l'Institut de Civilisation Indienne No. 24. Paris 1964

Bühnemann, G.: *Der allwissende Buddha*. Wiener Studien zur Tibetologie und Buddhismuskunde No. 4. Wien 1980

Bühnemann, G.: "Tarkarahasya and Vādarahasya." WZKS XXVIII 1984, 185-91

Burnyeat, M.: "Can the Sceptic live his Scepticism?" in *Doubt and Dogmatism*, ed. by M. Schofield, M. Burnyeat and J. Barnes. Oxford 1980, 20-53

Chakravarti, P.: *Origin and Development of the Sāṃkhya System of Thought*. 2nd ed., Delhi 1975

Chattopadhyaya, D.: *Lokāyata*. 4th ed., Delhi 1978

Chisholm, R.: *Theory of Knowledge*. 2nd ed., Delhi 1977

Cicero: *Academica*. Transl. by H. Rackham. Loeb Classical Library. Revised ed., London, Cambridge 1933

Collingwood, R.G.: *An Essay on Philosophical Method*. 6th ed., Oxford 1977

" *An Autobiography*. Repr., Oxford 1982

Dixit, K.: "The Ideological Affiliation of Jayarāśi, the Author of the Tattvopaplavasiṃha." Indian Studies Past and Present Vol. 4,1. Calcutta 1962, 98-104

Dravid, R.: *The Problem of Universals in Indian Philosophy*. Delhi 1972

D'Sa, F.: *Śabdaprāmāṇyam in Śabara and Kumārila*. Publications of the De Nobili Research Library No. 7. Wien 1980

Franco, E.: "Studies in the *Tattvopaplavasiṃha*. I. The Criterion of Truth." *JIP* 11 1983, 147-66

" "Studies in the *Tattvopaplavasiṃha*. II. The Theory of Error." *JIP* 12 1984, 105-37

Franco, E.: "On the Interpretation of *Pramāṇasamuccaya(vṛtti)* I,3d." *JIP* 12 1984, 389-400

" "Once again on Dharmakīrti's Deviation from Dignāga on *pratyakṣābhāsa*." *JIP* 14 1986, 79-97

" "The *Paurandarasūtra*." Forthcoming in *D. Malvania Felicitation Volume*

Frauwallner, E.: "Beiträge zur Apohalehre. I. Dharmakīrti. Zusammenfassung." *WZKM* 42 1935, 93-102

" "Beiträge zur Geschichte des Nyāya. I. Jayanta und seine Quellen." *WZKM* 43 1936, 263-78

" *Geschichte der indischen Philosophie*. Salzburg 1953, 1956

" "Die Reihenfolge und Entstehung der Werke Dharmakīrtis" in *Asiatica*, Festschrift Friedrich Weller, Leipzig 1954, 142-54

" *Die Philosophie des Buddhismus*. 2nd ed., Berlin 1958

" "Die Erkenntislehre des klassischen Sāṃkhya-Systems." *WZKSO* 2 1958, 84-139

" "Dignāga, sein Werk und seine Entwicklung." *WZKSO* 3 1959, 83-164

" "Sprachtheorie und Philosophie im Mahābhāṣyam des Patañjali." *WZKSO* 4 1960, 92-118

" "Landmarks in the History of Indian Logic." *WZKSO* 5 1961, 125-48

" "Kumārila's Bṛhaṭṭīkā." *WZKSO* 6 1962, 78-90

" *Materialien zur ältesten Erkenntnislehre der Karmamīmāṃsā*. Wien 1968

Frauwallner, E.: *Kleine Schriften*. Hrsg. von G. Oberhammer und E. Steinkellner. Wiesbaden 1982

Granoff, P.: *Philosophy and Argument in Late Vedānta*. Studies of Classical India No. 1. Dordrecht, Boston, London 1978

Hacker, P.: *Vivarta*. Akademie der Wissenschaften und der Literatur (Mainz), Abh. der geistes- u. sozialwissensch. Klasse Jahrgang 1953, Nr. 5

Halbfass, W.: "The Vaiśeṣika Concept of *guṇa* and the Problem of Universals." WZKS 24 1980, 225-38

" "Praśastapāda's Concept of Substance (*dravya*)" in *Dr. Ludwik Sternbach commemoration volume*. Torino 1981, 537-44

Hara, M.: "A Note on the Sanskrit-Phrase *devānāṃ priya*" in *Katre Felicitation Volume* Part II, *Indian Linguistics* 30 1969, 13-26

Hattori, M.: *Dignāga, On Perception*. Harvard Oriental Series 47. Cambridge 1968

" "Apoha and Pratibhā" in *Sanskrit and Indian Studies*, ed. by M. Nagatomi, B.K. Matilal, J.M. Masson and E. Dimock. Dordrecht 1979, 61-73

Hayes, R.: "Diṅnāga's Views on Reasoning (*svārthānumāna*)." *JIP* 8 1980, 219-77

Hume, D.: *An Enquiry Concerning Human Understanding*. Ed. by Selby-Bigge, rev. by P.H. Nidditch. Oxford 1975

Iyer, K.A.S.: *Bhartṛhari*. Poona 1969

Jayatilleke, K.N.: *Early Buddhist Theory of Knowledge*. London 1963

James, W.: *The Meaning of Truth*. New York 1909

Jha, G.: *The Prābhākara School of Pūrva Mīmāṃsā*. Allahabad 1911

": *Padārthadharmasaṅgraha of Praśastapāda with the Nyāyakandalī of Śrīdhara*. Translation. Chowkhamba Oriental Studies No. 4. Varanasi 1916

": *Pūrva-Mīmāṃsā in its Sources*. 2nd ed., Varanasi 1964

Johnston, E.: *Early Sāṃkhya*. London 1937

Kajiyama, Y.: *An Introduction to Buddhist Philosophy*. Kyoto 1966

": "Three Kinds of Affirmation and two Kinds of Negation in Buddhist Philosophy." WZKS 17 1973, 161-75

La Vallée Poussin, L. de: *L'Abhidharmakośa de Vasubandhu*. 6 vols. Paris, Louvain 1923-31

": "Le Bouddhisme et le Yoga de Patañjali." *Mélanges chinois et bouddhiques* V 1936-37, 223-42

Liebenthal, W.: *Satkārya in der Darstellung seiner buddhistischen Gegner*. Beiträge zur indischen Sprachwissenschaft und Religionsgeschichte 9. Stuttgart, Berlin 1934

Lindtner, Chr.: "Apropos Dharmakīrti - Two New Works and a New Date." AO 41 1980, 27-37

Matilal, B.K.: *The Navya-Nyāya Doctrine of Negation*. Harvard Oriental Series 46. Cambridge 1968

": *Logical and Ethical Issues of Religious Belief*. Calcutta 1982

Mayrhofer, M.: *Kurzgefasstes etymologisches Wörterbuch des Altindischen*. Heidelberg 1956-76

Mimaki, K.: *La Réfutation Bouddhique de la Permanence des Choses et La Preuve de la Momentanéité des Choses.* Publications de l'Institut de Civilisation Indienne No. 41. Paris 1976

Mookerjee, S.: *The Buddhist Philosophy of Universal Flux.* Calcutta 1935

" *The Jaina Philosophy of Non-Absolutism.* 2nd ed., Delhi 1978

Mookerjee, S. and Nagasaki, H.: *The Pramāṇavārttikam of Dharmakīrti.* An English Translation of the First Chapter. Patna 1964

MW *A Sanskṛit-English Dictionary* by Sir M. Monier-Williams. Oxford 1899

Naess, A.: *Scepticism.* London 1968

Nagatomi, M.: "Arthakriyā." *Adyar Library Bulletin* 31-32 1967-68, 52-72

Namai, M.: "A Survey of Bārhaspatya Philosophy." *Indological Review* 2 1976, 29-74

Passmore, J.: *Philosophical Reasoning.* 2nd ed., London 1970

Popkin, R.: *A History of Scepticism from Erasmus to Spinoza.* Berkeley, Los Angeles, London 1979

Potter, K.: *Encylopedia of Indian Philosophies.* Vol. I. Bibliography. Delhi 1983

" *Encyclopedia of Indian Philosophies.* Vol. II. Nyāya-Vaiśeṣika. Delhi 1977

Preisendanz, K.: *Vācaspati Miśra II. Nyāyatattvāloka* (Typescript). Forthcoming in Alt- und neu-Indische Studien

PW O. Böhtlingk und R. Roth: *Sanskrit-Wörterbuch.* St. Petersburg 1852/53-1875

Radhakrishnan, S. and Moore, C.: *A Source Book in Indian Philosophy*. 5th ed., Princeton 1973

Raja, K.: *Indian Theories of Meaning*. Adyar Library Series No. 91. 2nd ed., Madras 1969

Randle, H.: *Fragments from Dignāga*. Prize Publication Fund Vol. No. IX. London 1926

" *Indian Logic in the Early Schools*. Oxford 1930

Renou, L.: *Grammaire Sanscrite*. Paris 1975

Ruben, W.: "Über den Tattvopaplavasiṃha des Jayarāśi Bhaṭṭa, eine agnostizistische Erkenntniskritik." WZKSO 2 1958, 140-53

Ruegg, D.: "On Ratnakīrti." *JIP* 1 1970, 300-309

Sanghavi, S.: *Advanced Studies in Indian Logic and Metaphysics*. Indian Studies Past and Present. Vol. 2,2-3. Calcutta 1960-61, 189-201, 387-494

Schmithausen, L.: *Maṇḍanamiśra's Vibhramavivekaḥ*. Wien 1965

" "Sautrāntika-Voraussetzungen in Viṃśatikā and Triṃśikā." *WZKS* 11 1967, 109-36

" *Der Nirvāṇa-Abschnitt in der Viniścayasaṃgrahaṇī der Yogācārabhūmiḥ*. Wien 1969

Sextus Empiricus: *Outlines of Pyrrhonism* in *Sextus Empiricus*, with English translation by R.G. Bury. Loeb Classical Library. Cambridge, London 1933

" *Against the Ethicists* in ditto, 1936

Shastri, D.N.: *The Philosophy of Nyāya-Vaiśeṣika and its Conflict with the Buddhist Dignāga School*. Delhi 1976

Siderits, M.: "The Sense-Reference Distinction in Indian Philosophy of Language." *Synthese* 69 1986, 81-106

Sinha, J.: *Indian Psychology*. Vol. I. *Cognition*. 2nd ed., Calcutta 1958

Stcherbatsky, Th.: *Buddhist Logic*. Vol. I. St. Petersburg 1932. Vol. II. St. Petersburg 1930

Steinkellner, E.: "Die Literatur des älteren Nyāya." *WZKSO* 5 1961, 149-62

" cf. *HB*

" "New Sanskrit-Fragments of *Pramāṇaviniścayaḥ*, First Chapter." *WZKS* 16 1972, 199-206

" "Yogische Erkenntnis als Problem im Buddhismus" in *Transzendenzerfahrung, Vollzugshorizont des Heils*, hrsg. von G. Oberhammer. Wien 1978, 121-34

" cf. *PVin* II

Strawson, P.: *Skepticism and Naturalism*. London 1985

Striker, G.: "Sceptical Strategies" in *Doubt and Dogmatism*, 54-83, cf. Burnyeat

Vetter, T.: *Erkenntnisprobleme bei Dharmakīrti*. Wien 1964

" cf. *PVin* I

" "Die Gauḍapādīya-Kārikās: Zur Entstehung und zur Bedeutung von (A)dvaita." *WZKS* 22 1978, 95-132

Vidyabhushana, S.C.: *History of Indian Logic*. Calcutta 1922

Wezler, A.: "Die 'dreifache' Schlussfolgerung im *Nyāyasūtra* I.1.5." *IIJ* XI 1969, 190-211

Wezler, A.: "Zur Identität der 'Ācāryāḥ' und 'Vyākhyātāraḥ' in Jayantabhaṭṭas *Nyāyamañjarī*." WZKS 19 1975, 135-46

": "Studien zum Dvādaśāranayacakra des Śvetāmbara Mallavādin. I. Der *sarvasarvātmakatvavāda*" in *Studien zum Jainismus und Buddhismus*, Gedenkschrift für Ludwig Alsdorf, hrsg. von K. Bruhn und A. Wezler. Alt- und Neu-Indische Studien 23. Wiesbaden 1980, 359-408

Woods, J.: *The Yoga-System of Patañjali*. Harvard Oriental Series No. 17. Cambridge 1914

Index locorum*

---

*Numbers refers to pages and lines, superscripted numbers to notes.

Index of Sanskrit Terms